Intertemporal Macroeconomics

B

for Asimo: NYNKAIAEI

Intertemporal Macroeconomics

Costas Azariadis

BLACKWELL
Oxford UK & Cambridge USA

First published 1993
Reprinted 1993, 1994 (twice), 1995
Reprinted with revisions 1998, 2000

Blackwell Publishers Inc
350 Main Street
Malden, Massachusetts 02148, USA

Blackwell Publishers Ltd
108 Cowley Road
Oxford OX4 1JF, UK

Library of Congress Cataloging in Publication Data
Azariadis, Costas
Intertemporal macroeconomics / Costas Azariadis
p. cm.
Includes bibliographical references and index.
ISBN 1–55786–366–0
1. Macroeconomics. I. Title.
HB172.5.A93   1993
339—dc20   92–16498   CIP

British Library Cataloguing in Publication Data
A CIP catalogue record for this book is available from the British Library

Typeset in 10 on 12pt Times by TecSet Ltd, Wallington, Surrey
Printed and bound in Great Britain
by MPG Books Ltd, Bodmin, Cornwall

This book is printed on acid-free paper

Contents

Foreword

This textbook is addressed to graduate students in economics and finance and to practicing research economists; I hope other social scientists will find it of interest. But its main purpose is to collect between one pair of covers the building blocks of dynamical macroeconomics, to arrange them into a coherent framework, and to illustrate their uses in a variety of traditional and newer macroeconomic issues.

Intended primarily for first-year graduate students, the text is divided into four parts which are best read sequentially: Part I and the first four chapters in Part II lay the technical foundations needed to discuss the key macroeconomic issues in chapters 14 through to 30 Part III and Part IV. Starred sections contain advanced material suitable for second-year courses in macroeconomics, growth theory, monetary theory, or economic dynamics. The User's Guide offers suggestions about such courses.

Just like industrial organization, general equilibrium theory, and other established areas in economics, macroeconomics has been developing a central theoretical core. Sparked by the seminal contributions of Solow (1956) on growth theory, Diamond (1965) on national debt and Lucas (1972) on rational expectations, that core started forming rather slowly at first; it expanded rapidly in the 1980s to the point where most active research is now conducted with the tools of neoclassical growth theory and expressed in the symbolism of dynamical mathematics.

A profound change in methodology is taking place in a field that historical evolution has brought to close proximity with almost every other area in economics – from economic history to economic theory – and wedded to an eclectic toolkit intended to study the diverse component parts that make up macroeconomics. Macroeconomists study business cycles and capital accumulation, unemployment and inflation, consumption and investment, asset prices and financial intermediation, monetary theory and fiscal policy, expectations and price volatility, exchange rates and the balance of payments, fertility and economic development, and a variety of other issues. How could all of these fit into a common theoretical paradigm?

What appeared improbable ten years ago has become feasible today: neoclassical growth theory and related dynamical approaches have spilled out of their traditional long-run domain and became routinely employed in exploring short-run phenomena. They dominate current research on more than half of the topics listed in the previous paragraph, and are likely to expand into areas such as unemployment, financial intermediation, and the demand for money in which static models are still the rule.

As of this writing, a small and relatively uniform set of models have evolved into a *language* in which many macroeconomists, especially of the younger generation, choose to express their work and communicate their findings. There are good reasons to believe that this language, already preponderant in the better research and teaching institutions, will soon become a nearly universal medium of discourse in macroeconomics. To this author at least, the time seems ripe for a "manual" that will help teach the new language to future economists and strengthen the language skills of practicing ones.

What are the most important elements of the new paradigm? In what sequence should they be taught to graduate students and learned by practitioners? Do they improve our understanding of traditional macroeconomic issues? How do they help researchers with the problems of an integrating world economy?

One key lesson of the new paradigm is that macroeconomics is about *human interactions over time.* A familiar example calls for individuals, corporations, and governments to abstain from current consumption whenever they wish to raise future consumption; the resulting surplus is invested in education, plant and equipment, research and development, and items of public infrastructure such as bridges, highways, and health clinics. To describe the resulting time path of an economy, or any of its component parts, one needs to feel comfortable with dynamical mathematics. The theory of dynamical systems, in particular, is a research tool of enormous value in identifying both transitional and long-term responses of such endogenous economic variables as the trade balance, income per head, population, the rate of inflation, and many others to changes in policy, tastes, technological progress, the terms of trade, and a large variety of other outside forces acting on a national economy.

Dynamical systems have spread so widely into macroeconomics that vector fields and phase diagrams are on the verge of displacing the familiar supply–demand schedules and Hicksian crosses of static macroeconomics. If current trends continue, younger economists will find it sensible to learn a lot of dynamical mathematics *early* in their career. Accordingly, Part I of this textbook, written collaboratively with Angel de la Fuente, presents a detailed survey of dynamical systems designed especially for economists. The survey is self-contained (except for some proofs); it focuses on discrete-time systems rather than continuous-time systems because economic data come in discrete form; and the great majority of the examples and illustrations it contains (save for some drill questions) draw on economics and not on mechanics and other natural sciences which, up to this point, have been the chief beneficiaries of dynamical tools.

To emphasize the broad range of application for these tools, Part I is organized in *pairs* of chapters: a collection of related mathematical results is described in the first chapter and is applied to a number of well-known economic problems in the second chapter. Chapters (2, 3), (4, 5), (6, 7) and (8, 9) are four such pairs which explore insights from the theory of dynamical systems in a variety of settings – from asset prices to the study of human fertility.

The dynamical systems one tends to study most often in macroeconomics are mathematical descriptions of neoclassical growth models of various stripes or of growth "forms," that is, pure exchange economies that look like growth models without production. Part II of this text is an extensive survey of growth models and growth forms, and of their applications to foreign lending, economic development, and income taxation. Among dynamic macroeconomic models, two that have seen wide and expanding use in the last decade are the *overlapping generations model* and the *optimal growth model*. Part II covers them both in some detail, emphasizing the overlapping generations model for two reasons. First, the overlapping generations model is more readily adaptable than any other to extensions of its basic structure; it deals easily and authoritatively with consumer heterogeneity, unproductive paper assets, and the evaluation of public policies. The second reason is that, nine years after Woodford's (1984) excellent but inaccessible survey, the time is ripe for a comprehensive restatement of the overlapping generations model, from basic principles to policy implications, written primarily for macroeconomists.

Among active researchers, the optimum growth model remains at the moment slightly more popular than the overlapping generations model. Why is this so? What are the strengths and weaknesses of each model?

Readers who like analogies will find it useful to think of either model as a distinct dialect of the broad language we call "neoclassical growth theory." Each dialect has unique structural elements that make it better suited to express some syllogisms and not others, to describe certain features of real-world economies better than others. Optimum growth in particular refers to a class of economies that typically, though not necessarily, consist of a representative infinite-lived individual or of an equally representative dynastic family whose generations are bonded together by strong parental altruism. Overlapping generations models, too, study economies that extend into the infinite future; these, however, are made up of unending sequences of heterogeneous finitely lived households with weak or nonexistent dynastic links.

Both types provide similar analyses on a large number of questions in positive macroeconomics: lists of factors affecting interest rates, the broad outlines of economic growth and human fertility, the channels by which money exerts influence over prices and economic activity, and the answers to many other issues depend only slightly on which particular growth model we choose as our research instrument.

The similarities end when it comes to issues of intergenerational redistribution (social security, public debt), the importance of beliefs in equilibrium, and patterns of long-term growth. Here the two models offer distinct, and not equally sensible, answers to many key questions. The optimum growth model, for example, seems better suited to econometric work at business cycle frequencies than do existing versions of the overlapping generations model for it permits individuals to transact much more frequently. Suitably parametrized versions of this model track with a fair degree of accuracy postwar time-series movements in many US economic aggregates. This explains why "real business cycle" models, stochastic variants of the optimal growth model developed by Kydland and Prescott (1982) and Hansen (1985), enjoy considerable popularity among empirical researchers.

Another feature of that model that has endeared it to many economists is its parsimonious description of data. It has relatively few free parameters, admits a very small number of equilibria and therefore tends to make unequivocal predictions about how prices and production respond to changes in the economic environment. Sharp predictions are a two-edged sword that often lead representative–agent models into indefensible statistical corners: fluctuations in aggregate consumption and asset prices at business cycle frequencies turn out to be much larger than one would hypothesize from any reasonably parametrized optimal growth model.

More guarded predictions emerge out of the overlapping generations model which inherits more free parameters and a relatively large set of equilibria from the consumer heterogeneity and finite lifecycle that are built into it. The richer set of equilibria turns this model into a potent instrument whenever economic events come to depend on the distribution of wealth among individuals or generations, on swings in market psychology, or on the organization of market institutions.

The overlapping generations model seems better suited than do existing versions of the optimal growth model to explain why the exchange of fiat value money and other intrinsically worthless paper assets depends on how much "trust" households place in government liabilities; how deficit finance redistributes resources between generations; to what extent optimistic or pessimistic market anticipations influence a list of short-run phenomena, from the volatility of stock prices and foreign-exchange rates to the amplitude of business cycles; and precisely what role smoothly functioning factor markets play in the process of economic development. Last, but not least, the overlapping generations model does a better job of accounting for poverty traps, that is, explaining why truly poor countries so often seem unable to catch up with developed lands in per capita income.

Despite their differences in details, both the overlapping generations model and the optimal growth model are genuinely dynamic structures built on solid microeconomic foundations. In that respect alone they are significant improvements over the static IS–LM model which preceded them as the dominant macroeconomic paradigm in the postwar period. From the extensive list of strong and weak features that occupies the last few paragraphs, it is difficult to foretell if one of the two neoclassical "dialects" will displace the other and become the universal language of discourse in macroeconomics, as IS–LM used to be a scant 20 years ago.

Since each neoclassical dialect is spoken by a large number of active researchers, both good economic theory and plain horse sense suggest that young economists should become proficient in both of them. I intend this textbook for readers who aim to be fluent in the "optimal growth" idiom and native speakers of "overlapping generations."

Costas Azariadis

References

Diamond, P. 1965: National debt in a neoclassical growth model. *American Economic Review*, 55, 1126–50.

Hansen, G. 1985: Indivisible labor and the business cycle. *Journal of Monetary Economics*, 16. 309–27.

Kydland, F. and Prescott, E. 1982: Time to build and aggregate fluctuations. *Econometrica*, 50, 1345–70.

Lucas, R. 1972: Expectations and the neutrality of money. *Journal of Economic theory*, 4, 103–24.

Solow, R. 1956: A contribution to the theory of economic growth. *Quarterly Journal of Economics*, 70, 65–94.

Woodford, M. 1984: Indeterminacy of equilibrium in the overlapping generations model: a survey. Mimeo.

Acknowledgments

Writing this book has been more a collective effort than readers would guess by just counting the number of references to economists of generations neighboring my own. It drew on the support of colleagues and students, coworkers and secretaries, family members and editors, of more people than space permits to acknowledge. As successive drafts of my lecture notes circulated in the profession in 1984, 1986, 1988 and 1990–1, many colleagues and students volunteered helpful comments on substance or exposition.

For suggestions on these drafts I thank Patricio Arrau, Alan Auerbach, Kerry Back, Michele Boldrin, James Bullard, Jordi Caballe, Roberto Chang, Russell Cooper, Constantine Dafermos, Peter D'Antonio, Allan Drazen, Roger Farmer, Jean-Michel Grandmont, Fumio Hayashi, Satu Kähkönen, Yuval Michaely, Stephen O'Connell, James Peck, Aris Protopapadakis, Mikko Puhakka, Natalie Shapiro, Douglas Shuman, Bruce Smith, Robert Solow, Lawrence Summers, Alberto Trejos, and Michael Woodford. I am grateful to Oded Galor, Anne Sibert, and an unknown reviewer for closely and constructively reading parts of the text, to Paul Zak for drawing the diagrams, and to Angel de la Fuente for contributing so substantially to Part I that his name appears in the Contents list.

A number of people deserve credit for kindling my interest in dynamic macroeconomics, influencing the way I have come to think about the field, and tangibly shaping the contents of this textbook. Foremost among them is Robert Lucas whose work over the last quarter-century has revolutionized the methodology and redefined the subject matter of macroeconomics. The list also includes former teachers like Edward Prescott, such colleagues as David Cass, Roger Farmer, Herschel Grossman, and Karl Shell, and collaborators like Russell Cooper, Allan Drazen, Roger Guesnerie, Pietro Reichlin, and Bruce Smith. To them, and to many other economists whose names appear in the bibliography, I owe more than I can ever repay.

Successive drafts of the manuscript were typed, time and time again, with patience, diligence, and unflagging good cheer by Mrudu Patel, Audrey Buck, Mary Larue, Margaret Becerra, Susana Salazar, Polly Osell, Deborah Trejos, Kelly Bonner-Quinn, Leh-Teen Fogelquist, and Billie Raskin. The University of Pennsylvania and the University of California at Los Angeles provided generous secretarial support.

Blackwell Publishers were involved in this book from the outset and its editors helped at all stages of production. Rene Olivieri, Mark Allin and Judith Harvey deserve my thanks for coaxing the book through its long gestation period. I thank Jill

Landeryou for overseeing the editing process and Christine Sharrock for a thoroughly professional job of copy-editing.

Lisa Coffin and Rosalind Bennett were very helpful with the bibliography and proofreading; Angel de la Fuente, Luisa Fuster and M. Angeles de Fruitos wrote the index. My largest debt is to Asimo and Cleo, close relatives and good friends, for being so tolerant of an interminable writing project that crept into family evenings, holidays, and vacations.

For pointing out misprints thanks are due to Ahmet Akyol, Max Alier, Shanka Chakraborty, Carlos da Costa, Jang Ting Guo, Yannis Ioannides, Hiroyuki Kawakatsu, Randy O'Toole, Rob Plunkett, Mikko Puhakka, Andras Simonovits and Eduardo Urdapilleta; particularly useful in this regard were Lisa Boehmer, and Mich Tvede and his students at the University of Copenhagen.

User's Guide

The intended audience for this book is first-year graduate students in economics; starred sections contain much current research that I believe advanced graduate students and practicing research economists will find of some value. Among the features unique to this text are the following:

1 A self-contained survey of dynamical systems with extensive applications to macroeconomics – the survey includes ample material on the "new wave" of mathematical tools written especially for economists, that is, nonlinear dynamics, periodic equilibria, bifurcation theory and chaos, together with an extensive bibliography;
2 Up-to-date statements of the overlapping generations model that range from theoretical foundations to policy applications.
3 A unified and systematic exposition of the key issues in dynamic macroeconomics, both traditional and new, based on neoclassical growth theory in general and on the overlapping generations model in particular.
4 Extensive coverage of many interesting recent ideas in macroeconomics such as endogenous growth theory and its implications for economic development (externalities, increasing returns, human capital); intergenerational transfers and Ricardian equivalence; expectations, sunspots, and market volatility; laboratory experiments in monetary economies; and many others.
5 An emphasis on geometric tools of analysis such as vector fields and phase diagrams which permeate the text (there are over 100 figures in total).
6 30 solved examples sprinkled throughout the book to help readers check how well they understand what is before them.
7 Large problem sets (about 130 questions altogether) designed to take readers from simple drill exercises to creative questions on topics of current research.

All this material has been assembled slowly over the last dozen or so years from lectures I gave at the University of Pennsylvania, the University of California at Los Angeles, and elsewhere (Princeton, Instituto de Matematica Pura e Aplicada, Virginia Polytechnic Institute) to several generations of students. The exact contents of each course rarely followed fixed rules, adjusting according to need to the technical background, training objectives, and intellectual interests of the audience. Other colleagues have tried portions of the text on audiences at Brown, Cornell, New York

University, and elsewhere. The current version has seen use at both Penn and UCLA with generally happy results. Students have taken to the new mathematical tools in Part I without great difficulty and, on occasion, with gusto.

Happy results are more likely if the instructor takes some pain to engage the students' geometric intuition with qualitative instruments like phase diagrams and to quench their thirst for economic relevance by quickly putting mathematical results to work in growth theory, development, and other applied areas.

First-year graduate courses of semester length typically start with the mathematical material in Part I: we begin with chapter 1, and move to the nonlinear tools in chapters 6 and 7 as fast as the mathematical preparation of the audience allows. These two chapters are the nucleus of Part I on which we normally spend three to four weeks. Another four weeks are needed to develop basic skills in growth theory, that is, to master the internal logic and grasp the economic intuition of the three workhorses of neoclassical economic growth: the descriptive growth, optimum growth and overlapping generations models. The core of this material takes up chapters 11 and 12 plus the unstarred sections of 13; the first three sections of 14 illustrate how growth theory contributes to our understanding of economic development.

Parts III and IV explore the more traditional macroeconomic issues of money, national debt, asset prices, and economic policy. Standard issues such as social security, the equivalence of national debt to taxes, the allocative consequences of budget deficits, the determinants of asset prices, the neutrality of money, central banking, inflationary finance, and many others are discussed from the vantage point of a unified intertemporal general equilibrium paradigm – the overlapping generations model. We normally spend five to six weeks on chapters 17 through 19, section 20.1, chapters 23 through 25 plus sections 26.1 and 26.2.

Parts of this textbook have seen use in advanced graduate courses, suitable for second- and third-year students, in which they are supplemented liberally with technical monographs, surveys, and research articles from scientific journals. Courses in dynamics and economic growth, for instance, may start with chapters 6 and 7, then cover bifurcation theory and chaos in chapter 8 and the Technical Appendices (sections A.4 and A.5) survey economic applications in chapter 9 and section 13.5, and then study topics in growth theory from sections 13.3, 15.1, 15.4 and 15.5. I have used much of the material in Part IV, especially chapters 25 through 28, as the theoretical core of advanced courses in monetary economics.

Questions and problems are an integral part of learning any technical subject, and graduate macroeconomics is by now a fairly technical discipline. Students can test their command of basic tools and their grasp of key results against *unmarked* problems located at the end of each part. These are typically the easiest problems to do; more technical questions are marked (T), and starred ones relate to advanced material. A special group of problems, labeled (C), require some creative thinking and are often meant to give students a peek at the research frontier in macroeconomics. Many of these are distilled from plainly identified journal articles which readers may consult for details and additional references.

Finally a few words should be said about the subjective and practical reasons that kept some useful technical tools and a number of interesting conceptual ideas out of this textbook. A number of fairly important topics in private information and strategic behavior (search theory, principal–agent problems and the theory of contracts, signaling and screening, coordination failures, insider–outsider relations and union–labor bargains) of fundamental value in analyzing the markets for labor and capital were omitted because they do not fit at present into the expository framework of dynamical competitive general equilibrium that pervades the next several hundred pages.

Stochastic growth theory, imperfect competition, and much empirical work in macroeconomics were left out because of space limitations or because I am not quite sure they are appropriate for a beginning graduate text. Topics like open-economy and political-economy aspects of macroeconomics received less attention than they deserve because I did not feel sufficiently at home with the subject matter to convey it effectively to readers; the list of these topics is, I fear, embarrassingly long.

To make up for some of the gaps in the exposition, all bibliographies contain notes on *Further Reading* which steer interested users to survey articles, specialized monographs, and other relevant sources of material not adequately covered in the text.

Part I

Discrete Dynamical Systems

(written with the collaboration of Angel de la Fuente)

1 Introduction to Part I

1.1 Overview

Part I is a self-contained survey of the mathematical tools we need in order to analyze the behavior of dynamical systems, that is, of systems of differential and difference equations that have time as the independent variable. The chief conceptual distinction is that time is a continuous variable in differential equations and a discrete variable in difference equations. While this leads to some idiosyncrasies in solution methods and in the precise formulation of certain results, the basic theory is almost identical in both cases. Since economic data come in discrete form, we will lay more emphasis on discrete systems. Useful results on continuous-time systems are collected in the Technical Appendices.

The main results we survey are amply illustrated with economic applications frequently drawn from the theory of economic growth. Nevertheless, this part of the book is heavily mathematical in nature; readers should think of it as a set of tools whose usefulness will become apparent in Parts II, III and IV.

We begin with linear systems in which it is frequently possible to obtain explicit solutions; we do so for systems with constant coefficients and illustrate the results in the Dornbusch (1976) model of exchange-rate overshooting. We then turn to nonlinear systems for which closed form solutions are not generally available. We focus instead on the *qualitative* properties of solutions, often relying on graphical methods which provide a convenient way to visualize dynamics. We give several demonstrations of how these geometric tools can elucidate the workings of neoclassical growth models.

A fair amount of information concerning the behavior of a nonlinear system in the neighborhood of a rest point or steady state can be obtained by approximating it with a linear system. On a global scale, there are interesting results concerning the stability of steady states, the existence of periodic solutions, and the nature of changes in the qualitative behavior of the system as parameters change. Some of these results are applied to the analysis of business cycles and other economic fluctuations.

Until fairly recently, most applications of dynamical systems in economics were drawn from the theory of linear systems. Models were either explicitly linear or were linearized in order to analyze local behavior in the neighborhood of a steady state. Lately, however, the study of nonlinear systems has received a good deal of attention by economists. The main reason is that such systems have much richer dynamics than linear systems. In particular, they often admit several steady states or display periodic solutions that may be interpreted as business cycles. Models of this type, then, serve as supplements or alternatives to the more standard linear stochastic models in which economic fluctuations arise strictly as a result of exogenous random shocks in tastes or technology.

Nonlinear dynamical systems of particular interest to macroeconomics include descriptions of long-run economic growth like the one-sector models of Solow, Ramsey, and Diamond; investigations of money and inflation like Brock's; Tobin's *q* theory of investment; the endogenous business cycle models of Benhabib and Grandmont; the two-sector growth system of Uzawa; and many others.

To illustrate some economic applications of dynamical tools, we start with compact descriptions of the simplest one-sector and two-sector models of economic growth; later in chapter 7 we will analyze each of them in some detail.

The *descriptive one-sector*[1] *model* due to Solow (1956) and Swan (1956) may be written as a first-order system in either continuous time,

$$\dot{k} + (\delta + n)k = sf(k) \tag{1.1a}$$

or discrete time,

$$(1 + n)k_{t+1} = (1 - \delta)k_t + sf(k_t) \tag{1.1b}$$

In these equations as we interpret $\dot{k}$ as the time derivative of the amount k of capital per worker; f is a neoclassical net production function; and δ, n and s are parameters denoting, respectively, the depreciation rate of physical capital, the rate of population growth, and the fraction of national income saved.

Each equation says simply that the fraction of current output that is not consumed is invested to replace worn-out equipment and increase the stock of productive capital. This model captures explicitly a simple idea that is missing in static formulations: there is a tradeoff between consumption and investment or between current and future consumption. The implications of this ever-present competition for resources between today and tomorrow are central to macroeconomics and can be explored only in a dynamic framework. Time is clearly of the essence.

One aspect of Solow's model that is not entirely satisfactory is the assumption that a constant fraction of national income is saved each period. A few decades ago this was a perfectly acceptable simplification but recently the economics profession has been getting fussier in its insistence that models be derived from the assumption that all individuals pursue rational courses of action, maximizing something like utility or profits. In current terminology, Solow made an *ad hoc* assumption – and there are few sins as grave as this for a self-respecting economist.

The descriptive growth model was soon improved upon. There are now two standard versions of the neoclassical growth model and both derive saving from the assumption that households maximize lifetime utility. One version is the *optimal*[2] *economic growth* model pioneered by Cass (1965) and Koopmans (1965), who built on earlier work by Ramsey (1928). As we will see in more detail later, this line of work assumes that households live forever, and leads to a system of two dynamic equations,

$$k_{t+1} = f(k_t) + (1 - \delta)k_t - c_t \tag{1.2a}$$

$$u'(c_t) = \beta u'(c_{t+1})[f'(k_{t+1}) + 1 - \delta] \tag{1.2b}$$

in discrete time, and to something quite similar in continuous time. Here primes denote total derivatives; the symbols k, f, and δ have the same interpretation as in the Solow model; c is consumption per capita, u is an instantaneous utility function; and the parameter $\beta \in (0,1)$ is the rate at which agents discount utility from consumption that takes place one period hence.

The second model, rather more sensibly, features finitely lived agents. It is called the *overlapping generations model* of growth and its simplest version, due to Diamond (1965), assumes that agents live for only two periods. In this case, we again get a single equation

$$(1 + n)k_{t+1} = z[f'(k_{t+1}) + 1 - \delta, \, w(k_t)] \tag{1.3}$$

In equation (1.3) the symbols δ, n, and f have the same meaning as before; and $z(1+r,y)$ is the amount saved by a consumer who lives two periods, faces an interest rate r, and is endowed with income y in the first period, zero in the second period. The function $w(k)$ describes how wages depend on the capital–labor ratio in an economy that operates under perfect competition and constant returns to scale.

Finally, the two-sector extension of the overlapping generations model studied by Reichlin (1987), but inspired by earlier work of Uzawa (1961), is described by the linear first-order difference equation

$$(1 + n)k_{t+1} = A \, \frac{k_x - k_t}{k_x - k_y} \, k_y \tag{1.4}$$

whenever the technologies of producing the investment good and the consumption good are both Leontieff with fixed capital–labor ratios k_y and k_x, respectively. In equation (1.4) k_t is the economywide capital–labor ratio, A is a scale parameter, and n is again the rate of population growth. We study a general form of the two-sector model in chapter 15.

It would not be a gross misrepresentation to say that the business of mainstream macroeconomics amounts to "complicating" one of the dynamical systems (1.1), (1.2) or (1.3) and exploring what happens as new features are added. If we put in taxes and government debt, we can study the short- and long-run implications of fiscal policy. Introducing money (a surprisingly hard thing to accomplish without *ad hoc* assumptions) enables us to explore the effects of monetary policy. By adding a stochastic shock to the production function, we obtain equilibria that look like business cycles, etc.

More on this will follow in Parts II, III, and IV. The purpose of this digression is to whet the reader's appetite for mathematical enlightenment by suggesting how technical tools are of use to an economist. If we have succeeded, the not-so-mathematically-inclined student should find it easier to bear with us over the next few chapters.

The remainder of this chapter introduces some basic concepts and gives an overview of the remaining contents of Part I.

1.2 Dynamical systems, difference equations, and boundary-value problems

Many applications in economics and other disciplines focus on the behavior over time of certain systems. Typically, the state of a system at a given point in time is described by a dated n-vector of real numbers $x(t)$, called the *state vector*. The evolution of the system over time is given by a function $g(x^0, t; \alpha)$ that specifies the state of the system at time t given that its initial state at time 0 was x^0. The function g, called the *state transition function*, is an essential part of what we call a dynamical system. We allow the transition function to depend on the value of parameters $\alpha \in \mathbb{R}^p$ that summarize some relevant structural characteristics of the system or describe a set of policies in effect.

Definition 1.1 (Dynamical systems in $\mathbb{R}^n$) A parametrized dynamical system in $\mathbb{R}^n$ is a pair (X, g) where $g : X \times \mathbb{R} \times \mathbb{R}^p \to X$ is a rule that describes the current state as a function of time, initial position, and parameters; and the state space X is a subset of $\mathbb{R}^n$ that contains all feasible states of the system.

In most cases the transition function g is not known explicitly. Rather, it is implicitly defined as the solution to a system of difference or differential equations with time as the independent variable.

An ordinary *difference equation* or system of equations in a time-dependent variable $x_t \in \mathbb{R}^n$ is an equation of the form

$$F(t; x_t, x_{t+1}, \ldots, x_{t+m}; \alpha) = 0 \tag{1.5}$$

where 0 is a n-dimensional vector of zeros and F is a function that, for each t and α, maps points in $\mathbb{R}^{m+1+n}$ into $\mathbb{R}^n$. We sometimes refer to x as the *state variable* and think of it as a function of time. Time takes only integer values. The standard notation is to write t as a subscript of x rather than as a full argument. Solutions to equation (1.5) are sequences of vectors $\{x_t\} = \{x_0, x_1, \ldots\}$ rather than continuous functions of time, as they would be in differential equations.

In general, we will assume that equation (1.5) can be "solved" for x_{t+m}, and that we can rewrite it in the form

$$x_{t+m} = f(t; x_t, x_{t+1}, \ldots, x_{t+m-1}; \alpha) \tag{1.6}$$

where, for each t and α, f maps points in $\mathbb{R}^{m+n}$ into $\mathbb{R}^n$.

Difference equations are said to be *linear* if f is a linear function of the state variables and nonlinear otherwise. The *order* of a difference equation is the difference between the largest and the smallest time subscript appearing in the equation. We will study only systems of first-order difference equations. This is not a serious limitation, for it is easy to reduce a higher-order system to first order by introducing additional equations and variables. For example, in the equation

$$x_t = f(x_{t-1}, x_{t-2}) \tag{1.7}$$

we can define the new variable y by

$$y_t = x_{t-1} \tag{1.8a}$$

and rewrite (1.7) as

$$x_t = f(x_{t-1}, y_{t-1}) \tag{1.8b}$$

Note that the second-order equation (1.7) has been replaced by an equivalent system of two first-order equations, (1.8a) and (1.8b). With no loss of generality, then, we can concentrate on first-order systems of the type

$$x_{t+1} = f(t, x_t; \alpha) \tag{1.9}$$

where x_t is a vector in some, typically low-dimensional, Euclidean space.

An equation like (1.9) is said to be *autonomous* if time does not enter as a separate argument in f. In fact, the impact of t is likely to come through a time-dependent exogenous or "forcing" term. A typical example is the equation that describes the evolution of the capital stock over time:

$$K_t = (1-\delta)K_{t-1} + I_t \tag{1.10}$$

Here the stock of capital K at time t is equal to last period's stock net of depreciation, plus new investment. Investment is a time-dependent forcing term, and the equation is not autonomous.

Linear systems are relatively easy to investigate; chapter 2 explains how to study linear systems of certain types. In the remainder of this section we will discuss some indirect ways to obtain qualitative information about the solutions of nonlinear systems.

A *solution* to a difference equation like (1.9) is a sequence or time path $\{x_t\}$ of the state vector x that satisfies equation (1.9) for all integer values of t or for some interesting subset of these, say $t = 0,1...,\infty$. The sequence $\{x_t\}$ is often called an *orbit* or *trajectory*. Intuitively, an equation like (1.9) tells us how x evolves from period to period, while a solution sequence $\{x_t\}$ would describe the time path of x as a function of the exogenous variables in the model, rather than of x's own previous values.

If we are given an initial value for the state vector, say x^0, it is easy to construct a solution sequence, and in the process obtain the state transition function, by iterating (1.9) forward, that is,

$$x_1 = f(0, x^0; \alpha) \equiv g(0, x^0; \alpha)$$
$$x_2 = f(1, x_1; \alpha) = f[1, f(0, x^0; \alpha); \alpha] \equiv g(1, x^0; \alpha)$$
$$\vdots$$
$$x_{t+1} = f(t, x_t; \alpha) = f[t, g(t-1, x^0; \alpha); \alpha] \equiv g(t, x^0; \alpha)$$

Some basic properties of the transition function follow immediately from the observation that g is defined by the iterative composition of f with itself. If f is a well-defined function, a unique solution exists for any given x^0. Moreover, if f is a continuous function, so is g, and if f is differentiable, the solution x_t will depend smoothly on α and x^0.

It is apparent from this construction that the solution sequence to a given system of difference equations is not uniquely defined. In particular, if we start from two different initial values of the state vector, we will obtain two different sequences, both of which satisfy equation (1.9). For example, if we have $I_t = 1$ for each t in our investment example, each possible starting value of the capital stock K_0 will generate a different, although parallel, path of capital stocks as a solution to (1.10).

This leads us to the notion of a *boundary-value problem* defined by a difference equation like (1.9) together with a boundary condition which specifies that the value of the state variable x at some given time s is some known constant x^0:

$$x_s = x^0 \tag{1.9$'$}$$

In constructing a solution iteratively from a given value of x we have implicitly assumed a specific type of boundary condition, known as an *initial condition*, which specifies the value of the state variable at some "natural" starting point. In many cases, however, no obvious initial condition exists and we will need some other type of boundary condition in order to pin down the trajectory of the system. As we will see below, the choice of an appropriate boundary condition will often reflect important economic considerations rather than mathematical ones.

Even though a difference equation may have an infinite number of solutions, a boundary-value problem will have precisely one solution if f is a single-valued function in equation (1.9). Out of the family of trajectories that satisfy (1.9), a condition like (1.9)$'$ picks out the one member that goes through the point x^0 at time s. It is clear, moreover, that one such trajectory will always exist; given the starting point $x_s = x^0$, we can always compute x_{s+1}, x_{s+2} and so on simply by iterating equation (1.9) from time s onward.[3]

We will find it useful, then, to distinguish the general solution to a difference equation like (1.9) from particular solutions to the same equation. By the *general solution* x_t^g to a difference equation, we mean an expression that describes the entire family of sequences that satisfy the equation, that is, the set

$$x_t^g = x(t; c; \alpha) = \{\{x_t\} \mid x_{t+1} = f(t, x_t; \alpha) \quad \forall t \in D(c, \alpha)\}$$

where D is some subset of Z, the set of all integers; and c is an arbitrary constant vector that indexes the family of sequences $\{x_t\}$ that solve equation (1.9); some of these are shown in figure 1.1. A *particular solution* to a difference equation is a specific member of this set. Each particular solution corresponds to a boundary-value problem: imposing a boundary condition like (1.9)$'$, picks out *one* member of the family described by x_t^g.

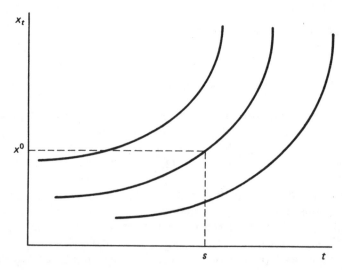

Figure 1.1 A family of solutions.

If an explicit form for the general solution can be found and an appropriate boundary condition is given, we will have a complete description of the behavior of the system over time. It will then be easy to see how the system responds to changes in parameter values. Such explicit solutions are available only for certain classes of linear systems, which we study in chapters 2 and 4. For nonlinear systems, however, closed form solutions are not available and we will have to rely on less direct methods to study qualitative aspects of the behavior of solutions.

1.3   Autonomous systems

An equation like (1.9) is said to be *autonomous* if time does not enter as a separate argument in f, that is, if we can write that equation in the form

$$x_{t+1} = f(x_t; \alpha) \tag{1.11}$$

Autonomous systems are models of situations in which behavior changes over time while "structural characteristics" remain the same. This simplifies things considerably and makes autonomous systems particularly easy to analyze by graphical methods in low-dimensional cases. Most of the material that follows concerns specifically the properties of autonomous systems.

To understand why equation (1.11) is much easier to work with than equation (1.9), we backtrack a little to give a geometrical interpretation of (1.9). Subtracting x_t from both sides of that equation, we can write

$$\Delta x_t = d(t, x_t; \alpha) \tag{1.12}$$

where $\Delta x_t \equiv x_{t+1} - x_t$ and $d(t, x_t; \alpha) \equiv f(t, x_t; \alpha) - x_t$. To summarize the information given by equation (1.9) we may think of affixing to each point x in the state space X a vector $d(t, x_t; \alpha)$ starting at x_t. In this context, the function d is sometimes referred to as a *vector field*.

The following physical interpretation then arises quite naturally. We may picture (1.9) as describing the motion of a particle that jumps once every period from one point to another in n-dimensional space. At a given point in time, the value of the state vector x_t describes the position of the particle and $\Delta x_t = d(t, x_t; \alpha)$ describes the next jump. Given the system's position at a certain time, we have only to follow the arrows to determine its future trajectory. Figure 1.2 illustrates this.

In the general case, of course, the direction and length of the arrows of motion depend on the time at which the particle reaches a certain position. When the system is autonomous, however, there is only one time-invariant arrow

$$\Delta x_t = d(x_t; \alpha)$$

affixed to each point in the state space. Since t is not an argument of d, all particles that ever reach a given point x in state space will follow exactly the same trajectory.

In analytical terms, the time invariance of the arrows of motion implies that the position of a particle that goes through x_0 at some point depends only on the time that has *elapsed* since x_0 was reached, and not on the time at which it reached this point. This also has implications for the structure of the transition function, which is now given by the iterated composition of a time-invariant map with itself.

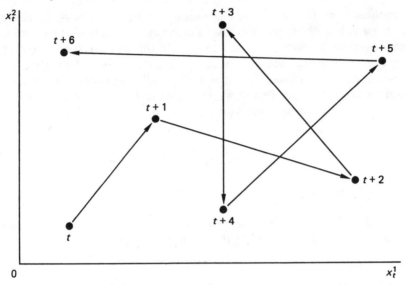

Figure 1.2 A particular trajectory.

Given an initial condition x^0 at $t = 0$, we iterate (1.11) to obtain a solution sequence:

$$x_1 = f(x^0; \alpha)$$

$$x_2 = f(x_1; \alpha = f[f(x^0);\alpha] \equiv f^2/x^0; \alpha)$$

$$\vdots$$

$$x_{t+1} = f(x_t; \alpha) = f[f^t(x^0); \alpha] \equiv f^{t+1}(x^0; \alpha)$$

where f^n denotes the nth iterate of the map f, not its nth power. The transition function

$$x(t, x^0; \alpha) = f^t(x^0; \alpha) \tag{1.13}$$

is sometimes called the *flow* of the system (1.11). It gives us the value of the state vector as a function of the parameters of the system, its initial position and time.

Some additional terminology will be useful below. We define the *positive orbit* of (1.11) through x^0 as the set

$$\gamma^+(x^0; \alpha) = \{x_t \in X \mid x_t = f^t(x^0; \alpha), t = 0,1,2...\}$$
$$= \{x^0, f(x^0; \alpha), f^2(x^0;\alpha)...\}$$

If the map f is invertible we can write $x_t = f^{-1}(x_{t+1})$ and, iterating backwards from the starting point, we construct the *negative orbit*

$$\gamma^-(x^0;\alpha) = \{x_t = X \mid x_t = f^t(x^0; \alpha), t = 0, -1,-2,...\}$$
$$= \{x^0, f^{-1}(x^0; \alpha), f^{-2}(x^0; \alpha)...\}$$

Finally, we can define the orbit of (1.11) through x^0 as the union of the sets γ^+ and γ^-:

$$\gamma(x^0; \alpha) = \gamma^+(x^0; \alpha) \cup \gamma^-(x^0; \alpha) = \{x_t \in X \mid x_t = f^t(x^0; \alpha), t = 0, \pm1, \pm2,...\}$$

provided that $\gamma^-(x^0)$ is well defined.

Most economic questions of interest can be put in terms of properties of solution sequences, flows, or orbits. Given an autonomous system $x_{t+1} = f(x_t; \alpha)$, we would like to determine first how the system behaves over time for a given value of α. We have noted that a complete answer to this question does not exist in general. For low-dimensional systems, however, the qualitative properties of the system's motion can be compactly summarized by a phase diagram, a convenient device that builds on the graphical interpretation of the concept of a vector field developed above. The construction of phase diagrams will be discussed in chapters 2 and 4 for linear systems and chapter 6 for nonlinear systems.

Of particular relevance to economists is the *asymptotic or long-run behavior* of solutions. We will see that in many cases at least some solution sequences $\{x_t\}$ of a given system approach very simple configurations as $t \to \infty$. The last section of this chapter describes the simplest of those configurations (steady states and periodic equilibria), and introduces the notion of stability. A detailed discussion of some useful results about stability for nonlinear systems appears in chapters 6 and 8.

Finally, we frequently need to know how the behavior of a given system responds to changes in the value of certain parameters that may describe existing policies or basic features of the technology and preferences that underlie the time map f. The *comparative dynamics* of certain simple policy changes are discussed at different points in the text, using both graphical and analytical techniques. The most general treatment of this problem appears in chapter 8, where we find that, in most cases, small changes in parameter values do not change the qualitative behavior of a dynamical system. On the other hand, chapter 8 shows that there are parameter values, called *bifurcation points*, near which very small changes in the "environment" as summarized by α have a drastic effect on the qualitative properties of the system. We defer until later a detailed discussion of these subjects, and finish this chapter by introducing certain concepts that will figure prominently in the remainder of Part I.

1.4 Steady states, periodic equilibria, and stability

Consider an autonomous system

$$x_{t+1} = f(x_t) \tag{1.14}$$

where f is a continuous function, and let $\{x_t\}$ be a solution sequence for it. If $\{x_t\}$ approaches a constant limit x^* as $t \to \infty$, it follows from the continuity of f that x^* itself must be a solution of (1.14), that is,

$$x^* = \lim_{t \to \infty} x_{t+1} = \lim_{t \to \infty} f(x_t) = f(\lim_{t \to \infty} x_t) = f(x^*)$$

Hence, constant solutions play a special role in the analysis of the dynamic behavior of autonomous systems. They deserve a special name.

Definition 1.2 (Steady state of fixed point) A point $\bar{x} \in X$ is a steady state of the system $x_{t+1} = f(x_t)$ if it is a fixed point of the map f, that is, if $\bar{x} = f(\bar{x})$.

Stationary states or fixed points of nonlinear autonomous dynamical systems are values of the state variables that will be preserved in perpetuity if they are achieved once. These rest points correspond naturally to the economic notion of long-run equilibria, that is, to asymptotic positions that the economy may reach in response to equilibria, that is, to asymptotic positions that the economy may reach in response to the sum of all the external forces acting on it. Note that, without further restrictions on f, there is no guarantee that long-run equilibria will be "attracting" or stable in any sense. We will derive conditions for stability in later chapters, but it will be useful to formalize the notion at this early stage.

There are two useful definitions of stability for a fixed point $\bar{x}$ of a dynamical system, the second one being stronger than the first. In particular, a stationary state $\bar{x}$ of a dynamical system $x_{t+1} = f(x_t)$ is called *stable* (or Liapunov stable) if all orbits that get near it stay close to it; and it is *asymptotically stable* if all nearby orbits tend to $\bar{x}$ asymptotically. The state $\bar{x}$ is unstable if it is not stable. Formal definitions follow together with illustrative pictures.

Definition 1.3 (Stability) The state $\bar{x}$ is a stable fixed point of the map f if for any $\epsilon > 0$ there exists some $\delta \in (0, \epsilon)$ such that

$$\| x_s - \bar{x} \| < \delta \Rightarrow \| x_t - \bar{x} \| < \epsilon$$

for all integers $t \geqslant s$.

The meaning of this definition is shown in figure 1.3(a). Consider a ball of radius δ around $\bar{x}$; $\bar{x}$ is stable if any orbit $\{x_t\}$ entering the δ-ball at some time s remains forever within a ball of (possibly larger) radius ϵ_x centered on $\bar{x}$.

Definition 1.4 (Asymptotic stability) The state $\bar{x}$ is asymptotically stable if it is stable and the constant δ in the last definition can be chosen so that, if $\|x_s - \bar{x}\| < \delta$ for any s, then $\|x_t - \bar{x}\| \to 0$ as $t \to \infty$.

In other words, trajectories that at some point reach the neighborhood of $\bar{x}$ not only stay close but asymptotically approach the steady state, as illustrated in figure 1.3(b). The largest neighborhood from which any entering orbit converges asymptotically to the steady state is called the *basin of attraction* or region of asymptotic stability of $\bar{x}$. If this region is the entire state space x, so that all feasible trajectories converge to $\bar{x}$, we say that the steady state is *globally asymptotically stable*.

Not all stable orbits are asymptotically stable; periodic trajectories, like those of the planets about the sun, are a good example of this distinction, shown in figure 1.3(d).

Periodic orbits are the simplest type of solutions of autonomous systems other than steady states. These trajectories will be discussed in more detail later, but it is worth noting now the close similarity between stationary and periodic solutions. If we take the pth iterate of the map f, we have

$$x_{t+p} = f^p(x_t) \tag{1.15}$$

which is completely analogous to (1.14) except for the length of the period. It can be shown that, if a constant solution to this equation exists, then p such solutions exist, each of which is an element of a periodic orbit of equation (1.14). The notions of stability introduced above can be extended to periodic solutions by replacing f by f^p in the appropriate definition.

Periodic orbits have attracted considerable interest in recent years because they can be interpreted as stylized business cycles. Hence, nonlinear models that display such solutions can provide an alternative to the more standard linear stochastic models in which economic fluctuations arise strictly as a result of exogenous random shocks in tastes or technology. Some results concerning the existence of periodic solutions are

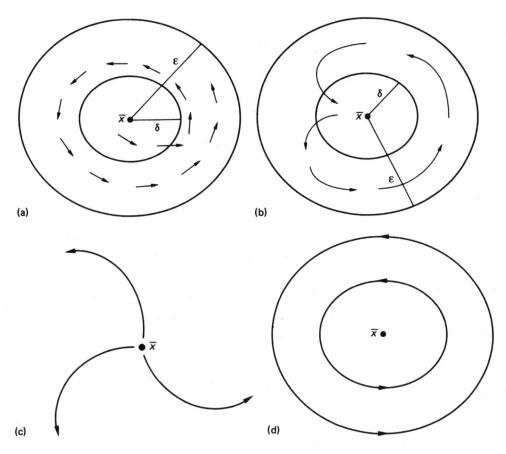

(a)

(b)

(c)

(d)

Figure 1.3 (a) $\bar{x}$ is stable; (b) $\bar{x}$ is asymptotically stable; (c) $\bar{x}$ is unstable; (d) $\bar{x}$ is stable but not asymptotically stable.

discussed in chapter 8, while 9 contains an introduction to the theory of endogenous fluctuations in economic models.

Notes

1 Called "one sector" because the consumption good and the capital good can be transformed into one another at a fixed ratio, typically equal to one, much like corn into seed. Multisector models, on the other hand, do not permit this immediate transformation.
2 Called "optimal" because it corresponds to the pattern of economic growth set by a benevolent, omnipotent and omniscient central planner.
3 This observation is the discrete equivalent of the existence and uniqueness theorem for differential equations; see the Technical Appendices.

2 Scalar linear equations

A first-order linear difference equation has the general form $x_t = a_{t-1}x_{t-1} + b_{t-1}$ where a and b are given sequences and x is an unknown function to be determined. We will typically assume that the coefficient a is a constant, but we will allow the forcing term b to change over time. Hence, the most general equation form with which we will be concerned in this section is

$$x_t = ax_{t-1} + b_{t-1} \tag{2.1}$$

It is easy to show that the general solution to a linear difference equation can be written as

$$x_t^g = x_t^c + x_t^p \tag{2.2}$$

where the *complementary function* x_t^c is the general solution to the corresponding homogeneous equation $x_t = ax_{t-1}$ obtained from (2.1) by setting $b_t = 0$ for all t; and x_t^p is any *particular solution* to the full non-homogeneous equation.

This result, sometimes known as the superposition principle (for a proof see the Technical Appendices, section A.2), will be very useful because it permits us to reduce the problem of solving equation (2.1) into two simpler problems. We will first study the homogeneous equation and develop its general solution. With the complementary function in hand, all we need is a particular solution. We will look, in particular, for simple solutions that may be interpreted as economic equilibria.

2.1 The homogeneous equation

Consider the homogeneous first-order linear equation

$$x_t = ax_{t-1} \tag{2.3}$$

where x_t is the value of some economic variable x at time t, x_{t-1} is the value of the same variable at time $t-1$, and a is a real number. While this simple dynamical system describes few cases of economic interest, studying it will shed some light on the behavior of more complicated difference equations and will help us interpret their solutions.

We will first investigate the dynamic behavior of the system described by (2.3) with the aid of a simple graphical method, and then find the complementary function iteratively.

A graphical approach

Let us trace the evolution of x_t over time, starting from some initial value x_0, with a geometric device called a *phase diagram*. We graph x_t as a function of x_{t-1} and use the diagonal (defined by the equation $x_t = x_{t-1}$) to project x_t to the x_{t-1} axis as time passes.

Suppose that the variable x has some given value x_0 at time $t = 0$. From equation (2.3) we can find the value of x for the next period, that is, $x_1 = ax_0$. To do this, we simply read x_1 off the graph of equation (2.3) in figure 2.1. At $t = 2$, then, x_1 becomes the starting value x_{t-1}; to project x_1 onto the x_{t-1} axis, we use the diagonal, and continue exactly as above. This is illustrated graphically in figures 2.1(a)–2.1(d) for four different cases, depending on the value of a.

Case 1: $a \in (0,1)$. The system converges smoothly to the origin, which is the only "steady state" of the equation; once x becomes zero, it remains zero forever. Suppose, for instance, that $a = 0.5$ and $x_0 = 16$. Then $x_1 = (0.5)(16) = 8$, $x_2 = 4$, $x_3 = 2$, $x_4 = 1$, etc. As $t \to \infty$, x_t clearly converges to zero.

The two panels of figure 2.1(a) plot the phase diagram and the time path of x_t, given an initial value of x_0.

Case 2: $a \in (-1,0)$. The system converges again to zero, but now positive and negative values of x_t alternate in a pattern of damped oscillations. See figure 2.1(b) for the phase diagram and time path.

Case 3: $a \in (1,\infty)$. Here the system "explodes." If $x_0 > 0$, then $x_t \to \infty$ as $t \to \infty$; if $x_0 < 0$, then $x_t \to -\infty$ as $t \to \infty$. See figure 2.1(c).

Case 4: $a \in (-\infty,-1)$. In this case, all solutions to equation (2.3) are explosive oscillations, as shown in figure 2.1(d).

To sum up: the dynamics of this system depend crucially on the size and the sign of the coefficient a. Table 2.1 describes the four main cases.

An exact solution

Equation (2.3) may also be solved by iteration, that is, by noting that $x_t = ax_{t-1}$, $x_{t-1} = ax_{t-2}$, and so on, which implies $x_t = a^2 x_{t-2} = a^2(ax_{t-3}) = a^3 x_{t-3}...$, and eventually

$$x_t = a^t x_0 \qquad (2.4)$$

Without an initial condition that fixes x at $t = 0$, we cannot think of x_0 as a known number. Equation (2.4) says instead that solutions to the homogeneous equation (2.1) must be of a certain form. It is easy to check that, for any arbitrary constant x_0, the function in (2.4) solves the homogeneous equation, because, for any such function, we may write

$$x_t = x_0 a^t = ax_0 a^{t-1} = ax_{t-1}$$

and immediately satisfy equation (2.3). In other words, equation (2.4) contains the

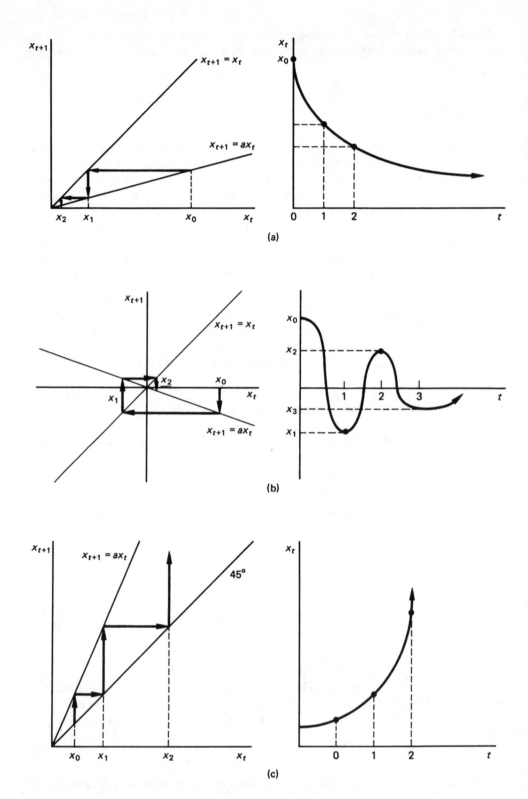

Figure 2.1 Solving autonomous equations.

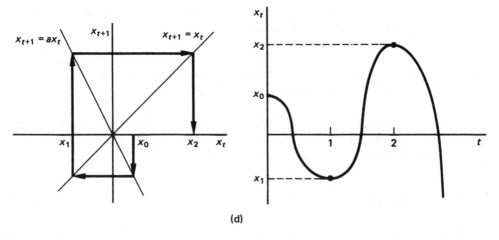

(d)

Figure 2.1 cont'd

Table 2.1 Qualitative behaviour in the scalar linear case

Stable solution	Explosive solution	
Monotone convergence to the origin $(0 < a < 1)$	Monotone divergence from the origin $(a > 1)$	Monotone
Damped oscillations converging to the origin $(-1 < a < 0)$	Explosive oscillations $(a < -1)$	Cyclical

entire family of functions that obey (2.3) and therefore must be the general solution to the homogeneous equation.

The dynamic properties of the system, displayed previously by graphical methods, follow directly from the general solution. Inspection of (2.4) reveals that

1 x_t changes monotonically if $a > 0$, and oscillates if $a < 0$ as t changes from odd to even values;
2 if $|a| > 1$, the absolute value of x_t increases without bound and the dynamical system explodes. If $|a| < 1$, on the other hand, x_t becomes smaller and smaller in absolute value, approaching the zero steady state as $t \to \infty$.

The general solution

$$x_t = ca^t \tag{2.4}'$$

describes a one-parameter family of functions, indexed on the arbitrary constant c, all of which satisfy the homogeneous equation (2.1). In most cases we will be interested in a single member of this family, that is, a particular solution that satisfies a boundary condition of the type $x_t = x_s$ at $t = s$. This means that x will take some specific value x_s at some specific point s in time.

Boundary conditions allow us to determine the appropriate value of the arbitrary constant c in the general solution. Since (2.4)' must hold at all times, it must also hold at $t = s$. Hence $x_s = ca^s$ and, solving for c, we obtain $c = x_s a^{-s}$. Substituting this into (2.4)', we obtain the particular solution

$$x_t = x_s a^{t-s} \tag{2.5}$$

which identifies that orbit of x that solves (2.3) and goes through x_s at $t = s$.

We summarize the results of this section in the following theorem.

Theorem 2.1 The general solution to the homogeneous first-order linear equation $x_t = ax_{t-1}$ is of the form $x_t = ca^t$. The particular solution corresponding to the boundary-value problem ($x_t = ax_{t-1}$ and $x_t = x_s$ at $t = s$) is of the form $x_t = x_s a^{t-s}$.

2.2 Autonomous equations

What happens to the homogeneous equation if we introduce a forcing term but require it to be constant over time? This yields the first-order autonomous equation

$$x_t = ax_{t-1} + b \tag{2.6}$$

By the superposition principle, we may write the general solution to (2.6) in the form $x_t^g = x_t^c + x_t^p$, where the complementary function x_t^c is the general solution of the homogeneous equation and x_t^p is any particular solution of the full non-homogeneous equation. In the last section we learned that the solution to the homogeneous equation is $x_t^c = ca^t$ and so the general solution of (2.6) must be

$$x_t^g = ca^t + x_t^p \tag{2.7}$$

A natural candidate for the role of the particular solution is a constant solution $x_t = \bar{x}$ for all t. This is known as a *steady state* or *stationary solution*. To solve for the steady state $\bar{x}$ we use (2.6) to obtain $\bar{x} = a\bar{x} + b$ which implies $\bar{x} = b/(1 - a)$ if $a \neq 1$. Thus a stationary solution will exist provided that $a \neq 1$, and the general solution to the autonomous equation (2.6) becomes

$$x_t^g = \bar{x} + ca^t \tag{2.8}$$

An alternative way to obtain (2.8) is to reduce the autonomous equation to a homogeneous equation by looking at deviations of x_t from the steady state. Starting with (2.6), we subtract $\bar{x} = b/(1-a)$ from both sides and, after some algebra, get

$$x_t - \bar{x} = a(x_{t-1} - \bar{x}) \tag{2.6}'$$

If we think of $x_t - \bar{x}$ as a single variable, we have a homogeneous equation whose solution

$$x_t - \bar{x} = ca^t$$

is equivalent to (2.8).

Proceeding exactly as in the previous section, we find that the boundary-value problem consisting of equation (2.6) plus the boundary condition $x_t = x_s$ at $t = s$ has the following particular solution:

$$x_t = \bar{x} + (x_s - \bar{x})a^{t-s} \tag{2.9}$$

The stability of the system depends crucially on the value of the coefficient a in the general solution (2.8). In particular:

1. if $|a| < 1$, the term ca^t vanishes as t gets larger and the system converges asymptotically to the steady state $\bar{x}$ for any value of c;
2. if $|a| > 1$, then $ca^t \to \infty$ as $t \to \infty$ and the system explodes unless $c = 0$;
3. the sign of a determines whether x_t oscillates around $\bar{x}$ ($a < 0$) or remains forever on the same side of the steady state ($a > 0$).

To understand how the system behaves outside the steady state, we write the general solution (2.8) for $t = 0$, observe that $x_0 = \bar{x} + c$, solve for $c = x_0 - \bar{x}$, and substitute back into (2.8) to obtain

$$x_t - \bar{x} = (x_0 - \bar{x})a^t \qquad (2.8)'$$

Equation (2.8)' says that the deviation of x_t from the steady state value $\bar{x}$ depends on the value of a, the time elapsed, and the deviation of x_t from $\bar{x}$ when the system was originally set in motion at $t = 0$. If x_t starts at its stationary equilibrium value ($x_0 = \bar{x}$), the deviation term is zero and x remains at its steady state forever.

For any $x_0 \neq \bar{x}$ the system starts from its sustainable equilibrium position. What happens then depends on the value of a. The term $(x_0 - \bar{x})a^t$ approaches zero as $t \to \infty$ if $|a| < 1$, and the system tends to return to its equilibrium value; if $|a| > 1$, however, we have $|(x_0 - \bar{x})a^t| \to \infty$ as $t \to \infty$, and the system explodes away from $\bar{x}$. No steady state exists in the special case $a = 1$ for which direct iteration yields the solution

$$x_t = x_0 \pm ct \qquad (2.10)$$

We sum up this section's findings in the following theorem.

Theorem 2.2 For any $a \neq 1$, the first-order autonomous linear equation $x_t = ax_{t-1} + b$ has a unique steady state $\bar{x} = b/(1 - a)$ and a general solution of the form $x_t^g = \bar{x} + ca^t$, where c is an arbitrary constant fixed by a boundary condition. Solutions are stable and converge asymptotically to $\bar{x}$ if $|a| < 1$, and are unstable if $|a| > 1$.

2.3   Non-autonomous equations

We return to the first-order difference equation

$$x_t = ax_{t-1} + b_t \qquad (2.11)$$

in which b_t represents an exogenous sequence of forcing variables, but these are not necessarily constant as in the previous section. The introduction of a time-dependent forcing term is necessary in many cases when we want to describe the behavior of an economic system over time. For example, x_t could conceivably represent the price level and b_t the money supply. While we may take the value of the money supply to be exogenous, it is seldom constant over time.

In Technical Appendices, section A.1, it is shown why the superposition principle holds for equation (2.11). We may then write out the general solution to (2.11) as the sum of the general solution $x_t = ca^t$ to the homogeneous equation and a particular solution to (2.11) itself, that is,

$$x_t^g = ca^t + x_t^p \qquad (2.12)$$

where c is an arbitrary constant and x_t^p is any solution to (2.11).

Choosing different particular solutions for x_t^P leads to different but equivalent ways of writing the general solution; regardless of which one we pick we can still obtain any solution to (2.11) by using the appropriate value for c. Some choices for x_t^P may, of course, be more convenient than others in certain cases. To be more specific, let us look at two particular solutions often referred to as the "forward-looking" and "backward-looking" solutions.

The forward-looking solution

The forward-looking solution refers to an initial-value problem consisting of equation (2.11) together with an appropriate initial condition. To derive it, we iterate equation (2.11) *backward* for n periods by recursive substitution (which explains why some economists call this the "backward" solution):

$$
\begin{aligned}
x_t &= ax_{t-1} + b_t \\
&= a(ax_{t-2} + b_{t-1}) + b_t \\
&= a^2 x_{t-2} + ab_{t-1} + b_t \\
&= a^2(ax_{t-3} + b_{t-2}) + ab_{t-1} + b_t \\
&= a^3 x_{t-3} + a^2 b_{t-2} + ab_{t-1} + b_t \\
&\;\;\vdots \\
&= a^n x_{t-n} + (a^{n-1} b_{t-n+1} + a^{n-2} b_{t-n+2} + \dots + ab_{t-1} + b_t)
\end{aligned}
$$

Equivalently, we have

$$
x_t = a^n x_{t-n} + \sum_{i=0}^{n-1} a^i b_{t-i} \tag{2.13}
$$

If the system was set in motion at time zero, we may have a natural initial condition of the form "x_0 is a known constant." For $n = t$, then, equation (2.13) reduces to

$$
x_t = a^t x_0 + \sum_{i=0}^{t-1} a^i b_{t-i} \tag{2.13$'$}
$$

which tells us that the state of the system at time t is a function of its initial state x_0 and of all the shocks $\{b_s\}$ received between time zero and the present. In some cases, there may be no natural starting point; then we may let $n \to \infty$ to express the state of the system at time t as a function of its whole past history:

$$
x_t = \sum_{i=0}^{\infty} a^i b_{t-i} + \lim_{n \to \infty} (a^n x_{t-n}) \tag{2.13$''$}
$$

Note, however, that this expression may not be well defined unless both the infinite sum and the limit exist. To ensure this we need to assume $|a| < 1$ and $|b_t| < B$ for all t and some finite B, that is, that the sequence of forcing terms is bounded. In this case the infinite sum in (2.13)″ will converge to a finite value. Also, if the sequence of "shocks" $\{b_t\}$ is bounded, it seems reasonable to require that the corresponding $\{x_t\}$ sequence be bounded as well; boundedness makes compelling economic sense for such economic variables as capital per worker, real national debt, income, etc. For any $|a| < 1$, this means that $a^n x_{t-n} \to 0$ as $n \to \infty$, and the limit term vanishes from (2.13)″. Then the forward-looking solution is well defined, and the general solution to equation (2.11) becomes

$$x_t^g = ca^t + \sum_{i=0}^{\infty} a^i b_{t-i} \qquad (2.14)$$

In sum, if the sequence of exogenous variables $\{b_t\}$ is bounded and $|a| < 1$, there is a bounded solution to (2.11) given by equation (2.14).

The backward-looking solution

Another particular solution results from iterating equation (2.11) forward rather than backward, that is, by treating it as a terminal-value problem. Proceeding exactly as before, we obtain after n recursive substitutions

$$x_t = \left(\frac{1}{a}\right)^n x_{t+n} - \frac{1}{a} \sum_{j=0}^{n-1} \left(\frac{1}{a}\right)^j b_{t+1+j} \qquad (2.15)$$

Equation (2.15) gives us an expression for the state of the system at time t as a function of its future state at time $t + n$ and all the future shocks between now and then. If we know where the system is headed n periods from now, that is, the value of x_{t+n} for some particular n, we can use (2.15) directly to describe the time path of x between t and $t + n$. In many cases, however, there is no natural endpoint for the system. Letting $n \to \infty$, we derive an expression for the state of the system at time t as a function of all future shocks:[1]

$$x_t = \lim_{n \to \infty} \left(\frac{1}{a}\right)^n x_{t+n} - \frac{1}{a} \sum_{j=0}^{\infty} \left(\frac{1}{a}\right)^j b_{t+1+j} \qquad (2.15)'$$

Like the corresponding forward-looking expression, equation (2.15)′ is not always well defined. In particular, we should expect trouble if $|a| < 1$; terms of the form $(1/a)^j$ then go to infinity as $j \to \infty$. If b is constant for all t, for example, the infinite sum will diverge. On the other hand, if $|a| > 1$, the boundedness assumptions we used in the forward-looking case will give us a well-defined solution. Specifically, if the sequence of exogenous variables $\{b_t\}$ is bounded, then $\lim_{n \to \infty} (a^{-n} x_{t+n}) = 0$, and equation (2.11) has the general solution

$$x_t^g = ca^t - \frac{1}{a} \sum_{j=0}^{\infty} \left(\frac{1}{a}\right)^j b_{t+1+j} \qquad (2.14f)$$

To sum up: the forward- and backward-looking solutions we have just derived are simply two particular solutions to the difference equation (2.11). We know that adding a term of the form ca^t, where c is an arbitrary constant, to any particular solution gives us another solution and also that by assigning different values to c we can obtain *all* possible solutions to (2.11). Therefore, we may write the general solution to the non-autonomous linear equation in two equivalent forms:

$$x_t^g = c_F a^t + x_t^F \qquad \text{where } x_t^F = \sum_{i=0}^{\infty} a^i b_{t-i} \qquad (2.14f)$$

$$x_t^g = c_B a^t + x_t^B \qquad \text{where } x_t^B = -\frac{1}{a}\sum_{j=0}^{\infty}(1/a)^j b_{t+1+j} \qquad (2.14b)$$

We will refer to (2.14f) as the forward-looking form of the general solution, and to (2.14b) as the backward-looking form of the general solution.

Stability

An autonomous system was previously called "stable" if any trajectory tended to approach the steady state as $t \to \infty$. We generalize this to non-autonomous equations by calling a system *asymptotically stable* if all its trajectories approach whichever particular solution, x_t^F or x_t^B, happens to be well defined for the system at hand as $t \to \infty$. As before, convergence depends on the value of the parameter a. In particular we have the following.

1. The forward solution is stable if $|a| < 1$: x_t converges to a "generalized steady state" x_t^F as $t \to \infty$ for any value of the arbitrary constant c_F, that is, for any boundary conditions. Deviations from x_t^F tend to disappear over time. An identical argument can be made about the convergence of the backward solution to x_t^B as $t \to \infty$ whenever $|a| > 1$.
2. If $|a| > 1$, then the forward solution is unstable. The absolute value of x "explodes" to $+\infty$ at $t \to \infty$ unless we impose the condition $c_F = 0$. Alternatively, any initial deviation from x_t^F, however small, will grow without bound over time. "Explosive" behavior can only be ruled out by assuming that the system starts on the equilibrium path, that is, $c_F = 0$. A similar argument applies to the backward solution if $|a| < 1$.

The analysis, then, is broadly analogous to the one in the last section – except that our point of reference is no longer a stationary solution or steady state, but the "moving" equilibrium of the backward- or forward-looking solution. As in section 2.1, there are four main patterns for the asymptotic behavior of solutions to equation (2.11), illustrated in figures 2.2(a)–2.2(d). These are drawn under the assumption that the sequence of exogenous terms approaches asymptotically a finite limit b. As a result, the forward-looking solution converges to $\bar{x} = b/(1-a)$ if $|a| < 1$; the backward-looking solution converges to $\bar{x}$ if $|a| > 1$.

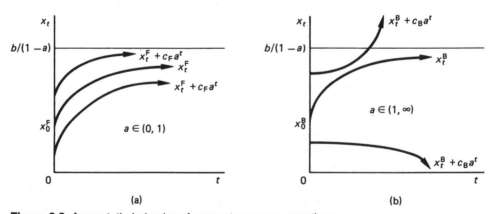

Figure 2.2 Asymptotic behavior of non-autonomous equations.

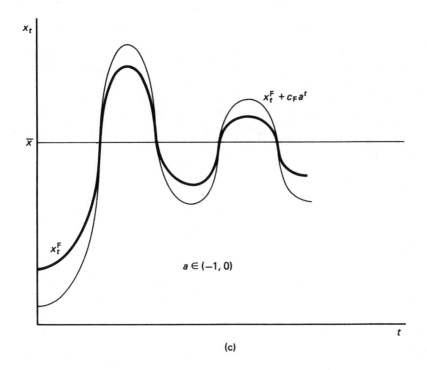

(c)

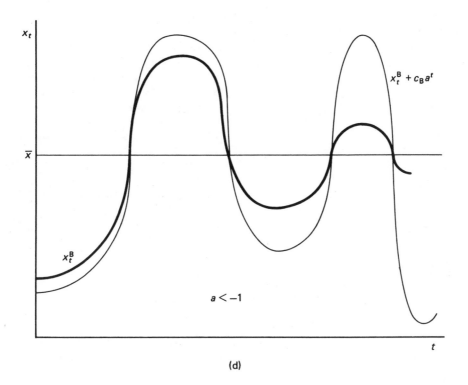

(d)

Figure 2.2 cont'd

Note

1 This solution makes less sense than the forward-looking solution in which the current state of the system is related to its past history. There are some economic systems, however, that we can naturally model as backward looking; an example is asset prices that reflect the present value of an infinite stream of (expected) future dividends. It is worth repeating that the term "backward solution" is occasionally used in macroeconomics to denote a forward-looking solution and, correspondingly, one finds the term "forward solution" to mean backward-looking equilibria.

3 Stockmarket bubbles

In this chapter we apply the results of the previous chapter to the study of stockmarket dynamics. Movements in share prices are one economic phenomenon for which a scalar linear dynamical system provides a tolerable approximation. The extended example below will explore the role of anticipations and other factors that cause fluctuations in stock prices, and serve as a training ground for non-autonomous linear difference equations.

3.1 Price dynamics with adaptive expectations

Suppose now that investors have available to them two, and only two, financial assets: a riskless bank deposit yielding a constant interest rate r in perpetuity; and a common share, that is, an equity claim on some firm, which pays out a known stream of dividends per share, $\{d_s\}_{s=t}^{\infty}$, where $s = t$ is the present period. Let p_s be the actual market price of a common share at the beginning of period s, before the dividend $d_s > 0$ is paid out; suppose also the future share prices are unknown but that all investors have the common belief at $t = s$ that the price is going to be p_{s+1}^e at the beginning of the following period.

Our example consists of two simple relations: an *arbitrage condition* that relates the rate of return on shares to the interest rate on bank deposits; and an *adaptive expectations mechanism* that describes how share-price expectations are revised over time in response to observed share prices. The arbitrage condition

$$(1 + r)p_t = d_t + p_{t+1}^e \tag{3.1}$$

says that, if a monetary sum of p_t dollars were invested in the stockmarket at time t, it should yield at $t + 1$ an amount whose expected value $d_t + p_{t+1}^e$ equals the principal plus interest on an equal sum invested in bank deposits. If, on the contrary, equation (3.1) did not hold, then one of the two assets would be expected by all savers to yield less than the other and hence would be avoided by all rational investors. Financial markets in which both equity and bank deposits are traded actively[1] ought to satisfy an arbitrage condition like equation (3.1).

Expectations of future share prices are assumed to conform to the adaptive expectations hypothesis

$$p^e_{t+1} = \lambda p_t + (1-\lambda)p^e_t \tag{3.2}$$

which amounts to fractional "error learning." This hypothesis simply asserts that, if a prediction error should occur at time t, then expectations for $t+1$ are revised in the direction of the error $p_t - p^e_t$ by only a fixed fraction $\lambda \in [0,1]$ of that error. The parameter λ describes the speed of learning, that is, the relative weight put on the latest price observation and, also, the rate at which older information depreciates. In particular, $\lambda = 1$ describes a prediction scheme that places all the weight on the last observation and none on earlier price history, while $\lambda = 0$ completely disregards the latest available information.

Using equation (3.1) to eliminate expected prices from (3.2), we obtain a non-autonomous linear equation:

$$p_{t+1} = ap_t + b_t \tag{3.3}$$

in which we have defined

$$R = 1 + r \qquad a = \frac{R(1-\lambda)}{R - \lambda} \tag{3.4}$$

$$b_{t-1} = \frac{d_t - (1 - \lambda)d_{t-1}}{R - \lambda}$$

The parameter a clearly lies in the interval $(0,1)$ whenever $r > 0$ and $\lambda \in (0,1)$. Proceeding as in the previous section, we take $t = 0$ as our natural starting point and write the solution to (3.3) in the particular form

$$p_t = a^t p_0 + \sum_{i=0}^{t-1} a^i b_{t-1-i} \tag{3.5}$$

In this equation we have solved backward to $t = 0$ to obtain the particular solution

$$\frac{1}{R - \lambda} \sum_{i=0}^{t-i} a^i d_{t-i} - \frac{1-\lambda}{R-\lambda} \sum_{i=0}^{t-1} a^i d_{t-1-i} \tag{3.6}$$

which appears on the right-hand side of equation (3.5). Equation (3.5) now becomes

$$p_t = a^t p_0 + p^*_t \tag{3.5'}$$

We already know that the right-hand side of equation (3.5)' converges to a finite sum, say p^*_t, if we make the economically sensible assumption that dividends are bounded. Therefore, our share price obeys asymptotically the familiar relation

$$p_t = p^* + ca^t \tag{3.4'}$$

in which the parameter c is fixed by an appropriate boundary value, say $p_t = p_0$ at $t = 0$. Equation (3.5)' is then the particular solution of (3.3) that conforms to this boundary condition.

As we might have expected, solutions to equation (3.3) are the sum of a complementary function ca^t that vanishes asymptotically because $a < 1$ and a particular solution p^*_t that converges to a well-defined value p^*. In the terminology of financial markets, the shrinking term is called a *bubble*; the persisting term is called the *fundamental value* because it closely approximates share prices in the long run. To understand this terminology, suppose that dividends are constant in perpetuity, that is, $d_t = d > 0$ for all t. Recalling that $\sum_{j=0}^{t-1} a^j = (1 - a^t)/(1 - a)$ we conclude after a little algebra that

$$p_t^* = \frac{(1-a^t)d}{r} \tag{3.7a}$$

The asymptotic value of this term

$$p^* = \frac{d}{r} \tag{3.7b}$$

simply equals the discounted value of the infinite dividend stream.

The boundary-value problem that consists of equation (3.3) together with the initial condition p_0 has the unique solution

$$p_t - p^* = a^t (p_0 - p^*) \tag{3.8}$$

which converges to p^* at a speed $a = R(1-\lambda)/(R-\lambda)$ that depends on the rate of interest and the rate at which the forecasting scheme depreciates historical share prices. High rates of information depreciation imply fast learning and rapid convergence to fundamentals. Suppose, for instance, that share prices begin above their fundamental value ($p_0 > p^*$) and adjust downward over time, as equation (3.8) dictates. If in the course of the adjustment process investors come to agree that recent price observations deserve greater weight in future forecasts (and past observations should be given correspondingly less weight), then the speed of convergence in equation (3.8) will go up, causing *an immediate drop* in share prices. The bubble term, $a^t(p_0 - p^*)$, then will shrink at a rapid pace which financial analysts and commentators will call a "burst" or even a "crash."

What happens if dividends change over time? Suppose, for example, that the dividend policy of firms follows the linear rule

$$d_t = \rho d_{t-1} + e \tag{3.9}$$

described by two positive parameters ρ and e, with $\rho < 1$. This rule says that dividends revert toward a particular stationary value d^*, increasing over time if $d_t < d^*$, and falling whenever $d_t > d^*$. Question I.33 asks you to define d^*, investigate the conditions under which stock prices converge to their fundamental value, and list the factors or parameters that affect the speed of convergence to fundamentals.

3.2   Price dynamics with perfect foresight

In the previous section we studied the behavior of stock prices under adaptive expectations. We now rework the model under the assumption that agents are able to forecast asset prices correctly. This assumption, often called *perfect foresight*, is a simple non-stochastic version of the rational expectations hypothesis that has revolutionized macroeconomic theory in the last two decades or so; see Part IV for additional material on rational expectations. We will use the simple stock price model as a vehicle to explore the logic behind the rational expectations hypothesis and as an introduction to the dynamics of perfect foresight models.

The first step is to understand why adaptive expectations may not be a good assumption. Let us go back to the model of section 3.1 and assume for simplicity that both the dividend and the interest factor R remain constant over time. We then have

$$Rp_t = d + p_{t+1}^e \tag{3.10}$$

$$p_{t+1}^e = \lambda p_t + (1-\lambda)p_t^e \tag{3.11}$$

Using (3.10) to eliminate *expected* prices from (3.11) we obtain

$$p_{t+1} = \frac{(1-\lambda)R}{R-\lambda}p_t + \frac{\lambda d}{R-\lambda} \tag{3.12}$$

This equation has a unique steady state

$$p^* = \frac{d}{r}$$

and, for a given initial value p_0, it is uniquely solved by

$$p_t = p^* + (p_0 - p^*)\left[\frac{(1-\lambda)R}{R-\lambda}\right]^t \tag{3.13}$$

Using equation (3.10) again, this time to eliminate *actual* prices from (3.11), we have

$$p_{t+1}^e = \frac{(1-\lambda)R}{R-\lambda}p_t^e + \frac{\lambda d}{R-\lambda} \tag{3.14}$$

which has exactly the same form and hence the same steady state as equation (3.13). For a given initial value p_0^e, in particular,

$$p_t^e = p^* + p_0^e\left[\frac{(1-\lambda)\,R}{R-\lambda}\right]^t \tag{3.15}$$

Combining (3.13) and (3.15), we may now calculate the difference between prices and price forecasts:

$$p_t - p_t^e = (p_0 - p_0^e)\left[\frac{(1-\lambda)R}{R-\lambda}\right]^t \tag{3.16}$$

The initial forecasting error, says equation (3.16), is gradually eliminated over time for any $\lambda > 0$ and $r > 0$. Both actual and expected prices approach the fundamental solution p^*, which represents the present value of the dividend stream.

Equation (3.16) has the troubling implication that agents make a predictable forecast error every period: they either overpredict the price each period or else they underpredict each period. This is difficult to reconcile with the assumption that agents are rational maximizers of utility or wealth. In the context of a model as simple as this, with no uncertainty or information problems, the simplest way to model the idea that agents are rational is to suppose that they know the model and all the relevant facts, such as the time path of dividends. But then they can compute the solution just as well as we can; there is no point in eliminating errors gradually if we can do it immediately and earn a nice profit doing it.

In short, given a world without uncertainty, adaptive expectations are inconsistent with the assumption of rationality. The theory works only as long as agents do not understand its full meaning!

One way out of this problem is to give up the assumption of certainty. Here we choose instead to use a forecasting rule that is compatible with the assumption that agents know the structure of the economy. We assume that individuals exploit the model and all the relevant information they have in order to forecast future prices. Since there is nothing stochastic here, the equilibrium path of prices will be correctly anticipated. We therefore replace (3.11) with the assumption of perfect foresight:

$$p^e_{t+1} = p_{t+1} \qquad \text{for all } t \tag{3.17}$$

Equation (3.17) looks peculiar at first sight, but remember that we are assuming complete certainty. More complicated versions of the rational expectations hypothesis are explored in Part IV.

Let us see where (3.17) takes us. Substituting it into (3.10) and solving for p_{t+1} we have

$$p_{t+1} = Rp_t - d \tag{3.18}$$

Like equation (3.3), equation (3.18) has a unique steady state given by the fundamental solution $p^* = d/r$. The dynamics implied by the two equations, however, are very different. Note that unlike (3.3), (3.18) has an unstable steady state because $R > 1$. The general solution is given by

$$p_t = p^* + cR^t = p^* + (p_0 - p^*)R^t \tag{3.19}$$

which stresses the fact that choosing a value for the arbitrary constant c is equivalent to picking an initial value for the stock price.

At first sight this does not look very promising. If we take the initial value of p as given, as we did in the last section, (3.19) implies that, unless $p_0 = p^*$, asset prices will explode as the bubble term cR^t goes to either plus or minus infinity as $t \to \infty$. This difficulty, common in models involving asset prices, almost led at one point to the abandonment of the perfect foresight assumption. Researchers such as Sargent and Wallace (1973) and Calvo (1978) were quick to point out that taking the initial asset price as given was probably not a reasonable thing to do. Since asset prices are often free to move and even jump at each point in time, at least half the problem is figuring out how the initial stock price should be set.

The general point is that it is not always economically legitimate to take the initial value of any state variable as a parameter fixed by history. The proper choice of boundary condition will generally require some thought about the economics of the problem. What equation (3.19) says is that the equilibrium of the model must be one of the family of solutions described by (3.19). The economic question is which one, and the answer to it will determine the appropriate boundary condition, that is, the proper choice of p_0.

Suppose we take some arbitrary value of p_0 as given. The instability of the system implies that, if the initial price is wrong, things will only get worse. Why is that so? To get an answer, go back to equation (3.18) and rearrange it to obtain the familiar arbitrage relation

$$\frac{p_{t+1} + d}{p_t} = R \tag{3.20}$$

Now suppose $p_0 > p^*$, that is, the stock price is higher than can be reasonably justified by the underlying dividend. But then, in order for equation (3.20) to hold, it must be that the price is increasing at such a rate that capital gains compensate for a dividend that is low relative to the price. Today's price increase, however, makes tomorrow's price even more unreasonable, and therefore requires an even greater capital gain two periods hence, and so on.

What is not so clear is the mechanism that drives tomorrow's price up in order to justify, *ex post*, today's excessively high share values. In fact, the only way to interpret an explosive path is as a speculative "bubble" in which unreasonable expectations become self-fulfilling. Although things of the sort certainly have happened from time to time, we may wish to rule out such behavior under "normal" circumstances. This leaves us only with the "fundamental" solution in which the stock price accurately reflects the present value of the underlying stream of dividends.

To attain the fundamental solution, we set $c = 0$ to "kill" the bubble term, making the initial stock price endogenous. In equilibrium, the stock price p jumps immediately to p^* and remains there forever, or until the system is disturbed in some way.

It is worth noting how perfect foresight eliminates the inconsistency we noted at the beginning of this section. If you know the structure of an economy in which everybody else uses an adaptive forecasting rule, you have a good incentive to predict prices accurately, rather than adaptively, because you will make a killing in the process. But the same will be true for everybody else, and hence the model cannot be "correct." Under perfect foresight, however, everybody uses the correct model to forecast prices, and nobody has an incentive to deviate. While perfect forecasting will not earn you an above-average rate of return, any alternative forecasting rule will lose money on average.

3.3 Dividend taxes

As an application of the material in section 3.2, we work out what happens to stock prices when taxes on dividends change. Initially, let us suppose that dividends are taxed at some known rate $\tau \in [0,1]$. Then equation (3.18) becomes

$$p_{t+1} = Rp_t - (1 - \tau)d \tag{3.21}$$

and its general solution is given by

$$p_t(\tau) = \bar{p}(\tau) + cR^t = \bar{p}(\tau) + [p_0 - \bar{p}(\tau)]R^t \tag{3.22}$$

where

$$\bar{p}(\tau) = \frac{(1 - \tau)d}{r}$$

We want to study the behavior of the system when the tax rate on dividends is increased from τ_0 to some new value τ_1. This exercise will serve as a check on the reasonableness of the model under the perfect foresight assumption and will provide a simple introduction to the method of comparative dynamics.

First suppose that the tax increase is unannounced and people expect that the new tax rate will be maintained forever. As shown in figure 3.1(a), the change in the tax parameter shifts the phaseline up and yields a new lower steady state at

$$\bar{p}(\tau_1) = \frac{(1 - \tau_1)d}{r} < \frac{(1 - \tau_0)d}{r} = \bar{p}(\tau_0)$$

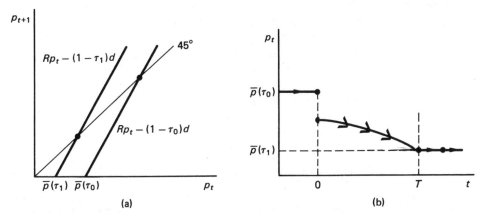

Figure 3.1 Stockmarket dynamics with perfect foresight.

If we rule out explosive paths, the equilibrium value of p immediately following the change is the new fundamental solution $\bar{p}(\tau_1)$. The model predicts, rather reasonably, a one-time capital loss following the policy change as the price drops from $\bar{p}(\tau_0)$ to $\bar{p}(\tau_1)$.

Next suppose that today (at time 0) the government announces, and everyone believes, that the tax rate will be increased to τ_1 at some future date T and will remain at the new level forever thereafter. To work out the equilibrium path of the system following the announcement, we go backward in time. If we rule out bubbles, the system can only be in equilibrium for $t \geq T$ at the new fundamental solution $\bar{p}(\tau_1)$. For $t < T$, the tax rate remains at the initial level τ_0, and so the system must still satisfy the "old" law of motion and the equilibrium path for $0 \leq t \leq T$ must be a member of the family described by

$$p_t(\tau_0) = \bar{p}(\tau_0) + cR^t = \bar{p}(\tau_0) + [p_0 - \bar{p}(\tau_0)]R^t \qquad (3.23)$$

The right solution is the one that will put us at the new equilibrium price $\bar{p}(\tau_1)$ precisely at the time of the change. Formally, the boundary condition we need is

$$p_T(\tau_0) = \bar{p}(\tau_1) \Rightarrow \bar{p}(\tau_0) + [p_0 - \bar{p}(\tau_0)]R^T = \bar{p}(\tau_1)$$

which can be solved to yield today's price

$$p_0 = \bar{p}(\tau_0) - \frac{1}{R^T}[\bar{p}(\tau_0) - \bar{p}(\tau_1)] \qquad (3.24)$$

Hence, prices drop immediately following the announcement and continue to decline until they reach the new fundamental solution precisely at the time of the change. Figure 3.1(b) illustrates the time path of stock prices.

During the transition period $t \in [0,T]$, prices follow what seems to be an explosive path of the "old" system. Question I.35 asks you to use the more general form of the solution and show that "killing" the bubble term there gives exactly the path described by equation (3.24).

Equation (3.24) is exactly what we should expect: if prices remained constant at $\bar{p}(\tau_0)$ until the tax increase actually took place, agents would be anticipating a capital loss of $\bar{p}(\tau_0) - \bar{p}(\tau_1)$ at time T. To avoid such a loss, people would try to sell stocks at

$T - 1$, driving p_{T-1} below $\bar{p}(\tau_0)$. In fact, the adjustment must begin even earlier, since the same logic implies that the equilibrium price cannot be $\bar{p}(\tau_0)$ at $T - 2$ and so on. Thus equilibrium is incompatible with rationally forecast prices that imply a rate of return lower than R at some point in the future. Hence, the whole burden of the adjustment must fall on the current owners of stocks who, caught by surprise, cannot do anything to avoid a capital loss. Note also from equation (3.24) that the unexpected capital loss at time zero is equal to the discounted value of the change in equilibrium stock prices as a result of the tax change.

Note

1 Recall that our arbitrage condition assumes equity to be *riskless*, just like insured bank deposits. That is not empirically true; over the last hundred years, equity returns have averaged 6 percent annually above the yield on safe assets. This rate-of-return differential, called the *equity premium*, is discussed by Mehra and Prescott (1985).

4   Linear systems

Next we study solutions to first-order linear systems with constant coefficients of the general form

$$z_{t+1} = Az_t + f_{t+1} \tag{4.1}$$

where A is an $n \times n$ matrix of time-invariant coefficients and z and f are $n \times 1$ vectors of dated variables. The variable z_t is typically the state vector of the system at time t, often interpreted as the vector of "endogenous" variables; f_t is a vector of (possibly time-dependent) forcing terms often thought of as independent or exogenous. For illustrative purposes, we will frequently work with a 2×2 system of the form

$$x_{t+1} = a_{11}x_t + a_{12}y_t + b_t$$
$$y_{t+1} = a_{21}x_t + a_{22}y_t + d_t$$

or

$$\begin{pmatrix} x_{t+1} \\ y_{t+1} \end{pmatrix} = \begin{pmatrix} a_{11} & a_{12} \\ a_{21} & a_{22} \end{pmatrix} \begin{pmatrix} x_t \\ y_t \end{pmatrix} + \begin{pmatrix} b_t \\ d_t \end{pmatrix} \tag{4.2}$$

The superposition principle holds in this higher-dimensional case as well, which entitles us to write the general solution to any linear system like (4.1) in the familiar form

$$z_t^g = z_t^c + z_t^p$$

as the sum of a complementary function that solves the relevant homogeneous system and any one particular solution to the full system. This result allows us to solve (4.1) in the usual two stages: we start with the homogeneous equation $z_{t+1} = Az_t$, and complete the task by finding a particular solution to the full system. Particular solutions are easy to find when the forcing term is time invariant because a steady state to the autonomous system $z_{t+1} = Az_t$ will exist in most cases.

The mathematical theory of linear difference equation systems is almost identical to that of linear differential equation systems which we briefly review in the Technical Appendices.

4.1 Homogeneous systems

In the homogeneous first-order system with constant coefficients

$$z_{t+1} = Az_t \tag{4.3}$$

A is an $n \times n$ coefficient matrix and z is an n-vector of dated variables. For $n = 2$ we rewrite (4.3) as

$$x_{t+1} = a_{11}x_t + a_{12}y_t$$

$$y_{t+1} = a_{21}x_t + a_{22}y_t$$

or

$$\begin{pmatrix} x_{t+1} \\ y_{t+1} \end{pmatrix} = \begin{pmatrix} a_{11} & a_{12} \\ a_{21} & a_{22} \end{pmatrix} \begin{pmatrix} x_t \\ y_t \end{pmatrix} \tag{4.4}$$

The basic difference between the equations in (4.3) and those we studied in earlier chapters is that now we have several state variables in each equation and hence we must solve simultaneously *all* the equations in the system.

There is a special case, however, in which the system reduces to a set of independent equations that may be solved separately. Note that, if $a_{12} = a_{21} = 0$, then the coefficient matrix is diagonal, and equation (4.2) reduces to two independent homogeneous equations in a single variable

$$x_{t+1} = a_{11}x_t \qquad y_{t+1} = a_{22}y_t$$

with general solutions given by

$$x_t = c_1 a_{11}^t \qquad y_t = c_2 a_{22}^t$$

In most cases the coefficient matrix of the system will not be diagonal, but it is often possible to find a way to diagonalize the coefficient matrix and obtain an "uncoupled" system by a suitable transformation of the original variables. We can then solve the transformed system and recover the solution to the original problem by inverting the diagonalizing transformation. Systems for which this approach works are said to be *diagonalizable*. We derive below the general solution for a diagonalizable system and discuss the complications that arise when some of the eigenvalues of the system are complex numbers.

Diagonalizable systems with distinct eigenvalues

In order to diagonalize the coefficient matrix A of the system (4.1) we need to find an invertible matrix P such that

$$P^{-1}AP = D$$

where D is a diagonal matrix. We know from linear algebra that a sufficient condition for a square matrix to be diagonalizable is that all its eigenvalues be distinct; see the Technical Appendices, section A.1. Moreover, we may use as a diagonalizing matrix the matrix E of eigenvectors of A, that is, set $P = E$, to transform A into a diagonal matrix with the eigenvalues of A, on the main diagonal.[1]

To see this in the 2×2 case, let λ_1 and λ_2 be the eigenvalues of the coefficient matrix A and assume $\lambda_1 \neq \lambda_2$. Then the corresponding column eigenvectors $e_1 = (e_{11}, e_{12})^T$ and $e_2 = (e_{21}, e_{22})^T$ will be linearly independent; the matrix $E = (e_1, e_2)$ is invertible and diagonalizes A, that is,

$$E^{-1}AE = \Lambda \Leftrightarrow AE = E\Lambda \tag{4.5}$$

where Λ is a diagonal matrix with the eigenvalues of A on the main diagonal.

We can take advantage of this result to uncouple the dynamic system described by equation (4.3). We premultiply both sides by E^{-1}, note that EE^{-1} equals the identity matrix I, and obtain

$$E^{-1}z_{t+1} = E^{-1}A(EE^{-1})z_t = \Lambda E^{-1}z_t$$

using equation (4.5) in the process. If we now define the transformed (vector) variable

$$\hat{z}_t = E^{-1}z_t \tag{4.6a}$$

we can rewrite the last expression as

$$\hat{z}_{t+1} = \Lambda \hat{z}_t \tag{4.6b}$$

This is an uncoupled system made up of independent homogeneous equations whose coefficients are the eigenvalues of the original system. In the 2×2 case we have

$$\begin{pmatrix} \hat{x}_{t+1} \\ \hat{y}_{t+1} \end{pmatrix} = \begin{pmatrix} \lambda_1 & 0 \\ 0 & \lambda_2 \end{pmatrix} \begin{pmatrix} \hat{x}_t \\ \hat{y}_t \end{pmatrix}$$

or

$$\hat{x}_{t+1} = \lambda_1 \hat{x}_t$$
$$\hat{y}_{t+1} = \lambda_2 \hat{y}_t \tag{4.7}$$

where λ_1 and λ_2 are the eigenvalues of the coefficient matrix A and $\hat{x}$ and $\hat{y}$ are artificial variables constructed from the original variables. Since the transformed system consists of two independent homogeneous equations, we can write its general solution immediately as

$$\hat{x}_t = c_1\lambda_1^t \qquad \hat{y}_t = c_2\lambda_2^t$$

To recover the solution to the original system, we invert the original transformation:

$$\hat{z}_t = E^{-1}z_t \Rightarrow z_t = E\hat{z}_t$$

This means

$$\begin{pmatrix} x_t \\ y_t \end{pmatrix} = \begin{pmatrix} e_{11} & e_{21} \\ e_{12} & e_{22} \end{pmatrix} \begin{pmatrix} c_1\lambda_1^t \\ c_2\lambda_2^t \end{pmatrix}$$

or equivalently

$$x_t = c_1 e_{11}\lambda_1^t + c_2 e_{21}\lambda_2^t \tag{4.8a}$$
$$y_t = c_1 e_{12}\lambda_1^t + c_2 e_{22}\lambda_2^t \tag{4.8b}$$

Equations (4.8a) and (4.8b) are the general solution to the original system. It contains two arbitrary constants c_1 and c_2, which means that we need *two* boundary conditions to pick a definite solution to the system. For the case of a system with n variables $z_t = (x_{1t}, ..., x_{nt})$, equations (4.8a) and (4.8b) generalize to

$$z_t = \sum_{i=1}^{n} c_i e_i \lambda_i^t \tag{4.9}$$

where e_{ij} is the jth component of the eigenvector e_i associated with the eigenvalue λ_i for each $i = 1, ..., n$.

The dynamical behavior of this solution depends crucially on the nature and absolute value of the eigenvalues $(\lambda_1, ..., \lambda_n)$.

Real eigenvalues

If all the eigenvalues of A are real, we need not go any further. The general solution of the system is given by

$$x_{jt} = \sum_{i=1}^{n} c_i e_i \lambda_1^t \qquad \text{for each } j = 1, ..., n \tag{4.9}'$$

This solution is stable, approaching the steady state vector $x = 0$ as $t \to \infty$, if and only if all eigenvalues of A are smaller than unity in absolute value. If, on the other hand, $|\lambda_i| > 1$ for any i, we have $\lambda_i^t \to \pm\infty$ as $t \to \infty$ and the system behaves explosively, except possibly for certain special boundary conditions.

Complex eigenvalues

If one or more of the eigenvalues of the coefficient matrix A are complex numbers, equations (4.8a) and (4.8b) still give the general solution to the system (4.3). However, with λ_1 and λ_2 complex, (4.8) now describes a family of sequences some of which are complex valued. This is not very informative, for it is not easy to visualize functions of a complex number. Instead, we would like to see a more descriptive real-valued expression as a solution to the system.

Since A is a real matrix, eigenvalues and eigenvectors must come in conjugate pairs[2] as in figure 4.1. In particular, if i is the square root of -1, we have:

$$\lambda_1 = \gamma + i\mu = r(\cos\theta + i\sin\theta) = re^{i\theta} \tag{4.10}$$

$$\lambda_2 = \gamma - i\mu = r(\cos\theta - i\sin\theta) = re^{-i\theta}$$

for the eigenvalues and

$$e_1 = d + if \qquad e_2 = d - if$$

for the corresponding eigenvectors, where d and f are also vectors. The elementary solutions in equations (4.8a), (4.8b) can then be written as complex conjugates:

$$
\begin{aligned}
z_t^1 &= e_1 \lambda_1^t \\
&= (d + if)(re^{i\theta})^t \\
&= (d + if)r^t[\cos(\theta t) + i\sin(\theta t)] \\
&= r^t[d\cos(\theta t) + id\sin(\theta t) + if\cos(\theta t) + i^2 f\sin(\theta t)] \\
&= r^t[d\cos(\theta t) - f\sin(\theta t)] + ir^t[d\sin(\theta t) + f\cos(\theta t)]
\end{aligned}
$$

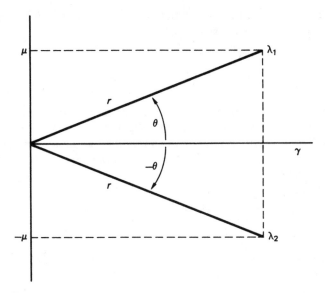

Figure 4.1 Complex eigenvalues.

Proceeding in a similar fashion we obtain

$$z_t^2 = e_2\lambda_2^t = r^t[d \cos(\theta t) - f \sin(\theta t)] - ir^t[d \sin(\theta t) + f \cos(\theta t)]$$

To express these solutions more compactly, we define

$$u_t = r^t [d \cos(\theta t) - f \sin(\theta t)] \qquad\qquad (4.11a)$$
$$v_t = r^t [d \sin(\theta t) + f \cos(\theta t)]$$

and obtain

$$z_t^1 = u_t + iv_t \qquad z_t^2 = u_t - iv_t \qquad\qquad (4.11b)$$

It is easy to show that the real-valued sequences u_t and v_t are independent solutions to the system, which entitles us to write the general solution in terms of the vectors d and f, that is,

$$z_t^g = c_1 u_t + c_2 v_t = c_1 r^t[d \cos(\theta t) - f \sin(\theta t)] + c_2 r^t[d \sin(\theta t) + f \cos(\theta t)] \qquad (4.12)$$

Compared with equation (4.9), this form of the general solution has the obvious advantage of being the sum of real-valued fundamental solutions. All the real-valued solutions to the dynamic system (4.3) follow by assigning numerical values to the free parameters c_1 and c_2.

From equation (4.12) we see that the polar coordinates (r,θ) of the conjugate pair of eigenvalues determine the qualitative properties of the system.

1. The stability of the system depends on the value of $r = (\gamma^2 + \mu^2)^{1/2}$, that is the modulus of the eigenvalues. If $r < 1$, z_t^g approaches the steady state $(0,0)$ asymptotically from any initial condition; if $r > 1$, the system explodes.
2. Complex roots generate oscillatory trajectories. As t changes, the sine–cosine terms produce a cycle in the interval $[-1,1]$ with frequency that depends on θ.

Recall that z_t is a vector; the time paths of its component variables will in general differ in size and timing over the cycles.

Repeated eigenvalues and non-diagonalizable systems

If some of the eigenvalues of the coefficient matrix A happen to be identical, the corresponding eigenvectors may be linearly dependent, and therefore A may not be diagonalizable. The procedure outlined above no longer applies. In this case, let λ_i be an eigenvalue of multiplicity $m_i \geq 1$; then the general solution to the homogeneous system is of the form

$$x_{jt} = \sum_i \sum_{k=1}^{m_k} c_{ik} \, t^{j-1} \lambda_i^t \qquad \text{for each } j = 1,\ldots,n \tag{4.13}$$

For a discussion of repeated eigenvalues in systems of differential equations, which applies to difference equations with the obvious changes, the reader is referred to Hirsch and Smale (1974, ch. 3).

4.2   Autonomous systems

General solutions to the non-homogeneous autonomous system

$$z_{t+1} = Az_t + b \tag{4.14}$$

where b is a vector of time-invariant constants, can be written as

$$z_t^g = z_t^c + z_t^p \tag{4.15}$$

Here again z_t^p is any particular solution to (4.14) and z_t^c is the general solution to the homogeneous equation $z_{t+1} = Az_t$. Since we already know how to solve the homogeneous equation, we only need to identify one particular solution to the full system to complete z_t^g. A natural choice for z_t^p is a stationary solution, $z_t = \bar{z}$ for all t. If a solution of this type exists, we can write the general solution to (4.14) simply as

$$z_t^g = z_t^c + \bar{z} \tag{4.16}$$

To find the steady state, we set $z_{t+1} = z_t \equiv \bar{z}$ in (4.14) and solve for $\bar{z}$, obtaining

$$\bar{z} = A\bar{z} + b \Rightarrow (I-A)\bar{z} = b \Rightarrow \bar{z} = (I-A)^{-1}b \tag{4.17}$$

provided that the matrix $I-A$ is invertible. If the system has real and distinct eigenvalues, (4.16) becomes

$$z_t^g = \sum_{i=1}^{n} c_i e_i \lambda_i^t + \bar{z} \tag{4.16}'$$

In the 2×2 case, $\bar{z} = (\bar{x}, \bar{y})$ and we have

$$x_t = \bar{x} + c_1 e_{11} \lambda_1^t + c_2 e_{21} \lambda_2^t$$
$$y_t = \bar{y} + c_1 e_{12} \lambda_1^t + c_2 e_{22} \lambda_2^t \tag{4.16}''$$

An alternative derivation of (4.16) transforms (4.14) into a homogeneous system and then solves it exactly as in equation (4.9).

Particular solutions to the system (4.14) follow if we specify n boundary conditions. For example, suppose we are given two initial conditions (x_0, y_0) for the two-dimensional system solved generally in equations (4.16)". Since (4.16)" holds for all t, it must hold for $t = 0$. Therefore

$$x_0 - \bar{x} = c_1 e_{11} + c_2 e_{21}$$
$$y_0 - \bar{y} = c_1 e_{12} + c_2 e_{22}$$

(4.18)

is a system of two equations in two unknowns, the arbitrary constants c_1 and c_2. After solving (4.18) for c_1 and c_2, we substitute these values back into (4.16)" to obtain the particular solution corresponding to the boundary conditions (x_0, y_0).

Stability in the two-dimensional case

Inspection of the general solution (4.16)" to the 2×2 system reveals that stability depends on the moduli of the two eigenvalues, λ_1 and λ_2. In particular, we have the following.

1. If $|\lambda_1| < 1$ and $|\lambda_2| < 1$, then the system is stable. For any value of c_1 and c_2 (that is, for any boundary conditions), we have λ_1^t and λ_2^t converging to zero; therefore the system approaches the steady state $(\bar{x}, \bar{y})$ as $t \to \infty$.
2. If $|\lambda_1| > 1$ and $|\lambda_2| > 1$, the system is dynamically unstable. Now λ_1^t and λ_2^t tend to $\pm\infty$; hence x_t and y_t go to infinity also unless $c_1 = c_2 = 0$, that is, unless the system starts exactly at the steady state itself.
3. If one of the eigenvalues has modulus above unity (say $|\lambda_1| > 1$ and $|\lambda_2| < 1$), then the system will still be unstable in the sense that the effect of the explosive root will prevail asymptotically, and the system diverges for almost all boundary conditions. On the other hand, there is one non-stationary solution, called the *saddlepath*, which converges to the steady state. To obtain it, we impose a boundary condition $c_1 = 0$ that eliminates the impact of the explosive root by setting the associated constant to zero; the behavior of the system is then determined by the stable root alone.

Saddlepath solutions are frequent in economic models. Suppose that x is a free variable (say, the flow of consumption or the price level) and y is a predetermined variable, such as the stock of capital or the money supply; assume also that we have $|\lambda_1| > 1$ and $|\lambda_2| < 1$. This corresponds to a situation like that depicted in the phase diagram of figure 4.2. (Section 4.3 following explains how to construct phase diagrams for linear systems.)

To find the saddlepath we set $c_1 = 0$ in the general solution (4.16)" to suppress the explosive root λ_1. The outcome is

$$x_t - \bar{x} = c_2 e_{21} \lambda_2^t$$
$$y_t - \bar{y} = c_2 e_{22} \lambda_2^t$$

(4.19)

which implies a linear relation between x and y. Eliminating $c_2 \lambda_2^t$ from equation (4.19), we obtain the equation of the saddlepath

$$x_t - \bar{x} = \frac{e_{21}}{e_{22}} (y_t - \bar{y})$$

(4.20)

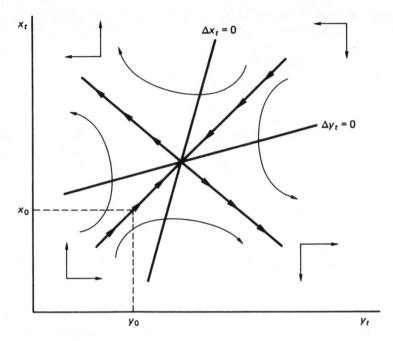

Figure 4.2 Phase diagram for a linear system.

Note that the slope of the saddlepath is the same as the slope of the eigenvector associated with the stable eigenvalue λ_2. The stable eigenvalue points in the direction of the saddlepath when we take the steady state as the origin of our coordinate system.[3]

Saddlepath solutions often make good economic sense. If y is a predetermined variable, then the value of y is some given amount y_0 at some initial time $t = 0$. Thus the system starts from some vertical line through y_0 in figure 4.2. Corresponding to y_0 there is a single value of x, given by equation (4.20), for which the system converges to the steady state; for all other initial values of x we have explosive behavior, a phenomenon without meaning under normal economic conditions. Since x is a free variable, the value x_0 is not strictly predetermined; it often makes sense to assume that x jumps at $t = 0$ precisely to the value needed to put the system on the saddlepath. Actual economies, after all, rarely display "explosive" behavior.

Systems with more than two equations

Both the solution method and the stability conditions described above generalize to systems with any finite number of equations. To solve large-dimensional linear dynamical systems, we start by computing the eigenvalues and eigenvectors of the relevant coefficient matrix. As before, we use the transformation $\hat{z} = E^{-1}z$ to obtain a diagonal system whose solution is easy to compute. We then recover the solution to the original system by using the inverse transformation $z = E\hat{z}$.

If all the eigenvalues of the system are real and distinct, the general solution will involve a linear combination of terms of the form $c_i \lambda_i^t$. The system will be stable if

$|\lambda_i| < 1$ for all i, and unstable if $|\lambda_i| > 1$ for all i. Instability means that all components of the solution vector explode to $\pm\infty$ from all initial positions except the steady state itself.

When some of the roots are complex, the solution will include sine–cosine terms that impart a cyclical pattern. The resulting oscillations will be damped, converging to the steady state if, and only if, the moduli of all complex eigenvalues are smaller than unity, that is, if all complex eigenvalues lie *within the unit circle* depicted in figure 4.3.

When some eigenvalues have moduli greater than unity and others do not, the system converges to the steady state from some locations in the state space and diverges from others; then the steady state is said to be a saddlepoint. The convergent and divergent subspaces are called, respectively, *the stable and unstable subspace* in linear systems, and the *stable and unstable manifold* in nonlinear systems. If the dimension of the convergent subspace turns out to be the same as the number of predetermined variables in the system, we can find the saddlepath solution exactly as above.

More generally, suppose we have n variables, s of which are predetermined, and a convergent subspace of dimension s. Then the predetermined variables pick off a unique point in the stable manifold and we may infer the unique convergent path from any date on by applying the difference equations that describe the state of the system at this initial point.

If the dimension of the stable manifold exceeds the number of predetermined variables, then we lack sufficient initial conditions to tie down a unique initial point in the convergent subspace, and the equilibrium path will not be unique. This is a serious problem for economic systems in which individuals are supposed to possess *perfect*

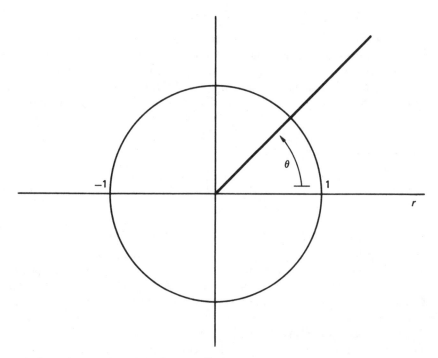

Figure 4.3 Complex numbers in polar coordinates.

foresight, that is, to be able to make unerring forecasts. If the equilibrium path is unique, agents may theoretically be assumed to know what will happen in the future, but this assumption sounds hollow when multiple equilibrium path are possible. Individuals in this case are required to guess perfectly which one from a variety of equilibrium paths the economy will settle on. Forecasts of this type presuppose a great deal of agreement and coordination among numerous, and otherwise independent, economic units.

Finally, if the dimension of the convergent subspace is smaller than the number of predetermined variables, the system has "too many" initial conditions and will start in the convergent subspace only by coincidence. In general that system has *no* stable solution.

4.3   Phase diagrams for linear systems

How does one construct a phase diagram like figure 4.2? Phase diagrams are convenient graphical devices showing the orbits of a two-dimensional dynamical system like equations (4.16)″ in the space of the relevant state variables. Trajectories are *sequences of points* in some Euclidean space if the system is discrete, *continuous curves* if time is continuous. The shape of these trajectories is easy to guess for linear systems by inspecting their general solution. For nonlinear systems we will find it difficult to draw orbits outside small neighborhoods that envelop steady states.

Consider now the first-order system

$$x_{t+1} = -a + \hat{b}x_t + cy_t \qquad (4.21)$$

$$y_{t+1} = d + ex_t - \hat{f}y_t \qquad (4.22)$$

which we will rewrite in terms of the first differences of x and y, $\Delta x_t = x_{t+1} - x_t$, $\Delta y_t = y_{t+1} - y_t$, to find out how the state variables change over time. Directions of change in y and x during the unit period are indicated by arrows pointing away from the origin (increase in absolute value) or toward the origin (fall in absolute value). Each point in the state space is associated with two such arrows and one resultant vector that represents the overall direction of the system at that point. The set of all resultant vectors in the plane is called the *vector field* of the dynamical system.

Subtracting x_t from both sides of (4.21) and y_t from both sides of (4.22), we can rewrite the system as

$$\Delta x_t = -a + bx_t + cy_t \qquad (4.21)'$$

$$\Delta y_t = d + ex_t - fy_t \qquad (4.22)'$$

where we define $b = \hat{b} - 1, f = \hat{f} + 1$ and assume that all the coefficients $a, \ldots, f$ are positive. To construct the phase diagram we "solve" the weak inequalities $\Delta x_t \geq 0$ and $\Delta y_t \geq 0$, that is, we obtain the sequence of points (x_t, y_t) that satisfy each inequality. Doing so will give us a precise idea of the regions in the state space in which state variables are weakly increasing and also of the complementary regions in which state variables will necessarily be strictly decreasing. If we set $\Delta x_t = 0$ and $\Delta y_t = 0$, we obtain equations describing *phaselines*, that is, combinations of state variables for which the vector field vanishes in one direction.

Note, in particular, that

$$\Delta x_t \geq 0 \Leftrightarrow y_t \geq \frac{a}{c} - \frac{b}{c} x_t \qquad (4.23)$$

$$\Delta y_t \geq 0 \Leftrightarrow y_t \leq \frac{d}{f} + \frac{e}{f} x_t \qquad (4.24)$$

Hence, x is increasing above the straight line implied by the equality form of (4.23), and decreasing below it (figure 4.4(a)). Similarly, y rises over time in the subspace that lies below the straight line in (4.24) and falls above it (figure 4.4(b)).

Next, we combine the two phaselines into figure 4.5 which draws the phase diagram for the entire system. If both phaselines had slopes of the same sign, we would need to

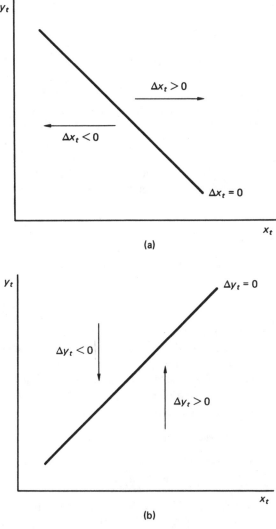

Figure 4.4 Components of a phase diagram.

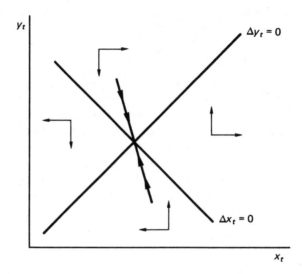

Figure 4.5 Assembly of a phase diagram.

compare their absolute values to see which was steeper. Figure 4.5 suggests the existence of a convergent saddlepath through the upper and lower quadrants and that all other paths diverge, most obviously paths starting in the left and right quadrants. If we did not assume that all the coefficients of the dynamical system (4.21)′ and (4.22)′ were positive, its vector field could differ greatly from figure 4.5. For instance, there could be a continuum of trajectories converging to the steady state s if *all* arrows pointed *toward* it, no converging trajectories if all arrows were to point *away* from it.

4.4 Non-autonomous systems

We will briefly review non-autonomous systems of the form

$$z_{t+1} = Az_t + f_t \tag{4.25}$$

with a constant coefficient matrix A and a time-varying vector f_t of forcing variables. We studied the scalar version of (4.25) in chapter 2. In principle, all we need to do to solve (4.25) is diagonalize the matrix A, that is, reduce (4.25) to a set of n independent equations in some transformation of the original variables.

To illustrate the procedure we will work with the two-equation case, assuming that the eigenvalues λ_1 and λ_2 of the coefficient matrix A are real and distinct. We know that the general solution to the equations

$$\hat{x}_{t+1} = \lambda_1 \hat{x}_t + \hat{b}_i \qquad \hat{y}_{t+1} = \lambda_2 \hat{y}_t + \hat{d}_i \tag{4.26}$$

in the transformed variables will be of the form

$$\hat{x}_t = c_1 \lambda_1^t + \hat{x}_t^p \qquad \hat{y}_t = c_2 \lambda_2^t + \hat{y}_t^p$$

where $\hat{x}_t^p$ and $\hat{y}_t^p$ are any particular solutions to the equations in the transformed variables, e.g. the forward- or backward-looking solution. We do not want to introduce boundary conditions at this stage because the variables $\hat{x}$ and $\hat{y}$ are composites of the original variables; it makes more sense to pick a unique solution by making assumptions directly about the original dependent variables.

To recover the solution to the original system we apply, as before, the inverse of the original transformation:

$$\hat{z}_t = E^{-1}z_t \Rightarrow z_t = E\hat{z}_t$$

Equivalently,

$$\begin{pmatrix} x_t \\ y_t \end{pmatrix} = \begin{pmatrix} e_{11} & e_{21} \\ e_{12} & e_{22} \end{pmatrix} \begin{pmatrix} c_1\lambda_1^t + \hat{x}_t^p \\ c_2\lambda_2^t + \hat{y}_t^p \end{pmatrix}$$

or

$$x_t = c_1e_{11}\lambda_1^t + c_2e_{21}\lambda_2^t + e_{11}\hat{x}_t^p + e_{21}\hat{y}_t^p \qquad (4.27a)$$

$$y_t = c_1e_{12}\lambda_1^t + c_2e_{22}\lambda_2^t + e_{12}\hat{x}_t^p + e_{22}\hat{y}_t^p \qquad (4.27b)$$

Equations (4.27) are the general solution to the original system (4.25).

Notes

1 See any good review of linear algebra, e.g. Anton (1981) or Hirsch and Smale (1974).
2 Recall from Euler's formula that a complex number c can be written $c = a + ib = r(\cos \theta + i \sin \theta) = re^{i\theta}$. Its conjugate is defined as $\bar{c} = a - ib = r(\cos \theta - i \sin \theta) = r\cos(-\theta) + i \sin(-\theta) = re^{-i\theta}$.
3 The connection between the saddlepath and the eigenvector associated with the stable root of the system is not accidental. For the homogeneous system $z_{t+1} = Az_t$, suppose that somehow the state vector z comes to point in the same direction as one of the eigenvectors e. Then we have $z_t = ke_i$ where k is some scalar constant. Note that if z points in the direction of an eigenvector now, it will still point in the same direction next period because $z_{t+1} = Az_t = A(ke_i) = k(Ae_i) = k\lambda_i e_i$ where, by the definition of an eigenvector, $Ae_i = \lambda_i e_i$. Once the state vector of the system comes to point in the direction of an eigenvector, it will continue to do so thereafter. The vector z is getting smaller with time and shrinks toward zero if $|\lambda_1| < 1$ but gets larger if $|\lambda_1| > 1$. Thus, eigenvectors associated with unstable roots define an explosive linear path. For non-autonomous systems, the same ideas will work if we express solutions in terms of deviations from the steady state. If the vector $z_t - \bar{z}$ is some scalar multiple of the eigenvector associated with the stable eigenvalue, the system is on the saddlepath, moving toward the steady state. The other eigenvector, associated with the explosive root, also defines a straight-line trajectory in the phase plane known as the anti-saddlepath.

5 Exchange-rate overshooting

This chapter presents an interesting application of the theory of linear dynamical systems to the phenomenon of overshooting exchange rates, that is, the tendency of exchange rates to fluctuate considerably more than financial market analysts think is justified by changes in the underlying economic "fundamentals." The model we shall study, due to Dornbusch (1976), is an open economy adaptation of the IS–LM structure that dates back to Keynes (1936) and Hicks (1937).

It is fair to warn the reader that the once very popular IS–LM framework by now belongs to the history of economic thought as an unsuccessful attempt to analyze purely short-run macroeconomic events, often by means of reasonable-looking behavioral relationships such as the aggregate consumption function, the investment function, and the liquidity preference schedule. Because none of these schedules follows from any small set of consistent axioms about rational economic behavior, economists often say that the IS–LM structure lacks *microeconomic foundations*. This is one reason why Keynesian methods are not found anywhere else in this book; another reason is that the methods are not very well suited to exploring low-frequency economic phenomena like the accumulation of physical and human capital, national debt, social security, or the long-run effects of various fiscal policies.

With this methodological caveat, we return to the Dornbusch exchange-rate model which consists of the following equations:

$$y_t^d = \delta(e_t + p^* - p_t) - \sigma(r_t - p_{t+1} + p_t) \tag{5.1}$$

$$p_{t+1} - p_t = \alpha(y_t^d - y) \tag{5.2}$$

$$m - p_t = \phi y - \lambda r_t \tag{5.3}$$

$$r_t = r^* + e_{t+1} - e_t \tag{5.4}$$

Here the parameters δ, σ, m, y, r^*, p^*, α, ϕ, λ are exogenous positive constants and y_t^d, p_t, r_t, e_t are endogenous variables whose interpretation is given below.

We start with the parameters: δ and σ are elasticities of aggregate demand with respect to the foreign-to-domestic price level ratio and to the domestic real interest rate respectively; ϕ and λ are elasticities of the liquidity preference (price-deflated demand for money) schedule with respect to real income and the nominal rate of interest; α is the elasticity of the home inflation rate with respect to excess aggregate demand; y, and p^* are the logarithms of the domestic commodity supply and foreign price level, which we take to be exogenous and constant; r^* is the foreign nominal rate of interest, also regarded as exogenous and constant. The parameter m is the logarithm of the nominal stock of money, assumed to be controlled by the central bank.

Next we define the endogenous variables: y_t^d and p_t are logarithms of domestic aggregate demand and the domestic price level at time t; r is the domestic nominal interest rate; and e_t is the logarithm of the exchange rate, that is, the price in home currency of one unit of foreign money. An increase in e means that domestic money depreciates.

Finally, we offer a few, admittedly less than fully convincing, words of explanation about the behavioral relations (5.1)–(5.4). The first states that home aggregate demand is a decreasing function of the home-to-foreign price ratio and of the expected real rate of interest; the latter rate is simply the difference between the nominal interest rate and the expected rate of inflation, $p_{t+1} - p_t$. We assume *perfect foresight* which means that the rate of inflation individuals expect equals the actual rate

$$p_{t+1} - p_t = \log\left(\frac{P_{t+1}}{P_t}\right) \approx \frac{P_{t+1}}{P_t} - 1 \tag{5.5}$$

for small changes in the actual level of prices P_t. Equation (5.2) is a Phillips curve, an *ad hoc* relation from the 1950s which describes price change out of equilibrium: excess demand for goods and services drives price inflation. Equation (5.3) is a standard Keynesian LM schedule that relates the demand for money to real income and the nominal rate of interest; and (5.4) is an arbitrage condition in asset markets which says that the home interest rate will exceed the foreign interest rate by an amount exactly equal to the expected rate of depreciation in the home currency.

Equations (5.1)–(5.4) describe the dynamical behavior of a small open economy with perfect foresight. To analyze this economy, we eliminate the endogenous variables (y_t^d, r) by substituting equation (5.1) into (5.2), and (5.4) into (5.3); the outcome is a two-dimensional autonomous linear dynamical system in the variables (e_t, p_t):

$$\lambda r^* + \lambda(e_{t+1} - e_t) = \phi y + p_t - m \tag{5.6a}$$

$$(1 - \alpha\sigma)(p_{t+1} - p_t) = \alpha\left[\delta(e_t + p^* - p_t) - y - \frac{\sigma}{\lambda}(\phi y - m + p_t)\right] \tag{5.6b}$$

Setting $e_t = \bar{e}$ and $p_t = \bar{p}$ for all t in (5.6a), (5.6b) we find the steady state of this system:

$$\bar{e} = \bar{p} - p^* + \frac{1}{\delta}(y - \sigma r^*) \tag{5.7a}$$

$$\bar{p} = \lambda r^* + m - \phi y \tag{5.7b}$$

Furthermore, in that state

$$r_t = r^* \qquad y_t^d = y \qquad \text{for all } t \tag{5.7c}$$

In other words, the domestic price level is an increasing function of the exogenous variables m and r^*, a decreasing function of y; the exchange rate is an increasing function of m and r^*, a decreasing function of p^*; the home rate of interest equals the corresponding foreign rate; and aggregate demand equals aggregate supply.[1]

To transform (5.6a), (5.6b) into a homogeneous system, we express variables in terms of deviations from the steady state:

$$\lambda(e_{t+1} - e_t) = p_t - \bar{p} \tag{5.8a}$$

$$p_{t+1} - p_t = \left[\delta(e_t - \bar{e}) - \left(\delta + \frac{\sigma}{\lambda} \right)(p_t - \bar{p}) \right] \frac{\alpha}{1 - \alpha\sigma} \tag{5.8b}$$

Equivalently we rewrite (5.8a), (5.8b) in the form

$$\begin{pmatrix} x_{t+1} \\ y_{t+1} \end{pmatrix} = A \begin{pmatrix} x_t \\ y_t \end{pmatrix} \tag{5.9}$$

where

$$x_t = e_t - \bar{e} \qquad y_t = p_t - \bar{p} \tag{5.10a}$$

$$A = \begin{pmatrix} 1 & 1/\lambda \\ \dfrac{\alpha\delta}{1 - \alpha\sigma} & 1 - \dfrac{\alpha(\delta + \sigma/\lambda)}{1 - \alpha\sigma} \end{pmatrix} \tag{5.10b}$$

To simplify matters, we restrict somewhat the parameters of this economy by assuming in what follows that

$$\alpha\sigma < 1 < \alpha\delta\left(1 + \frac{1}{\lambda} \right) \tag{5.11}$$

From equations (5.8a) and (5.8b) we construct the phrase diagram in figure 5.1 by observing that

$$e_{t+1} \geqslant e_t \Leftrightarrow p_t \geqslant \bar{p} \tag{5.12a}$$

$$p_{t+1} \geqslant p_t \Leftrightarrow p_t - \bar{p} \leqslant \frac{\delta}{\delta + \sigma/\lambda}(e_t - \bar{e}) \tag{5.12b}$$

Both the direction of the vector field and the sense of the trajectories drawn in figure 5.1 suggest that the steady state $s = (\bar{e}, \bar{p})$ may well be a saddle. We recall, once more, that the orbits of discrete systems are not continuous curves but collections of distinct points in the appropriate state space.

To ascertain the exact nature of the steady state S, we investigate the characteristic polynomial

$$z(\eta) = (\eta - \eta_1)(\eta - \eta_2) = \eta^2 - T\eta + D$$

where η_1 and η_2, the solutions to $z(\eta) = 0$, are the eigenvalues of the coefficient matrix A, while T and D are its trace and determinant. For a complete discussion of how the characteristic polynomial can be used to determine the stability properties of a steady state, the reader should refer to section 6.4. Continuing with $z(\eta)$, we have

$$T = \eta_1 + \eta_2 = 2 - \frac{\alpha}{1 - \alpha\sigma}\left(\delta + \frac{\sigma}{\lambda} \right) \tag{5.13a}$$

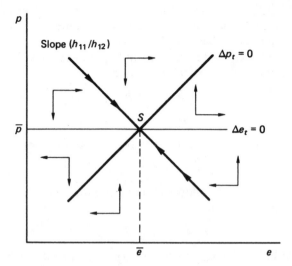

Figure 5.1 Exchange-rate dynamics.

$$D = \eta_1\eta_2 = 1 - \frac{\alpha}{1 - \alpha\sigma}\left(\delta + \frac{\alpha}{\lambda}\right) - \frac{\alpha\delta}{\lambda(1 - \alpha\sigma)} \tag{5.13b}$$

$$z(1) = (1 - \eta_1)(1 - \eta_2) = -\frac{\alpha\delta}{\lambda(1 - \alpha\delta)} \tag{5.14}$$

$$z(-1) = (1 + \eta_1)(1 + \eta_2) = 4 - \frac{\alpha}{1 - \alpha\sigma}\left[2\left(\delta + \frac{\sigma}{\lambda}\right) + \frac{\delta}{\lambda}\right] \tag{5.15}$$

$$\Delta = T^2 - 4D = \left[\frac{\alpha}{1 - \alpha\sigma}\left(\delta + \frac{\sigma}{\lambda}\right)\right]^2 + 4\frac{\alpha\delta}{\lambda(1 - \alpha\sigma)} \tag{5.16}$$

If $1 - \alpha\sigma > 0$, as assumed in (5.11), then the eigenvalues are real (because $\Delta > 0$), lie on opposite sides of 1 (because $z(1) < 0$) and their sum is less than 2 (since $T < 2$). In order to have a saddle, we need the eigenvalues to lie on different sides of -1, that is,

$$z(-1) > 0 \Leftrightarrow \alpha < \frac{4}{(2 + \lambda^{-1})(\delta + 2\sigma)}$$

In short, if the coefficient α is small enough (price adjustment is sufficiently slow), the steady state of the system is a saddle.

Figure 5.1 displays the phase diagram for the system when the steady state is indeed a saddle. The general solution may be written

$$e_t = \bar{e} + c_1 h_{11}\eta_1^t + c_2 h_{21}\eta_2^t \tag{5.17a}$$

$$p_t = \bar{p} + c_1\eta_1^t + c_2\eta_2^t \tag{5.17b}$$

where $h_i = (h_{i1}, 1)^T$ is the eigenvector associated with the eigenvalue η_i for $i = 1,2$ (assuming that $h_{12}h_{22} \neq 0$); by definition h_i solves the equation $Ah_i = \eta_i h_i$ in which A is the coefficient matrix in equation (5.10b). We will rule out explosive paths and assume that, for the given value of the price level, the exchange rate adjusts as needed to keep the system on the unique convergent path. This reflects the traditional view that asset prices are considerably more flexible than commodity prices.

To impose this condition, we set the constant c_1 associated with the explosive root ($\eta_1 > 1$) to zero, yielding the particular solution

$$e_t = \bar{e} + c_2 h_{21} \eta_2^t \qquad\qquad (5.17a)'$$

$$p_t = \bar{p} + c_2 \eta_2^t \qquad\qquad (5.17b)'$$

where the value of c_2 is determined by the given initial value of p, that is,

$$p_0 = \bar{p} + c_2 \eta_2^0 \Rightarrow c_2 = p_0 - \bar{p}$$

The equation of the saddlepath follows directly from these equations. Solving for $c_2 \eta_2^t$ in (5.17b)' and substituting into (5.17a)' we obtain

$$e_t = \bar{e} + h_{21}(p_t - \bar{p}) \qquad\qquad (5.18)$$

an equation that describes the negatively sloped straight line through S drawn in figure 5.1.

We apply this solution to study the effect on prices and exchange rates of a permanent change in the stock of money, say of an increase in the policy parameter m. Equations (5.7a), (5.7b) show that the steady state values of (e, p) will rise by an equal amount, from $S = (\bar{e}, \bar{p})$ in figure 5.2 to $\hat{S} = (\hat{e}, \hat{p})$; in the long run, the price level tends to rise and the home currency is devalued. It is interesting to consider how the economy reaches $\hat{S}$ from S.

To understand the adjustment path of the state variables, suppose the change in the money supply happens at $t = 0$ with the economy initially at the steady state S. By assumption, the price level is sticky, and so $p_0 = \bar{p}$, but the exchange rate is free to jump immediately to a new saddlepath, which is parallel to the old one and lies above it. Making use of the solution derived above, the transition path from the old to the new steady state is given by

$$p_t = \hat{p} - (\hat{p} - \bar{p})\eta_2^t \qquad \text{for } t \geq 0 \qquad\qquad (5.19a)$$

$$e_t = \hat{e} + \frac{\hat{p} - \bar{p}}{\lambda(1 - \eta_2)} \eta_2^t \qquad \text{for } t \geq 0 \qquad\qquad (5.19b)$$

Figure 5.2 graphs the path of the state variables from one long-run equilibrium to another. A monetary expansion results in an immediate depreciation of the currency and sustained inflation as the price level gradually adjusts upward from $\bar{p}$ to $\hat{p}$.

Note that the exchange rate *overshoots* its long-run equilibrium value, so that inflation is actually accompanied by a gradual appreciation of the currency during the transition. The reason for this is that the presumed stickiness of output prices puts the full burden of the immediate adjustment on the exchange rate. The instantaneous depreciation produces a "disequilibrium" in the goods market that is eliminated over time as output prices adjust. Following the sudden depreciation, and with output prices constant, domestic goods become cheaper relative to foreign goods. This leads to an excess demand for domestic output and to a gradual increase in domestic prices.

Since p is assumed to be predetermined, the increase in m is an increase in *real* money supply which leads to a reduction in domestic interest rates. This increases demand for output and generates additional inflationary pressures. Moreover, at the

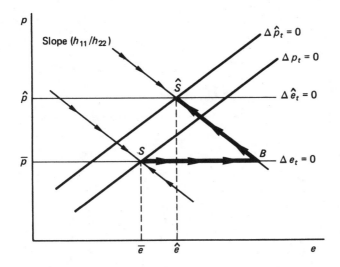

Figure 5.2 Overshooting adjustment process.

lower interest rate, the domestic currency will be held only if it is expected to appreciate in the future. Such an appreciation can only occur if the immediate adjustment puts S above its long-run level; that is why we have overshooting. As the adjustment proceeds, domestic prices rise, reducing the real money supply and increasing the interest rate. This leads to an appreciation of the domestic currency that offsets some of the first-round impact of the monetary expansion.

Note

1. Thus the Keynesian system regards a state of zero excess demand as a stationary or long-run equilibrium state. In the short run, inventory changes accommodate discrepancies between supply and demand.

6 Nonlinear systems

6.1 Introduction

Systems of nonlinear difference equations cannot be analyzed with the direct methods we have used on linear equations. In this chapter we are concerned with autonomous systems of the form

$$x_t = f(x_{t-1}) \tag{6.1}$$

where x_t is a vector in $\mathbb{R}^n$, typically a low-dimensional Euclidean space, and f is a continuously differentiable map $f: X \to \mathbb{R}^n$, where X is a subset of $\mathbb{R}^n$. Since explicit solutions to (6.1) are available only in rare and very special cases, we must rely on indirect qualitative methods to gather information about the dynamical behavior of nonlinear systems like equation (6.1). We develop graphical methods, called *phase diagrams*, which are useful in the study of low-order equations. The main result of this chapter is that, if (6.1) has a hyperbolic steady state $\bar{x}$ at which all eigenvalues of the matrix $Df(\bar{x})$ of partial derivatives have modulus different from unity, then we can study local dynamics near $\bar{x}$ by replacing the nonlinear equation (6.1) with its linear approximation. We explore in detail the stability of scalar and planar systems.

We discuss briefly an alternative method of assessing stability, Liapunov's direct method, which defines a function analogous to the "total energy" of the dynamical system f. Chapter 7 applies the techniques of this chapter to the study of simple neoclassical models of economic growth. Chapter 8 treats more complicated, and economically richer, types of asymptotic behavior such as periodic cycles and the non-repetitive patterns of strange attractors.

We recall from chapter 1 how to construct solutions to an initial-value problem for the system of equation (6.1). Given an initial condition x_0 at $t = 0$, we define a solution sequence as follows:

$$x_1 = f(x_0)$$
$$x_2 = f(x_1) = f[f(x_0)] = f^2(x_0)$$
$$\vdots$$
$$x_t = f(x_{t-1}) = f[f^{t-1}(x_0)] = f^t(x_0)$$

where f^n denotes the nth iterate of the map f, not its nth power. The function

$$x(t,x_0) = f^t(x_0) \tag{6.2}$$

is the *flow* of the system (6.1), giving us the value of the state vector as a function of initial conditions and time. Since t takes only integer values, (6.2) describes a discrete dynamical system. Finally, we can define the orbit of (6.1) through x_0 as the union of the positive and negative orbits γ^+ and γ^-, that is,

$$\gamma(x_0) = \gamma^+(x_0) \cup \gamma^-(x_0) = \{x_t \in X : x_t = f^t(x_0), t = 0, \pm1, \pm2,...\} \tag{6.3}$$

provided that $\gamma^-(x_0)$ is meaningfully defined.

Two dynamical systems that have qualitatively similar orbit structures are called *topologically equivalent*. Formally we have the following definition.

Definition 6.1 (Topological or flow equivalence) Let $\hat{f}$ and g be continuously differentiable maps from $X \subseteq \mathbb{R}^n$ into $\mathbb{R}^n$. Then we say that the discrete dynamical systems $x_{t+1} = f(x_t)$ and $x_{t+1} = g(x_t)$ are topologically equivalent if there exists a homeomorphism $h: \mathbb{R}^n \to \mathbb{R}^n$ (that is, a continuous change of coordinates with a continuous inverse) that maps f orbits into g orbits while preserving the sense of direction in time.

Topologically equivalent systems have many similar features: their phase diagrams, orbital structure, number of steady states, and other properties are closely related. Like systems of differential equations, discrete dynamical systems have certain simple orbits that are of special interest. The simplest case is a steady state or stationary equilibrium, corresponding to a constant solution of the system; the next simplest case is a periodic orbit. In the remainder of this chapter we study the behavior of nonlinear systems in the neighborhood of stationary equilibrium points, leaving periodic solutions for chapter 8.

Essential to any discussion of stability is the concept of *hyperbolicity* used in systems of differential equations to rule out eigenvalues with zero real parts. In discrete systems we frequently wish to exclude eigenvalues that fall on the boundary of the unit circle. The reason for this difference, already apparent in our discussion of the stability of linear systems, should become clearer below.

Definition 6.2 (Hyperbolic equilibrium) Let $\bar{x}$ be a steady state of the system $x_{t+1} = f(x_t)$. We say that $\bar{x}$ is hyperbolic if none of the eigenvalues of the Jacobian matrix of the partial derivatives $Df(\bar{x})$, evaluated at $\bar{x}$, falls on the unit circle in the complex plane, that is, if no eigenvalue has modulus exactly 1.

6.2 Geometric properties

Scalar systems

The general first-order difference equation may be written

$$x_{t+1} = f(x_t) \tag{6.4}$$

for some real-valued function $f: X \to \mathbb{R}$. Once we know f, we plot x_{t+1} as a function of x_t to obtain a phase diagram that can help trace the time path of the state variable. A steady state $\bar{x}$ corresponds to an intersection of the phaseline and the 45° line, that is, to a fixed point of the map f. This happens because $x_t = \bar{x}$ for all t implies $\bar{x} = f(\bar{x})$ at a steady state. In economic applications we often identify steady states with long-run equilibria. If we are given an initial value x_0, we can trace the subsequent values of x_t as shown in figure 6.1.

To start, note that $x_{t+1} = f(x_t)$ maps the initial value x_0 into x_1; hence we can go directly to point A on the phaseline and read its height as x_1. Now, when $t = 2$, x_1 becomes x_{t-i}; we can use the 45° line to translate x_1 back to the horizontal line, and so on. By this procedure we see that the system converges to a steady state S in the case illustrated above.

Next consider the example in figure 6.2. The phaseline $x_{t+1} = f(x_t)$ intersects the 45° line ($x_t = x_{t+1}$) at two points (S_1, S_2). Hence, the system has two steady states, $\underline{x}$

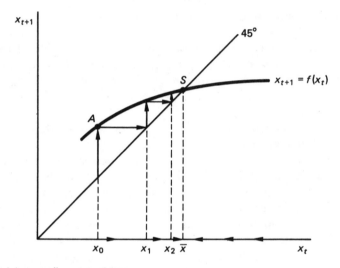

Figure 6.1 Solving nonlinear systems.

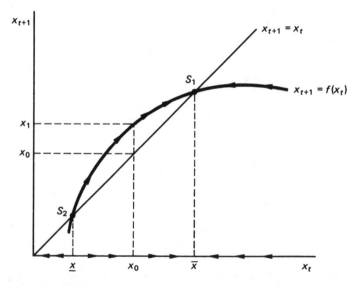

Figure 6.2 Nonlinear stability.

and $\bar{x}$, at which it will stay forever once it starts there. What happens if it starts away from the steady states? There are three possibilities.

1. $x_t < \underline{x}$: in this region the phaseline is below the 45° line. Since the height of the phaseline gives us the value of x_{t+1} and the height of the 45° line gives us the current value of x_t, we have that $x_{t+1} < x_t$, that is, the value of x is decreasing. This is shown by an arrow of motion pointing southwest, *away from S_2*.
2. $x_t > \bar{x}$: here we also have $x_{t+1} < x_t$, and so x is decreasing over time, only now the direction of motion takes us *toward* the steady state S_1 rather than away from it.
3. $\underline{x} < x_t < \bar{x}$: here the phaseline is above the 45° line. Hence, $x_{t+1} > x_t$ and x is increasing. This takes us again toward S_1, as shown by the arrows.

When the phaseline slopes upward, a steady state is asymptotically stable if the phaseline cuts the diagonal from above left, and unstable otherwise. Equivalently, the steady state is asymptotically stable if the slope of the phaseline at the steady state is less than 1 in absolute value, unstable if that slope is greater than 1.

This observation brings out the close connection between the geometric approach of figures 6.1–6.3 and earlier results on the stability of autonomous linear equations. What we are doing is equivalent to approximating the behavior of the nonlinear system $x_{t+1} = f(x_t)$ in the neighborhood of the steady state by a closely related linear system and studying the stability of the corresponding linear equation. To this end, we use a first-order Taylor approximation to f in the neighborhood of $\bar{x}$

$$x_{t+1} = \bar{x} + f'(\bar{x})(x_t - \bar{x}) \tag{6.5}$$

which describes the tangent to the phaseline at the steady state. As we shall see later, if $f'(\bar{x}) \neq 1$ then a mathematical result known as the Hartman–Grobman theorem allows us to judge the local stability properties of the nonlinear system (6.4) from the behavior of its linearized counterpart in equation (6.5). This enables us to employ results derived earlier for linear equations. As before there are four possible cases, shown also in figure 6.3.

If $f'(\bar{x}) \in (0,1)$, orbits that start near $\bar{x}$ converge monotonically to $\bar{x}$. Similarly, damped oscillations converging to $\bar{x}$ are a feature of all orbits near $\bar{x}$ if $f'(\bar{x}) \in (-1,0)$. Explosive oscillations occur if $f'(\bar{x}) < -1$, and monotone divergence away from $\bar{x}$ takes places if $f'(\bar{x}) > 1$.

Observe that the system may have several steady states, some of them stable, for example S_1 in figure 6.2, and some unstable, e.g. S_2 in the same figure.

Planar systems

Consider an autonomous first-order system of difference equations

$$x_{t+1} = f(x_t, y_t) \tag{6.6a}$$

$$y_{t+1} = g(x_t, y_t) \tag{6.6b}$$

in which time is not a separate argument of the scalar functions f or g. Assume that both f and g are continuously differentiable. In this simple setting we can construct a graphical representation of the system that will be of use in the study of its qualitative behavior. It should be noted that the phase diagram *alone* does not yield sufficient information to analyze many important aspects of the system's behavior. When

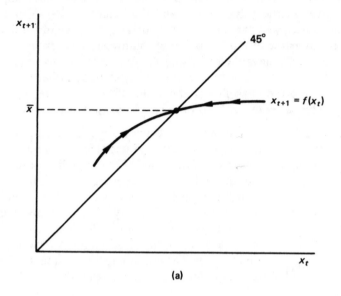

(a)

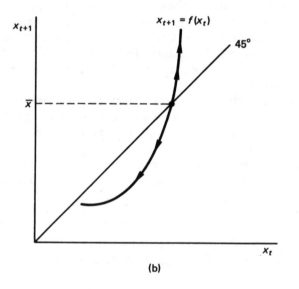

(b)

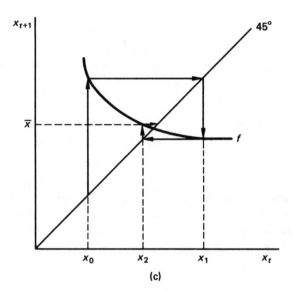

(c)

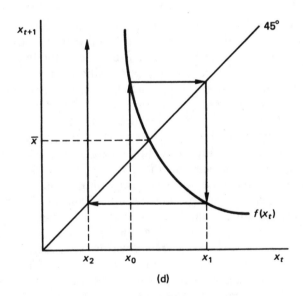

(d)

Figure 6.3 (a) Monotone convergence, $f'(\bar{x}) \in (0, 1)$; (b) monotone divergence, $f'(\bar{x}) > 1$; (c) damped oscillations, $f'(\bar{x}) \in (-1, 0)$; (d) explosive oscillations, $f'(\bar{x}) < -1$.

combined with some analytical results that we develop below, phase diagrams become a truly potent tool.

Steady states $(\bar{x}, \bar{y})$ of the dynamical system (6.6) are solutions to the system of equations

$$x = f(x,y) \qquad y = g(x,y) \tag{6.7}$$

in which each equation describes one phaseline. Let us approximate the nonlinear system (6.6) in the neighborhood of the steady state by the linear system

$$x_{t+1} = \bar{x} + \frac{\partial f(x_t,y_t)}{\partial x_t}(x_t - \bar{x}) + \frac{\partial f(x_t,y_t)}{\partial y_t}(y_t - \bar{y}) \tag{6.6a}'$$

$$y_{t+1} = \bar{y} + \frac{\partial g(x_t,y_t)}{\partial x_t}(x_t - \bar{x}) + \frac{\partial g(x_t,y_t)}{\partial y_t}(y_t - \bar{y}) \tag{6.6b}'$$

where all the partial derivatives are evaluated at the steady state. Note that the phaselines of the associated linear system will be tangent to those of the original system at the steady state. In some neighborhood of $(\bar{x},\bar{y})$, then, the phase diagram for equations (6.6a), (6.6b) can be approximated by that for equations (6.6a)', (6.6b)'. Chapter 4 outlines how to draw phase diagrams for linear systems.

6.3   Stability of equilibria

Stationary states or fixed points of nonlinear autonomous dynamical systems are values of the state variables that are preserved in perpetuity if they are achieved once. These rest points, we argued earlier, correspond naturally to the economic notion of long-run equilibria, that is, to asymptotic positions an economy may reach in response to the sum of all the external forces acting on it. As an economy approaches a long-run equilibrium, its propensity to change position gradually weakens, and it vanishes altogether when the rest point is reached.

Economically meaningful steady states must satisfy a stability criterion, that is, a notion of robustness that keeps perpetually in the neighborhood of a steady state at least *some* of the trajectories that start near it. This means that small deviations from long-run equilibrium are dampened by the self-correcting features of the economy or by cleverly designed policies. There are three useful definitions of stability for a fixed point $\bar{x}$ of a dynamical system; we introduced two of them in chapter 1. In particular, we called *stable* a stationary state $\bar{x}$ of the dynamical system $x_{t+1} = f(x_t)$ if all orbits that start near it stay near it; we called it *asymptotically stable* if all nearby orbits tend to $\bar{x}$ asymptotically. A steady state $\bar{x}$ is called *structurally stable* if the qualitative properties of orbits are invariant to small perturbations in the continuously differentiable map f. Specifically, we have the following.

Definition 6.3 (Structural stability) Let $f : \mathbb{R}^n \supseteq X \to \mathbb{R}^n$ be a C^1 map and $g : X \to \mathbb{R}^n$ be a perturbation of f, that is, a map close to f in the space of C^1 functions, in the sense that both $\|f(x) - g(x)\|$ and $\|Df(x) - Dg(x)\|$ are "small" for all $x \in X$. Then the dynamical system $x_{t+1} = f(x_t)$ is structurally stable if its orbits are topologically equivalent to those of any perturbation g of f that lies within some ball of positive radius around f in the space of C^1 functions.

Now that we have in place a number of definitions for judging the stability of the nonlinear system

$$x_{t+1} = f(x_t) \qquad f: \mathbb{R}^n \supseteq X \to \mathbb{R}^n \qquad f \in C^1 \qquad (6.8)$$

we introduce two diagnostic devices that permit us to do so. The first one was explained in chapter 4: we construct a linear approximation to f in the neighborhood of a fixed point and use results already known from the study of linear systems. The second criterion is Liapunov's direct method, which defines an energy-like function for the dynamical system f.

Linearization

Applying Taylor's formula to equation (6.8) we have

$$f(x) = f(\bar{x}) + Df(\bar{x})(x - \bar{x}) + O(\|x - \bar{x}\|)$$

where the remainder term $O(\cdot)$ is small in a well-defined sense. Hence, we expect the linear system

$$x_{t+1} = \bar{x} + Df(\bar{x})(x_t - \bar{x}) \qquad (6.9)$$

to be a good approximation to (6.8) near the steady state. This is indeed the case quite often. In fact, the next result supplies conditions under which the orbits of (6.8) can be mapped into those of (6.9) by a continuous change of coordinates in a sufficiently small neighborhood of $\bar{x}$.

Theorem 6.1 (Hartman–Grobman) Let $\bar{x}$ be a hyperbolic equilibrium of equation (6.8). If the Jacobian matrix $Df(\bar{x})$ is invertible, there is a neighborhood U of $\bar{x}$ in which the nonlinear system (6.8) is topologically equivalent to the linear system (6.9).

The theorem says that, if $\bar{x}$ is a hyperbolic fixed point of a nonlinear system f, then the nonlinear system is equivalent, up to a continuous change of coordinates, to a linear system with coefficient matrix $Df(\bar{x})$. Since topologically equivalent systems have the same qualitative dynamical properties, the stability of the fixed point under f can be determined by examining the eigenvalues of the Jacobian. Linearization works well around hyperbolic fixed points; in particular, we have the following.

Theorem 6.2 (Nonlinear stability) Let $\bar{x}$ be a steady state of (6.8).

(a) If all eigenvalues of $Df(\bar{x})$ have moduli strictly less than 1, $\bar{x}$ is asymptotically stable (a sink).
(b) If at least one eigenvalue has modulus greater than 1 then $\bar{x}$ is unstable. If this holds for all eigenvalues, $\bar{x}$ is a source, otherwise a saddle.
(c) If no eigenvalue of the Jacobian matrix is outside the unit circle but at least one is on the boundary (has modulus 1), then $\bar{x}$ may be stable, asymptotically stable, or unstable.

Non-hyperbolic equilibria are unstable if they have any eigenvalues with modulus greater than 1, but their stability type cannot be determined in case (c) of the theorem. Fortunately, non-hyperbolic equilibria are the exception in a well-defined sense. Given a parametrized system $x_{t+1} = f(x_t; \alpha)$ with $f \in C^1$, the moduli of the eigenvalues are continuous functions of the parameters α. If the fixed point of f is non-hyperbolic for a given value of α, then almost any small change in the value of α will yield a hyperbolic equilibrium, provided that the fixed point itself does not disappear, as we shall see when we discuss bifurcations in chapter 8. On the other hand, if the system has a hyperbolic fixed point for some value of α, any small perturbation of the parameters will leave us with a system that has a hyperbolic fixed point close to the old one.

Liapunov's direct method

We saw earlier that it is often possible to determine the local stability properties of an equilibrium in a nonlinear system by linearizing around the steady state. We found, however, that this method does not work in non-hyperbolic cases, and that the results it yields are valid only in a sufficiently small neighborhood of the equilibrium. Here we develop an alternative way to study the stability of equilibria. This method, known as Liapunov's second or direct method, generalizes the idea that, in certain physical systems, equilibrium points that correspond to a local minimum of the system's total energy are stable.

To study stability by Liapunov's direct method, we need no knowledge of the solutions of the system. We work instead with an auxiliary function called a Liapunov function, which possesses certain desirable properties. If such a function can be found, a simple and intuitive argument ensures the stability of the equilibrium. One advantage of the direct method relative to linearization is that it works for non-hyperbolic equilibria; another is that it often yields some information about the size of the basin of attraction. The major drawback is that there is no easy or general way to construct a Liapunov function.

We first define the concept of a Liapunov function and indicate in intuitive terms why the existence of such a function implies stability. Suppose $\bar{x}$ is an equilibrium point of the system of equation (6.8). A Liapunov function for that system is a function

$$V: X \supseteq U \rightarrow \mathbb{R} \text{ such that } \bar{x} \in U$$

that is, a scalar function defined on some region U of the state space X that contains the equilibrium $\bar{x}$. Moreover, V must satisfy three conditions.

1. It is a continuous function.
2. $V(\bar{x}) < V(x) \quad \forall x \in U$, that is, it has a unique minimum $\bar{x}$ in the region U.
3. Along the trajectory of the system contained in U, the value of V never increases.

The graph of V, then, may look as shown in figure 6.4(a). By conditions (1) and (2), it is an unbroken surface on $X \times \mathbb{R}$ that reaches its lowest point in U at $\bar{x}$. Condition (3) means that $V(x_t)$, the value of V evaluated along a solution to (6.8), decreases with time. In figure 6.4(a) the sequences $c_t = (x_t, V(x_t))$ must "run downhill."

Alternatively, we may want to think of V in terms of its level sets in the state space, that is, sets of the form

$$V^{-1}(c) = \{x \in X: V(x) = c\}$$

For a Liapunov function defined on a two-dimensional state space, the situation may look as depicted in figure 6.4(b): for c close enough to the minimum value of V, the level sets are concentric closed curves around the equilibrium. Then the requirement

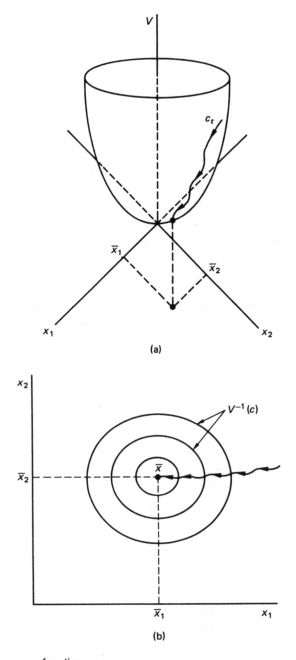

Figure 6.4 A Liapunov function.

that $V(x_t)$ be non-increasing implies that orbits of the system will cross the level curves from the outside in, and once inside will remain there.

The geometric interpretation of the Liapunov function makes it intuitively plausible that the equilibrium must be stable if such a function exists. The graph of V looks like a valley with a single minimum point. If the curves corresponding to the trajectories of the system cannot run uphill, orbits that get close enough to the bottom will never escape, and hence the system is stable. If, in addition, we require that the curves run strictly downhill, then they must approach the minimum and the equilibrium is asymptotically stable. We sum up in the following theorem.

Theorem 6.3 (Liapunov) Suppose $\bar{x}$ is an equilibrium point for the system $x_{t+1} = f(x_t)$. Let $V: X \rightarrow \mathbb{R}$ be a continuous function defined on a neighborhood U of X containing $\bar{x}$. Assume that V has a unique strict minimum in U at $\bar{x}$ and define $\Delta V(x_t) = V[f(x_t)] - V(x_t)$.

(a) If $\Delta V(x_t) \leqslant 0$ for all $x \neq \bar{x}$ in U, then $\bar{x}$ is stable.
(b) If $\Delta V(x_t) < 0$ for all $x \neq \bar{x}$ in U, then $\bar{x}$ is asymptotically stable.
(c) If $\Delta V(x_t) > 0$ for all $x \neq \bar{x}$ in U, then $\bar{x}$ is unstable.

Note that the theorem gives us sufficient conditions for stability and instability. In fact, the converse also holds under rather general conditions so that, for example, if $\bar{x}$ is asymptotically stable, an appropriate V will exist. On the other hand, we may not be able to find it, and nothing can be concluded about the stability of an equilibrium for which we are unable to find a Liapunov function.

Conjuring up a Liapunov function can be difficult, but if one is found it yields useful information concerning the region of stability of the equilibrium. In some simple cases the following method will work. Given a planar system

$$x_{t+1} = f(x_t, y_t) \qquad y_{t+1} = g(x_t, y_t)$$

with a steady state that for convenience we normalize to $(0,0)$, let us define the function

$$V(x,y) = \frac{x^2 + y^2}{2}$$

whose level sets are concentric circles around the steady state. Clearly, V has a unique minimum at the origin. Suppose, for instance, that $f(x,y) = \frac{1}{2}(x+y)$, $g(x,y) = xy$. Then the change in the Liapunov function at (x,y) is

$$\begin{aligned}
\Delta V(x,y) &= V[f(x,y), g(x,y)] - V(x,y) &\Rightarrow \\
2\Delta V(x,y) &= f^2(x,y) + g^2(x,y) - (x^2+y^2) \\
&= \tfrac{1}{4}(x+y)^2 + x^2y^2 - (x^2+y^2) \leqslant 0 &\Leftrightarrow \\
&3(x^2+y^2) \geqslant 4x^2y^2 + 2xy &\Leftrightarrow \\
&3(x-y)^2 \geqslant 4\,xy(xy-1) &(6.10)
\end{aligned}$$

Inequality (6.10) holds as a strict equality at the steady state $\bar{x} = \bar{y} = 0$, and as a weak inequality for any (x,y) in the region $xy \in [0,1]$ among others. Hence the stable region contains the origin.

6.4   Stability of planar systems

Planar autonomous systems of difference equations are quite common in dynamic economics. In this section we examine stability conditions for such systems from a geometric viewpoint.

We start with two continuously differentiable maps, $f : \mathbb{R}^2 \rightarrow \mathbb{R}$ and $g : \mathbb{R}^2 \rightarrow \mathbb{R}$, and a nonlinear system of the form

$$x_{t+1} = f(x_t, y_t) \tag{6.11}$$

$$y_{t+1} = g(x_t, y_t) \tag{6.12}$$

We know that the stability type of a steady state $s = (x, y)$ depends on the eigenvalues of the Jacobian matrix of partial derivatives

$$J(x,y) = \begin{pmatrix} f_x & f_y \\ g_x & g_y \end{pmatrix}$$

In particular, s is a *sink* if both eigenvalues have modulus less than 1, a *source* if both have modulus greater than 1, and a *saddle* if one eigenvalue is inside the unit circle in the complex plane and the other is outside.

The eigenvalues of J are obtained by solving the following equation:

$$p(\lambda) = |J - \lambda I| = \begin{vmatrix} f_x - \lambda & f_y \\ g_x & g_y - \lambda \end{vmatrix}$$

$$= (f_x - \lambda)(g_y - \lambda) - f_y g_x$$
$$= \lambda^2 - (f_x + g_y)\lambda + f_x g_y - f_y g_x = 0$$
$$= \lambda^2 - (\operatorname{tr} J)\lambda + \det J = 0$$

Eigenvalues are thus roots of the *characteristic polynomial* $p(\lambda)$. Rearranging, we obtain

$$p(\lambda) = \lambda^2 - (\operatorname{tr} J)\lambda + \det J = 0 \tag{6.13}$$

where $\operatorname{tr} J$ and $\det J$ are the trace and determinant of the Jacobian matrix.

Our aim is to draw a figure on a Cartesian plane, with $D = \det J$ on the vertical axis and $T = \operatorname{tr} J$ on the horizontal axis, and identify on that figure areas that correspond to various types of steady states. We proceed by defining first three auxiliary lines that divide the plane into a number of regions distinguished by the nature of the eigenvalues in each one. Let Δ be the discriminant of the characteristic polynomial. The first auxiliary line is defined by

$$\Delta = T^2 - 4D = 0 \tag{6.14}$$

This is a parabola with a minimum at the origin (cf. figure 6.5(a)). Clearly, the eigenvalues of J are real if and only if $\Delta \geq 0$, and are complex otherwise. The graph of $\Delta = 0$ then divides the plane in two regions, as shown in figure 6.5(a): we have $\Delta < 0$ and complex roots above the parabola, while the region below it is associated with real eigenvalues.

Let λ_1 and λ_2 be the eigenvalues of J. We can factor the characteristic polynomial and write it in the form $p(\lambda) = (\lambda - \lambda_1)(\lambda - \lambda_2)$. Suppose that the eigenvalues are real for the time being, and that we want to determine whether or not both of them fall on the same side of a given constant a on the real line. Evaluating p at a we have

$$p(a) = (a - \lambda_1)(a - \lambda_2) \tag{6.15}$$

Clearly, $p(a) > 0$ if and only if both factors on the right-hand side of equation (6.15) have the same sign, that is, if both λ_1 and λ_2 fall on the *same* side of a.

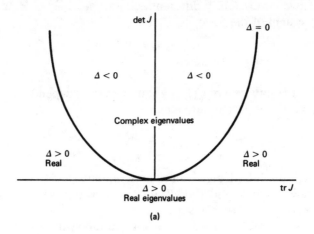

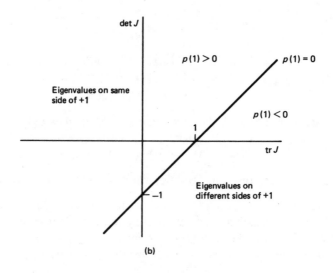

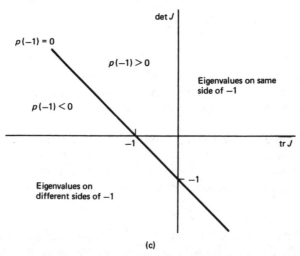

Figure 6.5 Planar systems.

In our case we are interested in determining whether or not the (real) eigenvalues of J fall on the same side of the numbers 1 and -1 on the real line. Thus, we draw the lines $p(1) = 0$ and $p(-1) = 0$. From (6.13) we obtain

$$p(1) = 0 \Leftrightarrow D = T - 1 \qquad (6.16)$$

This is a straight line that goes through the points $(0,-1)$ and $(1,0)$ as shown in figure 6.5(b). Note that in the region above the line $p(1) > 0$ both eigenvalues are on the same side of unity. The opposite is true below the line $p(1) = 0$.

Similarly,

$$p(-1) = 0 \Leftrightarrow D = - (T + 1) \qquad (6.17)$$

which goes through the points $(-1,0)$ and $(0,-1)$. Above this line we have $p(-1) > 0$, with both roots being on the same side of -1 (figure 6.5(c)).

The two lines that appear in figures 6.5(b) and 6.5(c) divide the plane into four regions, as shown in figure 6.6(a). We note, further, that the parabola $\Delta = 0$ is tangential to both the line $p(1) = 0$ at $(2,1)$ and the line $p(-1) = 0$ at $(-2,1)$. The parabola is therefore entirely contained in the upper quadrant of the plane, as partitioned by the two straight lines.

Figure 6.6(b) shows how the plane is divided into eight regions by the three reference lines described above and the horizontal line at $D = 1$. For each of these regions we discuss next the stability properties of the steady state.

First we concentrate on the regions of the plane that correspond to real eigenvalues; these are indicated in figure 6.6(b) by the circled numbers 1, 2, 3, 4, 7, and 8. The steady state is a sink if both roots are in the interval $(-1,1)$, a source if neither eigenvalue falls in this interval, and a saddle if one root is in $(-1,1)$ and the other is not. Taking each region in turn we have the following cases.

Region 1: $p(1) < 0$ and $p(-1) > 0$. Both eigenvalues are on the same side of -1 and on different sides of 1. The only possibility is one eigenvalue in $(-1,1)$ and the other in $(1,\infty)$. The steady state is a saddle.

Region 2: $p(1) < 0$ and $p(-1) < 0$. Eigenvalues of opposite sign outside the unit circle; the steady state is a source.

Region 3: $p(1) > 0$ and $p(-1) < 0$. Again a saddle.

Region 4: $p(1) > 0$ and $p(-1) > 0$. Both eigenvalues are on the same side of both 1 and -1. Moreover, we have $D > 0$ and so the eigenvalues have the same sign, and $T < -2$ so they are negative. Hence both are in $(-\infty,-1)$, and the steady state is a source.

Region 7: $p(1) > 0$ and $p(-1) > 0$. Here $\lambda_1 + \lambda_2 = T \in (-2,2)$ and $\lambda_1\lambda_2 = D \in (-1,1)$. Thus both eigenvalues fall in $(-1,1)$ and we have a sink.

Region 8: $p(1) > 0$ and $p(-1) > 0$. Now $D > 0$ and $T > 2$, and so the two eigenvalues are positive and fall on the same side of both 1 and -1; they must therefore lie in $(1,\infty)$. The steady state is a source.

In regions 5 and 6 the eigenvalues are complex. Complex eigenvalues come in conjugate pairs, for example

$$\lambda_1 = a + ib \qquad \lambda_2 = a - ib$$

We also know that $D = \lambda_1\lambda_2$ and $T = \lambda_1 + \lambda_2$. Expanding the right-hand side of this expression, we see that the determinant is equal to the square of the modulus of the eigenvalues. Stability depends on whether or not the eigenvalues fall inside the unit

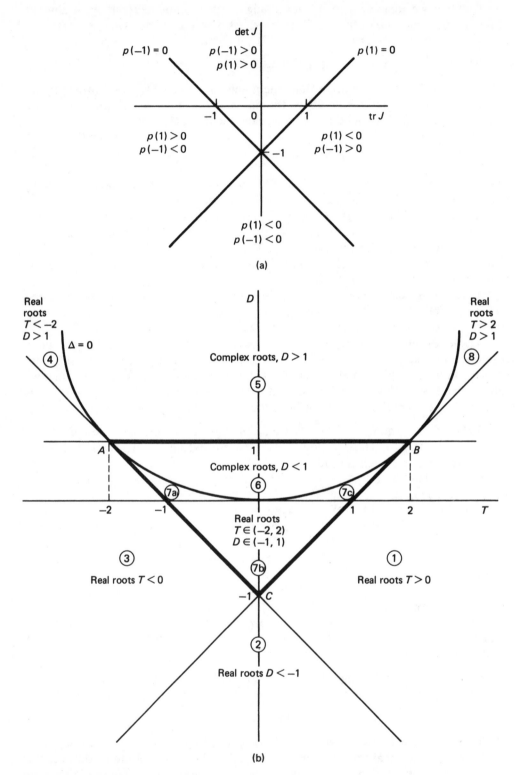

Figure 6.6 Asymptotic stability on the plane.

circle in the complex plane, that is, $|\lambda| < 1$. In *region 5* we have $D > 1 \Rightarrow |\lambda| > 1$ and so the steady state is a source, whereas in *region 6* we have $D < 1 \Rightarrow |\lambda| < 1$ and a sink.

To sum up we refer again to figure 6.6(b): the hyperbolic steady state $\bar{x}$ is an asymptotically stable sink if the Jacobian matrix $Df(\bar{x})$ of the relevant dynamical system has a trace–determinant combination inside the stability triangle ABC drawn in bold. The state $\bar{x}$ is unstable if it lies outside that triangle; specifically, it is a saddle if it lies in the interior of the conical regions marked 1 and 3, and a source if it is located in regions numbered 2, 4, 5 and 8.

Eigenvalues have real or imaginary parts of opposite sign in areas 2, 5, 6, and 7b which means that orbits in the neighborhood of $\bar{x}$ are oscillatory for these Jacobian matrices; regions 6 and 7b, therefore, correspond to *stable spirals*, while *unstable spirals* arise in regions 2 and 5.

In regions 4, 7a, 7c, and 8, eigenvalues have the same sign which means that orbits are monotone; in particular, we have *stable nodes* in areas 7a and 7c, *unstable nodes* in areas 4 and 8. We note finally that, if the Jacobian were somehow to move from inside the stability triangle ABC to outside, the dynamical system would lose stability and experience a qualitative change in trajectories near the steady state. We call this abrupt change a *bifurcation* and take up its study in chapter 8.

7   The structure of growth models

7.1   Introduction

The study of nonlinear dynamical systems was originally motivated by physical phenomena. Most real-world examples one finds in texts on ordinary differential equations arose in physics, continuum mechanics, and the life sciences,[1] just as Newtonian mechanics provided the first applications and, in fact, the very origin, of linear dynamical systems. Well-known nonlinear differential equations due to Duffing and van der Pol describe oscillations in solid media and electrical circuits respectively; the Lotka–Volterra equations explore interactions between predators and prey in animal populations; and the Lorenz equation arose in meteorology.

Despite this impressive chain of examples that date back more than a century to the work of Poincaré and Hamilton, nonlinear dynamics offers a wide variety of insights that ranges well beyond the natural sciences to economics and its many subfields, notably finance, industrial organization, human resources, and macroeconomics. Macroeconomics, in particular, is where dynamical concepts have gained prominence in recent years as research has come to rely ever more frequently on various types of neoclassical growth models. Economists use these to investigate not only the traditional long-term problems of growth, economic development, and population but, increasingly, for shorter-term phenomena like business cycles, for policy issues related to inflationary finance, social security, or national debt, and in a wide array of other applications.

There are three broad types of neoclassical one-sector growth models: the descriptive growth model of Solow (1956), the optimal growth model of Ramsey (1928), and the overlapping generations model of Diamond (1965). Equations (1.1b), (1.2a) (1.2b) and (1.3) in chapter 1 describe standard versions of these growth models, two of which are first-order systems. In the remainder of this chapter we examine in some detail the dynamical structure of the most common neoclassical growth models, both to see the theory of nonlinear systems "in action" and to grasp some of the elementary technological, demographic, and fiscal factors that influence economic growth.

We defer for Part II and, in some cases, for Parts III and IV the details of how one derives from first economic principles the behavioral equations of various growth models. For the time being we will be content to describe carefully the economic interpretation of all relevant time maps but otherwise to accept on faith the mathematical representation of one-sector growth models.

The Solow and Ramsey versions of neoclassical growth theory have a simple dynamical structure. Under certain mild technical conditions, the scalar Solow model turns out to possess one unstable and one stable steady state, while the planar Ramsey model has a unique saddlepoint.

A considerably richer set of equilibria characterizes the overlapping generations model. Given again some mild assumptions, the scalar version of this model which appears in equation (1.3) never has fewer than two steady states, at least one stable and one unstable. We shall also explore the simplest planar variant of that model whose state variables are physical capital per worker and national debt per worker; there we typically find *three* stationary points: one sink, one source, and one saddle.[2] When we consider standard issues of fiscal policy in Part III, we will discover that the *minimal* number of steady states for the planar Diamond model usually ranges from two to four depending on the sign and size of the government deficit.

7.2   Descriptive growth

We reproduce from chapter 1 the discrete variant of the model due to Solow (1956), which satisfies an autonomous nonlinear scalar first-order difference equation of the form

$$k_{t+1} = h(k_t) \tag{7.1a}$$

where

$$h(k) = \frac{(1 - \delta)k + sf(k)}{1 + n} \tag{7.1b}$$

In equation (7.1b), $h: \mathbb{R}_+ \to \mathbb{R}_+$ is a C^1 map inheriting all its properties from the continuously differentiable neoclassical production function $f: \mathbb{R}_+ \to \mathbb{R}_+$ and from the three parameters $n > -1$, $\delta \in [0,1]$ and $s \in [0,1]$, representing respectively the rates of population growth, depreciation, and saving. The production function maps capital per worker into output per worker. It is increasing, strictly concave, and satisfies two assumptions

$$f(0) = 0 \tag{7.2a}$$

$$0 \leqslant \lim_{k \to \infty} f'(k) < \frac{\delta + n}{s} < \lim_{k \to 0} f'(k) \leqslant +\infty \tag{7.2b}$$

which ensure, respectively, that production cannot occur without capital and that the marginal product of capital is sufficiently small when workers are saturated with capital and sufficiently large when workers are starved for capital.

To derive the basic difference equation (7.1a) of the Solow model, one starts from the equality of aggregate saving to gross investment, that is, from a statement of equilibrium in the asset or commodities market of a simplified macroeconomic structure. We denote by time-subscripted upper-case letters (Y_t, K_t, L_t) economywide aggregates such as output, capital, and labor; the corresponding lower-case letters $y_t = Y_t/L_t$ and $k_t = K_t/L_t$ stand for output and capital *per worker*.

Saving at time t is sY_t, a fixed fraction of aggregate income which is itself equal to the output $F(K_t,L_t)$ produced from the existing stocks of capital and labor. The aggregate production function is continuously differentiable, increasing in each input, strictly concave, linearly homogeneous; both inputs are essential for production, that is,

$$F(K,0) = 0 \text{ for all } K \geqslant 0 \qquad F(0,L) = 0 \text{ for all } L \geqslant 0$$

Linear homogeneity means that $F(K,L) = LF(K/L,1) = F(k,1)$, which allows us to write output per worker as a simple function of capital per worker:

$$y = \frac{Y}{L} = \frac{F(K,L)}{L} = F(k,1) = f(k) \tag{7.3}$$

At the end of this equation we simply define $f(k) = F(K,1)$ and conclude readily that f inherits *all* the properties of F except linear homogeneity.

Investment at t is simply the sum of net plus replacement investment, that is,

$$I_t = K_{t+1} - K_t + \delta K_t = K_{t+1} - (1-\delta)K_t$$

Investment per worker is then

$$\frac{I_t}{L_t} = \frac{K_{t+1}}{L_t}(1 - \delta)\frac{K_t}{L_t}$$

$$= \left(\frac{L_{t+1}}{L_t}\right)k_{t+1} - (1-\delta)k_t$$

$$= (1+n)k_{t+1} - (1-\delta)k_t$$

if we assume that population grows geometrically at the rate $n > -\delta$. The equality of investment and saving yields

$$(1+n)k_{t+1} - (1-\delta)k_t = sf(k_t)$$

which we solve for k_{t+1} to obtain equations (7.1a) and (7.1b). We have now come full circle back to the original statement of the Solow model. From equation (7.1b) we find that h is concave because f is, $h(0) = 0$ because $f(0) = 0$, and

$$\lim_{k \to 0} h'(k) = (1 + n)^{-1}[1 - \delta + s \lim_{k \to 0} f'(k)] > 1 \tag{7.4a}$$

because the marginal product of capital satisfies $f'(0) > (\delta+n)/s$ by assumption (7.2b) as $k \to 0$. Also note that any solution to the difference equation (7.1a) satisfies

$$\lim_{k \to \infty} \left(\frac{k_{t+1}}{k_t}\right) = (1 + n)^{-1}\left\{1 - \delta + s \lim_{k \to \infty}\left[\frac{f(k)}{k}\right]\right\}$$

This equals $(1 - \delta)/(1 + n)$ if f is bounded and, by L'Hôpital's rule, equals $(1+n)^{-1}[1-\delta + sf'(\infty)]$ if f is not bounded. In either case, any sequence (k_t) that solves equation (7.1a) also satisfies

$$\lim_{k_t \to \infty} \left(\frac{k_{t+1}}{k_t}\right) < 1 \tag{7.4b}$$

Putting together inequalities (7.4a) and (7.4b), we discover that the time map, or phaseline, of equation (7.1a) is an increasing concave function through the origin, as shown in figure 7.1; it is steeper than the diagonal at $k = 0$ and eventually falls below the diagonal. There are two steady states at $k = 0$ and $k = \bar{k} > 0$, where $\bar{k}$ is the unique positive fixed point of the map h, that is, the unique positive solution of the equation

$$(n + \delta)k = sf(k) \qquad\qquad (7.5)$$

The trivial steady state $k = 0$ is asymptotically unstable while $\bar{k}$ is *globally* asymptotically stable, attracting orbits that start at any initial value $k_0 > 0$.

Encapsulated in this descriptive model are some useful predictions about factors that affect economic growth. To understand them let us find out how the steady state $\bar{k}$ itself depends on the values of the parameters δ, n, s and also on the aggregate production function f. As one may expect both from the definition of the map h and from the underlying economic intuition, $\bar{k}$ increases whenever the parameter s or the function f shifts upward or the parameters δ and n fall. On the basis of the phaseline in figure 7.1, we would also predict that *the rate of change* in either capital per worker or output per worker would vary inversely with the size of an economy's initial conditions, that is, with k_0 or with $y_0 = f(k_0)$.

These predictions state that the rate of output in the stationary state responds favorably to thrift (high values of s), factor productivity, durability of capital (low values of δ), and low population growth. Convergence to the steady state is faster for economies that start far from it and slow for economies that start near it. It is interesting to note here that some, although by no means most or all, of the development data that economic historians have accumulated in the last century or so conform to the prognoses of the Solow model (see the economic development material in chapter 13). Among them are the very low incomes observed in the demographically explosive countries of Africa, South Asia, and Central America; the

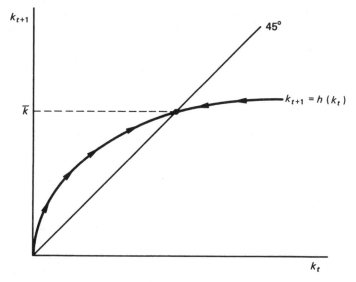

Figure 7.1 The descriptive growth model.

high incomes of those national economies in North America and Western Europe that
have been technological and industrial leaders; and the experience of several nations
(Germany in the previous century, Japan and Finland in this one) that caught up with
such technological leaders as the USA and Britain from an initial position of capital
inferiority.

Neoclassical growth models explain very well how some poorer economies catch up
with richer ones. They are not as good at figuring out why most less-developed
countries seem not to be catching up.

7.3   Optimal growth

Optimal growth theory is a shorthand name for a class of neoclassical growth models
starting with Ramsey's; these are populated by a single infinite-lived representative
individual (or a larger number of identical individuals) whose saving plans are
"optimal" because they are equivalent to the choices of a central planner who
maximizes a lifetime utility function of the form

$$V = \sum_{t=0}^{\infty} \beta^t u(c_t) \tag{7.6}$$

The function V, defined over countably infinite consumption sequences, is a weighted
sum of instantaneous utilities, evaluated by the flow utility function $u: \mathbb{R}_+ \to \mathbb{R}$ and
discounted to the present by powers of the constant discount factor $\beta \in (0,1)$. We
choose u to be a standard increasing concave function and $\beta < 1$ so that the sum on
the right-hand side of equation (7.6) converges if $u(c)$ is bounded.

Ramsey's original contribution to capital accumulation opened a large area of
fruitful research to which significant contributions were made later by Cass (1965) and
Koopmans (1965) on deterministic growth, Sidrauski (1967) and Brock (1974) on
growth with money, Brock and Mirman (1972) on growth under uncertainty, and
many other researchers. We postpone for Part II the details of deriving the
fundamental equations of the optimal deterministic growth model from utility and
profit maximization; here we simply copy these equations from chapter 1:

$$k_{t+1} = f(k_t) + (1 - \delta)k_t - c_t \tag{7.7a}$$

$$\beta u'(c_{t+1}) = \frac{u'(c_t)}{1 - \delta + f'(k_{t+1})} \tag{7.7b}$$

First we seek positive steady states $(\bar{k}, \bar{c})$, that is, nontrivial solutions to the system
of equations

$$c = f(k) - \delta k \tag{7.8a}$$

$$f'(k) = \rho + \delta \tag{7.8b}$$

The right-hand side of equation (7.8b) is the sum of two non-negative numbers: the
depreciation rate $\delta \geq 0$ and the *rate of time preference* $\rho = 1/\beta - 1 > 0$. Since f' is a
decreasing function, a positive steady state $(\bar{k}, \bar{c})$ exists if the marginal product of
capital schedule is sufficiently sensitive to changes in k, that is, if the limits $f'(0)$ and
$f'(\infty)$ satisfy

$$0 \leq f'(\infty) < \rho + \delta < f'(0) \leq + \infty \tag{7.9}$$

As in the Solow model, the origin $(0,0)$ is a steady state here because an economy that starts with zero capital remains forever at $(0,0)$. This steady state does *not* represent a tangency of a budget line with the appropriate indifference curve and therefore violates equation (7.8b).

Next we draw a phase diagram to gauge the qualitative properties of orbits in the state space (k,c). This requires that we identify the loci of points in the state space for which k is increasing and c is increasing. From equation (7.7a) we obtain

$$k_{t+1} \geq k_t \Leftrightarrow f(k_t) + (1 - \delta)k_t - c_t \geq k_t \Leftrightarrow c_t \leq f(k_t) - \delta k_t \qquad (7.10a)$$

Continuing with (7.7b) we observe that

$$c_{t+1} \geq c_t \Leftrightarrow \beta u'(c_{t+1}) \leq \beta u'(c_t)$$

$$\Leftrightarrow u'(c_t)/[1 - \delta + f'(k_{t+1})] \leq \beta u'(c_t)$$

$$\Leftrightarrow 1 \leq \beta[1 - \delta + f'(k_{t+1})]$$

$$\Leftrightarrow k_{t+1} \leq \overline{k} \qquad \text{by equation (7.8b)}$$

$$\Leftrightarrow f(k_t) + (1 - \delta)k_t - c_t \leq \overline{k} \qquad \text{by equation (7.7a)}$$

which leads to

$$c_{t+1} \geq c_t \Leftrightarrow c_t \geq f(k_t) - \delta k_t + k_t - \overline{k} \qquad (7.10b)$$

Applying to the optimal growth model the methods we used in section 4.3 to construct phase diagrams for discrete systems, we derive the planar vector field of figure 7.2 which consists of two concave phaselines and four pairs of arrows indicating the direction of the force field. In this figure it is obvious that the steady state $(\overline{k},\overline{c})$ is unstable since any orbit that starts at any (k_0,c_0) satisfying

$$(k_0 - \overline{k})(c_0 - \overline{c}) < 0 \qquad (7.11)$$

will continue to move away from $(\overline{k},\overline{c})$, either toward the northwest or toward the southeast. Given the direction of the arrows, it seems *likely* that the steady state is reachable through trajectories that lie on a path like the saddlepath drawn in figure 7.2.

To make *sure* that $(\overline{k},\overline{c})$ is a saddlepoint we have to evaluate at that point the Jacobian matrix of partial derivatives for the dynamical system (7.7a) and (7.7b). Eliminating k_{t+1} from equation (7.7b), we obtain

$$k_{t+1} = x(k_t,c_t) \qquad (7.12a)$$

$$\beta u'(c_{t+1}) = \frac{u'(c_t)}{1 - \delta + f'[x(k_t,c_t)]} \qquad (7.12b)$$

where we defined

$$x(k,c) = f(k) + (1 - \delta)k - c \qquad (7.12c)$$

At $(\overline{k},\overline{c})$ we compute the Jacobian matrix

$$J = \begin{pmatrix} x_k & x_c \\ \dfrac{\partial c_{t+1}}{\partial c_t} & \dfrac{\partial c_{t+1}}{\partial c_t} \end{pmatrix} = \begin{pmatrix} 1/\beta & -1 \\ \dfrac{f''(\overline{k})}{A(\overline{c})} & 1 - \dfrac{\beta f''(\overline{k})}{A(\overline{c})} \end{pmatrix} \qquad (7.13)$$

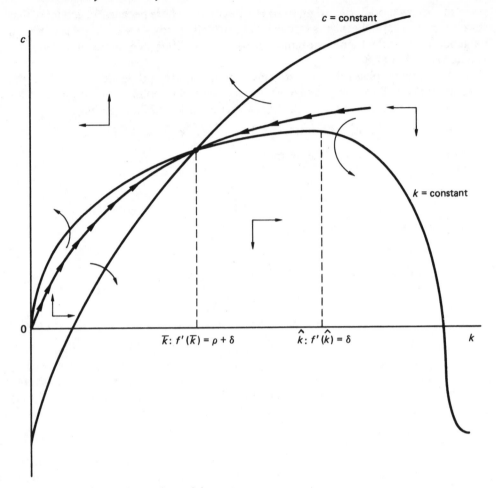

Figure 7.2 The optimal growth model.

which we express in terms of the positive function

$$A(c) = -\frac{u''(c)}{u'(c)}$$

This matrix has trace

$$T = 1 + \frac{1}{\beta} - \frac{\beta f''}{A} \geqslant 1 + \frac{1}{\beta} > 2 \qquad (7.14a)$$

and determinant

$$D = \frac{1}{\beta} > 1 \qquad (7.14b)$$

Hence, $T^2 - 4D \geqslant (1 + 1/\beta)^2 - 4/\beta = (1 - 1/\beta)^2 > 0$, and the characteristic polynomial $p(\lambda) = \lambda^2 - T\lambda + D$ has two positive real roots $\lambda_2 > \lambda_1 > 0$ whose sum exceeds 2 and whose product exceeds 1. Because

$$p(1) = 1 - T + D = \beta f''/A < 0$$

the two real eigenvalues lie on either side of unity, which means that $0 < \lambda_1 < 1 < \lambda_2$ and $(\overline{k},\overline{c})$ really is a saddle. One shows easily that the saddlepath slopes upward in the state space, and its slope near the steady state lies somewhere in the interval $(\rho, 1+\rho)$.

Equations (7.8b) and (7.5) reveal how closely optimal growth theory agrees with the Solow model on the long-run determinants of income per worker. Both affirm that steady state income is positively associated with the productivity of inputs, the durability of capital, and some parameter that depends on consumer patience. The Ramsey model, however, states that $(\overline{k},\overline{c})$ is independent of the instantaneous utility function u.

7.4 Overlapping generations: scalar systems

One way to relax the unrealistic demographic structure of optimum growth theory is to replace the single infinitely-lived consumer with a sequence of overlapping generations; one of these is assumed to be born each period, becomes an economic decision-maker over a fixed life-cycle of $T \geq 2$ periods, and dies out at the end of its natural life when its position is taken over by younger generations. This class of models, which we examine thoroughly in Part II, goes back to Samuelson's investigation (1958) of interest rates in pure exchange economies, and Diamond's seminal study (1965) of growth with national debt. Each time period there are alive at least two generations of possibly heterogeneous agents; the resulting gains from trade support a richer pattern of production and exchange possibilities than one finds in economies with one representative individual.

Equation (1.3) describes the simplest growth model in the overlapping generations tradition; it makes no provision for government and has only one state variable, capital per worker. We call this *the scalar Diamond model* and explore it immediately below. To introduce any kind of fiscal policy, we must augment the state space by one, adding national debt per worker as a second state variable; we refer to the enlarged structure as *the planar Diamond model* and examine its dynamical properties in section 7.5.

For the scalar model we copy equation (1.3) from chapter 1 in the form

$$(1 + n)k_{t+1} = z[R(k_{t+1}), w(k_t)] \tag{7.15}$$

in which n is the rate of population growth. The functions

$$R(k) = f'(k) + 1 - \delta \tag{7.16a}$$

$$w(k) = f(k) - kf'(k) \tag{7.16b}$$

explain how the capital–labor ratio affects, respectively, the *interest factor* (one plus the rate of interest) on safe bank loans and the *wage income* of each worker in competitive markets in which factors are paid their marginal products. The saving function $z: \mathbb{R}^2_+ \to \mathbb{R}_+$ is a continuously differentiable function that averages individual saving functions z_h over all workers $h = 1,\ldots,H$, that is,

$$z(R,w) = \frac{1}{H} \sum_{h=1}^{H} z_h(R,w) \tag{7.17}$$

As we shall see in Part II, each z_h represents the saving plan that maximizes lifetime utility for worker h. For the time being, we make certain assumptions directly on the aggregate production and savings functions f and z whose economic meaning is this: all individuals regard current and future consumption as normal goods and gross substitutes. We suppose, in other words, that

1. z is an increasing function of R and y;
2. $z(0,y) = 0$ for all $y \geqslant 0$ and $z(R,0) = 0$ for all $R \geqslant 0$; and
3. $(\partial/\partial y)z(R,y) \in (0,1)$.

Furthermore, it is easy to check that the interest factor and wage income functions R and w, defined in equations (7.16a) and (7.16b) are clearly positive and monotone in k provided that f is an increasing concave function such that $f(0) = 0$. In particular, R is decreasing in k and w is increasing in k, which means intuitively that a larger stock of capital per worker drives the cost of capital *down* and the cost of labor *up*.

Since the left-hand side of equation (7.15) is increasing in k_{t+1} while the right-hand side is decreasing in k_{t+1} and increasing in k_t, we may apply the implicit function theorem[3] to "solve" that equation to obtain the law of motion for capital per worker:

$$k_{t+1} = G(k_t) \tag{7.18}$$

The precise functional form of the continuously differentiable increasing map G: $\mathbb{R}_+ \to \mathbb{R}_+$ depends on how we specify the functions f and z. Some qualitative information about the general shape of G is contained in the normality and substitutability assumptions we have already made. We extract that information below in order to check whether the dynamical system (7.18) has any steady states and, if so, whether or not these are stable.

Note first that $G(0) = 0$ (since $k = 0$ implies $f(k) = 0$) and $w(k) = 0$, that is, zero capital means zero wages and zero saving. Hence $k = 0$ is always a steady state, just as in the Solow model, simply because zero capital means nothing is ever earned, saved, or invested. Next we find that[4]

$$\lim_{k \to \infty} \left[\frac{G(k)}{k} \right] = 0 \tag{7.19}$$

Hence, for sufficiently large k_t, we have $k_{t+1}/k_t = G(k_t)/k_t < 1$ which implies that the graph of G eventually falls below the diagonal in figure 7.3.

The function G, then, passes through the origin and lies below the 45° line for large k. Whether additional steady states with $k > 0$ exist depends on the slope of the time map at the origin.[5] There are two possibilities. If G is steeper than the diagonal and must eventually end up below it, continuity implies that it must cross the diagonal an odd number of times; hence at least one additional steady state with $k > 0$ exists. On the other hand, if G starts below the 45° line, we will have an even number of such equilibria, possibly zero. Some of the possibilities are illustrated in figure 7.3 and summed up in the following theorem.

Theorem 7.1 (Existence of steady states) The scalar Diamond model has a steady state $k = 0$. If, in addition, the time map (7.18) satisfies $G'(0) > 1$, then there is an odd number of positive steady states.

The stability properties of the positive steady states are easy to establish if G is steeper than the diagonal at the origin. Since G is a monotone map, it will intersect the

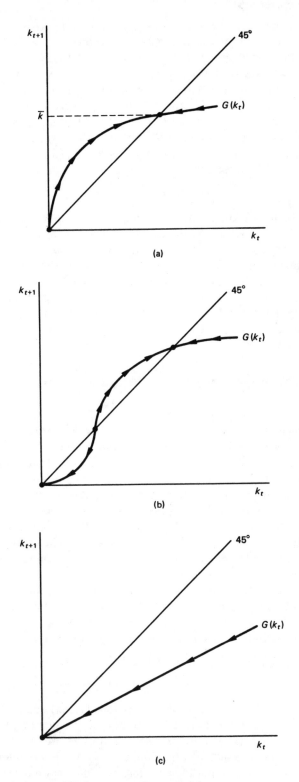

Figure 7.3 The scalar overlapping generations model.

diagonal $2j + 1$ times where j is some non-negative integer. Of these intersections, $j + 1$ will occur from above the diagonal at slopes in the interval $(0,1)$, and exactly j will occur from below the diagonal at slopes that exceed $+1$. Hence, we shall have *at least one* asymptotically stable stationary state if $G'(0) > 1$; we may or may not have other steady states. As a numerical example of a scalar system, consider an economy with production function $f(k) = k^{\frac{1}{3}}$ and a Solow-type saving function $z(R,y) = \frac{1}{2}y$ with constant propensity to save, equal to one-half, out of labor income y. For this economy we find readily from equation (7.16b) that the wage rate $w = \frac{2}{3}k^{\frac{1}{3}}$ equals two-thirds of output per worker. Aggregate saving becomes $\frac{1}{3}k^{\frac{1}{3}}$ and the dynamical system in equation (7.15) simplifies to

$$(1 + n)k_{t+1} = \tfrac{1}{3}k^{\frac{1}{3}} \tag{7.20}$$

where n is the population growth rate. This time map resembles that in figure 7.3(a) with an infinitely large derivative at the origin. It has two steady states: an unstable one at zero and an asymptotically stable one at $\bar{k} = [3(1 + n)]^{-\frac{3}{2}}$ where the slope of the time map equals one-third. If $n = 0$, the steady state value of capital per worker is approximately 0.19 and that of output per worker is about 0.58. Raising n to 1, that is, allowing every generation to be twice as large as the parent generation, lowers $\bar{k}$ to 0.07 and income per worker to 0.41. We shall continue with this example in the two-dimensional case.

7.5   Overlapping generations: planar systems

Suppose now that the economy described in equation (7.15) starts out at the beginning of its evolution not only with a given amount k_0 of capital per worker but also with some initial stock b_0 of national debt per worker which we may think of as the result of a deficit in the government budget at $t = 0$. It is simplest to think for the time being that all outstanding public debt matures in one period; the government must raise enough revenue to repay principal and interest on all public debt. We assume that the fiscal authority does so not by collecting taxes from households but, rather, through the familiar expedient of selling new debt to repay old debt. A given stock of national debt in our economy is perpetually refloated as long as households are willing to keep extending credit to the public sector. We assume that the government otherwise raises no taxes, consumes no goods or services, and invests no funds.

In Part III we analyze in detail several economies in which these assumptions are relaxed in order to understand how various fiscal policies interact with the production and distribution of resources over time. For now we simply write down the relevant dynamical system, a two-dimensional extension of equation (7.15):

$$(1 + n)(k_{t+1} + b_{t+1}) = z[R(k_{t+1}), w(k_t)] \tag{7.21a}$$

$$(1 + n)b_{t+1} = R(k_t)\,b_t \tag{7.21b}$$

where the functions R and w are defined in equations (7.16a) and (7.16b). Here b_t is the value of national debt per worker maturing at time t; equation (7.21a) expresses the equality of aggregate saving (more precisely, household wealth) to the sum of the stocks of physical capital and public debt. Equation (7.21b) is a budget constraint for the fiscal authority which states that the principal and interest on national debt due at any time t has to be financed by selling debt of equal principal value maturing at $t + 1$.

An *equilibrium* of this system is an infinite sequence $(k_t, b_t)_{t=0}^{\infty}$ of state variables that satisfies equations (7.21a) and (7.21b), keeps $k_t \geq 0$ for each t, and conforms to a given initial condition $k_0 \geq 0$ for capital and to some boundary condition for b_t. For the sake of exposition, let us assume that the saving function z satisfies all the normality and gross substitutability restrictions we placed on it earlier and, furthermore, that the scalar Diamond system has two steady states, $k = 0$ and $k = \overline{k} > 0$. Then we already know two of the three steady states (k, b) of the planar Diamond system: $(0,0)$ and $(\overline{k}, 0)$. To see this, note how $b_t = 0$ for all t turns equation (7.21b) into an identity, and check that both $k_t = 0$ and $k_t = \overline{k}$ for all t satisfy equation (7.21b) whenever $b_t = 0$ for all t. We call these states *inside-money equilibria* because in them households hold no government assets such as currency or national debt.

There is another steady state, $(k, b) = (k^*, b^*)$, associated with *non-zero national debt*. Following Phelps (1961), we call this state *the golden rule* for it corresponds to a particular kind of stationary welfare optimum, as we shall see in Part II. The golden rule solves the stationary form of equations (7.21a) and (7.21b), that is,

$$(1 + n)(k + b) = z[R(k), w(k)]$$

$$1 + n = R(k) = f'(k) + 1 - \delta$$

After a little manipulation, these expressions simplify to

$$f'(k^*) = n + \delta \tag{7.22a}$$

$$(1 + n)b^* = z[1 + n, w(k^*)] - (1 + n)k^* \tag{7.22b}$$

As in the Solow model, these equations have a meaningful solution $(k^*, b^*) \in \mathbb{R}_+ \times \mathbb{R}$ if the marginal product of capital is sufficiently sensitive to changes in the capital–labor ratio, that is, if

$$0 \leq f'(\infty) < n + \delta < f'(0) \leq +\infty \tag{7.23}$$

In what follows we assume $b^* > 0$, which means that aggregate saving exceeds the golden rule capital–labor ratio if the interest rate equals the population growth rate. The household sector is a net demander of government liabilities if $b^* > 0$, a net supplier of liabilities to the government if $b^* < 0$.

Qualitative *global* information on the stability properties of these three steady states comes from a phase diagram which we build up in the same way as in the Ramsey model; quantitative *local* information is contained in the relevant Jacobian matrix. We start with the phase diagram for which equation (7.21b) yields

$$b_{t+1} \geq b_t \Leftrightarrow (1 + n)b_t \leq (1 + n)b_{t+1} = R(k_t)b_t$$

$$\Leftrightarrow 0 \leq b_t[R(k_t) - 1 - n] = b_t[1 - \delta + f'(k_t) - 1 - n]$$

$$= b_t[f'(k_t) - f'(k^*)]$$

which means that

$$b_{t+1} \geq b_t \text{ if } b_t(k^* - k_t) \geq 0 \tag{7.24a}$$

Continuing, we substitute b_{t+1} from (7.21b) into (7.21a) and obtain

$$(1 + n)k_{t+1} = z[R(k_{t+1}), w(k_t)] - b_t R(k_t) \tag{7.21c}$$

Therefore

$$k_{t+1} \geq k_t \Leftrightarrow (1 + n)k_{t+1} \geq (1 + n)k_t$$

$$\Leftrightarrow b_t R(k_t) = z[R(k_{t+1}), w(k_t)] - (1 + n)\, k_{t+1} \qquad (*)$$

$$\leq z[R(k_t), w(k_t)] - (1 + n)k_t$$

because the right-hand side of (*) is a decreasing function of k_{t+1} for each fixed k_t. The upshot of all this algebra is summarized in the following statement:

$$k_{t+1} \geq k_t \text{ if } b_t \leq B(k_t) \qquad (7.24b)$$

where we define the single-valued function $B: \mathbb{R}_+ \to \mathbb{R}$ from

$$B(k) = \frac{z[R(k), w(k)] - (1 + n)k}{R(k)} \qquad (7.24c)$$

To draw the phase diagram for the planar system of equations (7.21a), (7.21b) or, equivalently, the system (7.21b), (7.21c), we need to know the shape of the function B. Note that, at $k = 0$, the numerator of B vanishes whereas the denominator $R = 1 - \delta + f'(k)$ is positive and possibly infinite; hence $B(0) = 0$. Recall next that the numerator of B resembles the time map (7.15) of the one-dimensional system, a function we assumed to have exactly two fixed points (0 and $\bar{k}$) and to look very much like the phaseline in figure 7.3(a). That map lies above the diagonal for $k \in (0,\bar{k})$ and below the diagonal if $k > \bar{k}$. Hence

$$k_t < \bar{k} \Leftrightarrow k_{t+1} - k_t = G(k_t) - k_t > 0$$

$$\Leftrightarrow 0 = (1 + n)k_{t+1} - z[R(k_{t+1}), w(k_t)] \qquad (**)$$

$$\Leftrightarrow 0 > (1 + n)k_t - z[R(k_t), w(k_t)]$$

because the right-hand side of (**) is an increasing function of k_{t+1} for each fixed k_t. Comparing this inequality with (7.24c) we obtain

$$(k - \bar{k})B(k) < 0 \text{ for all } k \neq \{0,\bar{k}\} \qquad (7.25)$$

In other words, B vanishes at $k = 0$ and $k = \bar{k}$, is positive for all $k \in (0,\bar{k})$ and becomes negative for $k > \bar{k}$. At the golden rule capital–labor ratio, in particular, we have $B(k^*) = b^* > 0$.

Figure 7.4 contains all the steps needed to construct a phase diagram for the planar overlapping generations economy. Figure 7.4(a) shows inequality (7.24a) which says that $b_{t+1} > b_t$ if *either* $b_t > 0$ and $k_t < k^*$ *or* $b_t < 0$ and $k_t > k^*$. Figure 7.4(b) does the same for inequality (7.24b), showing that the capital–labor ratio rises whenever b lies *below* the line $b_t = B(k_t)$ and falls whenever b lies *above* that line.

Figure 7.4(c) combines the first two and shows that their phaselines have three intersections at the points $0 = (0,0)$, $A = (\bar{k},0)$, and $G = (k^*, b^*)$. These are the three stationary states of our dynamical system, two of them having zero national debt and one, the golden rule state G, having non-zero national debt. Figure 7.4(c) also suggests that $(0,0)$ is unstable, possibly a source, that $(\bar{k}, 0)$ is asymptotically stable, and, finally, that (k^*, b^*) is unstable and may well be a saddle.

We recall, however, that orbits in discrete dynamical systems are sequences of points in the relevant state space, not continuous curves. The vector fields of discrete systems have more to say about the *direction of change* in state variables than about the *approximate position* of those variables next period. Qualitative information drawn from discrete phase diagrams is quite tentative and should be confirmed from the local information contained in Jacobian matrices.

A case in point is trajectories that start at the northwest corner of figure 7.4(c) from an initial position (k_0, b_0) with a large value of b_0. Figure 7.4(c) may suggest that such trajectories are asymptotically headed toward $k = 0$ and $b = +\infty$, but a perusal of equations (7.21a) and (7.21b) shows otherwise. A low value for k_0 means that $R(k_0)$ is large and hence national debt increases rapidly to the point where it drives capital down to zero in finite time; for a sufficiently low value of k_t and a sufficiently high value of b_t, equation (7.21a) cannot hold for *any* positive k_{t+1}. Thus no equilibria will exist if k_0 is "too small" relative to b_0.

Before we derive the Jacobian of the planar system, we compute the slope $T(k)$ of the phaseline for the original scalar system at any steady state $k \geqslant 0$. Referring back to equations (7.15) and (7.18), we take total derivatives and rearrange to obtain

$$T(k) = G'(k) = \frac{-kz_y f''(k)}{1 + n - z_R f''(k)} \tag{7.26}$$

for any fixed point of the map G. Here we define z_R and z_y to be the partial derivatives of the saving function $z(R, y)$ with respect to the interest factor R and first-period income y. Since we have already hypothesized G to be an increasing map with an unstable fixed point at $k = 0$ and a stable one at $k = \bar{k} > 0$, we assume that

$$0 < T(\bar{k}) < 1 < T(0) \tag{7.27}$$

where $T(0)$ denotes the limit of $G'(k)$ as $k \to 0$.

At any steady state (k, b) of the planar system that consists of equations (7.21b) and (7.21c), the Jacobian matrix of partial derivatives is easily computed:

$$J = \begin{vmatrix} \dfrac{R(k)}{1+n} & \dfrac{bf''(k)}{1+n} \\ -\dfrac{R(k)}{1+n-z_R f''(k)} & -\dfrac{(kz_y + b)f''(k)}{1+n-z_R f''(k)} \end{vmatrix}$$

Substituting $1 + n - z_R f''(k)$ from equation (7.26), this matrix reduces to

$$J = \begin{vmatrix} \dfrac{R(k)}{1+n} & \dfrac{bf''(k)}{1+n} \\ \dfrac{R(k)T(k)}{kz_y f''(k)} & \dfrac{T(k)(kz_y+b)}{kz_y} \end{vmatrix} \tag{7.28}$$

For any $(k,b) \geqslant 0$, its trace and determinant are

$$\operatorname{tr} J = \frac{1 - \delta + f'(k)}{1+n} + \frac{kz_y + b}{kz_y} T(k) > 0 \tag{7.29a}$$

$$\det J = \frac{R(k)T(k)}{1+n} > 0 \tag{7.29b}$$

It is easy to show that $(\operatorname{tr} J)^2 - 4 \det J > 0$ which means that J has two positive real eigenvalues at each steady state. At the two inside-money states we have $b = 0$,

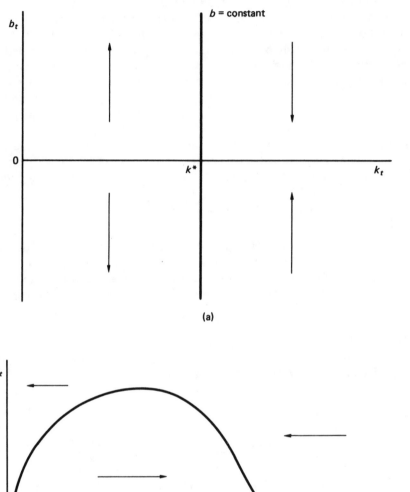

$b = \text{constant}$

(a)

$k = \text{constant}$

(b)

Figure 7.4 The planar overlapping generations model.

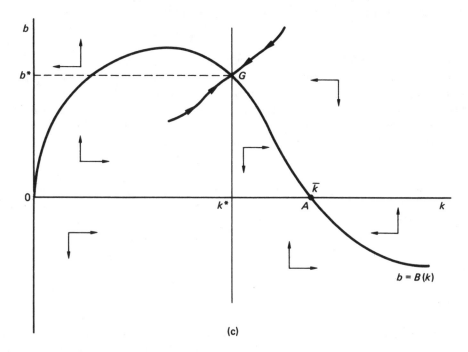

(c)

Figure 7.4 cont'd

tr $J = \lambda_1 + \lambda_2 = R/(1 + n) + T$, and det $J = \lambda_1\lambda_2 RT/(1 + n)$, which means that the eigenvalues are

$$\lambda_1 = \frac{R(k)}{1 + n} \qquad \lambda_2 = T(k) \tag{7.30}$$

at both $(0,0)$ and $(\overline{k},0)$. At $k = 0$ we have $\lambda_1 = [1 - \delta + f'(0)]/(1 + n) > 1$ by inequality (7.23), and $\lambda_2 = T(0) > 1$ by inequality (7.27). At $k = \overline{k} > k^*$, on the other hand, we have $1 - \delta + f'(\overline{k}) < 1 - \delta + f'(k^*) = 1 + n$ by the definition of the golden rule. Hence $\lambda_1 < 1$ and also $\lambda_2 = T(\overline{k}) < 1$ from (7.27).

The algebra of the last few paragraphs confirms the geometric intuition of the phase diagram about the inside-money steady states: *the trivial one is an unstable node; the nontrivial one is a stable node.* Trajectories do not oscillate in the immediate neighborhood of either state. What happens outside the neighborhood of each steady state is less clear and cannot be ascertained by the local analysis of this chapter.

What can we say about the positive golden rule state (k^*,b^*)? Evaluating the characteristic polynomial $p(\lambda)$ at $\lambda = 1$ we obtain

$$p(1) = 1 - \text{tr } J + \det J$$

$$\left[1 + \frac{(b^* + k^*z_y)T(k^*)}{k^*z_y}\right]$$

$$= -\frac{b^*T(k^*)}{k^*z_y} < 0$$

which means that the two positive eigenvalues straddle unity, that is,

$$0 < \lambda_1 < 1 < \lambda_2 \qquad \text{at } (k^*, b^*) \tag{7.31}$$

Hence *the golden rule is a saddle in the planar Diamond model.*

To acquire a feel for the magnitudes involved in this economy, we solve explicitly a parametric example similar to that used in the scalar case. This time we choose parameter values $\delta = 1$, $n = 0$, a constant saving rate $s \in (0,1)$ out of labor income, and pick the production function $f(k) = k^a$ for some $a \in (0,1)$. The inside-money states are fixed points of the one-dimensional time map

$$G(k) = s(1 - a)k^a$$

These states are readily found to be $k = 0$ and $k = [s(1 - a)]^{1/(1-a)}$. The golden rule capital–labor ratio solves $f'(k) = n + \delta = 1$ which implies $k^* = a^{1/(1-a)}$. If we pick any parameter values such that $0 < a < s(1 - a) < 1$, we have $k^* < \bar{k}$ and

$$b^* = s(1 - a)(k^*)^a - k^* = k^* \left[\left(\frac{\bar{k}}{k^*} \right)^{1-a} - 1 \right] > 0$$

Notes

1 The text by Hirsch and Smale (1974) is a good source of elementary nonlinear differential equations drawn from the natural sciences; the monograph by Guckenheimer and Holmes (1983) contains more advanced material. See the bibliography for details.
2 The planar version of the Diamond model may also produce, in some circumstances, solutions that converge to periodic orbits or limit cycles; see chapter 9 for economic examples of periodic equilibria, and also chapter 12 for a more detailed treatment.
3 See the Technical Appendices, section A.2 for a precise statement of this important mathematical result.
4 To see this, start from equation (7.15) and note that saving can never exceed wage income. Hence

$$\frac{(1 + n)k_{t+1}}{k_t} \leq \frac{w(k_t)}{k_t} \Rightarrow \lim_{k \to \infty} \left[\frac{G(k)}{k} \right] \leq \lim_{k \to \infty} \left[\frac{w(k)}{k} \right] = \lim_{k \to \infty} \left[\frac{f(k)}{k} - f'(k) \right]$$

by equation (7.16b). The expression in the last square brackets is non-negative by the concavity of f; it tends to zero, either directly (if f is bounded) or by L'Hôpital's rule (if f is not bounded).
5 Galor and Ryder (1989) examine the time map G thoroughly.

8 Periodic equilibria and bifurcations (*)

Periodic solutions of nonlinear dynamical systems are of particular interest from both a mathematical and an economic point of view. Periodic orbits generalize the concept of steady states and expand the set of solutions that deserve special attention in any thorough dynamical study of asymptotic behavior. In the field of macroeconomics, too, where the study of cyclical fluctuations is a long-standing concern, periodic solutions and limit cycles are of considerable importance for they resemble idealized business cycles.

This chapter and the next one are an elementary introduction to periodicity and related issues which arise when steady states lose stability in response to changes in the structure of a system. We introduce and illustrate the main mathematical results in this chapter, and look at some economic applications in chapter 9.

8.1 Periodic equilibria

Periodic points of maps are simply fixed points of their iterates which we defined at the very beginning of chapter 6. Formally we have the following definition.

Definition 8.1. (Periodic point) A point $x^* \in X$ is called a periodic point of period $p > 0$ for the dynamical system $x_{t+1} = f(x_t)$ if it is a fixed point for the pth iterate of f, that is, if $f^p(x^*) = x^*$ and p is the smallest integer for which this is true.

The set of all iterates of a periodic point

$$\Gamma = \{x_1^* = x^*, \ x_2^* = f(x^*), \ ..., \ x_p^* = f^{p-1}(x^*)\}$$

is called a *periodic orbit* of period p for this system or a *p-cycle*. Since periodic points are defined in terms of fixed points of iterated maps, the notion of stability generalizes naturally from steady states to periodic orbits.

Definition 8.2 (Stability of periodic orbits) A periodic point x^* of minimum period p is said to be stable, asymptotically stable, or unstable if x^* is respectively a stable, asymptotically stable, or unstable fixed point of f^p.

When do periodic cycles exist? We begin with a discussion of some results on the existence of two-cycles in scalar systems. Consider the dynamical system

$$x_{t+1} = f(x_t) \qquad \text{where } f: \mathbb{R} \supseteq X \to \mathbb{R}, \ f \in C^1 \tag{8.1}$$

and C^1 is the set of all continuously differentiable functions. A periodic point of period 2 for the system (8.1) is a fixed point x^* of f^2. A two-cycle for (8.1) is a set of two distinct periodic points $\{x_1^*, x_2^*\}$ such that $x_2^* = f(x_1^*)$ and $x_2^* \neq x_1^* = f(x_2^*)$. We would like to know under what conditions this system admits or rules out periodic orbits of period 2.

Let us start with a class of scalar systems that do not admit periodic solutions of *any* order. Recall that a scalar function f is said to be monotone nondecreasing if, for all (x,y) in its domain of definition X, we have that $x \geq y \Rightarrow f(x) \geq f(y)$. If f is differentiable, as we are assuming here, monotonicity is equivalent to the condition $f'(x) \geq 0$ for all x in X. It is easy to see (by doing question I.32 for instance) that monotone nondecreasing maps cannot exhibit cycles of any order since, along a periodic solution, the positive orbit $\gamma^+(x_0)$ that starts at any initial point x_0 cannot be a monotone sequence and must change direction at no fewer than *two* points; this simply means that a cycle must have a peak and a trough. Turning points, however, are not consistent with an increasing map and we have the following theorem.

Theorem 8.1 Let f be a monotone nondecreasing scalar map. Then the system $x_{t+1} = f(x_t)$ defined in equation (8.1) has no periodic solutions.

Figure 8.1(a) illustrates. A necessary condition for the existence of cycles is therefore that $f'(x)$ be negative in some part of the domain of f; this, however, is not sufficient. To see why intuitively recall that, if x_1^* and x_2^* are two periodic points, they must satisfy $x_2^* = f(x_1^*)$ and $x_1^* = f(x_2^*)$ because the system jumps from one to the other each period. Graphically, we can think of plotting f and its mirror image relative to the 45° line and looking for intersections. Intersections *on* the 45° line will then correspond to steady states, since $x_1^* = x_2^*$ will hold for these; intersections *off* the diagonal will come in pairs by symmetry and will correspond to periodic cycles.

Figure 8.1(b) suggests that cycles will exist provided that f slopes downward slowly enough near the steady state $\bar{x}$. Before we become more specific, we need to know more about the shape of the iterated map f^2.

Lemma 8.1 Let f be a C^1 map and let f^2 be its second iterate $f^2(x) = f[f(x)]$.

(a) If $\bar{x}$ is a fixed point of f, then it is also a fixed point of f^2.
(b) If $\bar{x}$ is a fixed point of f, then

$$\frac{df^2(\bar{x})}{dx} = \left[\frac{df(\bar{x})}{dx}\right]^2$$

Proof (a) By assumption, $f(\bar{x}) = \bar{x}$ which implies $f^2(\bar{x}) = f[f(\bar{x})] = f(\bar{x}) = \bar{x}$.

(b) $\dfrac{df^2(\bar{x})}{dx} = \dfrac{df[f(\bar{x})]}{dx} = f'[f(\bar{x})]f'(\bar{x}) = f'(\bar{x})f'(\bar{x}) = [f'(\bar{x})]^2$ ∎

This lemma helps establish the existence of two-cycles in certain cases. One of those is the following theorem (see Baumol and Benhabib (1989) and Grandmont (1985) for details).

Theorem 8.2 Suppose 0 and $\bar{x} > 0$ are fixed points of the scalar system $x_{t+1} = f(x_t)$ in which $f: \mathbb{R}_+ \supseteq X \to \mathbb{R}_+$ and $f \in C^1$. Suppose also that there exists an $a > \bar{x}$ such that

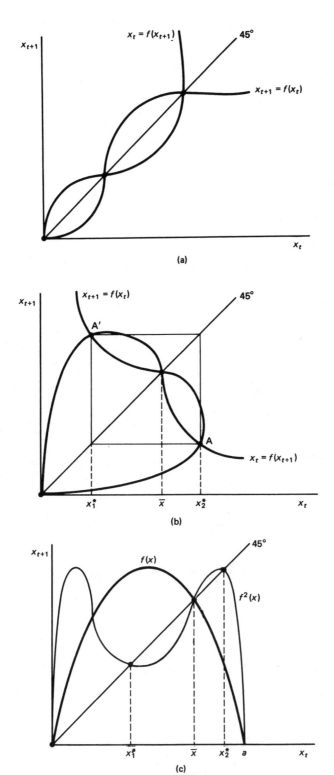

Figure 8.1 (a) Periodic points ruled out; (b) periodic points exist; (c) a map and its second iterate.

$a > f(a)$ and $a > f^2(a)$. Then $f'(\bar{x}) < -1$ is a sufficient condition for the existence of a two-cycle $\{x_1^*, x_2^*\}$ that satisfies $x_1^* < \bar{x} < x_2^* < a$.

Here is why this result holds true. If $\bar{x}$ is a fixed point for f, it is also a fixed point for f^2, as shown in figure 8.1(c). We want to prove that f^2 will have to cut the 45° line at two or more additional points that correspond to a two-cycle. By the previous lemma, the slope of f^2 at $\bar{x}$ exceeds unity and hence f^2 cuts the 45° line from below. By that lemma, however, $f^2(0) = 0$ and f^2 lies below the diagonal at $x = a$ so that the continuous map f^2 has to cross over once again somewhere in the interval $(\bar{x}, a)$.

8.2   A parametric example

We investigate the one-parameter family of discrete scalar systems

$$x_{t+1} = F(x_t,\lambda) = -(1 + \lambda)x_t - (3 + \lambda)x_t^2 \tag{8.2}$$

indexed by the real number λ. To find its steady states, we set $x_{t+1} = x_t$ and obtain $x = -(1 + \lambda)x - (3 + \lambda)x^2$. Clearly $\bar{x}^a = 0$ is a solution. For $x \neq 0$ we can divide by x to get the equation $1 = -(1 + \lambda) - (3 + \lambda)x$. The solution is another steady state $\bar{x}^b$, that is,

$$\bar{x}^b = \bar{x}(\lambda) = -\frac{2 + \lambda}{3 + \lambda}$$

To check stability we compute

$$\frac{\partial F(x_t,\lambda)}{\partial x_t} = -(1 + \lambda) - 2(3 + \lambda)x_t$$

and evaluate it at the steady states $\bar{x}^a = 0$ and $\bar{x}^b = \bar{x}(\lambda)$. This yields

$$\frac{\partial F(0,\lambda)}{\partial x_t} = -(1 + \lambda) \tag{8.3}$$

$$\frac{\partial F(\bar{x}(\lambda),\lambda)}{\partial x_t} = 3 + \lambda \tag{8.4}$$

We have, then, four possibilities for each fixed point, depending on the value of the parameter λ. Specifically,

$\bar{x}^a = 0$ is:
   an unstable spiral point if $\partial F(0,\lambda)/ \partial x_t \in (-\infty,-1) \Rightarrow \lambda > 0$
   a stable spiral point if $- (1 + \lambda) \in (-1,0) \Rightarrow \lambda \in (-1,0)$
   a stable node if $-(1 + \lambda) \in (0,1) \Rightarrow \lambda \in (-2,-1)$
   an unstable node if $-(1 + \lambda) \in (1,\infty) \Rightarrow \lambda \in (-\infty,-2)$

By the same token,

$\bar{x}^b = \bar{x}(\lambda) = -(2 + \lambda)/(3 + \lambda)$ is:
   an unstable spiral point if $\partial F[\bar{x}(\lambda),\lambda]/ \partial x_t \in (-\infty,-1) \Rightarrow \lambda \in (-\infty,-4)$
   a stable spiral point if $3 + \lambda \in (-1,0) \Rightarrow \lambda \in (-4,-3)$
   a stable node if $3 + \lambda \in (0,1) \Rightarrow \lambda \in (-3,-2)$
   an unstable node if $3 + \lambda \in (1,\infty) \Rightarrow \lambda \in (-2,\infty)$

A useful way to summarize this information is through a *bifurcation diagram* that shows how the parameter λ influences the qualitative properties of steady states $\bar{x}^a$ and $\bar{x}^b$. Solid line segments correspond to stable steady states, broken segments to unstable equilibria.

Note that $\bar{x}(\lambda)$ has a vertical asymptote at $\lambda = -3$ and tends to $\pm\infty$ as λ approaches -3 from above or below. Except for this discontinuity, $\bar{x}(\lambda)$ is a decreasing function that satisfies $\bar{x}(\pm\infty) = -\lambda/\lambda = -1$ and $\bar{x}(0) = -2/3$. In addition

$$\bar{x}(\lambda) = 0 \Rightarrow 2 + \lambda = 0 \Rightarrow \lambda = -2$$

and

$$\bar{x}(\lambda) > 0 \text{ if } 2 + \lambda < 0 < 3 + \lambda \Rightarrow \lambda \in (-2,-3)$$

To locate *two-cycles* we form the map $x_{t+1} = F^2(x_{t-1}) = F[F(x_{t-1},\lambda),\lambda]$, that is,

$$x_{t+1} = -(1 + \lambda)x_t - (3 + \lambda)x_t^2$$
$$= -(1 + \lambda)[-(1 + \lambda)x_{t-1} - (3 + \lambda)x_{t-1}^2] - (3 + \lambda)[-(1 + \lambda)x_{t-1} - (3 + \lambda)x_{t-1}^2]^2$$

After a bit of algebra we obtain

$$x_{t+1} = F^2(x_{t-1},\lambda) \tag{8.5}$$
$$= (1 + \lambda)^2 x_{t-1} - \lambda (1 + \lambda)(3 + \lambda) x_{t-1}^2 - 2(1 + \lambda)(3 + \lambda)^2 x_{t-1}^3 - (3 + \lambda)^3 x_{t-1}^4$$

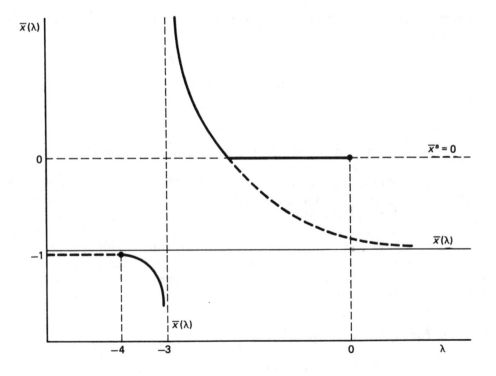

Figure 8.2 Bifurcation diagram for equation (8.2).

If a point x^* is an element of a two-period orbit, then it is a fixed point of F^2 and satisfies $x_{t+1} = x_{t-1}$. Two-cycles are thus solutions to

$$x = (1 + \lambda)^2 x - \lambda(1 + \lambda)(3 + \lambda)x^2 - 2(1 + \lambda)(3 + \lambda)^2 x^3 - (3 + \lambda)^3 x^4 \quad (8.6)$$

Clearly, $x = 0$ is a solution. For any $x \neq 0$ we divide equation (8.6) by x, collect terms, and get a third-degree polynomial equation in x:

$$p(x) = -(3 + \lambda)^3 x^3 - 2(1 + \lambda)(3 + \lambda)^2 x^2 - \lambda(1 + \lambda)(3 + \lambda)x + \lambda^2 + 2\lambda = 0 \quad (8.7)$$

To solve this equation we can try to factor out the polynomial. Note that if $p(x)$ is a third-degree polynomial and (x_1, x_2, x_3) are its roots, we can write $p(x)$ as

$$p(x) = A(x - x_1)(x - x_2)(x - x_3)$$

where A is the coefficient of its cubic term. If we happen to know any solution, say x_1, to $p(x) = 0$ we can divide $p(x)$ by $x - x_1$ to get a second-degree polynomial whose other two roots can be computed by the quadratic formula. In fact, we *do* know one such solution, the non-zero fixed point of F

$$\bar{x}(\lambda) = -\frac{2(2 + \lambda)}{3 + \lambda}$$

which, by definition, must also be a fixed point of F^2. Hence, we can divide $p(x)$ in equation (8.7) by $x - \bar{x}(\lambda)$, say, by the method of undetermined coefficients, to obtain

$$p(x) = [-(3 + \lambda)^3 x^2 - \lambda(3 + \lambda)^2 x + \lambda(3 + \lambda)][x - \bar{x}(\lambda)] \quad (8.8)$$

Solutions to $p(x) = 0$ that are not fixed points of the original map F must then satisfy the equation

$$- (3 + \lambda)^2 x^2 - \lambda(3 + \lambda) x + \lambda = 0 \quad (8.9)$$

After some algebra, the quadratic formula yields the periodic orbit

$$(x_1^*, x_2^*) = \frac{\lambda \pm (\lambda^2 + 4\lambda)^{1/2}}{-2(3 + \lambda)}$$

Note that x_1^* and x_2^* are real and distinct provided that $\lambda^2 + 4\lambda = \lambda(\lambda + 4) > 0$, that is, if λ is *outside* the closed interval $[-4,0]$.

To check whether the cycle is stable, we compute $\partial F^2(x^*,\lambda)/\partial x$ and check whether its absolute value, evaluated at the periodic orbit, is less than unity. Interested readers may pursue this issue in question I.13 which asks them to prove that the periodic orbit defined above is stable for parameter values $\lambda \in (-2 -2\sqrt{(1.5)}, -4)$ and $\lambda \in (0, 2\sqrt{(1.5)} -2)$. In other words, stable cycles arise if either steady state is a spiral that loses stability as a result of changes in the parameter λ. The critical values $\lambda = 0$ and $\lambda = -4$ are called *bifurcation points* for the dynamical system in equation (8.2). Below we explore such phenomena more closely.

8.3   Bifurcations of equilibrium

Consider a family of dynamical systems

$$x_{t+1} = F(x_t; \alpha) \qquad F: \mathbb{R}^n \times \mathbb{R}^m \supseteq X \times \Omega \to X \qquad F \in C^1 \qquad (8.10)$$

indexed on the parameter vector $\alpha \in \Omega$. As α varies so will the solutions of the system. In most cases small changes in α will not affect the qualitative structure of the orbits of the system. For some critical values of α, however, small perturbations can lead to qualitative changes in the system's orbit structure and its dynamic behavior. When this happens, we say that a *bifurcation* has occurred.

We will be interested here in bifurcations of equilibria when structural parameters change, that is, in changes in the number of steady states, their stability type, and the nature of orbits near a given equilibrium. To start, note that all stationary states of (8.10) are solutions to the parametrized system of equations

$$G(x; \alpha) = F(x_t; \alpha) - Ix = 0 \qquad (8.11)$$

where I is an appropriate identity matrix. Suppose that $(x^0; \alpha^0)$ is a solution to (8.11), that is, an equilibrium for $\alpha = \alpha^0$. If we change the value of α slightly away from α^0 the equilibrium will in general change. By the implicit function theorem we know that if

$$|D_x G(x^0; \alpha^0)| \neq 0 \qquad (8.12)$$

then x^0 is an isolated equilibrium. Moreover, we can write the equilibrium of the system locally as a function $\bar{x}(\alpha)$ of the parameters such that $\bar{x}(\alpha^0) = x^0$ and, for all α in some neighborhood of α^0, $\bar{x}(\alpha)$ is unique. Hence, *if bifurcations occur that involve either the appearance or the vanishing of equilibria, equation (8.12) and the implicit function theorem have to fail.*

We would like to relate condition (8.12) to the eigenvalues of the Jacobian matrix $D_x F(x^0; \alpha^0)$ for the system in equation (8.10). First we relate the eigenvalues of $D_x F$ to those of $D_x G$. Note that λ_f and λ_g are defined as the solutions to the following equations:

$$\lambda_f \text{ solve } |D_x F(x^0; \alpha^0) - \lambda_f I| = 0$$

$$\begin{aligned} \lambda_g \text{ solve } |D_x G(x^0; \alpha^0) - \lambda_g I| &= D_x F(x^0; \alpha^0) - I - \lambda_g I| \\ &= |D_x F(x^0; \alpha^0) - (\lambda_g + 1)I| = 0 \end{aligned}$$

It is clear that

$$\lambda_g = \lambda_f - 1 \qquad (8.13)$$

For each eigenvalue of the first system there is one in the second whose real part is lower by 1. Recall next that the determinant of a matrix is equal to the product of its eigenvalues. Hence, we can write

$$|D_x G(x^0; \alpha^0)| = \prod_i \lambda_g^i = \prod_i (\lambda_f^i - 1) \qquad (8.14)$$

where Π denotes the product operator. If the eigenvalues of $D_x F$ are real, equation (8.14) says that $D_x G$ vanishes and the implicit function theorem fails only if at least one of the eigenvalues of F is 1, that is, the system (8.10) is non-hyperbolic.

If some eigenvalues are complex, they come in conjugate pairs that we may write as $\lambda_f = a \pm jb$. Suppose we have just one pair of complex eigenvalues; then we can denote $j = \sqrt{(-1)}$ and have

$$\begin{aligned} |D_x G(x^0; \alpha^0)| &= \prod_{i=1}^{n} (\lambda_f^i - 1) \\ &= [(a - 1) + jb][(a - 1) - jb]\prod_{i=3}^{n}(\lambda_f^i - 1) \\ &= [(a-1)^2 + b^2]\prod_{i=3}^{n}(\lambda_f^i - 1) \end{aligned}$$

Note that the term in square brackets is positive except for the case $a = 1$, $b = 0$, again an eigenvalue with unit modulus. We conclude that the implicit function theorem can be used to guarantee smooth changes in a locally unique equilibrium under small perturbations in the parameters of a hyperbolic dynamical system.

Even if an equilibrium continues to exist and responds smoothly to changes in the parameters, we can still have bifurcations involving changes in the *stability type* of the steady state. Recall that the stability type of an equilibrium depends on the modulus of its eigenvalues $|\lambda_f(\alpha)|$. Under our assumptions $|\lambda_f(\alpha)|$ is a continuous function of the parameters. Hence, if the original equilibrium is hyperbolic, small changes in α will not take any eigenvalues across the boundary of the unit circle, and the stability type of the equilibrium will persist for small perturbations.

The upshot of this discussion is that bifurcations can occur only at non-hyperbolic equilibria. In the remainder of this section we will study the three typical bifurcations that can occur in *one-parameter families of discrete systems*.

We focus on the one-parameter family

$$x_{t+1} = F(x_t, \alpha) \qquad F: \mathbb{R}^n \times \mathbb{R} \supset X \times \Omega \to X \qquad F \in C^r \qquad (8.10)'$$

where α is a real number and r will generally be at least 2. Consider a pair $(x^0; \alpha^0)$ such that

$$F(x^0; \alpha^0) = x^0$$

and assume x^0 is a non-hyperbolic steady state. This means that one or more eigenvalues of the Jacobian matrix $D_x F(x^0; \alpha^0)$ lie on the boundary of the unit circle. There are generically three ways in which this can occur, giving rise to three "standard" bifurcations for one-parameter systems: the saddle-mode bifurcation, the flip bifurcation and the Hopf bifurcation.

The saddle-node bifurcation

The first possibility is that $D_x F(x^0; \alpha^0)$ has a single real eigenvalue on the boundary of the unit circle with value $+1$. As we have seen, the implicit function theorem fails in this case and we may expect a change in the number of equilibria. What actually happens is the merging and disappearance of two hyperbolic equilibria, one stable and one unstable, at the bifurcation point α^0, producing the typical "fold" pattern we illustrate in figure 8.3. A formal statement of what transpires is next; interested readers should consult Ruelle (1989, p. 64), for a proof.

Theorem 8.3 In the system defined by equation $(8.10)'$, assume that $(x^0; \alpha^0) \in X \times \Omega$, that x^0 is a non-hyperbolic equilibrium for α^0, and that the eigenvalues of the Jacobian $D_x F(x^0; \alpha^0)$ have moduli strictly less than unity with the exception of a single real eigenvalue $\lambda(\alpha^0) = 1$ on the boundary of the unit circle. Then, if we exclude unlikely choices of the parameter α, for any sufficiently small neighborhood of (x^0, α^0) in $X \times \Omega$ the system $(8.10)'$ has two hyperbolic steady states on one side of α^0, exactly one state at α^0, and none on the other side. Whenever two equilibria exist, one is stable and the other unstable, and the distance between them is of the order $(|\alpha - \alpha|)^{1/2}$.

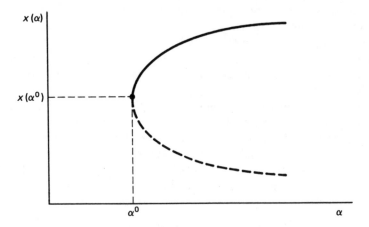

Figure 8.3 Saddle-node bifurcation diagram.

In planar systems, a saddle-node bifurcation occurs when one of the eigenvalues is unity and the other is less than unity in absolute value, say $\lambda_1 = 1$ and $|\lambda_2| < 1$. Hence

$$p(1) = (1 - \lambda_1)(1 - \lambda_2) = 0$$

Moreoever, the determinant and trace of the relevant Jacobian are $\det = \lambda_1\lambda_2 \in (-1,1)$ and $\mathrm{tr} = \lambda_1+\lambda_2 \in (0,2)$, and so saddle-node bifurcations can appear on the segment of $p(1) = 0$ between $(0,-1)$ and $(2,1)$. This occurs along the boldly drawn line segment BC of the stability triangle in figure 6.6(b), reproduced for convenience in figure 8.4.

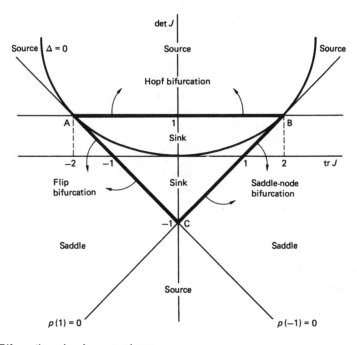

Figure 8.4 Bifurcations in planar systems.

Saddle-node bifurcations are examples of the "hard" loss of stability which takes place whenever the number of steady states changes as a parameter passes through some critical value; because equilibria vanish altogether in this case, it causes more concern than the "mild" loss of stability that occurs when steady states, which continue to exist as parameters change, lose their stability to another asymptotic orbit that has just appeared.

Parts III and IV contain several economic examples of the saddle-node bifurcation, many of which arise in a planar dynamical system when the central government's budget deficit exceeds a critical or sustainable value. To provide a simpler illustration, we return to the scalar Diamond model of chapter 7. Recall, in particular, equation (7.15) in which we assume a constant population (that is, $n = 0$), full depreciation ($\delta = 1$), a constant saving rate $s \in (0,1)$ out of wage income, and a family of production functions

$$f(k) = a \log(1 + k) \tag{8.15}$$

indexed on the parameter $a > 0$.

Note that f is a twice continuously differentiable production function that has all the standard properties: it is increasing, concave, and goes through the origin. Also $f'(k) = a/(1 + k)$, which equals a at $k = 0$ and tends to zero as $k \to \infty$. Saving is $sw = as[\log(1 + k) - k/(1 + k)]$ which reduces equation (7.15) to

$$k_{t+1} = asg(k_t) \tag{8.16a}$$

where

$$g(k) = \log(1 + k) - k/(1 + k) \tag{8.16b}$$

The phase diagram of equation (8.16a) resembles figure 7.3(b). There is a steady state at $k = 0$ and there may be an *additional pair* of positive steady states if the time map has additional fixed points, that is, if the equation

$$G(k) = asg(k) - k = 0 \tag{8.17}$$

has solutions other than zero. Recall that $G(0) = 0$ and that $[\log(1 + k)/k] \to 0$ as $k \to \infty$; hence $G(k) \to -\infty$ as $k \to \infty$. Note also that G has derivative $G'(0) = -1$ at $k = 0$. Because G is negative for both very low and very high values of k, a sufficient condition for the existence of two positive steady states is

$$G^* = \max_{k \geq 0} g(k) > 0 \tag{8.18}$$

as shown in figure 8.5(b).

The maximized value G^* varies directly with the parameter a; that much is obvious from equation (8.17). In fact G^* can be made arbitrarily large if a increases without bound, and will become negative if we pick a close enough to zero. By the intermediate value theorem, then, there exists a value a^0 for which $G^* = 0$. As the parameter a *falls toward* a^0, and G^* toward zero, the two positive steady states k_1 and k_2 of the dynamical system (8.16b) move closer to k^0 and to each other (see figure 8.5). When $a = a^0$, the stable state k_2 merges with the unstable state k_1 at the common value k^0, and both disappear when $a < a^0$.

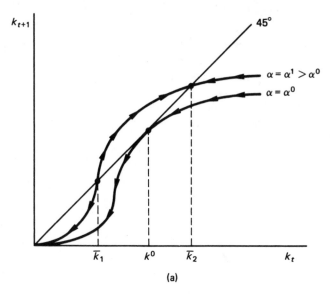

(a)

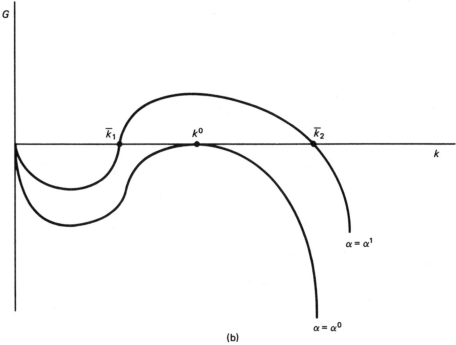

(b)

Figure 8.5 Analyzing saddle-node bifurcations.

The flip bifurcation

A second possibility is that $D_x F(x^0; \alpha^0)$ has a single real eigenvalue on the boundary of the unit circle with value -1. In this case, the hypotheses of the implicit function theorem hold, and the equilibrium persists and is locally unique under small perturbations of the parameter. On the other hand, small changes in α will generally take the eigenvalues across the unit circle's boundary, changing the stability type of the dynamical system. As the stationary equilibrium loses stability, a stable two-cycle will appear on one side of the bifurcation point. Figure 8.6 illustrates how the two periodic points $(x_1^*(\alpha), x_2^*(\alpha))$ envelope the steady state $\bar{x}$.

Flip bifurcations are called *period-doubling* because they give birth to stable periodic orbits whose period is twice that of the stability-losing equilibrium. We state below without proof the basic result on these bifurcations.[1]

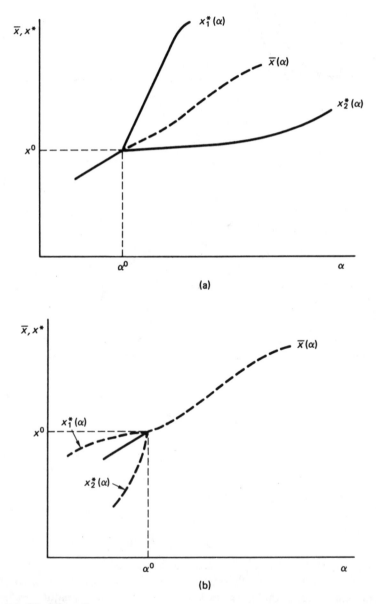

Figure 8.6 Flip bifurcations.

Theorem 8.4 Consider the system $x_{t+1} = F(x_t, \alpha)$ where $F: \mathbb{R}^n \times \mathbb{R} \supseteq X \times \Omega \to X$, $F \in C^r$ and $r \geqslant 3$. Assume that $(x^0; \alpha^0) \in X \times \Omega$, that x^0 is a non-hyperbolic equilibrium for α^0, and that the eigenvalues of the Jacobian $D_x F(x^0, \alpha^0)$ have moduli strictly less than unity with the exception of a single real eigenvalue $\lambda(\alpha^0) = -1$ on the boundary of the unit circle. Then, if $d\lambda(\alpha^0)/d\alpha \neq 0$ as the parameter crosses the bifurcation point α^0 in some direction, the equilibrium loses stability. Moreover:

(a) In a sufficiently small neighborhood of (x^0, α^0) in $X \times \Omega$, this system has a periodic orbit of period 2 on one side of the bifurcation point α^0. The distance between each of the periodic points and the stationary equilibrium $\bar{x}(\alpha)$ is of the order $|\alpha - \alpha^0|^{1/2}$.

(b) If $\bar{x}(\alpha)$ is asymptotically stable at $a = a^0$, then the periodic orbit is asymptotically stable and appears for values of the parameter for which the equilibrium $\bar{x}(\alpha)$ is unstable. Otherwise, the periodic orbit is unstable and "surrounds" the stable equilibrium.

This theorem does not tell us on *which side* of the bifurcation value α^0 periodic orbits will appear, nor does it reveal whether the non-hyperbolic steady state $x^0 = \bar{x}(\alpha^0)$ is stable. The eigenvalues of the Jacobian matrix at x^0 are not informative when a bifurcation takes place. Figures 8.6(a) and 8.6(b) illustrate the two possibilities described in part (b) of this theorem.

Planar dynamical systems undergo a period-doubling bifurcation when the eigenvalues satisfy $\lambda_1 = -1$ and $|\lambda_2| < 1$. Then $p(-1) = (-1-\lambda_1)(-1-\lambda_2) = 0$, det $= \lambda_1 \lambda_2 \in (-1,1)$, and tr $= \lambda_1 + \lambda_2 \in (-2,0)$, and so this bifurcation arises on the segment of $p(-1) = 0$ between $(0,-1)$ and $(-2,-1)$, as shown by the bold line segment AB in figure 8.4.

Flip bifurcations are a common source of endogenous business cycles in *scalar systems*, a topic we introduce in chapter 9 and take up more systematically in Part IV. Here we illustrate the phenomenon of "mild" stability loss in the *discrete logistic system*

$$y_{t+1} = ay_t(1 - y_t) \qquad 1 \leqslant a \leqslant 4 \qquad (8.19)$$

The logistic equation is indexed on the scalar parameter a and maps the interval $[0,1]$ into itself. It describes a quadratic map $f(y) = ay(1 - y)$ whose phaseline is symmetric about $1/2$, and achieves its maximum value $a/4$.

This system has two steady states $\{0, 1-1/a\}$ of which the zero state is an unstable node for any $a > 1$. From the derivative of the logistic map, we check readily that the positive steady state is a stable node for $a \in (1,2)$ and a stable spiral for $a \in (2,3)$; the spiral system and one converging orbit are drawn in figures 8.7(a) and 8.7(b). Equilibria become interesting once we pass the value $a = 3$ at which the positive state $y = 1-1/a$ becomes an *unstable spiral*.

What emerges then is a stable two-period limit cycle, as shown in figures 8.7(c) and 8.7(d). As the parameter becomes higher, at approximately $a = 3.4495$, the iterated logistic map f^2 loses stability; the two-period limit cycle loses stability to a four-period cycle, pictured in 8.7(e) and 8.7(f), which appears at that value of a.

This sequence of period-doubling bifurcations, from 1 to 2 to 4, continues to unfold as we raise the value of a; cycles with period 8, 16, etc. emerge as lower periodicity orbits lose stability but continue to be equilibria of the logistic system. Figure 8.7(g) contains the first and second iterates of the map for $a \in (3, 3.45)$, and makes plain why a stable two-cycle exists in that parameter range.

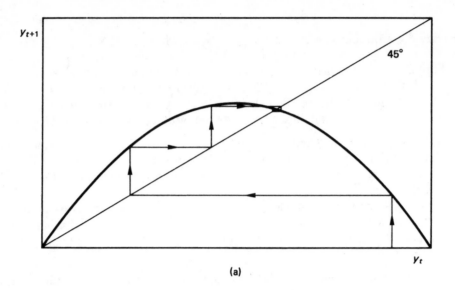

(a)

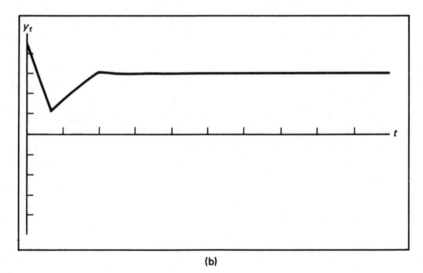

(b)

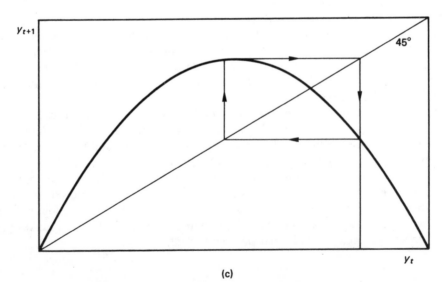

(c)

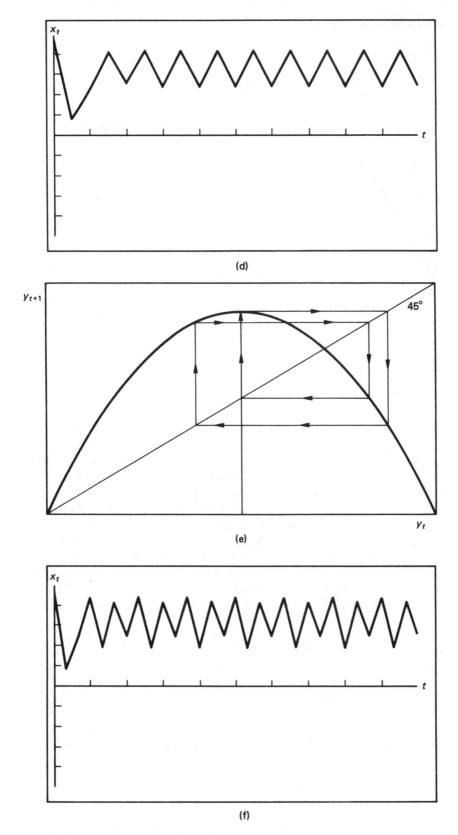

(d)

(e)

(f)

Figure 8.7 The logistic map. cont'd overleaf

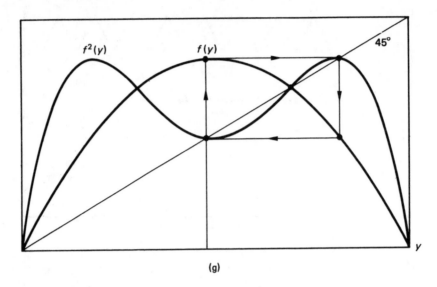

(g)

Figure 8.7 cont'd

The Hopf bifurcation

Another mild form of stability loss arises in planar systems when eigenvalues are complex conjugates with modulus 1, that is, $\lambda_1 = a + ib$ and $\lambda_2 = a - ib$ with $\det = \lambda_1\lambda_2 = a^2 + b^2 = |\lambda|^2 = 1$ which   requires $|a| < 1$, and   therefore $\text{tr} = \lambda_1 + \lambda_2 = 2a \in (-2,2)$. Hence, this bifurcation occurs at the horizontal line segment AB in figure 8.4; it is illustrated in figure 8.8.

In higher-dimensional systems, Hopf bifurcations take place when $D_xF(x^0; \alpha^0)$ has a conjugate pair of complex eigenvalues of modulus 1. By the implicit function theorem the equilibrium changes smoothly with the parameter and remains locally unique. However, small perturbations of α will change the stability of the equilibrium. As in the period-doubling bifurcation, this change is accompanied by the appearance of closed orbits for parameter values on one side of the bifurcation point.[2] The following result, due to Andronov (1933) and Hopf (1942), is proved in Ruelle (1989).

Theorem 8.5 For the system $x_{t+1} = F(x_t; \alpha)$ with $F: \mathbb{R}^n \times \mathbb{R} \supseteq X \times \Omega \rightarrow X, F \in C^r$, and $r \geqslant 3$, assume that $(x^0, \alpha^0) \in X \times \Omega$, x^0 is a non-hyperbolic equilibrium for α^0, and the eigenvalues of the Jacobian $D_xF(x^0; \alpha^0)$ have moduli strictly less than unity with the exception of a conjugate pair of complex eigenvalues $\lambda(\alpha^0)$, $\bar{\lambda}(\alpha^0)$ of modulus 1. We assume, in addition, that $|\lambda(\alpha^0)| = 1$, $\lambda^j(\alpha^0) \neq 1$ for $j = 1,2,3,4$, and $d|\lambda(\alpha^0)|/d\alpha \neq 0$. Then, near (x^0, α^0) and for either $\alpha > \alpha^0$ or $\alpha < \alpha^0$, there exists a manifold $H(\alpha)$ which is invariant to the map F. The manifold H is diffeomorphic to a circle (that is, there is a smooth invertible choice of coordinates that maps H into a circle) and consists of points at a distance of order $|\alpha - \alpha^0|^{1/2}$ from the stationary equilibrium $\bar{x}(\alpha)$.

If $x^0 = \bar{x}(\alpha^0)$ is asymptotically stable, then H is attracting (asymptotically stable) and appears for values of the parameter for which the equilibrium $\bar{x}(\alpha)$ is unstable. Otherwise, H is unstable and "surrounds" the stable equilibrium.

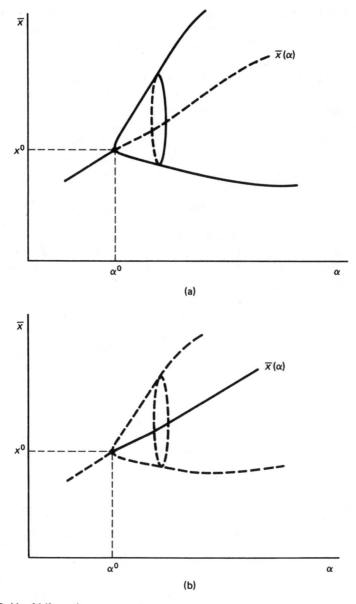

(a)

(b)

Figure 8.8 Hopf bifurcations.

The invariant manifold H is a higher-dimensional analog of a surface with the property that, if $x_0 \in H(\alpha)$ for some point $x_0 \in X$, then $F^n(x_0; \alpha) \in H(\alpha)$ for every iterate n of the map F.

Together with the Poincaré–Bendixson theorem (see the Technical Appendices, section A.3), the Hopf theorem is one of the most powerful tools for the detection of limit cycles. It is not an elementary result and its application requires several assumptions that exclude degenerate behavior; among these are that the complex eigenvalues not be roots of unity and, as in theorem 8.3, that they cross the unit circle with non-zero speed at $\alpha = \alpha^0$. The theorem does not say whether cycles emerge on the low or high side of the critical parameter value α^0 nor does it help with the stability of the steady state $\bar{x}$. Since $\bar{x}$ is not hyperbolic equilibrium, we do not learn anything about its stability from the eigenvalues of the relevant Jacobian. This is one case in which Liapunov's direct method may be quite useful.

Hopf bifurcations are common sources of limit cycles in *planar systems*, especially in the one-sector overlapping generations model of capital accumulation as well as in optimal growth models with two or more commodities. Two of the best illustrations[3] are due to Reichlin (1986) and Farmer (1986). Chapter 12 contains a summary account of Reichlin's work, which introduces elastic supply of labor into the scalar Diamond model and identifies bifurcations in the resulting planar system. Here we follow Farmer who found Hopf cycles in a specially calibrated case of the planar Diamond familiar to us from chapter 7.

To detect limit cycles, we pick a tractable parametrization of the overlapping generations economy described in equations (7.21a) and (7.21b). We assume $n = 0$, $\delta = 1$, and $z(R,y) = sy$, that is, a constant population, full depreciation of capital, and a constant savings rate $s \in (0,1)$. We retain considerable flexibility in choosing a linearly homogeneous production function from the constant elasticity of substitution (CES) family whose intensive form[4]

$$y = f(k) = (ak^{-\rho} + 1 - a)^{-1/\rho} \tag{8.20}$$

is defined for parameter values $\alpha \in (0,1)$ and $\rho \geqslant -1$.

Equation (8.20) describes how output per worker depends on capital per worker. Note that f is a standard increasing concave production function. The non-negative parameter

$$\sigma = \frac{1}{1 + \rho} \tag{8.21}$$

is called the *elasticity of substitution*. We define the function

$$\alpha(k) = \frac{kf'(k)}{f(k)} \tag{8.22a}$$

which may be interpreted as capital's share of output in an economy with linear homogeneous technology and competitive factor markets. After some tedious algebra,[5] equation (8.22a) simplifies to

$$\alpha(k) = \frac{a}{a+(1 + a)k^\rho} \tag{8.22b}$$

The planar overlapping generations system of equations (7.21a) and (7.21b) reduces in this case to

$$k_{t+1} + b_{t+1} = sw(k_t) \tag{8.23a}$$

$$b_{t+1} = b_t f'(k_t) \tag{8.23b}$$

We focus on orbits near the golden rule (k^*,b^*), that is, near the solution

$$f'(k^*) = 1 \qquad b^* = sw(k^*) - k^* \tag{8.24}$$

Without loss of generality, we choose units of measurement so that

$$k^* = 1 \qquad b^* = sw(1) - 1 \tag{8.25}$$

We also pick the particular value $a = 1/2$ for one of our technological parameters; capital's share of output at the golden rule becomes $\alpha(k^*) = 1/4$.

At the golden rule, the trace and determinant of the Jacobian matrix are given by equations (7.29a) and (7.29b), that is,

$$\text{tr } J = 1 + \left(1 + \frac{b^*}{sk^*}\right) T(1) \tag{8.26}$$

$$\det J = T(1) \tag{8.27}$$

Here $T(1)$ is the slope of the scalar Diamond map evaluated at the golden rule, a number we can compute from equation (7.26). The computation yields

$$T(k^*) = -sk^*f''(k^*) = \frac{s(1 - \alpha)}{\sigma} \tag{8.28}$$

To complete it we must invert the formula in note 5 to express $k^*f''(k^*)$ in terms of the elasticity of substitution σ and the marginal product $f'(k^*) = 1$.

Does the Hopf theorem apply to the golden rule equilibrium of the planar Diamond system that consists of equations (8.25) through (8.28)? Farmer found that it does for a suitable choice of the parameters $\sigma \geq 0$ and $s \in (0,1)$. Let us fix the elasticity of substitution at $\sigma = 3s^0/4$ and regard $s \in (0,1)$ as a free parameter which we must set at $s = s^0$ and hope that:

1. the system has two complex eigenvalues $u(s) \pm iv(s)$ of modulus 1;
2. neither eigenvalue is a second, third, or fourth root of unity; and
3. the modulus of the eigenvalues has non-zero derivative with respect to the free parameter s at $s = s^0$, that is, as the eigenvalues cross the unit circle.

Note that we have *already* picked σ so that, at the critical point $s = s^0$, $\det J = 1$ and the eigenvalues have modulus 1. Equations (8.27) and (8.28) show that $u^2 + v^2 = \det J = s/s^0$, which means that the modulus will change at non-zero speed when the eigenvalues cross the unit circle at the yet-to-be-determined critical parameter value s^0. These eigenvalues, we check easily, cannot be roots of unity if $u \neq 0$ and $v \neq 0$, which is true if the Jacobian matrix has a non-zero trace and a non-zero discriminant, $\Delta = (\text{tr } J)^2 - 4 \det J$.

All that remains now is to find an $s^0 \in (0,1)$ so that the system has complex eigenvalues and non-zero trace; in other words, s^0 should satisfy

$$(\text{tr } J)^2 < 4 \qquad \text{tr } J \neq 0 \tag{8.29}$$

From equation (8.24) we obtain

$$\frac{b^*}{k^*} = \frac{sw(k^*) - k^*}{k^*} \tag{8.30}$$

$$= \frac{sw(k^*) - k^*f'(k^*)}{k^*f'(k^*)}$$

$$= \frac{s(1 - \alpha) - \alpha}{\alpha}$$

Substituting this value into equation (8.26) yields

$$\operatorname{tr} J = 2 + \frac{s(1 - \alpha) - \alpha}{\alpha s}$$

whenever $T = 1$. Set $\alpha = 1/4$, as assumed earlier, to obtain

$$\operatorname{tr} J = \frac{5s - 1}{s} \tag{8.31}$$

which satisfies the conditions in (8.29) if $s \neq 1/5$ and $|5s - 1| < 2s$. In other words, we may choose the critical value s^0 *anywhere in the interval* (1/7, 1/3) *except at* $s = 1/5$. The corresponding elasticity of substitution $\sigma = 3s^0/4$ lies in the interval (3/28, 1/4), except at $\sigma = 3/20$.

   Low values of the elasticity of substitution in production, typically well below unity, are often required for Hopf bifurcations in overlapping generations models. This is a conclusion we will reach again in chapter 12 when we review Reichlin's work on growth with elastic labor supply.

8.4   Strange attractors and chaos

What are the asymptotic properties of a dynamical system $x_{t+1} = f(x_t)$? This question is of central importance to economists who care about the long-run impact of policies and institutions, as well as to mathematicians worried about limit behavior. The simplest, and must tractable, asymptotic solutions are steady states and closed or periodic orbits; but these are not the only possible outcome. Physicists already know that much from the van der Pol (1927) and Duffing (1918) equations that describe oscillations in circuits and continuous media, and from the Lorenz (1963) equations that govern convection in a heated fluid layer. All of these equations possess a rich set of asymptotic solutions, including unusual ones such as sets of uncountably many points that act as complicated "sinks" for all orbits that start within the set or in its immediate vicinity. We call these "sinks" *strange attractors*, and label *chaotic equilibria* the messy acyclic orbits that end up within strange attractors.

   To describe unusual types of asymptotic behavior we need to refine the concepts of stability we discussed in chapter 6. Suppose $f : \mathbb{R}^n \to \mathbb{R}^n$ is a locally invertible, continuously differentiable map and recall that the *positive orbit* or a point $x \in \mathbb{R}^n$ is the collection $\gamma^+(x) = \{f^q(x)\}_{q=0}^{\infty}$ of points reachable from x in $q = 0,1,2,...$ periods; we define iterations of the map f so that $f^0(x) = x$ and $f^1(x) = f(x)$. Similarly, the *negative orbit* $\gamma^-(x)$ of point x is the collection of points leading to x in $q = 0,1,2,...$periods. If there is a sequence of integers q_i such that $f^{q_i}(x_0) \to \hat{x} \in \mathbb{R}^n$ as $q_i \to \infty$, we say that $\hat{x}$ is a *positive limit point*, or ω-limit point, of the orbit $\gamma^+(x_0)$; similarly we define a *negative limit point*, or α-limit point, for the orbit $\gamma^-(x_0)$. The sets of all such limit points are the *positive and negative limit sets* of a given orbit.

   Asymptotically stable steady states and periodic orbits are good examples of limit sets for all solutions that start in their immediate neighborhood. The positive limit sets of planar dynamical systems in *continuous time* have a simple structure: they are either (i) fixed points, or (ii) closed orbits, or (iii) the unions of fixed points and the trajectories that connect them.[6] We refer to trajectories connecting a fixed point to itself as *homoclinic orbits*, to trajectories connecting distinct fixed points as *heteroclinic orbits*. These are illustrated in figure 8.9 along with *homoclinic cycles*, that is,

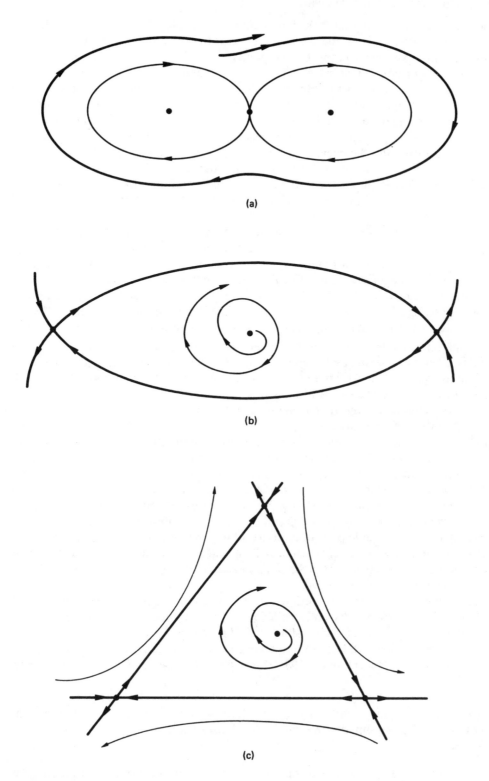

Figure 8.9 Limit sets for planar systems: (a) double saddle-loop; (b) homoclinic cycle; (c) homoclinic orbit.

closed trajectories resulting from heteroclinic orbits. Note that all connected fixed points are *saddles*; sinks or sources would either attract or repel trajectories, ruling out solutions that pass through those fixed points.

Limit sets of non-planar systems in either continuous or discrete time are not as simply or as easily categorized. Both scalar and higher-dimensional discrete structures may exhibit an extremely rich pattern of asymptotic behavior for which we need two extensions of the concept of a limit set: *the invariant set* and *the non-wandering set*. For a map $f: \mathbb{R}^n \to \mathbb{R}^n$, a subset S of the state space is an invariant set if, for any $x_0 \in S$, both the positive and the negative orbits $\gamma^+(x_0)$, $\gamma^-(x_0)$ are in S. Once an orbit starts in an invariant set, it never leaves in either forward or backward time. Closed invariant sets (for example, the stable and unstable manifolds of a stationary state or a periodic orbit) contain the positive and negative limit sets of all trajectories that start in them.

Non-wandering sets consist of non-wandering points which lie on or near orbits that return, but do not necessarily stay, within a specified distance of themselves. A point $x \in \mathbb{R}^n$ is non-wandering for the map f if, for any neighborhood U of x, there is a point $\hat{x} \in U$ and an integer $q > 0$ such that $f^q(\hat{x}) \in U$, that is, the orbit through $\hat{x}$ returns to U after q periods. The set of all non-wandering points for the map f is called the *non-wandering set*; it is a closed set that represents long-term or asymptotic paths in a very general sense, while wandering points characterize transient dynamic behavior.

A special example of both a non-wandering set and an invariant set is an *attractor*, that is, a generalized sink that eventually captures all orbits that start in it or near it. A closed invariant set $A \subset \mathbb{R}^n$ is an attractor if there is some neighborhood U of A such that, for all $x \in U$, $f^q(x) \to A$ as $q \to \infty$.

An attractor is *strange* if it contains chaotic solutions, that is, infinitely many periodic orbits of arbitrarily long period as well as completely *aperiodic trajectories* that never return to any point visited previously. These attractors are often present when the stable and unstable manifolds of a stationary state intersect.

To understand how chaotic equilibria arise, we return to the discrete logistic map $f(x) = ax(1 - x)$ which, as we saw earlier, produces a sequence of period-doubling bifurcations once the parameter a reaches or exceeds the value $a = 3$. As a is raised sufficiently (near 3.9), odd-period cycles appear not as bifurcations from pre-existing lower-period orbits but in pairs of periodic orbits, one of them unstable and the other stable. Chaotic orbits appear near $a = 3.94$ and are extremely sensitive to initial conditions; solutions that start in the same small neighborhood lose all resemblance to each other after a few iterations.[7]

How does one detect odd-period cycles and chaotic equilibria in a dynamical system? Two useful results are available in the literature: the Li–Yorke theorem (1975) and the less general Sarkovskii (1964) theorem apply to nonlinear scalar maps. We state these below without proof; interested readers should consult the monograph by Guckenheimer and Holmes (1983) for a proof outline, or Collet and Eckmann (1980).

Theorem 8.6 (Li and Yorke) Let $f:[a,b] \to [a,b]$ be a continuous map of the interval $[a,b]$ into itself, and suppose there is an $x \in [a,b]$ such that $f(x) > x$, $f^2(x) > x$, but $f^3(x) \leqslant x$. Then

(a) for any integer $q > 1$ there is some $x_0 \in [a,b]$ for which the positive orbit $\gamma^+(x_0)$ is a period-q cycle;

(b) there is a set S consisting of uncountably many initial points on $[a,b]$ such that no orbits that start in S will converge to one another or to any periodic orbits.

The maintained assumptions of this result are sufficient to produce a periodic orbit of period 3,[8] and the essence of the basic theorem is to show that cycles of period 3 imply the existence of chaotic equilibria. Another result, related to part (a) of the Li–Yorke theorem, is

Theorem 8.7 (Sarkovskii) Let f be a continuous map of the unit interval into itself. Consider the following ordering of all positive integers:

$$1 \leftarrow 2 \leftarrow 4 \leftarrow ... \leftarrow 2^k \leftarrow 2^{k+1} \leftarrow ...$$
$$\leftarrow 2^{k+1}(2l + 1) \leftarrow 2^{k+1}(2l - 1) \leftarrow ... \leftarrow 2^{k+1}5 \leftarrow 2^{k+1}3 \leftarrow ...$$
$$\leftarrow 2^k(2l + 1) \leftarrow 2^k(2l - 1) \leftarrow ... \leftarrow 2^k5 \leftarrow 2^k3 \leftarrow ...$$
$$\leftarrow 2(2l + 1) \leftarrow 2(2l - 1) \leftarrow ... \leftarrow 2 \times 5 \leftarrow 2 \times 3 \leftarrow ...$$
$$\leftarrow 2l + 1 \leftarrow 2l - 1 \leftarrow ... \leftarrow 5 \leftarrow 3$$

If f has a periodic orbit of period p and $p \rightarrow q$ in this order, then f has a periodic orbit of period q.

Hence orbits with low even periodic numbers are implied by those with higher even periodic numbers which, in turn, are implied by high odd periods and these are sequentially implied by low odd periods. As we saw earlier, a period-3 orbit guarantees that *all* periodic orbits are equilibria of the map f.

To evaluate how seriously we should take chaotic equilibria it would be useful to know what fraction of all possible initial conditions $x_0 \in X$ generate chaotic orbits $\gamma^+(x_0)$. For example, the Li–Yorke theorem mentions an uncountable set $S \subset [a, b]$ which generates chaotic equilibria, but tells us nothing about its size relative to the interval $[a, b]$. If S contains at least one line segment, it has the same dimension as $[a,b]$ and the probability of observing a chaotic path is positive; otherwise S is just a collection of disjoint points with measure zero, and we are not likely to observe chaotic orbits. Loosely speaking, we say that chaos is *ergodic* in the first case (if the asymptotic properties of solution sequences can be summed up by an absolutely continuous distribution that serves as an asymptotic sufficient statistic for the dynamical system) and *topological* in the second case; we take the ergodic or "observable" type of chaos more seriously than the other type.

Computer experiments may be quite helpful here because there are no mathematical results to guide us *a priori* as to when we should be really concerned about chaos. For chaotic equilibria have some properties that are particularly unfamiliar to economists, such as the extreme sensitivity of the trajectory to initial conditions, which makes tolerably accurate forecasting nearly impossible and therefore cripples many sequential or long-range economic decisions.

These considerations are not material to the physical sciences, in which chaotic orbits are more compelling objects of study than in dynamical systems that describe the behavior of forward-looking individuals. Nevertheless, macroeconomics has developed a fair number of examples exhibiting chaotic behavior in both multisector optimal growth models (see Boldrin and Montrucchio, 1986; Deneckere and Pelikan, 1986) and simple overlapping generations models of pure exchange (e.g. Benhabib and Day, 1982; Grandmont, 1985) like those we survey in the following chapter.

The richness of chaotic orbits has kindled a good bit of interest in empirical work. For instance, Brock and several collaborators have devised methods that test whether it is more convenient to describe business cycles as a low-order stochastic linear system or as a low-order deterministic nonlinear system (see Brock and Sayers (1988) for an application).

Notes

1　A proof is sketched in Guckenheimer and Holmes (1983, p. 157); see Devaney (1989, pp. 90–2) for a fuller treatment.
2　A closed orbit is an invariant manifold rather than a periodic orbit. In $\mathbb{R}^2$, for example, it is a closed curve around the steady state, and any orbit that starts on that curve remains on it forever. The resulting motion looks cyclical, but we cannot say much about periodicity.
3　The earliest application of bifurcation results like the Hopf theorem in economics that I am aware of are the articles by Torre (1977) on the IS–LM system and Benhabib and Nishimura (1979) on multisector Ramsey models, that is, on optimal growth with several consumption and capital goods.
4　See chapter 13 on linearly homogeneous production functions of the constant elasticity of substitution and other varieties. Here it is sufficient to define intuitively the elasticity of substitution as the logarithmic derivative $\sigma = $ d log $|\text{MRS}|$ of the capital–labor ratio with respect to the absolute value of the marginal rate of substitution between capital and labor in the production function.
5　Interested readers should consult Ferguson (1969, pp. 103ff) for this computation. Ferguson also shows how the elasticity of substitution of a linear homogeneous production function may be expressed in terms of its intensive form, that is, $\sigma = (1 - kf'/f)/(-kf''/f')$.
6　This result was proved by the Russian mathematician Andronov and his co-workers (1973) for the non-wandering set (non-wandering sets are defined later in this section) of a continuous planar dynamical system. It does not necessarily extend to discrete planar systems. For example, computer simulations indicate that the Hénon map, defined by $x_{t+1} = a - by_t - x_t^2$ and $y_{t+1} = x_t$, may possess a strange attractor when $a = 1.4$ and $b = -0.3$; see Devaney (1989, pp. 251–8). I am indebted to Michele Boldrin and Roger Farmer for bringing this to my attention.
7　Interested readers should consult the diagrams in Baumol and Benhabib (1989) which is the source of much of the material we present on the logistic map.
8　To understand more fully why $f(x) > x$, $f^2(x) > x$, and $f^3(x) \leqslant x$ for some $x \in [a,b]$ means that the map f has a cycle of period 3, see also theorem 9.2 in chapter 9.

9 Endogenous fluctuations (*)

In this chapter we illustrate elementary results from bifurcation theory in competitive economies whose periodic equilbria resemble idealized business cycles, growth cycles, or fertility cycles. These fluctuations occur in an overlapping generations setting with one individual per generation, one perishable commodity, and one durable asset, exactly the sort we shall examine more closely in Parts III and IV. The structure is simple enough to be captured by an *autonomous* scalar dynamic system $f: X \rightarrow X$, where f is a continuously differentiable map, X is the interval $[0,\overline{m}]$, and $\overline{m} > 0$ is a given number.

The word "autonomous" is italicized in the previous paragraph to warn readers that, as of this writing, most economists who regard business cycles and other fluctuations as equilibrium phenomena rarely think of them as *unforced oscillations in autonomous systems* but rather consider them to be household responses to *cyclical forcing variables*, for example to oscillating public policies or to possibly stochastic fluctuations in the structural characteristics of the economy[1] (tastes, endowments, or technology).

We suppose in what follows that tastes, endowments, technology, public policy – in fact, the entire structure of the economy – are completely stationary. Nevertheless, we will find that cyclical fluctuations cannot be excluded *a priori* even in an idealized completely autonomous environment. Investigators from Hicks (1950) and Goodwin (1951) to Grandmont (1985) and Benhabib and Nishimura (1985) have called cycles of this type *endogenous* because they are driven by history, market psychology, and the inner working of the economic mechanism rather than by time-dependent forcing terms like shocks to preferences, endowments, technology, or economic policy. These cycles are typically one of many equilibria that a given economy is capable of, rather than the unique reaction of markets to the outside forces that drive the economic system.

Self-driven oscillatory phenomena are commonplace in the natural sciences, for example in the work of Volterra, van der Pol, Lorenz, and many others. Early examples were known a century ago to Poincaré; a Russian mathematics group led by Andronov studied these oscillations systematically in the 1930s. Economists are just beginning to study endogenous cycles, one example of which is the Hopf cycle that Farmer found in the planar Diamond model (see section 8.3). This chapter focuses entirely on flip cycles in scalar systems.

9.1   Business cycles

A particularly simple example of endogenous fluctuations in a production economy comes from the two-sector model of growth with fixed proportions which we introduced briefly in section 1.1. We reproduce below equation (1.4) from that section,

$$k_{t+1} = \frac{Ak_y(k_x - k_t)}{k_x - k_y} \qquad (9.1)$$

and assume that population is constant ($n = 0$), the scale factor is large enough ($A > 1$), and the consumption good is produced under a more capital-intensive technology than the investment good ($k_x > k_y > 0$).

Equilibria are solution sequences (k_t) that satisfy

$$k_y \leq k_t \leq k_x \qquad (9.2)$$

for all t. As we shall see later in chapter 15, inequality (9.2) is needed to guarantee that both sectors employ labor, which will not happen unless the aggregate capital–labor ratio is a convex combination of the two sectoral ratios.

Equation (9.1) describes a scalar linear dynamical system of the form $k_{t+1} = a - bk_t$ with $a > 0$ and $b > 0$. It has a unique positive steady state

$$\bar{k} = \frac{Ak_x k_y}{k_x + (A - 1)k_y} \qquad (9.3)$$

in the interval (k_y, k_x) provided that $A > 1$. This state is *asymptotically stable* if $k_x/k_y > 1 + A$, and dynamical equilibria are damped oscillations converging to $\bar{k}$.

A period-doubling bifurcation appears at $k_x/k_y = 1 + A > 1$, a parameter value at which equation (9.1) reduces to

$$k_{t+1} + k_t = k_x \qquad (9.4)$$

Figure 9.1(d) illustrates. Here the steady state $\bar{k} = k_x/2$ becomes a *center*, and all trajectories starting in the interval $[k_y, k_x - k_y]$ are equilibrium cycles with period 2. No equilibria other than $k_t = \bar{k}$ for all t exist if $k_x/k_y < 1 + A$, for then orbits explode as the steady state loses stability.

What economic mechanism is responsible for these fluctuations in the economywide capital–labor ratio? A low value of k_t means a relatively low output for the capital-intensive consumption good and a relatively high output for the labor-intensive investment good, raising tomorrow's stock of capital *above* its steady state value and reversing the direction of the trajectory.

Flip bifurcations also appear in *nonlinear* economic systems, for example in pure-exchange overlapping generations models containing paper assets such as currency. As we shall see in Parts III and IV, the demographic structure of these models is rather primitive and their equilibria are described in terms of one non-negative state variable each period, the commodity value of the outstanding stock of fiat currency m_t. For historical reasons related to monetary economics, we sometimes call this variable "real currency balances."

Assuming that individuals possess *perfect foresight*, that is, the ability to make unerring forecasts, equilibria in this economy are solutions to a backward-looking difference equation[2] of the form

$$m_t = f(m_{t+1}) \tag{9.5}$$

where $f: [0,\overline{m}] \to [0,\overline{m}]$ is a C^1 map such that $f(0) = 0$, $\overline{m} > f(\overline{m})$, and $f(m) > m$ for sufficiently small m, and has at *most* one critical point c at which the derivative f' vanishes. The parameter $\overline{m} > 0$ reflects scarce resources and, hence, some upper bound on the willingness of society to hold savings in the form of currency balances. Note that we have *not* assumed f to be a *monotone* map or, equivalently, that a well-defined inverse map f^{-1} exists.

The phase diagrams of equation (9.5) and its iterates look a lot like figure 8.1. The map f starts at the origin as in figure 9.1(a), keeps above the diagonal for a while and eventually drops below it; it has at most one peak, no valleys, and two steady states at $m = 0$ and $m = m^* > 0$. To locate periodic equilibria, we construct the iterates f^q of the map for $q = 2,3,\dots$. Thus $f^2 = f(f)$ is the second iterate, $f^3 = f(f^2)$ is the third iterate, $f^k = f(f^{k-1})$ is the kth iterate. Note that f^2 is a single-valued continuously differentiable function that admits both steady states, $m = 0$ and $m = m^*$, as fixed points. Furthermore, f^2 has slope $[f'(0)]^2 > 1$ at $m = 0$, and $[f'(m^*)]^2$ at $m = m^*$. If the backward-looking competitive equilibrium at m^* is unstable, then $|f'(m^*)| > 1$.

Hence $f^2(m)$ has slope greater than unity at both $m = 0$ and $m = m^*$. The existence of a fixed point $\hat{m} \in (0,m^*)$ for f^2 follows by continuity (see figure 9.1(b)). Note that $f(\hat{m}) \geq m^*$ is also a fixed point of f^2. We have thus proved the following theorem.

Theorem 9.1 If the positive stationary equilibrium m^* is stable in the forward sense (unstable in the backward sense), an endogenous cycle with period 2 exists.

Endogenous fluctuations, says this result, may just be flip cycles of the type depicted in figure 8.1(b) which shows a map like f together with its image relative to the diagonal. Forward stability means that the original map is less steep than its mirror image at the positive stationary state. The two curves then intersect at $m = m^*$, at $m = 0$, and, by continuity, at least twice more: at point A and its mirror image A'.

To understand high-order cycles, we analyze a special case of the Li–Yorke theorem.

Theorem 9.2 Suppose the map in equation (9.5) satisfies $f'(0) > 1$. Then an endogenous cycle with period 3 exists if there is an $m \neq \{0,m^*\}$ such that $f^3(m) \leq m$.

Note first that f^3, the third iterate of the map f, is a function that admits zero and m^* as fixed points. Furthermore, $(d/dm)f^3 = [f'(0)]^3$ at $m = 0$, which exceeds unity; hence $f^3(m) > m$ for m in the neighborhood of $m = 0$. If, in addition, $f^3(m) \leq m$ for some other m, then continuity requires that the map f^3 has a fixed point m_3 either in $(0,m^*)$ or in $(m^*,\overline{m})$, as we can see in figure 9.1(c). We also easily see that m_3 differs from the fixed points of the map f^2.

What economic assumptions are responsible for endogenous business cycles and how credible are they? What would it take to prevent the bewildering variety of periodic equilibria implied by the Sarkovskii theorem once three-period cycles exist? We review some technical remedies in Part IV where we also discuss a number of policy options designed to avert endogenous business cycles. We continue with additional examples of the flip bifurcation drawn from the theory of economic growth and from demography.

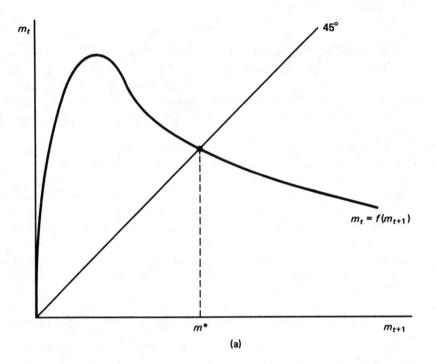

(a)

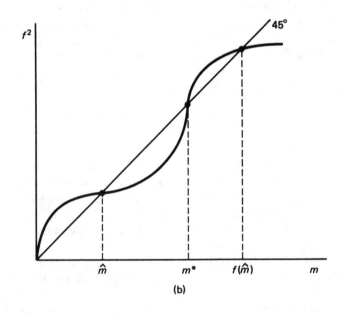

(b)

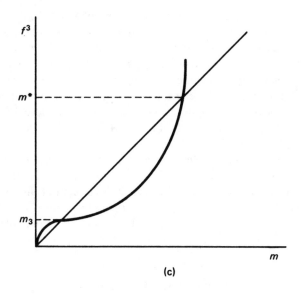

(c)

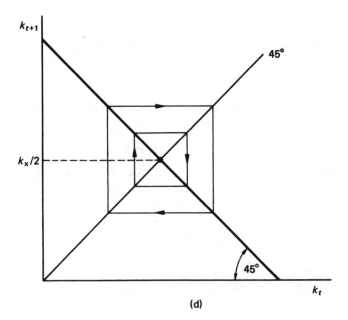

(d)

Figure 9.1 Endogenous business cycles.

9.2   Increasing returns and growth cycles

In this section we develop an example of a periodic equilibrium in the capital–labor ratio of an economy that produces under increasing returns to scale. Part II, section 14.5, examines in greater detail "learning by doing," the particular form of increasing returns we shall focus on. The underlying idea, however, is quite simple and worth explaining briefly: a given time endowment of labor may contain a smaller or larger amount of usable labor services depending on the state of "experience" or "knowledge" of the workforce. Individuals gain experience by actually working or, alternatively, by collecting useful tidbits of knowledge from their parents as a byproduct of family life.

One way to formalize this insight within a scalar Diamond model is to suppose that population is constant but the supply of *efficiency labor units*, that is, of labor services per unit time on the job, grows at a rate that depends on capital intensity. Workers who use a lot of capital become extremely knowledgeable about production and are able to impart this experience to their descendants at zero cost. The supply of efficiency labor units then evolves according to the law

$$L_{t+1}/L_t = \gamma(k_t) \tag{9.6}$$

where k_t is physical capital per efficiency unit and $\gamma: \mathbb{R}_+ \to [1,\bar{\gamma}]$ is a bounded nondecreasing function that is also bounded away from zero.

To simplify matters, suppose that the saving rate in this economy is a constant $s \in (0,1)$. Dynamical competitive equilibria are then sequences (k_t, L_t) that satisfy given initial conditions, equation (9.6), and the equality of savings to investment, that is,

$$k_{t+1}L_{t+1} = sw_t L_t \tag{9.7}$$

In equation (9.7) the wage rate per efficiency labor unit satisfies the well-known equation

$$w_t = f(k_t) - kf'(k_t) \equiv w(k_t) \tag{9.8}$$

which simply restates Euler's law: profits are zero if markets are competitive and production takes place under constant returns to scale.

Combining equations (9.6), (9.7) and (9.8), we obtain

$$k_{t+1} = \frac{sw(k_t)}{\gamma(k_t)} \tag{9.9}$$

To understand why this equation may admit periodic equilibria, suppose that all learning occurs within a band $k \in [k_a, k_b]$: γ is increasing in the interval $[k_a, k_b]$ and is constant outside it. Specifically we let

$$\gamma(k) = \begin{cases} 1 & \text{if } k \in [0,k_a] \\ \bar{\gamma} > 1 & \text{if } k \geq k_b \end{cases} \tag{9.10}$$

Figure 9.2(a) illustrates how the phase curve of (9.9) consists of two upward-sloped main branches connected by a decreasing segment. The first main branch applies to equilibria with no learning ($\gamma = 1$, $0 \leq k_t \leq k_a$), and the second one to equilibria with full learning ($\gamma = \bar{\gamma}$, $k_t \geq k_b$).

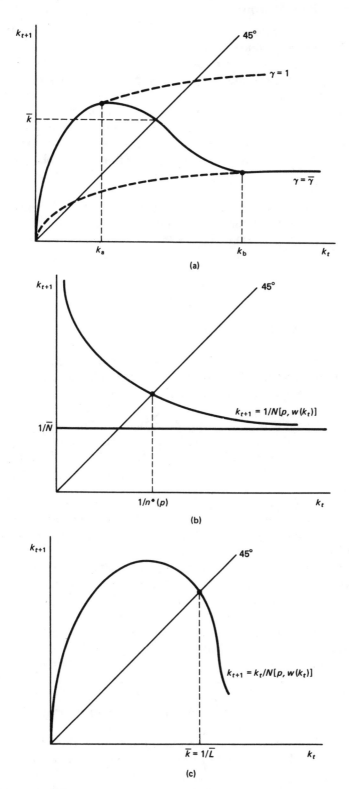

Figure 9.2 (a), (b) Growth cycles; (c) fertility cycles.

The decreasing segment of the phase curve describes the dynamics of transitional learning: there is a steady state $\overline{k} \in (k_a, k_b)$ around which appear a number of oscillating trajectories. If $k_t \geqslant \overline{k}$, then the endowment of efficiency labor units may grow faster than saving, which induces producers at $t + 1$ to choose a relatively *low* capital–labor ratio $k_{t+1} < \overline{k}$. This causes the growth of efficiency labor to decelerate at $t + 1$, and production becomes capital intensive again at $t + 2$.

As we know from chapter 8, a stable flip cycle will appear about $\overline{k}$ whenever the function w/γ becomes sufficiently steep at $\overline{k}$, that is, whenever γ becomes sufficiently elastic. From equation (9.9) we obtain readily that the slope of the phase curve at $\overline{k}$ is

$$T(\overline{k}) = \epsilon_w - \epsilon_\gamma \qquad (9.11)$$

where $(\epsilon_w, \epsilon_\gamma)$ are positive numbers representing the elasticities of the functions w and γ respectively. For a Cobb–Douglas production function, for instance, ϵ_w equals capital's share of output. Equation (9.11) shows that a flip bifurcation will occur as ϵ_γ exceeds the value $1 + \epsilon_w$.

9.3   Malthusian fertility cycles

Medium frequency oscillations in fertility and population growth rates have been known to demographers for quite some time (see Wrigley and Schofield, 1981). The population histories of England, France, and Sweden throughout the eighteenth and nineteenth centuries exhibit cyclical movements in population growth with a common average frequency of about six cycles per century, and a mean amplitude that varies from 0.13 percent in France and 0.25 percent in England to about 0.60 percent for Sweden. These movements continue, in a more damped fashion, into the twentieth century with a succession of active "baby booms" followed by demographically weaker "baby busts."

The traditional demographic explanation for fertility relies on the interplay between a variable stock of humans and a relatively fixed stock of material resources, along the lines originally suggested by Malthus (1798). Suppose that children are a normal consumption good produced mainly by peasant parents who draw income by working in agriculture. When the number of workers per acre of land is relatively low, the scarcity of labor raises agricultural wages above their "norm" and the resulting positive income effect increases the demand for all normal consumption goods, including children.

One immediate consequence of this change is earlier marriages and more births during each married couple's fertile years. A delayed outcome of the same process is a lessening of the initial scarcity of labor, a subsequent drop in real wages, and ultimately a reversal of the fertility rate.

It is not too hard to formalize the preceding verbal story into a scalar dynamical system whose equilibria are oscillatory or even periodic. Suppose that each household consists of one person who lives for one period and supplies one unit of labor services inelastically. Households are endowed with utility functions of the form $u^h: \mathbb{R}^2_+ \to \mathbb{R}$, expressed over a perishable consumption good and children, and are constrained by budget sets of the form $B_h = \{(c_t, n_{t+1}) \in \mathbb{R}^2_+ \mid c_t + pn_{t+1} \leqslant w_t\}$. Here we denote by w_t the wage rate at time t, by p the constant resource cost of bearing and raising each child, and by (c_t, n_{t+1}) the consumption bundle of household h. Ignoring the integral nature in the choice of family size, the demand for children

$$n_{t+1} = N(p, w_t) \tag{9.12}$$

may be expressed as a bounded continuous function which satisfies $N \leq \bar{n}$ for all w_t and $p(\partial/\partial w)N \in (0,1)$ if children are a normal good.

As in the previous section, we assume that production takes place under constant returns, now using labor and land as inputs hired in competitive factor markets. In this case the wage rate is given again by equation (9.8) with $k_t = K_t/L_t$ being the land-to-labor ratio and labor evolving endogenously at a variable rate n_t, that is,

$$L_{t+1}/L_t = n_{t+1} \tag{9.13}$$

There are two possible types of demographic steady states in this Malthusian economy, depending on how the endowment of land changes over time. A constant *rate* of population growth is possible if the stock of usable land each period is proportional to the number of workers in the *previous* period, a situation that makes sense if productive land is cleared and improved slowly. A constant population *stock* is a possibility if land is in fixed supply. We briefly analyze these two cases in turn.

Suppose first that $K_{t+1} = L_t$ which implies $k_{t+1} = L_t/L_{t+1} = 1/n_{t+1}$. Then equation (9.12) yields

$$k_{t+1} = \frac{1}{N[p, w(k_t)]} \tag{9.14}$$

Note that the right-hand side of this equation tends towards $+\infty$ as $k_t \to 0$ since $w(0) = 0$ and $N(p,0) = 0$ for all $p > 0$. The same expression tends to $1/\bar{n} < 1$ as $k_t \to 0$ because of our boundedness assumption. Hence, a stationary equilibrium exists at some $k^* \equiv 1/n^*(p)$ at which the constant fertility rate n^* is a decreasing function of p, the unit resource cost of bearing and raising children. Figure 9.2(b) illustrates this.

The figure also demonstrates the possibility for oscillations in fertility. Denote again by ϵ_n and ϵ_w, respectively, the income elasticity of the fertility rate and the elasticity of the wage rate with respect to the capital–labor ratio. Then the slope of the relevant phase curve at the steady state k^* is easily seen to equal $-\epsilon_n\epsilon_w$. After a little algebra, we can show that $\epsilon_w = \alpha/\sigma$ which is the ratio of land's share in total output and the elasticity of substitution in production (see also chapter 8, note 5). Damped fertility oscillations occur if

$$\epsilon_n < \sigma/\alpha \tag{9.15}$$

and stable periodic orbits appear when inequality (9.15) is reversed.

Next let us assume that the stock of land is constant for all time, that is, $K_t = 1 \; \forall t$. Then we have $k_t = 1/L_t$ and $n_{t+1} = L_{t+1}/L_t = N(p, w_t)$. Therefore, dynamical equilibria are sequences k_t that satisfy

$$k_{t+1} = H(k_t) \equiv \frac{k_t}{N[p, w(k_t)]} \tag{9.16}$$

It is easy to check that $H(0) = 0$, $H(k)/k \to \infty$ as $k \to 0$, and $H(k)/k \to 1/\bar{n} > 1$ as $k \to \infty$. As figure 9.2(c) shows, equation (9.16) possesses a trivial steady state $k = 0$ and at least one positive steady state $\bar{k}$ at which the fertility rate $n = N[w(\bar{k})] = 1$ is sufficient to maintain constant population. Oscillations in this case exist if $(1 - \epsilon_n \epsilon_w) \in (-1, 0)$, that is, if

$$\epsilon_n < 2\sigma/\alpha \tag{9.17}$$

Stable periodic cycles emerge when the steady state $n = 1$ loses stability, which occurs when $\epsilon_n \geq 2\sigma/\alpha$.

Inequalities (9.15) and (9.17) both support the established intuition of demographers: periodic equilibria in fertility rates are possible whenever childbearing decisions are sufficiently sensitive to changes in farm income.

Notes

1 Kydland and Prescott (1982) and Long and Plosser (1983) are leading proponents of "real" business cycle theory which regards business cycles as stochastic stationary responses of an optimum growth model shocked by exogenous technological disturbances. Building on work by Brock and Mirman (1972), this theory explains how the joint stationary distribution of the state variables, that is, money, income, factor inputs, prices, etc., depends on the probability distribution of exogenous shocks.
2 We defer until Part III a full statement of the economic reasons why we do not deal directly with a forward-looking difference equation.

Technical appendices (*)

These appendices review some technical material that is necessary for a thorough understanding of Part I, especially chapters 1, 2, 4, and 8. They comprise five short segments on linear algebra, difference equations, and differential equations, and a larger one on periodic solutions. Linear algebra, in particular, contains refreshers on complex numbers, eigenvalues and eigenvectors, and matrix diagonalization. The difference equation segment provides informal proofs of the superposition principle and the implicit function theorem.

Three refreshers on differential equations cover linear systems, and periodicity and bifurcations. We start with basic results on existence and stability, and then go on to nonlinear systems. Here we develop conditions for the existence of closed orbits (the Poincaré–Bendixson theorem) and for their nonexistence (the Bendixson and Dulac criteria). We also study the van der Pol equation which is particularly rich in asymptotic solutions, continue with bifurcation theory in continuous-time systems, and end with a brief presentation of catastrophe theory.

A.1 Linear algebra

We saw in earlier chapters that the eigenvalues of certain matrices, that is, the real or complex solutions to certain polynomial equations, play an important role in the theory of difference equations. This segment introduces the notion of a complex number and summarizes some important results on algebraic equations. We then define eigenvalues and eigenvectors and discuss their application to the problem of diagonalizing a square matrix.

Complex numbers

A *complex number* is a number of the form $c = a + bi$ where a and b are real numbers and i is the imaginary unit $i = \sqrt{(-1)}$. The number a is called the real part of c (Re c), and the number b is the imaginary part of c (Im c). The *complex conjugate* of a number $c = a + bi$ is the number $\bar{c} = a - bi$ with the sign of the imaginary part reversed. The notion of conjugate extends in a natural way to vectors with complex components.

Definition A.1 Let $x = (c_1,...,c_n)$ be a vector with complex-valued components; we define its complex conjugate to be vector $\bar{x} = (\bar{c}_1,..., \bar{c}_n)$ whose components are the conjugates of the components of the original vector.

It is useful to represent a complex number as a point with Cartesian coordinates (a,b) in a plane, called the *complex plane*, where the vertical axis measures the imaginary component and the horizontal axis the real component. Figure A.1 illustrates.

The *modulus r* of a complex number is the norm of the vector that represents it on the complex plane, that is,

$$r = |c| = \sqrt{(a^2 + b^2)}$$

Recall that multiplying a complex number by its conjugate yields the square of the norm:

$$(a + bi)(a - bi) = a^2 - b^2 i^2 = a^2 + b^2 = r^2 \Rightarrow r = |c| = \sqrt{(cc)}$$

Looking at figure A.1, we can see that

$$\cos \theta = a/r \Rightarrow a = r \cos \theta$$
$$\sin \theta = b/r \Rightarrow b = r \sin \theta$$

so that, in polar coordinates, we have the trigonometric form

$$c = a + bi = r \cos \theta + ir \sin \theta = r(\cos \theta + i \sin \theta)$$

Using the Maclaurin series representation for the sine, cosine, and exponential functions, we can get Euler's formula:

$$e^{i\theta} = \cos \theta + i \sin \theta \tag{A.1}$$

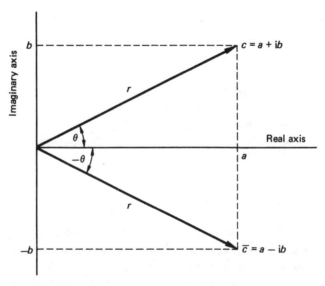

Figure A.1 The complex plane.

This allows us to write a complex number in yet another equivalent way:

$$c = a + bi = r(\cos \theta + i \sin \theta) = re^{i\theta} \qquad (A.2)$$

Note that the norm of $e^{i\theta}$ is $\sqrt{(\cos^2\theta + \sin^2\theta)} = 1$, so $e^{i\theta}$ falls on the unit circle in the complex plane. As θ varies from 0 to 2π, the number $e^{i\theta}$ circles around the origin at a constant distance equal to 1.

The close connection between complex numbers and circular functions is important. Differential equation systems with complex eigenvalues will have solutions with cyclical components.

Polynomials and algebraic equations

A polynomial of degree n in x is a scalar function

$$p(x) = a_0 x^n + a_1 x^{n-1} + \ldots + a_{n-1}x + a_n \qquad a_0 \neq 0 \qquad (A.3a)$$

whose coefficients a_i are complex constants. An equation of the form

$$p(x) = a_0 x^n + a_1 x^{n-1} + \ldots + a_{n-1}x + a_n = 0 \qquad a_0 \neq 0 \qquad (A.3b)$$

is called a polynomial or algebraic equation. The solutions or roots of the equation $p(x) = 0$ are called zeros or roots of the polynomial $p(x)$.

Algebraic equations arise often in applications, for example in computing the eigenvalues of a matrix. A basic problem is when solutions to (A.3b) exist. The following theorem tells us that a polynomial equation of degree n will always have n solutions, provided we allow for complex roots. In fact, complex numbers were "invented" to make sure that algebraic equations always had solutions.

Theorem A.1 (Fundamental theorem of algebra) An algebraic equation of the form

$$p(x) = a_0 x^n + a_1 x^{n-1} + \ldots + a_{n-1}x + a_n = 0 \qquad a_0 \neq 0 \qquad (A.4)$$

has exactly n complex or real roots.

It is possible that some of the n roots of (A.4) are repeated. A root that is repeated m times is said to have multiplicity m. Solutions of multiplicity one are called simple roots of equation (A.4). In all applications of interest to us, the coefficients of $p(x)$ will be real. In that case, we have the following result.

Theorem A.2 If the coefficients of a polynomial $p(x)$ are real, then any complex roots of the equation $p(x) = 0$ come in conjugate pairs.

Note that if $x_1, \ldots, x_n$ are the roots of (A.4) then we can write the polynomial $p(x)$ as the product of n binomial factors:

$$p(x) = a_0(x - x_1)(x - x_2)\ldots(x - x_n)$$

That is, if $p(x_i) = 0$ then $p(x)$ divides exactly by $x - x_i$, and we can write p as

$$p(x) = (x - x_i)q(x) \qquad (A.5)$$

where $q(x)$ is a polynomial of degree $n - 1$.

As we know, the solutions of second-order polynomial equations can be obtained directly by the quadratic formula. The equation $ax^2 + bx + c = 0$ had roots

$$x_1, x_2 = \frac{1}{2a}[-b \pm \sqrt{(b^2 - 4ac)}]$$

Whether these roots are complex or not depends on the sign of the expression $\Delta = b^2 - 4ac$, called the *discriminant* of the equation. A similar result is available for third-order equations of the form $z^3 + Az^2 + Bz + c = 0$. First, note that by putting $z = x - A/3$ this equation can be reduced to the form

$$x^3 + ax + b = 0 \tag{A.6}$$

Then, the nature of the solutions depends on the value of the discriminant $\Delta = 4a^3 + 27b^2$. As we know from elementary algebra, it turns out that

$\Delta < 0 \Rightarrow$ (A.6) has three different real roots
$\Delta = 0 \Rightarrow$ (A.6) has three real roots, at least two of which are equal
$\Delta > 0 \Rightarrow$ (A.6) has one real and two complex roots.

Moreover, the roots of (A.6) will satisfy the *Cardano formula*

$$x = \left[-\frac{b}{2} + \frac{1}{2}\sqrt{(4a^3 + 27b^2)} \right]^{1/3}$$

$$+ \left[-\frac{b}{2} - \frac{1}{2}\frac{1}{2}\sqrt{\frac{(4a^3 + 27b^2)}{27}} \right]^{1/3} \tag{A.7}$$

Note that there are more than three numbers that satisfy (A.7); only three of those will also satisfy (A.6).

An even more complicated formula exists for $n = 4$, and in general no explicit formulas exist for the solution of higher-degree equations. In applications the following method will sometimes work for finding the roots of a polynomial equation. We first look for integer solutions to $p(x) = 0$; if we find some we can use them to factor out the polynomial using (A.6) until we reduce it to one of the second or third degree; then we can use the quadratic or Cardano formulas to get the rest of the roots.

Most algebraic equations are solved by numerical methods. However, integer roots of a polynomial with integer coefficients are sometimes easy to find. We can rewrite

$$p(x) = a_0 x^n + a_1 x^{n-1} + \ldots + a_{n-1} x + a_n = 0 \qquad a_0 \neq 0$$

in the form

$$x(a_0 x^{n-1} + a_1 x^{n-2} + \ldots + a_{n-1}) = -a_n$$

Suppose the coefficients are integers and x^* is an integer solution of $p(x) = 0$. Then the expression inside the parentheses is an integer and x^* must be a factor of the constant term a_n.

If an integer solution of $p(x) = 0$ exists, it must be a factor of the constant term a_n. We can find all the integer factors of a_n and insert them in $p(x)$ to see if they are zeros of the polynomial. If an integer x^* is found such that $p(x^*) = 0$, we have a solution; we can then simplify $p(x)$ on dividing it by $x - x^*$ and so on.

We close this section with a result that may be useful when trying to determine how many of the solutions of a polynomial equation are real. Let p be a polynomial with real coefficients and consider the equation

$$p(x) = a_0 x^n + a_1 x^{n-1} + \ldots + a_{n-1} x + a_n = 0$$

Take the sequence $a_0, a_1, \ldots, a_n$ of coefficients and remove any zeros. If two successive coefficients in the resulting sequence have different signs, we say that a change of sign occurs. We then have the following theorem.

Theorem A.3 (Descartes' rule of signs) Assume all coefficients of a polynomial $p(x)$ are real, and let k be the total number of changes of sign in the sequence of coefficients. Then the number of positive real roots (including multiplicities) of $p(x) = 0$ is equal to k minus a non-negative even number. In particular, if $k = 1$, then the equation has exactly one positive real root.

Eigenvalues and eigenvectors

Multiplication by an $n \times n$ matrix A maps an n-vector x into another n-vector $y = Ax$. Vectors that are mapped into their own scalar multiples by A are known as *eigenvectors* of A. Let λ be a scalar. By definition, an eigenvector e of A must satisfy $Ae = \lambda e$ which implies

$$(A - \lambda I)e = 0 \tag{A.8}$$

for some scalar λ. Note, however, that (A.8) is a homogeneous system of equations that will have non-zero solutions if and only if λ is chosen so that

$$\det(A - \lambda I) = 0 \tag{A.9}$$

Equation (A.9) is the characteristic equation of A and the values of λ that satisfy it are called *eigenvalues* or characteristic roots of A. For each eigenvalue λ_i, we can then go back and solve the system (A.8) to extract the corresponding eigenvector e_i.

Example A.1 The column vector $e = (1, 2)^T$ is an eigenvector of

$$A = \begin{bmatrix} 3 & 0 \\ 8 & -1 \end{bmatrix}$$

corresponding to the eigenvalue $\lambda = 3$ because

$$Ae = \begin{bmatrix} 3 & 0 \\ 8 & -1 \end{bmatrix} \begin{bmatrix} 1 \\ 2 \end{bmatrix} = \begin{bmatrix} 3 \\ 6 \end{bmatrix} = 3e$$

When expanded, the determinant $|A - \lambda I|$ is a polynomial of degree n in λ, called the characteristic polynomial of A and denoted by $p(\lambda)$. Equation (A.9) is simply an nth degree polynomial equation and must therefore have n solutions, not all of them necessarily real or distinct from each other. If a given eigenvalue is repeated m times, we say that it has *multiplicity* m. If the coefficients of the matrix A are real, so will be the coefficients of $p(\lambda)$. In that case, theorem A.2 yields the following result.

Theorem A.4 If A is a real square matrix, then any complex eigenvalues must occur in conjugate pairs. Moreover, the corresponding eigenvectors are also conjugate pairs.

Example A.2 To find the eigenvalues of

$$A = \begin{bmatrix} 0 & 1 & 0 \\ 0 & 0 & 1 \\ 4 & 17 & 8 \end{bmatrix}$$

we form

$$p(\lambda) = |A - \lambda I| = 0 \Rightarrow$$

$$\det \begin{pmatrix} -\lambda & 1 & 0 \\ 0 & -\lambda & 1 \\ 4 & -17 & 8-\lambda \end{pmatrix} = \lambda^3 - 8\lambda^2 + 17\lambda - 4 = 0$$

Substituting the factors of the independent term 4 into $p(\lambda)$, we find that $p(4) = 0$, so that $\lambda = 4$ is a solution to the characteristic equation. To find the other two eigenvalues, we begin by dividing $p(\lambda)$ by $\lambda - 4$. By the method discussed previously, we obtain $p(\lambda) = (\lambda^2 - 4\lambda + 1)(\lambda - 4)$. Therefore, the eigenvalues are $\lambda_1 = 4$ and $\lambda_{2,3} = [4 \pm \sqrt{(16 - 4)}]/2 = 2 \pm 2\sqrt{3}$.

The following theorem, whose proof appears in all good texts on linear algebra, lists some useful properties of eigenvalues. Given an $n \times n$ matrix A, we define its *trace* as the sum of the diagonal entries of A, that is,

$$\text{tr } A = \sum_i a_{ii}$$

Theorem A.5 For any square matrix A, the sum of its eigenvalues is equal to its trace, and the product of the eigenvalues equals its determinant.

Once we know the eigenvalues of a matrix, we can find the corresponding eigenvectors. An eigenvector of A corresponding to an eigenvalue λ_i is a non-zero vector e_i that satisfies $Ae_i = \lambda_i e_i$, or equivalently $(A - \lambda I)e = 0$. In general, then, one has to look at the system of equations $(A - \lambda_i I)e_i = 0$ and find the vectors that satisfy it.

We should note that the eigenvectors of a matrix A are not uniquely defined. If e_i is an eigenvector for A associated with an eigenvalue λ_i, any vector ke_i, where k is an arbitrary number, will also be an eigenvector. To see this, multiply A by ke_i to obtain

$$A(ke_i) = k(Ae_i) = k(\lambda_i e_i) = \lambda_i(ke_i)$$

Example A.3 To find the eigenvectors of

$$A = \begin{bmatrix} 3 & -2 & 0 \\ -2 & 3 & 0 \\ 0 & 0 & 5 \end{bmatrix}$$

we form the characteristic equation and solve for the eigenvalues:

$$|A - \lambda I| = \begin{vmatrix} 3-\lambda & -2 & 0 \\ -2 & 3-\lambda & 0 \\ 0 & 0 & 5-\lambda \end{vmatrix}$$

$$= (3 - \lambda)(3 - \lambda)(5 - \lambda) - 4(5 - \lambda)$$
$$= 25 - 35\lambda + 11\lambda^2 - \lambda^3$$
$$= (\lambda - 1)(-\lambda^2 + 10\lambda - 25) = 0$$

whence $\lambda_1 = 1$ and $\lambda_2 = \lambda_3 = 5$ which shows that eigenvalues can be repeated.

By definition, $e = (e_1, e_2, e_3)^T$ is an eigenvector of A corresponding to λ if it is a nontrivial solution to $(A - \lambda I)e = 0$, that is, if

$$(A - \lambda I)e = \begin{bmatrix} \lambda - 3 & 2 & 0 \\ 2 & \lambda - 3 & 0 \\ 0 & 0 & \lambda - 5 \end{bmatrix} \begin{bmatrix} e_1 \\ e_2 \\ e_3 \end{bmatrix} = \begin{bmatrix} 0 \\ 0 \\ 0 \end{bmatrix}$$

With $\lambda = 1$ we have

$$\begin{bmatrix} -2 & 2 & 0 \\ 2 & -2 & 0 \\ 0 & 0 & -4 \end{bmatrix} \begin{bmatrix} e_1 \\ e_2 \\ e_3 \end{bmatrix} = \begin{bmatrix} 0 \\ 0 \\ 0 \end{bmatrix} \Rightarrow \begin{matrix} -2e_1 + 2e_2 + 0e_3 = 0 \\ 2e_1 - 2e_2 + 0e_3 = 0 \\ 0e_1 + 0e_2 - 4e_3 = 0 \end{matrix}$$

Clearly, the first and second equations are not linearly independent. This leaves us with an undetermined system of two equations in three unknowns:

$$\left(\begin{matrix} -2e_1 + 2e_2 = 0 \\ -4e_3 = 0 \end{matrix} \right) \Rightarrow \left(\begin{matrix} e_1 = e_2 = r \\ e_3 = 0 \end{matrix} \right)$$

where r is an arbitrary constant. Hence, the eigenvectors corresponding to $\lambda = 1$ are non-zero vectors of the form

$$e = \begin{bmatrix} e_1 \\ e_2 \\ e_3 \end{bmatrix} = \begin{bmatrix} r \\ r \\ 0 \end{bmatrix} = r \begin{bmatrix} 1 \\ 1 \\ 0 \end{bmatrix} \text{ for } r \neq 0$$

The 2 × 2 case

Since many systems of difference or differential equations that you are likely to encounter in economic applications will be planar systems with a 2 × 2 coefficient matrix, let us look a bit more closely into the problem of determining the eigenvalues and eigenvectors for a 2 × 2 matrix

$$A = \begin{bmatrix} a_{11} & a_{12} \\ a_{21} & a_{22} \end{bmatrix}$$

To find the eigenvalues, we solve $|A - \lambda I| = 0$, that is,

$$\begin{vmatrix} a_{11} - \lambda & a_{12} \\ a_{21} & a_{22} - \lambda \end{vmatrix} \begin{matrix} = (a_{11} - \lambda)(a_{22} - \lambda) - a_{12}a_{21} \\ \\ = (a_{11}a_{22} - a_{12}a_{21}) - (a_{11} + a_{22})\lambda + \lambda^2 = 0 \end{matrix}$$

We can write this equation as

$$p(\lambda) = \lambda^2 - (\text{tr } A)\lambda + \det A = 0 \tag{A.10}$$

and solve it by the quadratic formula.

This will yield two eigenvalues, λ_1 and λ_2. For each one we now want to find an associated eigenvector e_i. To simplify the calculation, we can take advantage of the fact that the eigenvectors are defined only up to a multiplicative constant; let us "normalize" the eigenvector e_i so that its second component is $e_{i2} = 1$. We then search for a vector $e_i = (e_{i1}, 1)^T$ such that $Ae_i = \lambda_i e_i$, that is,

$$\begin{bmatrix} a_{11} & a_{12} \\ a_{21} & a_{22} \end{bmatrix} \begin{bmatrix} e_{11} \\ 1 \end{bmatrix} = \lambda_i \begin{bmatrix} e_{i1} \\ 1 \end{bmatrix}$$

This yields a system of two equations in the single unknown e_{i1}:

$$a_{11}e_{i1} + a_{12} = \lambda_i e_{i1} \qquad \text{(A.11a)}$$
$$a_{21}e_{i1} + a_{22} = \lambda_i \qquad \text{(A.11b)}$$

We know that the system must be consistent and so both equations must yield the same value for e_{i1}. Hence, we choose to solve the easier equation (A.11b) to obtain

$$e_{i1} = (\lambda_i - a_{22})/a_{21} \qquad \text{(A.12)}$$

Example A.4

$$A = \begin{bmatrix} 3 & 0 \\ 8 & -1 \end{bmatrix} \Rightarrow |A - \lambda I| = \begin{vmatrix} 3 - \lambda & 0 \\ 8 & -1 - \lambda \end{vmatrix} = (3 - \lambda)(-1 - \lambda) = 0$$

whence $\lambda_1 = 3$, $\lambda_2 = -1$. Then, we have $Ae_i = \lambda_i e_i$ which means that

$$\begin{bmatrix} 3 & 0 \\ 8 & -1 \end{bmatrix} \begin{bmatrix} e_{i1} \\ 1 \end{bmatrix} = \lambda_i \begin{bmatrix} e_{i1} \\ 1 \end{bmatrix} \Rightarrow \begin{array}{l} 3e_{i1} = \lambda_i e_{i1} \\ 8e_{i1} - 1 = \lambda_i \end{array}$$

For $\lambda_i = 3$ we obtain an identity plus

$$8e_{i1} - 1 = 3 \Rightarrow e_{i1} = 1/2$$

Hence, the eigenvector associated with $\lambda_1 = 3$ is $e_1 = (1/2,1)^{\mathrm{T}}$. Similarly, with $\lambda_2 = -1$ the system to be solved becomes

$$\left(\begin{array}{l} 3e_{21} = -e_{21} \\ 8e_{22} - 1 = -1 \end{array} \right) \Rightarrow \left(\begin{array}{l} e_{21} = 0 \\ e_{22} = 0 \end{array} \right)$$

and the eigenvector associated with $\lambda_2 = -1$ is $e_2 = (0,1)^{\mathrm{T}}$ for any scalar multiple.

Diagonalizing a square matrix

We know that it is very convenient to be able to diagonalize the coefficient matrix of a linear system of difference equations. In this section we establish conditions under which this can be done and develop a procedure for diagonalizing square matrices.

Definition A.2 (Diagonalizable matrix) A square matrix A is said to be diagonalizable if there exists an invertible matrix P such that $P^{-1}AP$ is diagonal.

Theorem A.6 Let A be an $n \times n$ matrix. If the n eigenvectors of the square matrix A are linearly independent, then it is diagonalizable. Moreover, $E^{-1}AE = \Lambda$, that is, the "diagonalizing" matrix is the matrix of eigenvectors E, and the diagonal matrix that results from the transformation is the matrix Λ that has A's eigenvalues on the main diagonal and zeros elsewhere.

Proof E is the matrix that has as columns the eigenvectors of A, that is $E = [e_1,...,e_n]$ where e_i, the eigenvector associated with λ_i, is a column vector. Since the eigenvectors are linearly independent by assumption, $|E| \neq 0$, and E is invertible. Therefore, the expressions $E^{-1}AE = \Lambda$ and $AE = E\Lambda$ are equivalent. That this last expression holds true follows by the definition of eigenvectors and eigenvalues:

$$AE = A[e_1, ..., e_n] = [Ae_1,...,Ae_n]$$
$$= [\lambda_1 e_1, ..., \lambda_n e_n]$$

$$[e_1, \ldots, e_n] \begin{bmatrix} \lambda_1 & 0 \ldots 0 \\ \cdots & \cdots \cdots \\ 0 & 0 \ldots \lambda_n \end{bmatrix} = E\Lambda$$ ∎

Theorem A.7 If the n eigenvalues of the square matrix A are all different, then its eigenvectors $e_1, \ldots, e_n$ are linearly independent. It follows by theorem A.6 that A is diagonalizable.

Proof Recall that the vectors $e_1, \ldots, e_n$ are said to be linearly dependent if there exist scalar constants $c_1, \ldots, c_n$, not all zero, such that $c_1 e_1 + \ldots + c_n e_n = 0$. The vectors $e_1, \ldots, e_n$ are linearly independent if this equality does not hold, except in the trivial case where all the constants are zero.

Suppose first that $n = 2$ and some linear combination of the eigenvectors e_1, e_2 produces the zero vector, that is,

$$c_1 e_1 + c_2 e_2 = 0 \qquad\qquad\qquad (A.13a)$$

Multiplying (A.13a) by A we get $c_1 A e_1 + c_2 A e_2 = 0 \Rightarrow$

$$c_1 \lambda_1 e_1 + c_2 \lambda_2 e_2 = 0 \qquad\qquad\qquad (A.13b)$$

Subtracting λ_2 times the first equation from (A.13b) yields

$$c_1 \lambda_1 e_1 + c_2 \lambda_2 e_2 - c_1 \lambda_2 e_1 + c_2 \lambda_2 e_2 = 0 \Rightarrow c_1(\lambda_1 - \lambda_2)e_1 = 0$$

Since, by assumption, $\lambda_1 \neq \lambda_2$ and $e_1 \neq 0$, we must have $c_1 = 0$, and by a similar argument it can be shown that $c_2 = 0$. Hence, only the trivial combination $0e_1 + 0e_2$ yields the zero vector, and so the eigenvectors are linearly independent.

A similar argument will work for any number of vectors: assume that some linear combination produces zero, multiply by A, subtract λ_n times the original combination, and the vector e_n will disappear, leaving a combination of $e_1, \ldots, e_{n-1}$ that yields zero. By repeating the process, we end up with a multiple of e_1 that yields zero, forcing $c_1 = 0$ and eventually $c_i = 0$ for all i. Therefore, eigenvectors associated with distinct eigenvalues must be linearly independent. ∎

These two theorems tell us that, if the coefficient matrix A of a system of difference or differential equations has eigenvalues that are different from each other, we can use the matrix of eigenvectors to diagonalize the coefficient matrix. This procedure transforms the system into independent equations in transformed variables that are easier to solve. Then we can apply the inverse of the diagonalizing transformation to recover the solution in terms of the original variables. If A has some repeated eigenvalues, this procedure does not always work because A may not be diagonalizable. Recall that some (but not all) matrices with repeated eigenvalues are diagonalizable; the identity matrix is one example of this type.

A.2 Difference equations

The superposition principle

We shall prove that equation (2.2) contains all the solutions to the linear inhomogeneous equation (2.1). First we verify that, if x_t^p is any solution to (2.1), then $x_t^g = ca^t + x_t^p$ will also satisfy (2.1):

$$ax_{t-1}^g + b_t = a(ca^{t-1} + x_{t-1}^p) + b_t = ca^t + (ax_{t-1}^p + b_t) = ca^t + x_t^p = x_t^g$$

Thus, if we start with a solution and add ca^t we get another solution; but do we get all the solutions this way? The answer is yes. To see this, let x_t^p and x_t^g be two arbitrary solutions; by definition they both satisfy (2.1), that is,

$$x_t^p = ax_{t-1}^p + b_t \tag{A.14a}$$

$$x_t^g = ax_{t-1}^g + b_t \tag{A.14b}$$

Subtracting (A.14b) from (A.14a) we obtain

$$x_t^p - x_t^g = ax_{t-1}^p + b_t - ax_{t-1}^g - b_t = a(x_{t-1}^p - x_{t-1}^g) \tag{A.15}$$

If we define a new variable $y_t = x_t^p - x_t^g$, equation (A.15) can be written $y_t = ay_{t-1}$ and will have a general solution of the form $y_t = x_t^p - x_t^g = ca^t$. Therefore, the difference between any two arbitrary solutions has to be of the form ca^t, which completes our informal proof.

Bifurcations and the implicit function theorem

In this section we show how the bifurcation system problem is related to a more general problem that arises in many other areas of economics. To be more specific, note that practically every static economic model can be written as a parametrized system of equations of the form

$$F(x;\alpha) = 0 \qquad F: X \times \Omega \rightarrow \mathbb{R}^n, \ F \in C^1 \tag{A.16}$$

where $x \in X \subseteq \mathbb{R}^n$ is a vector of endogenous state variables and $\alpha \in \Omega \subseteq \mathbb{R}^m$ is a vector of parameters that summarize in some sense the larger environment in which the system is embedded. For a given value of α, the equations of the model will determine the equilibrium (or solution) values x^* of the state vector x. By solving the system for each possible value of the parameters we can construct a mapping $x^*: \Omega \rightarrow X$ that assigns to each given environment α the corresponding equilibrium value(s) $x^*(\alpha)$ of the endogenous variables. We will refer to this mapping as the *equilibrium or solution map*. In a rather general sense, the properties of this map capture the essence of the economic model in (A.16).

The situation is depicted in figure A.2(a). For a given value of α, say α^0, we can think of plotting $F(x;\alpha^0)$ as a function of x. A solution to the model is then an intersection of $F(x;\alpha^0)$ with the "horizontal axis" X. A change in the parameter vector, say to α^1, shifts the graph of F and yields a new equilibrium at $x(\alpha^1)$. The graph of the equilibrium mapping x^* is shown in the lower part the diagram. It is the locus of pairs $[\alpha, x(\alpha)]$ formed by a value of the parameter vector and a corresponding equilibrium.

Many interpretations of the system $F(x;\alpha) = 0$ are possible. In the present context $x_{t+1} - x_t = F$ is a vector field defining a dynamical system, and (A.16) is the set of equations we have to solve to find the steady states of the system. But many other models have exactly the same formal structure. For example, we may be trying to find the vector of demand functions for a consumer. We then have to solve the problem

$$\max_x \ U(x) \text{ subject to } px = y \tag{A.17a}$$

To solve (A.17a) we form the Lagrangean function

$$\mathcal{L} = U(x) + \lambda(y - px) \tag{A.17b}$$

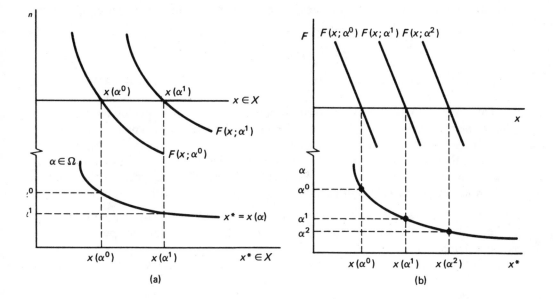

(a)

(b)

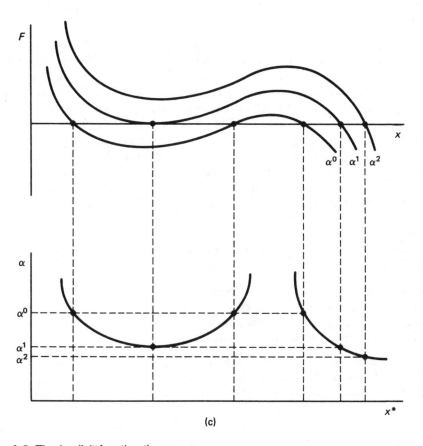

(c)

Figure A.2 The implicit function theorem.

which, on differentiation with respect to x and λ, yields the first-order conditions

$$D_x \mathcal{L} = DU(x) - \lambda pI = 0 \qquad\qquad (A.18a)$$

$$D_\lambda \mathcal{L} = y - px = 0 \qquad\qquad (A.18b)$$

In more compact notation, we may rewrite these as a version of (A.16), that is, $F(x, \lambda; p, y) = 0$.

The point is that, whatever interpretation (A.16) has in a specific context, some basic questions always come up. For example, we are interested in how the solution x^* changes as the parameters of the model change. Suppose, for instance, that for some given α^0 there is an equilibrium x^0 that is locally unique. Next, imagine a very small change in the parameter vector. We want to know what happens to the solution following the perturbation; in particular, we are concerned with the following issues.

1. *Number of equilibria, existence and local uniqueness*: Do we still have an equilibrium following the perturbation? Does the equilibrium disappear? Or do we get more than one?
2. *Continuity*: If only one equilibrium exists after the change, is it "close" to the old one?
3. *Comparative statics*: In which direction does the equilibrium position change following the shock?
4. *Are certain properties of the equilibrium (e.g. stability) preserved after the parameter change?*

Figures A.2(b) and A.2(c) should provide some intuition on what answers to expect to questions (1)–(3). Under "normal circumstances" the graph of F will cross the x axis with non-zero slope, and small changes in the environment should lead to small changes of equilibrium which preserve local uniqueness. Intuition says that, if F depends continuously on α, a small change in parameter values leaves the new picture looking very similar to the old one. On the other hand, there are certain special situations where we can expect "trouble", that is, bifurcations of equilibrium.

In figure A.2(b) for each α there is a unique equilibrium that changes continuously with α; the solution mapping $x(\alpha)$ is a continuous function. This is also true in figure A.2(c) for the right branch of the equilibrium mapping, but not for the left branch. At α^1 we have a bifurcation point: a small "decrease" in α would make the equilibrium vanish, whereas a small "increase" would result in the emergence of two distinct equilibria.

The intuition behind these figures – that tangency equilibria are in some sense fragile – is formulated more precisely in the following important result.

Theorem A.8 (The implicit function theorem) Let $f: \mathbb{R}^n \times \mathbb{R}^m \to \mathbb{R}^n$ be a C^1 map and consider the system of equations $F(x;\alpha) = 0$. Suppose (x^0, α^0) solves the system. If the Jacobian of endogenous variables does not vanish at (x^0, α^0), that is, if $|D_x F(x^0; \alpha^0)| \neq 0$, then we have the following.

(a) For all α in some neighborhood of α^0 there exists a unique x^* in some neighborhood of x^0 such that $F(x^*; \alpha) = 0$. In other words, the system defines locally the equilibrium values of the endogenous variables x^* as functions of α; hence we can write $x^* = x(\alpha)$.
(b) The function $x(\alpha)$ is continuously differentiable.

In this case, the comparative statics question can be answered by differentiation, since the solution mapping is a well-defined function in a neighborhood of α^0 and inherits the differentiability of F. Plugging the solution function $x(\alpha)$ back into the system yields the identity

$$F[x(\alpha);\alpha] \equiv 0 \tag{A.19}$$

Since (A.19) is an identity, it will continue to hold if we differentiate both sides totally with respect to α; thus

$$D_\alpha F(x^*;\alpha^0) + D_x F(x^*;\alpha^0)Dx(\alpha^0) = 0$$

which can be solved for the partial derivatives of the solution point with respect to the parameters:

$$Dx(\alpha^0) = -[D_x F(x^*;\alpha^0)]^{-1}D_\alpha F(x^*;\alpha^0) \tag{A.20}$$

This is basically the approach one follows to establish the comparative statics properties of supply and demand functions.

Perhaps more importantly, the implicit function theorem gives us sufficient conditions for the local uniqueness of the solution to the system and its continuous dependence on the parameters. This serves our purposes well because it tells us where to look for bifurcations, which are precisely those points at which uniqueness and continuity fail. To state this result more formally, we introduce the concept of critical point or singularity.[1]

Definition A.3 (Critical point or singularity)   Let $f: \mathbb{R}^n \to \mathbb{R}^n$ be a C^1 function. A point $x^c \in \mathbb{R}^n$ is a critical point or singularity of f if $Df(x^c)$ is not of full rank, that is, if $|Df(x^c)| = 0$. A point that is not critical is called a *regular* point of f.

With this definition, the implicit function theorem can be restated as follows.

Theorem A.9 (Implicit function theorem)   Given the system $F(x;\alpha) = 0$, consider the pair (x^c, α^c) where $F(x^c;\alpha^c) = 0$. A necessary condition for (x^c, α^c) to be a bifurcation point for $F(x;\alpha) = 0$, at which at least one steady state appears or disappears, is that x^c be a critical point of the function $f(x) \equiv F(x;\alpha^c)$.

A.3   Ordinary differential equations

An ordinary differential equation is an equation of the form

$$F[t, x(t), x'(t), x''(t), \ldots, x^{(n)}(t)] = 0 \tag{A.21}$$

where $x'(t) = dx/dt$, $x''(t) = d^2x/dt^2$, $\ldots$, $x^{(n)}(t) = d^nx/dt^n$.

Note that (A.21) is a functional equation, describing the behavior of an unknown function $x(t)$ and its derivatives. Solving a differential equation means finding functions $x: \mathbb{R} \to \mathbb{R}$ which, along with their derivatives, satisfy equation (A.21).

The *order* of a differential equation of this type is the order of the highest derivative that appears in the equation. Hence equation (A.21) is of order n. We will assume it is always possible to solve a differential equation for the highest derivative appearing in it to obtain

$$x^{(n)}(t) = G[t, x(t), x'(t), x''(t), \ldots, x^{(n-1)}(t)] \tag{A.22}$$

Ordinary differential equations can be classified as linear or nonlinear. An equation like (A.22) is said to be *linear* if G is a linear function of its arguments. Thus, the general linear differential equation of order n is given by

$$x^{(n)}(t) = a_0(t)x(t) + a_1(t)x'(t) + \dots + a_{n-1}(t)x^{(n-1)}(t) + b(t)$$

where the coefficients $a_i(t)$ and the independent term $b(t)$ are known functions of t.

First-order systems

In what follows we are concerned only with first-order equations and systems of differential equations. This involves little loss in generality because a higher-order system can always be reduced to a first-order system by introducing additional "dummy" variables and additional equations to eliminate higher-order derivatives, as one does with discrete systems. For example, consider the second-order linear equation

$$x''(t) = ax'(t) + bx(t) \tag{A.23}$$

Define $y(t) = x'(t)$ and rewrite (A.23) as a system of two first-order equations

$$x'(t) = y(t) \qquad y'(t) = ay(t) + b \times (t)$$

Consider now a vector-valued function $f: \mathbb{R}^n \times \mathbb{R} \supseteq X \times I \to \mathbb{R}^n$. The system of equations

$$x'(t) = f[x(t); t] \qquad t \in I \tag{A.24}$$

where I is an open interval in $\mathbb{R}$, is called a system of first-order differential equations. In less compact notation, we can write (A.24) as

$$x_1'(t) = f_1[x_1(t), x_2(t), \dots, x_n(t); t]$$
$$\vdots$$
$$x_n'(t) = f_n[x_1(t), x_2(t), \dots, x_n(t); t]$$

Systems like (A.24) are often used to describe the behavior of a set of economic variables $x_1, \dots, x_n$ over time, which we denote by the independent variable t. We typically assume that f is defined for all real values of t, with $t = 0$ referring to the "present" moment.

To give a graphical representation of the information given by the system (A.24), we may think of affixing to each point x in X the vector $f(x)$, which we should picture as starting from x. In this context, the function f is referred to as a *vector field*. The following physical interpretation arises, then, quite naturally. Imagine a system of differential equations that describe the motion of a particle in Euclidean n-space. At a given point in time the value of the state vector $x(t)$ describes the position of the particle, with the derivative $x'(t)$ indicating the direction and speed of the body. To "solve" the system would then mean to construct the set of trajectories that are compatible with the given set of velocity vectors.

Boundary-value problems are defined in the same way as in discrete systems. The following fundamental theorem tells us that every boundary problem will have a unique solution, provided that the function f has continuous partial derivatives. For a proof, see any of the standard references on differential equations in the bibliography.

Theorem A.10 (Cauchy-Peano-Picard-Lindelöf) Let the function $f: \mathbb{R}^n \times \mathbb{R} \supset X \times I \to \mathbb{R}^n$ have continuous partial derivatives in some neighborhood of (x^0, t_0). Then in some subinterval $[t_a, t_b]$ of I containing t_0 there is a unique solution $x[t;(x, t_0)]$ to the boundary-value problem $x'(t) = f[x(t), t]$, $x(t_0) = x^0$ for each $(x^0, t_0) \in X \times I$.

In fact, the continuity of f is sufficient to guarantee the *existence* of a solution; differentiability ensures uniqueness as well. This is convenient because it implies that solutions cannot "cross" each other in the sense that two different solutions cannot go through the same point in X at the same time.

An application of theorem A.10 is that we can identify each particular solution to $x' = f(x,t)$ with the solution to a specific boundary-value problem. In other words, choosing an appropriate boundary condition is equivalent to choosing a particular solution to this equation.

As in static systems of equations, the solution to a system of differential equations often depends on a set of exogenous variables or parameters that describe the wider environment in which the system is embedded. Thus, we may write the general first-order system as

$$x'(t) = f[x(t), t; \alpha] \tag{A.25}$$

where α is a vector of parameters in Ω, a subset of $\mathbb{R}^m$.

It is clear that a change in the value of the parameter vector will change the solution to the system. One may expect that small changes in the parameters will result in small changes in the solution, that is, that the solution to the system will be a continuous function of the parameter. The following result tells us that this is indeed the case, at least locally, provided that the conditions of the Cauchy–Peano theorem are satisfied. In fact, if f is continuously differentiable in α we get an even stronger result: the solution turns out to be a differentiable function of the parameter.

Theorem A.11 (Dependence of the solution on parameters) Consider the system (A.25), where f is a function $f: \mathbb{R}^n \times \mathbb{R} \times \mathbb{R}^m \supset X \times I \times \Omega \to \mathbb{R}^n$. Assume that f has continuous partial derivatives $\partial f/\partial x_i$ and $\partial f/\partial \alpha_j$ in some neighborhood of a point (x^0, t_0, α^0). Then, for any α in a neighborhood of α^0, there exists a unique solution $x(t; \alpha)$, defined in some subinterval $[t_a, t_b]$ of I containing t_0, which satisfies $x(t_0; \alpha^0) = x^0$. Moreover, the solution $x(t; \alpha)$ is a differentiable function of the parameter vector α.

As a byproduct of this theorem we get the result that the solution $x[t; (t_0, x^0)]$ of (A.23), seen as a function of the initial condition (t_0, x^0), is a differentiable in the initial condition.

Autonomous linear systems

We sum up some results on the homogeneous linear system

$$x'(t) = Ax(t) \tag{A.26}$$

where A is a matrix of real numbers. These are generally similar to what we know from discrete systems and are covered extensively in standard texts.

The first step in solving (A.26) is to find the eigenvalues $(\lambda_1, ..., \lambda_n)$ and eigenvectors $(e_1, ..., e_n)$ of the coefficient matrix. Then, depending on whether the eigenvalues are real or complex, or distinct or repeated, there are three cases.

1. *Real and distinct eigenvalues*: the coefficient matrix is diagonalizable, and the elementary solutions $x^i(t) = e_i \exp(\lambda_i t)$ are real valued. The general solution is

$$x^g(t) = c_1 e_1 \exp(\lambda_1 t) + \ldots + c_n e_n \exp(\lambda_n t)$$

2. *Complex eigenvalues*: now the elementary solutions associated with the complex eigenvalues are complex conjugates. Suppose there is a single pair of complex elementary solutions,

$$x^1(t) = u(t) + iv(t) \qquad x^2(t) = u(t) - iv(t)$$

The real and imaginary parts of these solutions, $u(t)$ and $v(t)$, are real-valued solutions to the system and can be used in conjunction with the rest of the elementary solutions to obtain a real basis for the solution space of (A.26). We write the general solution as

$$x^g(t) = c_1 u(t) + c_2 v(t) + c_3 x^3(t) + \ldots + c_n x^n(t)$$

where $x^i(t) = e_i \exp(\lambda_i t)$ are the elementary solutions corresponding to the real eigenvalues $\lambda_3, \ldots, \lambda_n$.

3. *Repeated eigenvalues*: we may not have enough linearly independent elementary solutions. Let μ_i be an eigenvalue of multiplicity m_i; in order to complete a fundamental set of solutions we consider functions of the form $P_i(t) \exp(\mu_i t)$ where $P_i(t)$ is a polynomial in t of degree $(m_i - 1)$. Solutions will then be of the form

$$x(t) = \sum_{i=1}^{k} P_i(t) \exp(\mu_i t) = \sum_{i=1}^{k} \sum_{j=1}^{m_i} p_{ji} t^{j-1} \exp(\mu_i t)$$

Note, however, that not all the functions of this form are solutions to (A.26); additional restrictions on the coefficients of P will have to be imposed so that $x(t)$ satisfies (A.26).

In all three cases, the stability of the system depends crucially on the sign of the real part of the coefficient-matrix eigenvalues; this is indicated by the following theorem.

Theorem A.12 (Stability of autonomous homogeneous systems)   Consider the autonomous homogeneous system (A.26) and assume that the eigenvalues of the coefficient matrix are all different from zero. Then the system has a unique steady states $\bar{x} = 0$; moreover, it is globally asymptotically stable if the real parts of all the eigenvalues are negative, and unstable otherwise.

Non-homogeneous autonomous systems like $x'(t) = Ax(t) + b$ behave quite like autonomous ones except that their steady state is not the zero vector. These systems are easily transformed into homogeneous systems and their qualitative properties are easy to ascertain.

Planar systems of the form

$$\begin{bmatrix} x'_1(t) \\ x'_2(t) \end{bmatrix} = \begin{bmatrix} a_{11} & a_{12} \\ a_{21} & a_{22} \end{bmatrix} \begin{bmatrix} x_1(t) \\ x_2(t) \end{bmatrix} + \begin{bmatrix} b_1 \\ b_2 \end{bmatrix} \tag{A.27}$$

with constant coefficients $(a_{11}, \ldots, a_{22}, b_1, b_2)$ are particularly instructive to study. The low dimensionality of these systems allows a convenient graphical representation that can be used to clarify some of the results discussed above.

As we already know, the nature and stability of the steady state of a planar autonomous linear system depends on the values of its characteristic roots, given by

$$\lambda_1,\lambda_2 = \frac{\text{tr } A \pm \sqrt{[(\text{tr } A)^2 - 4 \det A]}}{2} \tag{A.28}$$

which implies

$$\text{tr } A = \lambda_1 + \lambda_2 \tag{A.29a}$$

$$\det A = \lambda_1\lambda_2 \tag{A.29b}$$

Here it is easy to determine the nature of orbits near the steady state $\bar{x}$ just by looking at the coefficient matrix. We recall that

1. if $\det A < 0$, the eigenvalues of the system have opposite signs and $\bar{x}$ is a saddlepoint.
2. if $\det A > 0$, the roots have the same sign or else they are complex.
   In this case we have two possibilities: *either* tr $A < 0$ and the system is stable because the two eigenvalues are negative (if real) or have negative real parts (if complex); *or* tr $A > 0$ and the system is unstable because the eigenvalues have positive real parts.

Figure A.3 summarizes most of this information in a convenient diagram.

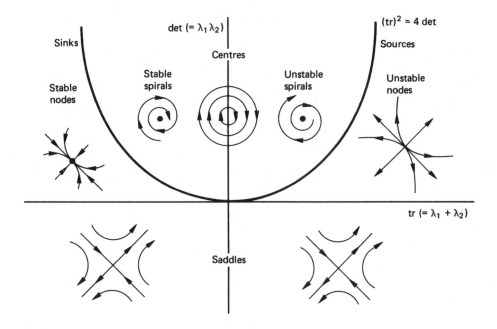

Figure A.3 Orbits in continuous planar systems.

A.4   Periodicity in continuous time

In this section we review periodic solutions for planar nonlinear systems of differential equations, with occasional excursions into higher dimensions and much illustration drawn from the natural sciences. Our chief concern is systems of the general form

$$x' = f(x) \tag{A.30}$$

where $f: \mathbb{R}^2 \to \mathbb{R}^2$ is typically a C^1 map.

Periodic solutions and cycles

A solution $x(t)$ of the system $x' = f(x)$ is called a *periodic solution with scalar period p* if it exists for all t and satisfies $x(t + p) = x(t)$ $\forall t$ and $x(t + m) \neq x(t)$ for all $m < p$.

It is clear that orbits that correspond to periodic solutions are closed curves in state space, called periodic orbits or cycles. Like stationary equilibria, closed orbits may be approached asymptotically by other orbits. This leads to the concept of a limit cycle.

Definition A.4 (Limit cycle)   A periodic orbit Γ is called a limit cycle if there are two points on $\mathbb{R}^2$, one in the interior of Γ and the other in the exterior, such that the ω- or α-limit set of the orbits through these two points is the periodic orbit Γ.

More intuitively, a limit cycle is a closed curve on the plane that has non-closed curves spiralling toward it or away from it from the inside and the outside as $t \to \infty$.

The concept of stability can be readily extended to periodic solutions. If all trajectories that start near a closed trajectory (both inside and outside) spiral toward the closed trajectory at $t \to \infty$, we say that the limit cycle Γ is asymptotically stable. If the trajectories on one side spiral toward Γ, while those on the other spiral away, the limit cycle is semi-stable. If trajectories on both sides are repelled by Γ, the cycle is unstable. If neighboring trajectories are neither attracted nor repelled, the closed trajectory is (neutrally) stable, like the concentric periodic orbits of a linear system with purely imaginary eigenvalues.

We have seen that a linear system on the plane has closed paths if and only if both eigenvalues are imaginary numbers, and in that case every path is closed. Thus, for a linear system either every path is closed or no path is closed. On the other hand, nonlinear systems can have both closed and non-closed paths. We now list some sufficient conditions for the existence and nonexistence of periodic solutions to the dynamical system (A.30).

The following three results guarantee that cycles do not exist.[2]

Theorem A.13 If $f \in C^1$, a closed trajectory of $x' = f(x)$ must necessarily enclose at least one equilibrium point. If it encloses only one equilibrium, that equilibrium cannot be a saddlepoint.

Hence, there can be no closed trajectory lying entirely in a region that contains no stationary states or just one saddle.

Theorem A.14 (Bendixson's criterion)   If $f: \mathbb{R}^2 \to \mathbb{R}^2$ has continuous partial derivatives in a simply connected domain D of the phase plane and if, in addition, the function

$$\text{div } f = \frac{\partial f^1}{\partial x_1} + \frac{\partial f^2}{\partial x_2}$$

called the divergence of f, is of constant sign and not identically zero on D, then the system $x' = f(x)$ has no periodic orbit lying entirely in the region D.

A "simply connected" domain is one with no holes in it. Note that the divergence of f is the trace of the Jacobian matrix. Intuitively, enough monotonicity of the components of f is sufficient to rule out cycles. On the other hand, this is not a necessary condition; if div f changes sign on D we may or may not have cycles. The following theorem provides a generalization of Bendixson's criterion.

Theorem A.15 (Dulac's criterion)   Let D be a simply connected open set in X, and let $B(x_1, x_2)$ be a real-valued C^1 function in D. Then, if the function

$$\text{div } Bf = \frac{\partial (Bf^1)}{\partial x_1} + \frac{\partial (Bf^2)}{\partial x_2}$$

is of constant sign and not identically zero on D, $x' = f(x)$ has no periodic solutions with orbit lying entirely in D.

The function B is called a Dulac function. As with Liapunov functions, the problem is that there is no simple or general way to find a B that will work. Note that Bendixson's criterion is a special case of Dulac's with $B \equiv 1$.

  These results are useful because they can sometimes keep us from looking for cycles where none exists. We would also like to have positive criteria telling us when cycles *do* exist. One of the few results of this type is stated below.

Theorem A.16 (Poincaré–Bendixson)   If the ω-limit set $\omega(x^0)$ of the planar system (A.30) through x^0 is a bounded set containing no equilibrium points, then $\omega(x^0)$ is a periodic orbit of $x' = f(x)$

To understand the logic of this result, refer to theorem A.18 below. That theorem tells us that if $\gamma^+(x^0)$ is a bounded positive orbit on the plane, then its ω-limit set is either a steady state, a periodic cycle, or a set formed by steady state and orbits joining them. By assuming that $\omega(x^0)$ contains no stationary equilibria, we are ruling out the first and third case and are left with the second: either $\gamma(x^0)$ is itself a cycle or it converges to a cycle as $t \to \infty$. In either case, a periodic solution exists.

  To apply theorem A.16, one must be able to construct a bounded positively invariant region in X that contains no equilibrium points. Roughly speaking, since the set is positively invariant, no solution that enters can escape it, and since it is bounded, so is $\gamma^+(x^0)$, which must therefore converge to one of the three types of limit sets for a planar system. Finally, since there are no equilibria in the region, the limit set must be a cycle. Hence, we may restate the theorem in a more "usable" form as follows.

Corollary   Let D be a bounded, positively invariant set for $x' = f(x)$ and let $\overline{D}$ denote the closure of D (that is, D plus its boundary). Suppose $\overline{D}$ contains no critical point of the system. Let $\gamma(x^0)$ be an orbit that begins in D and remains in D (since D is positively invariant). Then either $\gamma(x^0)$ is a periodic orbit or it spirals toward a limit cycle $\Gamma = \omega(x^0)$ as $t \to \infty$; in either case the system has a periodic orbit in D.

  Recall that a closed trajectory must necessarily enclose a stationary equilibrium. If D contains a cycle, it must enclose a steady state which cannot be in D. Hence, D

cannot be simply connected and must have a "hole." A typical situation in which the Poincaré–Bendixson theorem applies is shown in figure A.4(a). Let D be the region between the two closed curves; it is a doughnut-shaped region around an equilibrium. If the vector field $x' = f$ points into the region D at every boundary point, then every path that enters D remains in it and D is positively invariant. Hence, any orbit in D must converge to the limit cycle. A typical case arises when we can find a bounded positively invariant region that contains a single unstable equilibrium. If we remove a small neighborhood around this point, the rest of the region must contain a limit cycle that surrounds the equilibrium.

To obtain an appropriate D, we must remove a neighborhood around the equilibrium and not just $\bar{x}$ itself; otherwise, the boundary of D would contain an equilibrium and the theorem does not hold. Figure A.4(b) shows another situation in which the boundary condition is important. Suppose $\bar{x}$ is asymptotically stable and the region U bounded by the circle is part of its basin of attraction. Then the region $D = U - \{\bar{x}\}$ is bounded and positively invariant. However, $\bar{x}$ belongs to the closure of D and the theorem fails, as we know it must.

The Poincaré–Bendixson theorem has several important limitations. It only applies to planar systems, and it does not tell us anything about the number of orbits in the region. Perhaps most importantly from an operational point of view, there is no easy way to construct a region with the desired properties. Applying the theorem can be painful as we shall see below in connection with the van der Pol equation.

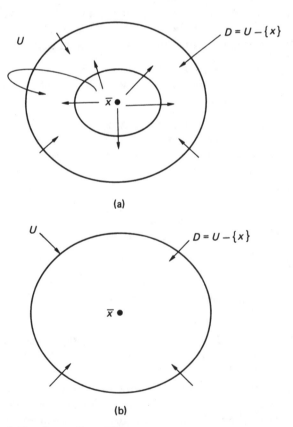

(a)

(b)

Figure A.4 The Poincaré–Bendixson theorem.

A more practical criterion has been developed for systems of the form

$$x'' + f(x)x' + g(x) = 0 \tag{A.31}$$

called the *generalized Lienard equation*. By a closed path of (A.31) we mean a closed orbit of the equivalent planar system

$$\begin{aligned} x' &= y \\ y' &= -g(x) - f(x)y \end{aligned} \tag{A.32}$$

Theorem A.17 (Lienard)   Let the functions f and g in (A.32) satisfy the following assumptions.

(a) Both are continuously differentiable for all x.
(b) $g(x)$ is an odd function $g(x) + g(-x) = 0$, with $g(0) = 0$ and $g(x) > 0$ for all $x > 0$.
(c) $f(x)$ is an even function, $f(x) - f(-x) = 0$.
   Moreover, the functions $F(x)$ and $G(x)$, defined from

$$F(x) = \int_0^x f(s)ds \qquad G(x) = \int_0^x g(s)ds$$

   are assumed to satisfy the following conditions.
(d) $G(x) \to \infty$ and $F(x) \to \infty$ as $x \to \infty$.
(e) There exists a positive number x_0 such that $F(x) < 0$ for $x \in (0,x_0)$ and $F(x) > 0$ for $x > x_0$.
(f) $F(x)$ is monotonically increasing for $x > x_0$.

   Then the generalized Lienard equation (A.31) has a unique periodic orbit around the origin, and all trajectories in the plane except that corresponding to the steady state $(0,0)$ spiral toward the closed trajectory as $t \to \infty$.

An important application of Lienard's theorem is the *van der Pol equation*

$$x'' + \mu(x^2 - 1)x' + x = 0 \qquad \mu > 0 \tag{A.33}$$

In this case, we have

$$f(x) = \mu(x^2 - 1) \qquad g(x) = x$$

Clearly, conditions (a)–(d) hold. To check (e), note that

$$F(x) = -\mu \int_0^x (1 - s^2)ds = -\mu\left(x - \frac{x^3}{3}\right)$$

which is less than zero for $x \in (0,\sqrt{3})$, is greater than zero for $x > \sqrt{3}$, and increases monotonically thereafter to infinity as $x \to \infty$. Thus the van der Pol equation has a stable periodic solution.

Limit sets in planar systems

We know that closed orbits and equilibria are examples of limit sets; other limit sets exist that are neither closed orbits nor equilibria. In higher dimensions we can find extremely complicated examples that are hard to describe. In planar systems, however, limit sets must have a very simple structure already alluded to in section 8.4:

besides closed orbits and stationary equilibria there is only one other possibility – a limit set formed by equilibria and trajectories joining them.

Theorem A.18 (Limit sets for planar systems) Consider the planar autonomous system

$$x' = f(x) \qquad f: \mathbb{R}^2 \supseteq X \to \mathbb{R}^2 \qquad X \qquad \text{open} \qquad f \in C^1 \qquad (A.34)$$

If the positive orbit $\gamma^+(x^0) = \{x(t,x^0) : t \geq 0\}$ is bounded, then the limit set $\omega(x^0)$ is a non-empty, compact, and connected invariant set. Moreover, one of the following statements holds true.

(a) $\omega(x^0)$ is a single point $\bar{x}$; then $\bar{x}$ is a steady state and $x(t,x^0) \to \bar{x}$ as $t \to \infty$.[3]
(b) $\omega(x^0)$ is a periodic orbit Γ, and either $\omega(x^0) = \Gamma$ or $\gamma^+(x^0)$ spirals toward Γ from one side at $t \to \infty$.
(c) $\omega(x^0)$ consists of equilibrium points and orbits that join them and whose α- or ω-limit sets are the equilibria.

These three possibilities apply to the α-limit set $\alpha(x^0)$ when $\gamma^-(x^0)$ is bounded. In other words, trajectories of a planar system that do not go off to infinity must converge either to a stationary equilibrium, to a cycle, or to a set formed by equilibria and orbits joining them. The first two possibilities are already familiar; figure 8.9 gives an example of the third.

The simplicity of the structure of limit sets for planar autonomous systems arises as a consequence of the following result, which is essential in any proof of Theorem A.18.

Theorem A.19 (Jordan curve theorem) A closed curve in $\mathbb{R}^2$ that does not intersect itself separates $\mathbb{R}^2$ into two connected components, one bounded (called the interior of the curve) and the other unbounded (called the exterior of the curve).

The intuitive idea is that orbits cannot escape cycles in two dimensions. To do so, they would have to cut them and thus violate the uniqueness theorem. This precludes the appearance of more complicated trajectories like those possible in higher-dimensional systems.

A.5   Bifurcations and catastrophe

Consider a family of dynamical systems parametrized by a vector α:

$$x' = F(x; \alpha) \qquad F: \mathbb{R}^n \times \mathbb{R}^m \supseteq X \times \Omega \to \mathbb{R}^n \qquad F \in C^1 \qquad (A.35)$$

For a given value of α, say α^0, (A.35) becomes a system of ordinary differential equations

$$x' = f(x) \equiv F(x; \alpha^0) \qquad (A.36)$$

of the type we have studied in these Technical Appendices.

In chapter 6 we introduced the notions of topological equivalence and structural stability. In the present context, these ideas can be summarized intuitively if we recall, in particular, definitions 6.1 and 6.3. Two members of the family (A.35) indexed by α^0 and α^1 respectively are said to be *topologically equivalent* if their orbit structures are qualitatively similar. More precisely, they have to be similar enough that it is possible to find a continuous change of coordinates $h: \mathbb{R}^n \to \mathbb{R}^n$ mapping the orbits of one system onto those of the other. Also, we say that the system $x' = F(x; \alpha^0)$ is *structurally stable* if all other members of the family (A.35) that are "close enough" to it (in the sense that $\|\alpha - \alpha^0\| < \epsilon$ for some $\epsilon > 0$) are topologically equivalent to this system.

With this background in mind, we can now discuss bifurcations. If the system $x' = F(x; \alpha^0)$ is not structurally stable, a small change in the parameters away from the critical value α^0 will change the qualitative nature of the system's orbit structure. The parameter value α^0 for which such a qualitative change takes place is called a *bifurcation* or *catastrophe point* for the system.

Note that we are using the words "bifurcation" and "catastrophe" interchangeably. In some cases, however, catastrophe means something slightly different. Let us return to the parametrized system (A.35) which we regard as describing the behavior over time of some system with a state vector x that is embedded in a certain "environment" governed by the parameter vector α. Imagine that the environment α changes very slowly and continuously over time and that, by comparison, the state variables are quick to adjust. Then, we can think of the state vector x as being almost always close to some sort of an attractor, for example a stable steady state.

For concreteness, imagine that at some time t_0 the state vector is very close to a stable equilibrium $\bar{x}(\alpha^0)$. Then, as time passes, α changes slowly; typically $\bar{x}(\alpha)$ will also change smoothly and the state vector x can be expected to follow suit, always lying close to $\bar{x}(\alpha)$. If at that point in time, say t_1, α hits a bifurcation point α^0, this pattern of smooth change can be disrupted by a "catastrophe."

Figure A.5(a) shows an example. The thick straight line traces the displacement of the equilibrium over time; it is continuous if the equilibrium is stable and broken otherwise. The curved middle line shows the evolution of the state vector. At t_1 the previously stable equilibrium loses its stability and a new stable equilibrium appears. The sharp change that starts when the system hits a bifurcation point at $t = t_1$ may be called a catastrophe.

This simple example should give you some idea of why catastrophe theory can be interesting. Generating abrupt responses to smooth changes in environmental conditions seems important for the modeling of a number of phenomena in which systems appear to "over-react" to external stimuli; examples are the extinction of a species, heart attacks, "take-offs" in economic development, depressions, etc.

Bifurcation and catastrophe are very general terms that may be used to describe any qualitative changes in the behavior of a system as parameters change. In what follows we will be concerned only with local bifurcations near equilibrium points of a dynamical system. Given a parametrized family of systems like (A.35), we are interested in finding pairs (x^0, α^0) for which the nature of the vector field near the equilibrium x^0 changes. In particular, we will look for values of α for which either *the number* of equilibria of the system in a neighborhood of x^0 changes or *the stability type* of the equilibrium changes, or both. Specifically, we will consider three different types of problems:

1. Where do bifurcations occur?
2. Given a specific system of differential equations, how can we find its bifurcation points and determine what kind of reorganization of the orbit structure takes place at the bifurcation point?
3. Can we classify most bifurcations and catastrophes into a small number of elementary types?

Next we analyze some simple examples of systems that display bifurcations. In addition to finding bifurcation points, we examine the nature of the changes that take place at such points by constructing a phase diagram for the system *before, after* and *exactly at* the bifurcation point. We will then show that some of these examples are typical in the sense that "most" bifurcations of certain kinds of systems look just like them.

We begin with some simple dynamical systems that exhibit bifurcations, particularly of types we did not explore in section 8.3. To study them, we need to determine the nature of the change in the system's orbit structure at the bifurcation point; this we typically do by drawing phase diagrams on both sides of each bifurcation point. In simple cases, a simple *bifurcation diagram* will summarize all the relevant pieces of qualitative information we need. This technique is illustrated with some specific examples below.

Given the system

$$x' = F(x; \alpha) \qquad F : \mathbb{R}^n \times \mathbb{R}^m \supseteq X \times \Omega \to \mathbb{R}^n \qquad F \in C^1$$

we define its set of stationary equilibria

$$M = \{(x, \alpha) \in X \times \Omega \mid F(x; \alpha) = 0\}$$

as a surface in $\mathbb{R}^n \times \mathbb{R}^m$ that corresponds to the parametrized equilibria of the system. We are interested in the subset at M at which bifurcations can occur, that is, pairs (x, α) in M that yield singularities of $f(x) = F(x; \alpha)$. Hence, we define the singularity set of the system as

$$S = \{(x, \alpha) \in X \times \Omega \mid F(x; \alpha) = 0 \text{ and } |D_x F(x; \alpha)| = 0\}$$
$$= \{(x, \alpha) \in M \mid D_x F(x; \alpha)| = 0\}$$

If we now project S onto the parameter space Ω by eliminating the state variables x from the equations $F(x; \alpha) = 0$ and $|D_x F(x; \alpha)| = 0$, we obtain the bifurcation set

$$B = \{\alpha \in \Omega \mid (x, \alpha) \in S \text{ for some } x \in X\}.$$

This is the set of parameter values at which the implicit function theorem fails and bifurcations of equilibrium occur. Geometrically, the bifurcation set B corresponds to a surface that divides the parameter space Ω into different regions. Members of the family $x' = F(x; \alpha)$ that lie within a given region have similar phase portraits, which change qualitatively as we cross the surface B into a different region. To describe the behavior of the family (A.35) completely, then, we only need to construct a phase diagram for a convenient point in each of the areas in which Ω is divided by B, including B itself.

Bifurcations of scalar one-parameter systems

Example A.5 (Hyperbolic system)   Consider the system

$$x' = F(x, a) = a + x \tag{A.37}$$

where a is a scalar constant. For $a = 0$ this system becomes

$$x' = F(x, 0) = x \tag{A.38}$$

The phase diagram for (A.38) is shown in figure A.5(b). The equation has a single unstable (hyperbolic) equilibrium point at $\bar{x} = 0$, and two orbits $(0, \infty)$ and $(-\infty, 0)$.

Introducing the parameter a will shift the phaselines of $F(0, x)$ upwards by a distance a. Instead of shifting the phaseline, it is more convenient to leave it fixed and shift the x axis in the opposite direction, as shown in figure A.5(c). In this manner we can display the phase diagram for the whole family of system (A.37) in a single figure. We observe that changes in the value of a do not change the qualitative features of the system's orbit structure: for each value of the parameter there are two orbits and a unique equilibrium point $\bar{x}(a)$ given by $\bar{x}(a) = -a$. This equilibrium is always unstable since

$$D_x F[a, \bar{x}(a)] = 1 > 0$$

Hence, the hyperbolic system (A.37) has *no* bifurcations, as we expected from the implicit function theorem.

Example A.6 (The fold bifurcation)   Next we study the system

$$x' = F(a, x) = x^2 - a \qquad\qquad (A.39)$$

where a is again a scalar. Proceeding as above, note that the graph of $F(0, x) = x^2$ is a parabola tangent to the x axis at the origin. By shifting the horizontal axis by a we can construct the flow of the system for each value of the parameter, as shown in figure A.5(d). Note that for $a > 0$ there are two steady states which merge into one at $a = 0$ and disappear for all $a < 0$. Hence this system *does* have a bifurcation.

Analytically, we set $x' = F(a,x) = 0$ to obtain the equilibria of the parametrized system:

$$x' = F(x, a) = x^2 - a = 0 \Rightarrow \bar{x}(a) = \pm\sqrt{a}$$

The equilibrium set for this system is therefore given by

$$M = \{(x, a) \in \mathbb{R}^2 | x^2 - a = 0\}$$

Its graph, as shown in figure A.5(e), is a parabola on the right half-plane, tangential to the vertical axis at the origin. The bullet-shaped figure in A.5(e) is called a *bifurcation diagram*. In addition to describing the equilibria of (A.39) as a "function" of the parameter, it tells us which equilibria are stable and which are not. Portions of M corresponding to stable equilibria are drawn as solid lines, whereas portions corresponding to unstable equilibria are shown as broken lines. The arrows indicate the direction of motion of the system around the equilibrium.

To check for stability we study the sign of $D_x F[a, \bar{x}(a)]$. We have

$$D_x F(x, a) = 2x \Rightarrow D_x F[a,\bar{x}(a)] = 2\bar{x}(a)$$

which is positive on the upper branch of the parabola $(\sqrt{a})$ and negative on the lower branch $(-\sqrt{a})$. Clearly, the only bifurcation point of this system is $(\bar{x}^c, a^c) = (0,0)$.

Note that (0,0) is the only solution to the system of equations

$$x' = F(x, a) = x^2 - a = 0$$

$$D_x F(x, a) = 2x = 0$$

that is, $\bar{x}^c$ is an *equilibrium* for a^c and a *singularity* of $f(x) = F(x, a^c)$.

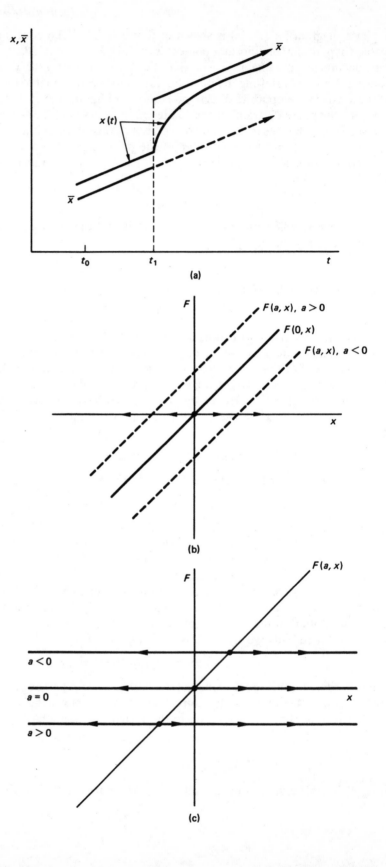

(a)

(b)

(c)

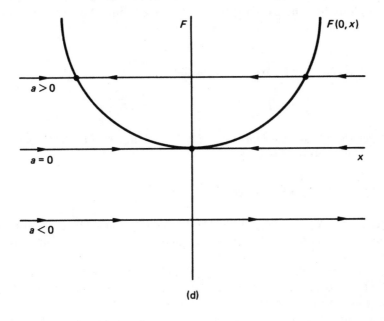

(d)

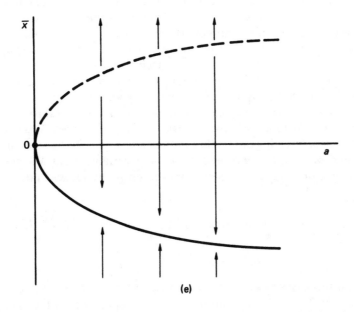

(e)

Figure A.5 (a) Catastrophe; (b), (c) hyperbolic systems; (d), (e) the fold bifurcation.

It turns out that the fold catastrophe described in this example is typical of systems with one parameter. The basic idea is that, around a bifurcation, most functions of the form $F(x, a)$ look like the parabola in this example point. We will return to this idea below.

Example A.7 (Hysteresis)   We are given the system

$$F(x; c) = -\frac{x^3}{3} - 2x^2 - 3x + c \qquad (A.40)$$

To construct the phase diagram note that $F(x;c)$ has two critical points, given by $D_x F(x;c) = -x^2 - 4x - 3 = 0 \Rightarrow$

$$x = -\frac{1}{2}[4 \pm \sqrt{(16 - 12)}] = \{-3, -1\}$$

Moreover, $D_x^2 F(x; c) = -2x - 4 \Rightarrow D_x^2 F(-3; c) > 0$ and $D_x^2 F(-1; c) < 0$. Therefore, F has a minimum at $x = -3$ and a maximum at $x = -1$. The corresponding extremal values are $F(-3; c) = c$ and $F(-1; c) = 4/3 + c$.

With this information we can plot $F(x;0)$ and construct the bifurcation diagram in figures A.6(a) and A.6(b) by the graphical method explained above. The diagram shows *two* fold bifurcations at $c = 0$ and $c = -4/3$.

Figure A.6(b) illustrates the phenomenon known as *hysteresis*. Imagine that we start out with a *very low* value of c and that the system is given enough time for the state variable x to get very close to the unique stable equilibrium. Initially, then, we are on the lower left branch of the equilibrium hyperbola. Next, imagine that the value of c is increased very slowly. The equilibrium of the system moves up along the curve maintaining its stability, and the state variable x will follow right along. When $c = 0$ we hit a bifurcation and the equilibrium loses its stability. A catastrophe occurs and the system jumps to the upper branch of the hyperbola.

Now imagine starting with a *very high* c and moving in the other direction. A similar phenomenon occurs, with a jump to the lower branch at $c = -4/3$; this is shown in figure A.6(b). The interesting part is that for any $c \in (-4/3,0)$ the state of the system does not depend only on the current environment variable c but also on where the system is coming from; this is precisely what the term "hysteresis" means.

Example A.8 (The pitchfork bifurcation)   For any real number d, consider the equation

$$x' = F(x, d) = dx - x^3 = x(d - x^2) \qquad (A.41)$$

Steady states of this system occur at points where $x^2 = d$. Hence, there is always an equilibrium at $x = 0$, and possibly up to two more depending on the value of d; for $d > 0$ we have two equilibria at $\pm\sqrt{d}$, whereas for $d < 0$ there are no other equilibria. At $d = 0$ three distinct equilibria merge into a single one that persists for negative values of d.

To draw the phase diagram, observe that

$$D_x F(x, d) = d - 3x^2 \qquad \text{and} \qquad D_x^2 F(x, d) = -6$$

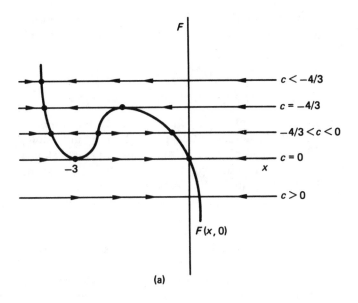

(a)

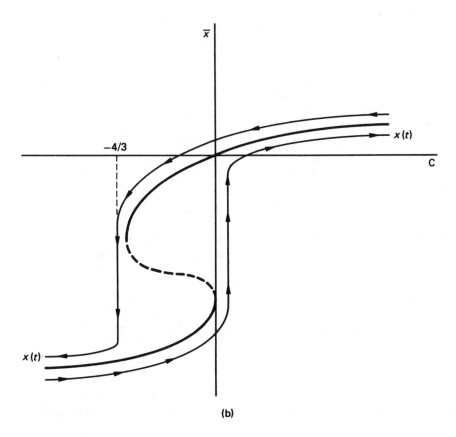

(b)

Figure A.6 Hysteresis.

The critical points of $F(x, d)$ are therefore at $x^2 = d/3$ which has two solutions $x = \sqrt{(d/3)}$ and $\sqrt{(d/3)}$ if $d > 0$, one solution $(x = 0)$ if $d = 0$, and none if $d < 0$. For $d > 0$ we have

$$D_x^2 F[\sqrt{(d/3)}, d] = -6\sqrt{(d/3)} < 0$$
$$D_x^2 F[-\sqrt{(d/3)}, d] = 6\sqrt{(d/3)} > 0$$

and so the first critical point corresponds to a local maximum and the second to a minimum. For $d = 0$, the unique critical point of F is an inflection point at the origin.

Stability can be checked directly in the phase diagrams shown in panels A.7(a) through A.7(c). The bifurcation diagram is figure A.7(d); its shape explains why this example is called the "pitchfork" bifurcation.

The classification of elementary catastrophes

One goal of catastrophe theory is to classify systematically the ways in which the behavior of a dynamical system can change at bifurcation points. In view of the examples we just saw, this may look like an impossible task. After all, we have already come up with *three* different examples of bifurcations using only simple polynomials in one state variable and a single parameter. One may expect that, with more state variables and parameters, things can only get worse.

Here we show that bifurcations display a great deal more regularity than appears at first sight. In fact, for certain simple types of systems, most bifurcations are qualitatively equivalent to a small number of standard examples we will call *elementary catastrophes*.

To make precise the meaning of this statement, we concentrate on systems with one parameter and one state variable. We will show that for such systems the fold catastrophe in example A.6 is typical. This result extends to systems with one parameter and more state variables, but a proof goes beyond our purposes here.

We return to bifurcations of the system

$$x' = F(x, a) = x^2 - a$$

and to the diagrams in figures A.5(d) and A.5(e). As the parameter crosses a critical value, two distinct equilibria "fold" into one and then disappear. We now want to show that this fold catastrophe is essentially the only one that can occur in the case of one-parameter scalar systems, except for *degenerate* cases of rare occurrence. The idea here is that if a scalar function with one parameter has a non-hyperbolic equilibrium, then it will in all likelihood look like a parabola near the equilibrium, and hence the bifurcation diagram will look like the one in example A.6.

Consider the scalar one-parameter family of dynamical systems

$$x' = F(x, \alpha) \tag{A.42}$$

where $F \in C^2$. We know that bifurcations can only occur at non-hyperbolic equilibria. Let $\bar{x}^c$ be a non-hyperbolic equilibrium for the system $x' = F(x, \alpha^0)$, that is, a pair $(\bar{x}^c, \alpha^c)$ is such that $F(\bar{x}^c, \alpha^0) = 0$ and

$$F_x(\bar{x}^c, \alpha^c) = 0 \tag{A.43}$$

We assume that $\bar{x}^c$ is a nondegenerate critical point of $F(x, \alpha^c)$ in the sense that

$$F_{xx}(\bar{x}^c, \alpha^c) \neq 0 \qquad (A.44a)$$

For concreteness, suppose $F_{xx}(\bar{x}^c, \alpha^c) > 0$, so $\bar{x}^c$ corresponds to a local *minimum* of $F(x,c)$. It is then obvious that the function F looks like a parabola around $\bar{x}^c$. To show this formally, consider the equation

$$F_x(x, \alpha) = 0 \qquad (A.44b)$$

which implicitly defines the critical points of F as a function of the parameter, that is, $x^c = c(\alpha)$. Since $F_{xx}(\bar{x}^c, \alpha^c) \neq 0$, the conditions of the implicit function theorem hold at $(\bar{x}^c, \alpha^c)$ $(\bar{x}^c, \alpha^c)$ and the function c is well defined and differentiable in a neighborhood of α^c. By continuity, moreover, for any α close enough to α^c, $F_{xx}[c(\alpha), \alpha]$ has the same sign as $F_{xx}(\bar{x}^c, \alpha^c)$, that is, it is positive. Hence F has a single isolated minimum at $c(\alpha)$ close to $\bar{x}^c$ and looks locally like a parabola. The number of equilibria around $\bar{x}^c$ is either two or zero, depending on whether the minimum value of the function $F[c(\alpha), \alpha]$ is negative or positive.

The critical assumption here is (A.44) which says that $\bar{x}^c$ is a *nondegenerate critical point* of $F(x, \alpha^c)$. This, however, is a very mild requirement. In a well-defined sense, degenerate critical points are rare and hence "most" bifurcations of systems like (A.42) will resemble the fold. Intuitively, the nondegeneracy assumption rules out inflection-point equilibria like that of figure A.5(b) and leaves us only with the relative maxima or minima of figure A.5(a) which generate folds in the neighborhood of the steady state. But then, what about the examples in the preceding section? The hysteresis example poses no problem; as we have already noted, its bifurcation diagram is made up of two standard folds. The pitchfork example

$$x' = F(x, d) = dx - x^3$$

is also easy to explain: the point $(\bar{x}^0, \alpha^0) = (0,0)$ is a *degenerate* critical point of $F(x, 0)$.

Planar one-parameter systems

We conclude this appendix with a survey of planar systems of the form

$$x' = F(x; \alpha) \qquad F : \mathbb{R}^2 \times \mathbb{R} \supseteq X \times \Omega \to \mathbb{R}^2 \qquad F \in C^2 \qquad (A.45)$$

For a given value of the parameter α^0, we can write the determinant of the Jacobian matrix of the system at an equilibrium $\bar{x}^0$

$$|D_x F(\bar{x}^0, \alpha^0)| = \lambda_1(\alpha^0)\lambda_2(\alpha^0) \qquad (A.46)$$

where λ_1 and λ_2 are the eigenvalues of the Jacobian matrix.

If $\bar{x}^0$ is a hyperbolic equilibrium, λ_1 and λ_2 have non-zero real parts and the Jacobian determinant does not vanish. We know that in such cases no bifurcations arise. Two possibilities remain.

1. If one of the eigenvalues is zero, the conditions of the implicit function theorem do not hold at $(\bar{x}^0, \alpha^0)$ and hence we may expect small perturbations of the system to lead to a change in the number of equilibria around $\bar{x}^0$.

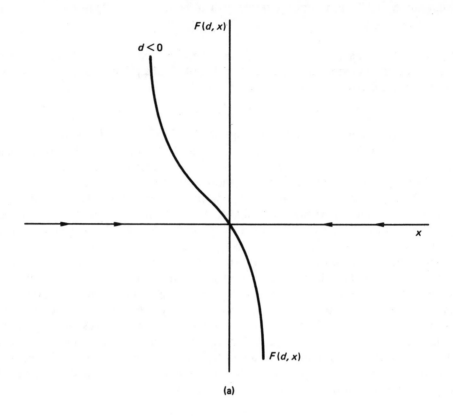

(a)

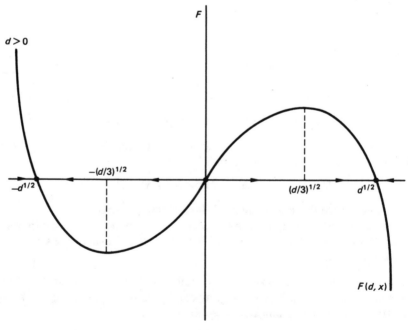

(b)

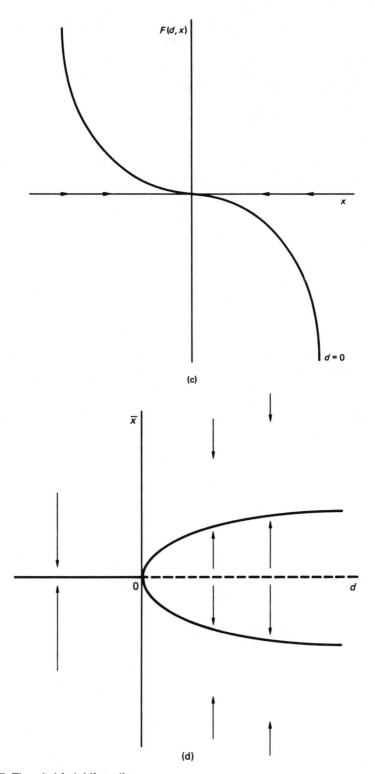

Figure A.7 The pitchfork bifurcation.

2. If the eigenvalues are pure imaginary numbers, their product is positive, and hence the Jacobian does not vanish and the implicit function theorem guarantees that small perturbations will leave the system with a unique equilibrium close to $\bar{x}^0$. On the other hand, such perturbations will almost surely make the real parts of the eigenvalues non-zero and change the stability type of the equilibrium.

These two cases will be discussed in turn, starting with an example of each.

Example A.9 (The saddle-node bifurcation)   We will analyze the one-parameter system

$$x' = f(x,y; a) \equiv x^2 - a \tag{A.47}$$

$$y' = g(x,y; a) \equiv -y \tag{A.48}$$

where $x = x(t)$, $y = y(t)$, $x' = dx/dt$ and $y' = dy/dt$. We begin by finding the steady states of the system. Setting $x' = 0$ and $y' = 0$ we obtain

$\{\bar{y} = 0, \bar{x}^2 = a\} \Rightarrow$ if $a > 0$ then $\bar{x} = \pm \sqrt{a}$
   if $a = 0$ then $\bar{x} = 0$
   if $a < 0$ then no real solution exists

Hence, there are three possibilities depending on the value of the parameter. If $a > 0$ we have two steady states; at $a = 0$ the two steady states merge into a single equilibrium $(0,0)$; and they disappear for $a < 0$.

To check the stability of the steady state we compute the eigenvalues of the Jacobian matrix:

$$J(x, y; a) = \begin{pmatrix} 2x & 0 \\ 0 & -1 \end{pmatrix}$$

Assuming $a \geq 0$ we evaluate $|J - aI|$ at the two steady states:

$$|J(\sqrt{a}, 0) - \lambda I| = \begin{vmatrix} 2\sqrt{a} - \lambda & 0 \\ 0 & -1-\lambda \end{vmatrix} = (-1-\lambda)(2\sqrt{a} - \lambda)$$

$$= \lambda^2 + (1 - 2\sqrt{a})\,\lambda - 2\sqrt{a} = 0$$

By the quadratic formula, we obtain

$$\lambda_1 = 2\sqrt{a} > 0 \qquad \lambda_2 = -1 < 0$$

Hence, the first equilibrium is a saddle. Similarly

$$|J(-\sqrt{a}, 0) - \lambda I| = \begin{vmatrix} -2\sqrt{a} - \lambda & 0 \\ 0 & -1-\lambda \end{vmatrix} = (-1-\lambda)(-2\sqrt{a} - \lambda)$$

$$= \lambda^2 + (1 + 2\sqrt{a})\lambda + 2\sqrt{a} = 0$$

Again, by the quadratic formula,

$$\lambda_1 = -2\sqrt{a} < 0 \qquad \lambda_2 = -1 < 0$$

Therefore the second equilibrium is a stable node. Moreover, it is clear that at $a = 0$ the two equilibria fold into a single equilibrium, with eigenvalues $\lambda_1 = 0$ and $\lambda_2 = -1$.

The phase diagram for this system is easy to construct; it appears without detailed explanation in figures A.8(c) through A.8(e) for different values of the parameter a.

The saddle-node bifurcation is typical of planar systems with one parameter in the same sense that the fold is typical for scalar systems with one parameter. In fact, the saddle node is essentially a fold embedded in a two-dimensional phase space. Note that in this example the direction of movement along the y axis is always the same; all the action takes place along the x axis. The same will be true for an arbitrary saddle-node bifurcation after an appropriate change of coordinates. Moreover, the one-dimensional pattern of change, shown below, is exactly the same as that which takes place in the fold catastrophe when a stable and an unstable equilibrium collide and disappear.

An important lesson of this example is that the nature of the bifurcation depends not on the number of state variables but on the number of parameters. In fact, for one-parameter systems with any number of state variables, bifurcations of equilibria with zero eigenvalues will look exactly like the saddle node, with the change in the direction of motion confined to one dimension.

Example A.10 (The Hopf bifurcation)   The system

$$x' = f(x, y; c) \equiv y + x(c - x^2 - y^2)$$
$$y' = g(x, y; c) \equiv -x + y(c - x^2 - y^2) \tag{A.49}$$

has a unique equilibrium $(0,0)$ for any value of c. Its Jacobian matrix, evaluated at the steady state, is

$$J(0, 0) = \begin{pmatrix} c & 1 \\ -1 & c \end{pmatrix}$$

with complex eigenvalues $\lambda = c \pm i$.

It follows that the equilibrium is a stable spiral point for $c < 0$ and an unstable spiral point for $c > 0$. For $c = 0$ the equilibrium is non-hyperbolic and its stability cannot be determined from the eigenvalues.

If we switch to polar coordinates by the transformation $r^2 = x^2 + y^2$, $\theta = \arctan(y/x)$, it is easy to check that (A.49) is equivalent to

$$r' = r(c - r^2)$$
$$\theta' = -1 \tag{A.50}$$

where r is the norm of the state vector (the distance from the origin) and θ is the angle it forms with the x axis. Inspection of (A.50) reveals the following.

1. If $c > 0$ we have $r' = 0$ whenever $r = \sqrt{c}$. Hence the system has a periodic orbit around the origin with radius $\sqrt{c}$. If $r < \sqrt{c}$ then $r' < 0$ and r decreases over time, whereas if $r > \sqrt{c}$ we have $r' > 0$ and r increases. It follows that the periodic orbit is a stable limit cycle: points starting inside it move away from the unstable equilibrium and toward the closed orbit; points starting outside it also approach the cycle.
2. If $c < 0$ we have $r' = 0$ only at the origin since r^2 cannot be negative. Moreover r' is always negative outside the origin, and so all orbits approach the stable steady state.
3. Finally, if $c = 0$, equation (A.50) reduces to $r' = -r^3$. Since r is positive outside the origin, r' is always negative and the steady state is still stable at the bifurcation point $c = 0$.

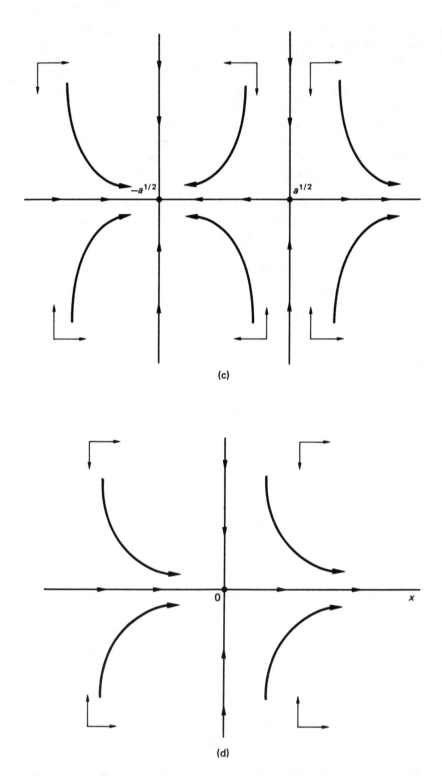

Figure A.8 (a) Nondegenerate critical points; (b) degenerate critical point; (c), (d), (e) saddle-node bifurcations. cont'd overleaf

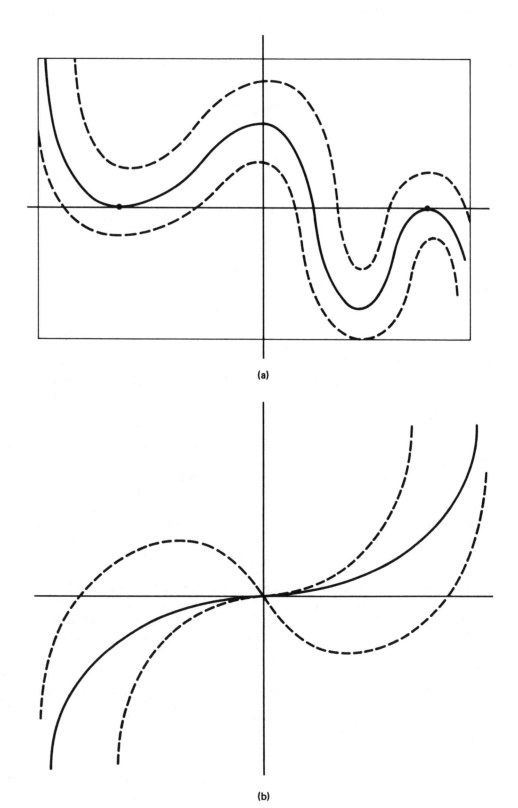

(a)

(b)

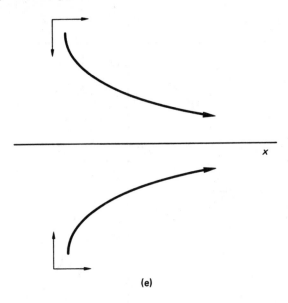

(e)

Figure A.8 cont'd

The corresponding phase diagram is shown in figures A.9(a)–A.9(c): as the parameter c crosses from a negative to a positive value, a stable spiral point loses stability and a stable limit cycle is "born" around it.

If initially $c < 0$ and the state vector is close to the stable equilibrium, then a one-time increase in c takes us across the bifurcation point. In this event, the behavior of the system over time is described in figure A.9(d). As it bifurcates, the system begins to increase amplitude and eventually converges to the stable cycle.

In addition to the phenomenon we have just described, there is another possible bifurcation at an equilibrium with purely imaginary eigenvalues. We could have a stable equilibrium point surrounded by an unstable limit cycle, as in figure A.9(e). As the value of the parameter changes in a certain direction, the cycle shrinks and, at a critical point of the parameter, collapses into the equilibrium which then becomes unstable.

Both these situations are examples of the Hopf bifurcation which occurs at equilibria with imaginary eigenvalues. The following theorem gives a precise statement of the conditions under which such bifurcations exist; the result is due to Poincaré (1880) and Andronov (1933) in the planar case. It was generalized to higher-dimensional spaces by Hopf (1942); see also the related theorem 8.5 for discrete systems.

Theorem A.20 (Hopf–Andronov)　Let the planar system (A.45) have an equilibrium $\bar{x}(\alpha)$ and eigenvalues $\lambda(\alpha) = \mu(\alpha) \pm i\eta(\alpha)$. Suppose that, for some value α^0 of the parameter, the equilibrium $\bar{x}(\alpha^0)$ is non-hyperbolic with purely imaginary eigenvalues $\mu(\alpha^0) = 0$. Moreover, as α crosses α^0 in some direction, $\mu(\alpha)$ changes from negative to positive and $\bar{x}(\alpha)$ changes from sink to source.

(a) Then, for all α on the side of α^0 and close enough to it, there is a periodic orbit surrounding the equilibrum $\bar{x}(\alpha)$ with radius of magnitude $|\alpha - \alpha^0|^{1/2}$

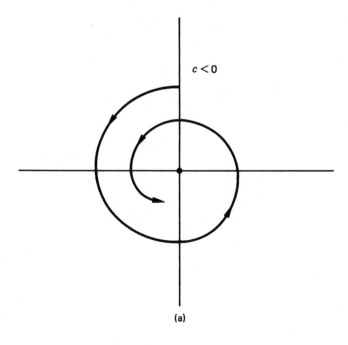

(a)

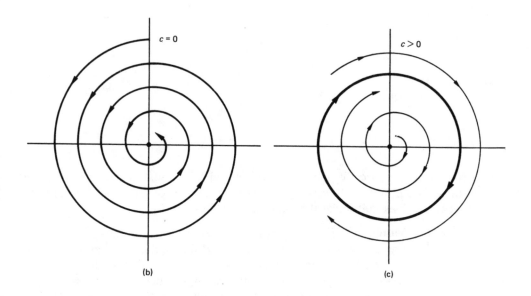

(b)   (c)

Figure A.9 The Hopf bifurcation. cont'd overleaf

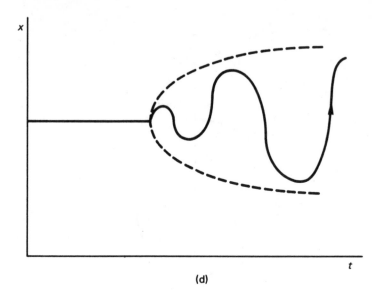

(d)

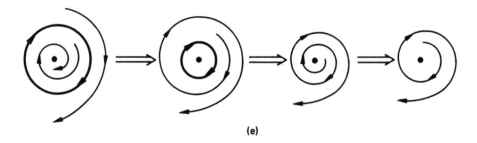

(e)

Figure A.9 cont'd

(b) If $\bar{x}(\alpha^0)$ is asymptotically stable, then the closed orbit is stable and surrounds the unstable equilibrium. Otherwise, the closed orbit is unstable and occurs for parameter values that make the equilibrium a sink.

As we saw in theorem 8.5, if the eigenvalues of (A.45) cross the imaginary axis at some point α^0, some periodic orbit will exist around the equilibrium, either on one side or the other of the bifurcation value of the parameter. The harder part is to determine on *which* side the cycle occurs and whether it is stable. The two issues come together, since a stable cycle must surround an unstable equilibrium and vice versa. The key to answering this question turns out to be whether the equilibrium is stable at the bifurcation point. In most cases this will not be easy to determine since $\bar{x}(\alpha^0)$ is by assumption non-hyperbolic and hence the eigenvalues tell us nothing about its stability.

Notes

1 Critical points are not exactly the same thing as singularities, but the more general definitions coincide for our purposes.
2 The proofs are elementary. Interested readers may consult Hirsch and Smale (1974, p. 252) on theorem A.13, and Wiggins (1990, p. 26) on theorem A.14.
3 This statement does not say that $\bar{x}$ is asymptotically stable. First, even though the orbit through x^0 approaches $\bar{x}$, others may not, for example x^0 may be on the stable branch of a saddle. Second, even if $x(t,x^0) \to \bar{x}$ for all x^0 close enough to the equilibrium, it is possible for the orbit to "go far away" first and then come back to $\bar{x}$. This makes $\bar{x}$ unstable, and hence not asymptotically stable.

Bibliography

Further reading

Arnold (1986) and Baumol and Benhabib (1989) are well-written intuitive overviews of catastrophe theory and chaos. Readers may consult Anton (1981) for a review of linear algebra and the classic text of Hirsch and Smale (1974) for the basic theory of dynamical systems in continuous time. Material that is roughly equivalent to chapters 1, 2, 4, and 6 of this text appears in chapters 3, 4, 8, and 9 of Hirsch and Smale.

Goldberg (1958) and Chiang (1974) provide elementary introductions to difference and differential equations. More advanced treatments of nonlinear dynamics are available in three excellent texts: Devaney (1989) concentrates on relatively low-order discrete systems while Guckenheimer and Holmes (1983) and Wiggins (1990) cover both continuous and discrete systems. The first 100 pages of Devaney are a lucid exposition of nonlinear dynamics for one-dimensional maps up to, and including, local bifurcation theory; chapters 1 and 3 in Guckenheimer and Holmes are thorough compilations of useful results for continuous and discrete dynamical systems. These books also review global bifurcations which produce homoclinic and heteroclinic orbits (cf. Devaney, 1989, chs 1.16, 2.7; Guckenheimer and Holmes, 1983, ch. 6).

Stokey and Lucas (1989) survey the dynamical properties of optimal growth models in a variety of settings: sections 2.1, 5.1, and 5.3 cover fundamentals while 5.4–5.8 deal with various extensions. Fairly thorough explorations of the structure of overlapping generations growth models are Galor and Ryder (1989) for the scalar case and Tirole (1985) for the planar case. Grandmont (1985), Farmer (1986), and Reichlin (1987) are leading illustrations of periodic and near-periodic equilibria in macroeconomics; Boldrin and Woodford (1990) offer a clear survey of chaotic equilibria in multisector optimal growth models. Diamond and Fudenberg (1989), Mortensen (1991), and Pissarides (1990) explore endogenous cycles in economies with search.

References

Andronov, A. 1933: *Mathematical Problems in the Theory of Self Oscillations* (in Russian). GTTI.
——, Leontovich, E., Gordon, I., and Maier, A., 1973: *Qualitative Theory of Second-Order Dynamic Systems*. New York: Halsted Press.
Anton, H. 1981: *Elementary Linear Algebra*. New York: Wiley.

Arnold, V. 1973: *Ordinary Differential Equations*. Cambridge, MA: MIT Press.
—— 1986: *Catastrophe Theory*, 2nd edn. New York: Springer.
Baumol, W. and Benhabib, J. 1989: Chaos: significance, mechanism and economic applications. *Journal of Economic Perspectives*, 3, 77–105.
Benhabib, J. and Day, R. 1982: A characterization of erratic dynamics in the overlapping generations model. *Journal of Economic Dynamics and Control*, 4, 37–55.
—— and Nishimura, K. 1979: The Hopf bifurcation and the existence and stability of closed orbits in multisector models of optimal economic growth. *Journal of Economic Theory*, 21, 421–44.
—— and —— 1985: Competitive equilibrium cycles. *Journal of Economic Theory*, 35, 284–306.
Boldrin, M. and Montrucchio, L. 1986: On the indeterminacy of capital accumulation paths. *Journal of Economic Theory*, 40, 26–39.
—— and Woodford, M. 1990: Equilibrium models displaying endogenous fluctuations and chaos: a survey. *Journal of Monetary Economics*, 25, 189–222.
Brock, W. 1974: Money and growth: the case of long-run perfect foresight. *International Economic Review*, 15, 750–77.
—— and Mirman, L. 1972: Optimal economic growth and uncertainty: the discounted case. *Journal of Economic Theory*, 4, 479–513.
—— and Sayers, C. 1988: Is the business cycle characterized by deterministic chaos? *Journal of Monetary Economics*, 22, 71–90.
Calvo, G. 1978: On the indeterminacy of interest rates and wages with perfect foresight. *Journal of Economic Theory*, 19, 321–37.
Cass, D. 1965: Optimum growth in an aggregative model of capital accumulation. *Review of Economic Studies*, 32, 233–40.
Chiang, A. 1974: *Fundamental Methods of Mathematical Economics*. New York: McGraw-Hill.
Collet, P. and Eckmann, J. 1980: *Iterated Maps on the Interval as Dynamical Systems*. Basel: Birkhauser.
Deneckere, R. and Pelikan, S. 1986: Competitive chaos. *Journal of Economic Theory*, 40, 13–25.
Devaney, R. 1989: *An Introduction to Chaotic Dynamical Systems*, 2nd edn. Reading, MA: Addison Wesley.
Diamond, P. 1965: National debt in a neoclassical growth model. *American Economic Review*, 55, 1026–50.
—— and Fudenberg, D. 1989: Rational expectations business cycles in search equilibrium. *Journal of Political Economy*, 97, 606–19.
Dornbusch, R. 1976: Expectations and exchange rate dynamics. *Journal of Political Economy*, 84, 1161–76.
Duffing, G. 1918: *Erzwungene Schwingungen bei Veränderlicher Eigenfrequenz*. Wiesbaden: F. Vieweg und Sohn
Ezekiel, M. 1938: The cobweb theorem. *Quarterly Journal of Economics*, 52, 255–80.
Farmer, R. 1986: Deficits and cycles. *Journal of Economic Theory*, 40, 77–88.
Ferguson, C. 1969: *The Neoclassical Theory of Production and Distribution*. Cambridge: Cambridge University Press.
Galor, O. and Ryder, H. 1989: On the existence of equilibrium in an overlapping generations model with productive capital. *Journal of Economic Theory*, 49, 360–75.
Goldberg, S., 1958: *Introduction to Difference Equations*. New York: Wiley.
Goodwin, R., 1951: The non-linear accelerator and the persistence of business cycles. *Econometrica*, 19, 1–17.
Grandmont, J.-M. 1985: On endogenous competitive business cycles. *Econometrica*, 53, 995–1045.
Guckenheimer, J. and Holmes, P. 1983: *Nonlinear Oscillations, Dynamical Systems and Bifurcations of Vector Fields*. New York: Springer.

Hicks, J. 1937: Mr. Keynes and the classics: a suggested interpretation. *Econometrica*, 5, 147–59.

—— 1950: *A Contribution to the Theory of the Trade Cycle*. Oxford: Clarendon Press.

Hirsch, M. and Smale, S. 1974: *Differential Equations, Dynamical Systems and Linear Algebra*. New York: Academic Press.

Hopf, E. 1942: Abzweigung einer Periodischen Lösung von einer Stationären Lösung eines Differentialsystems. Translated in J. Marsden and M. McCracken, *The Hopf Bifurcation and its Applications*, New York: Springer, 1976.

Keynes, J. M. 1936: *The General Theory of Employment, Interest and Money*. London: Macmillan.

Koopmans, T. 1965: On the concept of optimal growth. In *The Econometric Approach to Development Planning*, Skokie, IL: Rand McNally.

Kydland, F. and Prescott, E. 1982: Time to build and aggregate fluctuations. *Econometrica*, 50, 1345–71.

Li, T. Y. and Yorke, J., 1975: Period three implies chaos. *American Mathematical Monthly*, 82, 985–92.

Long, J. and Plosser, C. 1983: Real business cycles. *Journal of Political Economy*, 91, 39–69.

Lorenz, E. 1963: Deterministic non-period flow. *Journal of Atmospheric Science*, 20, 130–41.

Lotka, A. 1920: Undamped oscillations derived from the law of mass action. *Journal of the American Chemical Society*, 42, 1595–8.

Malthus, T. 1798: *Population: The First Essay*. Reprinted by The University of Michigan Press, 1959.

Mehra, R. and Prescott, E. 1985: The equity premium: a puzzle. *Journal of Monetary Economics*, 15, 145–61.

Metzler, L. 1941: The nature and stability of inventory cycles. *Review of Economics and Statistics*, 23, 113–29.

Mortensen, D. 1991: Equilibrium unemployment cycles. Mimeo, Northwestern University.

Phelps, E. 1961: The golden rule of accumulation: a fable for growthmen. *American Economic Review*, 51, 638–43.

Pissarides, C. 1990: *Equilibrium Unemployment Theory*. Oxford: Blackwell.

Poincaré, H. 1880: *Mémoire sur les Courbes Définies par les Equations Différentielles I*. Paris: Gauthier-Villars.

Ramsey, F. 1928: A mathematical theory of saving. *Economic Journal*, 38, 543–59.

Reichlin, P. 1986: Equilibrium cycles in an overlapping generations economy with production. *Journal of Economic Theory*, 40, 89–102.

—— 1987: Endogenous fluctuations in a two-sector overlapping generations economy. Mimeo, European University Institute.

Ruelle, D. 1989: *Elements of Differentiable Dynamics and Bifurcation Theory*. New York: Academic Press.

Samuelson, P. 1939: Interactions between multiplier analysis and the principle of acceleration. *Review of Economics and Statistics*, 21, 75–8.

—— 1958: An exact consumption–loan model of interest with or without the social contrivance of money. *Journal of Political Economy*, 66, 467–82.

Sargent, T. and Wallace, N. 1973: The stability of models of money and growth. *Econometrica*, 41, 1043–8.

Sarkovskii, A. 1964: Coexistence of cycles of a continuous map of a line into itself. *Ukrainian Mathematical Journal*, 16, 61–71.

Shannon, C. E., and Weaver, W. 1949: *The Mathematical Theory of Communication*. Urbana, IL: University of Illinois Press.

Sidrauski, M. 1967: Inflation and economic growth. *Journal of Political Economy*, 75, 796–810.

Solow, R. 1956: A contribution to the theory of economic growth. *Quarterly Journal of Economics*, 70, 65–94.

Stokey, N. and Lucas R., 1989: *Recursive Methods in Economic Dynamics*. Cambridge, MA: Harvard University Press.

Swan, T., 1956: Economic growth and capital accumulation. *Economic Record*, 22, 334–61.

Tirole, J. 1985: Asset bubbles and overlapping generations. *Econometrica*, 53, 1499–1528.

Torre, J. 1977: Existence of limit cycles and control in complete Keynesian system by theory of bifurcations. *Econometrica*, 45, 1457–66.

Uzawa, H. 1961: On a two-sector model of economic growth. *Review of Economic Studies*, 29, 40–7.

van der Pol, B. 1927: Forced oscillations in a circuit with nonlinear resistance. *London, Edinburgh and Dublin Philosophical Magazine*, 3, 65–80.

Volterra, V. 1931: *Leçons sur la Théorie Mathématique de la Lutte pour la Vie*. Paris: Gauthier-Villars.

Wiggins, S. 1990: *Introduction to Applied Nonlinear Dynamical Systems and Chaos*. New York: Springer.

Wrigley, E. and Schofield, R. S. 1981: *The Population History of England, 1541–1871: A Reconstruction*. Cambridge, MA: Harvard University Press.

Questions

Unmarked questions are the easiest to do while starred questions relate to advanced material. Other questions are labelled (T) if they are primarily technical and (C) if they require some creative thinking.

I.1 Study the riskless asset pricing model of chapter 3 *under perfect foresight.* To do that you need to replace the adaptive expectations forecasting rule in equation (3.2) with $p_{t+1}^e = p_{t+1}$ for all t.

(a) Does this change in expectation formation affect the stability of the steady state?
(b) Suppose now that at time $t = T$ dividends change suddenly and unexpectedly from $b_t = b > 0$ for all t to $b_t = b^* \neq b$ for all t. Describe how stock prices would adjust over time from the old to the new steady state.

I.2 (a) Draw phase diagrams for the linear system $x_{t+1} = Ax_t$ where

$$A = \begin{pmatrix} 2 & 1 \\ 1 & 1 \end{pmatrix} \qquad A = \begin{pmatrix} 1 & 0 \\ 0 & 2 \end{pmatrix} \qquad A = \begin{pmatrix} 0 & -1 \\ 1 & 0 \end{pmatrix}$$

(b) In each case find whether the steady state is hyperbolic.

I.3 Let c, c_1, c_2 be arbitrary constants and show that

(a) $y_t = c_1 + c_2 2^t$ solves $y_{t+2} - 3y_{t+1} + 2y_t = 0$
(b) $y_t = c_1 + c_2 (-1)^t$ solves $y_{t+2} = y_t$
(c) $y_t = c_1 + c_2 2^t - t$ solves $y_{t+2} - 3y_{t+1} + 2y_t = 1$
(d) $y_t = c/(1 + ct)$ solves $y_{t+1} = y_t/(1 + y_t)$

How could one derive these solutions without prior knowledge of them?

I.4 Metzler (1941) explored business cycles that arise from inventory movements. His model is described by the equation $y_{t+2} - 2cy_{t+1} + cy_t = b$, where y is gross national product (GNP) and the parameters $b > 0$ and $c \in (0, 1)$ represent "exogenous investment" and the "marginal propensity to consume."

(a) Show that the general solution to this equation is

$$y_t = A(\sqrt{c})^t \cos(t\theta + B) + b/(1 - c)$$

where A and B depend on initial conditions and $\theta \in (-\pi, \pi)$ is an angle whose cosine equals $\sqrt{c}$.

(b) What type of oscillation does your solution describe? What is the steady state value of GNP?

I.5 The Weber–Fechner law in experimental psychology relates a stimulus x and a response y in the following way: $\Delta y_t = c\Delta x_t/x_t$. Here $c > 0$ is a constant, $\Delta y_t = y_{t+1} - y_t$, $\Delta x_t = x_{t+1} - x_t$. What sequence of stimuli do we need in order to produce a sequence of responses that form an arithmetic progression with constant difference $h > 0$?

I.6 Samuelson (1939) proposed a model of economic fluctuations described by the equation $y_{t+2} - c(1 + b)y_{t+1} + bcy_t = 1$ for $t = 0, 1, 2,...$. Symbols here have the same interpretation as in question I.4 except that $b > 0$ is now the "acceleration coefficient," that is, the change in aggregate investment per unit change in aggregate consumption. Assume $c(1 + b) < 1$.

(a) Construct a phase diagram for this equation, find the steady states, and examine their asymptotic stability.
(b) Write out the general solution of the equation and find conditions under which equilibrium GNP oscillates.
(c) Are there any periodic equilibria in this model? If so, are they stable?

I.7 A sequence of positive integers is called a Fibonacci sequence if each term after the first two equals the sum of the two preceding terms, that is, if the nth term satisfies $y_{n+2} = y_{n+1} + y_n$. Show that the nth term of a Fibonacci sequence $(0,1,...)$ is given by the expression

$$y_n = \frac{1}{\sqrt{5}}\left[\left(\frac{1 + \sqrt{5}}{2}\right)^n - \left(\frac{1 - \sqrt{5}}{2}\right)^n\right]$$

for any $n \geqslant 2$.

I.8 Starting with Ezekiel (1938), a number of economists have studied output cycles as periodic solutions of first-order difference equations that arise from production lags.

Suppose, for example, that we have two linear schedules $D_t = a_0 - a_1 p_t$ and $S_t = b_0 + b_1 p_{t-1}$ which represent the demand and supply for a given commodity whose production must be decided one period in advance. The parameters (a_0, a_1, b_0, b_1) are all positive.

(a) For what values of these parameters does equilibirum correspond to a cycle of period 2 in the price and production of this good? How many periodic orbits are there?
(b) Draw a few periodic orbits in the appropriate phase space. Can you guess why early investigators called these orbits "cobweb cycles"?

I.9 (T) The theory of information transmission, originated by Shannon and Weaver (1949), explores how messages flow through communication channels. Suppose, in particular, that messages are sequences of variable length made up of two possible signals s_1 and s_2, like the dashes and dots of the Morse code in telegraphy. The signal s_1 requires 1 unit of time while s_2 needs 2 units of time. The number of messages, x_t, of duration t that a communication channel can transmit may be shown to satisfy the equation $x_{t+2} - x_{t+1} - x_t = 0$.

(a) Solve the equation given initial values $x_0 = 0$, $x_1 = 1$.
(b) Interpret the initial values in part (a). Are they a natural choice?
(c) Using logarithms to the base 2, Shannon defined the capacity of a channel as

$$\bar{x} = \lim_{t \to \infty} (\log_2 X_t/t)$$

Prove that $\bar{x}$ is approximately equal to 0.7 in this problem.

I.10 (T) Analyze the difference equation $x_{t+2} = \sin x_t$ for $x_t \in [-\pi, \pi]$. In particular:

(a) Draw its phase diagram on the plane and prove that $x = 0$ is the only steady state.

(b) From the vector field you drew in part (a) conjecture whether the steady state is asymptotically stable. Could you have made this conjecture by linearizing about $x = 0$ instead?

(c) Outline a proof to support your conjecture in (b).

I.11 (T) Consider the non-autonomous initial value problem $x_{t+1} = (t - 1/2 \, x_t^2)/(1 - x_t)$, $x_0 = t$. For what values of t does the solution x_t converge? What is the limit point?

I.12 (T) Study perfect-foresight equilibria in Brock's model of monetary dynamics which satisfies the following difference equation in the sequence m_t of real money balances.

$$u'(\overline{c})m_{t+1} = \frac{\mu}{\beta}[u'(\overline{c}) - v'(m_t)]\, m_t$$

Here consumption per capita is fixed at $\overline{c}$; $\beta > 0$ represents utility discounting; the policy parameter $\mu \geq 0$ equals 1 plus the rate of growth in nominal money balances; $u'(c)$ and $v'(m)$ are (positive, decreasing) marginal utilities for the consumption good and for money balances respectively.

(a) Assume that $v'(m) \to 0$ as $m \to \infty$ and $v'(m) \to \infty$ as $m \to 0$. Show that at most one steady state $\overline{m} > 0$ exists whenever $\mu > \beta$. Is it asymptotically stable?

(b) What assumption on the utility function v will rule out $m = 0$ as a steady state.

(c) Show that explosive equilibria starting at $m_0 > \overline{m} > 0$ and converging to infinity as $t \to \infty$ have the property that $lim(\beta^t m_t) > 0$ as $t \to \infty$, if the rate β of utility discounting is less than one.

I.13 (*) For the discrete scalar system $x_{t+1} = F(x_t, \lambda)$ we define $F(x, \lambda) = -(1 + \lambda)\, x - (3 + \lambda)x^2$.

where $\lambda \in \mathbb{R}$ is a parameter. Are there values of λ for which stable two-period orbits exist? Explain.

I.14 Investigate the equilibria of the descriptive growth model when the aggregate production function is $f(k) = \log(1 + k)$.

(a) Does this function satisfy the standard smoothness, monotonicity, and concavity assumptions required of neoclassical production functions?

(b) For what values of the parameters (δ, n, s) does a positive asymptotically stable steady state exist?

(c) If a positive steady state does not exist, what is the asymptotic behavior of the solutions?

(d) What basic assumption of section 7.2 is violated by the production function $f(k) = \log(1 + k)$?

I.15 Calculate the steady state values of consumption and capital per person in an optimal growth model with the production function $f(k) = \log(1 + k)$, rate of time preference 0.05, and depreciation rate 0.15.

I.16 (C) Dynamical equilibria in the optimal growth model with *variable* labor supply are described by three equations in the state variables (k_t, c_t, l_t) where l_t is labor supply in period t by the representative infinitely lived agent. These equations are

$$c_t = l_t[f(k_t) + (1 - \delta)k_t] - l_{t+1}k_{t+1}$$

$$\beta u'(c_{t+1}) = \frac{u'(c_t)}{1 - \delta + f'(k_{t+1})}$$

$$u'(c_t)w(k_t) = h'(l_t)$$

where $w(k) = f(k) - kf'(k)$ is the wage rate and $h: \mathbb{R}_+ \to \mathbb{R}$ is a smooth, increasing, convex function that measures the disutility of work. Recall that the utility of consumption $u: \mathbb{R}_+ \to \mathbb{R}$ is a smooth, increasing, concave function.

The first two equations in this dynamical system are the same as in the standard optimal growth model with fixed labor supply. The third equates the wage rate to the marginal rate of substitution between leisure and consumption.

(a) Find a way to reduce this system to two dimensions by eliminating one of the state variables.
(b) Suggest how to proceed with the analysis in two dimensions.

I.17 Consider a scalar Diamond model like the one of section 7.4 in which $\delta = 1$ and $z(R,y) = 1/2\,y$ for all R.

(a) Suppose the production function is $f(k) = \sqrt{k}$. Compute the steady states of this system and examine their asymptotic stability with the help of a phase diagram.
(b) Repeat your analysis for $f(k) = \mu k(2 - k)$ assuming that $k \in [0,1]$ and the parameter μ is in the interval $[1/2,1]$.

I.18 Analyze the planar Diamond model that corresponds to the economy of question I.17(a). Specifically, compute all the steady states and examine their stability in a phase diagram. What are the equations defining the constant-capital and constant-debt phaselines?

I.19 (*) (a) Does the scalar difference equation $x_{t+1} = f(x_t)$ have any equilibria of period 2 when $f(x) = 2x - x^3$?
(b) If so, can you compute at least one of them? If not, explain why.

I.20 (*) Study the difference equation $x_{t+1} = f(x_t)$ where $f(x) = 4x - 4x^2$. In particular:

(a) Show that f maps the interval $[0,1]$ into itself.
(b) Find the steady states of this dynamical system. Are they asymptotically stable?
(c) Compute the second iterate f^2 of the map f and prove that a two-cycle exists. Is this cycle asymptotically stable? Explain briefly.

I.21 (*) Find all the periodic points of the following one-dimensional maps:

(a) $f(x) = x^3$, $f(x) = x^2 - 1$, $f(x) = -x/2$, $f(x) = -x^3$ for x real.
(b) $f(x) = 1/2\,(x + x^3)$ for $x \in [-1,1]$.

I.22 (*) Prove that homeomorphisms on $\mathbb{R}$ cannot have periodic orbits with period greater than 2.

I.23 (*) Consider the tent map $f(x) = 2x$ for $x \in [0, 1/2]$, $f(x) = 2(1 - x)$ for $x \in [1/2,1]$.

(a) Draw its nth iterate $f^n(x)$ and show that, for any $n \geqslant 2$, f has exactly 2^n periodic points with period n.
(b) Are the trajectories of the implied dynamical system $x_{t+1} = f(x_t)$ sensitive to initial conditions? If so, provide a numerical example.
(*Hint*: Period n here does not necessarily mean "minimum period n"; it may include periodic points of lower order.)

I.24 (*) For $\mu > 0$ we define the tent map

$$f(x;\mu) = \begin{cases} \mu x & \text{for } x \in [0,1/2] \\ \mu(1 - x) & \text{for } x \in [1/2,1] \end{cases}$$

(a) Prove that f has a unique fixed point and no periodic points if $\mu < 1$.
(b) Show that f has periodic points with period 2^j for any $j = 1, 2, \ldots$ if $\mu > 1$.
(c) Show that $f(x; \sqrt{2})$ has periodic points with period 2^j for any $j = 1, 2, \ldots$.
(d) Suppose now that $\mu > \sqrt{2}$ and prove that f has a periodic point with period 3. What other periodic orbits does this particular map have?

I.25 (*) Consider the dynamical system

$$x'_1 = x_2 + x_1(1 - x_1^2 - x_2^2)$$
$$x'_2 = -x_1 + x_2(1 - x_1^2 + x_2^2)$$

(a) Show that $(x_1, x_2) = (0,0)$ is the only steady state and that it is unstable.
(b) Switch to polar coordinates $x_1 = r \cos\theta$, $x_2 = r \sin\theta$ for $r > 0$. Show that every solution satisfies

$$r(t) = \frac{r_0}{\sqrt{r_0^2 + (1 - r_0^2)\exp(-2t)}}$$

(c) What happens to $r(t)$ as $t \to \infty$? Does this dynamical system have a stable equilibrium?

I.26 (*) Sketch the phase diagram and analyze the stability of the following dynamical systems:

(a) $x' = 2\sin x$
(b) $x' = x - x^3$
(c) $x' = ax(1 - x/b)$ for $a > 0$, $b > 0$
(d) $x'_1/x_1 = a - bx_2$, $x'_2/x_2 = -c + dx_1$ for $a > 0$, $b > 0$, $c > 0$, $d > 0$

(*Note*: (c) is a logistic equation, (d) is a simple "predator–prey" system.)

I.27 (*) The second-order differential equation $x'' + x = 0$ describes trajectories of the harmonic oscillator.

(a) Reduce that equation to a system of two first-order equations and draw the relevant phase diagram.
(b) What are the stability properties of its steady state?
(c) Show that trajectories are concentric circles in the appropriate phase space.

I.28 (*) Repeat question I.27 for the equation $x'' - x = 0$ and show that its orbits are a family of parabolas.

I.29 (*) The second-order equation $x'' + \sin x = 0$ for $x \in [-\pi, \pi]$ describes in mechanics the motion of a pendulum. Draw a phase diagram for it on the plane, and locate all the steady states on that diagram.

I.30 (*) Apply the Bendixson criterion to the planar system $(x' = -x + y^2, y' = x^2 - y^3)$ and show that it has no periodic orbits.

I.31 (*,C) Students of search unemployment describe economies in which unemployed workers and vacant jobs are randomly matched with each other in various bargaining contexts. To be specific, we normalize aggregate labor supply to unity and denote by $e \in [0, 1]$ aggregate employment; $\delta > 0$ is the exogenous value of the separation frequency, that is, the rate at which job–worker matches dissolve per unit time; r is the exogenous interest rate; $u = 1 - e$ is the unemployment rate; $J > 0$ is the discounted value of the worker to an employer; and $\pi(J, e)$, $\eta(J, e)$ are two functions that represent instantaneous profit per worker and the equilibrium hiring frequency per worker.

If returns to production and search are decreasing, the functions π and η have the following properties:

(i) π is decreasing in each argument;
(ii) η is increasing in each argument;

(iii) $\eta(0, e) = 0$ for all e;

(iv) $\lim_{e \to 1} \eta(J, e) = \infty$ for all J; and

(v) $(1 - e)\eta(J, e)$ is decreasing in e for all J.

Mortensen (1991) shows that economies with search unemployment satisfy the following pair of differential equations:

$$\dot{e} = (1 - e)\eta(J, e) - \delta e$$

$$\dot{J} = (r + \delta)J - \pi(J, e)$$

(a) Draw a phase diagram for this system and show that it has *at most* one steady state.

(b) Assuming a unique steady state exists, what are its stability properties?

(c) What is the correlation between employment e and per worker profit J along an equilibrium path?

I.32 Prove theorem 8.1 by contradiction. Suppose an increasing map $f: X \to \mathbb{R}$ *did* admit a periodic orbit which necessarily must have a turning point, that is, contain a subsequence (x_1^*, x_2^*, x_3^*) of points such that $(x_1^* - x_2^*)(x_2^* - x_3^*) < 0$. Show that this is inconsistent with f being a nondecreasing map.

I.33 Investigate the dynamics of stock prices under adaptive expectations when the dividend policy of firms follows equation (3.9) (in section 3.1) for $e > 0$ and $\rho \in (0,1)$. In particular:

(a) Find the steady state value of dividends d^* and define the stationary fundamental stock price p^*.

(b) Under what conditions does p_t converge to p^*?

(c) What factors affect the speed of convergence to p^*?

I.34 Assume dividends increase at a geometric rate g, that is, $d_{t+1}/d_t = g$ for all t. Using the general solution for the non-autonomous equation and the "no bubbles" assumption of perfect foresight, derive an expression for the stock price as a function of the current dividend, the interest rate, and g.

I.35 Assume that the following time path of tax rates

$$\tau = \tau_0 \quad \text{for} \quad 0 < t < T$$
$$\tau = \tau_1 \quad \text{for} \quad t \geq T$$

is known in advance by all agents. Derive the equilibrium path of the system shown in equation (3.24) by using the backward-looking solution to the resulting linear difference equation.

I.36 Work out the equilibrium path for an anticipated temporary tax surcharge, that is,

$$\tau = \tau_0 \quad \text{for} \quad 0 < t < T_1$$
$$\tau = \tau_1 \quad \text{for} \quad T_1 \leq t < T_2$$
$$\tau = \tau_0 \quad \text{for} \quad t \geq T_2$$

I.37 Assume agents are risk neutral and dividends follow a *random walk*, that is,

$$d_{t+1} = d_t + \epsilon_{t+1}$$

where ϵ_t is an independent and identically distributed random variable with mean zero for all t. Rewrite the no-arbitrage condition in expected value terms, and use it to describe how stock prices are set if expectations are rational.

I.38 Suppose that an increase in the stock of money is announced, and believed, T periods before it occurs in the overshooting model of chapter 5. Work out the adjustment of the system toward its new steady state.

Intertemporal Allocation

10 Introduction to Part II

Interactions between the present and the future underlie many of the topics that make up macroeconomics and monetary theory. Anticipations of the future are influential in shaping the present while, simultaneously, current observations are useful predictors of future events. Saving, portfolio selection, and the acquisition of job skills are leading examples of household decisions in which time plays a substantive role, as investment planning is a corresponding example for firms.

To study the problems of intertemporal allocation, we describe next the *overlapping generations* model, proposed by Paul Samuelson in 1958 and developed by Peter Diamond and many others.[1] The overlapping generations model is distinguished from other dynamical general equilibrium structures by its realistic assumptions about demography which prevent living individuals from trading with the unborn or the dead. As we shall see later in chapter 12, an unbounded time horizon along with limited exchange opportunities may interfere with the operation of the invisible hand: competitive equilibria lose their automatic efficiency properties even if markets function perfectly in other respects.

In chapter 11 we examine the simplest sort of competitive equilibrium that arises in a pure-exchange economy when there is one perishable consumption good, private debt is the only store of value, and everyone's endowment or income is publicly known. We study such *inside-money equilibria* to find out two things: (i) what factors affect real interest rates; and (ii) how well a private-ownership economy can distribute resources over time without the help of institutions like social security or government liabilities like currency and interest-bearing national debt. Borrowing and lending become more difficult if information about incomes, especially future ones, is restricted or private; chapter 11 takes a first look at the effect of market imperfections on the exchange of credit. Chapter 12 presents criteria for judging the intertemporal optimality of a stationary competitive equilibrium – in fact, of any feasible stationary allocation – by looking at the implied price system.

Next we study neoclassical one-sector growth theory both from the overlapping generations viewpoint and from the optimal growth viewpoint: physical capital is introduced in chapter 13 as a factor of production whose use results in intertemporal equilibria with genuinely dynamic properties. Among the topics we discuss are the existence, stability, and uniqueness of stationary equilibria, the q theory of investment, and capital accumulation with elastic labor supply. The welfare properties of various growth paths are examined in chapters 13 and 15 with the aid of criteria invented by Malinvaud, Phelps, Koopmans, and Cass.

Neoclassical growth theory is used in chapter 14 to address some elementary issues in economic development. That chapter sums up the predictions that growth theory makes about development, compares them with historical data recorded in the USA and elsewhere, and reviews in detail some of the factors that affect long-term economic growth other than the accumulation of physical capital. The factors we survey include demography, technical progress, human capital, various forms of increasing returns to scale, and the evolution of financial markets.

In chapter 15 we discuss advanced topics in intertemporal allocation, in particular, criteria for judging the welfare properties of nonstationary allocations; the behavior of economies that consist of dynastic families linked by parental altruism; how growth is affected by the taxation of labor and capital income; and two-sector growth theory.

Note

1 Among the original contributors were Diamond (1965), Shell (1971), Lucas (1972), and Gale (1973). Since then the field has expanded enormously; see Woodford (1984) for a fairly complete bibliographical list of early work.

11 Exchange equilibrium

11.1 Inside money

For expositional ease, we start with the simplest pure-exchange version of the overlapping generations model, one that abstracts from uncertainty, production, durable goods, and assets originating outside the household sector.[1] We suppose, accordingly, that calendar time is discrete, extending forward from one to infinity. For any $t = 1, 2, \ldots$ we label "period t" the time interval between t and $t + 1$. Population grows geometrically at a constant rate $n > -1$; at time t a new group of individuals appears which we denote "generation t" or G_t.

Generation $t = 1, 2, \ldots$ consists of $H(1 + n)^t$ households or individuals who belong to H distinct "types," indexed by $h = 1, 2, \ldots, H$; the proportion of all households that belongs to a given type stays fixed over time. All households survive for two periods, "youth" and "old age." Thus, a generation-t household is born at time t, considers itself "young" in period t, "old" in period $t + 1$, and dies at time $t + 2$. In addition to the ordinary generations numbered $1, 2, \ldots$, there is a "special" generation, numbered zero, which consists of H households; this one is born "old" at $t = 1$ and dies at $t = 2$. Thus, total population in period t is $H[(1 + n)^{t-1} + (1 + n)^t]$ households. The pattern is shown in figure 11.1.

There is one physical commodity, a consumption good, which can be neither produced nor stored at any finite cost. Household h is endowed with an amount $e_{1h} \geq 0$ of this good in youth and with $e_{2h} \geq 0$ of it in old age. Endowments are assumed to be stationary: the vector $e_h = (e_{1h}, e_{2h})$ may depend on the household type but not on time. In other words, we permit *intra*generational variations in tastes and endowments but constrain generations $G_1, G_2, \ldots$ to be scaled replicas of each other; the resulting economic equilibria are described by autonomous dynamical systems that unfold free from time-dependent impulses.

To maintain a stationary structure, we suppose that all households of type h have the same utility index $u^h : \mathbb{R}^2_+ \to \mathbb{R}$, which is a function of youthful consumption c^t_{1h}, and old-age consumption c^t_{2h}. The consumption vector $c^t_h = (c^t_{1h}, c^t_{2h})$ of every household is non-negative. For each h, we make the following assumptions.

Assumption 11.1 Neither youthful nor old-age consumption is an inferior good.[2]

Assumption 11.2 The function u^h is increasing in the vector c^t_h, twice continuously differentiable and strictly quasi-concave.[3]

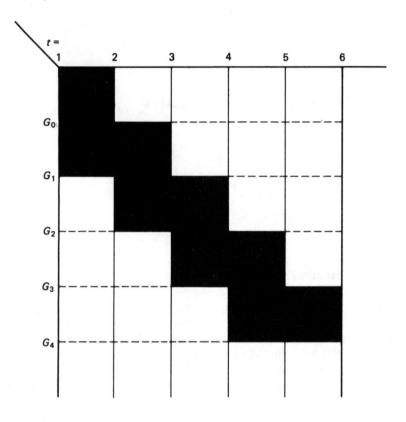

Figure 11.1 Demographic structure.

Without any opportunity to trade endowments, households would be limited to *individual autarky*, that is, to consuming their own endowment each period. Yet an individual who is relatively patient or well endowed in youth may be willing to give up youthful consumption in return for old-age consumption. This could attract another individual, particularly one who is relatively impatient or well endowed in old age. An agreement between two such individuals to exchange consumption in two successive periods is called a *loan*; loans are private securities the stock of which we call *inside money* or *credit*. We make here the extreme assumption that all individual net trades, current and future, are publicly observed: loans are to be thought of as binding contracts, enforced by the legal system at no cost, which constitute the sole store of value in this economy. We examine in section 11.2 below what happens if information about future incomes is not so readily available. Note, meantime, that as long as all endowments and trades are public knowledge, individuals can easily borrow up to the present value of their future income.

Intergenerational lending is not possible here because of the two-period life-cycle. Lending would require either individuals of different generations to coexist for two successive periods or the intermediation of a unit with a longer lifespan, for example a government. We examine the latter possibility in Part III in connection with fiscal policy, as well as in questions II.25 and II.26 of this part in connection with a multiperiod life-cycle. Transactions in the credit market, even though they exclude members of the oldest living generation, result in a net welfare improvement because they replace individual autarky with *generational autarky*.

To study the operation of the loan market, we divide each period $t = 1, 2, \ldots$ into three subperiods – early, middle, and late. In the "early" stage of period t young households of type $h = 1, \ldots, H$ receive endowments $(e_{11}, e_{12}, \ldots, e_{1H})$ while old households receive endowments $(e_{21}, e_{22}, \ldots, e_{2H})$. In the "middle" stage new loan contracts are negotiated, and all debts outstanding from the previous full period are settled. A new loan contract, which can be traded in fractions, exchanges one unit of consumption at t for $R_{t+1} > 0$ units of consumption in period $t + 1$. The gross yield (one plus the interest rate) R_{t+1} is taken as given by each individual. Finally, consumption takes place in the "late" stage of each period.

Households of generation t have excess demands $x_{1h}^t = c_{1h}^t - e_{1h}$ in youth and $x_{2h}^t = c_{2h}^t - e_{2h}$ in old age. These are related by the budget constraint

$$x_{1h}^t + x_{2h}^t / R_{t+1} \leqslant 0 \tag{11.1}$$

Together with the non-negativity of the consumption vector c_h^t, the budget constraint (11.1) defines a budget set, shown as the shaded triangle in figure 11.2. Each point in the budget set corresponds to a consumption vector and therefore to a particular value $u^h(c_h^t)$ of the numerical function that represents the preference ordering of household h. For instance, point E in figure 11.2 corresponds to individual autarky for the household in question, while point M is the maximal (utility-maximizing) element in the budget set defined by the gross interest rate R_{t+1}.

As R_{t+1} changes from 0 to $+\infty$, the budget set changes as well, yielding a unique maximal element for each value of R_{t+1} if indifference curves have no flat parts (see

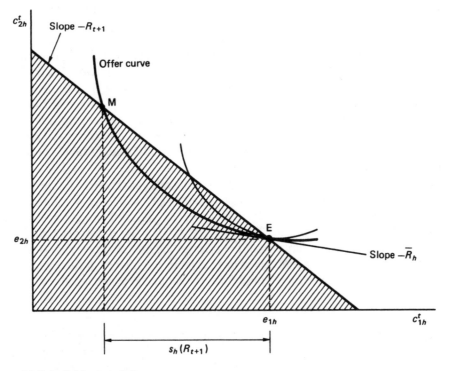

Figure 11.2 Individual saving.

question II.1(a)). The set of individually maximizing choices of a given household at each price ratio is called *the offer curve*; it is drawn with a bold line in figure 11.2. On the offer curve of each household lies its own endowment point, which becomes the utility-maximizing consumption bundle at some non-negative interest factor, $\bar{R}_h$ called the *autarkic interest factor*.

For a given R_{t+1}, each individual consumer's choice may be expressed in terms of the vector of excess demands (x_{1h}^*, x_{2h}^*) that satisfy the budget constraint (11.1) with equality. Because this choice is unique, individual excess demands are single-valued functions of the interest factor. Youthful excess supply, in particular, is called the *saving function*, s_h of household h. Thus we have

$$-x_{1h}^* = s_h(R_{t+1}) \tag{11.2a}$$

Figure 11.2 plainly shows that individual h saves when the market interest factor R exceeds $\bar{R}_h$ and dissaves otherwise. In other words

$$s_h(R) > 0 \text{ if } R > \bar{R}_h \qquad s_h(R) < 0 \text{ if } R < \bar{R}_h \tag{11.2b}$$

The normalized aggregate (or average) saving function in period t is $(1 + n)^t s(R)$, where

$$s(R) = \frac{1}{H} \sum_{h=1}^{H} s_h(R) \tag{11.3}$$

A competitive equilibrium with inside money is now simply defined as one interest factor $\bar{R}$ and H consumption vectors $(c_1, c_2,...,c_H)$ with the following properties.[4]

1. Each generation's excess demand vanishes at $R = \bar{R}$, that is, $s(\bar{R}) = 0$.
2. For $t = 1,2,...$ and $h = 1,2,...,H$ the consumption vectors satisfy

$$c_{1h}^t = e_{1h} - s_h(\bar{R}) \qquad c_{2h}^t = e_{2h} + \bar{R}s_h(\bar{R})$$

The term "inside-money equilibrium" refers to the zero net asset position of the household sector; in this economy every security held by an individual is the liability of another, which implies zero net financial assets and zero aggregate saving. *More generally, net household assets* (that is, the cumulated value of principal and interest saved by all surviving generations) *should equal the sum of net corporate plus net government liabilities, that is, the value of the entire stock of physical capital plus public debt.* We introduce physical capital in chapter 13; Parts III and IV take up economies with non-zero public debt.

The number of inside-asset equilibria is generally odd, as shown in figure 11.3. This is because of the continuity of $s(R)$ and also because $s(R) < 0$ for $R < \min(\bar{R}_1,..., \bar{R}_H)$ and $s(R) > 0$ for $R > \max(\bar{R}_1,..., \bar{R}_H)$. Moreover, if youthful and old-age consumption are *strict gross substitutes* for each household (that is, if the demand for each dated good is an increasing function of the price of the other) at every interest factor, then every individual saving function is increasing in the interest factor, and so is the aggregate function s. Therefore equilibrium is unique. We sum up these existence results in the next theorem.

Theorem 11.1 Given assumption 11.2, a competitive equilibrium with inside assets exists and satisfies $\min(\bar{R}_1,..., \bar{R}_H) \leq R \leq \max(\bar{R}_1,..., \bar{R}_H)$. The equilibrium is unique if youthful and old-age consumption are strict gross substitutes for all h.

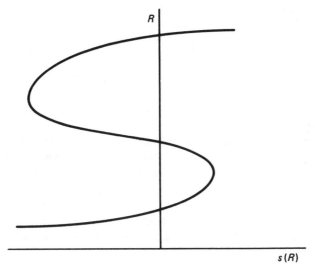

Figure 11.3 Aggregate saving.

Question II.2(a) asks the reader to prove this result. One property of it is the removal of all static gains from trade; members of a given generation face an identical marginal rate of substitution between current and future consumption. Therefore a central planner cannot Pareto-improve the equilibrium referred to in theorem 11.1 (that is, raise the utility of at least one household without simultaneously lowering that of any other) simply by redistributing resources *within* a generation. This property is called *static optimality* or efficiency; allocations that possess it can still be dynamically inefficient, that is, can be improved if the planner transfers resources *between* generations. Chapters 12 and 13 contain several examples of allocations that are statically efficient yet dynamically inefficient.

Another noteworthy feature of the equilibrium described here is that members of the oldest living generation simply carry out existing loan contracts, exchanging no assets with subsequent generations. Asset exchange of that type presupposes inter-generational trust or a social contract that binds generations to honor the commitments of their predecessors. A familiar example of intergenerational trust is an unbacked *outside* asset like currency or national debt, so called because it represents liabilities of governments to the household sector. Trust enables such securities to have positive commodity value even when they are just stamped pieces of paper denominated in an arbitrary unit of account rather than promises to pay given quantities of some consumption good. Social security, on the other hand, exemplifies a more formal social contract between generations enforced by the authority of government to tax.[5]

We conclude this section with an extended parametric example highlighting some of the factors that affect the real rate of interest in an inside-money equilibrium of a pure-exchange economy populated by identical households. We suppose, in particu- lar, that the representative household has an *isoelastic utility function* with a constant rate of time preference, namely

$$u(c_1,c_2) = (1 - \sigma)^{-1}(c_1^{1-\sigma} + \beta c_2^{1-\sigma}) \tag{11.4}$$

where $\beta > 0$ is a discount factor and $\sigma > 0$ is a parameter $(\sigma \neq 1)$ which we may interpret as the reciprocal of the intertemporal elasticity of substitution. This interpretation follows from the marginal rate of substitution

$$\frac{u_1}{u_2} = \frac{1}{\beta}\left(\frac{c_2}{c_1}\right)^\sigma \tag{11.5}$$

which shows that the consumption ratio c_2/c_1 has elasticity $1/\sigma$ with respect to the marginal rate of substitution.

To capture the impact of income growth on the rate of interest we endow households with geometrically expanding endowment vectors. Specifically, we suppose that each generation $t = 1, 2 \ldots$ receives an income stream

$$e^t = (e_1^t, e_2^t) = (e_1(1 + \gamma)^t,\ e_2(1 + \gamma)^{t+1}) \tag{11.6}$$

Inside-money equilibria are uniquely defined by the equality of interest factors to the relevant marginal rate of substitution at the initial endowment point. Equation (11.5), in particular, yields

$$\beta R_t = (e_2^t/e_1^t)^\sigma$$

which reduces to

$$R_t = \frac{1}{\beta}\left[\frac{(1 + \gamma)e_2}{e_1}\right]^\sigma \qquad \forall t \tag{11.7}$$

As we should have expected from theorem 11.1, this equation reiterates that the two main determinants of the real rate of interest in a simple exchange economy are consumer patience and the steepness of the income profile. Interest rates tend to be large when households desire to consume early, either because they are impatient (low β) or because they experience rapid income growth over their life-cycle (high γ).

11.2   Foreign lending and borrowing

In this section we apply the insights of section 11.1 to elementary open economy issues, and specifically to the balance of international payments in a simple world economy made up of two countries, one physical commodity and one asset. Following Buiter (1981), suppose we index by $i = $ A,B the two countries which we call colorfully the "home" country and the "foreign" country. Each country is a pure-exchange economy populated by a representative household that lives for two periods and is endowed with a standard utility function $v^i : \mathbb{R}_+^2 \to \mathbb{R}$ and an endowment vector $e^i \in \mathbb{R}_+^2$.

The two countries have identical populations both growing at the rate n. Each one has an autarkic interest factor $\bar{R}_i = v_1^i(e^i)/v_2^i(e^i)$ which, for $i = $ A,B, describes the domestic interest rate in a competitive closed economy equilibrium.

We suppose

$$\bar{R}_A > \bar{R}_B \tag{11.8}$$

or, roughly, that foreigners are "more patient" than domestic residents.

What would happen if the two national economies were to open themselves to trade in commodities and assets, permitting their residents access to foreign goods and securities free from tariffs, quotas, and other distortionary impediments to trade? What would be the pattern of exports and capital flows? Ignoring costs of transportation, competition among sellers would drive to equality the price of domestic and foreign goods as well as the domestic and foreign interest rates. Theorem 11.1 assures us that an equilibrium, not of necessity a unique one, will exist at some interest factor $\bar{R} \in (\bar{R}_B, \bar{R}_A)$. At $\bar{R}$ the relatively impatient young generation in the home country will dissave, importing goods from abroad and issuing liabilities that require the payment of interest to foreign residents.

In this one-good model there is only one independent market for assets and goods: imports must be financed by foreign debt. We denote by X the *trade account* surplus of the home country and by F the corresponding *current account* surplus. X is an economywide measure of excess supply for goods, which equals the excess of domestic endowment over domestic consumption in a pure-exchange economy and the excess of gross domestic product over domestic demand (consumption plus gross investment plus government purchases) in an economy with production. F is simply X plus *net factor income from abroad*; it equals the difference between national income and domestic demand.

In the pure-exchange home economy we are studying, we have per member of the young generation

$$X = e_1^A + \frac{e_2^A}{1 + n} - \left(c_1^A + \frac{c_2^A}{1 + n} \right) \tag{11.9a}$$

$$F = X + \frac{\bar{R}s^A}{1 + n} \tag{11.9b}$$

Here s^A is the saving per member of the young generation in the home country, reckoned at the world interest factor $\bar{R} = 1 + \bar{r}$; and $(\bar{r} - n)s^A$ is per capita net interest income from abroad after a correction for population growth.

Recalling that $s^A = e_1^A - c_1^A$ and $\bar{R}s^A = c_2^A - e_2^A$, we may rewrite equations (11.9a) and (11.9b) in the form

$$X = \left(\frac{1 + n - \bar{R}}{1 + n} \right) s^A \tag{11.10a}$$

$$F = s^A \tag{11.10b}$$

The less patient home country must by definition dissave at the open economy interest rate $\bar{r}$; hence $s^A < 0$ which means a current account deficit for the home country.

This economy has equilibria with *permanent* imbalances in international payments because budget constraints bind households and generations, not countries that consist of overlapping mortal individuals. The home country's trade account depends very much on whether its foreign debt increases faster or slower than its population. If the world rate of interest is above the rate of population growth, foreign debt service requires $X > 0$, that is, the home country is a net *exporter* of goods. If $\bar{r} < n$, on the other hand, the home country is a net *importer* because the young generation borrows abroad more goods than the older generation is shipping out to retire foreign debt. The balance of trade becomes less favorable the larger is the natural rate of growth n.

11.3   Credit rationing

Anybody who has tried to obtain an unsecured loan knows that borrowing against future income, especially future labor earnings, is often rationed. Lenders seem to consider human capital as poor debt collateral for reasons that are partly legal and partly economic. Among the former is the reluctance of courts of law to seize the earnings of defaulting borrowers, especially if such attachment results in financial hardship. The economic reasons, on the other hand, relate to the ability of individuals to misrepresent their income flow, if income is unearned or exogenous, or to alter their income by varying labor supply, if it is earned or endogenous. These two phenomena, termed *adverse selection* and *moral hazard*,[6] respectively, stem from the fact that individuals are better informed about their own private circumstances than are outsiders. We take in this section a preliminary look at the microeconomic underpinnings of these phenomena, and leave for subsequent chapters the task of figuring out their aggregate implications on consumption and investment.

Potential lenders do try, as a matter of course, to ascertain the circumstances of loan applicants. Credit histories, employment records, and completed loan applications are valuable sources of information about the past and the present, but cannot be considered as the best available predictors of future income or future actions; that predictor is the individual himself or his employer.

How does *private* or *asymmetric* information of the type we have just mentioned change the working of the credit market relative to the public (or symmetric) information case of the previous section? More precisely, how does the activity of borrowing and lending respond to the cost of collecting accurate information about potential borrowers? To capture this effect, one has to specify what individual characteristics of potential borrowers can be learned by lenders and at what cost. Borrowers may attempt to convey information about themselves by holding easily observable stocks of durables (for example housing) or by revealing credible evidence of their past income (for example tax records). Lenders, too, will collect such information either directly from credit histories, completed loan applications, and the like, or indirectly by observing current decisions that are correlated with estimated future income (for example asset holdings, current consumption patterns, etc.).[7]

A simple way to figure out the general equilibrium consequences of asymmetric information is to divide each household's old-age endowment in two parts: one part is publicly observed (at no cost) by all potential lenders; another part cannot be observed at finite cost by anyone other than the receiving household itself. Accordingly, we supplement each household's lifetime endowment vector (e_{1h}, e_{2h}) by a non-negative number $\omega_h \leq e_{2h}$ which describes how much of its old-age income is public information. Dividends, interest, and rent are good examples of income that is relatively easy to observe; labor income, on the other hand, is less easily ascertained.

If individual consumption and tastes are not publicly known, lenders cannot extract reliable estimates of old-age income from observations of consumption which might convey information about that income. Credit histories and threats of cutting off future credit are not much use either, for the households in our economy only borrow once. There is nothing, in other words, to induce individual h to repay any loan in excess of ω_h because nobody can prove in a court of law that individual h can afford to. Unless the act of bankruptcy has significant deadweight losses (that is, costs of counting assets and liabilities, transferring ownership, etc.), a declaration of bankruptcy nets debtors a handsome bonus in the form of increased consumption, and inflicts a capital loss on creditors.

To avoid such losses, creditors will lend debtors sums that the latter can afford to repay and which also are within the debtors' publicly known future income. In other words, households face a lifetime budget constraint like (11.1) and, in addition, a *borrowing constraint* of the form

$$x_{1h}^t \leqslant \omega_h / R_{t+1} \tag{11.11}$$

Borrowing constraints have straightforward economic consequences in our simple pure-exchange economy (see also chapter 15). First, some borrowers may suffer from credit rationing, especially if the unobserved portion of their old-age endowment is large. Second, less borrowing and lending occurs at a constrained private-information equilibrium than in an unconstrained public-information one. Third, borrowing constraints reduce the demand for loanable funds at every interest rate; under some technical assumptions, this means that credit rationing will *lower* the equilibrium rate of interest. In more complicated economies, credit rationing will generally tend to discourage consumption and leisure (that is, encourage work) and induce rationed individuals to shift these activities towards periods in which they are not rationed.

To demonstrate some of the elementary consequences of rationing, we denote by $z_h(R) = \max[s_h(R), -\omega_h/R]$ the savings function of household h subject to a borrowing constraint, and display the relevant truncated budget set in figure 11.4. Let also $z(R) = (1/H)\Sigma_{h=1}^{H} z_h(R)$ be the corresponding normalized aggregate savings function. *A competitive equilibrium with credit rationing* consists of an interest factor $\bar{R}_c$ and H consumption vectors $(c_1, c_2, ..., c_H)$ with the following properties.

1. Each generation's excess demand vanishes at $\bar{R}_c$, that is, $z(\bar{R}_c) = 0$.
2. For $t = 1, 2, ...$ and $h = 1, 2, ..., H$, the consumption vectors satisfy

$$c_{1h} = e_{1h} - z_h(\bar{R}_c) \qquad c_{2h} = e_{2h} + \bar{R}_c z_h(\bar{R}_c)$$

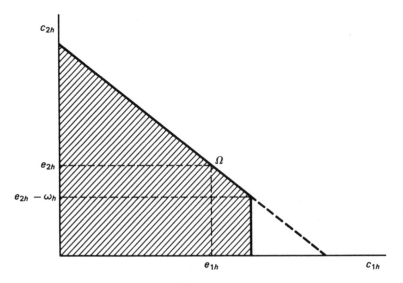

Figure 11.4 Individual borrowing constraints.

By analogy with theorem 11.1 we can demonstrate the existence of an odd number of constrained equilibria with interest factors lying between the lowest and highest possible autarkic factors (see figure 11.5). Credit is rationed for at least one household if old-age endowment is sufficiently unobservable, that is, if at some unconstrained equilibrium interest factor $\bar{R}$ the inequality

$$\omega_h + \bar{R}s_h(\bar{R}) < 0 \qquad\qquad (11.12a)$$

holds for some h. On the other hand, no household is rationed if old-age incomes are sufficiently observable, that is, if

$$\omega_h + \bar{R}s_h(\bar{R}) \geq 0 \qquad \text{for all } h \qquad\qquad (11.12b)$$

Credit rationing reduces the demand for loanable funds and therefore shifts the aggregate savings function: *it increases net saving at each interest factor*. From figure 11.5 we see that for each constrained-equilibrium interest factor $\bar{R}_c$ there exists an unconstrained competitive equilibrium with interest factor $\bar{R} > \bar{R}_c$. If equilibrium is unique, credit rationing lowers both the amount of borrowing and the rate of interest in equilibrium. We summarize in the next theorem.

Theorem 11.2 Suppose assumption 11.2 and inequality (11.12a) both hold. Then a competitive equilibrium exists in which at least one household faces credit rationing; less lending occurs, and at a lower interest rate, than in the unconstrained case. The equilibrium is unique if youthful and old-age consumption are gross substitutes for every household.

The consumption plans of credit-constrained households depend not only on the interest rate and the present value of their endowment stream, but also on the *timing* of endowments. This is brought out in example 11.1 below as well as in figure 11.6 which demonstrates how borrowing constraints change individual consumption plans. In figure 11.6 we depict two households that are identical in everything (including lifetime wealth and indifference maps) except the timing of their endowment: initial

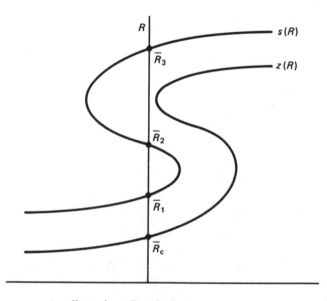

Figure 11.5 The aggregate effect of credit rationing.

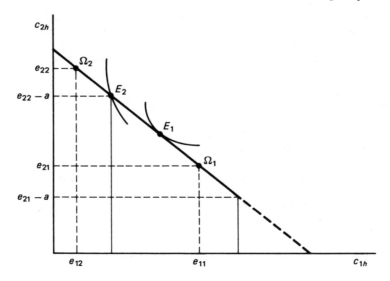

Figure 11.6 The timing of income.

endowment vectors are Ω_1 and Ω_2. Household 1 is sufficiently well endowed in youth to avoid credit rationing in equilibrium and reach an individual optimum at E_1; household 2, however, can only reach point E_2 because of credit rationing.

The same figure brings out in sharp relief the welfare consequences of private information. Without verifiable public information, unconstrained static efficiency is no longer the automatic property of competitive equilibria; equilibrium allocations can always be improved by a fully informed central planner and, on occasion, by an incompletely informed planner as well. The reason, figure 11.6 says, is that private information makes it quite possible to find two members of the same generation who face different marginal rates of substitution in equilibrium.

Example 11.1 Suppose the economy consists of three households with endowment vectors $e_1 = (4, 2)$, $e_2 = (0, 2a)$, $e_3 = (0, 2b)$, where $0 < a < b < 1$, and a common utility function of the form $u^h = c_{1h} c_{2h}$. With no borrowing constraints, household 1 saves $2 - 1/R$; household 2 saves $-a/R$; household 3 saves $-b/R$. The equilibrium interest factor is $\bar{R} = (1 + a + b)/2$, and the amount of funds borrowed and lent is $\bar{B} = 2(a + b)/(1 + a + b)$.

Suppose now that only a units of future income are publicly observed for each household. Individuals now must obey a borrowing constraint of the form $c_{1h} - e_{1h} \le a/R$, which will be binding on $h = 3$. Constrained saving plans are then $e_{1h} - c_{1h} = 2 - 1/R$ for $h = 1$ and $-a/R$ for both $h = 2$ and $h = 3$. At equilibrium we have an interest factor $R_c = (1 + 2a)/2 < \bar{R}$, and borrowing equals $\bar{B}_c = 4a/(1 + 2a) < \bar{B}$, that is, it falls short of the corresponding public-information figure.

Notes

1. Many of these assumptions are inessential. For instance, storage is treated in question II.4; production in chapters 13 and 14; "outside" assets are covered in Parts III (interest-bearing national debt) and IV (currency).

2. A commodity is *inferior* if the demand for it is a decreasing function of income at constant prices. Note also that a real-valued function $f: \mathbb{R}^n \to \mathbb{R}$ is *strictly quasi-concave* if, for every pair (x^1, x^2) of distinct points in $\mathbb{R}^n$ and any $\lambda \in (0,1)$ we have $f[\lambda x^1 + (1 - \lambda)x^2] > \min[f(x^1), f(x^2)]$. The indifference curves that correspond to a strictly quasi-concave utility function are strictly convex, containing no flat parts.

3. See note 2.

4. This definition of equilibrium includes all household *types* and omits G_0; each member of G_0 clearly consumes his or her own endowment.

5. Question II.3 takes a first look at the effect of social security on interest rates. Additional material on social security appears in Part III.

6. For good introductory treatments of adverse selection and moral hazard, see Arrow (1963), Akerlof (1970), Rothschild and Stiglitz (1976), Grossman and Hart (1983), and Guesnerie (1990).

7. Inferences of this type underlie partial equilibrium treatments of loan contracts by Stiglitz and Weiss (1981) and Gale and Hellwig (1985).

12 Intertemporal optimality

Under some technical conditions that need not concern us here, competitive equilibrium in a static economy possesses socially desirable properties which we identify with the popular phrase "invisible hand" and with the scientific term "Pareto optimality."[1] Do these socially desirable properties of competitive equilibrium extend to dynamic infinite-horizon economies in which the living are physically unable to trade with the unborn or the dead? And, if not, how can we tell whether a potential equilibrium is optimal?

From the immediately preceding chapter we know that private information will typically result in *laissez-faire* equilibria with static inefficiencies which an omniscient central planner can cure by redistributing resources within a cohort. What concerns us in this chapter is how to evaluate the welfare properties of competitive equilibria and, more generally, of any economically feasible allocation of resources when information about the characteristics of individuals' households is easy to verify.

A society willing to reallocate resources between generations may on occasion find ways to improve the working of undisturbed competitive markets. The following straightforward example of social security shows that the invisible hand does not work automatically in economies that extend to infinity. Specifically, we consider a competitive equilibrium with private credit, of the type discussed in chapter 11, for an economy consisting of identical households with endowment vector $e = (e_1, e_2)$. All these households are assumed to have an individually *autarkic interest rate* $\bar{r}$ which is lower than the rate n of population growth.

The *laissez-faire* equilibrium, which occurs naturally at the interest rate $\bar{r}$, turns out to be dynamically inefficient. To demonstrate this, we consider how that equilibrium responds to a social security system that, from some finite time T onward, begins to transfer resources from the young to the old.[2] Let $\tau \in [0, e_1]$ be a lump-sum tax levied on each young household at $t = T, T + 1,...$ and $(1 + n)\tau$ be the subsidy paid to each aging household; then the budget of the social security system is in perpetual balance.

Interventionist equilibria with social security are again autarkic: generations $T + 1$, $T + 2,...$ simply consume their *after-tax* endowment vector $\hat{e} = (e_1 - \tau, e_2 + (1 + n)\tau)$; one plus the equilibrium rate of interest equals the marginal rate of substitution at the after-tax endowment point. Thus $1 + \hat{r} = u_1(\hat{e})/u_2(\hat{e})$ where u_1 and u_2 are partial derivatives of the utility function u; we assume u to be strictly concave in this example.

No generation before T is affected by the social security system; T itself is clearly favored, receiving a subsidy but making no contribution. Generations subsequent to T participate fully in social security, obtaining from it utility which we denote by $v(\tau)$. The function $v(\tau) = u[e_1 - \tau, e_2 + (1 + n)\tau]$ is increasing in the social security parameter for small τ. To see this, we denote by $u_1(e), u_2(e)$ the partial derivatives of the utility function at the initial endowment, and evaluate the derivative $v'(\tau)$ at $\tau = 0$. This yields

$$
\begin{aligned}
v'(0) &= -u_1(e) + (1 + n)u_2(e) \\
&= u_2(e)[-u_1(e)/u_2(e) + 1 + n] \\
&= u_2(e)[-(1 + \bar{r}) + 1 + n] \\
&= u_2(e)(n - \bar{r}) \\
&> 0 \text{ if } \bar{r} < n
\end{aligned}
$$

As long as the equilibrium rate of interest falls short of the growth rate n, *the material wealth* (more precisely, the present value of total resources) *of this economy is infinite.* Then it is possible to improve on the competitive outcome here by expanding the social security system or otherwise transferring income from the earlier to the later stage of the lifecycle.

To discuss more generally how and when the invisible hand operates in a dynamic setting, we return to the pure-exchange economy with heterogeneous households which we studied in chapter 11. What commodity allocations are technically feasible in that economy? How do we judge the social desirability of each one?

An allocation of commodities over households is technically *feasible* if it can be achieved by a hypothetical fully informed central planner who can tax away and redistribute endowments at zero cost. A competitive equilibrium is an example of a feasible allocation. Intertemporal optimality extends to dynamic settings the concept of Pareto optimality which is familiar in static microeconomics. We label a feasible allocation *intertemporally optimal or efficient* (equivalently, dynamically optimal or efficient) if the planner cannot find another that makes at least one member of some generation better off without reducing the welfare of any member of any generation.

In mathematical language, an allocation is an infinite sequence of $2 \times H$ matrices $(C^t)_{t=0}^{\infty}$ whose columns describe how much consumption a particular household of a particular generation t is permitted in youth and old age. Elements of the sequence (C^t) are of the form

$$
C^0 = \begin{pmatrix} 0 & 0 & \cdots & 0 \\ c_{21}^0 & c_{22}^0 & \cdots & c_{2H}^0 \end{pmatrix} \tag{12.1}
$$

$$
C^t = \begin{pmatrix} c_{11}^t & c_{12}^t & \cdots & c_{1H}^t \\ c_{21}^t & c_{22}^t & \cdots & c_{2H}^t \end{pmatrix} \qquad t = 1, 2, \ldots
$$

The allocation (C^t) is called *feasible* if the component vectors c_h^t are non-negative for all h and t and the planner never commits more resources than are available, that is, if, for all t, the following inequality holds:

$$
\sum_{h=1}^{H} [(1 + n)(c_{1h}^t - e_{1h}) + c_{2h}^{t-1} - e_{2h}] \leq 0 \tag{12.2}
$$

We call a feasible allocation (C^t) intertemporally optimal (or dynamically efficient) if there is no other feasible allocation $(\tilde{C}^t)$ with the property that $u^h(\tilde{c}_h^t) \geq u^h(c_h^t)$ for all t and h and $u^h(\tilde{c}_h^t) > u^h(c_h^t)$ for at least one combination of t and h.

Formalism aside, how does one recognize whether or not a feasible allocation – in particular, a competitive equilibrium – is optimal? There are two important results to discuss in this connection. One, due to Balasko and Shell (1980), says that the invisible hand works well under public information if the time horizon is finite; all competitive inefficiencies of inside-money equilibria must then have something to do with the infinite horizon. The other proposition, conceived by Malinvaud (1953), Phelps (1965), and Koopmans (1965), and expressed more generally by Cass (1972), shows an allocation to be intertemporally inefficient if, and only if, it is associated with a summable sequence of appropriately defined relative prices (equivalently, of multiperiod interest factors or marginal rates of substitution). We discuss here only a special case of that general proposition, leaving a fuller treatment of it for chapters 13 and 15.

We begin with a heuristic discussion of the finite case; question II.7 is a useful supplement for readers who seek more detail. Let us start the economy at time $t = 1$ and cut it off at $t = T + 1$, that is, at the end of period $T \geqslant 2$. Generation T dies "young" and no subsequent generations appear. This changes only slightly the nature of the competitive inside-money equilibrium from the infinite case: as before, generation G_0 is individually autarkic and G_1, G_2,..., G_{T-1} are generationally autarkic. The difference from the infinite-horizon case is the last generation, G_T, which is individually autarkic because, like G_0, it consists entirely of individuals with a single-period horizon.

Any intertemporally optimal allocation has two rather obvious properties (see also question II.7): no resources are left unconsumed in any period, and all individuals of a *given* generation are faced with the same marginal rate of substitution between youthful and old-age consumption. Both of these are also properties of the competitive allocation since, at an individual optimum, the competitive interest factor equals the marginal rate of substitution of each household.

Therefore, whatever improvement a central planner may achieve over a competitive allocation must come from changing the common marginal rate of substitution of some generation, that is, from the redistribution of resources *between* successive generations. However, if a particular generation G_t is to be favored by the planner at the expense of another, say G_{t+1}, so that the former becomes better off than under some competitive equilibrium, then G_{t+1} will become worse off unless it is compensated at the expense of G_{t+2}.

Following this chain, we end up with G_T being worse off under the planned allocation than in competitive equilibrium. If the chain were to unfold backward instead of forward, G_0 would become worse off. We summarize in the next theorem.

Theorem 12.1 Every competitive equilibrium with inside money is intertemporally optimal in the finite economy case.

The social welfare properties of competitive equilibrium are not harmed in this case by *limited market participation*, that is, by the mere inability of the living to exchange loan contracts with the dead or the unborn. A finite-horizon economy, we should note, has finite resources for any well-defined system of positive prices.

Things become quite different if the economy does not have *a known finite end*. A completely specified allocation requires the planner to distribute over time a potentially infinite amount of resources: even though goods are perishable, the planner may "borrow" from the future by transferring resources to a particular generation from the next one, compensating the latter at the expense of the one after it, and so on *ad infinitum*. This is technically impossible in a finite economy but is achievable by a social security system or by other means when the horizon is infinite and total resources grow faster than the (actual or shadow) rate of interest. Any infinite-horizon economy in which resources grow faster than the rate of interest possesses infinite wealth, that is, it cannot attach a finite value to its total resources even if all prices are well defined.

As an illustrative special case, we analyze first *quasi-stationary allocations* of the form

$$C = \begin{pmatrix} c_{21}^0 & c_{22}^0 & \cdots & c_{2H}^0 \\ c_{11} & c_{12} & \cdots & c_{1H} \\ c_{21} & c_{22} & \cdots & c_{2H} \end{pmatrix}$$

which treat households of the same type in an identical manner, *irrespective* of the generation to which they belong. The only exception is the "special" generation 0 which receives special treatment in the matrix C: it occupies the top row.[3] A feasible quasi-stationary allocation C is *equal-treatment optimal* (ET-O) if (i) it treats identical individuals the same way and (ii) there is no other feasible quasi-stationary allocation $\tilde{C}$ that makes at least one household better off without making any household worse off.

It is quite easy to see (by doing question II.8 for example) that an ET-O allocation is intertemporally optimal, and a quasi-stationary allocation that is not ET-O must be dynamically inefficient. Readers who do question II.8 as well will convince themselves as easily that, for a suitable choice of the non-negative weights $(\beta_1, \beta_2,..., \beta_H)$ and $(\lambda_1, \lambda_2,..., \lambda_H)$, any ET-O allocation maximizes the social welfare function

$$W = \sum_{h=1}^{H} [\beta_h c_{2h}^0 + \lambda_h u^h(c_{1h}, c_{2h})] \tag{12.3a}$$

subject to the resource constraints

$$\sum_{h=1}^{H} [(1 + n)(c_{1h} - e_{1h}) + (c_{2h} - e_{2h})] \leq 0 \tag{12.3b}$$

$$\sum_{h=1}^{H} [(1 + n)(c_{1h} - e_{1h}) + (c_{2h}^0 - e_{2h})] \leq 0 \tag{12.3c}$$

This social welfare function assigns a combined weight λ_H to all type-h households of generations "one" through "infinity"; weight β_h goes to household h of generation 0.

In formal language, then, optimal quasi-stationary allocations are saddlepoints of the Lagrangean function

$$\mathcal{L} = W - \mu \sum_{h=1}^{H} [(1 + n)(c_{1h} - e_{1h}) + c_{2h} - e_{2h}] - \theta \sum_{h=1}^{H} [(1 + n)(c_{1h} - e_{1h}) +$$

$$c_{2h}^0 - e_{2h}]$$

(where $\mu \geq 0$ and $\theta \geq 0$ are multipliers) and must therefore satisfy the Kuhn–Tucker theorem.[4] Suppose there is at least one household of type h with weight $\lambda_h > 0$ in the social welfare function for whom marginal utilities satisfy the boundary conditions

$$u_1^h(c_1, c_2) \to \infty \text{ as } c_1 \to 0 \qquad u_2^h(c_1, c_2) \to \infty \text{ as } c_2 \to 0 \tag{12.4}$$

Then the first-order conditions of the Kuhn–Tucker theorem hold with equality for that household, that is,

$$\lambda_h u_1^h(c_{1h}, c_{2h}) - (1 + n)(\mu + \theta) = 0 \qquad (12.5a)$$

$$\lambda_h u_2^h(c_{1h}, c_{2h}) - \mu = 0 \qquad (12.5b)$$

These two imply that $\mu > 0$ and that all households face a common marginal rate of substitution equal to $(1 + n)(\mu + \theta)/\mu$. With that marginal rate of substitution we can associate an implicit interest rate r such that $1 + r = u_1^h/u_2^h$. Then, on eliminating the multiplier λ_h from the first-order conditions, we obtain

$$1 + r = (1 + n)(\mu + \theta)/\mu \geq 1 + n \qquad (12.5c)$$

because $\theta > 0$. Optimality here reduces to a relationship between the (implied) interest rate r and the growth rate n. In particular, we have the following.

Theorem 12.2 A quasi-stationary allocation is intertemporally optimal if it is statistically optimal (that is, it equalizes the appropriate marginal rates of substitution) *and* the associated interest rate is equal to or greater than the growth rate; it is suboptimal if it is *either* statically suboptimal *or* the associated interest rate is less than the growth rate.

The resources disposed by the central planner in period t are $\omega_t = \Sigma_{h=1}^H[(1 + n)^t e_{1h} + (1 + n)^{t-1} e_{2h}]$. Note that the intertemporal resource vector for this economy $(\omega_t)_{t=1}^\infty$ has a finite present value $\Sigma_{t=0}^\infty[\omega_t/(1 + r)^t]$ if, and only if, the interest rate exceeds the growth rate.

An extension of theorem 12.2 to economies with production appears in chapter 13. The underlying intuition is not hard to understand: any quasi-stationary allocation that results in both a well-defined interest rate and a well-defined present value of the aggregate endowment stream is intertemporally optimal. If the interest rate is not well defined, not all relevant marginal rates of substitution are equalized, and intertemporal optimality is ruled out by the underlying static inefficiency. Lastly, if the interest rate is well defined but the present value of resources is not (because it is infinite), then the quasi-stationary allocation in question may be suboptimal; as we shall see in chapter 15, however, dynamical allocations with a well-defined sequence of interest rates may be (but are not necessarily) intertemporally optimal *even if* they are associated with infinitely valued resources.

For a geometric explanation of theorem 12.2, we consider allocations that equalize the marginal rate of substitution between youthful and old-age consumption for all households. Let point B in figure 12.1 be what household h gets from such an allocation, and draw through B a straight line with slope $-(1 + n)$. The resource constraints (12.3b) and (12.3c) show that $-(1 + n)$ represents the "terms of trade" that a central planner faces between youthful and old-age consumption.

At point B, of course, $r < n$ as the relevant indifference curve is flatter than the resource constraint. The central planner can transfer consumption from youth to old age and, in the process, increase the utility of every generation. Therefore, the allocation associated with B is dynamically inefficient. A similar argument *cannot* be made about point A where $r > n$. A central planner who transfers resources from old age to youth, starting from the allocation A, will raise the utility of all generations except one: generation 0 will suffer in this process. Hence the initial allocation at A is dynamically efficient unless generation 0 carries no weight in the social welfare function.

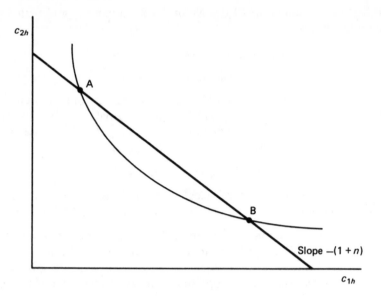

Figure 12.1 Intertemporal optimality.

Theorem 12.2 is of immediate use in establishing the welfare properties of competitive inside-money equilibria, like those we studied in chapter 11. All those equilibria were generationally autarkic because different age groups did not trade with each other, and stationary because the demographic structure was constant. We begin by ranking the individually autarkic interest factors: without loss of generality, we assume that $\bar{R}_h \leq \bar{R}_{h+1}$ for $h = 1, ..., H - 1$.

Following Gale (1973), we classify pure-exchange economies like that of chapter 11 into two possible types:

1. the *Samuelson type* if aggregate saving is positive when the interest rate equals n;
2. the *classical* type if aggregate saving is negative when the interest rate equals n.

This classification scheme calls "Samuelson" an economy whose household sector is a net saver when the interest rate equals the natural growth rate and "classical" an economy whose household sector dissaves under the same conditions. In broader terms, *an economy is of the Samuelson type if the household sector is a net creditor when the rate of interest is at its natural value.* Debtors in this definition may be the government or, possibly, foreigners.

Question II.12 asks readers to use theorem 11.2 on each type of economy and prove the following.

Corollary 12.1 If the vector of autarkic interest factors $(\bar{R}_1,...,\bar{R}_H)$ does not consist of identical elements, then there exists at least one suboptimal inside-money equilibrium in the Samuelson case, and at least one optimal inside-money equilibrium in the classical case.

The intuition for this result is shown in figure 12.2 which depicts multiple inside-money equilibria for a Samuelson and a classical economy. A special case of corollary 12.1 is a result of Gale (1973) that applies to economies consisting of identical households. For such economies, of course, equilibrium is uniquely defined

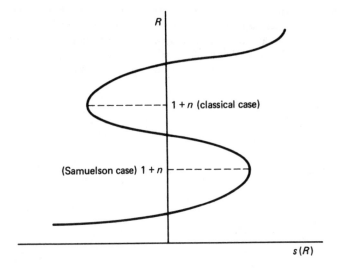

Figure 12.2 Samuelson economies and classical economies.

by the marginal rate of substitution of the representative household at its initial endowment point.

Corollary 12.2 If all households are identical, then the inside-money competitive equilibrium is individually autarkic and unique, with an interest factor equal to the marginal rate of substitution at the initial endowment point (e_1, e_2). This equilibrium is intertemporally optimal in the classical case, suboptimal in the Samuelson case.

The range of theorem 12.2 is limited to stationary allocations: it does not help us evaluate nonstationary allocations in economies with stable structures and does not apply at all to time-varying economic structures. For example, how does one evaluate a feasible nonstationary allocation when the associated interest rate is above the population growth rate in odd periods and below the growth rate in even periods? And what meaning can we give to equal-treatment allocations when generations differ fundamentally from one another because, say, endowments or utility functions change over time?

The welfare properties of nonstationary allocations, it turns out, cannot be expressed by a single interest rate; one has to look instead at the *entire* infinite sequence $(R_t)_{t=1}^{\infty}$. We take up this issue once more in chapters 13 and 15.

Notes

1. Classic general statements of the connection between competitive equilibria and Pareto optima are Arrow (1951) and Debreu (1959) for static economies; Hart (1975) on the finite-horizon case; and Malinvaud (1953), Koopmans (1957), and Radner (1967) for infinite-horizon economies.
2. Note that transfers in the opposite direction cannot possibly improve everyone's lot for they would leave worse off than before the first generation ever to experience the social security system; that generation would contribute to the system but would draw nothing from it.

3. It is for this reason that the allocation is called "quasi" rather than "fully" stationary.

4. Note that the first-order conditions are necessary and sufficient here: the constraint set is convex and non-empty, and the objective function is continuously differentiable and strictly quasi-concave. See Chiang (1974, ch. 20) for an elementary discussion of the Kuhn–Tucker theorem, and Luenberger (1969) for material on optimization in infinite-dimensional spaces.

13 Neoclassical growth theory

13.1 The overlapping generations model

This chapter is concerned with production economies and, in particular, ones in which consumption goods can be produced from capital and labor under constant returns to scale. We study capital accumulation with three aims in mind: (i) to allow per capita income to grow in our model economies, much as it does in real-world economies; (ii) to study how durable goods interact with credit markets; and (iii) to begin to learn something about the factors that affect economic development.

As a vehicle for this effort we use the neoclassical growth model due to Diamond (1965), appropriately modified to conform with the overlapping generations model of chapter 11; we called this the "scalar Diamond model" in chapter 7. As before, we have one physical commodity, households indexed by $h = 1, \ldots, H$, with two-period lives, and population growing geometrically at the rate n. Since H is an integer and n is any number above -1, the number of households in each type is not strictly integral.

The timing of events remains the same as previously. Unlike the previous chapter, however, the consumption good must be produced from capital and labor. All individuals are price takers. Members of the same cohort can in principle exchange loans to smooth consumption or to invest in physical capital; in what follows all young people are savers because no income is earned in old age.

Households in this section are best thought of as workers in youth and producers (or owners of a firm) in old age. They are endowed with no physical commodities (except for members of generation 0, each of whom comes to the world endowed with an amount $k_1 > 0$ of capital) but possess instead 1 unit of labor in youth all of which they supply inelastically to producers. Demand for labor comes from old individuals (or firms), each of whom is endowed with the stationary constant-returns-to-scale technology[1] $Y = F(K,L)$ that converts capital (K) and labor services (L) into the consumption good. The function F is increasing in each argument and concave, and (because of constant returns) satisfies

$$F(K,L) = LF(K/L,1) \equiv Lf(k) \tag{13.1}$$

where $k = K/L$ is capital intensity. Define $f(k) = F(k,1)$ and assume that capital is *essential* in production, that is,

$$f(0) = 0$$

Capital saved in one period becomes an input in the production process of the following period; it is physically identical to the consumption good and depreciates during production at the rate $\delta \in [0,1]$.[2] Because capital is essential in the production process, we need to endow generation 0 with some of it, sinking into the production process an amount $k_1 > 0$ of capital on behalf of each of its members. If $k_1 = 0$, or if generation 0 were to consume its endowment on the spot, production would never get off the ground in this model; income as well as saving would remain zero forever.

Constant returns to scale and atomistic competition taken together mean that payments to factors of production will exhaust every profit-maximizing producer's revenue, leaving nothing for profit. This is a straightforward application of Euler's theorem for homogeneous functions (see Chiang, 1974, p. 407). In particular, output per laborer employed in period t satisfies

$$f(k_t) = \rho_t k_t + w_t \tag{13.2}$$

where w_t is the wage rate expressed in terms of the consumption good, ρ_t is the rental rate (or user cost) of capital, and $R_t = 1 + r_t$ is the interest factor on loans. Since the markets for renting and purchasing physical capital are competitive, the opportunity cost of owning equipment for one period should equal the relevant rental rate. Then an arbitrage condition of the form

$$\rho_t = \delta + r_t \tag{3.3}$$

should hold in equilibrium where r_t, the opportunity cost of funds invested in physical capital, is also the yield on loans made at $t-1$ and maturing at t. Note in addition (from question II.13(a)) that the first-order conditions for maximal profit imply factor demands such that

$$\rho_t = f'(k_t) \tag{13.4a}$$

$$w_t = f(k_t) - k_t f'(k_t) \tag{13.4b}$$

Figure 13.1 illustrates the relationship between factor prices and capital intensity.

In view of the zero profit that accrues to producers, the lifetime budget constraint for household h is $c_{1h}^t + c_{2h}^t / R_{t+1} \leq w_t$. Equivalently, we have two sequential budget constraints $c_{1h}^t + s_h^t \leq w_t$ and $c_{2h}^t \leq R_{t+1} s_h^t$, where s_h^t is the saving by household h. Denote by $z^h(R, w)$ the savings function of household h, and by

$$z(R, w) = \frac{1}{H} \sum_{h=1}^{H} z^h(R, w) \tag{13.5}$$

the (normalized) aggregate savings function. Each $z^h : \mathbb{R}_+^2 \to \mathbb{R}_+$ is a single-valued function that describes how much is saved by a household with utility function $u^h : \mathbb{R}_+^2 \to \mathbb{R}$ and income vector $(w, 0)$ when the interest factor is greater than zero. In other words, $z^h(R, w)$, the most preferred (or maximal) point in that household's budget set, is single valued if u^h is strictly monotone and strictly quasi-concave. Formally, we have the following definition:

$$z^h(R, w) = \operatorname*{argmax}_{0 \leq z \leq w} u^h(w - z, Rz) \tag{13.6}$$

Because leisure has no value for the young, the economy we are studying is perpetually in full employment with labor services growing geometrically at the rate of population growth. Therefore, the income accounting identity for generation t,

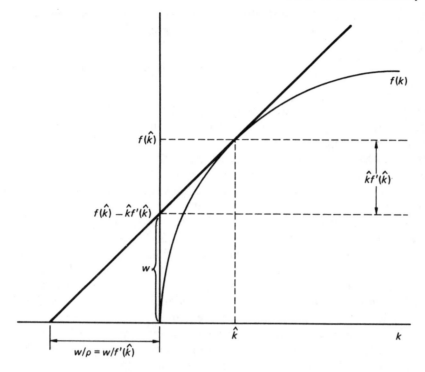

Figure 13.1 Factor pricing under constant returns.

$$Hw_t = \sum_{h=1}^{H} c_{1h}^t + H(1 + n)k_{t+1} \qquad (13.7)$$

says that total labor earnings in any period equal the aggregate consumption by the young plus their "investment", that is, the total capital stock available in the subsequent period.

Equations (13.5) and (13.7), taken together, imply that the normalized aggregate supply of capital in period $t + 1$ is the corresponding aggregate saving of the previous period, that is, $z(R_t, w_t)$. From equations (13.3) and (13.4a), on the other hand, we conclude that the aggregate demand for capital at t is $(1 + n)^t Hk^d(\delta + r_t)$, where k^d is the inverse of the marginal product function $f'(k)$ evaluated at $\delta + r_t$.

We can define a *dynamic competitive equilibrium* in terms of *either* the equilibrium sequence (R_t) of yields *or* the equilibrium sequence (k_t) of capital stock per worker; each sequence is a *state variable* that completely describes events. If the capital intensity sequence is known, equilibrium interest factors, wage rates, and factor incomes are defined uniquely from equations (13.4a) and (13.4b); and individual consumption vectors are easily computed from the appropriate savings functions:

$$c_{1h}^t = w_t - z^h(R_{t+1}, w_t) \qquad c_{2h}^t = R_{t+1} z^h(R_{t+1}, w_t) \qquad (13.8)$$

for $h = 1, ..., H$.

The sequence $(k_t)_{t=1}^{\infty}$ is an equilibrium if the price sequences associated with it by equations (13.3), (13.4a), and (13.4b) clear the capital market, that is, if for all $t \geq 0$ the equation

$$(1 + n)k_{t+1} - z[1 - \delta + f'(k_{t+1}), f(k_t) - k_t f'(k_t)] = 0 \qquad (13.9)$$

holds, given some initial capital stock per worker equal to $k_1 > 0$. Equation (13.9) means that excess demand for capital vanishes for all t. Recall that the number of workers in an overlapping generations economy with constant population is one-half the number of living persons.

This is an ordinary first-order difference equation whose solution we have already explored in section 7.4. Here *we no longer assume* that the two dated consumption goods are gross substitutes and therefore we allow the saving function to be locally *decreasing* in the interest factor R. The solution to (13.9) tells us how the economy may behave at any point in time if it starts from a given initial position k_1.

To grasp the nature of that solution, it is sufficient to draw equation (13.9) in (k_t, k_{t+1}) space, that is, to construct a phase diagram like those of figure 7.3. To do this we take k_t as given and solve for k_{t+1}. It is natural to do this rather than to take k_{t+1} as given and solve for k_1 because the starting position k_1 is a historical datum. If this type of equilibrium exists, it is called a *forward-looking temporary competitive equilibrium*.[3] Similarly, if we took k_{t+1} as given in equation (13.9) and solved for k_t instead, we would obtain a *backward-looking temporary competitive equilibrium*.

We have already done some of the necessary work in section 7.4. More precisely, one can show (see the Technical Appendix) the following.

Theorem 13.1 If the two dated consumption goods are normal, then a backward-looking temporary competitive equilibrium exists and is unique. Under the same assumption, a forward-looking temporary competitive equilibrium exists, but it is not necessarily unique; a sufficient condition for uniqueness is that saving be an increasing function of the interest rate.

For this theorem, it is actually sufficient that old-age consumption be a normal good which ensures that saving is an increasing function of youthful income.

Figure 13.2(c) illustrates this result in a phase diagram that shows k_t to be a single-valued function of k_{t+1} but not the other way around; *diagrams like that in 13.2(b) are ruled out by the normality assumption*. The reason is that youthful and old-age consumption are normal goods but *not necessarily* gross substitutes; that makes aggregate saving at t monotone in w_t or k_t, not perforce in R_{t+1} or k_{t+1}. To see why we argue as follows. Suppose that a diagram like 13.2(b) were indeed to represent equilibrium; then a given value of k_{t+1} would correspond to two distinct values of k_t and hence to two different values of wage income at t, say $w_t^1 \neq w_t^2$. For this to be true, a representative household facing a given interest factor $1 - \delta - f'(k_{t+1})$ would have to save in equilibrium the same amount, k_{t+1}, when its youthful income was w_t^1 as it would if income were instead w_t^2.

From equation (13.9) we see that $k_{t+1} = 0$ whenever $k_t = 0$ (because $k_t = 0$ implies that both labor income and saving out of it are zero); furthermore, we recall from section 7.4 and especially note 4, that $(k_{t+1}/k_t) \to 0$ as $k_t \to \infty$.

Any phase diagram of equation (13.9), therefore, will show a map that starts at the origin, lies below the 45° line for large values of k_t, and slopes upward for small values of k_t. These bits of information still allow a rich variety of dynamical equilibrium behavior; some of the possibilities are shown in figure 13.2 and in figure 7.3 also.

Note first that $k_t = 0$ for all t is always a trivial equilibrium that represents zero production and factor incomes in an economy that has shut down; this steady state exists whenever $f(0) = 0$. Are there any nontrivial steady states $\bar{k} > 0$? Suppose temporarily that saving is increasing in the interest rate which means that a unique forward-looking temporary competitive equilibrium exists. Then we can solve equation (13.9) for k_{t+1}:

$$k_{t+1} = G(k_t) \tag{13.10}$$

where $G : \mathbb{R}_+ \to \mathbb{R}_+$ is an increasing continuously differentiable time map such that $G(0) = 0$, and $[G(k)/k] \to 0$ as $k \to \infty$. If $G'(0) > 1$, this map is steeper at the origin than the 45° line and has an *odd number $2j + 1$ of nontrivial steady states*, as shown in figures 13.2(a) and 7.3(a). Of these states $j + 1$ are asymptotically stable and j are unstable. On the other hand, if $G'(0) < 1$, the map is flatter than the 45° line at the origin and there is an *even number $2j = 0, 2, 4, \dots$ of nontrivial steady states*, as shown in figures 7.3(b), 7.3(c), and 13.2(d); an example of a nonexistent positive steady state is furnished by the saddle-node bifurcation example in equations (8.16a) and (8.16b) as well as by figure 8.5(a). If nontrivial steady states do exist here, exactly half of them will be asymptotically stable and half will be unstable.

What happens if saving is not everywhere increasing in the interest rate? Then equation (13.9) may be solved for k_{t+1} only locally; the time map G is in general set valued, as in figure 13.2(c). As before, these figures show that there will be $2j + 1$ positive steady states if $G'(0) > 1$ and $2j$ states if $G'(0) < 1$, where j is some *non-negative* integer. The difference from the monotone case is that here we can no longer be sure that asymptotically stable states like A and C in figure 13.2 are separated by unstable states. In fact, state B is unstable in 13.2(a) but not necessarily so in 13.2(c).

To evaluate the crucial parameter $G'(0)$ we need a more precise idea of the map implicit in equation (13.9). Let us differentiate it totally with respect to k_t and k_{t+1} to obtain its derivative evaluated at any steady state $k \geqslant 0$, that is,

$$G'(k) = \frac{(-kf'')z_y}{1 + n - f''z_R} \tag{13.11a}$$

In this expression, z_y and z_R denote the partial derivatives of the saving function $z(R, y)$. Let ϵ_y and ϵ_R stand for the corresponding elasticities;

$$\omega = -\frac{d \log k}{d \log \rho} = -\frac{f'}{kf''} \tag{13.11b}$$

denote the elasticity of the demand for capital with respect to the rental rate $\rho = f'(k)$; and $\alpha = kf'/f$ be capital's share of output. Then, after a little algebra, equation (13.11a) is rearranged into

$$G'(k) = \frac{\alpha}{1 - \alpha} \frac{\epsilon_y / \omega}{1 + A\epsilon_R / \omega} \qquad \text{for } k > 0 \tag{13.12}$$

where

$$A = \frac{f'}{1 - \delta + f'} \tag{13.13}$$

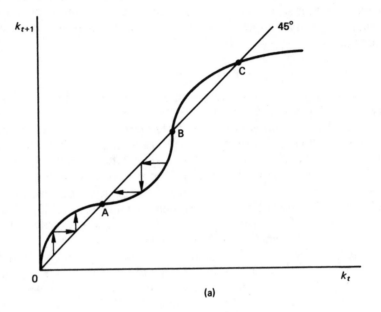

(a)

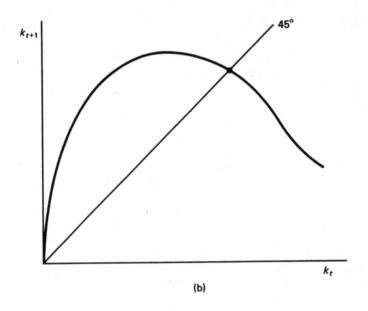

(b)

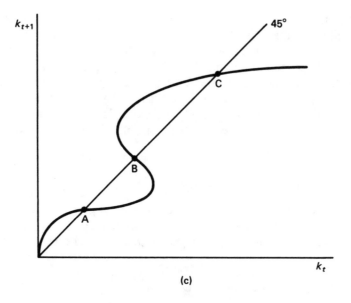

(c)

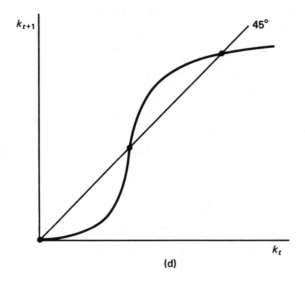

(d)

Figure 13.2 Existence of steady states: (a), (b), (c) $G'(0) > 1$; (d) $G'(0) < 1$.

From equation (13.12) we see straightaway that

$$G'(0) > 1 \quad \Leftrightarrow \quad \lim_{k \to 0} \frac{- kf''z_y}{1 + n - f''z_R} > 1 \qquad (13.14)$$

The second inequality in (13.14), due to Galor and Ryder (1989), amounts to a sufficient condition for the existence of at least one asymptotically stable positive steady state, like those exhibited in figures 13.2(a) and 13.2(c).

Equation (13.12), on the other hand, will yield conditions that guarantee the uniqueness of the nontrivial steady state, as for example in figure 7.3(a), or the existence of a flip cycle like the one we may easily imagine about point B in figure 13.2(c). From figures 13.2(a) and 13.2(c), for example, we see immediately that sufficient conditions for a unique asymptotically stable positive steady state are that

1. the map G be monotone;
2. $G'(0) > 1$; and
3. $G'(k) < 1$ at each fixed point $k > 0$ of G.

The first requirement is met automatically if aggregate saving is increasing in the rate of interest and second-period consumption is a normal good; the second can be checked with the help of inequality (13.14); and equation (13.12) reduces the third to

$$\frac{\alpha \epsilon_y}{(1 - \alpha)\omega} < 1 + \frac{A\epsilon_R}{\omega} \qquad \text{for all } k > 0 \qquad (13.15)$$

To discuss flip cycles, let us recall from theorem 13.1 that we can always solve backward the scalar overlapping generations model in equation (13.9) to express k_t as a single-valued function of k_{t+1}, that is, we can write the inverse time map

$$k_t = \phi(k_{t+1}) \qquad (13.16)$$

A flip cycle is a collection of points, all of which are fixed points of the even-order iterate ϕ^{2j} of this map, for some positive integer $j = 1, 2, ...$; and $2j$ is the smallest integer for which this orbit is a solution of equation (13.16).

Flip cycles have even period; as we know from theorem 8.2, a cycle with period 2 will occur in the scalar Diamond model when a steady state like point B in figure 13.2(c) loses stability in the *backward* dynamics, that is, just as $\phi'(k)$ falls below -1. A sufficient condition for this is $G'(k) \in (-1, 0)$ for some fixed point $k > 0$, that is, that there should be a spiral sink in the ordinary forward dynamics of equation (13.9). From equation (13.12) we check immediately that

$$G'(k) \in (-1, 0) \quad \Leftrightarrow \quad 1 + \frac{A\epsilon_R}{\omega} < \frac{- \alpha \epsilon_y}{(1 - \alpha)\omega}$$

Thus a flip cycle, which is stable in the backward dynamics and unstable in the ordinary forward dynamics, will appear if

$$A\epsilon_R < - \frac{\omega(1 - \alpha) + \alpha \epsilon_y}{1 - \alpha} \qquad (13.17)$$

This occurs if aggregate saving drops sufficiently fast when the interest rate rises in the neighborhood of *some* steady state; it is more likely to happen if the elasticity parameter ω (and the capital–labor elasticity of substitution on which ω depends) is small.[4]

To illustrate some of the dynamical equilibria that are possible solutions to equation (13.9), we look at a special case of it, namely

$$(1 + n)k_{t+1} = s[f(k_t) - k_t f'(k_t)] \equiv sw(k_t) \tag{13.18}$$

Here s is no longer a function but a given constant in the interval $(0,1)$, representing the economywide average propensity to save out of wage income.[5] The following two are examples of the dynamic behavior illustrated in figure 7.3.

Example 13.1 (A unique stable nontrivial steady state)   Suppose the technology is Cobb–Douglas with $f(k) = k^a$, $0 < a < 1$. Then equation (13.18) becomes $(1 + n)k_{t+1} = s(1 - a)k_t^a$ with a single asymptotically stable positive stationary equilibrium $k = [s(1 - a)/(1 + n)]^{1/(1-a)}$. The time map is exactly as in figure 7.3(a).

Example 13.2 (Positive stationary equilibria do not exist)   Assume now $f(k) = \log(1 + k)$, $n = 0$, and $s = 1/2$. Then $kf'(k) = k/(1 + k)$, and stationary solutions to equation (13.18) are roots of the function $g(k) = 2k + k/(1 + k) - \log(1 + k)$. Note, however, that $g(0) = 0$ and g is strictly increasing for all $k \geqslant 0$. Hence, the only stationary equilibrium is $k = 0$; all dynamical equilibria converge asymptotically to the autarkic state $k = 0$.

Another class of interesting illustrations for the phase portraits of figure 13.2 emerges from constant-elasticity-of-substitution production functions like those described by equation 8.20 (section 8.3). Intensive production functions in this class are of the general form

$$f(k) = A[ak^{-\rho} + (1 - a)]^{-1/\rho} \tag{13.19}$$

where $A > 0$, $a \in (0,1)$, and $\rho \geqslant -1$ are technological parameters that capture the scale of production, factor shares, and factor substitutability respectively. The elasticity of substitution is $\sigma = 1/(1 + \rho)$. The marginal products of capital and labor for any function of this class are (see question II.11)

$$\text{MPK} = aA^{-\rho}[f(k)/k]^{1+\rho} \tag{13.20a}$$

$$\text{MPL} = (1 - a)A^{-\rho}[f(k_t)]^{1+\rho} \tag{13.20b}$$

If the economywide propensity to save is constant, equation (13.18) reduces to

$$(1 + n)k_{t+1} = s(1 - a)A^{-\rho}[f(k_t)]^{1+\rho} \tag{13.21}$$

Depending on the elasticity of substitution parameter $1/(1 + \rho)$ and the scale factor A, *this difference equation may have none, one, or two positive steady states*. One positive steady state exists if $\rho = 0$ in which case the constant-elasticity-of-substitution production function reduces to the Cobb–Douglas form of example 13.2. The existence of a positive steady state is guaranteed for all $\rho \leqslant 0$ because the wage function $w(k)$ satisfies the inequality $G'(0) > 1$ whenever $\rho \leqslant 0$.
   In particular, we have

$$\lim_{k \to 0} f'(k) = +\infty \tag{13.22a}$$

$$\lim_{k \to 0} w'(k) = +\infty \tag{13.22b}$$

For constant elasticities of substitution below unity, a positive steady state is almost never unique, as the following examples illustrate.

Example 13.3 (Two positive steady states)   Suppose $\rho > 0$ in equation (13.21). Then it is easy to show, by doing question II.11, that $f(k)/k$ and $f'(k)$ are both bounded, and we then use equation (13.20b) to demonstrate that

$$\lim_{k \to 0} w'(k) = 0 \qquad (13.23)$$

This means that the time map of equation (13.21) looks like figure 13.2(d): it starts below the 45° line at the origin and eventually dips below the 45° line again. Whether or not it crosses the diagonal depends on total factor productivity, that is, on the value of the scale factor A. For large A, there will be at least two steady states; one will be asymptotically stable and the other will be unstable. (Can you guess why the phase diagram is shaped that way? Verify that, for a low elasticity of substitution, the marginal product of labor is very sensitive to changes in the capital–labor ratio.)

Example 13.4 (No positive steady state)   Suppose now that $\rho > 0$ and the scale factor A is small; the smaller A is the lower will be the time map of equation (13.21) relative to the diagonal in figure 13.2(d). For sufficiently low total factor productivity, the origin $k = 0$ is the only steady state, and it will possess global asymptotic stability. All equilibrium paths will contract this economy into the lowest level at which it can operate (as in figure 7.3(c)). We can interpret this situation as a kind of inescapable poverty trap.

13.2   Welfare issues

How good are the stationary competitive equilibria we just studied? Do durable goods aid or hinder the intertemporal working of the invisible hand? To find out, we pick up the thread from chapter 12 and look at the equal-treatment optimal (ET-O) allocations that are available to a central planner. As we saw previously, ET-O allocations maximize a social welfare function of the type

$$W = \sum_{h=1}^{H} [\beta_h c_{2h}^0 + \lambda_h u^h(c_{1h}, c_{2h})]$$

subject to resource constraints (or national income accounting constraints) of the form

$$\sum_{h=1}^{H} \left[c_{1h} + \frac{c_{2h}}{1+n} \right] \leq H[f(k) + (1 - \delta)k - (1 + n)k] \qquad (13.24)$$

$$\sum_{h=1}^{H} \left[c_{1h} + \frac{c_{2h}^0}{1+n} \right] \leq H[f(k_1) + (1 - \delta)k_1 - (1 + n)k] \qquad (13.25)$$

Aggregate consumption, says each of these, cannot exceed output, $f(k)$, net of investment, $(n + \delta)k$. The first constraint applies to all time periods except the very first; the second constraint refers solely to the first time period which contains the special generation 0. Each member of that generation is endowed with $k_1 > 0$ units of capital, in order to start off the production process, and is assigned an entry in the consumption vector $(c_{21}^0, c_{22}^0, \ldots, c_{2H}^0)$.

Given the initial capital endowment k_1, the central planner chooses a non-negative consumption matrix

$$C = \begin{pmatrix} c_{21}^0 & c_{22}^0 & \cdots & c_{2H}^0 \\ c_{11} & c_{12} & \cdots & c_{1H} \\ c_{21} & c_{22} & \cdots & c_{2H} \end{pmatrix}$$

and a capital stock k in the interval $[0,(f(k_1) + (1 - \delta)k_1)/(1 + n)]$. Proceeding as in chapter 12, we find from the first-order conditions to the planning problem that an ET-O allocation satisfies the following relation for $h = 1,...,H$:

$$\frac{u_1^h(c_{1h}, c_{2h})}{u_2^h(c_{1h}, c_{2h})} = 1 - \delta + f'(k) \geq 1 + n \tag{13.26}$$

with equality holding if generation 0 carries no weight in the social welfare function. In this event, the social planner is no longer bound by inequality (13.25) and will choose capital intensity in order to maximize aggregate consumption. The outcome k^* equalizes the net marginal product of capital to the growth rate:

$$\delta + n = f'(k^*) \tag{13.27}$$

Following Phelps (1961), we refer to k^* as the *golden rule*.

Once we allow generation 0 some weight, inequality (13.26) identifies dynamic inefficiency with situations of *oversaving* or *overaccumulation of capital*, that is, with any choice of capital intensity $k > k^*$. This valuable result, discovered by Phelps (1965) and Koopmans (1965), adapts theorem 12.2 to an economy with production. We recapitulate below.

Theorem 13.2 Given an initial endowment of capital $k_1 > 0$, a feasible quasi-stationary allocation (k,C) is equal-treatment optimal if the associated net interest rate is equal to or greater than the rate of population growth, suboptimal otherwise.

Stationary competitive equilibria will fit the golden rule only by accident, and they will be outright suboptimal on occasion. Consider, for instance, the economy of example 13.1. There, the unique stationary non-autarkic competitive equilibrium is $\bar{k} = [s(1 - \alpha)/(1 + n)]^{1/(1-a)}$ while the golden rule allocation is $k^* = [\alpha/(\delta + n)]1/(1-a)$. The two are identical if, and only if, $s = \alpha(1+n)/[(1-\alpha)(\delta+n)]$. The competitive equilibrium is dynamically efficient if $s \leq a/(1 - a)$, inefficient otherwise. Inefficiency occurs when the saving rate is "too big."

There is a small policy lesson in that realization: economies with inherently high saving rates (like those of the Far East) may not achieve for their citizens as high a sustained consumption path as they are capable of while other economies (such as those of North America and Western Europe), with naturally lower saving rates, can perform much better in that regard. In any event, a high propensity to save does not *automatically* imply dynamic efficiency in the steady state, nor is a low rate necessarily a cause for remedial public policy.

How saving relates to welfare is a complex policy issue that needs to be explored more carefully. Until then, it is prudent to keep in mind the message of question II.12, namely, that high saving and large asset holdings may well be a response to credit rationing and, more generally, to poorly developed credit markets.

13.3   Adjustment costs (*)

We continue this chapter with the *q-theory of investment*, an extension of the one-sector growth model that has seen much use in empirical investment studies. This extension picks up a suggestion by Tobin (1969) that the flow of investment should depend on q, the ratio of the price of physical capital to its replacement cost. In a strictly one-sector growth model, q is clearly equal to unity because both the opportunity cost of physical capital and its price are unity when expressed in terms of the consumption good.

This situation will change if the costs of producing new capital goods are augmented by costs of installing them on the factory floor. Putting new investment in place on a production line involves adjustment costs which earlier writers like Lucas (1967), Lucas and Prescott (1971), Abel (1982), and Hayashi (1982) have recognized as playing a leading role in the timing of investment. These costs enrich the one-sector model with asset-price dynamics by permitting q_t, the price of capital goods at time t, to differ on occasion from unity.

In the remainder of this section we extend the overlapping generations model of capital accumulation to include adjustment costs and explore how investment is related to the equilibrium price of capital goods; this relation forms the core of the q theory of investment. Our presentation draws heavily on unpublished work by Carlos Budnevich (1990). Changes from the standard one-sector model include the specification of the adjustment cost function and two arbitrage relations for users of capital goods.

Suppose that a firm wishes to change its capital stock from K_t this period to K_{t+1} the following period. The total costs of the resulting net investment $I_t^n = K_{t+1} - K_t$ are not only I_t^n units of forgone consumption but also additional installation or adjustment costs

$$A_t = K_t c(I_t^n/K_t) \tag{13.28}$$

incurred at t. Adjustment costs are proportional to the starting capital stock K_t and depend also on the net investment rate I_t^n/K_t. The function $c:\mathbb{R} \to \mathbb{R}_+$ is assumed to be twice continuously differentiable and convex and attains a minimum at zero. In other words

$$c(0) = 0 \qquad c'(0) = 0 \qquad c''(x) > 0 \qquad \text{for all } x \tag{13.29}$$

There are two arbitrage relations we must consider: the first says that producers should be indifferent between using at time t capital goods rented at t or capital goods purchased at $t - 1$; the second states that producers should make no profit from producing new capital goods and selling them to others. These arbitrage conditions may be written in the form

$$\rho_t = R_t q_{t-1} - (1 - \delta)q_t \tag{13.30a}$$

$$q_t = 1 + c'\left(\frac{K_{t+1} - K_t}{K_t}\right) \tag{13.30b}$$

where ρ is the rental cost of capital, R is the gross yield on bank loans, δ is the depreciation rate and q is the price of capital. Note how the price of capital equals the direct production cost of unity plus the marginal cost of adjustment.

At any competitive equilibrium labor is fully employed; the marginal products of capital and labor equal the competitively determined rental and wage rates respectively, that is,

$$\rho_t = f'(k_t) \tag{13.31a}$$

$$w_t = f(k_t) - k_t f'(k_t) \equiv w(k_t) \tag{13.31b}$$

From equations (13.30) and (13.31) we obtain

$$f'(k_t) = R_t q_t - (1 - \delta)q_t$$

which may be solved for R_t to yield

$$R_t = \frac{f'(k_t) + (1 - \delta)q_t}{q_{t-1}} \tag{13.32}$$

To simplify matters, let us assume away population growth and define a dynamic competitive equilibrium for this economy to be any non-negative sequence (q_t, k_t) that satisfies two relations: the arbitrage condition (13.30b) plus the usual equality between saving and wealth. In other words, the state variables satisfy

$$q_t k_{t+1} = z(R_{t+1}, w_t)$$

$$q_t = 1 + c'\left(\frac{k_{t+1}}{k_t} - 1\right)$$

for all t, where $w_t = w(k_t)$ and $q_t R_{t+1} = f'(k_{t+1}) + (1 - \delta)q_{t+1}$ from equation (13.32). Together with appropriate boundary conditions, the resulting planar system

$$q_t k_{t+1} = z\left[\frac{f'k_{t+1}) + (1 - \delta)q_{t+1}}{q_t}, w(k_t)\right] \tag{13.33a}$$

$$q_t = 1 + c'\left(\frac{k_{t+1}}{k_t} - 1\right) \tag{13.33b}$$

contains all the information we need on dynamical equilibria.

Before we proceed with the planar case, let us return to the standard scalar overlapping generations growth model, which is a special case of equation (13.33a) with $q_t = 1$ for all t, and make whatever assumptions are necessary (see the material preceding equation (13.15)) to guarantee a unique, positive, asymptotically stable steady state $\bar{k} > 0$. Note now from equations (13.33a) and (13.33b) that the steady states of the adjustment-cost economy are isomorphic to those of the scalar Diamond economy, with *identical* capital stock, that is,

$$(q,k) = \{q_0, 0), (1,(\bar{k})\} \tag{13.34}$$

where

$$q_0 = 1 + \lim_{k_t \to 0} c'\left(\frac{k_{t+1}}{k_t} - 1\right) \tag{13.35}$$

The easiest case to study is when $\delta = 1$: in this case the system (13.33a), (13.33b) reduces to a scalar system as the term q_{t+1} drops from the right-hand side of equation (13.33a); that equation becomes

$$q_t k_{t+1} = z \left[\frac{f'(k_{t+1})}{q_t}, w(k_t) \right] \tag{13.33a}'$$

Assuming gross substitutes in consumption, we see that for any fixed k_t, k_{t+1} is a decreasing function of q_t. For $q_t = 1$, adjustment costs are irrelevant and the time map of (13.33a)' coincides with the scalar Diamond model. As $q_t > 1$ (< 1), on the other hand, this time map falls below (rises above) that of the scalar model, an event that occurs whenever $k_{t+1} > k_t$ ($k_{t+1} < k_t$).

Figure 13.3(a) compares the phase diagram of the simplest adjustment-cost economy with the phase diagram that is free from such costs. As one might expect, installation costs slow down the process of converging to the stable steady state. This is easily verified by substituting q_t from equation (13.33b) into (13.33a)', computing the slope T of the time map at the positive steady state $\bar{k}$, and comparing with equation (13.12).

We return next to the two-dimensional adjustment-costs economy described by equations (13.33a) and (13.33b) for any $\delta \in [0,1)$. Since the function $c : \mathbb{R} \to \mathbb{R}_+$ is strictly convex, we can use the implicit function theorem to invert equation (13.33b) and solve for k_{t+1}. We define an increasing function $h : \mathbb{R}_+ \to \mathbb{R}_+$ such that $h(1) = 1$ and

$$k_{t+1}/k_t = h(q_t) \tag{13.36}$$

From equations (13.33a) and (13.36) we should be able to construct a phase diagram for the planar dynamical system we are exploring. In particular, either (13.33b) or (13.36) says that

$$k_{t+1} \geqslant k_t \quad \text{iff} \quad q_t \geqslant 1 \tag{13.37a}$$

We call KK the constant-capital locus in figure 13.3(b). Substituting (13.36) into (13.33a), we obtain

$$q_t h(q_t) k_t = s \left\{ \frac{f'[k_t h(q_t)] + (1 - \delta)q_{t+1}}{q_t}, w(k_t) \right\}$$

Given gross substitutes in consumption, we have $q_{t+1} \geqslant q_t$ iff

$$q_t h(q_t) k_t \geqslant s \left\{ \frac{f'[k_t h(q_t)]}{q_t} + 1 - \delta, w(k_t) \right\} \tag{*}$$

Because h is an increasing function, the left-hand side of inequality (*) is increasing in q_t and the right-hand side is decreasing. Therefore there exists a single-valued function $Q : \mathbb{R}_+ \to \mathbb{R}_+$ which "solves" inequality (*), that is, (*) is equivalent to

$$q_{t+1} \geqslant q_t \quad \text{iff} \quad q_t \geqslant Q(k_t) \tag{13.37b}$$

By construction the graph of $q = Q(k)$, labeled QQ in figure 13.3(b), passes through both steady states, $(q_0, 0)$ and $(1, \bar{k})$, of the dynamical system (13.33a) and (13.33b). Furthermore, if $k/w(k) \to +\infty$ as $k \to \infty$, the line QQ eventually slopes downward, falling below $q = 1$, and intersecting the horizontal line of constant k only

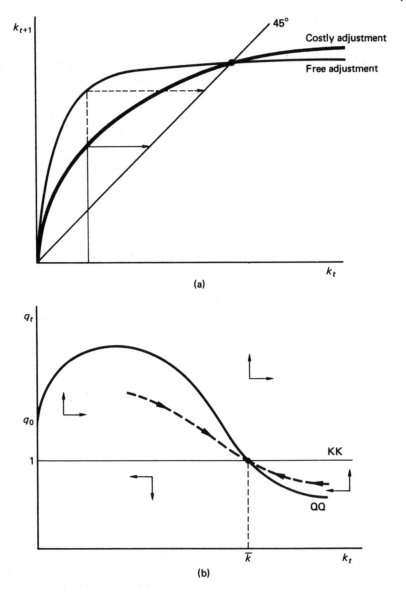

Figure 13.3 Adjustment cost dynamics.

once. The arrows on figure 13.3(b) define a vector field that is likely to have a saddle at $(1, \overline{k})$, a fact that is easy to verify from the eigenvalues of the relevant Jacobian.

A saddlepath appears in the figure as a broken line; it is a unique trajectory which requires that each historically given initial value k_1 of the capital stock be associated with a suitably chosen price q_1 of physical capital. One interesting empirical statement we can extract from the phase diagram is the negative correlation between physical capital and its price along the saddlepath. Along that path, positive net investment is associated with a high and falling price of capital while negative net investment is associated with a low and rising price of capital.

13.4   Optimal economic growth

We return now to the Ramsey model of one-sector growth, introduced in section 7.3, in order to explore the relationship of planning optima to competitive equilibria and also to derive in detail the dynamical system of equations (7.2a) and (7.2b) that describes equilibrium trajectories in that model. The equations are the first-order conditions for a planning optimum in an economy inhabited by a single infinitely lived individual born at $t = 0$. Each period this individual is endowed with one unit of labor which he supplies inelastically to production. There is one perishable consumption good produced from capital and labor under constant returns to scale, using an intensive production function $f: \mathbb{R}_+ \to \mathbb{R}_+$ that maps capital per worker into output per worker. The individual's resource constraint is

$$c_t \leqslant f(k_t) + (1 - \delta)k_t - k_{t+1} \qquad (13.38a)$$

and his lifetime utility function is

$$V = \sum_{t=0}^{\infty} \beta^t u(c_t) \qquad (13.38b)$$

where β and δ are two parameters in the interval $[0,1]$ called the subjective discount rate and the depreciation rate. The related parameter $\rho = 1/\beta - 1$ is called *the rate of time preference*. Inequality (13.38a) says that, in each period, the sum of consumption c_t and gross investment $k_{t+1} - (1 - \delta)k_t$ cannot exceed output.

Imagine now a benevolent all-knowing and all-powerful central planner who comes to be in charge of this economy. If no output is ever wasted, (13.38a) becomes an equality, and the representative individual's utility function reduces to an object that depends only on the infinite sequence k_t:

$$V = \sum_{t=0}^{\infty} \beta^t v(k_t, k_{t+1}) \qquad (13.39a)$$

where

$$v(k_t, k_{t+1}) = u[f(k_t) + (1 - \delta)k_t - k_{t+1}] \qquad (13.39b)$$

What sequence k_t^* should the planner pick if he wants to maximize the representative individual's lifetime utility? Denoting by (v_1, v_2) the partial derivatives of the function v, we obtain from (13.39a) a first-order condition of the form

$$\beta^t v_2(k_t, k_{t+1}) + \beta^{t+1} v_1(k_{t+1}, k_{t+2}) = 0 \qquad (13.40)$$

for each t by differentiating with respect to k_{t+1}. Note now that $v_1 = [1 - \delta + f'(k_{t+1})]u'(c_{t+1})$ and $v_2 = -u'(c_t)$; dividing (13.40) by β^t yields $\beta v_1 + v_2 = 0$ or

$$\beta[1 - \delta + f'(k_{t+1})]u'(c_{t+1}) = u'(c_t) \qquad (13.41a)$$

$$k_{t+1} = f(k_t) + (1 - \delta)k_t - c_t \qquad (13.41b)$$

This is precisely the dynamical system we analyzed in section 7.3; its phase diagram appears in figure 7.2 and shows that its unique steady state $(\bar{k}, \bar{c}) > 0$ is a saddle. The stationary optimum capital stock $\bar{k}$ (if it exists) satisfies the relation $f'(\bar{k}) = \rho + \delta$ and is sometimes referred to as *the modified golden rule*. Question II.9 explores an economy in which $\bar{k}$ does not exist.

Not every solution to equations (13.41a) and (13.41b) is a planning optimum or, for that matter, a competitive equilibrium. Solutions that do not lie on the stable manifold of the saddle (k, c) either become infeasible in finite time or violate the *transversality condition*

$$\lim_{t \to \infty} [\beta^t u'(c_t) k_t] = 0 \qquad (13.41c)$$

which is necessary for an optimum. This additional restriction is needed because the first-order conditions (13.41a) and (13.41b) by themselves describe a second-order difference equation in the capital stock. Given an initial condition that fixes k_0, the second-order equation in the capital stock has a different solution sequence for each *terminal value* of the capital stock.

The transversality condition means that the social welfare function, that is, discounted lifetime utility, is maximal when the terminal value of the capital stock is zero. More precisely, equation (13.41c) states that the present value of capital at t, reckoned in terms of intertemporal marginal rates of substitution, tends to zero as time goes to infinity.

Extensions of optimal growth models that allow for uncertainty in the technology, money in the utility function (see Part IV), and other generalizations of the basic Ramsey structure have found wide use in macroeconomics, especially in the "real business cycle" models mentioned in chapter 9, note 1. One reason is that the "number" of equilibrium trajectories is small: the steady state is typically unique in one-sector models,[6] and its stable manifold is small relative to the state space. A more serious reason is that competitive equilibria are planning optima and hence are fully described by the first-order conditions to some suitably defined, and often tractable, planning problem.

To show how equations (13.41a) and (13.41b) correspond to a competitive equilibrium, let us think of the representative agent as a consumer-worker who supplies to producers 1 unit of labor each period, earning a sequence w_t of wages. If x_t is this person's wealth at the *beginning* of period t, then wealth evolves according to the identity

$$x_{t+1} = R_t x_t + w_t - c_t \qquad (13.42)$$

which we call the *flow budget constraint* of the representative individual. In this equality R_t is one plus the rate of interest on one-period loans contracted at $t - 1$ and repaid at t. Wealth may be positive or negative at each period. To prevent individuals from becoming perpetual debtors or from rolling over debt forever, we impose a transversality condition like equation (13.41c):

$$\lim_{t \to \infty} \frac{x_t}{\Pi_{s=1}^{t} R_s} \geq 0 \qquad (13.43)$$

This equation prevents the asymptotic value of household wealth from becoming negative in present-value terms. If the left-hand side of (13.43) *were* negative, then the household could borrow at the beginning of time and never repay its debt, consuming its entire income each period and refinancing this debt in perpetuity.

Consumption plans that maximize the lifetime utility function (13.38a), subject to the flow budget constraint (13.42) for each t and to the transversality condition

(13.43), are equivalent to wealth sequences $(x_t)_{t=0}^{\infty}$ that for each price sequence (w_t, R_t) maximize lifetime utility

$$\sum_{t=0}^{\infty} \beta^t u(R_t x_t + w_t - x_{t+1}) \tag{13.44}$$

subject to $x_0 = 0$ (that is, to zero initial wealth), to inequality (13.43), and to the non-negativity restriction $w_t \geq x_{t+1} - R_t x_t$ for all t. The first-order conditions for this problem are similar to equation (13.40) above, that is,

$$\beta R_{t+1} u'(c_{t+1}) = u'(c_t) \tag{13.44a}$$

In any competitive equilibrium, firms will hire capital according to the well-known equality

$$f'(k_t) = \rho_t = \delta + r_t \tag{13.44b}$$

of the marginal product of capital to the rental rate ρ_t, that is, to the sum of the depreciation and interest rates. This equality implies that $R_t = 1 - \delta + f'(k_t)$, which reduces the consumer optimum in (13.44a) to the planner's optimum in (13.41a). Furthermore, the competitive wage rate will be $w_t = f(k_t) - k_t f'(k_t)$ and the wealth of the representative consumer in equilibrium will equal the capital stock. Hence, the individual flow budget constraint (13.42) in any competitive equilibrium becomes

$$k_{t+1} = R_t k_t + w_t - c_t$$
$$= [1 - \delta + f'(k_t)] + f(k_t) - k_t f'(k_t) - c_t$$
$$= f(k_t) + (1 - \delta)k_t - c_t$$

which is simply the resource constraint (13.41b) of the central planner.

It is easy to check that the transversality condition (13.43) reduces to (13.41c) if we set $x_t = k_t$ and $R_s = u'(c_{s-1})/\beta u'(c_s)$. Hence, *competitive equilibria and centrally planned optima are completely equivalent in the Ramsey model.*

13.5   Elastic labor supply and Hopf cycles (*)

We conclude this chapter with Reichlin's (1986) extension of the scalar Diamond model to endogenous labor supply, that is, to situations in which the aggregate supply of labor varies when the wage rate or the interest rate changes. Specifically, we study dynamical equilibria in an otherwise standard Diamond model with constant population ($n = 0$), a representative household ($H = 1$), no technical progress, and fully depreciating capital ($\delta = 1$). Each household is endowed with 1 unit of leisure in youth, part of which it consumes and the remainder it supplies to the labor market. The household also consumes, in its old age only, one perishable consumption good manufactured by firms under constant returns to scale; none of this good is desired or consumed in youth.

All households evaluate leisure–consumption bundles by a common well-behaved utility function $u : I \times \mathbb{R}_+ \to \mathbb{R}$ where I is the unit interval. Both leisure and consumption are assumed to be normal goods. If L_t is the labor supply of a young individual at t, his old-age consumption is $c_{t+1} = w_t R_{t+1} L_t$ where (w_t, R_t) have the usual interpretation. Labor supply, and saving, is $L_t = s(w_t R_{t+1})$ where

$$s(p) = \underset{0 \leqslant s \leqslant 1}{\text{argmax }} u(1 - s, ps) \tag{13.45}$$

Given full depreciation and constant returns to scale, factor demands satisfy the usual relations $f'(k_t) = R_t$ and $w_t = w_t(k_t) = f(k_t) - k_t f'(k_t)$.

A *competitive equilibrium* is an infinite sequence (L_t, k_t) that clears the labor and capital markets for given initial conditions $L_1 \in [0,1]$ and $k_1 \geqslant 0$, that is, that satisfies

$$L_t = s[w(k_t)f'(k_{t+1})] \tag{13.46a}$$

$$L_{t+1}k_{t+1} = L_t w(k_t) \tag{13.46b}$$

The first of these conditions describes equilibrium in the labor market; the second equates planned investment with saving, that is, with the *entire wage income* of non-consuming young workers.

Assuming that consumption and leisure are gross substitutes and that the marginal rate of substitution between them is zero at the initial endowment point $(1,0)$, we conclude that the saving function $s: \mathbb{R}_+ \to I$ is monotone and $s(0) = 0$. This means that we can solve equation (13.46a) for k_{t+1} and write

$$k_{t+1} = \phi(k_t, L_t) \tag{13.47a}$$

Then (13.46b) reduces to

$$L_{t+1} = \frac{L_t w(k_t)}{\phi(k_t, L_t)} \tag{13.47b}$$

To draw a phase diagram for the dynamical system (13.46a) and, (13.46b) or, equivalently, (13.47a) and (13.47b), we recall that both s and w are increasing functions and quickly verify that a positive steady state $(\bar{k}, \bar{L})$ will exist if $\bar{k} > 0$ is a solution to $w(k) = k$ and $\bar{L} = s[w(\bar{k})f'(\bar{k})]$. Let us assume that $\bar{k}$ is uniquely defined.[7] From (13.46a) we obtain

$$k_{t+1} \geqslant k_t \Leftrightarrow f'(k_{t+1}) \leqslant f'(k_t)$$
$$\Leftrightarrow L_t \leqslant p(k) \equiv s[w(k_t)f'(k_t)] \tag{13.48a}$$

Equations (13.46a) and (13.46b) together imply that

$$L_{t+1} \geqslant L_t \Leftrightarrow w(k_t) \geqslant k_{t+1}$$
$$\Leftrightarrow f'[w(k_t)] \leqslant f'(k_{t+1})$$
$$\Leftrightarrow L_t \geqslant \pi(k) \equiv s\{w(k_t)f'[w(k_t)]\} \tag{13.48b}$$

Note that $p(k) \geqslant \pi(k) \Leftrightarrow f'(k) \geqslant f'[w(k)] \Leftrightarrow k \leqslant w(k) \Leftrightarrow k \geqslant \bar{k}$. We call LL and KK, respectively, the constant-labor and constant-capital phaselines. Furthermore we observe that $\pi(0) = 0$ since $s(0) = 0$ by assumption, and π is increasing in k if $kf'(k)$ is, that is, if the elasticity of substitution between capital and labor exceeds labor's share of output. Not much can be said about the function p except that $p(\bar{k}) = \bar{L}$ and that p is increasing (decreasing) if capital's share of output is above (below) one-half.

Two possible phase diagrams are given in figure 13.4, depicting the most likely vector fields. In figure 13.4(a) both phaselines slope upward, crossing at the origin and at $(\bar{k}, \bar{L})$; steady states seem to be unstable. In figure 13.4(b) the phaselines slope down in the neighborhood of the positive steady state which may be a saddle, an unstable spiral, or even a stable spiral.

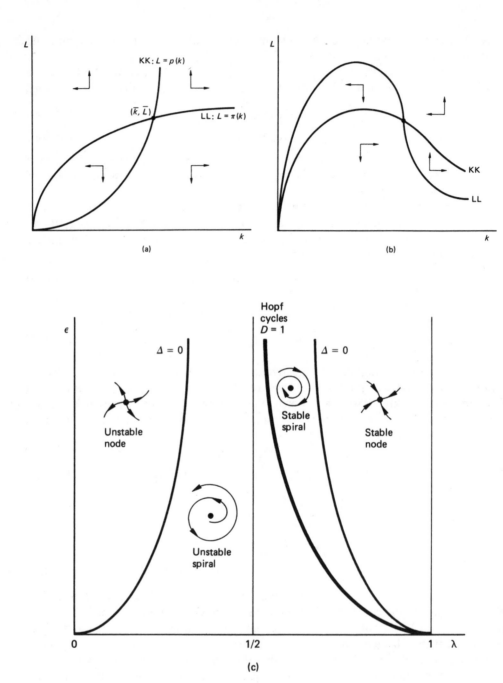

Figure 13.4 Variable labor supply; (a) unstable equilibrium; (b) saddle or spiral; (c) bifurcation diagram.

To ascertain the local stability properties of $(\bar{k}, \bar{L})$ we calculate the Jacobian of the dynamical system contained in equations (13.47a) and (13.47b). We rewrite that system in the form

$$k_{t+1} = \phi(k_t, L_t) \tag{13.49a}$$

$$L_{t+1} = \Lambda(k_t, L_t) \equiv \frac{L_t w(k_t)}{\phi(k_t, L_t)} \tag{13.49b}$$

Next we denote by ϵ, α, and σ respectively the elasticity of labor supply, capital's share of output, and the elasticity of substitution in production, all of them evaluated at the steady state. After a little algebra, we find the Jacobian to be

$$J = \begin{pmatrix} \phi_k & \phi_L \\ \Lambda_k & \Lambda_L \end{pmatrix} = \begin{pmatrix} \dfrac{\alpha}{1-\alpha} & -\dfrac{\sigma/\epsilon}{1-\alpha}\dfrac{k}{L} \\ \dfrac{L}{k}\left(\dfrac{1-\alpha}{\sigma}-1\right)f' & 1+\dfrac{\sigma/\epsilon}{1-\alpha} \end{pmatrix}$$

Recalling that $f'(k) = kf'(k)/k = kf'(k)/w = \alpha/(1-\alpha)$ in any steady state, we obtain the determinant and trace of this matrix:

$$D = \left(1 + \frac{1}{\epsilon}\right)\frac{\alpha}{1-\alpha} > 0 \tag{13.50a}$$

$$T = \frac{1 + \sigma/\epsilon}{1-\alpha} > 0 \tag{13.50b}$$

The local dynamical behavior of this system about the steady state $(\bar{k}, \bar{L})$ is governed by the roots of the characteristic polynomial

$$y(\lambda) = \lambda^2 - T\lambda + D$$

whose discriminant is

$$\Delta = T^2 - 4D = \frac{(1 + \sigma/\epsilon)^2}{(1-\alpha)^2} - \frac{4\alpha(1 + 1/\epsilon)}{1-\alpha} \tag{13.50c}$$

Furthermore

$$y(1) = 1 - T + D = \frac{\alpha - \sigma}{(1-\alpha)\epsilon} \tag{13.50d}$$

Below we provide some examples of local dynamics drawn from familiar parametric economies and then go on to examine general conditions for the existence of Hopf cycles.

Example 13.5 (Cobb–Douglas technology) Here $\sigma = 1$ and $\alpha = $ constant. Then

$$\Delta = \frac{1 + 1/\epsilon}{(1-\alpha)^2}\left[1 + \frac{1}{\epsilon} - 4\alpha(1-\alpha)\right]$$

$$\propto 1 + \frac{1}{\epsilon} - 4\alpha(1-\alpha)$$

$$> 1 - 4\alpha(1-\alpha) \geq 0 \text{ for all } \alpha \in [0,1]$$

Hence we have two positive eigenvalues that straddle $+1$ because $y(1) = -1/\epsilon < 0$; the steady state is necessarily a saddle.

Example 13.6 (Leontieff technology)   Suppose, as Reichlin (1986) did in his original piece, that $f(k) = \min\{1, k/\lambda\}$ where $\lambda \in (0,1)$ is some given parameter. Here the elasticity of substitution is zero and efficient production requires $k_t = \lambda \ \forall t$, which means that all dynamical behavior amounts to movements in employment, not in the capital–labor ratio. From the zero profit condition $1 = w + \lambda R$, we obtain a factor-price frontier that permits us to write $wR = w(1 - w)/\lambda$. Positive steady states $(\bar{k}, \bar{L})$ satisfy

$$k = \lambda \qquad kL = s\,\frac{w(1 - w)}{\lambda}\,w \tag{13.51}$$

These relations yield $w = \lambda$ and $\bar{L} = s(1 - \lambda)$, which imply that capital's share of output is

$$\alpha = \lambda R = 1 - w = 1 - \lambda \tag{13.52a}$$

From (13.50a), (13.50c), and (13.52a) we obtain

$$\Delta \geq 0 \quad \text{iff} \quad \epsilon \geq \frac{4\lambda(1 - \lambda)}{1 - 4\lambda(1 - \lambda)} \tag{13.52b}$$

$$D = 1 \quad \text{iff} \quad \epsilon = \frac{1 - \lambda}{2\lambda - 1} \tag{13.52c}$$

As the capital–labor ratio λ varies in $[0,1]$ the expression on the right-hand side of (13.52b) rises continuously from zero at $\lambda = 0$ towards infinity as $\lambda \to 1/2$, has a discontinuity at $\lambda = 1/2$, and then falls back towards zero as $\lambda \to 1$. The resulting graph corresponds to the branches of the curve $\Delta = 0$ in figure 13.4(c).

The characteristic polynomial has two positive real roots if inequality (13.52b) holds. These roots sum to $1/\lambda$ by equation (13.50b) and lie on the *same* side of unity because, says equation (13.50d),

$$y(1) = \frac{1 - \lambda}{\lambda\epsilon} > 0$$

Therefore, both roots are in the unit interval if $\lambda > 1/2$ and in $(1,\infty)$ if $\lambda < 1/2$. We conclude that $(\bar{k}, \bar{L})$ is a *stable node* if $\lambda > 1/2$ and $\Delta \geq 0$, and an *unstable node* if $\lambda < 1/2$ and $\Delta \geq 0$.

Suppose now that $\Delta < 0$ which means that $(\bar{k}, \bar{L})$ is a spiral that is stable if the determinant is less than unity, that is if $1/\epsilon < (2\lambda - 1)/(1 - \lambda)$, and unstable otherwise. The situation is summed up in the bifurcation diagram of figure 13.4(c), which also shows that a Hopf bifurcation takes place as the steady state changes stability along the line

$$\epsilon = \frac{1 - \lambda}{2\lambda - 1} \qquad \lambda \in (0,1) \tag{13.53}$$

If some technical conditions mentioned in theorem 8.5 are fulfilled, then a closed orbit will appear near values (ϵ, λ) that satisfy equation (13.53), and its stability will be the opposite of the steady state $(\bar{k}, \bar{L})$ which it surrounds.

To understand the range of economies for which Hopf cycles are likely to appear, we return to equations (13.50a)–(13.50d) and apply the Hopf bifurcation theorem 8.5 to them in order to find out what parameter values (σ,ϵ) are likely to generate closed orbits.

A Hopf bifurcation will occur in the neighborhood of some parameter vector (σ,ϵ) if $D = 1$, $\Delta < 0$, and a few technical side conditions are met.[8]

Solving $D = 1$ for α we obtain

$$\alpha = \frac{1}{2 + 1/\epsilon} \tag{13.54a}$$

and, on substituting this into $\Delta < 0$, we see after some algebra that

$$\Delta < 0 \;\Leftrightarrow\; \sigma < \frac{\epsilon}{1 + 2\epsilon} \tag{13.54b}$$

The right-hand sides of these relations are drawn in figure 13.5 and the shaded area satisfies the sufficient conditions we need in order to guarantee that a closed orbit exists in an overlapping generations model of capital accumulation with variable labor supply. These are as follows:

1 capital's share of output is an increasing function of the elasticity ϵ, which measures how close a substitute consumption is for leisure; and
2 the technical elasticity of substitution should be quite close to zero which means that capital and labor should be highly complementary inputs.

For example, if $\epsilon = 1/4$ we need $\alpha = 1/6$ and $\sigma < 1/6$ to support a closed orbit in this economy. As $\epsilon \to \infty$ and consumption goods become perfect substitues, closed orbits will occur for values $\sigma < 1/2$.

What do we conclude from the elastic-labor-supply version of the Diamond model about the likelihood of cycles in one-sector overlapping generations models? The message seems to be that cycles are *possible* even if consumption goods are gross substitutes (that is, $\epsilon > 0$) but not *probable* because they require consumption goods to be moderately substitutable *and* factor inputs to be highly complementary.

Notes

1. Constant returns to scale mean that $F(\lambda k,\lambda) = \lambda F(k,1)$ for any $\lambda > 0$. Stationarity means no technical progress or retrogression; see chapter 14 on technical progress, and Chiang (1974, pp. 403–7) on the properties of homogeneous functions.
2. Question II.14 explores some of the consequences on economic growth of changing the durability of physical capital.
3. The idea goes back to Hicks (1946) who coined the term. A more complete coverage of temporary equilibrium, together with additional references, appears in Part IV.
4. From chapter 8, note 5 recall that $\sigma = (1 - kf'/f)/\omega$ and hence $\omega = \sigma/(1 - \alpha)$.
5. In the standard Solow model of descriptive growth theory that we studied in Part I, a fraction s of all income is saved, so that the right-hand side of equation 13.18 is just $sf(k)$ (see Solow, 1956). The propensity to save in the overlapping generations model is a constant, independent of income and interest rates, if all utility functions are of the form $\log u^h = (1 - a_h) \log c_{1h} + a_h \log c_{2h}, 0 < a_n < 1$. Then s is just the population average of a_h.

6. If this were not true, we would get a contradiction to (13.40), taken as an equality, if we divided both sides by k_t and let $k_t \to \infty$. Then q would remain finite and so would the left-hand side of (13.40), while the right-hand side, bounded by w/k, would necessarily tend to zero.

7. Multisector optimal growth models do not possess unique positive steady states, except when the discount rate is sufficiently close to unity. See Benhabib and Nishimura (1979) for some examples and Boldrin and Woodford (1990) for a general survey.

8. A sufficient condition for the uniqueness of $\bar{k}$ is that $w(k)$ have slope above unity at $k = 0$ and elasticity below unity at all $k > 0$.

14 Economic development

14.1 The sources of economic growth

This chapter is a conceptual and historical extension of the previous one: it sums up the predictions of neoclassical growth theory about the process of economic development, compares them with historical data recorded in the USA and elsewhere, and reviews in detail some of the factors that affect long-run economic growth.

Chapter 13 focused on one of these factors, the accumulation of physical capital, which has been the traditional subject of growth theory since the 1950s. The remainder of this chapter is an elementary discussion of the role that a number of other sources play in economic development; in these we include population growth, technological progress, human capital, increasing returns to scale, and the state of financial markets. There are several important factors that we do *not* discuss, for example international trade, product innovation, public health, fiscal incentives, the quality of public administration, political stability, family and cultural factors, and many others.[1]

What do neoclassical one-sector growth models, of the sort we studied in chapters 7 and 13, predict[2] about economic development in the long run? Figure 14.1(a) suggests that *history does not matter in the long run*. Countries with basically similar physical environments and apparent access to similar technologies may show temporary differences reflecting different initial conditions, but should not exhibit wide or persistent dispersion in growth rates. On the contrary, many of the growth models with which we are by now familiar (that is, the descriptive growth model, the optimal growth model, and, occasionally, the overlapping generations model as well) imply convergence to a unique steady state if we strengthen standard convexity assumptions with appropriate limit conditions like inequality (13.15). Figure 14.1(a) sums up the growth path implied by neoclassical models which satisfy these stronger assumptions.

What is the mechanism that impels neoclassical growth models eventually to converge to the same level of per capita income irrespective of starting conditions? How are national economies supposed to reach identical asymptotic levels of wealth per capita if the initial distribution of income over countries is very uneven? Changes in interest rates are at the heart of this convergence. Capital-poor countries have very high rates of interest which provide a strong incentive to invest for both domestic and foreign lenders. As these economies become richer, returns to capital decline along

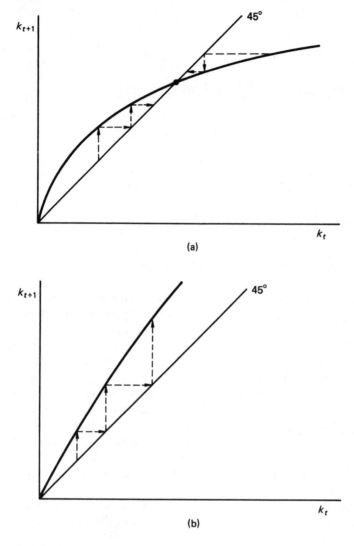

Figure 14.1 (a) Convergent growth with constant returns to scale; (b) unbounded growth with constant returns to scale.

with the marginal product of capital, incentives to invest are progressively weakened, growth slows down and eventually vanishes.

If the marginal product of capital does not vanish asymptotically but stabilizes instead at a sufficient high level, then perpetual growth without convergence is possible under constant returns to scale. This strikingly simple idea, worked out by Jones and Manuelli (1990), is easiest to illustrate in a descriptive growth model without technical change. Solow (1956) was clearly aware of this possibility; questions II.9 and II.16 ask the reader to construct optimal growth and overlapping generations economies with the same property.

Consider the asymptotic behavior of the dynamical system

$$k_{t+1} = sf(k_t) \tag{14.1}$$

where $F(K,L) = K^{\alpha}L^{1-\alpha} + bK$, and $\alpha \in [0,1]$, $b > 0$ $s \in (0,1)$ are constants. Rewriting (14.1) in closed form, we obtain

$$k_{t+1} = s(k_t^{\alpha} + bk_t) \qquad (14.2)$$

and observe that $(k_{t+1}/k_t) \rightarrow sb$ as $k_t \rightarrow \infty$.

If $sb > 1$, then equation (14.2) has a unique unstable steady state at $k = 0$ and *no* stable steady state. This economy is so productive that the capital–labor ratio rises without bound. Figure 14.1(b) shows how orbits starting at $k_1 > 0$ permit capital and output to grow without bound. The example above is not of great empirical relevance for it implies that labor's share of output will vanish in the limit; it does, however, stress that *long-run growth is hard to account for unless the marginal product of physical or human capital is bounded sufficiently far away from zero*.

A bound of the general type suggested by Jones and Manuelli seems a necessity because international evidence on growth rates in per capita income reveals that striking inequalities persist in the development patterns of nations. Some countries are able to sustain high growth rates over long periods of time, others advance at acceptable if not spectacular rates, while still others seem to stagnate in low-growth "traps," exhibiting persistently slow rates of growth or relatively modest levels of economic development, or both. Tables 14.1–14.5 illustrate the relative economic performance in the last two centuries of several developed and less developed countries, with special reference to Britain whose historical records seem to be the oldest.

These persistent differences are not explained by faster growth in early stages of development, that is, by poorer countries growing faster as they converge to the steady state and catch up with richer countries. From table 14.4 we see, for instance, that Norway experienced accelerating growth for a whole century (1867–1965) while Egypt and India grew more slowly than the richer countries of Western Europe and North America. Table 14.5 shows that each of the three countries in the sample which grew fastest between 1940 and 1970 (Japan, Greece, and Finland) started out with higher per capita income than any of the three slowest growing countries (Egypt, Thailand, and India).

Data compiled by Baumol (1986) and Baumol and Wolff (1988) indicate that "growth miracles" tend to occur most often among middle income countries, thus lending support to the suspicion that history may matter for economic growth, as in figures 13.2(a),(b), or (d). In fact, upper middle income countries as a group have been expanding a good deal more rapidly than the very poorest countries since 1965. For example, six of the world's slowest growing nations (that is, those with per capita gross national product (GNP) growth rates below *minus* 1.5 percent per annum in 1965–85) were in sub-Saharan Africa, and already belonged among the very poorest in 1965.

One explanation, of course, is that persistent differences in national economic performance are due entirely to systematic variations across countries in culture, religion, national character, economic policies, or broadly defined social institutions, that is, to economically "exogenous" factors. This chapter explores the alternative possibility that sustainable differences in per capita growth rates may appear even among economies with similar social and institutional structures.

To understand why the long-term growth paths of different nations may not converge, we shall explore in sections 14.2–14.6 several extensions of the elementary one-sector neoclassical growth model developed in chapter 13.

Table 14.1 Development indices for the UK (1751 = 100)

Year	Population	GNP per capita
1701	93	81
1751	100	100
1791	131	117
1831	222	192
1871	354	301
1911	554	455
1985	765	1,238

Table 14.2 Early Britain versus contemporary Kenya

Britain (1751 = 100)			Kenya (1964 = 100)		
Year	Population	GNP	Year	Population	GNP
1751	100	100	1964	100	100
1771	114	120	1969	117	130
1791	131	153	1974	139	174
1811	164	217	1979	165	201
1831	222	426	1984	209	232

Sources: Deane and Cole, 1969; *International Financial Statistics*, various years; World Bank, World Development Report 1987

Table 14.3 Share of agriculture in national income (%)

	1870	1970
Britain	15	3
France	45	6
USA	30	3
Japan	63	7
Sweden	43	4

Source: Cipolla, 1974

Table 14.4 Comparative long-run rates of growth

Country	Time period	GNP per capita (beginning of period)	GNP per capita (end of period)	Growth rate
Britain	1922–65		1,870	16.9
France	1896–1965		2,047	18.6
Germany	1910–65		1,939	20.5
Italy	1897–1927	271		16.9
	1927–52			14.3
	1952–65		1,100	60.4
Japan	1890–1910	79		25.5
	1910–27			32.8
	1927–53			9.9
	1953–65		876	128.4
USA	1800–40			13.5
	1840–74			13.9
	1874–94			20.3
	1890–1910			20.1
	1905–27			16.5
	1927–52			19.2
	1952–65		3,580	20.8
Norway	1867–90			10.8
	1890–1910			14.3
	1910–27			21.4
	1927–52			29.1
	1952–65			38.0
Australia	1902–65	930	2,023	13.1
Argentina	1902–65		811	10.1
Mexico	1897–1965		461	18.2
Ghana	1901–65		312	15.6
Philippines	1902–65		255	10.3
Egypt	1897–1965		185	4.8
India	1905–65		84	6.8

All GNP figures are in constant (1965) US dollars. Growth rates are percent per decade.
Source: Azariadis and Drazen, 1990a

Table 14.5 Comparative medium-run rates of growth

Country	Percentage literacy		Per capita output		Growth in per capita output	
	1940	1960	1940[a]	1960[b,c]	1940–70[a]	1960–80[b]
Australia	98	99	1,128	5,182	2.88	2.41
Belgium	96	98	715	4,375	4.11	3.80
Canada	97	98	1,041	6,069	3.81	3.17
Chile	72	84	371	2,932	1.70	1.90
Colombia	56	63	190	1,362	2.13	3.19
Denmark	99	99	971	5,490	3.71	2.83
Egypt	15	26	167	496	0.64	3.54
Finland	91	99	419	4,073	5.35	3.68
Greece	67	80	187	1,474	5.91	5.60
Guatemala	35	32	78	1,268	5.06	2.18
Honduras	34	45	109	748	2.95	1.83
India	14	28	67	533	1.01	0.71
Ireland	99	99	665	2,562	2.11	3.33
Japan	80	98	260	2,237	6.32	6.66
Korea	31	71	–	700	–	6.28
Mexico	49	65	138	2,157	5.32	3.55
Netherlands	99	98	889	4,690	3.25	3.33
New Zealand	99	98	1,055	5,571	2.25	1.40
Nicaragua	37	53[d]	105	1,588	4.76	1.19
Panama	65	73	374	1,255	1.84	4.11
Peru	48	61	89	1,721	4.04	1.79
Philippines	62	72	113	885	2.33	2.84
Portugal	51	63	–	1,429	–	4.92
Spain	77	87	361	2,426	3.03	4.74
Sweden	99	99	1,091	5,149	4.17	2.75
Switzerland	99	100	1,246	6,834	2.92	1.93
Thailand	54	68	128	688	0.88	4.61
Turkey	21	38	212	1,255	1.66	3.12
UK	99	99	1,334	4,970	1.36	2.39
USA	96	98	1,549	7,380	3.45	2.20

[a] Real GNP in 1970 US dollars.
[b] Real GDP as computed by Summers and Heston (1988) in "international dollars," computed to take account of purchasing power differences.
[c] Columns for a given variable using World Bank versus Summers–Heston data are not easily comparable. The conversion factor from "international dollars" to real US dollars varies with the level of development. See Summers and Heston (1988).
[d] 1970 literacy.

Sources: World Bank, 1987; Summers and Heston, 1988; Azariadis and Drazen, 1990a

14.2 Demographic factors

One possible reason why the standard one-sector growth model with an exogenously fixed rate of population growth gives an oversimplified picture of the development process is that it ignores the determinants of population growth and its interaction with economic growth. Both the descriptive and the overlapping generations growth model suggest that per capita income in any stable steady state is a decreasing function of the rate of population growth. Let us examine how large a discrepancy in per capita income these growth models can justify on the basis of differences in purely exogenous population growth rates.

It is easiest to think now in terms of a specific parametrization of the Diamond model; readers who do question II.13 will draw similar conclusions from the descriptive growth model. Assume that the production function and the utility function are both Cobb-Douglas (the first in capital and labor, the second in youthful and old-age consumption), that capital depreciates fully, that labor supply is inelastic, and that the rate of population growth is exogenously fixed at $n \geqslant 0$.

The equality of saving and investment then yields

$$(1 + n)k_{t+1} = bk_t^\alpha \tag{14.3}$$

where k_t is the capital–labor ratio at t; α is capital's share of output; and $b = s(1 - \alpha)$ is a constant that has to do with the saving rate s.

Some discrepancies in per capita output can be attributed to differences in fertility. The steady state per capita income implied by equation (14.3) for a given value of n is $y(n) = (\bar{k})^\alpha$, where $\bar{k}$ is the stationary capital intensity. Hence

$$y(n) = \left(\frac{b}{1 + n}\right)^{\alpha/(1-\alpha)} \tag{14.4}$$

The ratio of per capita incomes of a country with constant population ($n = 0$) to one whose population doubles within a generation ($n = 1$), corresponding to an annual growth rate of close to 2.5 percent, is *not* very large. From (14.4) we see that

$$\frac{y(0)}{y(1)} = 2^{\alpha/(1-\alpha)} \tag{14.5}$$

Since α is typically one-half or less, this hypothetical income ratio equals 2 at most. The *World Development Report* lists per capita GNP figures that imply ratios as large as 150.

Actual populations do not grow at constant rates, and there is quite a bit of evidence that demographic growth interacts with both economic growth and scientific progress in many dimensions. The population of Britain, for example, rose by a modest 55 percent over the eighteenth century, expanded by a whopping 247 percent in the nineteenth, and by some 56 percent so far (1900–85) this century.[3] Historical population data often are of doubtful quality. As far as one can judge from available data, however, population growth seems to have spurted upward in several countries during the eighteenth century. The accelerating phase, or *first demographic transition*, begins about the year 1700 in China and Holland, nearer 1750 in Britain and Japan, about 1800 in India and Germany, and only very recently in sub-Saharan Africa.[4] The decelerating phase, or *second demographic transition*, begins about 1880 in Britain, is already complete in all developed countries, and shows signs of taking hold in the Third World. Once the two phases are complete, the evolution of population over time often looks like an S-shaped curve.

The experience of Europe illuminates the underlying causes of this S-shaped or "logistic" population growth pattern. In pre-industrial Europe, moderate fertility rates balanced mortality to keep population growth close to zero; given the level of technology, traditional economies could not support any significant expansion in the population. Changes in fertility induced changes in mortality in the same direction, keeping population growth close to zero. Similarly, a decrease in mortality led to reduced fertility via later marriages and fewer children.

With industrialization, life expectancy shot up in response to scientific and technological advances; both mortality and fertility declined. Even though earlier movements in fertility were at first responses to mortality changes, the reduction in fertility after industrialization seems to have been brought about by the desire to bear fewer children.

This decline in fertility, however, occurred only with a lag, so that population growth rates initially increased sharply in Western Europe and East Asia with the improvement in medical technology and public health. As fertility continued to decline in Europe and North America, the slowdown in life expectancy increases after 1900 meant that net population growth rates began to decline, resulting in the observed flattening of the population curve.

For many of the least developed countries, however, demographic variables have moved so fast as to completely overwhelm economic growth during the first demographic transition. Among the ten slowest-growing countries from 1965 to 1985 (that is, those whose per capita real income *declined* on average by 1 percent or more per year), seven were in the poorest income group. For low income countries as a whole, the annual growth rate in per capita GNP averaged about 0.4 percent or about *one-sixth* of the corresponding figure for industrial market economies. The aggregate GNP figures of these two groups do not appear to be growing at substantially different rates; it seems simply that too much of total growth is absorbed by population change in the very poorest economies.

Rapid changes in the size of national populations and in their sectoral distributions began in the eighteenth century. The expansion of industry and services attracted millions away from farming in small relatively isolated communities to work in urban centers (see table 14.3). This movement has lost some of its momentum in the most developed countries but continues to dominate many Third World economies and is swelling the population of conurbations like Cairo, Mexico City, and Seoul to figures that have no historical precedent.

Our understanding of how demography and development interact is hindered by the fact that neoclassical growth models with endogenous population growth are still in their earliest infancy;[5] some particularly simple cases are explored in Part I, section 9.3. It is still too early to reach any conclusions on that score. However, it makes little sense to take the rate of population growth as an exogenous datum in the longest of long runs. Doing so leaves unexplained too many regularities in recorded development history and may well hide from us some features of economic growth shared by widely dissimilar countries.

Table 14.2, for instance, shows that the development history of Kenya from 1964 to 1984 has tantalizing similarities to that of Britain from 1751 to 1831. Population and

GNP growth look similar until the British economic "take-off" that took place in the early nineteenth century. In both countries population expands much faster than per capita income; the population of Britain grows as fast every 20 years as the Kenyan population does in five. Of course, any similarity in development histories of two countries that are two centuries apart and one-and-a-half continents distant may very well be superficial or even a pure coincidence. The similarity, however, raises the question of whether these phenomena may reflect properties of economic growth that transcend time and geographic location, and are at least partly amenable to a common theoretical explanation. Can we learn something about the recent past of developing countries by looking at the economic history of developed ones?

14.3 Technical progress

Much of modern economic development stems from the invention and adoption of new products and production processes in farming, manufacturing, and services. From the cotton gin and the steam engine to the green revolution and microchips, economic improvements are the fruits of improved technology and, ultimately, of shared advances in scientific knowledge.

Technical progress raises the effectiveness of the services that society draws from physical and human capital, enabling one motor car to do the work of several horses, one word processor to do the work of several typewriters, and one educated person to perform the job of several untrained ones. The easiest way to explore the effect of technical progress on economic growth is to suppose that it is completely exogenous to the working of an economy, arising at some constant rate dictated by scientific advances. Alternative ways of thinking about technical progress are explored briefly in section 14.5 when we discuss increasing returns.

Until then, we continue to work with a standard constant-returns-to-scale aggregate production function $Y = F(K, L)$ whose inputs are the labor services and capital services hired by the representative producer. These services we now choose to measure in efficiency units rather than in physical units. Specifically, let us define efficiency-unit coefficients $(A_t, B_t)_{t=0}^{\infty}$ for capital and labor respectively. These are positive numbers that describe how many units of services can be extracted in each period from one physical unit of capital and labor.

A producer who hires an input vector (K_t, L_t) of physical units at t has available to him a vector $(A_t K_t, B_t L_t)$ of input services. As the coefficients (A_t, B_t) change over time, the resulting technical progress is called *neutral* because it preserves the ratio of factor shares if factor markets are competitive and factor prices are constant (see question II.30(a)). In particular, technical progress is called

Harrod-neutral (or labor-augmenting) if $A_t = A_0$ and $B_t > B_{t-1}$ for all t;
Hicks-neutral if $A_t > A_{t-1}$ and $B_t > B_{t-1}$ for all t;
Solow-neutral (or capital-augmenting) if $A_t > A_{t-1}$ and $B_t = B_0$ for all t.

Certain types of steady technical progress permit perpetual economic growth, converting the steady states of neoclassical growth models from constant sequences into geometric sequences in which all quantities grow at a common rate. We call such steadily growing sequences *balanced growth paths*. The main result here is the following.

Theorem 14.1 If technical change is Harrod-neutral at a constant rate γ and the utility function is homothetic, then steady states in the scalar Diamond model are balanced growth paths. Along these paths all quantities grow at the rate γ and all relative prices are constant.

Proving this result is quite simple. One begins from the fact (see question II.29) that homothetic utility functions, like the Cobb–Douglas, generate saving functions that are linearly homogeneous in the income vector. In the scalar Diamond model of the previous section, we may write the savings function

$$z(R,y) = s(R)y \tag{14.6}$$

where $s: \mathbb{R}_+ \to [0, 1]$ is the average propensity to save out of labor income. The income of a representative worker at time t

$$y_t = (1 + \gamma)^t w_t \tag{14.7}$$

is the product of the number of efficiency units this worker possesses and the wage rate per efficiency labor unit.

If we normalize to unity the stocks of both physical capital and labor at $t = 0$, the equality of the value of capital to household financial wealth at each t requires

$$(1 + \gamma)^{t+1}(1 + n)k_{t+1} = s(R_{t+1})y_t \tag{14.8}$$

Here k_t stands for *capital per efficiency labor unit*. Recalling that $R_t = 1 - \delta + f'(k_t)$ and $w_t = w(k_t) = f(k_t) - k_t f'(k_t)$ in any competitive factor-market equilibrium, we combine equations (14.7) and (14.8) to obtain

$$(1 + n)(1 + \gamma)k_{t+1} = w(k_t)s[1 - \delta + f'(k_{t+1})] \tag{14.9}$$

This is a nonlinear scalar system whose dynamical structure is very similar to the standard scalar Diamond model. To any positive steady state $\overline{k}$ of equation (14.9) corresponds a balanced growth path along which labor income is given by the geometric sequence $y_t = (1 + \gamma)^t w(\overline{k})$, capital per worker equals $(1 + \gamma)^t \overline{k}$, and output per worker is simply $(1 + \gamma)^t f(\overline{k})$.

Similar results will hold in the descriptive growth model for all three types of neutral technical progress (see question II.14). What is essential for the existence of balanced growth paths is that *both* the production function *and* the saving function be linearly homogeneous in the appropriate sense. Otherwise the steady state of the system will require all quantities, including income per worker, to be constant sequences.

Readers who have invested long years and large amounts of material resources to earn advanced degrees may wish to question the assumption that increases in labor productivity come about automatically with the passage of time. We explore next the more realistic alternative that improved human skills are the outcome of deliberate and costly investment in human capital.

14.4 Human capital (*)

The theory of human capital is a branch of labor economics, developed by Gary Becker (1964) and many other contributors, which studies the accumulation of marketable human skills by heredity, formal education, on-the-job training and other methods, and tries to explain how these skills influence earnings and job patterns.[6]

Unlike labor economists, we are interested in human capital purely as an engine of growth. Growth accountants like Denison (1974) attribute a large fraction of US economic growth to improvements in the quality of labor services; and capital theorists like Uzawa (1965) and Razin (1972) have studied the accumulation of human capital in the optimal growth model of Ramsey.

In this section we follow the footsteps of Uzawa and Razin with a twist: we recognize that people pick up useful skills not only at school and in job-training programs but also from other less formal sources like books, family members, experienced coworkers, etc. Our basic presumption is that the stock of skills that an individual possesses depends both on how much time he has invested in formal training and on what he has learned from others by osmosis, mainly as an automatic byproduct of social interactions.

The engine of economic growth in what follows comes directly from the *external effect* of these social interactions: a person who has acquired valuable skills by formal education or hard work manages to transmit some of them to a family member, colleague, or relative in a way that involves little time or resource cost.

To explore this particular source of growth, we return to the scalar Diamond model with constant population, full depreciation of physical capital, and one type of household per generation. Departing somewhat from chapter 13, we endow individual workers with 2 units of time, one in youth and one in old age, both of which are supplied inelastically to gainful activities. The quantity of labor services in efficiency units per unit time of work we call "human capital" and denote by the variable x. Human capital is simply an index of labor quality.

To keep things simple, we assume that all individuals have access to a common training technology which requires no pecuniary costs. This technology converts time investments when young to subsequent labor quality, enhancing the stock of knowledge, skills, or even the state of health, and thereby permitting a higher flow of labor services per unit time when workers are older. In particular, the flow of efficiency units of labor services from any old worker supplying labor at $t + 1$ is

$$x_{t+1} = x_t h(\tau_t) \tag{14.10}$$

where $\tau_t \in (0,1)$ is the fraction of time this worker invested at t in labor quality, that is, in formal education, training, or health maintenance. The remainder, $1 - \tau$, of each worker's youthful time endowment is supplied to the labor market. We assume h to be a weakly increasing and concave function of τ such that $h(x) \geq 0$ for all $x > 0$; and x_t is the quality of labor services achieved in old age by generation $t - 1$ and transmitted by osmosis to *all* young households of generation t.

A noteworthy feature of this specification is that different steady state values of τ, the fraction of time devoted to training, will yield different *rates of growth* in both human capital and labor services. This appears to be a natural assumption as long as educational attainment does not fully depreciate from one period to the next. Next period's stock of knowledge, x_{t+1}, attained by any individual should depend on currently available knowledge, and the change in x will depend on τ, that is, on how much time this individual has invested in improving his or her quality. The expression on the right-hand side of equation (14.10) is linearly homogeneous in x to help sustain balanced growth.

A young individual's labor supply decision is not trivial as in the models of chapter 13, for he must decide what fraction of his time to invest in training when young.

Assuming that training provides zero non-pecuniary benefits, τ is simply chosen to maximize discounted lifetime income:

$$(1 - \tau_t)w_t x_t + \frac{w_{t+1} x_t h(\tau_t)}{R_{t+1}} \tag{14.11}$$

Maximizing over τ_t leads to a first-order condition

$$R_{t+1} = \frac{w_{t+1}}{w_t} h'(\tau_t) \tag{14.12}$$

which equates the yields on human and physical capital at any interior maximum.

Because all individuals in this model have equal ability and equal access to credit (facing the same schedule h and the same rate of interest), they will choose identical investments. As a result, equations (14.10) and (14.12) describe the evolution of "average" labor quality x_t. Total labor supply in effective units is then $L_t = (1 - \tau_t) x_t + x_t$, that is, the sum of quality-adjusted labor supply by the young and the old.

The market clearing conditions which a dynamic equilibrium must satisfy are equations (14.10) and (14.12) plus the usual equality of saving to investment. Recall now that the saving function $z(R, y_1, y_2)$ for an individual who has income y_1 in youth and y_2 in old age, and may borrow or lend at an interest factor R, is

$$z(R, y_1, y_2) = \underset{z}{\text{argmax}} \; u(y_1 - z, y_2 + Rz) \tag{14.13}$$

This saving function is linearly homogeneous in (y_1, y_2) whenever the utility function $u:\mathbb{R}_t^2 \to \mathbb{R}$ is homothetic, that is,

$$z(R, \lambda y_1, \lambda y_2) = \lambda z(R, y_1, y_2) \text{ for all } \lambda > 0 \tag{14.14}$$

Given a homothetic preference map, then, we may easily write down the market clearing conditions for the human capital extension of the overlapping generations growth model once we understand that the net labor income vector of a typical worker in generation t,

$$y^t = (y_1^t, y_2^t) = [(1 - \tau_t)x_t w_t, x_{t+1} w_{t+1}] \tag{14.15}$$

is the product of wage rates for efficiency units of labor with the number of efficiency units the worker supplies to the labor market. In other words, we have

$$L_{t+1} k_{t+1} = z[R_{t+1}, w_t x_t (1 - \tau_t), w_{t+1} x_{t+1}] \tag{14.16a}$$

$$R_{t+1} = f'(k_{t+1}) \tag{14.16b}$$

$$w_t = f(k_t) - k_t f'(k_t) \tag{14.16c}$$

$$L_t = (2 - \tau_t) x_t \tag{14.16d}$$

$$R_{t+1} = \frac{w_{t+1}}{w_t} h'(\tau_t) \tag{14.16e}$$

$$x_{t+1} = x_t h(\tau_t) \tag{14.16f}$$

These equations describe dynamical competitive equilibria in which k_t denotes capital *per unit of efficiency labor services*. Specifically, (14.16a) balances investment with saving; equations (14.16b) and (14.16c) are factor demands while (14.16d) and (14.16f) trace the evolution of physical and human capital inputs.

The role of human capital in the growth process is described by equations (14.16e) and (14.16f); (14.16e) is the first-order condition for individual choice of labor quality by homogeneous individuals while (14.16f) gives the evolution of aggregate skills implied by individual decisions. A steady state of the economy that evolves according to these equations is a competitive equilibrium in which intensive variables such as τ and k are constant over time while extensive variables like c_t^1, c_t^2, x_t, K_t, L_t, and Y_t will typically grow at constant rates. Below we focus exclusively on steady states.[7]

If the utility function is homothetic, steady states are balanced growth paths compactly described by the equations

$$(2 - \tau)h(\tau)k = z[f'(k), (1 - \tau)w(k), h(\tau)w(k)] \tag{14.17a}$$

$$R = h'(\tau) = f'(k) \tag{14.17b}$$

$$x_t = [h(\tau)]^t \tag{14.17c}$$

where x_0, the beginning-of-time labor quality, has been normalized to unity.

The homotheticity assumption means that the savings function is linearly homogeneous in the income profile, so that equations (14.17a) and (14.17b) reduce to

$$\frac{k}{w(k)} = z\left[f'(k), \frac{1 - \tau}{(2 - \tau)h(\tau)}, \frac{1}{2 - \tau}\right] \tag{14.18a}$$

$$h'(\tau) = f'(k) \tag{14.18b}$$

On the usual assumption that consumption when young and old are both strict normal goods and gross substitutes, the savings function z is increasing in its first and second arguments, decreasing in the third. This implies that the right-hand side of equation (14.18a) is decreasing in both k and τ, because increases in τ are easily shown to depress first-period and raise second-period income. Thus a sufficient condition for (14.18a) to describe a downward-sloping frontier in (k, τ) space is that $k/w(k)$ be an increasing function for k, or (as we know from chapter 13, note 6) that $(kf'/f)(1 - kf''/f') < 1$. This inequality requires the elasticity of substitution between capital and labor services, $\sigma = -(f'/kff'')(f - kf')$, to exceed capital's share of output at every capital–labor ratio.

Equation (14.18b), on the other hand, traces an upward-sloping line in (k, τ) space when both sorts of capital exhibit diminishing returns, so that at most one solution to (14.18a), (14.18b) exists. A sufficient condition for existence is that both f and h are continuous functions satisfying appropriate boundary conditions in their respective arguments.[8] In this case, equations (14.18a) and (14.18b) possess a unique solution, that is, a balanced growth path supported by labor-augmenting technical progress in the accumulation of human capital. This progress stems from external effects in the transmission of marketable skills among members of successive generations.

14.5 Increasing returns

One reason why the long-term growth rates of different nations fail to converge may well be that economic development provides its own stimulus to the production possibilities of a given economy: as product per capita rises, state variables like physical capital and the stock of knowledge become more favorable to economic expansion and are, in turn, stimulated by that expansion. Underlying this line of thinking[9] is some form of production externalities such as interactions among different types of physical capital or even of human capital like the ones we saw in section 14.4. All of these externalities lead to increasing returns to scale in production.

Let us recall the definition of constant and increasing returns. Suppose $F: \mathbb{R}_+^2 \rightarrow \mathbb{R}_+$ is a twice differentiable map that describes how a (capital, labor) input vector is transformed into output. For a given input vector $(K_0, L_0) > 0$ and a number $\lambda > 0$, we define output as

$$Y(\lambda) = F(\lambda K_0, \lambda L_0) \tag{14.19}$$

Then returns to scale are *constant* if $Y(\lambda) = \lambda Y(1)$ for all $\lambda > 0$, *increasing* if $Y(\lambda) > \lambda Y(1)$ for all $\lambda > 1$, *decreasing* if $Y(\lambda) < \lambda Y(1)$ for all $\lambda > 1$. Figure 14.2(a) illustrates this.

The most convenient way to understand increasing returns is through a distinction between the *current private inputs* (K_t^i, L_t^i) hired by producer i and a vector A_t of *social or predetermined* inputs which this producer cannot affect at time t. In A_t we may in principle count economywide averages of private inputs (learning from peers), lagged values of private inputs or output (learning by doing), or intangible but variable factors of production (the stock of useful knowledge). Output at firm i may now be written as

$$Y_t = H(K_t, L_t, A_t) \tag{14.20}$$

where $H: \mathbb{R}_+^{2+n} \rightarrow \mathbb{R}_+$ is a production function with many inputs which is still linearly homogeneous in (K, L) but also depends on an n-vector of exogenous or predetermined variables A_t.

Four of the more compelling stories that we have for increasing returns to scale are of particular relevance to economic development. We review these in turn.

Infrastructure

The exposition here draws heavily on a paper by Murphy et al. (1989) but the basic idea goes back to Rosenstein-Rodan's (1943) investigation of the proper role for government capital in economic development (see also section 21.3). By government capital we mean objects such as bridges, highways, and health clinics which may increase the productivity of private factor inputs.

For any given vector of private inputs (K, L), suppose that private output is an increasing function of government capital G, that is

$$H(K, L, G) = A(G)F(K, L) \tag{14.21}$$

where F is a constant-returns-to-scale production function and the scale factor $A: \mathbb{R}_+ \rightarrow \mathbb{R}_+$ is an increasing function of G. Government capital in this specification causes Hicks-neutral technical progress. If public capital is produced from private output at the ratio 1:1, net output is $H(K, L, G) - G$. For any G, aggregate returns to scale may be defined with the aid of the net output function

$$Y(\lambda, G) = A(G)F(\lambda K_0, \lambda L_0) - G \tag{14.22}$$

How should the government choose G? One way is to maximize net output, that is, to compute the envelope

$$Y^*(\lambda) = \max_{G \geq 0} Y(\lambda, G) \tag{14.23}$$

of $Y(\lambda, G)$ as the parameter G varies. Figure 14.2(b) shows that this envelope exhibits increasing returns to scale: as production or trade grow, the government builds up the infrastructure which, in turn, stimulates economic activity more than in proportion.

For a parametric example, we suppose that the government can choose to invest $G = \{0, G_1, G_2\}$ on a road linking two villages. At $G = 0$ it simply maintains a dirt road cleared by private interests; a simple asphalt road costs $G_1 > 0$, and a modern two-lane highway costs $G_2 > G_1$. The proper public investment plan is for the government to spend nothing if the index of net economic activity is in the low interval between zero and $Y(\lambda_1, G_1)$; to spend G_1 if that index is in the middle interval between $Y(\lambda_1, G_1)$ and $Y(\lambda_1, G_2)$; and to spend G_2 if the index is above $Y(\lambda_1, G_2)$.

Learning by doing

Arrow (1962) reasoned that "experience" was a legitimate factor of production since the productivity of labor inputs tends to grow markedly after they become familiar with the production process in which they are engaged.

To explore the implication for growth of the link between past work and current productivity, we investigate a scalar Diamond model with a constant population of identical households possessing homothetic preferences. Let us assume that the current supply of efficiency labor units depends positively on past input use, that is,

$$L_t = \Gamma(K_{t-1}, L_{t-1}) \tag{14.24a}$$

where $\Gamma: \mathbb{R}_+^2 \to \mathbb{R}_+$ is an increasing linearly homogeneous function. An example is $\Gamma = bF$ for some constant $b > 0$, which says that current labor services are proportional to output in the previous period. Linear homogeneity means that

$$\frac{L_t}{L_{t-1}} = \gamma(k_{t-1}) \tag{14.24b}$$

where $\gamma(k) \equiv N(k, 1)$ is also an increasing function.

The familiar equality of saving and investment for an economy with homothetic preferences becomes

$$k_{t+1} L_{t+1} = L_t w(k_t) s[f'(k_{t+1})] \tag{14.25}$$

where $s: \mathbb{R}_+ \to [0,1]$ is the average propensity to save out of labor income, k_t is the capital per efficiency labor unit and w_t is wage per efficiency labor unit. Combining (14.24b) and (14.25) we obtain the difference equation

$$k_{t+1} = \frac{s[f'(k_{t+1})] w(k_t)}{\gamma(k_t)} \tag{14.26}$$

Every stationary equilibrium $\bar{k} > 0$ of this equation is a balanced growth path, that is, a competitive equilibrium in which all extensive variables (incomes, output, capital, consumption, saving, etc.) grow at the rate $\gamma(\bar{k})$. Section 9.3 in Part I shows that asymptotically stable balanced growth paths exist if γ is "not too sensitive" to

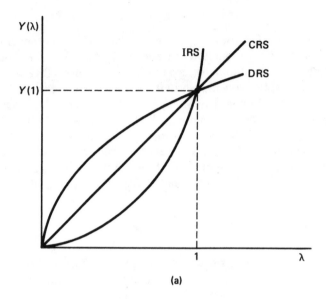

(a)

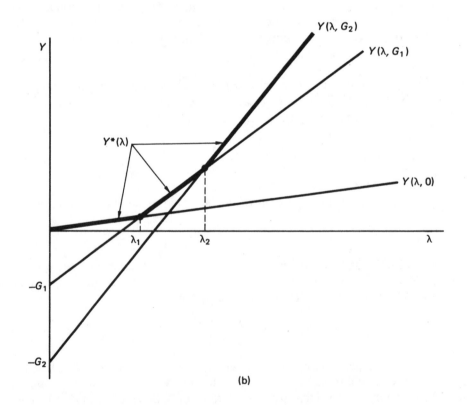

(b)

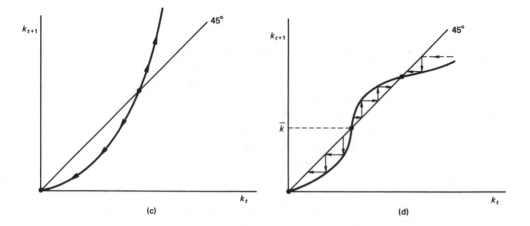

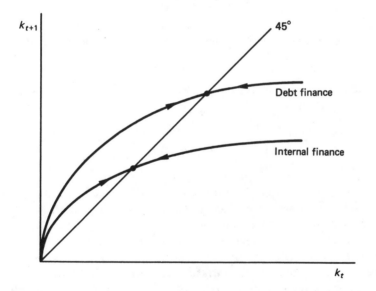

Figure 14.2 Decreasing (DRS), constant (CRS), and increasing (IRS) returns to scale; (b) increasing returns from infrastructure; (c) wealth-dependent growth with increasing returns to scale; (d) a development trap; (e) intermediated versus unintermediated growth.

changes in the capital–labor ratio. If it is, then limit cycles will appear and, in extreme cases, even chaotic paths of equilibrium growth.

Technological spillovers

What happens if the production possibilities of one firm depend on what inputs another firm employs? Technological externalities from pollution and congestion are one familiar example of such *negative* spillovers. A *positive* production externality with direct relevance to economic development is the social productivity of private factors of production. If workers at the Acme Hardware Store are in good health they will have few sick days but, in addition, they will not transmit any contagious diseases to their friends who work next door at the Superfresh Fruit Market. The number of sick days in the two stores is positively correlated and so, to some extent, must be overall labor productivity.

Romer (1986) and Lucas (1988) develop the idea of technological externalities (from knowledge and the quality of human capital, respectively) into an engine of growth in neoclassical growth models of the Ramsey type. Their formulations combine individually constant returns to scale with increasing returns at the aggregate level. To be specific, suppose that $F: \mathbb{R}_+^2 \to \mathbb{R}_+$ is a standard linearly homogeneous production function and $A: \mathbb{R}_+^2 \to \mathbb{R}_+$ and $B: \mathbb{R}_+^2 \to \mathbb{R}_+$ are two increasing functions that represent scale factors or efficiency unit coefficients. Then the output of firm i at time t is

$$Y_t^i = F[A(K_t, L_t)K_t^i, B(K_t, L_t)L_t^i] \tag{14.27}$$

where (K_t^i, L_t^i) is the vector of inputs hired by firm i and (K_t, L_t) is a vector of economywide averages. Assuming that all producers are identical, we shall have

$$K_t^i = K_t \qquad L_t^i = L_t \qquad \text{for all } t, i \tag{14.28}$$

in any equilibrium. The aggregate production function clearly exhibits increasing returns because, for any $\lambda > 1$:

$$Y(\lambda) = F[A(\lambda K_0, \lambda L_0)\lambda K_0, B(\lambda K_0, \lambda L_0)\lambda L_0]$$
$$> F[A(K_0, L_0)\lambda K_0, B(K_0, L_0)\lambda L_0] = \lambda Y(1) \tag{14.29}$$

since A and B are monotone and F is linearly homogeneous.

The reason is quite simple: if all firms were to double their input use they would cause themselves a direct effect that doubles their output and an indirect effect that raises all scale factors and boosts output even more. In other words, *there are constant private returns to scale and increasing social returns to scale.*

To grasp the consequences of this phenomenon for growth, we work out the dynamical equilibria of a parametrized economy in which an increasing-returns technology powers an otherwise standard scalar overlapping generations system. Suppose, in particular, that the number of workers is constant (normalized to 1), the depreciation rate is 1, the saving rate is another constant $s \in (0,1)$, and producers $i = 1,\ldots, H$ use an identical technology:

$$Y_t^i = (K_t^\gamma L_t^\beta)(K_t^i)^\alpha (L_t^i)^{(1-\alpha)} \tag{14.30}$$

where $A(K, L) = B(K, L) = K^\gamma L^\beta$ are scale factors which depend on aggregate input use and (K^i, L^i) are private inputs. The constants α, β, γ satisfy $\alpha \in [0,1]$, $\beta > 0$, $\gamma > 0$.

Full employment requires that $L_t = 1$ for all t; hence the wage rate at time t is

$$w_t = A_t(1 - \alpha)k_t^\alpha = (1 - \alpha)k_t^{\alpha+\gamma} \tag{14.31}$$

Dynamical equilibria equate saving with investment in each period and are described by sequences (k_t) that satisfy $k_{t+1} = sw_t$, that is,

$$k_{t+1} = s(1 - \alpha)k_t^{\alpha+\gamma} \tag{14.32}$$

This equation describes an increasing time map through the origin.

If the degree γ of aggregate increasing returns to physical capital is not too large, then $\alpha + \gamma < 1$ and the time map is concave, exactly like figure 14.1(a). There is an unstable steady state at $k = 0$ and an asymptotically stable steady state $k > 0$. Increasing returns *do not affect* the qualitative behavior of equilibrium trajectories and, in particular, cannot support unbounded growth.

On the other hand, particularly strong increasing returns will mean $\alpha + \gamma > 1$, and a convex map. As figure 14.2(c) shows, increasing returns affect the qualitative properties of growth paths in a substantive way. There are two steady states, an asymptotically stable one at $k = 0$ and an unstable one at some $\bar{k} > 0$. Furthermore, the asymptotic behavior of equilibrium trajectories depends on the initial wealth of the economy. If $k_1 \in (0, \bar{k})$, the economy starts with an insufficient stock of wealth and converges to $k = 0$ which we may interpret as a primitive form of a *development or poverty map*. Given a large enough stock of wealth, that is, $k_1 > \bar{k}$, the economy will experience unbounded growth, as in the Jones–Manuelli model depicted in figure 14.1(b).

Threshold externalities

Azariadis and Drazen (1990a) propose another mechanism that delivers wealth-dependent growth and, specifically, multiple asymptotically stable steady states the worst of which has the natural interpretation of a development map. Suppose, for example, that output per worker is $y = A(k)f(k)$, again the product of a standard intensive production function and a scale function that embodies social increasing returns to scale.

The key idea here is that returns to scale are constant except for a threshold region $k \in [k_a, k_b]$ over which they are rapidly increasing. We may think of that interval as a hurdle area on which state variables (for example physical capital, human capital, the stock of knowledge, the division of labor, product variety, the state of health) achieve a *critical mass* that sustains the process of economic development.

If the threshold region contains an unstable steady state, it should divide the state space into two regions: one is $[0, k_a]$ and the other is $[k_b, \infty]$. Each of these regions will typically include at least one asymptotically stable state. The lowest of these states may be thought of as a development trap attracting all trajectories that start with a sufficiently small capital stock. An example is the origin in figure 14.2(d) which traps all orbits starting in the region $(0, \bar{k})$.

14.6 The role of financial markets (*)

This section contains an elementary exploration of a phenomenon that Gurley and Shaw (1967), McKinnon (1973), and others have called "financial deepening," that is, the observed tendency of the financial sector to grow faster than the economy as a whole along any respectable growth path.[10] How important are financial markets to economic development as a whole?

By "financial deepening" we generally mean the evolution of credit markets toward the ideal mode of operation assumed in the theory of competitive general equilibrium: borrowers and lenders of the same risk type face the same interest rate, and everyone may borrow up to the present value of his lifetime income.

Judging how close actual credit markets come to being perfect is not a trivial matter; one may use various yardsticks to measure the efficiency of financial intermediaries, for example the gap between the yield on low-risk bank loans and bank deposits, the ratio of loans to GNP, the incidence of credit rationing, etc. For the time being we suppose that financial deepening is driven by a secular reduction in the costs of verifying the riskiness of individual borrowers, that is, by improvements in the ability of intermediaries to assess correctly the true risk of each loan.

What are banks supposed to do in a growing economy? What is the unique service performed by intermediaries that makes the credit market so important to economic development? The very term "intermediary" means a go-between, in this case one that links ultimate borrowers with ultimate lenders. If this link were broken, producers would be unable to go into debt and all investment would have to be financed by retained earnings and other internal sources of funding.

Another important function of banks, pointed out by Tobin (1963), is to spread the risks of individual investment projects over a large and diverse asset portfolio, much as insurance companies spread the risks of individual accidents over a large number of policy holders. Each loan finances an investment project that will go bankrupt with some probability and force the intermediary to forgo interest income or even the principal amount originally lent out. Banks allow for these losses by adjusting their loan rates to reflect the risk of bankruptcy, exactly as insurance companies adjust the premiums of their auto insurance policies for risks of fire, collision, and other accidents.

If the risks of bankruptcy for individual projects are independent, an intermediary that finances many relatively small projects (that is, one that does not tie up a significant fraction of its loans with any single borrower) is assured *by the law of large numbers* that the actual rate of return on its loan portfolio will be very close to the rate it expected to earn before it learned the outcome of the investment projects it was funding. This means that well-diversified loan portfolios will earn normal rates of return.

Economies with highly developed credit markets enable financial institutions to hold loan portfolios that are free from idiosyncratic risks specific to individual borrowers. These banks are able, in turn, to offer their depositors private deposit insurance in the form of contracts that guarantee the yield on deposits. Such guarantees are not possible in economies with imperfect credit markets; in these, borrowers must finance some fraction of their investment costs out of their own income from equity, from retained earnings, or from current cash flow, and are thereby obliged to bear some or all of their individual investment risks.

To grasp what smoothly operating financial markets mean for economic development, we shall compare the operating properties of two benchmark dynamic economies: a fairly standard scalar Diamond economy of heterogeneous producers with a perfect credit market, and an otherwise similar economy in which financial intermediaries have been *artificially removed*. Investment projects will be financed by debt in the first economy, purely by internal funds in the second one. Heterogeneity is essential to this comparison: any lack of financial intermediation is unlikely to affect a representative–agent economy in which the typical worker saves in youth exactly as much as he will need to borrow in old age, when he becomes the typical entrepreneur.

Perfect financial markets

We start with a simple generalization of the overlapping generations one-sector model of capital accumulation to which we add heterogeneous producers. As usual, we have one consumption good produced under constant returns to scale from two inputs, capital and labor. Population is constant, consisting of overlapping cohorts, each with unit mass and (with the exception of the very first) a lifespan of two periods.

Cohorts are identical replicas of each other and contain a *continuum* of heterogeneous households. Within each cohort, in particular, there is a mass $1 - \lambda$ of individual workers (called L-types) who are endowed in old age with the safe constant-returns-to-scale technology $F(K, N)$, whereas the remaining fraction λ of workers are high risk (H-type) producers in old age; their output is $F(K/p, N)$ with probability $p \in (0, 1)$ and zero with probability $1 - p$. The vector (K, N) denotes the inputs of capital and labor services, and production risks of individual projects are assumed to be independent of each other.

The production function $F: \mathbb{R}_+^2 \to \mathbb{R}_+$ has all the standard properties we discussed in chapter 13. Capital is identical to the consumption good and depreciates completely on production, which means that the capital rental rate is equal to one plus *some* rate of interest. All individuals are assumed to be price takers.

Producers borrow capital in "youth," one period before their individual uncertainty is resolved, and hire labor in "old age" after the resolution of uncertainty. In particular, L-type firms will always hire labor, repay debts, and make zero profits, just like producers in standard risk-free neoclassical growth theory. H-type firms operate exactly like L-types if their factor productivity turns out to be positive. If, on the other hand, factor productivity is zero, high risk firms are unable to repay their loans, hire any labor, or make any profit. Their entire capital is forgone without any damage to them; the loss is borne by financial intermediaries which possess reliable advance information as to the type of each borrower.

As we discussed earlier, the large number (literally, continuum) of producers allows banks fully to diversify individual project uncertainty. Assuming free entry in banking, financial intermediaries will exploit the law of large numbers and make zero economic profit by holding diversified loan portfolios and offering *safe* deposit contracts to savers. These savers are merely workers at firms operating "today" whose loans will finance production by successful firms "tomorrow." No uncertainty whatsoever remains at the aggregate level.

Assume that financial intermediaries incur no operating costs in transforming deposits into loans. In order to pay depositors a safe gross yield r, banks that earn zero profits must charge r on safe loans to L-type firms and r/p on risky loans to H-type firms. This kind of price "discrimination" is made possible by the full knowledge that banks possess about borrower types. Each risky loan will then return zero *expected* profit: intermediary revenues per unit of risky loan will be r/p with probability p and zero with probability $1 - p$.

The law of large numbers ensures that each bank will make very close to zero *actual* profit from a well-diversified portfolio. In fact, the bank's expected revenue per unit lent out is r while the variance of revenue, $p(r/p - r)^2 + (1 - p)(0 - r)^2$, is easily shown to equal $r^2(1/p - 1)$. Low values of p thus correspond to risky loans.

Individuals have a common lifetime leisure endowment $(1,0)$ which they supply inelastically to producers and a cardinal utility function $u(c_1) + p_i v(c_2) + (1 - p_i)v(\hat{c}_2)$ where the probability p_i of solvency in old age for agent $i = H, L$ satisfies

$$p_H = p \in (0,1) \qquad p_L = 1 \tag{14.33}$$

We also denote c_1, consumption in youth; c_2, consumption when solvent in old age; $\hat{c}_2$, consumption when bankrupt in old age; R_i, loan rate (that is, gross yield on solvent loans) for type $i = H, L$; D, debt; B, bank deposit; and Q, internal finance or "equity" investment.

Zero bank profits imply that the interest factor charged to a borrower of type i satisfies

$$R_i = r/p_i \tag{14.34}$$

Given factor prices (w, r), an individual whose investment project will succeed with probability p faces a consumption vector

$$c_1 = w - B - Q \tag{14.35a}$$

$$\hat{c}_2 = rB \tag{14.35b}$$

$$c_2 = rB + \pi(D, Q, p) \tag{14.35c}$$

Here $B + Q$ is total saving and $\pi(D, Q, p)$ is the maximal profit of an entrepreneur with debt D, internal investment Q, and probability of success p. Note that

$$\pi = \max_{N \geq 0} \left[F\left(\frac{Q + D}{p}, N \right) - RD - wN \right]$$

$$= \max_{N \geq 0} \left[\left(\frac{Q + D}{p} \right) F_K - RD + N(F_N - w) \right] \qquad \text{by Euler's law}$$

$$= \max_{N \geq 0} \left[\left(\frac{Q + D}{p} \right) F_K\left(\frac{Q + D}{p}, N \right) - \frac{rD}{p} \right]$$

because $F_N = w$ and $pR = r$ in equilibrium. Since $F_K = r$ also holds true in equilibrium, entrepreneurial profit is

$$\pi = rQ/p \tag{14.36}$$

For given (w, r, p) each consumer will choose $(B, Q, D) \geq 0$ to maximize $V = u(c_1) + pv(c_2) + (1 - p)v(\hat{c}_2)$ subject to

$$c_1 = w - B - Q \geq 0 \tag{14.37a}$$

$$c_2 = rB + rQ/p \geq 0 \tag{14.37b}$$

$$\hat{c}_2 = rB \geq 0 \tag{14.37c}$$

Equation (14.37c) says that bank deposits are needed to ensure positive consumption in bankruptcy states. The higher $1 - p$ is, the more important this objective becomes; individuals with low p will thus look more like depositors and less like entrepreneurs.

Internal finance, on the other hand, is not very desirable for it is an asset dominated by bank deposits. Recall from equation (14.36) that internal funds yield r/p with probability p (solvency) and zero with probability $1 - p$ (bankruptcy); the expected rate of return on *risky* internal funds is therefore r, exactly equal to the yield on *riskless* bank deposits. In fact, setting $Q = 0$ allows entrepreneurs to exploit the diversifying role of financial intermediaries, shifting all investment risk to banks and ensuring that their old-age consumption is completely riskless.[11]

With this observation, the first-order conditions for the consumer's problem become

$$r[pv'(c_2) + (1 - p)v'(\hat{c}_2)] = u'(c_1) \tag{14.38a}$$

$$F_K(D/p, N) = r \tag{14.38b}$$

$$c_1 = w - B \tag{14.38c}$$

$$c_2 = rB = \hat{c}_2 \tag{14.38d}$$

We rewrite these in the form

$$rv'(c_2) = u'(c_1) \tag{14.39a}$$

$$f'(k/p) = r \tag{14.39b}$$

$$c_1 = w - z \tag{14.39c}$$

$$c_2 = rz = \hat{c}_2 \tag{14.39d}$$

where $k = D/N$ is the debt-to-labor ratio. Because all individuals face the same deposit yield r, equation (14.39b) implies the following equality between effective capital–labor ratios:

$$k^H/p = k^L \tag{14.40}$$

If K_t^i denotes debt (capital investment) contracted by type i at $t - 1$, then total loans at t are

$$\lambda K_{t+1}^H + (1-\lambda)K_{t+1}^L = \lambda k_{t+1}^H N_{t+1}^H + (1 - \lambda) k_{t+1}^L N_{t+1}^L$$
$$= k_{t+1}^L[\lambda p N_{t+1}^H + (1 - \lambda)N_{t+1}^L] \qquad \text{by equation (14.40)}$$
$$= k_{t+1}^L$$

by normalizing total labor supply to unity.

In equilibrium, loans and deposits are equal at each t. If we define

$$k_t = k_t^L = k_t^H/p \tag{14.41}$$

then every dynamical equilibrium solves the familiar scalar Diamond relation

$$k_{t+1} = z[f'(k_{t+1}), w(k_t)] \tag{14.42}$$

Output per worker, the yield on bank deposits, and all consumption vectors are independent of (λ, p). In fact, *equilibrium allocations are independent of personal attributes* because the law of large numbers operates perfectly here; it neutralizes the higher moments of all random variables and permits projects to be evaluated by their expected yield alone.

Purely internal finance

What damages would the economy described by equation (14.42) suffer if we abolished the credit market arbitrarily but still kept a competitive labor market? Lacking a credit market, individuals may not hold safe bank deposits and must save instead by financing their own risky investment project. Individual asset portfolios thus consist entirely of risky assets, and the resulting uncertainty in the rate of return will influence household saving.

As Leland (1968) and Sandmo (1971) demonstrated some time ago, an *increase* in the riskiness of interest rates is certainty-equivalent to a *reduction* in expected yields, lowering the flow of saving whenever individual households exhibit decreasing absolute risk aversion. Hence, we should expect that a switch from debt finance to internal finance will diminish saving, reduce the capital–labor ratio and depress income in the steady state.

To see this more clearly, we denote by Q_i the amount of internal capital, by $k_i = Q_i/N_i$ the capital–labor ratio, and by N_i the employment of type $i = $ H,L. Then consumers would have no way of providing for consumption in bankruptcy states either by bank deposits or otherwise. Each individual will instead be solving a problem of the form

$$(P) \max_{(k_i, N_i)} \{u(w - k_i N_i) + p_i v[N_i f(k_i/p_i) - N_i w]\}$$

where w is the common wage rate. Euler's law yields

$$w = f\left(\frac{k_i}{p_i}\right) - \frac{k_i}{p_i} f'\left(\frac{k_i}{p_i}\right) \qquad i \equiv \text{H, L} \tag{14.43}$$

which implies that equation (14.41) still holds. Call k_t the value of this common ratio for period t. From the first-order conditions for (P) we have

$$\frac{u'(c_{1i})}{v'(c_{2i})} = f'\left(\frac{k_i}{p_i}\right) \tag{14.44}$$

With explicit time subscripts, (14.44) yields

$$f'(k_{t+1}) = \frac{u'(w_t - p_i k_{t+1} N_{t+1}^i)}{v'[N_{t+1}^i k_{t+1} f'(k_{t+1})]} \qquad i = \text{H, L} \tag{14.45}$$

Define a modified saving function

$$\hat{z}(R, y, p) = \underset{z}{\operatorname{argmax}} \, [u(w - z) + pv(Rz)] \tag{14.46}$$

and rewrite (14.45) as

$$p_i N_{t+1}^i k_{t+1} = \hat{z}\left[\frac{f'(k_{t+1})}{p_i}, w(k_t), p_i\right] \tag{14.47}$$

Labor market equilibrium requires

$$\lambda p N_t^H + (1 - \lambda) N_t^L = 1 \qquad \text{for all } t \tag{14.48}$$

Combining (14.47) and (14.48) we obtain

$$k_{t+1} = \lambda \hat{z}\left[\frac{f'(k_{t+1})}{p_i}, w(k_t), p_i\right] + (1-\lambda)\hat{z}[f'(k_{t+1}), w(k_t), 1] \qquad (14.49)$$

Equation (14.49) describes dynamical equilibria in an economy of *purely internal finance*, that is, of unintermediated credit. We shall compare it with equation (14.42) which governs the corresponding economy with fully intermediated credit. Recalling that $\hat{z}(R, y, 1) = z(R, y)$, we rewrite (14.42) as

$$k_{t+1} = \hat{z}[f'(k_{t+1}), w(k_t), 1] \qquad (14.42)'$$

From the first-order conditions defining the function $\hat{z}(R, y, p)$ we note the following.

1. Additive separability implies normality and hence that $\hat{z}$ is increasing in y, p.
2. $-cv''(c)/v'(c) < 1$ for all c implies gross substitutability, that is, that $\hat{z}$ is increasing in R.
3. Normality implies that $\hat{z}(R, y, p)$ is increasing in p with elasticity in the interval (0,1).

Given gross substitutes, equations (14.42)' and (14.49) yield monotone time maps of the form

$$k_{t+1} = \phi(k_t) \qquad (14.50)$$
$$k_{t+1} = \psi(k_t, p, \lambda) \qquad (14.51)$$

where

$$\psi(k, 1, \lambda) = \phi(k) \qquad \forall \lambda \in [0,1] \qquad (14.52)$$

For these maps we see readily that

1 ψ is increasing in p for fixed λ and
2 ψ is decreasing in λ for any $p < 1$.

As figure 14.2 shows, economies with a perfect, fully intermediated credit market (that is, pure debt finance) have a broad tendency toward higher per capita income and higher capital intensity than do economies with a nonexistent credit market (pure internal finance). Poor credit markets are unable to exploit fully the law of large numbers: incomplete diversification of investment projects allows risky yields to reduce saving, hinder investment, and hold back per capita income.

To assess the empirical importance of "financial depth" we compute steady state incomes in a fully intermediated and an unintermediated economy.

Example 14.1 Consider a standard overlapping generations growth model of representative households with Cobb–Douglas production and utility functions, that is, $f(k) = k^a$, $u(c) = (1-b)\log c$, $v(c) = b\log(\gamma + c)$ for some $a \in (0,1)$ and $b \in (0,1)$. Then $\hat{z}(R, y, p) = pby/(1-b+pb)$; for small γ, equations (14.50) and (14.51) reduce to

$$k_{t+1} = b(1-a)k_t^a \qquad (14.53a)$$
$$k_{t+1} = Ab(1-a)k_t^a \qquad (14.53b)$$

where

$$A = \frac{\lambda p}{1 - b + bp + 1 - \lambda} \tag{14.54}$$

Note that $A \in (0,1)$ and

$$A \to 1 \text{ as } p \to 1 \qquad \text{(vanishingly low risks)}$$

$$A \to 0 \text{ as } p \to 0 \qquad \text{(high risks)}$$

In the steady state, capital intensity and output per worker are

$$k_D = [b(1 - a)]^{1/(1-a)} \qquad y_D = (k_D)^a \tag{14.55}$$

in the fully intermediated economy and

$$k_I = [Ab(1 - a)]^{1/(1 - a)} \qquad y_I = (k_I)^a \tag{14.56}$$

for the unintermediated one. The ratio of per capita incomes in the steady state is

$$\frac{y_I}{y_D} = A^{a/(1-a)} \tag{14.57}$$

This ratio approaches unity as $p \to 1$; approaches zero as $p \to 0$; and equals approximately 0.84 if $\lambda = 1/2$, $a = 1/4$, and $p = 1/2$.

In other words, y_I is small relative to y_D whenever the undiversified risks facing savers in the internal-finance economy become large. A similar income disparity would arise for relatively modest risks if households became more risk averse.

Notes

1. Readers who are interested in broad surveys of economic development should consult some of the classic early papers collected in Meier and Seers (1984).
2. Sections 14.1 and 14.4 are partly based on Azariadis and Drazen (1990a).
3. See Deane and Cole (1969, pp. 6–8) and the *World Development Report* (1987); these percentages are not corrected for migration into and out of the UK. Wrigley and Schofield (1981) report data taken from a large sample of English parishes which date as far back as 1541.
4. See McEvedy and Jones (1978).
5. See Barro and Becker (1989) for one effort in the optimal growth tradition, and Azariadis and Drazen (1990b) for another in the overlapping generations tradition.
6. Surveys of this enormous literature are Becker (1967) on the theoretical side, Rosen (1977) on the empirical research, and Behrman (1990) on implications for economic development.
7. de la Fuente (1990) examines the dynamics of joint human–physical capital accumulation and explores low development traps in which no human investments occur in equilibrium.
8. Note that this implies that along (14.18b) $k \to 0$ as $\tau \to 0$, while $k \to \infty$ as $\tau \to 1$. Along (14.18a), since $\tau = 1$ implies negative saving (and hence $k < 0$), s and k will be zero for some $\bar{\tau} < 1$. Continuity then ensures an interior intersection of (14.18a) and (14.18b).
9. The main ideas are traced to the work of Arrow (1962) on learning by doing, and Romer (1986) and Lucas (1988) on technological spillovers.
10. Much of this section is based on joint work done with Bruce Smith and reported in Azariadis and Smith (1991).
11. It is easy to check that $Q > 0$ is inconsistent with the first-order condition for a consumer maximum.

15 Advanced topics (*)

15.1 Intertemporal optimality

The notion of capital overaccumulation in theorem 13.2 led a number of economists to related results that characterize the welfare properties of dynamical allocations. First, Phelps (1965) and Koopmans (1965) demonstrated that, if the path of capital per head associated with some allocation stays bounded away from the golden rule after some finite point in time, then that allocation is dynamically inefficient. The precise statement is as follows.

Theorem 15.1 (Phelps and Koopmans) Given an initial endowment of capital $k_1 > 0$, a feasible allocation $(k_t, C^t)_{t=1}^{\infty}$ is dynamically inefficient if it satisfies $k_t \geq k^* + \epsilon$ for some $\epsilon > 0$ and all $t \geq \tau$, where τ is any positive integer.

A Pareto-superior allocation is very easy to find in this case: the planner reduces the capital stock by ϵ at time τ, contributes that amount to the consumption of existing generations and assures higher aggregate future consumption for the economy as a whole at every point after τ.

What can we say about the welfare properties of dynamical allocations that allow the capital stock to oscillate about the golden rule, dipping below it on occasion and rising above it from time to time? Examples of this type point out that the Phelps–Koopmans theorem is incomplete, having little to say about the welfare properties of many feasible dynamical allocations. A more complete description, of course, needs to rely on the entire capital path or, equivalently, the whole sequence of the associated interest rates. The fundamental result here is due to Malinvaud (1953): finite aggregate wealth implies dynamic efficiency. More precisely, we have the following.

Theorem 15.2 (Malinvaud) Suppose an allocation is dynamically inefficient in an economy with zero population growth. Then

$$\lim_{t \to \infty} R^t \equiv \lim_{t \to \infty} \prod_{s=1}^{t} R_s = 0$$

This result is proved in the Technical Appendix; the intuitive meaning of it is that dynamic inefficiency corresponds to real interest rates that become negative when they are averaged over an infinite horizon.

A corollary of this theorem is that the normalized aggregate resource stream $(e_1 + e_2, e_1 + e_2, \ldots)$ of this economy has infinite present value. Thus *inefficiency implies infinite wealth and finite wealth implies dynamic efficiency*. This statement does not hold in reverse: the golden rule allocation shows that infinite wealth does not perforce imply inefficiency.

To sum up, we should not expect the converse of theorem 15.2 to hold. In other words, dynamic inefficiency is not implied by the statement $R_t \to 0$ as $t \to \infty$. Cass (1972) showed that dynamic inefficiency is not guaranteed if the sequence R^t goes to zero, but only if it goes to zero "sufficiently fast," that is, if it satisfies the following summability condition:

$$\sum_{t=1}^{\infty} R^t < +\infty \tag{15.1}$$

where R^t is defined in the statement of Theorem 15.2. This result generalizes previous work by Malinvaud and Phelps–Koopmans in the following manner.

Theorem 15.3 (Cass)   Suppose population is constant. Then a feasible allocation $(k_t, C^t)_{t=1}^{\infty}$ is intertemporally suboptimal if, and only if, inequality (15.1) holds.

The summability condition (15.1) is easy to understand if we define p_t to be the price of the consumption good at t in terms of an arbitrary unit of account. Normalizing prices by setting $p_0 = 1$, we have single-period interest factors $R_{t+1} = p_t/p_{t+1}$ and multiperiod interest factors $R^t = 1/p_t$. Then intertemporal suboptimality obtains if, and only if, $\sum_{t=1}^{\infty} (1/p_t) < \infty$.

All three preceding results apply, strictly speaking, to the one-sector model of economic growth or to a pure-exchange economy under certain assumptions. Among these are (i) one consumption good, (ii) a zero rate of population growth, and (iii) a stationary economic structure that includes time-invariant endowments, utility functions, and production functions.

It is a simple matter to extend the intertemporal optimality results to non-zero or nonconstant rates of population growth as well as, more generally, to nonstationary economic structures (see also question II.28). If the rate of population growth is a constant (say n) then theorems 15.2 and 15.3 apply to time-varying utility functions, technologies, and endowments if interest factors are divided by $1 + n$. On the other hand, if population does not grow geometrically, then each interest factor in theorem 15.3 ought to be deflated by the corresponding population growth factor.

It is a good deal more difficult to derive dynamic efficiency criteria for economies with an arbitrary finite number L of physical goods. Any efficient allocation, of course, will have to equate the marginal rates of substitution between any pair of goods consumed by any pair of individuals who are alive simultaneously. Therefore, we may represent these common marginal rates of substitution by price ratios, just as we did before. In particular, let $(p_t)_{t=1}^{\infty}$ be an infinite sequence of vectors, with each element $p_t = (p_t^1, p_t^2, \ldots, p_t^L)$ representing prices of all commodities in period t. These prices are again expressed in an arbitrary unit of account.

The easiest result to be found here is one that applies to quasi-stationary allocations of the kind that we studied in chapter 12. Because there are now L physical goods, an allocation is equal-treatment optimal if it maximizes a social welfare function that generalizes the expression in equation (12.3a) under resource constraints that generalize inequalities (12.3b) and (12.3c). In particular, there are L such constraints (one for each good) at time $t = 1$, and L more for all periods subsequent to the very first. The social welfare function is a weighted average of H utility functions (one for each type of household) for generation 0 and H utility functions for subsequent generations. Generation 0 indifference maps are naturally expressed over an L-dimensional Euclidean space while those for subsequent generations are defined over a $2L$-dimensional space. From the first-order conditions to the planner's problem (see question II.29), one proves the following equivalent to theorem 12.2.

Theorem 15.4 A quasi-stationary allocation is intertemporally optimal if it is statically optimal *and* it is associated with a price system such that for all $t \geq 1$ and all $j = 1,\ldots,$ L we have

$$p_t^i = R p_{t+1}^j \qquad (15.2)$$

where R is any number at least equal to $1 + n$.

This means, roughly speaking, that all prices shrink at the same rate over time and that the rate is at least as large as the growth rate.

What about non-stationary allocations? We state below without proof a result due to Balasko and Shell (1980) which extends the summability condition in (15.1) to an economy with many physical commodities.

Theorem 15.5 (Balasko and Shell)   Suppose the rate of population growth is zero. Then a feasible dynamical allocation is intertemporally suboptimal if, and only if, the associated price sequence satisfies

$$\sum_{t=1}^{\infty} \frac{1}{||p_t||} < +\infty$$

In this theorem $||p_t||$ is the Euclidean norm $[\Sigma_{i=1}^{L}(p_t^i)^2]^{1/2}$. Question II.20(b) asks the reader to show that theorem 15.5 reduces to theorem 15.3 if $L = 1$.

Finally, theorem 15.3 extends naturally to economies with stochastic production. Zilcha (1990), in particular, considers a standard overlapping generations economy with random technology captured by a variable ω_t which takes on values in some finite set Ω for all t. The intensive production function in this economy is $f(k, \omega)$ where f is endowed with the standard neoclassical properties for each ω. Here we denote the interest factor in period t by $R_t(\omega_t)$ to convey the intuitive idea that the marginal rate of substitution between past and current consumption depends on the current value of the technological disturbance ω. Zilcha shows that a feasible allocation is dynamically inefficient for an economy with constant population if, and only if, inequality (15.1) holds for all realizations of ω on some set $A \subseteq \Omega$ with positive measure; in other words, inefficiency occurs if the present-value price of physical capital goes to infinity "sufficiently fast" with positive probability.

15.2   Altruistic households: pure exchange

We study in this section and the next the implications for competitive equilibrium and dynamic efficiency in an exchange economy of doing away with generational overlap and allowing every pair of households to exchange goods in every period. We have already explored an economy with infinitely lived agents in the optimal growth model of section 13.4. The simplest pure-exchange economy we can deal with consists of a single infinitely-lived household (equivalently, of finitely many identical households). As we shall see in section 15.3, this economy comes very close to an overlapping generations model of identical households who bequeath resources to their progeny out of concern for their welfare.[1] If all individuals are sufficiently altruistic in this sense and if, in addition, all households have ancestors in the same evolving economy, then finitely-lived households are replaced by infinitely lived dynasties.

A childless household in this scenario will act as selfishly as one in the ordinary overlapping generations model. So will parents who are blessed with children but whose bequest motive is dulled by heavy discounting of their descendants' utility or by the firm expectation that their progeny will dispose of much greater lifetime resources than do they (see Abel, 1987). In either case older households choose to will nothing to their heirs, and the bequest motive is said to "inoperative."

If the bequest motive *does* operate for one family, it injects in effect an individual (strictly speaking, a dynasty) with an infinite planning horizon into an otherwise standard overlapping generations economy. The trading opportunities of finitely lived households expand radically as these may now trade indirectly with each other across the span of time by the intermediation of the infinitely-lived individual. Dynamically inefficient equilibria, in particular, vanish when there is one person who is endowed in the infinite future and can trade forever, provided his or her resources are of positive measure compared with the economy as a whole (see question II.18 and the paper by Muller and Woodford, 1988).

Inefficient equilibria with low rates of interest, like those of chapter 11 for instance, are no longer viable. They are subverted because the infinitely lived household may borrow arbitrarily large amounts of resources and then roll over the debt forever until it depreciates down to "nothing" if the real interest rate is negative or, more precisely, to an amount that is within the (arbitrarily small) endowment of the borrower. Other inefficient equilibria with a positive interest rate that is below the growth rate disappear for subtler reasons: an infinitely lived person may borrow from everyone early, roll over the ensuing debt, and spread it among a growing population of lenders until, asymptotically, his indebtedness to each finitely lived family drops to zero.

Another way to understand the nonexistence of low-interest-rate equilibria is through the market price of a hypothetical claim that pays off $(1 + n)^t$ units of consumption in any single time period $t = 1, 2,...,$ *ad infinitum*; the claim may represent a storage technology that produces $1 + n$ units of consumption next period out of each unit of investment (or forgone consumption) today. If the market rate of interest is below the growth rate, the price of that claim will be unbounded!

We return now to a pure-exchange economy that consists of a finite number H of households indexed by $h = 1,..., H$. All of these are born at $t = 0$ and live forever. There is a single nonstorable consumption good, of which household h is endowed with an amount e_t^h in period t. Both the endowment and consumption vectors, e^h and c^h, of household h are points in the non-negative orthant of a countably infinite-dimensional Euclidean space. In this space the preference orderings of households are captured by numerical functions of a form familiar from section 13.4:

$$v_h(c^h) = \sum_{t=0}^{\infty} \beta^t u_h(c_t^h)$$

where $u_h \colon \mathbb{R}_+ \to \mathbb{R}$ is a well-behaved instantaneous utility function and $\beta \in (0,1)$ is a subjective discount factor common to all households.[2]

We assume that total resources are stationary, that is,

$$\sum_{h=1}^{H} e_t^h = e \qquad t = 0, 1, \dots$$

and we discuss first competitive equilibrium with private loans, which are possible here between distinct households. As in chapter 11, a *competitive equilibrium with inside money* consists of an infinite sequence of interest factors $(\bar{R}_t)_{t=0}^{\infty}$ together with H consumption vectors $(\bar{c}_t^h)_{t=0}^{\infty}$, $h = 1,\dots, H$, with the following properties.

1. Given $(\bar{R}_t)$, the vector $(\bar{c}_t^h)$ is the maximal element in the relevant budget set of each h:

$$B_h = \left\{ c_t^h \middle| c_t^h \geq 0 \;\forall t; \lim_{t \to \infty} \left(\frac{D_t^h}{R^t} \right) \geq 0 \right\}$$

where R^{t-1} is the product of the interest factors $R_0 R_1 \dots R_{t-1}$; and $D_t^h = R_{t-1} D_{t-1}^h + e_t^h - c_t^h$ is the net asset position of household h at the end of period t.

2. $\displaystyle\sum_{h=1}^{H} c_t^h - e = 0 \qquad t = 0, 1, \dots$

The last equation is the national income accounting identity, which we may interpet either as equilibrium in the goods market or as equilibrium in the credit market, that is, as equality between lending and borrowing. The inequality $\lim_{t\to\infty} (D_t^h/R^t) \geq 0$ is a *transversality* condition that prevents individuals from becoming perpetual debtors and from rolling over debt in perpetuity. The weaker terminal condition $\lim_{t\to\infty} D_t^h \geq 0$ would prevent perpetual indebtedness but still allow a borrower who faces a negative interest rate to roll over liabilities until they depreciate down to zero.

From the first-order conditions of the consumer's choice problem we have

$$\beta^t R^{t-1} u_h'(c_t^h) = u_h'(c_0^h) \qquad h = 1,\dots, H; \qquad t = 1,\dots \tag{15.3}$$

Note from (15.3) that, if $\beta^t R^{t-1} > 1$ for some t, then $c_t^h > c_0^h$ for all h. Conversely, $\beta^t R^{t-1} < 1$ for some t implies $c_0^h < c_0^h$ for all h. Therefore, if $\beta R^{t-1} \neq 1$ for any t, we necessarily have $\sum_{h=1}^{H}(c_t^h - c_0^h) \neq 0$ and the credit market cannot clear in *both* period t *and* period 0. It follows that the rates of interest and of time preference are identical in equilibrium. In addition, the marginal utility of consumption is time invariant for each household.

Equilibrium consumption vectors obey here a simple form of the *permanent income hypothesis*.[3] For each household we define permanent income y_h as a constant sequence (y_h) that has the same present value as the actual endowment sequence (e_t^h). Then

$$y_h = (1 - \beta) \sum_{t=0}^{\infty} \beta^t e_t^h \tag{15.4}$$

Given that $R_t = 1/\beta$ for all t, the first-order conditions yield $c_t^h = c_0^h$ for all t and h. The budget constraint then instructs households to set $c_t^h = y_h$ for each t.

Is this equilibrium intertemporally optimal? As in chapter 12, the answer is obviously yes if households are identical: an autarkic equilibrium that wastes no resources is *necessarily* optimal. To find out what happens when households are not identical, we let a central planner maximize the social welfare function

$$W = \sum_{h=1}^{H} \lambda_h \sum_{t=0}^{\infty} \beta^t u_h(c_h^t)$$

subject to the resource constraints

$$\sum_{h=1}^{H} (c_t^h - e_t^h) \leq 0 \qquad t = 0, 1, \ldots \tag{15.5}$$

Here we try to ascertain whether the competitive equilibrium we have just described satisfies the first-order conditions of this planning problem for *some* choice of the non-negative weights $(\lambda_1, \ldots, \lambda_H)$. The first-order conditions are easily seen to be

$$\lambda_h \beta^t u_h'(c_t^h) = \mu_t \tag{15.6}$$

for an interior maximum, where $(\mu_t)_{t=0}^{\infty}$ is a non-negative sequence of Lagrange multipliers associated with the resource constraint (15.5). The choice $\mu_t = \beta^t$ and $1/\lambda_h = u_h'(y_h)$ reduces equation (15.6) to $c_t^h = y_h$ for all t and h, which is just what happens in competitive equilibrium. Competitive equilibrium is therefore an intertemporal optimum, and we sum up in the following theorem.

Theorem 15.6 Assume a finite number of infinitely-lived households with additive utility functions, a common rate of time preference, and stationary aggregate resources. Then there is a unique competitive equilibrium with inside money which satisfies the following three properties:

(a) equality of the interest and time-preference rates;
(b) the permanent income hypothesis;
(c) intertemporal optimality.

Without stationary aggregate resources, the permanent income property of equilibrium is modified, and the equality between the time preference and equilibrum interest rates disappears. As an example, consider the case of a single household (or a finite number of identical households). Let $(c_t)_{t=0}^{\infty}$ be the consumption vector, which does not necessarily consist of identical elements. The first-order conditions for the consumer are again given by equation (15.3); credit market clearing means individual autarky, that is, $c_t = e_t$ for all t. Accordingly, competitive equilibrium equates interest factors with marginal rates of substitution at the initial endowment point, that is,

$$\beta R_t = \frac{u'(e_t)}{u'(e_{t+1})} \qquad \forall t \tag{15.7}$$

This is different from unity whenever $e_t \neq e_{t+1}$. However, competitive equilibrium remains unique and optimal (see question II.19) even if aggregate resources do change over time.

In the following section we explore the precise circumstances under which households are equivalent to infinitely lived dynasties (see also chapter 21).

15.3   Altruistic households: growth

Life-cycle theories of saving, like those advanced by Ando and Modigliani (1963) and others in the same tradition, predict that finitely lived individuals will run out of assets as their date of death draws near, bequeathing nothing to succeeding generations. It is possible, in the absence of social security or of complete annuity markets, to conceive of older persons rationally maintaining positive asset balances as insurance against an uncertain length of life or an uncertain state of health. Nevertheless the amount of resources passed down by wealthy individuals to their descendants, and even the asset balances kept by middle-class persons at age 80,[4] seem to cast serious doubt on an assumption that we have maintained throughout this text, namely that individuals do not care about the welfare of their descendants.

Can we amend the neoclassical growth models of chapter 13 to allow altruistic bequests of resources from parents to children? And if we do, what changes should we expect once we replace saving driven by the life-cycle motive of selfish individuals with saving driven by the bequest motive of a benevolent family?

The easiest way to find out is to reinterpret slightly the scalar Diamond model of section 13.1 in the way suggested by Abel (1987) and Weil (1988). Suppose that all households are identical; each one consists of one adult and some children. Individuals thus live for two periods, "childhood" and "adulthood." Children make no economic decisions and their consumption is subsumed in that of their parent. Each adult is endowed with an exogenous number, $1 + n$, of children; with one unit of labor which he supplies inelastically to production; with some capital bequeathed by a benevolent parent; and with a constant-returns-to-scale technology which combines capital and labor to produce the consumption good. Production and discretionary consumption take place in adulthood.

Suppose now that all adults have a common utility index $v : \mathbb{R}_+^2 \to \mathbb{R}$ expressed over their own scalar consumption as well as over the consumption of their children which they influence by leaving bequests of physical capital. All bequests are assumed to be shared evenly by heirs, and nobody provides directly for grandchildren or other more distant generations. If the utility and production functions v and f have all the standard properties, a stationary planning optimum for this economy is simply the golden rule $k^* = \text{argmax}_{k \geqslant 0}[f(k) - (n + \delta)k]$.

Dynamical equilibria are slightly more complicated. Adults consume c_t in period t but are also concerned about the consumption c_{t+1} of their heirs in the immediate future. A representative adult at t has received a bequest $k_t \geqslant 0$ in the form of productive capital and must choose how much of an inheritance $k_{t+1} \geqslant 0$ to pass on to the next generation. Given (k_t, k_{t+1}) and n, the consumption of our altruistic adult

$$c_t = f(k_t) + (1 - \delta)k_t - (1 + n)k_{t+1} \tag{15.8a}$$

is fixed while that of his heirs

$$c_{t+1} = f(k_{t+1}) + (1 - \delta)k_{t+1} - (1 + n) k_{t+2} \tag{15.8b}$$

depends on how much they choose to bequeath to the generation following them. Notice that wage income does not appear in either budget constraint simply because hiring outside labor or using one's own work makes no difference to any producer; all workers are perfect substitutes for each other.

Adults of generation t maximize their utility index $v(c_t, c_{t+1})$ subject to the constraints (15.8a) and (15.8b), taking k_t, k_{t+2}, and n as given. The first-order conditions for an interior consumer maximum are

$$c_t = f(k_t) + (1 - \delta)k_t - (1 + n)k_{t+1} \tag{15.9a}$$

$$(1 + n)v_1(c_t, c_{t+1}) = [1 - \delta + f'(k_{t+1})]v_2(c_t, c_{t+1}) \tag{15.9b}$$

where (v_1, v_2) are partial derivatives. Denote by $M(c_t, c_{t+1})$ the absolute value of the marginal rate of substitution at (c_t, c_{t+1}), and note that M is decreasing in c_t and increasing in c_{t+1} if goods are normal. We may now rewrite (15.9b) in the form

$$1 - \delta + f'(k_{t+1}) = (1 + n)M(c_t, c_{t+1}) \tag{15.9c}$$

Equations (15.9a) and (15.9b) define a dynamical system whose solutions are competitive equilibria that describe fully how our altruistic economy evolves. The most glaring difference between the standard overlapping generations model of growth in section 13.1 and the altruistic model in equations (15.9a) and (15.9b) is in their mathematical representation: even though the commodity space of the representative agent is $\mathbb{R}^2_+$ in each case, a scalar dynamical system describes the standard model while a planar system is needed for the altruistic economy. Why is growth fully characterized by a first-order difference equation when individuals are selfish and by a second-order equation when they leave bequests? Readers are asked to provide an answer in question II.31.

In particular, let us assume that population and the rate of time preference are both constant, that is, $n = 0$ and $v(c_1, c_2) = u(c_1) + \beta u(c_2)$ for some $\beta > 0$. The system (15.9a) and (15.9b) reduces to

$$c_t = f(k_t) + (1 - \delta)k_t - k_{t+1} \tag{15.10a}$$

$$u'(c_t) = \beta[1 - \delta + f'(k_{t+1})]u'(c_{t+1}) \tag{15.10b}$$

that is, to a pair of equations that describe the optimal growth model in section 13.4. This identity is legitimate only if $\beta \in (0,1)$; the altruistic overlapping generations economy continues to have well-defined equilibria if $\beta > 1$, that is, the rate of time preference is negative;[5] this situation makes no sense in the optimal growth model where the consumer's utility function and budget constraint are not defined unless $\beta < 1$. We summarize in the next theorem.

Theorem 15.7 In an altruistic overlapping generations economy, assume that population is constant and that the rate of time preference is a positive constant. Then interior dynamical equilibria in this economy are equivalent to those of an optimal growth model with identical preference structure.

Among the equilibria of this economy is the steady state $(\bar{k}, \bar{c})$ of the corresponding optimal growth model, the entire saddlepath that converges to $(\bar{k}, \bar{c})$, plus any *non-interior* equilibria we may think of. The usual shut-down state $k_t = 0$ for all t continues to be a competitive equilibrium; a generation that inherits nothing from its parents cannot produce anything and therefore must bequeath nothing to its own heirs.[6] Any sufficiently altruistic generation that inherits a positive stock of capital will typically transfer at least some of it to its descendants.

More generally, we may allow for constant rates, ρ and n, of time preference and population growth for which the dynamical system (15.9a) and (15.9b) yields a slight generalization of (15.10a) and (15.10b):

$$(1 + n)k_{t+1} = f(k_t) + (1 - \delta)k_t - c_t \qquad (15.11a)$$

$$(1 + n)u'(c_t) = \beta[1 - \delta + f'(k_{t+1})]u'(c_{t+1}) \qquad (15.11b)$$

These equations reveal that the steady state is again a saddle and the capital–labor ratio $\bar{k}$ satisfies

$$1 - \delta + f'(\bar{k}) = \frac{1 + n}{\beta} = (1 + n)(1 + \rho)$$

which implies

$$f'(\bar{k}) = \delta + n + (1 + n)\rho = f'(k^*) + (1 + n)\rho \qquad (15.12)$$

by the definition of the golden rule k^*. Hence a positive rate of time preference means that $\bar{k}$ lies below the golden rule and the equilibrium interest rate exceeds the growth rate; a negative rate of time preference means that $\bar{k}$ exceeds the golden rule and the rate of interest falls below the growth rate. We have thus completed an informal proof of the next theorem.

Theorem 15.8 In an altruistic overlapping generations economy with a constant rate of time preference ρ and a constant rate of population growth n, there is a continuum of equilibria $(k_t, c_t)_{t=1}^{\infty}$, indexed on the initial capital stock k_1, which lie on a unique saddlepath that converges to the steady state $(\bar{k}, \bar{c})$. These equilibria are intertemporally optimal if $\rho \geq 0$, suboptimal if $\rho < 0$.

When the rate of time preference is not a constant, one can extract all the necessary information about dynamical equilibria from equations (15.9a) and (15.9c). For instance, it is easy to check that the qualitative properties of the vector field implied by (15.9a) and (15.9c) are quite similar to those of the optimal growth model. The phase diagrams of figure 15.1 suggest that the positive steady state $(\bar{k}, \bar{c})$ is a saddle (readers are asked to prove this in question II.30) whose welfare properties depend on the value $\bar{M} = M(\bar{c}, \bar{c})$ of the marginal rate of substitution function at the steady state. For any homothetic utility function, $\bar{M}$ simply depends on the (unitary) ratio of the stationary consumption flows accruing to two successive generations. In particular, $\bar{M}$ plays in the homothetic case the same role that $1/\beta$ does in the constant-time-preference case; equilibria are dynamically efficient if $\bar{M} \geq 1$, inefficient if $\bar{M} < 1$.

When the bequest motive is operating, *altruistic steady states have a broad tendency to be saddles even if the rate of time preference is not a positive constant* but, rather, a negative constant or even a function of actual consumption. It is not difficult to show, for instance, that if $v(c_t, c_{t+1}) = u_1(c_t) + u_2(c_{t+1})$ where (u_1, u_2) are isoelastic functions of the form

$$u_i(c) = -(1 - r_i)^{-1}c^{-(1-r_i)} \qquad r_i \geq 0, \qquad i = 1, 2$$

for given parameters (r_1, r_2), then the dynamical system (15.9a), (15.9c) has a unique positive steady state $(\bar{k}, \bar{c})$. This state is a saddle if

$$\min\left[\frac{r_1}{r_2}, M(\bar{c}, \bar{c})\right] \leq 1 \leq \max\left[\frac{r_1}{r_2}, M(\bar{c}, \bar{c})\right] \qquad (15.13)$$

Note that, if $u_2(c) = \beta u_1(c)$ for all c and some $\beta > 0$, then $r_1 = r_2$ and $M(c, c) = 1/\beta$ for all c; equation (15.13) obviously holds and $(\bar{k}, \bar{c})$ is a saddle as we know already.

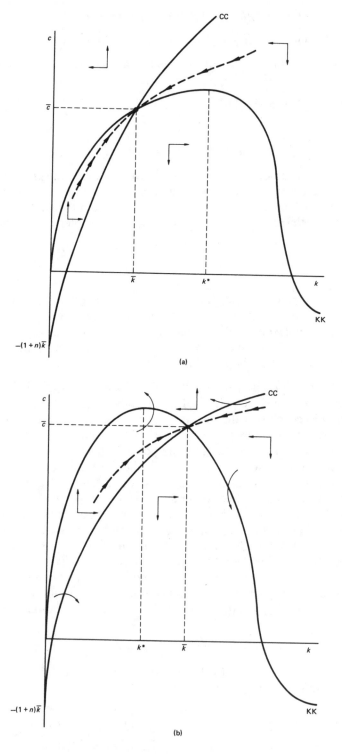

Figure 15.1 Homothetic altruism: (a) efficient equilibria, $\bar{M} \geq 1$; (b) inefficient equilibria, $\bar{M} < 1$.

15.4 The taxation of factor incomes

How should taxes be raised to finance government purchases when lump-sum taxes cannot be collected because of, say, private information about individual incomes? Suppose the government spends a fixed amount per capita g on goods and services each period and desires to raise an equal amount by proportional, and therefore distorting taxes on commodities and/or factors of production. Assuming that public consumption does not affect the indifference map of any household or the production set of any firm, who should bear the required tax burden and to what extent?

This question is at the heart of the theory of *optimal income taxation*. It was first solved by Ramsey (1927) who proposed to set indirect tax rates on commodities so as to maximize the utility of a representative consumer given total taxes. The Ramsey solution, extended by Diamond and Mirrlees (1971) and many subsequent writers to economies with heterogeneous consumers, minimizes the "excess burden" of taxation, that is, the damage to social welfare done by taxes that alter the marginal rates of substitution for all consumers and all taxed commodities.

Neoclassical growth models have one physical commodity and two factors of production, so that the natural extension of the question at the beginning of this section becomes one about *direct* income taxes. Given total taxes g to be raised, how much should come from labor income and how much from capital income? This question is explored in original contributions to public finance by Chamley (1981) and Summers (1981), and has been reviewed recently by Lucas (1990a). Chamley's work is in the optimal growth tradition started by Ramsey; Summers' is in the overlapping generations framework.

Stripped to the barest essentials, the issue is to pick fixed proportional taxes (θ, τ) on net capital and labor income that satisfy the government budget constraint

$$\tau w(k_t) + \theta k_t f'(k_t) = g \qquad (15.14)$$

for all t. Since the value of the capital–labor ratio is set competitively, the government has only one degree of freedom. For any relatively small flow of tax revenue, there is a continuum of feasible tax-rate combinations: at one extreme $\theta = 0$ forces the entire burden of the tax on labor; at the other, $\tau = 0$ exempts labor income from all taxes.

In what follows, we do not search for optimal structures, even though it is not too hard to solve a planning problem subject to the government budget constraint in (15.14). One may ask, for example (see question II.31), whether there is a stationary choice (θ, τ) that will collect the required amount of per capita taxes and will support the golden rule capital intensity as a competitive equilibrium.

We opt instead to investigate the positive issue of what it is that different tax structures imply for growth and income per capita in the steady state. We do so in full-employment models with inelastic labor supply which means that we ignore any disincentive effects wage taxes may have on labor supply. Still, any tax structure (θ, τ) must balance two opposing forces: capital income taxation tends to encourage consumption by reducing the after-tax yield on saving while wage taxation shrinks the pool of after-tax income out of which individuals save. Both taxes may have adverse effects on saving; which one is most hurtful depends on the structure of the economy in question, mainly on tastes and technology. The examples below illustrate two extreme cases.

Example 15.1 (Perfect substitutes in consumption)   Take a scalar Diamond model in which the representative household's utility function is $u(c_1, c_2) = c_1 + \beta c_2$ for some $\beta > 0$. Then, at every interior solution to the consumer's planning problem we have

$$\frac{1}{\beta} = 1 - \delta + (1 - \theta)f'(k_t) \tag{15.15}$$

for all t. This relation equates the consumer's marginal rate of substitution with the gross yield as loans, that is, with the sum "salvage value of capital plus the after-tax rental rate." Recalling that $1/\beta = 1 + \rho$, where ρ is the representative household's rate of time preference, we may rewrite equation (15.15) in the form

$$f'(k_t) = \frac{\rho + \delta}{1 - \theta} \tag{15.15'}$$

Hence the capital–labor ratio is a constant sequence that is a decreasing function of the capital income tax rate θ. Policymakers who find high income per capita a desirable aim should tax labor income only. As we shall see below, this policy conclusion extends to all economies in which the supply of capital is highly interest elastic, an event that occurs whenever the real rate of interest is virtually fixed by preferences or technology.

Example 15.2 (Equality of income and substitution effects)   In the economy of the preceding example, we change the utility function to $u(c_1, c_2) = c_1^{1-s}c_2^{s}$ for some $s \in (0, 1)$. This specification fixes the saving rate at s independently of how heavily we tax capital income. After-tax wage income in period t is

$$(1 - \tau)w(k_t) = w(k_t) - \tau w(k_t) = w(k_t) + \theta k_t f'(k_t) - g$$

by the government budget constraint. The scalar Diamond model in this case is described by the following difference equation:

$$(1 + n)k_{t+1} = s[w(k_t) - g + \theta k_t f'(k_t)] \tag{15.16}$$

For any fixed g and k_t, the value of k_{t+1} is an increasing function of the parameter θ. Therefore, any stable stationary solution $\hat{k}(g,\theta)$ to (15.16) should be an *increasing* function of θ, achieving its minimal value, for a fixed g, at $\theta = 0$ and its maximal value at $\tau = 0$. As figure 15.2 shows, the set of steady states that may be reached when all taxes fall on capital in this Cobb–Douglas economy is the same as that of the underlying tax-free economy. Therefore, income per capita is largest when wages are not taxed.

What we should conclude from these two examples is that the interest and income elasticities of saving have a lot to do with the ultimate impact of factor income taxes on growth. A practical rule of thumb is not to tax capital if its supply is highly interest elastic and if saving from capital income is a significant fraction of aggregate saving. One case in point is the optimal growth model in which a social planner will choose proportional tax parameters (θ, τ) on factor incomes satisfying the budget constraint (15.14) and the resource constraint

$$c_t + k_{t+1} + g \leq f(k_t) + (1 - \delta)k_t \tag{15.17}$$

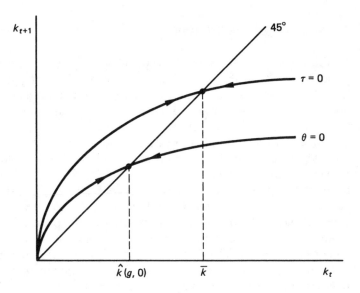

Figure 15.2 Taxing factor incomes.

One of the first-order conditions for a competitive equilibrium is the equality of factor prices to after-tax marginal products, that is,

$$R_t = (1 - \theta) f'(k_t) + 1 - \delta \qquad (15.18)$$

In a stationary equilibrium, the interest rate coincides with the rate of time preference and the capital–labor ratio is given by equation (15.15) exactly as in example 15.1.

Real rates of interest are harder to pin down in an overlapping generations economy. Generalizing readily from example 15.2, we modify the Diamond model to take account of factor income taxes. The fundamental difference equation becomes

$$(1 + n)k_{t+1} = z[1 - \delta + (1 - \theta)f'(k_{t+1}), w(k_t) + \theta k_t f'(k_t) - g] \qquad (15.19)$$

If g is relatively small, and the two dated consumption goods are normal and gross substitutes, we may write equation (15.19) in the form

$$k_{t+1} = G(k_t; \theta) \qquad (15.20)$$

where $G: \mathbb{R}_+ \times [0,1] \to \mathbb{R}_+$ is monotone in its first argument. Direct differentiation of (15.20) will yield information on G_θ, the partial derivative of the time map with respect to its second argument. After some algebra, we compute G_θ at any positive steady state to be proportional to the expression

$$G_\theta \sim \frac{(1 - \theta)\alpha}{(1 - \tau)(1 - \alpha)} - \frac{\epsilon_R}{\epsilon_y} \qquad (15.21)$$

where α is capital's share of output and ϵ_R, ϵ_y are respectively the elasticities of aggregate saving with respect to the interest factor and income.

For any fixed g and k_t, therefore, the time map G is increasing in θ, exactly as figure 15.2 illustrates, if and only if the ratio of after tax factor incomes exceeds the ratio of corresponding aggregate saving elasticities. In this case, shifting taxes from labor to capital improves per capita income in any stable stationary equilibrium.

15.5   Two-sector growth theory

We conclude this chapter with a brief account of the two-sector overlapping generations model of growth, based to a large extent on a recent paper by Galor (1991) to which the reader may refer for a fuller treatment. Different forms of the two-sector model have found wise use in the theory of international trade and in the dual-economy contributions of development economists.[7] The two sectors of concern are typically traded versus nontraded goods in international trade, and family-oriented farming versus the market-driven production of services or industrial goods in economic development.

In growth theory it is found useful for some purposes to distinguish investment goods from consumption goods. We made a distinction of this sort when we discussed adjustment costs in chapter 13 and found out how those costs permitted the price of capital to deviate from its cost of reproduction in an otherwise standard one-sector overlapping generations model. That deviation is one reason for being interested in multisector growth. The prices of various pieces of capital equipment are among the most important economic variables; one-sector growth theory has nothing to say about how those prices are set.

In addition to answering a need for a simple general equilibrium theory of capital asset prices, multisector growth models provide a much richer menu of dynamical behavior than do their one-sector counterparts.[8] What follows is an extension of the pioneering work by Uzawa (1961, 1964) to the overlapping generations setting: we explore sufficient conditions for the existence of a steady state and provide parametric examples to illustrate the main results.

If producing the consumption good is uniformly *more* capital intensive than producing the investment good then, under some additional technical assumptions, an asymptotically stable steady state exists in the overlapping generations model exactly as Uzawa (1961) proved for the descriptive growth model. If we suppose, on the other hand, that the consumption good is uniformly *less* capital intensive than the investment good then this leads to a saddle steady state.

To examine the dynamical behavior of the two-sector model in the simplest possible setting, we imagine a standard overlapping generations economy with a constant population of identical households endowed with a homothetic utility function and a unitary, inelastic supply of labor services in youth. Capital depreciates fully on use. We denote by the subscripts x and y, respectively, the consumption good and investment good; each is produced by constant-returns technologies from capital and labor. In particular, the output of the consumption good is

$$X_t = F^x(K_t^x, L_t^x) = L_t^x f_x(k_t^x) \tag{15.22a}$$

while that of the investment good is

$$Y_t = F^y(K_t^y, L_t^y) = L_t^y f_y(k_t^y) \tag{15.22b}$$

Here F^i, f_i, and k^i stand for the extensive production function, the intensive production function and the capital–labor ratio in sector $i = $ x, y. Denote by (w, ρ) the wage and rental rates in terms of the investment good, by $\omega = w/\rho$ the wage–rental ratio, and by p the price of the consumption good – again in terms of capital. All these prices will be common to both sectors if we assume that factors of production can move costlessly and freely from one sector to another.

Equilibrium conditions in this economy will require that

1. aggregate saving equal investment;
2. aggregate consumption equal the output of the consumption good;
3. aggregate investment equal the output of the investment good;
4. aggregate employment equal the inelastic supply of labor; and
5. factor prices be the same in both sectors and lie on the factor-price frontier.

Denoting by $w_i(k) = f_i(k) - kf_i'(k)$ the wage function of sector i, any competitive equilibrium will equalize the marginal product of each factor in the two sectors. This equalization requires

$$p_t = p_t f_x'(k_t^y) = f_y'(k_t^y) \tag{15.23a}$$

$$w_t = p_t w_x(k_t^x) = w_y(k_t^y) \tag{15.23b}$$

Dividing either of these lines into the other, we obtain the following expression for the wage–rental ratio:

$$\omega_t = \frac{w_t}{\rho_t} = \frac{w_x(k_t^x)}{f_x'(k_t^x)} = \frac{w^y(k_t^y)}{f_y'(k_t^y)} \tag{15.24}$$

The last two expressions in equation (15.24) are monotone functions of k_t^x and k_t^y, respectively. Each of them equals zero when $k_t^i = 0$ and becomes very large as $k_t^i \to \infty$ for $i = x, y$. By inverting the expressions, we obtain two increasing functions $k_i : \mathbb{R}_+ \to \mathbb{R}_+$ such that

$$k_i(0) = 0 \qquad k_t^i = k_i(\omega_t) \qquad i = x,y \tag{15.25}$$

In addition, we assume that there are *no factor-intensity reversals*, that is, we have

$$[k_x(\omega_2) - k_x(\omega_1)][k_y(\omega_2) - k_y(\omega_1)] \geq 0 \qquad \forall(\omega_1, \omega_2) \tag{15.26}$$

In other words, either $k_x(\omega) < k_y(\omega)$ for all ω or $k_x(\omega) > k_y(\omega)$ for all ω; one of the two goods requires a more capital-intensive technique than the other *at all factor-price ratios*.

Let $\gamma_t \in [0,1]$ be the fraction of the total labor force employed in the consumption goods sector. If both goods are produced, then the economywide capital–labor ratio must be a convex combination of the two sectoral ratios, that is,

$$K_t = K_t^x + K_t^y \Rightarrow k_t = \gamma_t k_t^x + (1 - \gamma_t) k_t^y \tag{15.27a}$$

Figures 15.3 and 15.4 illustrate the two main cases which correspond to the consumption good being more capital intensive and the investment good being more capital intensive.

We rewrite equation (15.22b) in the intensive form

$$y_t = \frac{Y_t}{L_t} = \frac{L_t^y}{L_t} \frac{Y_t}{L_t^y} = (1 - \gamma_t) f_y(k_t^y) \tag{15.27b}$$

Solving equation (15.27a) for $1 - \gamma_t = (k_t^x - k_t)/(k_t^x - k_t^y)$ and substituting into equation (15.27b), we obtain an equation that describes how the per capita output of the investment good depends on the variables k and ω:

$$y_t = \frac{k_x(\omega_t) - k_t}{k_x(\omega_t) - k_y(\omega_t)} f_y[k_y(\omega_t)] \equiv y(k_t, \omega_t) \tag{15.28}$$

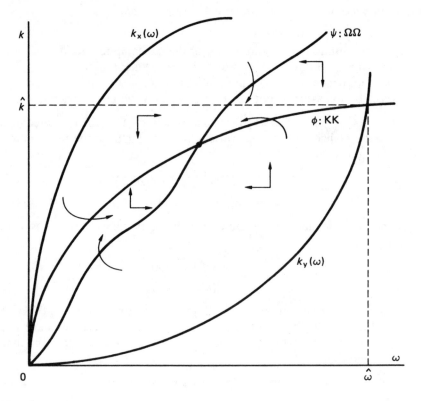

Figure 15.3 Two-sector growth: $k_x > k_y$.

The *Rybczynski theorem*, a well-known result in international trade theory, sums up some useful properties of the function $y: \mathbb{R}^2_+ \to \mathbb{R}_+$ defined in equation (15.28). Question II.32, in particular, asks you to prove that y is decreasing in k for each fixed ω if $k_x(\omega) > k_y(\omega)$ for all ω; and y is increasing in k with elasticity greater than unity if $k_x(\omega) < k_y(\omega)$ for all ω. This happens because a rise in the economywide capital–labor ratio increases the output of the capital-intensive good more than in proportion due to a scale effect: labor shifts away from the contracting sector of the economy.

Saving is the other variable we must study before we discuss equilibrium. The consumer's budget constraints are

$$(c_1^t, c_2^t) \in \mathbb{R}^2_+ \qquad p_t c_1^t + s_t \leqslant w_t \qquad p_{t+1} c_2^t \leqslant p_{t+1} s_t \qquad (15.29)$$

with everything denominated in terms of the investment good. From these constraints, it is obvious that

$$c_1^t = \frac{w_t - s_t}{p_t} \qquad c_2^t = \frac{R_{t+1} S_t}{p_t} \qquad (15.30)$$

where

$$R_{t+1} \equiv \frac{p_t p_{t+1}}{p_{t+1}} \qquad (15.31)$$

It follows immediately that, given an income vector $(y, 0)$ and a gross yield R, the representative household's homothetic utility function is maximized by a savings

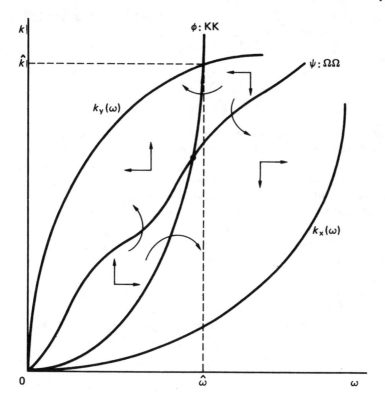

Figure 15.4 Two-sector growth: $k_x < k_y$.

function that is linearly homogeneous in income. More precisely, $y - c_1 = y\theta(R)$ where $\theta: \mathbb{R}_+ \rightarrow [0,1]$ is a saving rate that depends only on the rate of return.

From the budget constraints in equations (15.30) and (15.31), we have

$$s_t = w_t \theta(R_{t+1}) \tag{15.32}$$

where

$$w_t = w_y(k_t^y) \qquad \text{from equation (15.23b)}$$

$$R_{t+1} = \frac{p_t p_{t+1}}{p_{t+1}} = p_t f'_x(k_{t+1}^x) \qquad \text{from equation (15.23a)}$$

$$= \frac{f'_y(k_t^y)}{f'_x(k_t^x)} f'_x(k_{t+1}^x) \qquad \text{from equation (15.23a) again.}$$

This transforms equation (15.32) into an expression connecting saving with the wage–rental ratio alone:

$$s_t = w_y(k_t^y)\theta \left[\frac{f'_y(k_t^y)f'_x(k_{t+1}^x)}{f'_x(k_t^x)} \right] \tag{15.33}$$

Dynamical equilibria must equalize the capital stock at $t+1$ to both saving and the output of the investment good in the previous period, that is,

$$k_{t+1} = y_t = s_t \tag{15.34}$$

Combining equations (15.28), (15.33), and (15.34) we obtain the following planar dynamical system in the state variables (k, ω):

$$k_{t+1} = y(k_t, \omega_t) \qquad (15.35a)$$

$$\theta \left\{ f'_y[k_y(\omega_t)] \frac{f'_x[k_x(\omega_{t+1})]}{f'_x[k_x(\omega_t)]} \right\} w_y[k_y(\omega_t)] = y(k_t, \omega_t) \qquad (15.35b)$$

Orbitally equivalent dynamical systems could be expressed in terms of the state-variable vectors (k, k^x), (k, k^y), or (k, p) because k^x, k^y, and p are all continuous monotone functions of the wage–rental ratio. The equivalence of ω to either k^x or k^y is evident from figures 15.3 and 15.4. How the consumption good price relates to factor prices is spelled out in the *Stolper–Samuelson theorem*, another well-known result in international trade theory. Question II.33 asks readers to show that (i) if $k_x(\omega) > k_y(\omega)$ for all ω, then ω and w are decreasing functions of p, and ρ is increasing in p with elasticity above unity; (ii) if $k_x(\omega) < k_y(\omega)$ for all ω, then ω and w are increasing in p (the latter with elasticity greater than unity), and ρ is a decreasing function.[9]

The vector field of the dynamical system (15.35a) and (15.35b) consists of four regions defined by the loci $KK = \{(k_t, \omega_t) \in \mathbb{R}^2_+ \mid k_{t+1} = k_t\}$ and $\Omega\Omega = \{(k_t, \omega_t) \in \mathbb{R}^2_+ \mid \omega_{t+1} = \omega_t\}$. For the first locus, equation (15.35a) yields

$$k_{t+1} \geq k_t \quad \text{iff} \quad \frac{(k_x - k_t)f_y}{k_x - k_y} \geq k_t$$

$$\text{iff} \quad 1 + \frac{f_y}{k_x - k_y} k_t \leq \frac{k_x f_y}{k_x - k_y}$$

Hence

$$k_{t+1} \geq k_t \quad \text{iff} \quad k_t \leq \phi(\omega_t) \equiv \frac{k_x(\omega_t)f_y[k_y(\omega_t)]}{k_x(\omega_t) - k_y(\omega_t) + f_y[k_y(\omega_t)]} \qquad (15.36)$$

Proceeding in a similar fashion, we obtain

$$\omega_{t+1} \geq \omega_t \quad \text{iff} \quad k_x(\omega_{t+1}) \geq k_x(\omega_t)$$

$$\text{iff} \quad f'_x[k_x(\omega_{t+1})] \leq f'_x[k_x(\omega_t)]$$

$$\text{iff} \quad \frac{(k_x - k_t)f_y}{(k_x - k_y)w_y} \leq \theta[f'_y(k_y)]$$

assuming that θ is a monotone function. Therefore

$$\omega_{t+1} \geq \omega_t \quad \text{iff} \quad k_t f_y \geq k_x f_y - \theta(\cdot)(k_x - k_y)w_y$$

which implies

$$\omega_{t+1} \geq \omega_t \quad \text{iff} \quad k_t \geq \psi(\omega_t) \equiv [1 - g(\omega_t)]k_x(\omega_t) + g(\omega_t)k_y(\omega_t) \qquad (15.37a)$$

where

$$g(\omega) \equiv \frac{\theta[f'_y(k_y(\omega))]w_y[k_y(\omega)]}{f_y[k_y(\omega)]} \qquad (15.37b)$$

A steady state $(\overline{k}, \overline{\omega}) \in \mathbb{R}^2_+$ is a pair that satisfies $\overline{k} = \phi(\overline{\omega}) = \psi(\overline{\omega})$. Noting that $w_y = f_y - k_y f'_y < f_y$ and $\theta \in [0,1]$, it follows that $g(\omega) \in [0,1]$; hence ψ must be a convex combination of the functions k_x and k_y. In particular,

$$\psi(0) = 0 \tag{15.38}$$

Let us look now into the properties of the function ϕ. Rewrite this function in the form

$$\phi(\omega) = \frac{f_y(k_y)}{1 - k_y/k_x + f_y/k_y} \tag{15.39}$$

Starting with the case $k_x(\omega) > k_y(\omega)$ for all ω, we make the following assumptions.

Assumption 15.1 $\lim_{k \to 0} f'_y(k) = \infty$.
Assumption 15.2 $g(\omega)$ is bounded away from zero.
Assumption 15.3 $k_y(\omega)/k_x(\omega)$ is bounded by a number $\beta < 1$.
Assumption 15.4 There is a unique $\hat{k} > 0$ such that $f_y(k_y) > k_y$ iff $k_y < \hat{k}$.
Assumption 15.5 Equivalently, there is a unique $\hat{\omega} > 0$ such that $k_y(\hat{\omega}) = \hat{k}$ and $f_y[k_y(\omega)] > k_y(\omega)$ iff $\omega < \hat{\omega}$.

Then we have immediately that

$$\phi(0) = 0 \tag{15.40a}$$

$$\phi(\omega) < k_x(\omega) \qquad \forall \omega > 0 \tag{15.40b}$$

$$\phi(\omega) > k_y(\omega) \qquad \text{iff } \omega < \hat{\omega} \tag{15.40c}$$

These inequalities imply that $\psi(\hat{\omega}) > \phi(\hat{\omega})$ because ψ always lies in the interval $[k_y(\omega), k_x(\omega)]$; figure 15.3 illustrates. This figure also suggests that a positive steady state will exist if $\psi(\omega) < \phi(\omega)$ for very small ω or, equivalently, if

$$\lim_{\omega \to 0} \frac{\psi(\omega)}{\phi(\omega)} \equiv \lim_{\omega \to 0} z(\omega) < 1 \tag{15.41}$$

Define

$$A(\omega) \equiv \frac{k_y(\omega)}{f_y[k_y(\omega)]} \tag{15.42a}$$

$$\beta(\omega) \equiv \frac{k_y(\omega)}{k_x(\omega)} \in (0,1) \tag{15.42b}$$

and observe that

$$z(\omega) = [1 - g(\omega) + \beta(\omega)g(\omega)]\left[1 + \frac{1 - \beta}{\beta} A(\omega)\right] \tag{15.43}$$

Assumption 15.1 implies that $A(\omega) \to 0$ as $\omega \to 0$ and hence

$$\lim_{\omega \to 0} z(\omega) = 1 - \lim_{\omega \to 0} \{[1 - \beta(\omega)]g(\omega)\} < 1$$

if $g(\omega)$ is bounded away from zero and $\beta(\omega)$ has an upper bound below unity. If that is the case, then the vector field drawn in figure 15.3 suggests that at least one asymptotically stable steady state exists; see Galor (1991) for a detailed proof. We summarize in the next theorem.

Theorem 15.9 Suppose that $k_x(\omega) > k_y(\omega)$ for all ω, that assumptions 15.1 through 15.4 hold, and that the two dated consumption goods are normal and gross substitutes. Then there exists at least one, asymptotically stable, positive steady state $(\bar{k}, \bar{\omega})$.

This result is a *sufficient condition* for the existence of an asymptotically stable steady state in economies with smooth technologies. If the production functions are of the fixed-proportions variety, for instance, theorem 15.9 does not apply. Equation (9.1) (section 9.1) suggests that the positive steady state of the two-sector model with Leontieff technologies will be unstable unless $k_x/k_y > 1 + A$, that is, unless the consumption good is *substantially* more capital intensive than the investment good.

Solow (1961) demonstrated some time ago by a counterexample that $k_x(\omega) > k_y(\omega)$ cannot be a *necessary* condition for asymptotic stability. Here is how he did it.

Example 15.3 (The triple Cobb–Douglas economy) Suppose that $F^y(K,L) = (KL)^{1/2}$, $F^x(K,L) = K^\alpha L^{1-\alpha}$, $u(c_1, c_2) = c_1^{1-\theta} c_2^\theta$ for constant $\alpha \in (0, 1)$ and $\theta \in (0, 1)$. Then equation (15.22) yields

$$\omega = k^y = (1 - \alpha)k^x/\alpha \tag{15.44}$$

which implies

$$k_y(\omega) = \omega \qquad k_x(\omega) = \alpha\omega/(1 - \alpha) \tag{15.45}$$

The consumption good is produced more capital intensively if $\alpha > 1/2$, less capital intensively if $\alpha < 1/2$. Notice also that

$$y(k,\omega) = \frac{\alpha\omega - (1 - \alpha)k}{(2\alpha - 1)\sqrt{\omega}} \tag{15.46a}$$

Aggregate saving is given by equation (15.3), that is,

$$s = \frac{\theta}{2}\sqrt{k_y} = \frac{\theta}{2}\sqrt{\omega} \tag{15.46b}$$

The dynamical system (15.35a) and (15.35b), that is,

$$k_{t+1} = y(k_t, \omega_t) = s_t$$

now reduces to

$$\omega_t = Ak_t \tag{15.47a}$$

$$k_{t+1} = \frac{\theta}{2}(Ak_t)^{1/2} \tag{15.47b}$$

where

$$A \equiv \frac{2(1 - \alpha)}{2\alpha(1 - \theta) + \theta} > 0 \tag{15.47c}$$

Clearly, equation (15.47b) has one positive stable steady state, $\bar{k} = A\theta^2/4$, which is asymptotically stable irrespective of the value of A, that is, *even if the consumption good is less capital-intensive than the investment good.*

Reversing our capital intensity ranking, *we assume now that $k_x(\omega) < k_y(\omega)$ for all ω.* Proceeding as before, we end up reversing inequalities (15.36) and (15.37a). We have now

$$k_{t+1} \geq k_t \quad \text{iff} \quad k_t \geq \phi(\omega_t) \tag{15.48}$$

$$\omega_{t+1} \geq \omega_t \quad \text{iff} \quad k_t \leq \psi(\omega_t) \tag{15.49}$$

Continuing, we obtain

$$k_x(\omega) \leq \psi(\omega) \leq k_y(\omega) \tag{15.50a}$$

$$\phi(\omega) \geq k_x(\omega) \qquad \forall \omega > 0 \tag{15.50b}$$

$$\phi(\omega) \leq k_y(\omega) \quad \text{iff} \quad \omega \leq \hat{\omega} \tag{15.50c}$$

These inequalities imply that $\phi(\omega) > \psi(\hat{\omega})$, and a positive steady state will exist if

$$\lim_{\omega \to 0} z(\omega) \equiv \lim_{\omega \to 0} \frac{\psi(\omega)}{\phi(\omega)} > 1 \tag{15.51}$$

To find a set of conditions that guarantees (15.51), we replace assumption 15.3

Assumption 15.3′ $k_y(\omega)/k_x(\omega)$ is bounded below by a number $B > 1$.

Then equation (15.42) yields

$$z(\omega) \geq 1 - g(\omega) + B(\omega)g(\omega) \geq 1 + (B + 1)g_0 > 1 \tag{15.52}$$

where g_0 is a lower bound on $g(\omega)$. This inequality implies (15.51) and hence ensures the existence of a positive steady state $(\bar{k}, \bar{w})$. The vector field in figure 15.4 suggests that $(\bar{k}, \bar{w})$ is a saddle, and Galor (1991) proves this conjecture to be correct. We sum up in the following theorem.

Theorem 15.10 Suppose that $k_x(\omega) < k_y(\omega)$ for all ω, that assumptions 15.2, 15.3′ and 15.4 hold, and that the two dated consumption goods are normal and gross substitutes. Then there exists at least one saddle steady state $(\bar{k},\bar{w}) > 0$.

The main difference between the cases covered in theorems 15.9 and 15.10 is the correlation they predict along an equilibrium path between the stock of capital and factor prices. Theorem 15.10, in particular, asserts that, if $k_x < k_y$ for all ω, then along the stable manifold we should observe k and ω to change in the same direction. Consulting the Stolper–Samuelson theorem leads us to conclude that the stock of capital k and its price $1/p$ must change in opposite directions along an equilibrium trajectory. Exactly the same prediction comes out of the q theory of investment explored in section 13.3.

Theorem 15.9 makes a more guarded prediction on how the stock of capital correlates with its price. *Any* correlation, says that theorem, is possible in the neighborhood of an asymptotically stable steady state. This is one reason why economists frequently call *indeterminate* equilibria that converge to stable steady states and *determinate* equilibria that converge to saddles.

We conclude with a brief discussion of factor-intensity reversals, a possibility that we have excluded up to this point. Readers who combine figures 15.3 and 15.4 may imagine a critical value ω_c such that $k_x(\omega) > k_y(\omega)$ for $\omega \in (0,\omega_c)$ and $k_x(\omega) < k_y(\omega)$ for $\omega > \omega_c$. One way to understand what happens in the case of factor reversals is to investigate an economy in which one technology has fixed proportions and the other has variable proportions.

Example 15.4 (Factor-intensity reversals) Suppose that $F^y(K,L) = \min(K,\lambda L)$, $F^x(K,L) = (KL)^{1/2}$, and $u(c_1,c_2) = c_1^{1-\theta}c_2^{\theta}$ for some $\theta \in (0,1)$ and $\lambda \in (0,1)$. Then $k_y(\omega) = \lambda$, $k_x(\omega) = \omega$, and the consumption good is more capital intensive if, and only if, $\omega > \lambda$.

The basic building blocks of this dynamic economy are the two functions y and s that describe investment goods, output, and saving. From equation (15.28) we obtain

$$y(k,\omega) = \frac{\omega - k}{\omega - \lambda} \tag{15.53}$$

From the zero-profit condition in the investment goods sector and the factor demand schedules in the consumption goods sector, we also have

$$p = (p/2)k_x^{-1/2} \quad w = \rho k_x^{1/2}/2 \tag{15.54}$$

$$1 = \rho + \lambda w \tag{15.55}$$

Therefore

$$2/p = k_x^{1/2} + \lambda k_x^{-1/2} = \omega^{1/2} + \lambda \omega^{-1/2} \tag{15.56a}$$

Combining equations (15.54) and (15.56a), we obtain

$$w = \frac{\omega}{\lambda + \omega} \tag{15.56b}$$

which leads to the following expression for saving

$$s = \theta w = \frac{\theta\omega}{\lambda + \omega} \tag{15.57}$$

The dynamical system of equations (15.35a) and (15.35b) reduces to

$$k_{t+1} = \frac{\omega_t - k_t}{\omega_t - \lambda} = \frac{\theta\omega_t}{\lambda + \omega_t} \tag{15.58}$$

Since the saving rate is fixed, this is a scalar system fully described by a scalar variable – either k_t or ω_t. To see this, we assume $\omega_t \neq \lambda$, solve equation (15.58) for the capital–labor ratio

$$k_t = q(\omega_t) \equiv \omega_t + \theta\omega_t \frac{\lambda - \omega_t}{\lambda + \omega_t} \tag{15.59}$$

and substitute into $k_{t+1} = \theta\omega_t/(\lambda + \omega_t)$ to obtain

$$\omega_{t+1} \frac{1 + \theta(\lambda - \omega_{t+1})}{\lambda + \omega_{t+1}} = \frac{\theta\omega_t}{\lambda + \omega_t} \tag{15.60}$$

These equations reveal that there are two steady states: a trivial one $(k,\omega) = (0,0)$; and an interior positive steady state $(\bar{k},\bar{\omega})$ associated with the fixed point of equation (15.60). This one satisfies

$$\bar{\omega} = \frac{\theta - \lambda(1 + \theta)}{1 - \theta} \tag{15.61a}$$

$$\bar{k} = \frac{\theta - \lambda(1 - \theta)}{1 - 2\lambda} \qquad (15.61b)$$

It is a meaningful steady state if $\bar{\omega} > 0$ and $\bar{k} \in (\lambda, 1)$. After a little algebra, it can be shown that these two inequalities hold if

$$\lambda < \frac{\theta}{1 + \theta} \qquad (15.62)$$

Local stability properties of the states $(0,0)$ and $(\bar{k}, \bar{\omega})$ follow from equation (15.60). In particular, solving (15.60) backward we obtain

$$\omega_t = J(\omega_{t+1}) \qquad (15.63a)$$

where

$$J(\omega) = \frac{\lambda\omega[\theta + (1 - \theta)(\omega - \bar{\omega})]}{\theta\lambda + (1 - \theta)(\bar{\omega} - \omega)\omega} \qquad (15.63b)$$

As a diagnostic check, we observe that both zero and $\bar{\omega}$ are fixed points of the map J. In the forward dynamics, the origin is unstable while $\bar{\omega}$ is asymptotically stable; in fact, we see readily that, if (15.62) holds,

$$J'(0) = \frac{\lambda(1 + \theta)}{\theta} < 1$$

and

$$J'(\bar{\omega}) = \frac{\lambda\theta + (1 - \theta)\bar{\omega}(\lambda + \bar{\omega})}{\lambda\theta} > 1$$

Relative factor intensities do not affect the local stability properties of steady states in this economy: the positive steady state is asymptotically stable even if the consumption good is less capital intensive than the investment good at $(\bar{k}, \bar{\omega})$.

Notes

1. Among potential reasons for bequests of wealth are altruism on the part of the parent (see Barro, 1974); the provision of incentives that induce prospective heirs to behave in a way the testator finds desirable (see Bernheim et al., 1985); and accidental death of retired individuals who cannot purchase actuarially fair annuities (see Kotlikoff and Spivak, 1981).
2. If rates of time preference differ among individuals, the more patient individuals will tend over time to keep accumulating as assets the liabilities of the less patient ones. The issue is addressed in question II.22.
3. The hypothesis is due to Milton Friedman (1957) who also coined the term; see Bewley (1977) for a rigorous exposition. Hall (1978) and King (1983) provide literate overviews of a vast empirical literature.
4. Data on life-cycle saving by Japanese households, contained in Hayashi et al. (1988), reveal that the median surviving family continues to accumulate assets well beyond the age of 70, with a modest drop-off for those who reach 80.
5. Recall that $\beta > 1$ simply defines the Samuelson case in a pure-exchange economy whose representative household has a level endowment profile and additive utility.

6. This broken chain is an example of an *inoperative* bequest motive which occurs whenever a particular dynasty chooses to pass nothing down the line because one cohort is under-endowed or insufficiently altruistic. See Abel (1987) and Kimball (1987) for more on altruistic transfers.

7. See Jones (1965) for an early contribution to international trade and Drazen and Eckstein (1988) for a more recent one on migration in a dual economy. Dual-economy models on migration date back to the work of Lewis (1954) and Ranis and Fei (1964).

8. See the review article by Boldrin and Woodford (1990).

9. The intuitive meaning of this result becomes more transparent if one realizes that an increase in the price of the consumption good must reduce the relative size of the investment goods sector by attracting resources to the consumption goods sector. If $k_x > k_y$ then the rental rate will rise and the wage rate will fall in response to an increase in p.

16 Summing up

In Part II we studied the simplest types of dynamical equilibria in economies whose only store of value is *inside* money or private loans. The study of these economies, which operate without an *outside* asset such as currency or interest-bearing national debt, provides valuable information on how physical capital and private credit influence the allocation of resources over time, and shape the process of economic development. We also developed several criteria for judging the welfare properties of competitive equilibria and, more generally, of any resource-distributing scheme.

An economy with stationary preferences, endowments, and technology will typically possess an odd number of nontrivial stationary competitive equilibria if its structure satisfies certain technical assumptions about continuity, convexity, monotonicity, and non-satiation of preferences. But not all "nicely behaved" economies necessarily admit unique or stable stationary equilibria; uniqueness and/or stability in this sense are guaranteed if one restricts economic behavior with *stronger* assumptions like normality or gross substitutability in consumption, monotonicity or sufficient variability in factor rewards, and the like.

Some non-uniqueness of equilibrium is unavoidable in dynamical economies whose steady states are sinks or saddles. These states are associated with a well-defined *equilibrium manifold* which includes a continuum of convergent equilibrium sequences indexed on initial conditions. Economists typically dislike large equilibrium manifolds, and often refer to the limit points of such manifolds as "indeterminate" steady states. The Cauchy–Peano theorem and related results (see Part I, section A.3) assure us that appropriately defined boundary-value problems have unique solutions and therefore that indeterminacy in economics arises in part from a shortage of initial conditions.

Section 28.5 discusses indeterminacy in some detail because this is a potential source of confusion to any forecaster attempting to predict the course of an economy that admits several equilibrium sequences. Some of the indeterminacy eventually disappears if all equilibria approach each other as they converge to the same limit point. Nevertheless, dynamic economies often admit a large number of equilibrium price sequences, and thus stand in stark contrast with static economies where general equilibria are locally unique (see Debreu, 1970). In other words, if $p^* \in \mathbb{R}_+^L$ is an equilibrium price vector for an Arrow–Debreu economy and (p_t^*) is a countably infinite equilibrium price sequence for an overlapping generations economy, then under very mild assumptions one can show that there is no other static equilibrium price vector $\hat{p} \in \mathbb{R}_+^L$ in the neighborhood of p^* but typically there is another equilibrium price sequence $\hat{p}_t$ near p_t^*.

What is unusual about overlapping generations economies is not only the potentially large number of dynamical equilibria but, also, the existence of competitive equilibria that are not intertemporal Pareto optima, even without externalities or increasing returns. That property sets overlapping generations economies apart from both the atemporal constructions of general equilibrium theory and the infinitely lived dynasties of optimal growth theory. In fact, we found a class of economies, collectively identified as "Samuelson," which admit suboptimal inside-money equilibria.

Where does the suboptimality come from? One obvious source may be the kind of externalities or spillovers discussed in chapter 14: individuals choose selfishly without reckoning how their decisions will affect the welfare of other households – contemporaneous or subsequent ones. Setting these externalities aside, what element in the description of a standard overlapping generations economy of the Samuelson type must one change in order to restore to competitive equilibria their "invisible hand" property? This issue is worth reviewing with some care. Observe first that in a typical Samuelson economy all households of a given generation face identical prices and a single lifetime budget constraint; in this context *suboptimality has nothing to do with incomplete or imperfect markets*. Next recall from chapter 12 that competitive equilibria are optimal in finite economies, which means that the suboptimality we found in other chapters must relate to the *infinite number* of households and dated commodities.

The double infinity, to be sure, does not by itself guarantee the suboptimality of equilibria in smoothly functioning competitive markets. "Classical" economies, we recall, possess optimal inside-money equilibria; and we discused in chapter 15 how the injection of one infinitely lived household in a Samuelson economy eliminates all inefficient equilibria. In an infinite-horizon economy, however, competitive equilibria are unusually large objects: the total resources of the economy may not have finite value even if all commodity prices are finite. Thus a distinction exists between "valuation equilibria," in which resources have finite value, and competitive equilibria in general (see Debreu, 1954). It turns out that valuation equilibria are Pareto optimal, while competitive equilibria with an infinite resource value may or may not be optimal.

Malinvaud's fundamental result (proved in the Technical Appendix) has a similar interpretation: if a competitive equilibrium is dynamically inefficient, then it *must* assign infinite value to society's total resources. The contrapositive statement is also true: finite-wealth equilibria are efficient. Golden rule equilibria, in which the interest and growth rates coincide, are examples of optimal allocations with an infinite resource value.

Returning now to a question asked a few paragraphs earlier, we outline some remedies for inefficient competitive equilibria; some of them we have already discussed in Part II while others will play a prominent role in Parts III and IV. We begin with infinitely lived households of the type discussed in chapters 13 and 15. Any economy that consists of finitely many identical individuals with infinite planning horizons does not admit competitive equilibria with infinite resources simply because the consumption possibilities of the economy are *identical* to those of the representative household; infinite wealth is meaningless here for it would mean an infinitely "large" budget set for some household and hence ill-defined individual behavior.

Similar considerations apply to an economy of overlapping generations that contains one or more infinitely lived individuals born at the beginning of time. These individuals serve as bridges over time – they intermediate among households with finite lifespans, allowing sequences of individuals to trade indirectly with each other. The end result is to restore the property of *complete market participation* to overlapping generational structures, converting them in effect to economies in which all generations can meet in the beginning of time to exchange forward commodity claims of any maturity desired. We discussed in chapter 15 how these expanded trading possibilities may rule out competitive equilibria with low interest rates.

From the vantage point of economic policy, it is of more interest to examine the extent to which suboptimal equilibria have something to do with the asset structure of the economy and in particular with the availability of durable goods. There are two kinds of durables that one should consider: one includes consumption goods (housing) and factors of production (physical capital); the other consists of paper assets (currency, national debt) that do not directly affect consumption or production possibilities. We conclude with a brief look at each class of durables.

The simple overlapping generations model of capital accumulation originally studied by Diamond (1965) does not guarantee that equilibria will be optimal. Roughly speaking, optimality is more likely to occur if the economy begins with a relatively small capital stock, that is, below the "golden rule" level. The situation changes considerably if there is a nondepreciating input, like land, whose services can be converted to a consumption good by a constant-returns technology (see Part IV and also Woodford, 1984, pp. 15ff.). Assuming that the marginal factor product is a constant independent of use means that the constant output stream attributable to a unit of the input has infinite present value when the interest rate is negative. This is not consistent with equilibrium because, when the interest rate is negative, any competitive market would surely assign an infinite price to the durable input we have just described.

But this is not a robust property of durable goods. As we know from our study of growth theory in chapters 13 and 14, the mere *existence* of durables like productive capital and inventories is not sufficient to ensure dynamic efficiency. For that purpose we turn to *outside assets*, that is, government liabilities that are valued in exchange even though they are of no direct use as commodities or factors of production. Parts III and IV take up the study of outside-asset equilibria and of the policy options that such assets make available to central bankers and other policymakers.

Technical appendix (*)

Proof of Theorem 13.1

First we demonstrate the existence of a backward-looking temporary competitive equilibrium by fixing $k_{t+1} > 0$, letting k_t vary continuously from zero to infinity, and watching what happens to the excess demand for capital $\text{ED}_t = (1 + n)k_{t+1} - z(R_{t+1}, w_t)$. Note that, at $k_t = 0$, wages and saving are necessarily zero, which means $\text{ED}_t > 0$. As $k_t \to \infty$, on the other hand, $\text{ED}_t < 0$ because normality makes z a strictly increasing function of k_t. The intermediate value theorem says that, for a given k_{t+1}, there is a k_t such that $\text{ED}_t = 0$; this value is unique since ED_t is monotone in k_t.

To show that a forward-looking temporary competitive equilibrium exists, we now fix $k_t > 0$ and let k_{t+1} vary. Because

$$\text{ED}_t > (1 + n)k_{t+1} - w_t = (1 + n)k_{t+1} - [f(k_t) - k_t f'(k_t)]$$

it is clear that $\text{ED}_t > 0$ as $k_{t+1} \to \infty$. Also note that

$$\begin{aligned} \text{ED}_t &\sim (1 + n)k_{t+1}R_{t+1} - R_{t+1}z(R_{t+1}, w_t) \\ &= (1 + n)k_{t+1}[1 - \delta + f'(k_{t+1})] - R_{t+1}z(R_{t+1}, w_t) \end{aligned}$$

Therefore, as $k_{t+1} \to 0$, ED_t becomes negative: the first term goes readily to zero while the second one, which is increasing in R_{t+1} whenever goods are normal, becomes very large.

Continuity implies that a forward-looking temporary competitive equilibrium exists, and it is unique if ED_t is monotone in k_{t+1} which is true when the function z is increasing in the interest factor R.

Proof of Theorem 15.2

Because population growth, production, and consumer heterogeneity do not change proofs to any appreciable extent, we deal with a pure-exchange economy with a fixed number of identical households. Suppose that a feasible allocation $C^t = (c_1^t, c_2^t)_{t=0}^{\infty}$ is inefficient, that is, it is dominated by another feasible allocation

$\bar{C}^t = (\bar{c}_1^t, \bar{c}_2^t)_{t=0}^{\infty}$. This means that there exists a non-negative sequence $(\epsilon_t)_{t=1}^{\infty}$ of inter-generational transfers such that

$$\bar{c}_1^t = c_1^t - \epsilon_t \qquad \bar{c}_2^t = c_2^t + \epsilon_{t+1} \tag{A.1}$$

and $\epsilon_t > 0$ for all $t \geq \tau$. With no loss of generality, we set $\tau = 1$ and write out the utility gain from the intergenerational transfer of resources as

$$\delta_t = u(\bar{c}^t) - u(c^t) = -\epsilon_t u_1(c^t) + \epsilon_{t+1} u_2(c^t) - \Delta^2 \tag{A.2}$$

Equation (A.2) is a Taylor-series expansion of $u(\bar{c}^t)$ about the point $c^t = (c_1^t, c_2^t)$, in which the residual Δ^2 contains higher-order derivatives and is non-negative because of concavity. Recalling that the interest factor R_t equals the ratio u_1/u_2 of marginal utilities evaluated at c^t, we obtain from (A.2)

$$\delta_t = u_2(c^t)(\epsilon_{t+1} - \epsilon_t R_t) - \Delta^2 \tag{A.3}$$

Because (c_1^t, c_2^t) is a dominated allocation, we have by definition that $\delta_t > 0$ for all $t \geq 1$. Hence

$$u_2(c^t)(\epsilon_{t+1} - \epsilon_t R_t) \geq \Delta^2 \geq 0$$

which implies $\epsilon_{t+1} \geq R_t \epsilon_t$ for all $t \geq 1$. The multiperiod interest factor $R^t = \Pi_{s=1}^t R_s$ then satisfies

$$R^t \leq \frac{\epsilon_2}{\epsilon_1} \frac{\epsilon_3}{\epsilon_2} \cdots \frac{\epsilon_{t+1}}{\epsilon_t} = \frac{\epsilon_{t+1}}{\epsilon_1} \tag{A.4}$$

Since the transfer $\epsilon_t > 0$ is bounded above by the finite resources available to society in period t, *the factor R^t associated with the inefficient allocation C_t is bounded above.*

To prove that $R^t \to 0$ as $t \to \infty$, we assume

$$\lim_{t \to \infty} R^t > 0 \tag{A.5}$$

and obtain a contradiction. Consider, in particular, the allocation $\hat{C}_t = (c_1^t - \hat{\epsilon}_t, c_2^t)$ where the positive sequence $(\hat{\epsilon}_t)_{t=1}^{\infty}$ is chosen so that the resulting marginal rate of substitution $\hat{R} = u_1(\hat{c}^t)/u_2(\hat{c}^t)$ is a constant multiple, γR_t with $\gamma > 1$, of the marginal rate $R_t = u_1(c^t)/u_2(c^t)$ that corresponds to the original dominated allocation c_t. This is something we can always do if, for each fixed $c_2 > 0$, the marginal rate of substitution at (c_1, c_2) tends to infinity as c_1 goes to zero.

Then the allocation $\hat{c}_t$ is inferior to c_t, and hence dynamically inefficient. However, the associated multiperiod interest factor $\hat{R}^t$ equals $\gamma^t R^t$, where $\gamma > 1$. Hence $\lim_{t \to \infty} R^t > 0$ necessarily implies $\lim_{t \to \infty} \hat{R}^t = \infty$; therefore $\hat{R}^t$ is not bounded above even though it corresponds to a dynamically inefficient allocation. This is the contradiction we need to the assumption made by inequality (A.5). Thus $R^t \to 0$ as $t \to \infty$, and the theorem is proved.

Bibliography

Further reading

Of particular value here are Diamond (1965), Gale (1973), and Balasko and Shell (1980) as introductions to the overlapping generations model. Malinvaud (1953), Cass (1972), and Zilcha (1990) are excellent on intertemporal efficiency. Kehoe and Levine (1984, 1990) and Woodford (1984) contain a number of useful extensions of the overlapping generations model to many physical goods and longer lifespans, as does Galor (1991) on two-sector growth.

Stiglitz and Weiss (1981) explain how private information causes credit rationing in a partial equilibrium setting. General equilibrium analyses of credit rationing in pure exchange economies are in Wallace (1980) and Azariadis and Smith (1992). Credit rationing tends to affect households and firms in different ways; empirical work since Meyer and Kuh (1957) has tried to sort out the various mechanisms at work on net borrowers and lenders. Among recent contributions we note Hayashi (1987), Zeldes (1989), Jappelli and Pagano (1992), as well as the more theoretical work of Gertler (1988).

Solow (1956) remains a highly readable introduction to capital-oriented neoclassical growth theory. Much of the traditional development literature, from Lewis (1954) to Drazen and Eckstein (1988), focuses greater attention on "dual labor markets" and other institutional features of the development process.

Behrman (1990) surveys several modern theories of economic development, many of them based on increasing returns. Romer (1986) and Lucas (1988) are key contributors here. Greenwood and Jovanovic (1990) and Bencivenga and Smith (1991) have done much to revive scholarly interest in financial aspects of economic development. Interesting data on British, European, and American development history are summed up in Kaldor (1961), Deane and Cole (1969), Braudel (1981), Wrigley and Schofield (1981), and Summers and Heston (1988). For other interesting applications of neoclassical growth theory, see Buiter (1981) and Persson (1985) on the balance of payments, and Chamley (1981) on capital income taxation.

Infinitely lived agents with a constant rate of time preference have been common in the economics literature since Ramsey (1928). Uzawa (1964) and McKenzie (1976) have studied multisector growth theory in this framework. Brock and Mirman (1972) investigate growth with technological uncertainty; see Stokey and Lucas (1989) for a thorough treatment of this topic. For extensions of the optimal growth model to idiosyncratic rates of time preference, consult Becker and Foias (1987). Yaari (1965) has done fundamental work on consumers with uncertain lifetimes; see Kotlikoff and Spivak (1981) and Blanchard (1985) for two instructive illustrations.

Macroeconomic externalities of the general type we found in chapter 14 are common in settings outside growth theory. Searching for trading partners, for instance, changes the size or "thickness" of a market, as in Diamond (1982), and influences the terms of trade for the average participant. Self-seeking behavior in strategic environments causes "coordination failures" among agents who do not take account of how their decisions influence the welfare of their fellow traders; Cooper and John (1988) are a good reference here.

References

Abel, A. 1982: Dynamic effects of permanent and temporary tax policies in a Q model of investment. *Journal of Monetary Economics*, 9, 353–73.

—— 1987: Operative gift and bequest motives. Working Paper 2331, National Bureau of Economic Research.

Akerlof, G. 1970: The market for 'lemons': qualitative uncertainty and the market mechanism. *Quarterly Journal of Economics*, 84, 488–500.

Ando, A. and Modigliani, F. 1963: The life cycle hypothesis of saving: aggregate implications and tests. *American Economic Review*, 53, 55–84.

Arrow, K. 1951: An extension of the basic theorems of classical welfare economics. In J. Neyman (ed.), *Proceedings of the Second Berkeley Symposium on Mathematical Statistics and Probability*, Berkeley, CA: University of California Press.

—— 1962: The economic implications of learning by doing. *Review of Economic Studies*, 29, 155–73.

—— 1963: Uncertainty and the welfare economics of medical care. *American Economic Review*, 53, 941–69.

Azariadis, C. and Drazen, A. 1990a: Threshold externalities in economic development. *Quarterly Journal of Economics*, 105, 501–26.

—— and —— 1990b: Demographic transitions in a dual economy. Mimeo, University of Pennsylvania.

—— and Smith, B. 1991: Growth with adverse selection. Mimeo, University of Pennsylvania.

—— and —— 1992: Adverse selection in the overlapping generations model: the case of pure exchange. *Journal of Economic Theory*, forthcoming.

Balasko, Y. and Shell, K. 1980: The overlapping generations model, I: The case of pure exchange without money. *Journal of Economic Theory*, 23, 281–306.

Barro, R. 1974: Are government bonds net wealth? *Journal of Political Economy*, 82, 379–402.

—— and Becker, G. 1989: Fertility choice in a model of economic growth. *Econometrica*, 57, 481–501.

Baumol, W. 1986: Productivity growth, convergence and welfare. *American Economic Review*, 76, 1042–85.

—— and Wolff, E. 1988: Productivity growth, convergence and welfare: reply. *American Economic Review*, 78, 1155–9.

Becker, G. 1964: *Human Capital*, New York: National Bureau of Economic Research.

—— 1967: Human capital and the personal distribution of income: an analytical approach. Woytinsky Lecture, University of Michigan.

Becker, R. and Foias, C. 1987: A characterization of Ramsey equilibrium. *Journal of Economic Theory*, 41, 173–84.

Behrman, J. 1990: *Human Resource Led Development?* New Delhi: ILO-ARTEP.

Bencivenga, V. and Smith, B. 1991: Financial intermediation and endogenous growth. *Review of Economic Studies*, 58, 195–209.

Benhabib, J. and Nishimura, N. 1979: The Hopf bifurcation and the existence and stability of closed orbits in multisector models of economic growth. *Journal of Economic Theory*, 21, 421–44.

Bewley, T. 1977: The permanent income hypothesis: a theoretical formulation. *Journal of Economic Theory*, 16, 252–92.

Blanchard, O. 1985: Debt, deficits, and finite horizons. *Journal of Political Economy*, 93, 223–47.

Boldrin, M. and Woodford, M. 1990: Equilibrium models displaying endogenous fluctuations and chaos: a survey. *Journal of Monetary Economics*, 25, 189–222.

Braudel, F. 1981: *The Structure of Everyday Life*, vol. 1. New York: Harper and Row.

Brock, W. and Mirman, L. 1972: Optimal economic growth and uncertainty: the discounted case. *Journal of Economic Theory*, 4, 479–513.

Budnevich, C. 1990: International capital mobility in a general equilibrium model of asset prices, investment, saving and external debt. Mimeo, University of Pennsylvania.

Buiter, W. 1981: Time preference and international lending and borrowing in an overlapping-generations model. *Journal of Political Economy*, 89, 769–97.

Cass, D. 1972: On capital overaccumulation in the aggregative, neoclassical model of economic growth: a complete characterization. *Journal of Economic Theory*, 4, 200–23.

Chamley, C. 1981: The welfare cost of capital income taxation in a growing economy. *Journal of Political Economy*, 89, 468–96.

Chiang, A. 1974: *Fundamental Methods of Mathematical Economics*, 2nd edn. New York: McGraw-Hill.

Cipolla, E. 1974: *The Economic History of World Population*, 6th edn. London: Penguin.

Cooper, R. and John, A. 1988: Coordinating coordination failures in Keynesian macroeconomics. *Quarterly Journal of Economics*, 103, 441–64.

Deane, P. and Cole, W. 1969: *British Economic Growth 1688–1959*. Cambridge: Cambridge University Press.

Debreu, G. 1954: Valuation equilibrium and Pareto optimum. *Proceedings of the National Academy of Sciences*, 40, 588–92.

—— 1959: *The Theory of Value*. New York: Wiley.

—— 1970: Economies with a finite set of equilibria. *Econometrica*, 38, 387–92.

de la Fuente, A. 1990: On the dynamics of low-level development traps. Mimeo, University of Pennsylvania.

Denison, A. 1974: *Accounting for United States Economic Growth 1929–1969*. Washington, DC: Brookings Institution.

Diamond, P. 1965: National debt in a neoclassical growth model. *American Economic Review*, 55, 1026–50.

—— 1982: Aggregate demand management in search equilibrium. *Journal of Political Economy*, 90, 881–94.

—— and Mirrlees, J. 1971: Optimal taxation and public production (parts I and II). *American Economic Review*, 61, 8–27, 261–78.

Drazen, A. and Eckstein, Z. 1988: On the organization of rural markets and the process of economic development. *American Economic Review*, 78, 431–43.

Friedman, M. 1957: *A Theory of the Consumption Function*. Princeton, NJ: Princeton University Press.

Gale, D. 1973: Pure exchange equilibrium of dynamic economic models. *Journal of Economic Theory*, 6, 12–36.

—— and Hellwig, M. 1985: Incentive-compatible debt contracts: the one-period problem. *Review of Economic Studies*, 52, 647–63.

Galor, O. 1991: A two-sector overlapping generations model: a characterization of the dynamical system. Mimeo, Brown University.

—— and Polemarchakis, H. 1987: International equilibrium and the transfer paradox. *Review of Economic Studies*, 54, 147–56.

—— and Ryder, H. 1989: On the existence of equilibrium in an overlapping generations model with productive capital. *Journal of Economic Theory*, 49, 360–75.

Geanakoplos, J. and Polemarchakis, J. 1986: Walrasian indeterminacy and Keynesian macroeconomics. *Review of Economic Studies*, 53, 755–79.

Gertler, M. 1988: Financial structure and aggregate economic activity: an overview. *Journal of Money, Credit and Banking*, 20, 559–88.

Greenwood, J. and Jovanovic, B. 1990: Financial development, growth and the distribution of income. *Journal of Political Economy*, 99, 1076–107.

Grossman, S. and Hart, O. 1983: An analysis of the principal–agent problem. *Econometrica*, 51, 7–45.

Guesnerie, R. 1990: The Arrow–Debreu paradigm faced with modern theories of contracting. Mimeo, DELTA.

Gurley, J. and Shaw, E. 1967: Financial development and economic development. *Economic Development and Cultural Change*, 15, 257–68.

Hall, R. 1978: Stochastic implications of the life cycle–permanent income hypothesis: theory and evidence. *Journal of Political Economy*, 86, 971–87.

Hart, O. 1975: On the optimality of equilibrium when markets are incomplete. *Journal of Economic Theory*, 11, 418–43.

Hayashi, F. 1982: Tobin's marginal q and average q: a neoclassical interpretation. *Econometrica*, 50, 213–24.

—— (1987): Tests for liquidity constraints: a critical survey. In T. Bewley (ed.), *Advances in Econometrics*, vol. 2, Cambridge: Cambridge University Press.

——, Ando, A., and Ferris, R. 1988: Life cycle and bequest savings. A study of Japanese and U.S. households based on data from the 1984 NSFIE and the 1983 Survey of Consumer Finances. *Journal of Japanese and International Economics*, 2, 450–91.

Hicks, J. 1946: *Value and Capital*, 2nd edn. Oxford: Clarendon press.

International Financial Statistics (various years). Washington, DC: International Monetary Fund.

Japelli, T. and Pagano, M. 1992: Saving, growth and liquidity constraints. Mimeo: University of Naples.

Jones, L. and Manuelli, R. 1990a: Finite lifetimes and growth. *Journal of Economic Theory*, forthcoming.

—— and—— 1990b: A convex model of equilibrium growth. *Journal of Political Economy*, 98, 1008–38.

Jones, R. 1965: The structure of simple general equilibrium models. *Journal of Political Economy*, 73, 557–72.

Kaldor, N. 1961: Capital accumulation and economic growth. In F. Lutz and D. Hague (eds), *The Theory of Capital*, New York: St Martin's Press, 177–222.

Kehoe, T. and Levine, D. 1984: Regularity in overlapping generations exchange economies. *Journal of Mathematical Economics,* 13, 69–93.

—— and —— 1990: The economics of indeterminacy in overlapping generations models. *Journal of Public Economics*, 42, 219–43.

Kimball, M. 1987: Making sense of two-sided altruism. *Journal of Monetary Economics*, 20, 301–26.

King, M. 1983: The economics of saving. Working Paper 1247, National Bureau of Economic Research.

Koopmans, T. 1957: *Three Essays on the State of Economic Science*. New York: McGraw-Hill.

—— (1965): On the concept of optimal growth. In *The Econometric Approach to Development Planning*, Chicago, IL: Rand McNally, 225–87.

Kotlikoff, L. and Spivak, A. 1981: The family as an incomplete annuities market. *Journal of Political Economy*, 89, 372–91.

Leland, H. 1968: Saving and uncertainty: the precautionary demand for saving. *Quarterly Journal of Economics*, 82, 465–73.

Lewis, W. A. 1954: Economic development with unlimited supplies of labor. *The Manchester School*, 22, 139–91.

Lucas, R. 1967: Adjustment costs and the theory of supply. *Journal of Political Economy*, 75, 321–34.

—— 1972: Expectations and the neutrality of money. *Journal of Economic Theory*, 4, 103–24.

—— 1988: On the mechanics of economic development. *Journal of Monetary Economics*, 21, 3–32.

—— 1990a: Supply-side economics: an analytical review. *Oxford Economic Papers*, 42, 293–316.

—— 1990b: Why doesn't capital flow from rich to poor countries? *American Economic Review (Papers and Proceedings)*, 80, 92–6.

—— and Prescott, E. 1971: Investment under uncertainty. *Econometrica, 39*, 659–81.

Luenberger, D. 1969: *Optimization by Vector Space Methods*. New York: Wiley.

Malinvaud, E. 1953: Capital accumulation and efficient allocation of resources. *Econometrica*, 21, 233–68.

McEvedy, C. and Jones, R. 1978: *Atlas of World Population History*. London: Penguin.

McKenzie, L. 1976: Turnpike theory. *Econometrica*, 44, 841–55.

McKinnon, R. 1973: *Money and Capital in Economic Development*. Washington, DC: Brookings Institution.

Meier, G. and Seers, D. (eds) 1984: *Pioneers in Economic Development*. Washington, DC: World Bank.

Meyer, J. and Kuh, E. (1957): *The Investment Decision*. Cambridge: Harvard University Press.

Muller, W. and Woodford, M. 1988: Determinacy of equilibrium in stationary economies with both finite and infinite lived agents. *Journal of Economic Theory*, 46, 255–90.

Murphy, K., Shleifer, A. and Vishny, R. 1989: Industrialization and the big push. *Journal of Political Economy*, 97, 1003–26.

Persson, T. 1985: Deficits and intergenerational welfare in open economies. *Journal of International Economics*, 19, 67–84.

Phelps, E. 1961: The golden rule of accumulation: a fable for growthmen. *American Economic Review*, 51, 638–43.

—— 1965: Second Essay on the golden rule of accumulation. *American Economic Review*, 55, 793–814.

Radner, R. 1967: Efficiency prices for infinite horizon production programmes. *Review of Economic Studies*, 34, 51–66.

Ramsey, F. 1927: A contribution to the theory of taxation. *Economic Journal*, 37, 47–61.

—— 1928: A mathematical theory of saving. *Economic Journal*, 38, 543–59.

Ranis, G. and Fei, J. H. C., 1964: *Development of the Labor Surplus Economy*: Theory and Evidence, Homewood, IL: Irwin.

Razin, A. 1972: Investment in human capital and economic growth. *Metroeconomica*, 24, 101–16.

Reichlin, R. 1986: Equilibrium cycles in an overlapping generations economy with production. *Journal of Economic Theory*, 40, 89–102.

Romer, P. 1986: Increasing returns and long-run growth. *Journal of Political Economy*, 94, 1002–37.

Rosen, S. 1977: Human capital: a survey of empirical research. In R. Ehrenberg (ed.), *Research in Labor Economics*, vol. I, Greenwich, CT: JAI Press.

Rosenstein-Rodan, P. 1943: Problems of industrialization of Eastern and Southeastern Europe. *Economic Journal*, 53, 202–11.

Rothschild, M. and Stiglitz, J. 1976: Equilibrium in competitive insurance markets. *Quarterly Journal of Economics*, 90, 629–50.

Sandmo, A. 1971: The effect of uncertainty on saving decisions. *Review of Economic Studies*, 37, 353–60.

Shell, K. 1971: Notes on the economics of infinity. *Journal of Political Economy*, 79, 1002–12.

Solow, R. 1956: A contribution to the theory of economic growth. *Quarterly Journal of Economics*, 70, 64–94.

—— 1961: Note on Uzawa's two-sector model of economic growth. *Review of Economic Studies*, 29, 48–50.

Stiglitz, J. and Weiss, A. 1981: Credit rationing in markets with imperfect information. *American Economic Review*, 71, 393–410.

Stokey, N. and Lucas, R. 1989: *Recursive Methods in Economic Dynamics*, Cambridge, MA: Harvard University Press.

Summers, L. 1981: Capital income taxation and accumulation in a lifecycle growth model.

American Economic Review, 71, 533–44.

Summers, R. and Heston, A. 1988: A new set of international comparisons of real product and price levels: estimates for 130 countries, 1950–85. *Review of Income and Wealth*, 34, 1–25.

Tobin, J. 1963: Commercial Banks as creators of "money". In D. Carson (ed.), *Banking and Monetary Studies*, Homewood, IL: Irwin.

—— 1969: A general equilibrium approach to monetary theory. *Journal of Money, Credit and Banking*, 1, 15–29.

Uzawa, H. 1961: On a two-sector model of economic growth. *Review of Economic Studies*, 29, 40–7.

—— 1964: Optimal growth in a two-sector model of capital accumulation. *Review of Economic Studies*, 31, 1–24.

—— 1965: Optimum technical change in an aggregative model of economic growth. *International Economic Review*, 6, 18–31.

Wallace, N. 1980: Integrating micro and macroeconomics: an application to credit controls. *Federal Reserve Bank of Minneapolis Quarterly Review*, Fall, 16–29.

Weil, P. 1988: Love thy children: reflections on the Ricardian equivalence theorem. Mimeo, Harvard University.

Woodford, M. 1984: Indeterminacy of equilibrium in the overlapping generations model: a survey. Mimeo, Columbia University.

World Bank 1987: *World Development Report*. Washington, DC: Oxford University Press.

Wrigley, E. and Schofield, R. 1981: *The Population History of England, 1541–1871: A Reconstruction*. Cambridge: Cambridge University Press.

Yaari, M. 1965: Uncertain lifetime, life insurance, and the theory of the consumer. *Review of Economic Studies*, 32, 137–50.

Zeldes, S. 1989: Consumption and liquidity constraints: an empirical investigation. *Journal of Political Economy*, 97, 305–46.

Zilcha, I. 1990: Dynamic efficiency in overlapping generations models with stochastic production. *Journal of Economic Theory*, 52, 364–79.

Questions

Unmarked questions are the easiest to do while starred ones relate to advanced material. Other questions are labeled (T) if they are primarily technical and (C) if they require some creative thinking.

II.1 (a) (T) What assumption in the text guarantees that individual budget sets have unique maximal elements?

(b) Investigate how a household's endowment affects its autarkic interest rate. In particular, suppose two households are identical in everything but their endowment in either youth or old age. Which one has the higher autarkic rate of interest?

II.2 Prove theorem 11.1 [*Hint*: Show that aggregate saving is negative if $R = \min (\bar{R}_1, ..., \bar{R}_H)$, positive if $R = \max (\bar{R}_1, ..., \bar{R}_H)$].

II.3 Making the same assumptions as in chapter 12, investigate how lump-sum social security taxes affect the nature of an equilibrium with inside assets. In particular, what conclusions do you draw about the impact of a balanced social security system on the rate of interest and on aggregate borrowing and lending?

II.4 Suppose that the consumption good is durable and, in particular, that it can be stored for future use at a constant proportional rate of depreciation γ, where $0 \leqslant \gamma \leqslant 1$. Find out whether, and how, the availability of the constant-returns-to-scale storage technology changes the equilibria of an economy with inside assets.

II.5 (C) Suppose that potential borrowers have an *infinite* lifespan with endowment sequence $(e_t)_{t=1}^{\infty}$; the utility function is $\sum_{t=1}^{\infty} \beta^{t-1} u(c_t)$, where $0 < \beta < 1$; and the interest factor $R = 1/\beta$ is constant over time. Assume that (i) lenders know the future endowment of borrowers but cannot prove it to a third party, for example a court of law; (ii) financial assets are publicly observable; and (iii) bankrupt lenders forfeit their financial assets as well as all future participation in the credit market (that is, they are condemned to autarky).

(a) Give an example of a borrower (that is, a utility function and endowment profile) who never finds it in his own interest to go bankrupt. What endowment profiles are consistent with such a good credit record?

(b) Can you find an example of a borrower who will go bankrupt in finite time? How, if at all, can lenders identify borrowers of this type? (Here reputation is the *only* means of enforcing loan contracts).

II.6 (T) A static economy consists of H households, $h = 1, 2, ..., H$, living one period, and L commodities, $\ell = 1, 2, ..., L$. Each household has a non-negative endowment vector $\omega_h = (\omega_{1h}, \omega_{2h}, ..., \omega_{Lh})$ and a preference ordering expressed by an increasing, strictly concave, twice continuously differentiable numerical function $u^h: \mathbb{R}_+^L \to \mathbb{R}$ defined over consumption vectors of the form $x^h = (x_{1h}, x_{2h}, ..., x_{Lh})$. Prove that a suitable choice of a vector of non-negative weights $\lambda = (\lambda_1, \lambda_2, ..., \lambda_H)$ turns any Pareto-optimal allocation of resources over households, $\hat{x} = (\hat{x}^1, \hat{x}^2, ..., \hat{x}^H)$ into a maximal element of the central planner's budget set

$$B = \{x \geqslant 0 \mid \sum_{h=1}^{H} (x_{\ell h} - \omega_h) \leqslant 0, \ell = 1, 2, ..., L\}$$

if allocations are evaluated according to the *social welfare function* $W = \Sigma_{h=1}^{H} \lambda_h u^h(x^h)$. Also show that no generality is lost if the vector λ is normalized so that its components sum to unity.

II.7 (T) For a finite-horizon economy with inside money prove formally the following.

(a) Every intertemporally optimal allocation exhausts all resources in each period, and leaves all households of a given generation with the same marginal rate of commodity substitution.

(b) Every competitive equilibrium with private loans is intertemporally optimal (*Hint:* Assume the contrary and obtain a contradiction).

II.8 (T) Prove that every equal-treatment optimal (ET-O) allocation is intertemporally optimal, and every stationary allocation that is not ET-O fails to be intertemporally optimal.

II.9 In the optimum growth model of section 13.4 suppose that $f'(k)$ is bounded away from zero; specifically let $\lim_{k \to \infty} f'(k) > \rho + \delta$.

(a) Show that a positive steady state does not exist for this economy.

(b) What are the asymptotic properties of equilibrium sequences (k_t)?

II.10 Describe the equilibria of an optimum growth model in which production takes place without labor and the instantaneous utility function is isoelastic. In particular, assume full depreciation of capital, $f(k) = Ak$, and $u(c) = c^{1-\sigma}/(1-\sigma)$ where the parameters β, A, σ satisfy $\sigma > 0, \sigma \neq 1$, and $\beta A < A^\sigma$. In particular

(a) From the first-order conditions for this economy, show that equilibrium consumption grows at the gross rate $\gamma \equiv (\beta A)^{1/\sigma}$.

(b) Prove that the gross rate of growth of capital $x_t = k_t/k_{t-1}$ satisfies the difference equation $x_{t+1} = A + \gamma - \gamma A/x_t$ with two steady states, $\bar{x} = \{\gamma, A\}$.

(c) Explain why only one of the two stationary values for $\bar{x}$ in part (b) makes good economic sense.

II.11 (T) In the economy of chapter 13 demonstrate the following:

(a) Factor demand schedules do indeed satisfy equations (13.4a), (13.4b). [*Hint:* Exploit the homogeneity of the production function F].

(b) For any constant-returns-to-scale production function with constant elasticity of substitution $\sigma \geqslant 0$ described in equation (13.19), verify that the elasticity of substitution between capital and labor is indeed $\sigma = 1/(1 + \rho)$. (*Hint:* Begin with the definition $\sigma = d\log k/d\log|MRS|$ where $|MRS|$ is the absolute value of the marginal rate of substitution between capital and labor in the production function.)

(c) For any $\sigma > 1$ show that $f(0) > 0$ and that both $f'(k)$ and $f(k)/k$ tend to $+\infty$ as $k \to 0$. In addition, prove that $w'(k) \to +\infty$ as $k \to 0$.

(d) Let $\sigma \in (0,1)$ in part (c) and prove that $f(0) = 0; f'(k)$ and $f(k)/k$ are bounded; and $w'(k) \to 0$ as $k \to 0$.

II.12 An individual lives for T periods, indexed by $t = 1, ..., T$, and consumes a single perishable good. He is endowed with a vector $(e_1, ..., e_T)$ of that good and a utility function of the form $\Sigma_{t=1}^{T} u(c_t)$. The rate of interest is permanently zero.

(a) Suppose the individual may borrow at any time, at a zero rate of interest, up to the value of his remaining endowment. Describe his optimal consumption plan and the implied path of asset holdings.

(b) Assume, instead, that the individual is severely credit constrained. He may lend at a zero rate of interest but cannot borrow from others at any finite rate of interest. What is the optimal consumption plan and the implied asset holdings if his endowment profile rises over time? If it falls over time?

(c) (T) Repeat (b) for a single-peaked endowment profile that rises monotonically early in life, reaches a peak somewhere in the middle, and then falls monotonically.

II.13 Analyze the dynamical equilibria of an overlapping generations economy with a constant population of identical households, a Cobb–Douglas utility function $u(c_1, c_2) = c_1^{1-s} c_2^s$, $0 < s < 1$, a fixed proportions technology $f(k) = A \min(k, \bar{k})$ for given $A > 0$ and $\bar{k} > 0$, and a depreciation rate $\delta = 1$. In particular:

(a) Show that $k_t < \bar{k}$ means that a labor surplus exists and $w_t = 0$; $k_t > \bar{k}$ means that a capital surplus exists and $\rho_t = 0$. What does this reasoning imply for the size of k_{t+1} when $k_t < \bar{k}$? When $k_t > \bar{k}$?

(b) Show that this economy always has the trivial steady state $k_t = 0$ $\forall t$. Under what conditions is $\bar{k}$ a steady state? Is there a positive steady state other than $\bar{k}$?

(c) Draw a phase portrait for this economy. Explain how this portrait is a special case of figure 13.2d.

II.14 (T) Explore what happens to the descriptive model of economic growth if we add to it:

(a) Hicks-neutral technical progress, with output being $(1 + g)^t F(K, L)$ (here F is homogeneous of degree one, and $g > 0$ is the exogenous constant rate of technical progress);

(b) Harrod-neutral technical progress, with output being $F[K, (1 + g)^t L]$, and F again homogeneous of degree one.

For each change in specification of the basic model, write down the fundamental difference equation; explore the existence and stability of stationary states; and discuss how your results respond to changes in the exogenous parameters δ and g, where δ is the depreciation rate of capital.

II.15 Suppose that the indifference map of the representative household in the scalar overlapping generations model of growth contains a *subsistence* consumption vector $(\bar{c}_1, \bar{c}_2) > 0$ with the property that the marginal utility of consumption near either $\bar{c}_1$ or $\bar{c}_2$ becomes very large. In particular, suppose that $u_1(c_1, c_2) \to + \infty$ as $c_1 \to \bar{c}_1$ for any $c_2 > \bar{c}_2$, and $u_2(c_1, c_2) \to + \infty$ as $c_2 \to \bar{c}_2$ for any $c_1 > \bar{c}_1$. Can a sequence (k_t) converging to zero be an equilibrium of this economy?

II.16 Examine the possibility of unbounded growth in a scalar overlapping generations growth model with constant population, a constant saving rate, full depreciation of capital and the constant-returns-to-scale technology described in equation (14.2).

(a) Show that, unlike the descriptive growth model, the overlapping generations model *does not permit unbounded growth* in equilibrium if taxes and subsidies are zero.

(b) Can you devise a balanced system of taxes and transfers that will induce unbounded growth? Explain in detail.

II.17 (*) Explore dynamical equilibria in a production economy with variable labor supply. Begin with Diamond's model of capital accumulation in chapter 13 and add the following special features: There is no population growth. All households are identical, working in youth, producing and consuming in old age. All youthful labor income is saved, becoming productive capital for use in old age. The utility function of a member of generation t is

$$u(c_{t+1}, n_t) = \frac{1}{1 - \gamma} c_{t+1}^{1-\gamma} - n_t$$

where c_{t+1} is old-age consumption, n_t is youthful labor supply and $\gamma = 0$ is a parameter. The production function is $y_t = (k_t \, n_t)^{1/2}$, where k_t is the total capital available to each producer in period t (*not* capital intensity).

(a) Show that equilibrium satisfies the following *pair* of first-order difference equations

$$k_{t+1} = R_t k_t \qquad R_{t+1}^{1-\gamma} = 4k_t^\gamma \, R_t^{1+\gamma}$$

where R_t is the gross yield on loans contracted at $t - 1$ and paid at t.
(b) Describe stationary competitive equilibria and investigate their stability.
(c) Given some initial value $k_1 > 0$ for the capital stock, how many dynamical equilibria are there in this economy? (*Hint*: This example is due to Geanakoplos and Polemarchakis (1986), where the assiduous reader can find it fully worked out).

II.18 (*) Trace out the consequences of injecting one infinitely lived person into the economy of the previous question. Specifically, suppose there is no capital, output being instead equal to the labor input. The infinitely lived agent supplies no labor, has stationary endowment ω of the consumption good, and has utility function $\Sigma_{t=1}^T \beta^{t-1} \log c_t$, where $0 < \beta < 1$ and $\omega > 0$.

(a) Investigate the existence, dynamic efficiency, and stability of stationary equilibria.
(b) Describe the stationary-equilibrium consumption and asset holdings of the infinitely lived agent. (*Hint*: This question appears as example 8 in Woodford (1984)).

II.19 "In the one-sector overlapping generations model of capital accumulation due to Diamond (1965), all stationary equilibria with zero national debt are Pareto optimal if physical capital does not depreciate." Explain why this statement is true or false.

II.20 (*)(a) Investigate the intertemporal optimality of a feasible allocation that corresponds to an interest-factor sequence $R_t = 1$ for $t \leq T$; $= 1 - 1/2^t$ for all $t > T$. What does the Phelps–Koopmans theorem have to say about this allocation? Assume there is no population growth.
(b) Find out how theorems 15.1, 15.3, 15.4, and 15.5 are related. In particular, show that theorem 15.3 implies 15.1 for stationary allocations; 15.5 reduces to 15.3 if there is one physical good; and any allocation that satisfies equation (15.2) violates the summability condition of theorem 15.5.

II.21 (T) What can you say about the welfare properties of a periodic equilibrium with interest factor R_1 in all odd periods and R_2 in all even periods? Suppose there is no population growth and $0 < R_1 < 1 < R_2$.

(a) Is this equilibrium optimal if $R_1 R_2 = 1$? What if $R_1 + R_2 = 2$?
(b) What can you say about optimality if *all* you know is that $0 < R_1 < 1 < R_2$?

II.22 (C) Consider an economy consisting of finitely many, say H, infinitely lived individuals who are born simultaneously and have constant but unequal rates of time preference $\beta_h \in (0, 1)$, for $h = 1, ..., H$. Suppose the aggregate endowment is stationary and show that the equilibrium rate of interest equals the rate of time preference of the *most patient* individual. (*Hint*: Suppose H is the most patient individual. Assume $R\beta_H \neq 1$ and obtain a contradiction between first-order conditions, like equation (15.3), and asset market clearing).

II.23 Can generationally autarkic allocations be competitive equilibria if the life-cycle exceeds two trading periods? Take up this question in the one-good overlapping generations model of pure exchange. Show that the answer is generally negative, but could become affirmative for specially chosen preferences and endowments.

II.24 (C) How would you modify the dynamic efficiency criteria of section 15.1, specifically theorems 15.1 and 15.3, to discuss the intertemporal optimality of competitive equilibrium in the presence of borrowing constraints?

II.25 (C)(T) Investigate the equilibria of a simple exchange economy with one perishable commodity and a constant population of identical households living for *three* periods. Assume the endowment to be (e_0, e_1, e_2) and a utility function of the form

$$V = u(c_0) + \beta u(c_1) + \beta^2 u(c_2) \qquad 0 < \beta < 1$$

(a) Write down and interpret a general asset-market clearing condition that describes inside-money equilibria.

(b) Assume now that $e_1 = 1$ and $u(c_i) = \log c_i$ for $i = 0, 1, 2$. Describe stationary inside-money equilibria. What factors affect the rate of interest here?

(c) Does a stationary equilibrium exist for a general endowment profile? If so, is it unique? Assume again that $u(c) = \log c$.

(d) Show that, for any period after $t = 1$, dynamical equilibria satisfy the difference equation

$$\frac{\beta e_1[(1 + \beta)(1 + R_{t-1}) - \beta R_{t-1} R_t] + \beta e_2(1 + \beta - \beta R_t) - \beta^2 e_3}{e_2 + e_3} + \frac{e_3}{R_t R_{t+1}} =$$

II.26 (T) Generalize part (a) of the previous question to households that consume in $T \geq 3$ periods. In particular, how does the length of life T affect the order of the difference equation that is satisfied by a cleared asset market?

II.27 A pure-exchange economy consists of two types of households ($h = 1, 2$). Type 1 has utility function $c_1 c_2$ and endowment vector (e_1, e_2); type 2 has the same utility function as 1 and endowment vector (y_1, y_2). The two groups are equally numerous, and their number grows geometrically at the rate $n > -1$.

(a) For what values of the parameters (e_1, e_2, y_1, y_2, n) is this economy Samuelson? Classical?

(b) What would happen to your answers if the two groups were initially of equal size (in period $t = 1$), but their population growth rates were unequal (say, zero for type 1 and $n \neq 0$ for type 2)?

II.28 (*) Does theorem 15.2 apply to a pure-exchange economy with constant population in which all endowments grow geometrically at the rate n? To one with constant endowments and population but utility functions that change over time? Outline how the proof of this result would change in each case.

II.29 (T) Prove that homothetic utility functions generate saving functions that are linearly homogeneous in the income vector, that is, $s(R, \lambda y_1, \lambda y_2) = \lambda s(R, y_1, y_2)$.

II.30 (*) Prove that the unique positive steady state $(\bar{k}, \bar{c})$ of the dynamical system described by equations (15.9a) and (15.9c) in section 15.3 is a saddle.

II.31 (*) Consider the overlapping generations economy with taxed factor incomes described in section 15.4. Is there a choice of linear tax rates (θ, τ) that will collect a specified constant tax revenue and simultaneously support the golden rule capital intensity as a competitive equilibrium? Explain your answer intuitively.

II.32 (*) Prove the statement of the Rybczynski theorem contained in section 15.5.

II.33 (*) Prove the Stolper–Samuelson theorem, as stated in section 15.5. [*Hint:* Use the factor-price equations (15.23a), (15.23b) and (15.25)].

II.34 (*) Analyze a two-sector growth model with a constant saving rate $s \in (0, 1)$ and fixed proportions technologies $f_x(k) = \min(k, \lambda_x)$ in the consumption goods sector, $f_y(k) = A \min (k, \lambda_y)$ in the investment goods sector, where $A > 0$ is a scale factor.

   (a) Write out the dynamical system for this economy in terms of the economywide capital–labor ratio and the price of the consumption good. Show that there is a unique positive steady state $(\bar{k}, \bar{p})$.

   (b) Investigate the stability of $(\bar{k}, \bar{p})$. Prove that, depending on the parameter values $(s, A, \lambda_x, \lambda_y,)$ the state can be an unstable node, a stable node, or a spiral. Is it ever a saddle?

   (c) Are there conditions under which this economy has a flip bifurcation? A Hopf bifurcation?

II.35 (*) Examine how the behavior of the economy in the previous question would be changed by the existence of national debt. Assume, in particular, that there are no government purchases or taxes, and that the treasury perpetually refinances an inherited stock of public debt (b_t).

   Write out a dynamical system in the state variables k_t, p_t, b_t, identify carefully all steady states, and study their stability properties.

II.36 This question explores some potential reasons why international differences in per capita output persist over long periods of time; a good companion article for this material is Lucas (1990b). Suppose that the world consists of two countries – a rich country A and a poor country B – each having a constant population of identical two-period-lived households that satisfy the standard assumptions of the overlapping generations model of growth. In particular, each country $i \equiv$ A,B is endowed with a constant-returns-to-scale technology $F_i : \mathbb{R}_+^2 \to \mathbb{R}_+$ and physical capital that depreciates fully on use.

   In addition, we assume that the saving rate $s_i \in (0, 1)$ in each country is constant; each worker in country B is endowed with one (efficiency) unit of labor services in youth, while each worker of country A owns $n \geqslant 1$ units of labor. There is no technical progress.

   (a) Suppose that neither capital nor labor can move across international borders. Write down two separate growth models, one for each country, and focus on their positive steady states. In particular, list the factors that affect steady state output per worker in each country and explain what makes country A "richer" than country B.

   (b) How would steady state outputs change if capital were perfectly mobile but labor was still immobile? Would factor prices be equalized? What would happen to factor incomes? To the income per capita differential in the steady state? Assume that each country may use only its own technology.

   (*Hint*: Perfect capital mobility implies that the two countries share a *common* interest rate. Here you need one growth model describing the evolution of the world economy, plus one arbitrage condition equating interest rates.)

   (c) Suppose now that *both* capital and labor are perfectly and costlessly mobile but country A has acccess to a better technology than country B. Does labor mobility tend to shrink income differentials in the steady state?

II.37 This question and the next two, taken from Galor and Polemarchakis (1987), are about the implications of foreign aid for economic growth. In the economy of question II.36 we suppose that the two countries have a common technology $(F = F_A = F_B)$ but different saving rates $(s_A \neq s_B)$ and efficiency labor endowments $(n > 1)$. The "rich" country A gives away each period a fixed amount of aid $\tau > 0$ to the "poor" country B: τ is a lump-sum tax on working households in the donor country, and a gift to working households in the recipient country.

    (a) Explore the effect of permanent foreign aid on economic growth in each country if both factors of production are completely immobile. In particular, what happens to per capita output in the steady state? To income in the steady state?

    (b) Rework part (a) assuming instead that foreign aid subsidizes retired households in the recipient country.

II.38 What happens to the economy of question II.37 if capital is perfectly mobile across national borders? Suppose, once more, that labor is immobile and that foreign aid benefits working households in the recipient country.

    (a) Show that, if $s_B > s_A$, then foreign aid is likely to increase steady state output per capita in *both* countries.

    (b) Using a symmetric argument, prove that foreign aid is likely to *decrease* steady state income per capita in both countries if $s_B < s_A$. What is the economic intuition behind this result?

II.39 (C) Can you think of any strictly economic (as distinct from moral or humanitarian) reasons why rich nations would extend temporary aid to developing countries? In particular, can you imagine circumstances for which short-lived development aid confers long-lasting benefits to the recipient country? To the donor country?

Part III

National Debt and Fiscal Policy

17 Introduction to Part III

Governments purchase goods and services from firms and transfer income to households by collecting taxes, selling interest-bearing debt of various maturities, and creating high-powered money. As government spending has come to be a substantial fraction of aggregate spending,[1] the study of public consumption plans and the manner in which they are financed now occupies center stage in macroeconomics. One frequently hears concern voiced over how interest rates will respond to a particular fiscal policy as legislators, the press, and the public at large grapple with the implications of that policy for private consumption, investment, the balance of payments, and social welfare.

The study of government spending and finance is a task for which the dynamical apparatus developed in Parts I and II is well suited. In Part III we emphasize geometric descriptions of dynamical economies as we try to understand the *limits* of fiscal policy. What types of fiscal policies can be sustained as dynamical competitive equilibria? Specifically, does the smooth functioning of competitive credit markets place any upper bound on the flow of government deficits? How much national debt can a competitive credit market absorb if left to its own devices? And what sort of interventionist policies are governments likely to pursue when they wish to exceed that bound?

Chapter 18, in particular, introduces transfer payments in the form of a balanced social security system, and examines their impact on the rate of interest, aggregate saving, and capital accumulation; we then go on to explore government purchases of goods financed entirely by lump-sum taxes. Chapters 19 and 20 shift the focus to deficit finance, its similarities to and differences from taxation, and study national debt as a mechanism for transferring resources between generations. Among other topics, we describe the general class of fiscal policies consistent with *laissez-faire* competitive equilibrium; examine the capacity of a competitive credit market to absorb public debt; study the relationship of budget deficits to the stock of domestic debt; and look at the impact of national debt on the interest rate, capital accumulation, and economic welfare.

In chapter 21 we explore capital accumulation in an economy with bequests and study dynamic interactions between public investment and private capital accumulation; we also investigate legal restrictions as a form of policy intervention available to governments that wish to market more national debt than a closed economy is willing to absorb in a regime of *laissez-faire* competition.

Note

1. In the USA, a country with a relatively small government sector, purchases of goods and services by federal, state, and local governments rose from 8.7 percent of gross national product (GNP) in 1929 to 19.8 percent in 1989; see the *Economic Report of the President*, 1990. Government spending (including transfer payments) rose from about 10 percent of GNP in 1929 to about 34 percent in 1989.

18 Balanced Policies

18.1 Social security

Unfunded social security and related programs are the largest existing mechanism of transfer payments as well as a primary source of retirement income in most industrial economies. Employed individuals contribute a fraction of their earned income[1] to a pool of funds out of which retirees draw pensions and health benefits, and injured workers receive disability pay. The whole system produces no saving in the aggregate; it simply operates on the ancient principle of caring for one's elders, enforced by the tax-gathering authority of the government. Distortionary taxes are exacted from persons who are relatively young to fund old-age pensions plus a social insurance system designed to cover accidents, disability, and the like.

In what follows we abstract from several important aspects of social security: we ignore its insurance function (see Diamond and Mirrlees, 1978); omit altogether its impact on labor supply (see Blinder et al., 1980); assume away whatever distortions are introduced by the direct substitution effect of the social security tax (see Atkinson and Stiglitz (1980) or any other good text on public finance); and ignore the possibility of fully funded social security systems like those prevailing in certain Western European countries (see, however, question III.14). We concentrate, instead, on how a pay-as-you-go social security system influences aggregate saving and capital accumulation.

The issue, raised first in an influential paper by Feldstein (1974), concerns the allocative implications of any social security system that simply transfers resources from the young to the old. As we saw in the example that started chapter 11, intergenerational transfers of this type erode individual incentives to save, reducing the supply of loanable funds and putting upward pressure on the rate of interest. And we also know from Part II that these are welcome developments in an economy whose *laissez-faire* equilibrium tends toward low interest rates; in fact, one motivation for establishing a social security system is to improve the pattern of resource allocation over the life-cycle.

It is difficult to say what the "right" flow of intergenerational transfers is for a given economy. Carried to extremes, a social security system that soaks the young and maintains the elderly in handsome style is Pareto optimal, for the simple reason that any lowering of taxes and benefits will hurt at least one transitional generation, say, generation 0. However, if one is prepared to ignored transitional generations that contribute little to the system yet draw full benefits from it, then it becomes clear from chapter 13 that excessive intergenerational transfers may well *decapitalize* the economy. When labor works with less capital then the golden rule recommends, it will produce less per capita consumption than the economy is capable of in the steady state.

A pure-exchange economy with inside assets, like that described in chapter 11, affords the simplest setting in which to study how social security changes interest rates and individual saving. Let $n > -1$ be the rate of population growth and H be the number of different household types indexed $h = 1, \ldots, H$, with utility functions $u^h: \mathbb{R}_+^2 \to \mathbb{R}$ and pre-transfer endowment vectors $e^h \in \mathbb{R}_+^2$. Individuals may save by extending private loans to members of their own cohort; they are also obliged to participate in a social security system that levies on everyone a per capita tax τ in youth and pays out a pension $(1 + n)\tau$ in old age.

Introducing a social security system has no income effect, and does not affect individual consumption plans if $r = n$, that is, the interest rate and the growth rate are equal. Saving declines by the exact amount of the social security tax; see figure 18.1(a) where Ω is the initial endowment point without social security and S is the corresponding after-tax point. A positive income effect appears if $n > r$ and a negative effect if $n < r$. If youthful and old-age consumption are normal goods, then the positive (negative) income effect will cause individual saving to decline in absolute value by more than (less than) the social security tax. Note that saving falls in each case, *independently* of how r and n compare. Figures 18.1b and 18.1c illustrate this idea, which may also be demonstrated as follows. Let (c_{1h}, s_{1h}) be the youthful consumption and saving of household h without a social security system and $(\hat{c}_{1h}, \hat{s}_{1h})$ be the corresponding magnitudes with social security. Then we can relate c_{1h} and $\hat{c}_{1h}$ by

$$\hat{c}_{1h} = c_{1h} + \theta\left(\frac{1 + n}{1 + r}\tau - \tau\right) \tag{18.1a}$$

where $\theta \in [0, 1]$ if goods are normal. This relationship says that $\hat{c}_{1h}$ will differ from c_{1h} by a proper fraction of the contribution that the social security system makes to the present value of the household's endowment. From (18.1a) we easily obtain

$$\hat{s}_{1h} - s_{1h} = -\tau\left[\frac{\theta(1 + n)}{1 + r} + 1 - \theta\right]$$

which implies that

$$-\frac{\Delta s}{\Delta \tau} = \theta\frac{1 + n}{1 + r} + 1 - \theta \tag{18.1b}$$

We have thus provided the following theorem.

Theorem 18.1 Let $x_{1h} = -s_{1h}$ be the excess demand in youth of a household h for which youthful and old-age consumption are normal goods. Then $dx_{1h}/d\tau > 0$ at an individual optimum. Furthermore, $dx_{1h}/d\tau < 1$ if $r > n$, $dx_{1h}/d\tau = 1$ if $r = n$, $dx_{1h}/d\tau > 1$ if $r < n$.

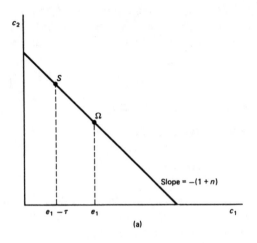

(a)

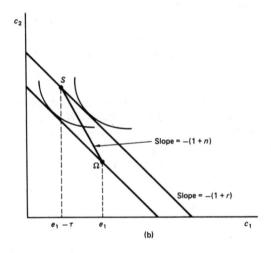

(b)

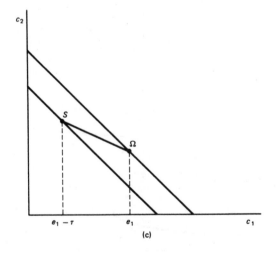

(c)

Figure 18.1 Social security: (a) $r = n$; (b) $r > n$; (c) $r < n$.

A consequence of this theorem is that *higher social security contributions* shift individual and aggregate saving functions to the left and *put upward pressure on the equilibrium rate of interest*. In fact, we may define individual saving functions in the usual way from

$$s_h[R, e_1 - \tau, e_2 + (1 + n)\tau] = \underset{z}{\text{argmax }} u^h[e_1 - \tau - z, e_2 + (1 + n)\tau + Rz]$$

$$\text{subject to } z \leq e_1 - \tau$$

and the normalized aggregate saving function from

$$z(R, \tau) = \frac{1}{H} \sum_{h=1}^{H} s_h$$

Theorem 18.1 says that z is a decreasing function of the social security tax τ (figure 18.2). In other words, the equilibrium rate of interest is *locally* an increasing function of the tax: starting from any equilibrium, an infinitesimal boost in social security contributions raises the rate of interest.

To gauge the impact of pay-as-you-go social security on aggregate saving and on the equilibrium capital stock, we turn to an economy that *does* do some net saving, as in the scalar Diamond model with production that is familiar to us from Parts I and II. To simplify matters, we assume that the two dated consumption goods are normal and gross substitutes.

Imagine that all individuals are identical. As before, the government levies a per capita tax τ on each young worker and uses the proceeds to make a transfer payment to old households. Since there are $1 + n$ young agents per old person, each retired worker receives $(1 + n)\tau$ units of output.

A member of generation t has a net income vector $y' = (y_1', y_2')$, where

$$y_1' = w_t - \tau \qquad y_2' = (1 + n)\tau$$

which yields aggregate saving of the form

$$s_t = s[R_{t+1}, w_t - \tau, (1 + n)\tau] \tag{18.2}$$

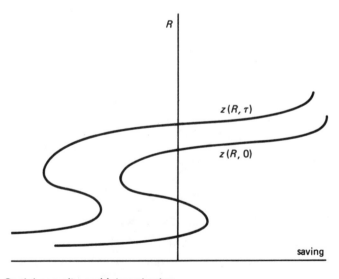

Figure 18.2 Social security and interest rates.

Profit maximization yields the familiar relations

$$R_{t+1} = f'(k_{t+1}) \tag{18.3a}$$

$$w_t = w(k_t) = f(k_t) - k_t f'(k_t) \tag{18.3b}$$

Finally, since the government has no need to borrow, the market clearing condition is simply

$$(1 + n)k_{t+1} = s_t \tag{18.4}$$

Substituting the conditions from individual optimization into the market clearing condition, we obtain a first-order difference equation of the form $k_{t+1} = G(k_t; \tau)$ implicitly given by

$$(1 + n)k_{t+1} = s[\, f'(k_{t+1}), w(k_t) - \tau, (1 + n)\, \tau] \tag{18.5}$$

The equation

$$k = G(k; \tau) \tag{18.6}$$

indirectly defines the steady state capital stock $\bar{k}(\tau)$ as a function of the social security parameter (figure 18.3). Comparative statics results can be obtained in the standard way by applying the implicit function theorem to equation (18.6). Graphically, we try to determine how a change in τ will shift the phaseline, and this tells us how the equilibrium is displaced. Equivalently, we can write (18.6) more explicitly as

$$(1 + n)k = s[\, f'(k), w - \tau, (1 + n)\, \tau] \tag{18.7}$$

and plot the two sides of (18.7) as functions of k. Then we ask how a change in τ shifts the steady state savings function, that is, we compute $(\partial/\partial\tau)s$ which is negative by theorem 18.1. A rise in τ shifts s up, as in figure 18.2. The effect of this on the steady state capital stock depends on whether we are initially at a stable or an unstable steady state. We have seen above that, if a steady state is stable, then the phaseline cuts the diagonal from above, as at point A of figure 18.3. In this case, the incrase in τ leads to a reduction in the steady state value of capital.

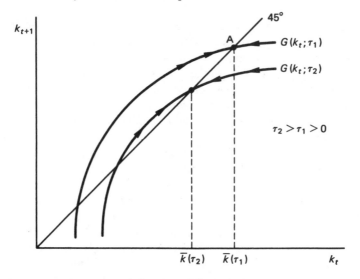

Figure 18.3 Social security and capital accumulation.

To obtain comparative statics results about an equilibrium, we need to know whether it is stable or not. The case of a stable steady state is clearly more relevant; for such states we have the following.

Theorem 18.2 Assume that first- and second-period consumption are normal goods and gross substitutes and that the economy is initially at a stable steady state. Then a balanced-budget increase in social security taxes and benefits shifts the savings function down and yields a new stable steady state with a lower per capita stock and a higher interest rate. Following the policy change, the economy converges monotonically to the new steady state.

Equation (18.7) also reveals that the rate of population growth affects steady state equilibria, quite possibly in the same way as social security taxes. A high rate of population growth may well detract, locally at least, from capital deepening, that is, it may lead to the adoption of a *less-capital-intensive* technology, to less saving per head and a higher rate of interest. The reason for this result is, quite simply, that faster population growth raises the per capita transfer to the old for a given lump-sum tax on the young. The higher future income leads to a shrinkage of saving at any given interest rate. On the other hand, if we have to take as given the social security benefit $(1 + n)\tau$, then faster population growth would reduce the tax on the young and hence raise both saving and capital intensity in the steady state.

18.2   Balanced budgets

We return to the pure-exchange economy described at the beginning of the previous section and introduce a government that purchases a sequence $(g_t)_{t=1}^{\infty}$ of the consumption good, levies lump sum taxes $(\tau_1^t)_{t=1}^{\infty}$ on the young and $(\tau_2^{t-1})_{t=1}^{\infty}$ on the old. More precisely, the symbols g_t, τ_1^t, and τ_2^t, respectively, refer to government consumption, youthful taxes, and old-age taxes per member of generation t. Total government purchases at t are than $H(1 + n)^t g_t$ and total tax collection is $H(1 + n)^t \tau_1^t + H(1 + n)^{t-1} \tau_2^{t-1}$.

Future taxes are assumed to be known to all individuals, which means that governments are able to bind or precommit their successors to a specific fiscal policy.[2] We also suppose that the government transforms at zero cost whatever it purchases into a proportional quantity of public goods, without affecting any household's marginal rate of substitution between private goods. *Preference orderings over private goods, then, are assumed to be independent of government purchases.*[3]

Taxes aside, we suppose that government spending can also be funded by selling national debt denominated in terms of commodities and hence *indexed* against fluctuations in the unit of account. Households regard public debt to be a perfect substitute for private debt and, like any other borrower, the government takes interest rates as given. All public debt instruments, called government bonds, are assumed to mature in one period, just like private loans, with principal and interest due on maturity. Not all of these assumptions are satisfied in actual credit markets. Public debt is often denominated in monetary units of account rather than goods; it is frequently safer, that is, a better "risk," than private debt; public borrowing often dwarfs private borrowing and affects interest rates so greatly that one cannot safely assume the treasury to take interest rates as given; governments typically have a longer horizon than individuals and do choose on occasion to issue bonds with long maturities, an extreme example being the British government perpetuity called a "consol."

The empirical relationship between the yield and the maturity of a security is called the "yield curve," and theories that study this relationship are collectively referred to as "the term structure of interest rates."[4] In a riskless economy with fully informed individuals, like that considered here, the connection of long-term and short-term yields is very simple; debt instruments of all maturities issued by all agents are perfectly safe and perfectly substitutable for each other (see question III.2). All securities have the same real yield per period.

Another fact of life, which we choose to ignore here, is that not even the safest of government obligations is completely safe for it is expressed in units of account; its future purchasing power is not known when the price level is itself uncertain. An interesting example of a risky government debt instrument was the medieval "tally of receipt," known in England and Flanders in the twelfth and thirteenth centuries. That was an obligation of the ruling monarch which was not always honored by his successor. Tallies quickly become negotiable, selling at discount.

Denoting by b_t the national debt maturing at t per member of generation t and by $R_t = 1 + r_t$ the interest factor on that debt, we have a government budget constraint of the form

$$(1 + n)b_{t+1} = R_t b_t + g_t - \tau_1^t - \frac{\tau_2^{t-1}}{1 + n} \tag{18.8}$$

We call $g_t - \tau_1^t - \tau_2^{t-1}/(1 + n) = q_t$ the *primary budget deficit* per member of generation t.

A *fiscal policy* is an infinite sequence $P = (g_t, \tau_1^t, \tau_2^{t-1})_{t=1}^{\infty}$. We call P *feasible* if it allows all after-tax endowments to be non-negative, that is, if, for all h and t, $e_{1h} - \tau_1^t \geq 0$, $e_{2h} - \tau_2^{t-1} \geq 0$. P is *stationary* if it consists of constant elements, and *balanced* if it specifies a zero primary budget deficit at all times, that is, if

$$\tau_1^t + \frac{\tau_2^{t-1}}{1 + n} = g_t \qquad \text{for all } t \tag{18.9}$$

Not every fiscal policy is consistent with a *laissez-faire* equilibrium; for instance, there is no equilibrium whatever if planned government purchases exceed the entire resources of the economy, or if the per capita tax exceeds the resources of some household. A more relevant example is large and persistent government deficits that drive up interest rates and national debt in an ever-rising spiral, until national debt exceeds the maximal flow of saving that a competitive market can sustain without outside intervention. This is studied in chapters 19 and 20; here we confine ourselves to balanced fiscal policies and therefore to zero public debt as well.

We begin again with individual households ranking feasible consumption bundles c_h of private goods in an ordinary budget set like that of figure 18.4 according to the utility index u^h. The only difference here from what happened in the pure-exchange economies of Part II is that the initial endowment vector of household h is $(e_{1h} - \tau_1^t, e_{2h} - \tau_2^t)$ because of taxes and/or subsidies. Once more, loan contracts with other households are the only store of value. The choice of each household is unique given the parameter vector $\theta_t = (R_{t+1}, \tau_1^t, \tau_2^t)$; it is expressed in terms of a single-valued savings function s_h with the property that

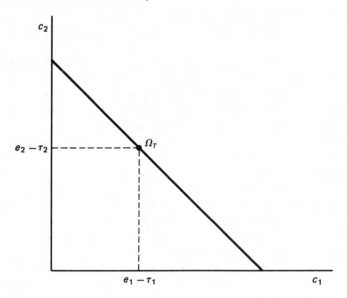

Figure 18.4 Lump-sum taxes.

$$e_{1h} - \tau_1^t - c_{1h}^t = s_h(R_{t+1}, e_{1h} - \tau_1^t, e_{2h} - \tau_2^t) \qquad h = 1, ..., H; t = 1, ...$$

at an individual maximum. If goods are not inferior, individual saving is clearly a decreasing function of the youthful tax parameter τ_1^t, and an increasing function of the old-age tax τ_2^t. Furthermore, if youthful and old-age consumption are gross substitutes, individual saving is an increasing function of the interest factor R. These properties are inherited as well by the (normalized) aggregate savings function $z = (1/H)\Sigma_{h=1}^H s_h$, which expresses the excess supply of loans.

Letting the interest factor vary from the lowest existing individually autarkic value to the highest, we can establish that at least one equilibrium exists, exactly as in theorem 11.1. Figures 18.5(a) and 18.5(b) illustrate this situation as well as the fact that the saving function shifts *upward* when youthful taxes rise or old-age taxes fall. The same figures confirm what we found in the previous section: the equilibrium rate of interest is locally an increasing function of social security benefits when these are financed by taxes on young individuals.

By the same token, the equilibrium rate of interest increases in response to either a rise in *current* government purchases financed at least in part by taxing the young, or a *decline* in future government spending that helps lower the taxes (or increase the social security benefits) of the old. The first situation is illustrated in figure 18.5(c) for an economy consisting of identical households. The equilibrium interest factor is simply (the absolute value of) the marginal rate of substitution at the after-tax endowment point Ω_0 when current government purchases are low, and at the point Ω_1 when youthful taxes rise to match the higher flow of public consumption. Normality of goods implies that the marginal rate of substitution is higher at Ω_1 than at Ω_0. Similarly, any reduction in future public consumption that is used to lower old-age taxes moves the after-tax endowment point from Ω_0 to Ω_2 in figure 18.5(d) and, because of normality, raises the rate of interest. We sum up in the following theorem.

Theorem 18.3 Given standard assumptions on preference orderings, a competitive equilibrium exists for each feasible balanced fiscal policy. If youthful and old-age consumption are normal goods, then at each competitive equilibrium the rate of interest is locally:

(a) an increasing function of *contemporaneous* government purchases, if these are financed at least in part by taxing the young;
(b) an increasing function of *contemporaneous* social security benefits; and
(c) a decreasing function of *subsequent* government spending, if changes in public consumption are at least partly financed by taxes on the old.

A numerical illustration is given in the following example.

Example 18.1 Suppose there are two equally numerous types of households: lenders, indexed by $h = 1$, with utility function $c_{11}c_{21}$ and endowment $(e_1, 0)$; and borrowers, indexed by $h = 2$, with the same utility function as borrowers but with a different endowment $(0, e_2)$. The government knows the type of each individual, and levies in period t a per capita tax g_t on young lenders and nothing on anyone else. Public consumption per young person is exactly equal to $g_t/2$. Each lender at t saves $1/2 (e_1 - g_t)$, and each borrower at t borrows the entire amount of current consumption $e_2/2R_{t+1}$. The equilibrium interest factor is therefore $R_{t+1} = e_2/(e_1 - g_t)$, an increasing function of g_t.

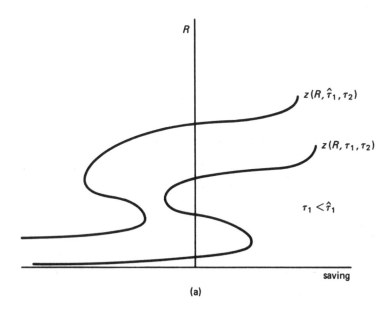

(a)

Figure 18.5 Fiscal policy and interest rates.

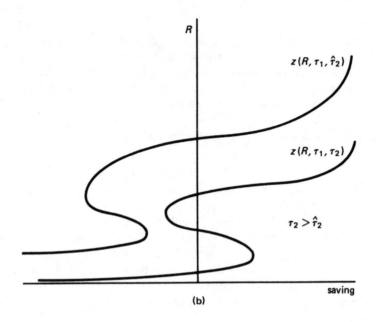

(b)

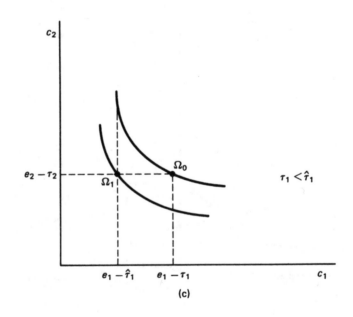

(c)

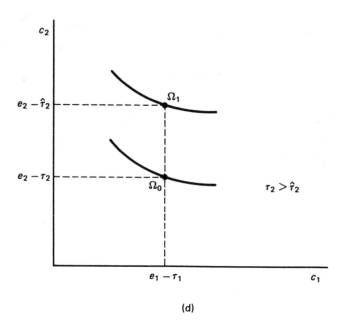

$$c_2$$

$$e_2 - \hat{\tau}_2 \quad \quad \quad \quad \quad \quad \Omega_1$$

$$e_2 - \tau_2 \quad \quad \quad \quad \Omega_0 \quad \quad \quad \quad \quad \tau_2 > \hat{\tau}_2$$

$$e_1 - \tau_1 \quad \quad \quad \quad \quad \quad c_1$$

(d)

Figure 18.5 Fiscal policy and interest rates (cont.)

Notes

1. As of 1989, aggregate social security and related transfer payments amounted to the hefty sum of approximately $632 billion in the USA, that is, about 12 percent of GNP, a figure that dwarfs interest payments on national debt.
2. The adjective "fiscal" stems from the Latin "fiscus" for basket, which also came to mean "treasury." Precommitment is an unrealistic but very convenient simplification. Real-world governments frequently exercise their privilege to change the policies of their predecessors in order to serve the interests of whatever coalition happens to dominate the political landscape. Policy plans that turn out to be not in the best interest of subsequent governments are said to suffer from *time inconsistency*. This issue is raised in Calvo (1978a) and Kydland and Prescott (1977).
3. The same purpose is achieved by the less realistic assumption that the government drops everything it buys into the sea, or otherwise disposes of it at no additional cost. Lump-sum taxes are another unrealistic assumption that we make for simplicity. Organized states first levied proportional taxes in preclassical antiquity on the leisure time of individuals and on crops of primary products. Citizens of the Aztec Empire, for instance, worked one day a week for the state (Webber and Wildavsky, 1986, ch. 2). Conscripted labor also financed the building of the great pyramids of Egypt of which one, that of Cheops, appears to have required approximately 1 billion man-hours of labor! Tax rates on crops appeared to have been moderated in peacetime: from 10 percent in Mesopotamia to about 25 percent in Mauryan India. Some cultures, however, exempted farmers from income taxes, preferring instead indirect taxes. Examples are classical Athens and Rome, which collected revenue primarily from import duties and excise taxes; income taxes were levied in purely discriminatory fashion on prostitutes and aliens in Athens, on the plebeian orders in

Rome.Interestingly enough, farm income is, once again, almost entirely exempt from taxation in modern Greece. The popularity of the income tax is a fairly recent phenomenon in Western countries. England was the first country to impose this tax in 1799, and France the last in 1909. Income taxes were initially quite small; in fact, all through the nineteenth century customs and excise taxes amounted to at least 50 percent of all government revenue in the UK.

4. Malkiel (1970), and Modigliani and Shiller (1973) give an elementary exposition and some suggestive empirical tests of term-structure theories.

19 Deficits in exchange economies

19.1 Ricardian equivalence

Balanced government budgets, the fiscal norm of the nineteenth and early twentieth century, became increasingly rare in the postwar period,[1] especially after 1960, as deficit finance gained wider acceptance among the public, the press, and mainstream political parties. What explains the relatively new-found faith in borrowing[2] as a method to fund current government consumption rather than one confined to the finance of extraordinary expenditure items or public investment?

Deficit finance is a pervasive economic phenomenon that may very well defy a simple, and narrowly economic, interpretation. Its spread undoubtedly has something to do with the ascendancy of simple Keynesian ideas in the 1950s and 1960s; deficit spending was widely regarded as the instrument that could achieve and maintain full employment. Others have argued that the public prefers deficit finance to taxation for any number of conceivable reasons: it is politically simpler for a parliamentary democracy to run a deficit than to raise taxes; citizens do not understand that inflation finance is a tax on money holdings or that servicing the public debt requires some form of taxation, etc.

In this section we view national debt as a potential mechanism for transferring resources between generations, and we study how deficit finance differs from taxation as a method of raising revenue for the government. We denote by $c_1^t = (1/H)\Sigma_{h=1}^H c_{1h}^t$ and $c_2^t = (1/H)\Sigma_{h=1}^H c_{2h}^t$ the average consumption per capita by members of generation t, and by $e_1 = (1/H) \Sigma_{h=1}^H e_{1h}$ and $e_2 = (1/H)\Sigma_{h=1}^H e_{2h}$ the corresponding average endowments per capita. One way to measure how well a particular generation, say t, does in the aggregate when it faces a system of taxes and subsidies is to calculate the net lifetime subsidy $\sigma_t = c_1^t + c_2^t - (e_1 + e_2)$ that it receives in competitive equilibrium.

Given government purchases, the subsidy to the private consumption of generation t depends on how taxes and public debt evolve over time. The faster national debt grows while that generation is alive, the larger the subsidy accruing to the cohort; national debt, after all, represents savings planned by the young to service government liabilities held by the old. The taxes borne by the young have an effect on generational subsidies exactly identical to that of public debt; in fact, what turns out to be of importance to any generation is the evolution of the sum "national debt plus youthful taxation," and not the size of each individual component.

A growing national debt, therefore, confers on any generation the same advantage as would secularly rising taxes on the young: it shifts the burden of financing a given path of government purchases onto succeeding generations. Debt and lump-sum taxes seem so similar to each other as intergenerational transfer mechanisms that one may question whether the financing of public consumption has *any* allcoative consequences whatsoever.

The issue was raised a very long time ago by David Ricardo (1817, ch. 17) who conjectured that equilibrium responds to the flow of government purchases alone, not to the precise mix of debt and taxes by which purchases are financed. In a remarkably prescient passage he wrote:

> It is not, then, by the payment of the interest on the national debt that a country is distressed, nor is it by the exoneration from payment that it can be relieved. It is only by saving from income, and retrenching in expenditure, that the national capital can be increased; and neither the income would be increased, nor the expenditure diminished by the annihilation of the national debt.
>
> (Ricardo, 1817, p. 254)

The idea was put on the back burner by the Keynesian revolution and resurfaced under the name of *Ricardian equivalence* in a stimulating paper by Barro (1974); it is easiest to illustrate in an exchange economy with identical, simultaneously born and infinitely lived individuals.

Before we illustrate Ricardian equivalence, it is perhaps useful to offer a word of caution. Recent discussions of this issue are needlessly clouded by emphasis on "parental altruism" as a motive for leaving bequests and as a device for converting a finitely lived household into an infinitely lived dynasty. We discussed in chapters 14 and 15 some of the pitfalls which attend this conversion; to deny that parental love is a factor affecting inheritances would make it quite difficult to explain why individuals, especially very wealthy ones, tend to maintain large asset balances at death.

It is equally true that, except in very special cases, bequests do not transform an economy of overlapping generations into one populated by identical infinitely lived agents. For instance, children marry, thus linking every parent with the descendants of many contemporaries and, perhaps, of everyone alive today. If there is a positive probability, however small, that my child will wed one among a large number of her contemporaries, then the number of my potential descendants ten generations from now is extremely large; many of these descendants are shared by ancestors who are members of a given cohort, say the one alive today. Fiscal perspective vanishes quickly in the resulting web of consumption externalities which may link any two persons one cares to name (see Bernheim and Bagwell, 1988). To avoid this confusing state of affairs, it is simpler to treat the "bequest motive" as an interesting side issue.

Nevertheless, it is a fundamental insight of Ricardo and his epigones that bequests do lengthen individual planning horizons and that one way to capture the effects of longer horizons is to study infinitely lived households. Suppose now that $(e_t)_{t=1}^{\infty}$ is the endowment vector of each household, and $(g_t)_{t=1}^{\infty}$ is a sequence of government purchases per capita with the property that $0 \leq g_t < e_t$ for each t. Competitive equilibrium here is individually autarkic and satisfies the national income accounting identity (or resource constraint)

$$c_t + g_t = e_t \qquad t = 1, 2, \ldots \qquad (19.1)$$

The equilibrium interest factor R_{t+1} equals the marginal rate of substitution at the net endowment point $(e_t - g_t, e_{t+1} - g_{t+1})$. Whatever method the government chooses to finance public consumption in this economy has no bearing whatever on competitive equilibrium. Any tax cut accompanied by an equal increase in the stock of national debt is matched, at the prevailing interest rate, by a rise in private saving of equal magnitude. Net savings remain zero, and all the consequential properties of equilibrium remain intact.[3] National debt does not have any of the attributes of wealth, for a greater or lesser quantity of it has no economic significance.

Ricardian equivalence holds in the previous example for a very simple reason. Intergenerational transfers are not feasible in an economy of infinitely lived persons born simultaneously at the beginning of time: all who benefit temporarily from a tax cut will have subsequently the obligation of greater interest payments on the public debt. In fact, *what seems crucial here is not the length of life but, rather, the identity of the individuals who draw the benefits, and bear the costs, of a tax cut.*

To grasp how national debt differs from taxation, we return to the overlapping generations model of pure exchange and study how an explicitly temporary issue of public debt disturbs its equilibrium. In other words, we compare an economy in which the government budget is in perpetual balance, and national debt is always zero, with an otherwise identical economy in which a temporary one-period budget deficit is funded by selling national debt to households. This is followed immediately by a budget surplus large enough to retire the entire national debt; the government issues no additional debt thereafter.

In the economy without national debt, we denote by $P = (g_t, \tau_1^t, \tau_2^{t-1})$ the fiscal policy which is balanced by definition, that is, we have $g_t = \tau_1^t + \tau_2^{t-1}/(1 + n)$ for all t. Each household h faces in period t a budget constraint of the form

$$c_{1h}^t + \frac{c_{2h}^t}{R_{t+1}} \leq e_{1h} - \tau_1^t + \frac{e_{2h} - \tau_2^t}{R_{t+1}}$$

Equilibrium interest factors satisfy $z(R_{t+1}, \tau_1^t, \tau_2^t) = 0$, where the aggregate saving function z is defined exactly as in the previous section.

Temporary national debt in this example stems from a fiscal policy that is identical to P in all periods except for changes in taxation at $t = T$ and $t = T + 1$. Specifically, at $t = T$ we lower taxes relative to the balanced budget case by $b > 0$, and sell an equivalent amount of national debt to households. At $t = T + 1$ we correspondingly raise taxes above those of the balanced budget case by an amount sufficient to repay principal and interest on the debt b. All we need do now is describe whose taxes are cut and whose are raised.

Suppose first that the tax cut benefits the same group of people hit later by the tax surcharge, namely generation T. All other generations face the same situation no matter what the economy in which they find themselves. Generation T, on the other hand, has its youthful taxes reduced to $\tau_1^T - b$ and its old-age taxes increased to $\tau_2^T + R_{T+1}b$, where R_{T+1} is the interest factor on loans contracted at T. The present value of the after-tax endowment for member h of generation T

$$e_{1h} - (\tau_1^T - b) + \frac{e_{2h} - \tau_2^T - R_{T+1}b}{R_{T+1}} = e_{1h} - \tau_1^T + \frac{e_{2h} - \tau_2^T}{R_{T+1}}$$

is the same as it would have been in the balanced case. Unless household h is subject to some sort of borrowing constraint or credit market imperfection, its excess demand function does not respond to the financial policy of the government, and neither does the equilibrium interest rate. All that deficit finance accomplishes is to shift forward the endowment of generation T, from point B to point D in figure 19.1, with no change in present value. National debt does not add to household wealth.

Equilibrium behavior changes drastically if the benefits of a tax cut accrue to persons other than those who bear the subsequent surcharge. Suppose, in particular, that taxes on the young remain as in the original balanced fiscal policy, but those on the old are reduced to $\tau_2^{T-1} - b$ at $t = T$ and lifted to $\tau_2^T + R_{T+1}b$ at $t = T + 1$. Then each member h of generation $T - 1$ disposes of lifetime wealth $e_{1h} - \tau_1^{T-1} + e_{2h} - \tau_2^{T-1}/R_{T+1} + bR_T$, which exceeds what would have been available to him under a balanced budget regime by an amount equal to the present value of b, the national debt per capita. Correspondingly, each member h of generation T owns lifetime wealth $e_{1h} - \tau_1^T + e_{2h} - \tau_2^T/R_{T+1} - b$, which falls short of what would have been the case under a balanced fiscal policy by the full amount of the national debt. *National debt thus raises the wealth of the generation whose taxes are cut, and lowers the wealth of the generation that pays for debt retirement.*

If consumption is a normal good, one outcome of this intergenerational redistribution of resources will be to shift excess demand functions, lowering the saving of generation $T - 1$ at any given interest rate and raising saving by generation T. Upward pressure is put on the rate of interest at $T - 1$ and downward pressure at T. The end result of this pressure is that every equilibrium of the balanced economy will respond to the temporary national debt at $T - 1$ by a local upward adjustment in the balanced budget rate of interest, and to the retirement of national debt of T by a local downward adjustment in the balanced budget rate of interest.

The intuition of a once-and-for-all budget deficit generalizes quite easily to more complicated fiscal policies. In fact, one may obtain the following result (see question III.12).

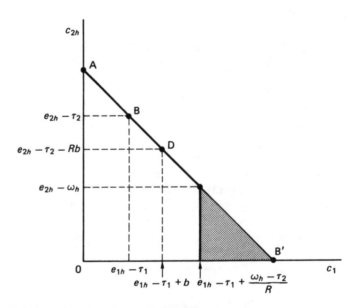

Figure 19.1 Deficit finance with no redistribution.

Theorem 19.1 (Ricardian equivalence) National debt is equivalent to lump-sum taxation if it does not redistribute resources between generations. In particular, any equilibrium under the fiscal policy $P = (g_t, \tau_1^t, \tau_2^{t-1})_{t=1}^\infty$ is also an equilibrium under any policy $\hat{P} = (g_t, \hat{\tau}_1^t, \hat{\tau}_2^{t-1})_{t=1}^\infty$ which specifies the same path of government purchases and the same present value of lifetime taxes as does P. At each equilibrium, P and $\hat{P}$ are associated with the same value of the sum "national debt plus taxes on the young."

Question III.11 applies this result to stationary fiscal policies. Figures 19.1 illustrates Ricardian equivalence in a simple way; B is the after-tax endowment point for a stationary balanced fiscal policy $P = (g, \tau_1, \tau_2)$ while D is the corresponding point for a policy $\hat{P} = (g, \tau_1 - b, \tau_2 + Rb)$ that permits constant per capita public debt $b > 0$. The government budget identity is $g = \tau_1 + \tau_2/(1 + n)$ for policy P, and $b + \tau_1 - b + (\tau_2 + Rb)/(1 + n) = g + Rb/(1 + n)$, that is, $g = \tau_1 + \tau_2/(1 + n)$ again, for policy $\hat{P}$.

Deficit finance then shifts the initial endowment point, changing the timing of lifetime income but not its discounted value. If endowments are public information and individuals can readily borrow up to the present value of after-tax future income, then the budget set of household h in figure 19.1 is the full triangle A0B' independently of how much national debt there is. We are assuming, of course, that total tax contributions plus debt service do not exceed anybody's gross endowment. Therefore, the saving function of household h is independent of per capita national debt; the competitive equilibrium of the economy does not respond to the manner in which public consumption is financed, only to the flow of that consumption.

Suppose, however, that at least some households suffer from borrowing constraints and cannot draw from the credit market loans up to the full discounted value of their future earnings. Does not deficit finance relax borrowing constraints as it shifts income towards youth and dampens the demand for loans?

This possibility, suggested by Tobin (1980), depends a great deal on how credit market constraints respond to fiscal policy. If borrowing constraints are largely independent of the stock of public debt, then deficit finance is an intelligent way to cure imperfections in the credit market: the government essentially borrows on behalf of individuals with unknown credit records, and taxes everyone to service the public debt created in the process.

Public debt by itself, however, does have a tendency to displace private debt and thus may restrict the access to credit of the very individuals whom the government is trying to aid. Unless the government has better information about future incomes than do private lenders, the act of raising old-age taxes by Rb in order to service public debt will reduce by b the credit line of each household, thus offsetting completely the original effect of national debt. Figure 19.1 demonstrates the idea by recalling the gist of section 11.3: if individual endowments cannot be verified, no household is allowed to accumulate claims (that is, loans and tax liabilities) against unobservable future income which exceed the smallest possible value of that income. Therefore, the budget set of household h is the *unshaded* trapezoidal area in figure 19.1, independently of how government purchases are financed.

To expand this budget set, the government needs to do more than the relabeling of claims accomplished by the sale of national debt. It must move resources *within* generations: from lenders to credit-rationed borrowers in youth, and in the opposite sense in old age.

19.2   Sustainable policies

Must governments eventually retire public debt or can they keep refinancing it in
perpetuity, issuing new liabilities to repay maturing debt? Must the government
budget be in balance over time, the surplus in good years canceling the deficits of
adverse years? Or is it possible that governments, quite unlike ordinary households,
can maintain a permanent deficit? These are questions that occur naturally to anyone
who has witnessed the rapid worldwide growth of deficit finance, especially since the
oil shocks of the 1970s, and wondered whether budget constraints are as meaningful to
the state as they are to individuals.

The answer is rather simple in an economy with a finite time horizon, or in one
populated by identical infinitely lived agents in which the government budget is simply
the mirror image of individual budgets. Terminal or transversality conditions in such
economies rule out competitive equilibria with permanent government deficits,
however small these may be; permanent budget deficits would imply that households
behave suboptimally by agreeing to accumulate in perpetuity liabilities that are never
exchanged for consumption goods. A strong transversality condition, like that in
section 13.4, dictates that the present value, reckoned at time zero, of all government
deficits cannot be positive; a weaker one states that the stock of real national debt will
vanish asymptotically in present-value terms. Neither condition prevents national
debt, a liability of the government to households, from being positive in any finite
time period; every transversality condition, however, states that government liabilities
must be *matched* by corresponding claims on households, that is, by current or future
taxes.

Permanent government deficits are easier to visualize in economies with a more
realistic demographic structure in which the state is possibly infinitely lived but
households are not. Whatever way one chooses to describe the modern state, one is
forced to include in any definition of it a social compact between successive
generations. Unwritten social agreements as well as written constitutions provide
governments with a sense of economic continuity that one cannot easily experience as
a member of an evolving family. For instance, the British government to this day pays
interest on consols issued almost 200 years ago to finance the Napoleonic wars.

Unlike mere mortals, modern states are not endowed with finite lives or, more
precisely, with a definite date in the future beyond which they surely will be unable to
meet economic obligations incurred today. As we shall see in Part IV, this is one
reason why governments are able to market completely unbacked liabilities like
currency or claims on currency. Another consequence of a potentially infinite
planning horizon is that resource constraints do not have the same meaning for a
government as they do for an ordinary household or even for a large privately held
firm.

Because governments possess both the legal authority and the administrative
machinery to tax resources away from individuals, they are constrained more by the
quality of their information about the household sector (and by the mobility of
resources across national borders) and less by formal budget constraints like equations
(18.8) and (18.9) of section 18.2. Within certain limits, the government budget
constraint is an accounting *identity*, a name that we have already used for it, which
holds for a large variety of fiscal policies.

In theory, governments are only restricted by the aggregate endowment of the economy within which they operate: if the tax authorities possessed detailed knowledge of individual incomes, they could in principle expropriate the entire resources of the economy. As a matter of fact, the authorities do not know enough to design a tax system tailored on individual characteristics, and must rely instead on relatively anonymous methods of raising revenue like income taxes, commodity taxes, and the sale of public debt; all these revenue-raising devices have distortionary side effects on the allocation of resources.

Anonymous taxation relies necessarily on the competitive mechanism, that is, on the working of the markets that determine prices and individual incomes. Does the competitive mechanism in itself place tighter bounds on fiscal policy than one might expect from a personalized tax system? The answer seems to be in the affirmative, for the borrowing requirements of the government cannot exceed (and likely will fall far short of) the maximal flow of savings that households are willing to set aside at any one rate of interest. Nor can a hypothetical per capita tax surpass the resources of the poorest taxpayer.

Competition from private borrowers, too, will hinder the finance of very large or persistent government deficits and restrict the size of real per capita national debt. Attempts to raise public debt, if carried beyond a certain point, will put enough upward pressure on interest rates to destroy competitive equilibrium: the requirements of debt service will grow past the lending capacity of the economy in finite time.

How does one measure the lending capacity of an economy? What size fiscal deficit can a credit market absorb if it is free of government intervention? How are governments likely to intervene when they find it necessary to expand private demand for public debt beyond the limits placed on it by competition from other debtors? We explore these questions in a variety of settings, beginning with a pure-exchange economy of selfish overlapping generations in the remainder of this chapter, and moving on to issues of production and growth in chapter 20, and to altruistic households in section 21.1.

First, we return to the pure-exchange model of section 18.1. We begin with a stationary fiscal policy $P = (g, \tau_1, \tau_2)$ defined in per capita terms, and satisfying $\tau_1 \leqslant e_{1h}$ and $\tau_2 \leqslant e_{2h}$ for all h. Let $q = g - \tau_1 - \tau_2/(1 + n)$ be the primary budget deficit per head and $b_{t+1} = R_t b_t/(1 + n) + q$ be the government budget identity. Also define $z_h(R, \tau_1, \tau_2) = \mathrm{argmax}_z u^h(e_{1h} - \tau_1 - z, e_{2h} - \tau_2 + Rz)$, the savings function of household h, and $z = (1/H)\Sigma_{h=1}^{H} z_h$, the normalized aggregate savings function. Then, we look for an ordinary competitive equilibrium in that economy, which we describe as follows.

Definition 19.1 Given a fiscal policy $P = (g, \tau_1, \tau_2)$ and the historical level b_0 of national debt per capita, a *competitive equilibrium* is a sequence of vectors $(c_1^t, c_2^t,..., c_H^t)$, a sequence of interest factors R_t and a sequence b_t of per capita national debt such that, for $h = 1,..., H$ and $t = 1, 2,...$ *ad infinitum*, we have

(a) $R_t = (1 + n)(b_{t+1} - q)/b_t$　　　　　　　(c) $b_t = z(R, \tau_1, \tau_2)$

(b) $c_{2h}^0 = e_{2h} - \tau_2$

　　$c_{1h}^t = e_{1h} - \tau_1 - z_h(R_{t+1}, \tau_1, \tau_2)$

　　$c_{2h}^t = e_{2h} - \tau_2 + R_{t+1} z_h(R_{t+1}, \tau_1, \tau_2)$

Part (a) of this definition is the government budget identity; (b) says that individuals choose maximal elements in their budget sets, given taxes and the price system (R_t); and (c) represents equilibrium in the credit market. From parts (a) and (c) we conclude that public debt satisfies the following first-order difference equation in equilibrium:

$$b_t = z \left[\frac{(1 + n)(b_{t+1} - q)}{b_t}, \tau_1, \tau_2 \right] \tag{19.2}$$

The pure-exchange economy we are studying here has a competitive equilibrium if, and only if, (19.2) has a solution $(b_t)_{t=1}^{\infty}$ given b_0. We begin with the case of primary budget balance in this section, leaving the dynamics of budget deficits for the section immediately following this.

Suppose that direct taxes equal government purchases, that is, $\tau_1 + \tau_2/(1 + n) = g$, which means $q = 0$. Then equation (19.2) reduces to

$$b_t = z \left[\frac{(1 + n)b_{t+1}}{b_t}, \tau_1, \tau_2 \right] \tag{19.3}$$

If $\bar{R}$ is an equilibrium interest factor for an economy with zero public debt, then $\bar{R}$ satisfies $z(R, \tau_1, \tau_2) = 0$. Theorem 18.3 says that such an R exists and depends functionally on the tax parameters, that is, $R = \bar{R}(\tau_1, \tau_2)$. We suppose for the time being that $\bar{R}(\tau_1, \tau_2)$ is a single-valued function; readers who do question III.4 will find out what happens to equation (19.3) if single-valuedness does not hold.

Equation (19.3) has two stationary solutions, both familiar to us from Part II. One of them is an *inside-asset equilibrium* with zero national debt and interest factor equal to $\bar{R}(\tau_1, \tau_2)$ for all t. The other is an *outside-asset equilibrium* of the golden rule type, with interest rate equal to the growth rate n and per capita national debt $b^* = z(1 + n, \tau_1, \tau_2)$ generally not equal to zero. Dynamical equilibria are readily described once we draw the phase diagram, that is, graph the difference equation (19.3) in national debt space for a given fiscal policy. This is done in figure 19.2 for the Samuelson case $(b^* > 0)$ and in figure 19.3 for the classical case $(b^* < 0)$. In each case the stationary equilibrium with inside money is at the origin while the outside-money equilibrium lies at the intersection of the 45° line with the phaseline of equation (19.3).

For a better grasp of the geometric structure of dynamical equilibria, let us assume temporarily that population is stationary and there is only one type of household. This special structure will reduce the aggregate equilibrium dynamics of national debt to the intertemporal consumption plan of the representative household. The phaselines of equation (19.3) in figures 19.2 and 19.3 become *reflected offer curves* that relate the equilibrium excess supply in youth by a generation-t household with the equilibrium excess demand in old age of the same household.

Excess supply in youth is simply the saving by generation t, which in equilibrium equals both national debt per capita and the excess demand by generation $t - 1$. We attach to these offer curves the appellation "reflected" to indicated that they connect *excess supply* of one dated good with *excess demand* for another, instead of relating two excess demands, as does an ordinary offer curve.

An individual offer curve is much like a savings function: any point on it maps a particular interest factor, measured by the slope of the ray that goes through that point, into a flow of savings, denoted by the relevant abscissa. Because saving is positive for interest factors above the autarkic value $\bar{R}(\tau_1, \tau_2)$ and negative below $\bar{R}(\tau_1, \tau_2)$, the offer curve is tangent at the origin to the ray with slope $\bar{R}(\tau_1, \tau_2)$.

The economic interpretation of the phase diagram is complicated slightly once the population becomes heterogenous or grows at a non-zero rate. Population growth means that the interest factor at a particular point is measured by $1 + n$ times the slope of the ray through that point; and heterogeneity means that the graph of equation (19.3) is a weighted average of individual reflected offer curves. Furthermore, its slope at the origin equals the ratio $\bar{R}(\tau_1, \tau_2)/(1 + n)$.

For specific examples we turn to the Samuelson case shown in figure 19.2. Here one demonstrates easily (see question III.5) that the graph of equation (19.3) intersects the diagonal from above at the origin and from below at the golden rule point. This means that $\bar{R}(\tau_1, \tau_2) < 1 + n$ and therefore that the inside-money equilibrium is both *dynamically inefficient* (as we already know from Part II) *and asymptotically stable if it is unique.*

The *outside-money equilibrium*, on the other hand, *is dynamically efficient but may or may not be stable.* For instance, if youthful and old-age consumption are gross substitutes for all households (equivalently, if all individual saving functions are increasing in the rate of interest), then the stationary outside-money equilibrium is of necessity unstable, as in figure 19.2(a). However, if the aggregate income effect of an interest rate change were greatly to outweigh the corresponding substitution effect when the interest rate equals n, then the aggregate savings function might bend backward sufficiently to ensure the asymptotic stability of the golden rule equilibrium. Figure 19.2(b) illustrates this possibility.

Exactly where the phaseline of equation (19.3) lies will depend on some extent on fiscal policy, that is, on the parameters τ_1 and τ_2. When goods are normal, a rise in τ_1 depresses saving, rotating the frontier counterclockwise about the origin; an increase in τ_2, on the other hand, raises saving and rotates the frontier in the opposite sense. Figure 19.2(c) illustrates.

The classical case is given in figure 19.3 which reveals two stationary equilibria: an inside-money equilibrium that is obviously dynamically efficient and asymptotically unstable because $\bar{R}(\tau_1, \tau_2) > 1 + n$; and an outside-money equilibrium that is dynamically efficient and asymptotically stable (see also question III.5).

We sum up the properties of stationary equilibria under a policy of primary budget balance in the following theorem.

Theorem 19.2 If the generationally autarkic factor $\bar{R}(\tau_1, \tau_2)$ is a single-valued function of fiscal policy, then a stationary policy of primary budget balance is consistent with two stationary equilibria, an inside-money equilibrium with interest factor $\bar{R}(\tau_1, \tau_2)$ and an outside-money equilibrium with interest factor $1 + n$. The former is an intertemporally suboptimal sink in the Samuelson case, an intertemporally optimal source in the classical one. The outside-money equilibrium is intertemporally optimal in both cases; its local stability is assured in the classical case but depends on the relative strength of the intertemporal income and substitution effects in the Samuelson case.

Note that the offer curve, and the phaseline of the difference equation (19.3), are *monotone* in the classical case in which the representative or average household is a borrower whenever $r = n$. This is because the income and substitution effects of an

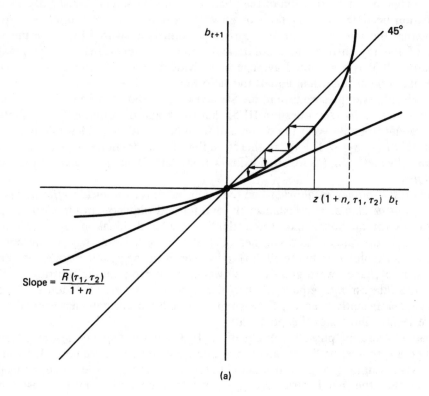

$$\text{Slope} = \frac{\bar{R}(\tau_1, \tau_2)}{1 + n}$$

b_{t+1}

$45°$

$z(1 + n, \tau_1, \tau_2) \; b_t$

(a)

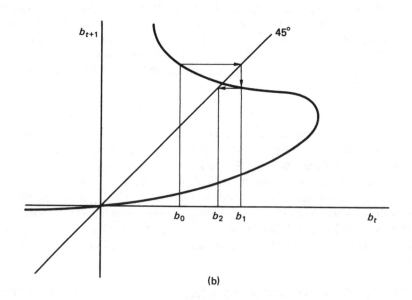

b_{t+1}

$45°$

$b_0 \quad b_2 \; b_1$

b_t

(b)

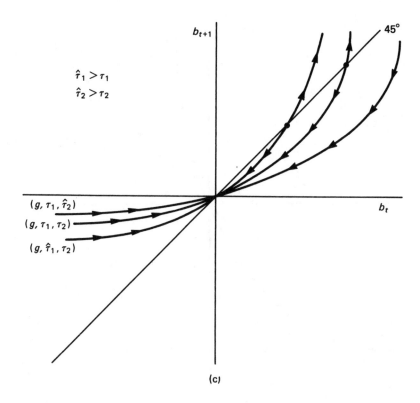

$\hat{\tau}_1 > \tau_1$
$\hat{\tau}_2 > \tau_2$

b_{t+1}

45°

$(g, \tau_1, \hat{\tau}_2)$
(g, τ_1, τ_2)
$(g, \hat{\tau}_1, \tau_2)$

b_t

(c)

Figure 19.2 National debt with a balanced budget: the Samuelson case.

interest rate change are in the *same* direction for borrowers (but not necessarily for lenders) whenever goods are normal. For instance, an increase in the rate of interest reduces the lifetime income of a borrower and implies a reduction in the demand for all normal goods, including youthful consumption.

One interesting thing to notice here is that equilibrium is *indeterminate* whenever there exists an asymptotically stable stationary state. Then any sequence b_t beginning in the neighborhood of the stationary state is a competitive equilibrium. As Calvo (1978b) points out, this means that there is a *continuum of competitive equilibria*, that is, a one-dimensional family indexed on beginning-of-time national debt b_0; see chapter 16 for a discussion of indeterminate equilibria.

This concludes our discussion of dynamical equilibria in pure-exchange economies with national debt, and we return to sustainable financial policies. How much national debt per capita can the credit market absorb in competitive equilibrium without any sort of government intervention? To be more precise, let us run a primary budget deficit b_0 per capita at the beginning of time and preserve primary budget balance thereafter. *How big can initial debt[4] be?*

If we take the subsequent fiscal policy $P = (g, \tau_1, \tau_2)$ as given and assume youthful and old-age consumption to be gross substitutes for every household, the offer curve is monotone. Figure 19.2(a) says that, in the Samuelson case, b_0 cannot exceed $z(1 + n, \tau_1, \tau_2)$, the golden rule stock of per capita public debt. For if $b_0 > z(1 + n, \tau_1, \tau_2)$, then the interest rate needed to induce households voluntarily to hold b_0 would

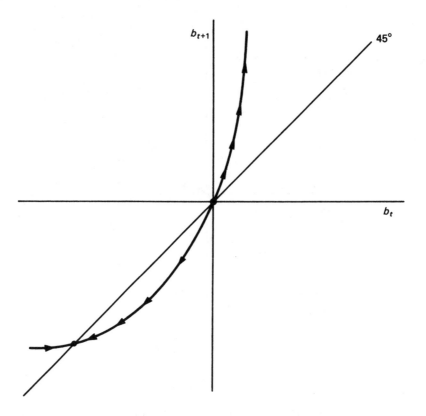

Figure 19.3 National debt with a balanced budget: the classical case.

exceed the growth rate n in each period. National debt would grow faster than the economy, with debt service surpassing in finite time the maximal flow of saving which the household sector is capable of. However, if $b_0 < z(1 + n, \tau_1, \tau_2)$, then public debt grows more slowly than the economy and, asymptotically, debt per capita tends to become zero.

It is not impossible that per capita public debt initially may even *exceed* the golden rule value. Figure 19.2(b) illustrates a Samuelson-type economy in which the income effect of an interest rate change is strong enough to guarantee the asymptotic stability (indeterminacy) of the golden rule. Then any b_0 in the neighborhood of $z(1 + n, \tau_1, \tau_2)$ supports a competitive equilibrium. Of course the critical value of per capita national debt depends on the fiscal policy itself, and can be raised if we decrease taxes in youth and/or raise them in old age (see figure 19.2(c)). This may be accomplished, for instance, by lowering social security benefits and taxes, and shows why social security, even when it is balanced, is a close substitute for public debt.

We note from figure 19.3 that, in the classical case, public debt cannot exceed zero, and collect our findings in the following.

Theorem 19.3 Suppose youthful and old-age consumption are gross substitutes for all households, fiscal policy is (g, τ_1, τ_2), the primary budget deficit is zero and the generationally autarkic interest factor $\bar{R}(\tau_1, \tau_2)$ is a single-valued function of fiscal policy. Then the largest amount of per capita public debt that is consistent with competitive equilibrium is either zero or $z(1 + n, \tau_1, \tau_2)$, whichever is greater.

The following example illustrates theorem 19.3.

Example 19.1 Consider an exchange economy with constant population; identical households with utility function $c_1^t c_2^t$; endowment vector $(1, e)$, where $e < 1$; fiscal policy (g, τ_1, τ_2), where $\tau_1 + \tau_2 = g$, $\tau_1 < 1$, $g < e$; and beginning-of-time national debt $b_0 > 0$. The budget constraint of the representative household is $c_1^t + c_2^t/R_t \leqslant 1 - \tau_1 + (e - \tau_2)/R_t$ which implies a savings function of the form $s_t = 1 - \tau_1 - c_1^t = 1/2\ [1 - \tau_1 - (e - \tau_2)/R_t]$; the equilibrium sequence of national debt must then satisfy the equation $2b_t = 1 - \tau_1 - (e - \tau_2)b_t/b_{t+1}$. Stationary solutions are $b = 0$ at $R = (e - \tau_2)/(1 - \tau_1)$ and $b = 1/2\ [1 - \tau_1 - (e - \tau_2)]$ at $R = 1$. The former is an asymptotically stable inefficient inside-asset equilibrium in the Samuelson case, that is, if $1 - \tau_1 > e - \tau_2$.

The outside-asset equilibrium is dynamically efficient for all parameter values; it is stable in the classical case, unstable in the Samuelson case. Given public consumption g per capita, the largest sustainable value of public debt per capita is attained if τ_1 is as small as possible, that is, at $\tau_1 = 0$, $\tau_2 = g$. Then $b = 1/2\ (1 - e + g)$.

19.3 Budget deficits and the national debt

This section focuses on two topics. The first continues the examination of the limits to fiscal policy begun in section 19.2: How large a permanent budget deficit can be sustained by a pure-exchange economy in a *laissez-faire* competitive equilibrium? What is the relationship between the flow of government deficits and the stock of national debt? The second topic concerns the burden of the national debt, that is, the potentially adverse impact it may have on the consumption and welfare of households.

Fiscal policies that call for a positive and constant primary deficit q in the government budget correspond to competitive equilibria that satisfy the difference equation (19.2) of the previous section. The phase diagram for this situation is similar to figures 19.2 and 19.3, with the graph of equation (19.2) translated upward from the zero-primary-deficit case by a vertical amount equal to q.

Figure 19.4(a) illustrates the equilibrium dynamics of budget deficits for a Samuelson-type economy in which youthful and old-age consumption are gross substitutes; question III.18 looks at budget deficits in classical economies. The rightmost phaseline of figure 19.4(a), denoted by $q = 0$, is similar to the non-negative orthant of figure 19.2(a). For modest values of the primary deficit, such as $q = \bar{q}$, there are always two stationary equilibria, $b^1(\bar{q})$ and $b^2(\bar{q})$; the former is asymptotically stable while the latter may well be unstable.[5]

As we raise purchases keeping taxes constant, the primary budget deficit increases up to a critical value q^* at which a saddle-node bifurcation takes place: the steady states b^1 and b^2 collide and vanish when the phaseline of the difference equation (19.2) ceases to have common points with diagonal. For any $q > q^*$, then, stationary states do not exist and neither does any competitive equilibrium. *The bifurcation value q^* represents the largest permanent primary budget deficit consistent with* laissez-faire *equilibrium*. It is measured simply by the vertical distance between the diagonal and

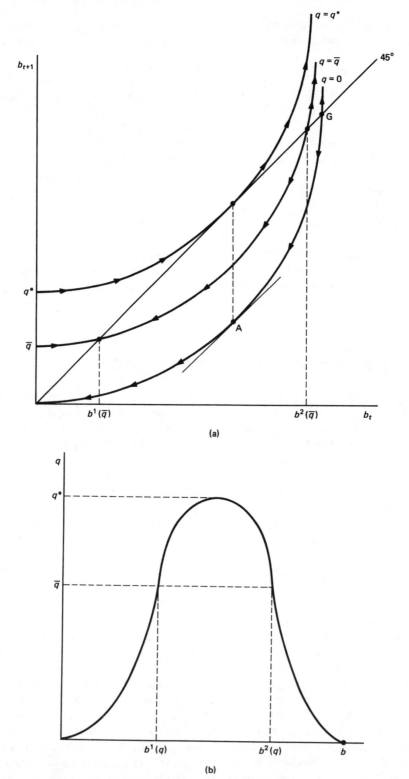

Figure 19.4 National debt with a primary budget deficit.

that point A on the zero-deficit frontier at which the frontier has slope exactly equal to unity.[6]

The precise size of q^* depends, among other things, on tax parameters. Given normal goods, for instance, a revenue-neutral realignment of taxes that lightens the taxation of the young at the expense of the old will encourage private saving at each rate of interest, shift the zero-deficit frontier to the right and raise q^*.

Figure 19.4(b) is an elementary illustration of the complex relationship of per capita budget deficit to national debt for a fixed tax policy (τ_1, τ_2). As we shall see in section 20.2, this relationship is even more complicated in economies with capital. The main message one should draw from this figure is that any permanent primary budget deficit $q \in (0, q^*)$ corresponds to *at least two* stationary values of per capita public debt; this is so even under stringent assumptions, like universal gross substitutability, which make aggregate saving everywhere an increasing function of the interest rate. For any given q, the lower value $b^1(q)$ of public debt corresponds to an asymptotically stable equilibrium and increases faster than the budget deficit, that is, $db^1/dq > 1$. The higher value $b^2(q)$ of stationary per capita debt may be an increasing or decreasing function of the deficit, depending on the relative strengths of the income and substitution effects at $R = 1 + n$. In either case, national debt increases more slowly than the budget deficit, that is $db^2/dq < 1$.

We summarize our findings in the next theorem.

Theorem 19.4 Let fiscal policy be stationary in a Samuelson-type pure-exchange economy and suppose that the generationally autarkic interest factor is a single-valued function of that policy. Given the tax parameters τ_1, τ_2, there is an upper bound $q^* > 0$ on the primary budget deficit such that competitive equilibrium fails to exist whenever $q > q^*$. For any $q \in (0, q^*)$ there is one stable stationary competitive equilibrium, with associated value of per capita debt $b^1(q) > 0$ such that $b^1(0) = 0$ and $db^1/dq > 1$. There is an additional stationary competitive equilibrium, which may or may not be stable; this is associated with a value $b^2(q)$ of per capita national debt such that $b^2(q) > b^1(q)$, $db^2/dq < 1$, and $b^2(0) = z(1 + n, \tau_1, \tau_2)$.

Each stationary state corresponds to a particular interest factor: a relatively low one, $(1 + n)[1 - q/b^1(q)]$, goes with the lower stationary stock of public debt $b^1(q)$; a higher one, $(1 + n)[1 - q/b^2(q)]$, prevails at the higher value $b^2(q)$. If the primary budget is in deficit, then both stationary equilibria are dynamically inefficient in the Samuelson economy; each of them corresponds to an interest rate below n. This inefficiency, as we shall see again in Part IV, is an inevitable consequence of all deficit finance: when the government prints new claims, it lowers the yield on existing claims and taxes indirectly all security holders.

The distortion from deficit finance disappears if the budget is balanced or in surplus, that is, if all government purchases can be financed by an appropriate system of nondistorting lump-sum taxes; see question III.15. Therefore, we have demonstrated the following rather obvious result.

Theorem 19.5 Consider a stationary fiscal policy in a Samuelson-type economy in which the generationally autarkic interest factor is a single-valued function of that policy. If the primary government budget is in deficit, then both stationary competitive equilibria are dynamically inefficient, and so are all convergent dynamical equilibria. The optimal way to finance any flow of government purchases is by nondistorting lump-sum taxes.

Question III.18 takes a look at permanent budget surpluses. A fiscal policy of that type, of course, is a curiosum for anyone familiar with actual national income accounts, the reality being large and growing stocks of national debt. Nineteenth-century British economists became concerned about the long-term economic consequences of public debt issued to pay for the Napoleonic Wars. David Ricardo, for instance, writes:

> From what I have said, it must not be inferred that I consider the system of borrowing as the best calculated to defray the extraordinary expenses of the state. It is a system that tends to make us less thrifty – to blind us to our real situation.

(Ricardo, 1817, p. 247)

The "real situation," of course, refers to the long-run consequences of public debt. What does it do to aggregate consumption and the economic welfare of households? To what extent does national debt displace or "crowd out" private investment? Chapter 20 examines these questions in some detail.

Notes

1. On an unweighted arithmetic basis, the US federal deficit averaged about 0.4 percent of GNP in the 1950s, 0.8 percent of GNP in the 1960s, rising to an average of 3.1 percent in the 1970s and 4.1 percent in the 1980s. Readers who are not impressed with these numbers might consider Greece, where the central government deficit grew from 2.8 percent of GNP in 1970 to 18.4 percent of GNP in 1985, or Guyana where the public sector deficit rose from 13 percent of gross domestic product (GDP) in 1978 to 60 percent in 1984. Other interesting fractions (all as percentages of GDP in 1983) are 36 percent for Israel, 27 percent for Nicaragua, and 21 percent for Suriname. I am indebted to Anne Sibert for these figures.
2. The word "relatively" should be stressed here. Since antiquity governments have known how to collect revenue by borrowing or debasing the currency. Deficits seem in fact to be the rule rather than the exception in monetized economies. Among the few rulers who consistently balanced the government budget, we mention Pericles, Augustus, and Hadrian (Webber and Wildavsky, 1986, ch. 3). Alesina (1988) and Alesina and Tabellini (1990) survey some of the strategic reasons for the political popularity of deficit finance.
3. This invariance property extends to any economy with finitely many infinitely lived individuals born simultaneously and sharing a common rate of time preference.
4. The ability of any government to roll over its debt perpetually brings to mind the notorious Boston financier Charles Ponzi who used to pay, *c.* 1920, exhorbitant interest to lenders out of an ever-expanding pool of deposits, without ever "investing" one penny. Mr Ponzi, who had a finite but eventful life, was indicted in Federal Court in November 1920, and his bank collapsed (see Russell 1973). O'Connell and Zeldes (1988) offer a theoretical study of "Ponzi schemes."
5. Stability is attained under a dominant income effect as in figure 19.2(b).
6. Point A certainly exists for any continuously differentiable aggregate savings function: the zero-debt frontier has slope less than unity at the origin, and more than unity at the golden rule point G.

20 Deficits in growing economies

20.1 The burden of the national debt

To investigate the long-run consequences of public debt, we return to the scalar Diamond model with constant-returns-to-scale production to which we add "internal" public debt, assuming all of it is held by domestic residents. Question III.9 deals with "external" debt, that is, with foreign holdings of domestic debt. Given a feasible fiscal policy $P = (g_t, \tau_1^t, \tau_2^t)_{t=1}^{\infty}$ a dynamical competitive equilibrium satisfies four equalities for each t: two factor demand schedules

$$R_t = R(k_t) = f'(k_t) + 1 - \delta \qquad (20.1)$$

$$w_t = w(k_t) = f(k_t) - k_t f'(k_t) \qquad (20.2)$$

a government budget identity

$$(1 + n)b_{t+1} = R_t b_t + q_t \qquad (20.3)$$

in which $q_t = g_t - \tau_1^t - \tau_2^{t-1}/(1 + n)$ is the primary budget deficit; and one asset-market clearing condition

$$(1 + n)(k_{t+1} + b_{t+1}) = s(R_{t+1}, w_t - \tau_2^t, - \tau_2^t) \qquad (20.4)$$

where $s(R, y_1, y_2) = \text{argmax } u(y_1 - s, y_2 + Rs)$ is the saving function of the representative household.

Combining equations (20.1)–(20.4) we obtain

$$(1 + n)(k_{t+1} + b_{t+1}) = s[R(k_{t+1}), w(k_t) - \tau_1^t, -\tau_2^t] \qquad (20.5a)$$

$$(1 + n)b_{t+1} = R(k_t)b_t + q_t \qquad (20.5b)$$

This non-autonomous system, a generalization of the familiar autonomous planar Diamond model of equations (7.1a) and (7.1b), describes fairly generally the dynamical impact of national debt on the stock of capital for an *arbitrary* feasible fiscal policy. In the remainder of this section, we concentrate on *constant-stock fiscal policies* that maintain constant per capita debt, just as Diamond did in his original work. Section 20.2 looks at *constant-flow fiscal policies* which fix the size of the primary deficit per capita.

Consider, in particular, a fiscal policy of the form $g_t = \tau_1^t = 0$ for all t, and

$$\tau_2^{t-1} = b(1 + n)[R(k_t) - 1 - n] \qquad (20.6)$$

where b is the constant stock of per capita public debt. This stock, says equation (20.3), is kept constant by continuously refloating the principal and raising from the old enough tax revenue to pay the interest. For this fiscal policy, the government's budget identity holds automatically; equation (20.5a) becomes

$$(1 + n)(k_{t+1} + b) = s\{R(k_{t+1}), w(k_t), -b(1 + n)[R(k_{t+1}) - 1 - n]\} \tag{20.7}$$

where $b \geqslant 0$ is a policy parameter. The taxes borne by the old are within their resources if the present value of their lifetime income, $R_{t+1}w_t - \tau_2^t$, is positive for all t. A look at equation (20.6) shows this to be the case if

$$R_{t+1}w_t \geqslant (1 + n)(R_{t+1} - 1 - n)b \tag{20.8}$$

that is, whenever b or R_{t+1} are "not too big."

For $b = 0$, equation (20.7) reduces to the familiar scalar Diamond model. What happens to the phaseline of that model as b rises above zero? Assuming that the utility function is of the class C^2 and that consumption goods are normal and gross substitutes, we rewrite the time map (20.7) in the form

$$k_{t+1} = G(k_t; b) \tag{20.9}$$

where $G: \mathbb{R}_+^2 \to \mathbb{R}_+$ is an increasing C^1 map and b is a parameter. By direct differentiation, then, we readily find that G is decreasing in b for each fixed k_t if, and only if,

$$1 > \frac{\tau_2}{b} \frac{|s_2|}{1 + n} \tag{20.10}$$

where s_2 is the partial derivative of $s(R, y_1, y_2)$ with respect to its last argument. Normality means $-1 < s_2 < 0$, and (20.10) is implied by $1 > \tau_2^t/b = R_{t+1} - (1 + n) = f'(k_{t+1}) - (n + \delta)$. Therefore

$$\frac{\partial k_{t+1}}{\partial b} < 0 \quad \text{if} \quad 1 > f'(k_{t+1}) - f'(k^*) \tag{20.11}$$

where k^* is the golden rule capital–labor ratio.

This relation implies that, if k_{t+1} is *not too far* below the golden rule, an increase in b shifts the phaseline of equation (20.9) downward, *just as an increase in the social security tax τ did in figure 18.3*. There will be typically *two* steady states for each parameter value $b > 0$, provided that b is not too big: a stable state $\bar{k}(b)$ in which k is a decreasing function of b, and an unstable state.

In fact, a comparison of equation (20.7) with (18.5) leads to the inescapable Ricardian conclusion that national debt and unfunded social security are very similar in their influence on capital accumulation. Social security simply dulls individual incentives to save. National debt, on the other hand, contributes both to the direct demand for loanable funds by the government and to saving through higher debt-service taxation; *excess* demand for funds is always positive when goods are normal.

The outcome in each case is an upward shift in excess demand for loans, upward local pressure on the rate of interest, and a tendency towards lower capital intensity in the stationary state. In fact, theorem 18.2 holds here almost exactly as it stands, once we substitute the term "per capita national debt" for "social security." Thus we have the following.

Theorem 20.1 Suppose consumption goods are normal and gross substitutes, government purchases are zero, and a constant stock of per capita public debt is serviced by taxes on old individuals. Then at any asymptotically stable stationary equilibrium, capital intensity and per capita saving are decreasing functions of per capita national debt, and the rate of interest is an increasing function of that debt.

Under the assumptions of theorem 20.1, capital intensity varies inversely with per capita debt in stationary equilibrium. Since aggregate consumption is proportional to $f(k) - (\delta + n)k$, it is an increasing function of national debt whenever k exceeds the golden rule capital intensity k^*, and a decreasing function of national debt otherwise. The case $k < k^*$ corresponds to dynamically efficient competitive equilibria, and it is here that national debt is a *burden* because of its adverse impact on the aggregate consumption possibilities of the economy.[1] Similar considerations apply to lifetime utility in the steady state; in fact, question III.10 asks readers to demonstrate the following proposition.

Theorem 20.2 Suppose goods are normal, government purchases are zero, and a constant stock of per capita public debt is serviced by taxing old individuals. Then an increase in the stock of per capita national debt decreases aggregate consumption and lifetime utility in the steady state if, and only if, the original competitive equilibrium is intertemporally optimal.

To illustrate the allocative and welfare implications of national debt, we use an example of stationary equilibrium in a pure-exchange economy.

Example 20.1 We return to a pure-exchange economy with constant population consisting of identical individuals. The utility function is $c_1 c_2$; endowment is (e_1, e_2) with $e_1 > e_2$; government purchases are zero; national debt is constant at $b < e_1$; and old individuals bear the entire burden of debt service. Saving per young household, then, is $e_1 - 1/2 \{e_1 + (1/R)[e_2 - b(R - 1)]\}$, and equals national debt in equilibrium. Asset-market clearing therefore implies

$$2b = 2e_1 - e_1 - \frac{1}{R}[e_2 + b(1 - R)]$$

Solving for R we obtain

$$R = \frac{e_2 + b}{e_1 - b} \tag{20.12}$$

which says that the equilibrium interest factor varies directly with per capita public debt. Because this is an economy without production, aggregate consumption does not respond to changes in national debt or in the transfer payments that constitute debt service. However, the *lifetime pattern* of consumption does vary in reaction to national debt. In particular, we have $c_1 = e_1 - b$ and $c_2 = e_2 + b$. Lifetime utility as a function of national debt is then

$$u(b) = e_1 e_2 + b(e_1 - e_2) - b^2 \tag{20.13}$$

which is a decreasing function of national debt if, and only if, $b < 1/2 (e_1 - e_2)$. From this and equation (20.12) we see easily that national debt is a burden if $1/2 (e_1 - e_2) < (e_1 R - e_2)/(R + 1)$, that is, if $R > 1$. As we know, this inequality holds true for dynamically efficient competitive equilibria and fails for inefficient equilibria.

20.2   Constant-flow budget policies (*)

We explore in this section the role of *permanent* budget deficits in an economy with production, placing particular emphasis on how public consumption influences the accumulation of privately owned physical capital and productive capacity in the long run. The material we present, an extension and refinement of the pure-exchange results developed in section 19.3, examines how the planar Diamond model behaves if we inject a constant government budget deficit $q > 0$ into it.

Fiscal policies that do this are termed "constant-flow" policies because they augment the principal value of public debt by a constant amount each period. The resulting dynamical system

$$(1 + n)(k_{t+1} + b_{t+1}) = z[R(k_{t+1}), w(k_t)] \tag{20.14a}$$

$$(1 + n)b_{t+1} = R(k_t)b_t + q \tag{20.14b}$$

is the autonomous form of the system contained in equation (20.5a) and (20.5b) if we set $\tau_1^i = 0$ and $\tau_2^i = 0$. For simplicity, then, we ignore taxes and let q stand for both government purchases per capita and deficit per capita.

Figure 7.4 shows a phase diagram for this system in the case $q = 0$ when equations (20.14a) and (20.14b) reduce to the standard planar Diamond model. To construct the corresponding diagram for $q \neq 0$, we retrace the procedure followed in section 7.5. Assume gross substitutability in consumption; define k^* to be the golden rule value of capital intensity; recall the factor-price relations $R(k) = 1 - \delta + f'(k)$, $w(k) = f(k) - kf'(k)$; define a function $B: \mathbb{R}_+ \times \mathbb{R} \to \mathbb{R}$ from

$$B(k, q) = \frac{z[R(k), w(k)] - (1 + n)k - q}{R(k)} \tag{20.15}$$

and end up with a vector field that satisfies the following inequalities:

$$b_{t+1} \geq b_t \Leftrightarrow [R(k^*) - R(k_t)]b_t \leq q \tag{20.16a}$$

$$k_{t+1} \geq k_t \Leftrightarrow b_t \leq B(k_t, q) \tag{20.16b}$$

Inequality (20.16a) means that $b_{t+1} \geq b_t$ if

$$\text{either} \quad k_t \geq k^* \text{ and } b_t \leq \frac{q}{f'(k^*) - f'(k_t)}$$

$$\text{or} \quad k_t \leq k^* \text{ and } b_t \geq \frac{q}{f'(k^*) - f'(k_t)}$$

It also reveals that, for any $q > 0$, the stationary value of national debt cannot be positive unless $k > k^*$. Figure 20.1(a) shows the national debt component of the vector field, which is quite straightforward if we assume that the marginal product of capital is sufficiently variable, that is,

$$f'(0) = +\infty \qquad f'(\infty) = 0 \tag{20.17}$$

The capital component of the force field is harder to draw because it depends on the shape of the complicated-looking function $B(k, q)$ defined in equation (20.15). Fortunately for us, the sign and size of that function are closely related to the properties of the scalar dynamical system.

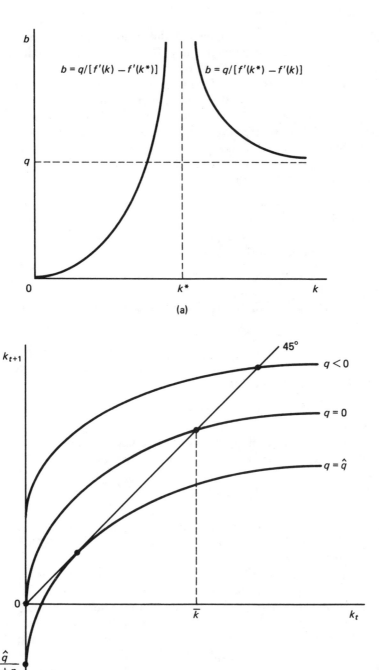

Figure 20.1 Growth with a budget deficit: preliminaries.

$$(1 + n)k_{t+1} = z[R(k_{t+1}), w(k_t)] - q \tag{20.18}$$

whose phaseline is that of the familiar one-dimensional Diamond model translated *downward* by a distance that depends on q. If saving is independent of the rate of interest, the vertical distance is $q/(1 + n)$ for all k_t.

Suppose now that the basic data of the economy, that is, the functions $f \colon \mathbb{R}_+ \to \mathbb{R}_+$ and $z \colon \mathbb{R}_+^2 \to \mathbb{R}_+$, are such that the scalar Diamond model has two steady states $k = \{0, \bar{k}\}$ if $q = 0$. Section 13.1 lists sufficient conditions for the existence of a unique positive steady state. If q lies in some bounded interval $[0, \hat{q}]$, equation (20.18) will typically have two fixed points $k^1(q)$ and $k^2(q)$ for each value of the deficit. From the geometry of figure 20.1(b) it is clear that the functions $k^1 \colon [0, \hat{q}] \to \mathbb{R}_+$ and $k^2 \colon [-\infty, \hat{q}] \to \mathbb{R}_+$ will satisfy

1. $k^1(0) = 0 \qquad k^2(0) = \bar{k}$;
2. $k^1(\hat{q}) = k^2(\hat{q}) \in (0, \bar{k})$
3. $0 < k^1(q) < k^2(q) < \bar{k}$ for $q \in (0, \hat{q})$;
4. k^1 is increasing in q; k^2 is decreasing in q.

As q rises in the interval $[0, \hat{q}]$, the two fixed points get closer until they merge into one at $q = \hat{q}$, and disappear altogether for $q > \hat{q}$. The saddle-node bifurcation value $\hat{q} > 0$ is one for which the map (20.18) has a unique steady state, that is, the equation

$$\hat{q} = \psi(k) = z[R(k), w(k)] - (1 + n)k \tag{20.19}$$

holds for *exactly one* $k > 0$. Figure 20.1(b) makes plain that $\psi(k) = 0$ at $k = \{0, \bar{k}\}$, $\psi(k) > 0$ for $k \in (0, \bar{k})$, and $\psi(k) < 0$ for $k > \bar{k}$. Therefore equation (20.19) holds for a unique k if, and only if, $\hat{q}$ satisfies

$$\hat{q} = \max_{k \geq 0} \psi(k)$$

This equation provides a precise definition of the upper bound $\hat{q}$.

We return now to inequality (20.16b) and rewrite it as

$$k_{t+1} \geq k_t \quad \Leftrightarrow \quad b_t \leq \frac{\psi(k_t) - q}{R(k_t)} \tag{20.20}$$

Recall that $R(k)$ is a positive decreasing function and, as we saw earlier, $\psi(k) - q > 0$ iff $k^1(q) < k < k^2(q)$. Then the function B looks exactly as shown in figures 20.2(a) and 20.2(b), with $B(0, q) \leq 0$.

Figures 20.1, 20.2(a) and 20.2(b) contain all the ingredients we need to put together a phase diagram for the dynamical system (20.14a) and (20.14b). This is done in figure 20.2(c) for "small" deficits: we call BB the constant-debt phaseline, and KK the constant-capital phaseline. This phase diagram reveals no fewer than two outside-money steady states plus the usual two inside-money states $(0, 0)$ and $(\bar{k}, 0)$ which prevail if households refuse to accept public debt as a store of value.

That two is the *minimal* number of steady states for sufficiently small q follows from the fact that the constant-debt phaselines $b = \pm q/[f'(k) - f'(k^*)]$ both tend to the vertical asymptote $k = k^*$ as $k \to k^*$, and to horizontal asymptotes $b = q/[f'(0) - f'(k^*)]$ as $k \to 0$ and $b = q/[f'(k^*) - f'(\infty)]$ as $k \to \infty$. As q becomes very small, the rightmost constant-debt phaseline shifts arbitrarily close to the L-shape defined by the horizontal axis and the straight line $k = k^*$. Hence, that line must intersect the constant-capital phaseline at least twice.

The properties of the two outside-money steady states are closely related to those of stationary equilibria in the standard zero-deficit planar Diamond model. The state

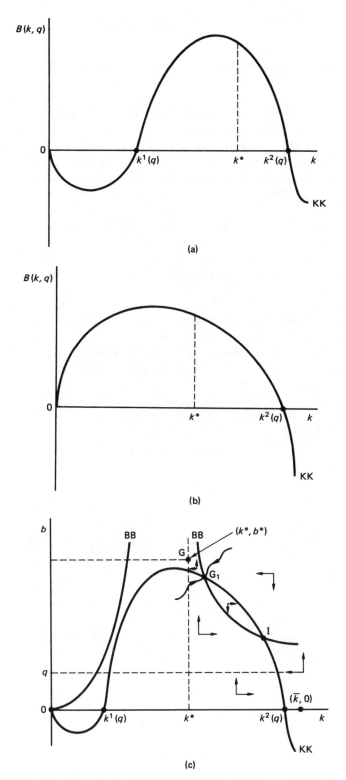

Figure 20.2 Growth with a budget deficit: (a) $q \in (0, \hat{q})$; (b) $q < 0$; (c) phase diagram for $q > 0$.

denoted I in figure 20.2(c) corresponds to the inside-money state $(\bar{k},0)$ in the no-deficit economy and reduces to that state for $q = 0$. More interestingly, the golden rule state (k^*, b^*) reduces to the steady state, denoted G_1 in figure 20.2(c), when the government abandons budget balance; this equilibrium has more capital and less debt than (k^*, b^*).

For relatively small deficits, the two outside-money steady states of the constant-deficit economy have stability properties similar to those of the underlying no-deficit case. Figure 20.2(c) confirms that point I could well be a sink and G_1 seems to be a saddle. Any dynamical equilibrium sequence (k_t, b_t) converging to G_1 would exhibit a positive correlation between capital and national debt, as both would be falling or rising. But sequences converging to the stable state I may, in principle, have any correlation pattern – positive if they converge from the southwest or northeast of point I, negative if they converge from northwest or southeast.

As q increases, the constant-capital phaseline shifts down while the constant-public-debt line shifts upward. This movement will force capital down and national debt up at the stable state I, producing all the symptoms of *crowding out*. Another process takes place at the saddle G_1 in which a higher deficit produces the counterintuitive outcome of more capital and less public debt.

The message from this economy is that *there is no simple rule* that relates the size of government deficits to the steady state values of capital and debt or, for that matter, the statistical correlation of physical capital and national debt. This relationship, rather straightforward for stable steady states, is quite subtle for the saddles that are quite often the most economically interesting stationary equilibria. What does seem clear in growing economies, as well as in pure-exchange economies, is that outside-money equilibria cease to exist if the government attempts to run permanent budget deficits that exceed a well-defined upper bound q^*. This bound allows equations (20.14a) and (20.14b) to have *exactly one* steady state. Repeating for the planar system (20.14a), (20.14b) what we did for the scalar system (20.18), we obtain a similar expression

$$q^* = \max_{k \geq 0} \phi(k) \tag{20.21a}$$

where

$$\phi(k) = (1 + n)^{-1}[f'(k^*) - f'(k)]\{z[R(k), w(k)] - (1 + n)k\} \tag{20.21b}$$

Note

1. See Modigliani (1961) and Phelps and Shell (1969) for a detailed treatment of this issue.

21   Advanced topics (*)

21.1   Fiscal policy with altruistic households

Does intergenerational altruism diminish the ability of government to finance budget deficits? Does the bequest motive dull or nullify the willingness of credit markets to hold national debt in perpetuity? This section repeats for dynastic families the standard exercises of fiscal policy conducted in chapters 18 and 20 for selfish households. The framework for this exercise is the altruistic growth economy of section 15.3 augmented by a fiscal policy and one outside asset – national debt.

Parents, the only independent agents in this economy, may now bequeath resources to their children in the form of either a physical investment or a claim on the government. Each claim matures one period later, when today's children are grownups, as both principal and interest become due. We examine two types of fiscal policies, constant-stock and constant-flow.

Constant-stock policies

The government purchases no goods or services; it simply maintains a constant principal b of national debt per capita by levying taxes T_t on income earners at time t to repay the interest due to bondholders at t. A typical altruistic parent maximizes a utility function $v(c_t, c_{t+1})$, expressed over his own consumption and that of *each* child, subject to the resource constraints

$$c_t = f(k_t) + R_t b_t - T_t - (1 + n)(b_{t+1} + k_{t+1}) \qquad (21.1a)$$

$$c_{t+1} = f(k_{t+1}) + R_{t+1} b_{t+1} - T_{t+1} - (1 + n)(b_{t+2} + k_{t+2}) \qquad (21.1b)$$

The parent picks (k_{t+1}, b_{t+1}) taking as given the number $(1 + n)$ of children he bears, the type (b_t, k_t) of the bequest he receives, the amount (b_{t+2}, k_{t+2}) left by his children to his grandchildren, plus the appropriate prices and tax parameters $(R_t, R_{t+1}, T_t, T_{t+1})$. Assuming the depreciation rate for physical capital is $\delta = 1$, first-order conditions at an interior consumer optimum are

$$1 + r_t \equiv R_t = f'(k_t) \qquad (21.2a)$$

$$(1 + n)v_1(c_t, c_{t+1}) = f'(k_{t+1})v_2(c_t, c_{t+1}) \qquad (21.2b)$$

Equation (21.2a) is a portfolio balance condition that equates the yields of two safe and perfectly substitutable assets; equation (21.2b) is a description of maximal consumption plans familiar to us from chapter 15. In addition, we have the individual budget constraint (21.1a), a government budget constraint

$$(1 + n)b_{t+1} + T_t = R_t b_t \tag{21.2c}$$

and the fiscal policy $b_t = b > 0$ for all t. These imply

$$T_t = (r_t - n)b \tag{21.3}$$

As in section 15.3, we define the marginal rate of substitution in consumption to be

$$M(c_t, c_{t+1}) = \frac{v_1(c_t, c_{t+1})}{v_2(c_t, c_{t+1})}$$

We substitute equation (21.3) into (21.1a) and obtain the following dynamical system:

$$(1 + n)k_{t+1} = f(k_t) - c_t \tag{21.4a}$$

$$M(c_t, c_{t+1}) = \frac{f'(k_{t+1})}{1 + n} \tag{21.4b}$$

We note straightaway that the stock of national debt is *not* a parameter in this system and hence exerts no effect on dynamical equilibria. The reason is rather obvious: interest on national debt accrues to the same group of people, for example parents, whose taxes finance the transfer payment. This pattern of incidence prevents intergenerational redistribution and leads to the following result which should be contrasted with theorem 20.1.

Theorem 21.1 Equilibrium allocations are independent of the stock of national debt in an overlapping generations economy of altruistic households with positive bequests.

Constant-flow policies

Suppose now that the government purchases a constant amount $g \geq 0$ of goods and services per capita each period, collects a lump-sum tax $\tau \geq 0$ from each adult, and sells national debt to finance the resulting budget deficit. Bequests consist of physical capital and national debt.

Budget constraints for the government and the representative altruistic household are

$$(1 + n)b_{t+1} = R_t b_t + q \tag{21.5a}$$

$$c_t = f(k_t) + R_t b_t - \tau - (1 + n)(b_{t+1} + k_{t+1}) \tag{21.5b}$$

where $q = g - \tau$ is the primary government budget deficit. Combining equations (21.5a) and (21.5b), we obtain the standard identity

$$c_t = f(k_t) - (1 + n)k_{t+1} - g \tag{21.6a}$$

Given the fiscal policy (g, τ), dynamical equilibria satisfy equation (21.6a) plus the first-order condition (21.2b) to the consumer's problem

$$M(c_t, c_{t+1}) = \frac{f'(k_{t+1})}{1 + n} \tag{21.6b}$$

and, lastly, the government budget constraint

$$(1 + n)b_{t+1} = f'(k_t)b_t + q \qquad (21.6c)$$

This is a three-dimensional system in the vector (k_t, c_t, b_t) of state variables. It dichotomizes naturally into equations (21.6a) and (21.6b) which alone determine the sequence (k_t, c_t) from appropriate initial conditions, and equation (21.6c) which describes the evolution of national debt *given* the sequence of physical capital. Since the budget constraint of the representative individual in (21.6a) depends on government purchases but not on how they are financed, Ricardo's intuition about the irrelevance of government financial policy is confirmed in this economy of operative bequests. A quick look shows that government spending has a direct impact on consumption and capital while the deficit affects only the stock of national debt. We sum up in the following theorem:

Theorem 21.2 Equilibrium allocations are independent of the primary budget deficit in an overlapping generations economy of altruistic households with positive bequests.

Stationary equilibria are easy to describe in this economy, especially if the marginal rate of substitution function $M : \mathbb{R}_+^2 \to \mathbb{R}_+$ is independent of the consumption vector in the steady state. This happens, for instance, whenever the utility index v is homothetic or exhibits a constant rate of time preference. In either case we can write $M(c, c) = \bar{M}$ independent of c; equations (21.6a) – (21.6c) then reduce to

$$\bar{c} = f(\bar{k}) - (1 + n)\bar{k} - g \qquad (21.7a)$$

$$\bar{M} = \frac{f'(\bar{k})}{1 + n} \qquad (21.7b)$$

$$\bar{b} = \frac{q}{(1 + n)(1 - \bar{M})} \qquad (21.7c)$$

As we know from chapter 15, homotheticity or constant time preference imply that the steady state $(\bar{k}, \bar{c})$ is likely to be a saddle, with $\bar{k}$ independent of government purchases and $\bar{c}$ a decreasing function of them. The stationary value $\bar{b}$ of national debt is an asymptotically stable positive increasing function of the deficit q if $\bar{M} < 1$; it is an unstable negative decreasing function of q if $\bar{M} > 1$. Recall that $\bar{M} < 1 + n$ defines a Samuelson-type economy in the standard overlapping generations model of pure exchange.

21.2   Legal restrictions

As we found in chapter 19, any government that relies on the anonymity of the competitive mechanism faces certain well-defined bounds on the amount of credit it can expect to raise from the private sector. *Laissez-faire* equilibria in financial markets restrain the stock of per capita public debt and also the flow of the primary budget deficit by the willingness of households to save. In order to exceed these upper bounds, modern-day governments must take steps to lessen competition from private borrowers and thereby lower the cost of credit to the public sector.

In the brutish climate of the Middle Ages governments favored direct approaches. For instance, Western European monarchs who became hopelessly indebted to their financiers simply found a religious pretext to avoid payment. To preserve the king's reputation, efforts were made to conceal royal bankruptcies by accusing creditors of heresy, satanism, and other deviations from orthodox christianity (Webber and Wildavsky, 1986, ch. 4). Victims of this practice were Jewish moneylenders, Italian bankers, and members of knightly orders like the Templars; these creditors were on occasion hanged individually, burned at the stake, or expelled *en masse* from the debtor's domain.

Fortunately for lenders, things have improved a bit recently. Today the regulation of financial institutions is a widely accepted form of nonviolent government intervention whose stated aim is to ensure the orderly working of credit markets. In the USA this intervention means that the Federal Reserve System and the Federal Deposit Insurance Corporation examine on a regular basis the balance sheets of commercial banks to guard against the danger of illiquidity, which may cause bank runs, and of excessively risky loan portfolios which may wipe out the net worth of, and undermine public trust in, the banking system. Public control is more stringent elsewhere, for instance in Southern Europe and Latin America, where it is not uncommon for governments to place a number of legal restrictions on loan portfolios or even to own large commercial banks outright.

Reserve requirements are a ubiquitous legal restriction on the operation of financial institutions.[1] In this section we examine how these requirements can be used to encourage the demand for public liabilities at the expense of private liabilities, and to reduce their mutual substitutability in private portfolios. We start with the standard pure-exchange overlapping generations economy with a two-period life-cycle, in which we require households to hold a fixed fraction $\theta \in [0, 1]$ of all positive saving in the interest-bearing government liabilities we have called national debt. It is more realistic to think of this requirement as applying to the *liabilities* of financial institutions; here we have no essential role for deposit intermediaries, and impose the restriction directly on the *assets* of households.[2]

Reserve requirements prop up the demand for public liabilities and may in principle differentiate them from private liabilities; these two liabilities then become imperfect substitutes in asset portfolios and do not have identical yields, even if both are completely safe. To dramatize the impact of legal restrictions, we compare the capacity of the pure-exchange economy to absorb public debt in the two polar cases, $\theta = 0$ and $\theta = 1$. We begin at time zero with debt per capita b_0 which we roll over in perpetuity; there are no government purchases or taxes at any time subsequent to period zero.

With no legal restrictions, $\theta = 0$ and we already know that, in an exchange economy, the sequence of per capita national debt satisfies the difference equation

$$b_t = s\left[(1 + n)\frac{b_{t+1}}{b_t}\right] \tag{21.8}$$

where $s_h(R) = \operatorname{argmax}_x u^h(e_{1h} - x, e_{2h} + Rx)$ subject to $-e_{2h}/R \leqslant x \leqslant e_{1h}$; $s = (1/H) \sum_{h=1}^{H} s_h$ denotes aggregate saving; and the government budget identity is $(1 + n)b_{t+1} = R_t b_t$.

At the other extreme, the full-reserve restriction $\theta = 1$ means that no household can dissave. The only possible form of private participation in the credit market is the purchase of government liabilities. If we define by $s_h^+(R) = \max[0, s_h(R)]$ the larger of planned individual saving and zero, and by $s^+ = (1/H)\Sigma_{h=1}^{H}s_h^+$ the relevant aggregate magnitude, then equilibrium in the credit market obtains whenever the sequence of per capita public debt satisfies

$$b_t = s^+\left[(1 + n)\frac{b_{t+1}}{b_t}\right] \tag{21.9}$$

Both the no-reserve and the full-reserve economy admit two stationary equilibria, one with inside assets and one with outside assets. The inside-money equilibrium corresponds to zero public debt in each case; it is achieved at the generationally autarkic interest rate $\bar{R}$ when $\theta = 0$, and at the lowest of all individually autarkic interest rates, say $\bar{R}_1$ when $\theta = 1$. Non-zero public debt is generally a feature of stationary outside-asset equilibria: the per capita figure is $s(1 + n)$ with no reserve requirements and $s^+(1 + n) \geq s(1 + n)$ with 100 percent reserves. Figure 21.1 illustrates the two polar cases for an economy of the Samuelson type when youthful and old-age consumption are gross substitutes for every household.

The following proposition sums up results.

Theorem 21.3 Suppose goods are normal and gross substitutes, government purchases and taxes are zero, and public debt is rolled over in perpetuity in a Samuelson-type economy. If a 100 percent reserve requirement were to apply to private asset portfolios, then the largest per capita stock of debt that the economy can absorb is $s^+(1 + n)$.

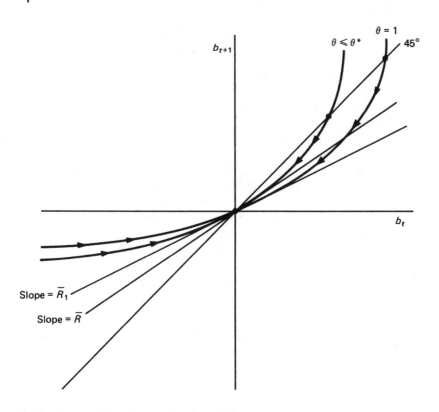

Figure 21.1 National debt with restricted portfolios.

Less extreme situations arise under a system of *fractional reserve requirements*, which prevails whenever $\theta \in (0, 1)$ and permits asset portfolios to contain both private and public liabilities. Some public debt, of course, is held in asset portfolios as a perfect substitute for private debt even if $\theta = 0$. To describe the composition of asset portfolios, we recall that $\bar{R}_h$ is the autarkic interest factor of household h whose net endowment is (e_{1h}, e_{2h}); without loss of generality, we assume that $\bar{R}_h \leq \bar{R}_{h+1}$ for $h = 1,..., H - 1$ and denote by $j(a)$ the number of household types whose autarkic interest factor is less than or equal to a. By this definition, then, we have for any $\epsilon > 0$

$$j(\bar{R}_1 - \epsilon) = 0 \qquad j(\bar{R}_H) = H \qquad (21.10)$$

Any no-reserve equilibrium obeys equation (21.9) which we may rewrite as

$$b_t = \sum_{h=1}^{j(R_t)} s_h(R_t) + \sum_{h=j(R_t)}^{H} s_h(R_t)$$

$$= \sum_{h=1}^{j(R_t)} s_h^+(R_t) + \sum_{h=j(R_t)}^{H} s_h(R_t) \qquad (21.11)$$

Here $R_t = (1 + n)b_{t+1}/b_t$; the first term on the right-hand side of equation (21.11) is the supply of loanable funds by savers; the last term of the same side is the private demand for loanable funds by dissavers.

Savers, therefore, hold portfolios in which the fraction of national debt to total asserts in period t equals $b_t/s^+(R_t)$ or, equivalently,

$$\theta^* (b_{t+1}/b_t) = \frac{s[(1 + n)b_{t+1}/b_t]}{s^+[(1 + n)b_{t+1}/b_t]} \qquad (21.12)$$

Reserve requirements have no essential bearing on the private demand for public debt unless they exceed the critical value θ^* that applies to the relevant time period. In the stationary state, for instance, the effect of such legal restrictions will not be felt until the requirement surpasses $s(1 + n)/s^+(1 + n)$. When that happens, private liabilities cease being perfect substitutes for public liabilities, and individual budget sets grow a "kink" at the initial endowment point.

To grasp this idea more clearly, we denote by R_t the gross yield on private liabilities and by $R_t^g < R_t$ the gross yield on government liabilities; the average yield on an asset portfolio is then $R_t^D = \theta R_t^g + (1 - \theta)R_t$. More commonly, we may use the term *loan rate* in connection with R_t (because it represents the cost of credit to a borrower) and *deposit rate* for R_t^D (because it describes the lender's unit revenue). A typical budget set is shown in figure 21.3, which implies that saving is positive if $\bar{R}_h < R_t^D$, negative if $\bar{R}_h > R_t$, and zero otherwise. Thus, the supply of loanable funds in period t is $\sum_{h=1}^{j(R_t^D)} s_h$, a fraction θ of which is lent to the government and the remainder is borrowed by households. Private borrowing totals $\sum_{h=j(R_t)}^{H} s_h(R_t)$; the market clearing conditions are

$$(1 - \theta) \sum_{h=1}^{j(R_t^D)} s_h(R_t^D) + \sum_{h=j(R_t)}^{H} s_h(R_t) = 0 \qquad (21.13a)$$

for private loans, and

$$\theta \sum_{h=1}^{j(R_t^D)} s_h(R_t^D) = b_t \qquad (21.13b)$$

for government loans. In addition, the government budget identity becomes

$$R_t^g = (1 + n) \frac{b_{t+1}}{b_t} \tag{21.13c}$$

If goods are gross substitutes for all households, then the left-hand side of equation (21.13a) is an increasing function of R and R^D, and a decreasing function of θ. Among others, equation (21.13a) admits the following pairs of (R, R^D) as solutions: $(\bar{R}_H, a)$ when $\theta = 1$, $(\bar{R}, \bar{R})$ when $\theta < 1$, and also $(\bar{R}_H, \bar{R}_1)$ when $\theta < 1$. Here $\bar{R}$ is the generationally autarkic factor satisfying $s(\bar{R}) = 0$; a is any number in the interval $(\bar{R}_1, \bar{R})$. Figure 21.2 illustrates some of these solutions.

Suppressing time subscripts temporarily, we may solve equation (21.13a) for any θ to obtain $R = T(R^D, \theta)$ where the single-valued function T is increasing in R^D and decreasing in θ. From the definition of the deposit rate, we have $R^g = (1/\theta)[R^D - (1 - \theta)R] = (1/\theta)[R^D - (1 - \theta)T(R^D, \theta)]$. This may be thought of as another single-valued function, $R^g = G(R^D, \theta)$, increasing in R^D and decreasing in the reserve parameter θ.

From the government budget identity and the market for public loans, we obtain

$$(1 + n) \frac{b_{t+1}}{b_t} = G(R_t^D, \theta) \tag{21.14a}$$

$$b_t = \theta \sum_{h=1}^{j(R_t^D)} s_h(R_t^D) \tag{21.14b}$$

Given any θ, equation (21.14a) says that R_t^D is increasing in b_{t+1}/b_t, while (21.14b) says that b_t is increasing in R_t^D. Therefore b_t is an increasing function of b_{t+1}/b_t at any θ. By the same token, R_t^D is an increasing function of θ for any given b_{t+1}/b_t, and b_t is similarly increasing in R_t^D. Given b_{t+1}/b_t, then, b_t is an increasing function of θ for any sufficiently large value of θ.

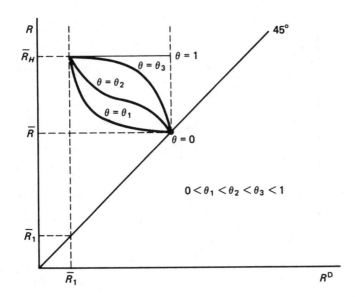

Figure 21.2 Deposit and loan rates of interest.

The upshot of all this analysis is that there exists an aggregate demand function W for public debt in terms of which one can describe the impact of reserve requirements on dynamical equilibrium in a pure-exchange overlapping generations economy. We formalize that description in the next theorem.

Theorem 21.4 Consider a reserve requirement $\theta \in [0, 1]$ on private asset portfolios in a Samuelson-type economy in which youthful and old-age consumption are normal goods and gross substitutes for every household. Assume government purchases and taxes to be zero, and public debt to be rolled over in perpetuity. Then there exists a single-valued function $W: \mathbb{R}_+ \times [0,1] \to \mathbb{R}_+$ such that per capita national debt satisfies $b_t = W[(1 + n)b_{t+1}/b_t,\theta]$ for all t. For any fixed θ, the function W is increasing in the interest factor $(1 + n)b_{t+1}/b_t$. For a fixed interest factor, W is independent of θ if $\theta \leqslant \theta^*[(1 + n)b_{t+1}/b_t]$, increasing in θ otherwise. Furthermore, $W(R, 0) = s(R)$ and $W(R, 1) = s^+(R)$.

As θ is raised from zero, the dynamical behavior of the economy does not change at first because savers are willing voluntarily to hold in their asset portfolios more public debt than reserve regulations require; see figure 21.1 for instance. This is true of the entire interval $[0, \theta^*]$ in which private and government liabilities are perfect substitutes. When θ surpasses the critical value θ^*, however, private and government liabilities cease to be perfect substitutes, private loans yield more than government loans, and the credit market is compelled to absorb more public debt.

Greater absorptive capacity towards national debt comes at a social cost: as lenders and borrowers no longer face the same terms of trade in the credit market, their marginal rates of substitution differ in the way shown in figure 21.3. The marginal lender's indifference curve is I_L while I_B is that of the marginal borrower. Therefore, any successful attempt to raise per capita debt above its *laissez-faire* maximum by the use of reserve requirements will cause an interest rate distortion and produce a short-run inefficiency.

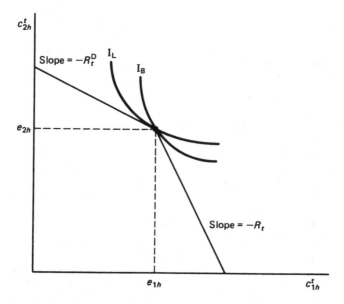

Figure 21.3 Consumer choice under legal restrictions.

The following example illustrates concretely how reserve requirements raise the capacity of an economy to absorb public debt and, simultaneously, drive a wedge between the loan and deposit rates.

Example 21.1 We look at a pure-exchange economy with no government purchases or taxes, zero population growth, and two types of households. Household 1 has utility function c_1c_2 and endowment vector $(2, 0)$; household 2 has the same utility function as 1 but a different endowment vector $(0, 1)$. Clearly the first household is a natural "lender," the second one a natural "borrower." When faced with an interest factor R, lenders consume 1 unit in youth, borrowers $1/2R$ units. Saving is 1 unit by lenders, $-0.5/R$ units by borrowers.

When fractional reserve requirements become sufficiently large, government debt yields less than private debt and the two asset markets separate. In the market for government loans, we have $\theta = 2b_t$, while the one for private loans clears if $1 - \theta - 1/2R_t = 0$. Therefore for any $\theta \in (0.5, 1]$ we obtain $R^g = 1$, $R = 1/2(1 - \theta) > 1$, and $b = 0.5\theta$. On the other hand, for small values of $\theta \in [0, 0.5]$ we have the zero-reserve-requirement solution $R^g = R = 1$, $b = 0.25$. The situation is shown in figure 21.4.

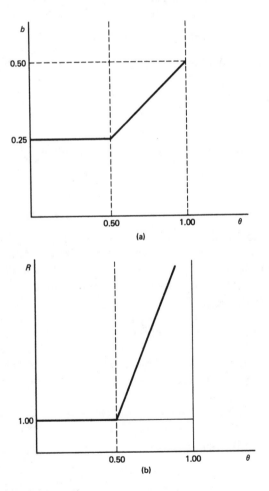

Figure 21.4 A parametric example.

21.3   Public investment

We discuss briefly the dynamical behavior of economies in which the stock of *government capital* directly affects the productivity of privately employed inputs such as labor and private physical capital. The term government capital refers to health facilities, public works (canals, highways, railroads, bridges), or any other form of productive infrastructure of the type Rosenstein-Rodan (1943) considered a prerequisite for economic development. Chapter 14 and particularly figure 14.2(b) show how infrastructure may be responsible for increasing returns in production.[3]

The easiest thing we can do here is add public investment to a one-sector neoclassical growth model and figure out how the properties of long-run equilibria respond to this change. To that end, we denote by G_t the stock of government capital at t, by $g_t = G_t/L_t$ the corresponding value per worker, and wᵉ assume that each producer's output depends on a vector (K, L) of private inputs plus the intensive value g of the public input. The production function $F(K, L, g)$ exhibits *increasing* returns to scale: it is assumed to be linearly homogeneous in (K, L), increasing in g, and concave in all inputs. All three inputs are *essential* in production: output is zero if *any* input is zero.

We define, as usual, a continuously differentiable intensive production function

$$f(k, g) = F(K/L, 1, g) \tag{21.15}$$

and assume that its partial derivatives f_k, f_g, f_{kg} satisfy the following assumptions for all $(k, g) \in \mathbb{R}_+^2$.

Assumption 21.1 $f_k > 0$ $f_g > 0$ $f_{kg} > 0$

Assumption 21.2 $f_g - kf_{kg} > 0$

In other words, both the marginal product of capital and $f - kf_k$ are increasing functions of g. Since

$$R_t = f_k(k_t, g_t) \tag{21.16a}$$

$$w_t = w(k_t, g_t) = f(k_t, g_t) - k_t f_k(k_t, g_t) \tag{21.16b}$$

in any economy with competitive factor markets, assumptions 21.1 and 21.2 mean that government capital is complementary with both private capital and labor; public investment tends to raise both wages and interest rates. Question III.19 looks at some alternative assumptions about the degree of complementarity between public and private factors of production.

Public investment is an activity which we suppose transforms 1 unit of the consumption good (to be precise, one unit of lump-sum taxes on labor income) into 1 unit of infrastructure capital, much as private investment produces 1 unit of private capital for each unit of forgone private consumption. Government capital depreciates at the same rate $\delta \in [0, 1]$ as private capital, and the public investment program is in continuous budget balance.

Given some constant government investment rate $i \geq 0$, the evolution of the system may be described in terms of the state variables (k_t, g_t) which satisfy the following relations in any competitive equilibrium:

$$(1 + n)g_{t+1} = (1 - \delta)g_t + i \tag{21.17a}$$

$$(1 + n)k_{t+1} = z[R(k_{t+1}, g_{t+1}), w(k_t, g_t) - i] \tag{21.17b}$$

Substituting g_{t+1} from (21.17a) into (21.17b), we obtain

$$(1 + n)k_{t+1} = z\left\{R\left[k_{t+1}, \frac{(1 - \delta)g_t + i}{1 + n}\right], w(k_t, g_t) - i\right\} \qquad (21.17c)$$

The phase diagram for this dynamical system follows directly from equations (21.17a) and (21.17c) in the usual manner. Specifically, we assume that $z(R, w)$ is increasing in R and get

$$g_{t+1} \geqslant g_t \Leftrightarrow g_t \leqslant \frac{i}{\delta + n} \qquad (21.18a)$$

$$k_{t+1} \geqslant k_t \Leftrightarrow H(g_t, k_t, i) \leqslant 0 \qquad (21.18b)$$

where

$$H(g, k, i) = (1 + n)k - z\left\{R\left[k, \frac{(1 - \delta)g + i}{1 + n}\right], w(k, g)\right\} \qquad (21.19)$$

Assumptions 21.1 and 21.2 guarantee that H is decreasing in g. For any fixed g, $-H$ looks quite similar to the function B defined in equation (20.15); in particular, if the functions z and f are sufficiently well behaved, then the scalar time map

$$(1 + n)k_{t+1} = z\left\{R\left[k_{t+1}, \frac{(1 - \delta)g + i}{1 + n}\right], w(k_t, g) - i\right\} \qquad (21.20)$$

has two positive steady states $k^1(i, g)$, $k^2(i, g)$ for any small $i > 0$, as shown in figure 21.5(a). This figure also shows that k^1 is unstable, k^2 is stable, and furthermore

$$H < 0 \text{ if } k \in (k^1, k^2)$$
$$H > 0 \text{ if } k \notin (k^1, k^2) \qquad (21.21)$$

Individual phaselines that correspond to the equality form of (21.18a) and (21.18b) are given in figures 21.5(b) and (21.5c); figure 21.5(d) contains the complete phase diagram in which GG is the constant-government-capital phaseline and KK is the constant-private-capital phaseline. The diagram combines the scalar system of figure 21.5(a) with equation (21.17a) whose steady state is unique. In particular, the equilibrium labeled A in figure 21.5(a) corresponds to A' in figure 21.5(d) and B corresponds to B'.

Both the force field in figure 21.5(d) and the one-dimensional intuition of figure 21.5(a) suggest that *the steady state A' is a saddle while B' is a stable node.* This is easily verified from the Jacobian matrix of (21.17a) and (21.17c) which contains one zero element (because g_{t+1} is independent of k_t) and hence has two real eigenvalues $\lambda_1 = \partial g_{t+1}/\partial g_t$ and $\lambda_2 = \partial k_{t+1}/\partial k_t$, both evaluated at the steady state. Of these $\lambda_1 = (1 - \delta)/(1 + n) \in (0,1)$ and λ_2 is simply the steady state slope of the scalar map (21.20) evaluated at $\bar{g} = i/(\delta + n)$ and $\bar{k} = k^i(i, \bar{g})$ for $i = 1, 2$. For $i = 1$ we have $\lambda_2 > 1$ which means that A' is a saddle; for $i = 2$ we have $\lambda_2 \in (0,1)$ which makes B' a stable node, exactly as intuition suggested earlier.

Given the flow of public investment, private and government capital change in the *same* direction along the saddlepath converging to the stationary state A', but may vary in opposite directions along trajectories that converge to B'. Another policy exercise we can perform with figure 21.5(d) is to find out what happens as public

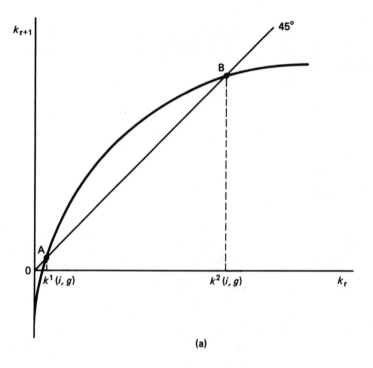

(a)

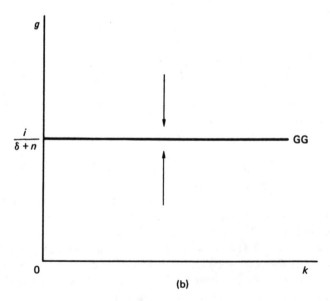

(b)

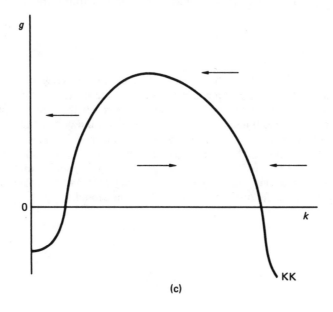

(c)

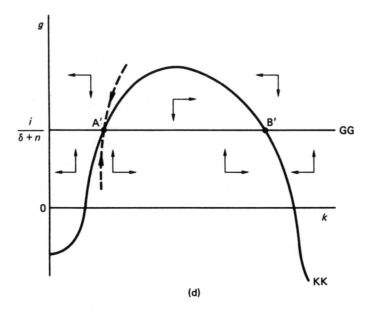

(d)

Figure 21.5 Private and government capital.

investment rises. If i goes up, both phaselines move up toward larger values of g; what happens to the stationary values of k is not immediately obvious and should depend to a certain extent on how much private and government capital one starts with.

Notes

1. Sargent and Wallace (1982) study how the demand for currency responds to a legal requirement that fixes a minimal denomination for private debt.
2. Direct quantity rationing of private borrowers serves much the same purpose. Puhakka (1985) and Bertocchi (1989) analyze how rationing affects the demand for public debt.
3. There is a shortage of work on how private and public capital interact in the process of economic growth. Arrow and Kurz (1970) are among the first to combine these two capital inputs in a decreasing-returns-to-scale technology; Barro (1990) studies increasing returns in a Ramsey model whose single consumer has isoelastic utility; and Aschauer (1989) presents interesting evidence on the productivity of government capital.

22 Summing up

We have explored the consequences of government purchases and transfer payments, in particular the working of commodity-denominated national debt as an intergenerational allocative device. Part III takes as given the existence of indexed debt and leaves for Part IV the reasons why governments of low-inflation countries (Western Europe, Japan, North America) prefer to denominate public debt in units of account.

Social security is one common device for transferring resources between generations. It is a mandatory institutional arrangement patterned after the voluntary transfers found among extended families in traditional societies: adults care for their elderly parents and are, in turn, cared for by their own offspring. These transfers smooth out disposable income over the life-cycle and, under weak assumptions about normality, erode life-cycle saving. If, in addition, the demand for capital services is relatively interest elastic, expanding a pay-as-you-go social security system slows down capital accumulation and raises equilibrium rates of interest.

Interest rates also respond to changes in government purchases in a way that depends on the intergenerational distribution of the tax burden. The standard Keynesian result, that a balanced budget increase in these purchases will put upward pressure on interest rates, holds if taxes fall primarily on young savers because the reduction in their disposable income reduces saving at each interest rate. It is possible in principle, however, for the opposite correlation to emerge in equilibrium. A fully expected balanced budget increase in government purchases may result in a lower rate of interest if the added tax levy falls on the old, who must set aside additional sums to meet their higher tax liability.

Next we explored the allocative consequences of public *financial policies* which define how debt and taxes are combined to pay for a given flow of government purchases. If the government can raise lump-sum taxes, what difference does it make whether a given sequence of purchases is financed by concurrent lump-sum taxes or by the deferred taxes which correspond to national debt? David Ricardo (1817) and Robert Barro (1974) found there was no difference: equilibrium allocations should depend exclusively on purchases (fiscal policy) and not at all on how these are funded (financial policy). Keynesian models, on the other hand, claim a big difference; deficit-financed spending is supposed to be much more expansionary than the equivalent amount of balanced budget government purchases.

The precise answer depends again on how different generations share in the tax burden. In a society of selfish households, the Ricardian equivalence of national debt to lump-sum taxes holds if future national debt service falls on the *exact* individuals whose reduced current taxes create the need for issuing public debt. When households are altruistic towards their descendants, national debt is equivalent to taxes under the restrictive assumption of operative bequests for all families.

If, however, the group of people whose future taxes will be raised is not the same as those whose current taxes are lowered, then the Keynesian intuition is not too far off the mark. Deficit finance works like social security, transferring resources from the young generation to the older one, raising the welfare of the latter, eroding life-cycle saving, and putting some upward pressure on interest rates. We also established the allocative equivalence of all financial policies which maintain unchanged the sum "national debt plus taxes on the young."

Voluntary exchange places definite upper bounds on both the stock of per capita national debt and the flow of deficits which can be absorbed by any economy in a *laissez-faire* equilibrium. When the primary government budget deficit is zero, existing national debt can be rolled over in perpetuity if the stock of per capita debt is "not too large." The stock of debt becomes "too large" if the real rate of interest at which current savers would willingly hold it surpasses the natural growth rate of the economy, that is, the sum of the population and productivity growth rates. Maximal sustainable per capita debt service simply equals the flow of saving at the natural rate of interest. We note that stationary equilibria with zero primary deficit and constant per capita national debt are dynamically efficient in an economy with a perfect credit market.

Laissez-faire equilibrium also places on upper bound, say q^*, on how large a permanent budget deficit a Samuelson-type economy can soak up. Competitive equilibria do not exist if the deficit always exceeds q^*, but may very well exist for *temporary deficits* considerably above q^*. Increases in the stock of per capita public debt become a *burden*, reducing both aggregate consumption and the representative household's utility in the steady state, if and only if the original equilibrium is dynamically efficient.

Upper bounds on government deficits and public debt arise partly from natural limits on household saving, and partly from competition with private debtors. When all loans are perfectly safe, government and private debt are perfect substitutes in private asset portfolios. This substitutability is lessened by reserve requirements and related legal restrictions on asset portfolios, which discriminate in favor of government liabilities. Legal restrictions support equilibria in which government debt yields less than equally safe private debt, and thereby raise the debt-absorbing capacity of any economy.

Parental altruism and the resulting positive bequests to one's offspring lessen the ability of national debt to redistribute resources between generations. Finitely-lived households in this case cease to be the effective decision units; they are replaced in that role by longer-lived dynastic families whose saving plans weaken the impact of intergenerational government transfer payments (public debt service, social security) by voluntary private transfers in the opposite direction.

Finitely lived altruistic households bequeath positive sums under circumstances similar to those which would induce selfish infinitely lived agents to save: inheritances are left by individuals who either are well endowed relative to their children or weigh their children's well-being almost as heavily as their own. Relatively underendowed or uncaring parents will ideally plan to leave "negative" bequests, that is, borrow from their progeny. Immigration, childless households, as well as laws disallowing negative bequests tend to enfeeble some of the allocative manifestations of altruistic parenthood, and effectively break up the similarities of extended dynastic families to infinitely lived agents.

Bibliography

Further reading

Useful summary data on US government finance appear in the *Economic Report of the President* (Council of Economic Advisers, 1990), and on that of other countries in *International Financial Statistics*. The geometric tools that we have found so suitable for the study of dynamical equilibria are due to Cass et al. (1979). Feldstein (1974) remains a useful introduction to current issues in social security, with the exception of the empirical results which are dated. On Ricardian equivalence, see Ricardo (1817, ch. 17), and Barro (1974); various departures from this result are noted by Drazen (1978), Tobin (1980), Weil (1985), and Bernheim (1987). Buiter (1981) and Persson (1985) are elementary introductions to fiscal policy in open economies; Chamley (1981), Summers (1981), and Lucas (1990) are excellent introductions to fiscal policy in growing economies. Finally, Aschauer (1989) is a good starting point for the rapidly expanding literature on the importance of public infrastructure.

References

Alesina, A. 1988: Macroeconomics and Politics. In *NBER Macroeconomics Annual*, Cambridge: MIT Press, 13–52.
—— and Tabellini, G. 1990: A positive theory of fiscal deficits and government debt. *Review of Economic Studies*, 57, 403–14.
Arrow, K. and Kurz, M. 1970: *Public Investment, the Rate of Return, and Optimal Fiscal Policy*. Baltimore, MD: Johns Hopkins University Press.
Aschauer, D. 1989: Is public expenditures productive? *Journal of Monetary Economic*, 23, 177–200.
Atkinson, A. and Stiglitz, J. 1980: *Lectures on Public Economics*. New York: McGraw-Hill.
Barro, R. 1974: Are government bonds net wealth? *Journal of Political Economy*, 82, 1095–118.
—— 1990: Government spending in a simple model of endogenous growth. *Journal of Political Economy*, 98 (Supplement), S101–25.
Bernheim, D. 1987: Ricardian equivalence: an evaluation of theory and evidence. In *NBER Macroeconomics Annual*, Cambridge, MA: MIT Press, 263–304.
—— and Bagwell, K. 1988: Is everything neutral? *Journal of Political Economy*, 96, 308–38.
Bertocchi, G. 1989: Marketing public debt: the fixed-priced technique. Mimeo, Brown University.

Blinder, A., Gordon, R., and Wise, D. 1980: Reconsidering the work disincentive effects of social security. *National Tax Journal*, 33, 431–42.

Böhm, V. and Keiding, H. 1985: Inflation and welfare in international trade. Mimeo, University of Mannheim.

Buiter, W. 1981: Time preference and international lending and borrowing in the overlapping-generations model. *Journal of Political Economy*, 89, 769–97.

Calvo, G. 1978a: On the time consistency of optimal policy in a monetary economy. *Econometrica*, 46, 1411–28.

—— 1978b: On the indeterminacy of interest rates and wages with perfect foresight. *Journal of Economic Theory*, 19, 321–37.

Cass, D., Okuno, M., and Zilcha, I. 1979: The role of money in supporting the Pareto optimality of competitive equilibrium in consumption–loan type models. *Journal of Economic Theory*, 20, 41–80.

Chamley, C. 1981: The welfare cost of capital income taxation in a growing economy. *Journal of Political Economy*, 89, 468–96.

Council of Economic Advisers 1990: *Economic Report of the President*. Washington, DC: US Government Printing Office.

Diamond, P. and Mirrlees, J. 1978: A model of social insurance with variable retirement. *Journal of Public Economics*, 10, 295–336.

Drazen, A. 1978: Government debt, human capital and bequests in a life-cycle model. *Journal of Political Economy*, 86, 505–16.

Feldstein, M., 1974: Social Security, induced retirement and aggregate capital accumulation. *Journal of Political Economy*, 82, 905–26.

International Financial Statistics (various years). Washington, DC: International Monetary Fund.

Kotlikoff, L. 1986: Deficit delusion. *Challenge*.

Kydland, F. and Prescott, E. 1977: Rules rather than discretion: the inconsistency of optimal plans. *Journal of Political Economy*, 85, 473–91.

Lucas, R. 1990: Supply-side economics: an analytical review. *Oxford Economics Papers*, 42, 292–316.

Malkiel, B. 1970: *The Term Structure of Interest Rates: Theory, Empirical Evidence and Applications*. New York: Silver Burdett.

Modigliani, F. 1961: Long-run implications of alternative fiscal policies and the burden of the national debt. *Economic Journal*, 71, 730–55.

—— and Shiller, R. 1973: Inflation, rational expectations and the term structure of interest rates. *Economica*, 40, 12–43.

O'Connell, S. and Zeldes, S. 1988: Rational Ponzi games. *International Economic Review*, 29, 431–50.

Persson, T. 1985; 1985: Deficits and intergenerational welfare in open economies. *Journal of International Economics*, 19, 67–84.

Phelps, E. and Shell, K. 1969: Public debt, taxation, and capital intensiveness. *Journal of Economic Theory*, 1, 330–46.

Puhakka, M. 1985: Credit rationing in a model of national debt. Chapter 4 of an unpublished doctoral dissertation, University of Pennsylvania.

Ricardo, D. 1817: *On the Principles of Political Economy and Taxation*. Reprinted from the 3rd edn, Cambridge: Cambridge University Press.

Rosenstein-Rodan, 1943: Problems of industrialization of Eastern and Southeastern Europe. *Economic Journal*, 53, 202–11.

Russell, F. 1973: Bubble, bubble – no toil, no trouble. *American Heritage*, 24, 74–80.

Sargent, T. and Wallace, N. 1982: The real-bills doctrine versus the quantity theory: a reconsideration. *Journal of Political Economy*, 90, 1212–36.

Summers, L. 1981: Capital taxation and accumulation in a life cycle growth model. *American Economic Review*, 71, 533–44.

Tobin, J. 1980: *Asset Accumulation and Economic Activity*. Chicago, IL: University of Chicago Press.

Webber, C. and Wildavsky, A., 1986: *A History of Taxation and Expenditure in the Western World*. New York: Simon and Schuster.

Weil, P. 1985: Love thy children: reflections on the Barro neutrality theorem. Mimeo, Harvard University.

Questions

Unmarked questions are the easiest to do while starred questions relate to advanced material. Other questions are labeled (T) if they are primarily technical and (C) if they require some creative thinking.

III.1 (T) Prove theorem 18.2

III.2 In a pure-exchange overlapping generations economy in which individuals live for $T \geqslant 2$ periods, we suppose that individuals and the government may issue liabilities maturing in $1, 2, \ldots, T - 1$ periods.

    (a) What relationship is there between the *short* interest rate at time t (that is, the yield on a security issued at t and maturing at $t + 1$) and some *long* interest rate (that is, the per-period geometric average yield on a security issued at t and maturing at least two periods later)?

    (b) Under what conditions will we observe a *normal* yield curve (that is, one for which the short rate is below the long rate)? An *inverted* yield curve (one which has the opposite configuration of interest rates)?

    (c) Can you think of any factors missing from your model which may affect the shape of the yield curve?

III.3 If the economy is definitely known to have a specific finite end, show that the present value of government deficits must be zero. Do your conclusions change if everyone just *believes*, perhaps mistakenly, that the human race will disappear for sure by a specified finite date?

III.4 (T) Draw the phase diagram for the difference equation (19.3) under the assumption that it possesses several autarkic equilibria (*Hint*: If you cannot do this question, consult Cass et al. (1979).)

III.5 (a) For a Samuelson economy with a unique autarkic interest factor, show that the graph of equation (19.3) intersects the diagonal from above at the origin and from below at the golden rule point.

    (b) For a classical economy with a unique autarkic interest factor, show that the sense of the two intersections described above is completely reversed.

III.6 (a) Find the competitive inside-asset equilibria of an overlapping generations model with inventories. Assume that all young households may lend or borrow and, in addition, possess a common decreasing-returns-to-scale storage technology of the form $x^t_{1h} = f(K^t_h)$. Here k^t_h is the amount of good household h of generation t stores in youth, and x_{h}^{i} is the corresponding amount available for consumption in old age; f is an increasing concave function such that $f(0) = 0$. Suppose there is no government spending, taxes or national debt.

(b) How would you define the Samuelson and classical cases for this economy?

III.7 (T) Consider the effects of national debt in the economy of question III.6. Specifically, let b_0 be the per capita stock of public debt at the beginning of time, refloated anew every period by a government which otherwise levies no taxes and purchases no goods.

　　Show that dynamical competitive equilibria are completely described by a difference equation of the form

$$b_t = s \left[(1 + n)\frac{b_{t+1}}{b_t} \right] - k^{\mathrm{d}} \left[(1 + n)\frac{b_{t+1}}{b_t} \right]$$

where s is the normalized aggregate savings function and k^{d}, the demand schedule for inventories, is the inverse of the marginal product f'.

III.8 (T) (a) In the preceding question, are there inside-asset stationary states such that $b = 0$? Outside-asset stationary states such that $b \neq 0$? What can you say about their local stability?

(b) How is your answer to part (a) affected by changes in the marginal cost of storage, that is, when we multiply the function f by a factor $\lambda > 0$.

III.9 (C) This question looks at the interplay of foreign debt and fixed domestic investment within Diamond's model of capital accumulation. Suppose, in particular, that financial capital is perfectly movable across national borders, and we are dealing with a *small* open economy that takes as given the "world" rate of interest.

(a) Describe the competitive dynamical equilibrium of a small open economy that faces a constant interest factor R and operates under a stationary fiscal policy of the form $P = (g, \tau_1, \tau_2)$. Assume there is no domestic public debt.

(b) How does national debt evolve in this economy? Is there a relationship between per capita deficit and capital intensity?

(c) What factors determine whether this economy is an importer or exporter of capital? Assume again a balanced government budget and zero domestic debt.

III.10 (T) Demonstrate theorem 20.2.

III.11 Apply theorem 19.1 to an economy with a stationary fiscal policy. In particular, find a balanced budget policy (g, τ_1, τ_2), with $g = \tau_1 + \tau_2/(1 + n)$, that supports the same equilibrium allocations as a policy of deficit finance (g, τ_1, τ_2), with $g > \tau_1 + \tau_2/ (1 + n)$. Government purchases per capita are the same in each case, and the beginning-of-time national debt per capita is $b_0 = 0$ in each case.

III.12 (T) Prove theorem 19.1. In particular show that

(a) every equilibrium under the fiscal policy P is an equilibrium under the fiscal policy $\hat{P}$;
(b) at each of these equilibria, P and $\hat{P}$ yield the same value for the sum "national debt plus taxes on the young."

III.13 (C) Redo question III.12 for a balanced stationary fiscal policy. In particular, write down the fundamental difference equation, study the existence and stability of stationary equilibria, and find out how these are affected by balanced budget changes in the fiscal parameters g, τ_1, τ_2.

III.14 Explore the effect on intertemporal equilibrium of a *fully funded* social security system, that is, an arrangement under which the government uses tax revenue collected from the young to purchase private liabilities in the stock or bond market, for example claims on capital or private loans. The yield from that portfolio is distributed to the old in the form of pensions.

(a) How does a change in the social security tax (assumed here to be a lump-sum tax) influence the equilibrium interest rate and capital accumulation?

(b) What fundamental differences are there between a funded and an unfunded social security system?

III.15 (C) Explore the general conditions under which a given constant flow of government purchases per head should be financed by taxes or by selling public debt. Specifically:

(a) Is it dynamically efficient to run a constant per capita budget deficit in a Samuelson-type economy? In a classical one?

(b) Repeat part (a) for a constant per capita primary budget surplus.

(c) Can we always find lump-sum taxes that support dynamically efficient equilibria at a zero budget deficit?

(d) How do your answers to parts (a), (b), and (c) change if the object of fiscal policy is to finance a given flow of government expenditure in a way that maximizes the lifetime utility of the representative consumer? Assume, for this part alone, that all households are identical.

(e) Which policy, budget balance or deficit finance, will a democratically elected government follow in an economy with growing population? Assume that every household has one vote.

(f) How do your conclusions in part (e) change if the young cannot vote? If the old cannot vote?

III.16 The world economy consist of two countries, A and B. Each country is described by a standard overlapping generations economy of pure exchange, one good, identical households, and zero population growth. The utility is $u = c_1 c_2$ in each country, and endowment vectors are $(3,1)$ in country A and $(2,1)$ in country B. Populations are equal.

(a) Describe the competitive equilibria that are possible in each country in the absence of international trade (closed economies).

(b) Do the same with completely free international trade and asset movement (open economies).

(c) Does international trade improve steady state welfare in the world economy? Explain. (*Hint*: Both inside and outside-money equilibria are possible in both the closed and the open case. A similar problem is the subject of a paper by Böhm and Keiding (1985).

III.17 Kotlikoff (1986) has estimated the unfunded social security liability in the USA (that is, the present value of benefits owed current contributors to the system less its current fund balance) and found it to exceed one year's GNP. Does this liability compromise the ability of the US economy to absorb ordinary national debt and to finance primary budget deficits? Explain.

III.18 Extend theorem 19.4 to an economy of the classical type. Do such economies admit permanent budget deficits? If so, explain the economic intuition and propose a way to determine an upper bound on permanent budget deficits.

III.19 (*) In the public investment economy of section 21.3 suppose that producers are endowed with the constant-returns-to-scale technology $Y_t = F(A_t K_t, B_t L_t)$ where (K_t, L_t) are private inputs and (A_t, B_t) are coefficients that measure the efficiency of private inputs and depend on government capital per worker. In particular, let $A_t = A(g_t)$ and $B_t = B(g_t)$ for some well-behaved nondecreasing functions $A: \mathbb{R}_+ \to \mathbb{R}_+$ and $B: \mathbb{R}_+ \to \mathbb{R}_+$.

(a) Describe dynamical equilibria if A is an increasing function and $B(g) = 1$ for all g, that is, if government capital improves the productivity of private capital only, not of labor services. How do changes in public investment affect steady states?

(b) Repeat the exercise if $A(g) = 1$ for all g, B is linearly homogeneous in g, and saving is linearly homogeneous in income. What are the steady states of this economy? How do they depend on the policy parameter i?

Money and Asset Prices

23 Introduction to Part IV

23.1 Overview

The national debt we studied in part III consisted of interest-bearing loans to the government which were denominated in terms of commodities, matured at a predetermined date, and were backed by the power to levy taxes. Indexed bonds are such a form of debt. Another kind of public liability, *currency* or *fiat money*, is denominated in arbitrary units of account, matures at the discretion of the lender, bears no interest, and is not backed by any formal government promise of redemption in commodities.

The adjective "fiat" means "relating to government permission or decree" and implies a liability that is not convertible into or backed by commodities. The noun "money" itself comes from the Latin word "moneta," meaning mint, which is derived from an appellation of the Roman goddess Juno. Romans originally used to strike their coins at the temple of *Juno Moneta*.

Among the "arbitrary" units of account in which money is denominated, we may mention the dollar, peso, franc; the reader may add any other well-known units. These were picked fairly late in a process of historical evolution which began with commodity money. In ancient Mesopotamia, for instance, the unit of account was one "gur" (that is, bushel) of barley; the medieval Mayas counted in cocoa beans. During the fifteenth or sixteenth century, West Africans used seashells called "zimbos," Icelandics defined value in terms of dried fish, sub-Saharan Africans counted in blocks of salt, etc.

Backed paper money has been in limited use for a considerable period of time (see Braudel, 1981, ch. 7). Promissory notes circulated in Babylon *c.* 2000 BC; banknotes were known in China from the ninth century AD and were observed in use there by Marco Polo in the thirteenth century.

Today unbacked paper money is normally accepted in trade against commodities, and its price is defined against every good and service sold. That unsecured government liabilities should exchange far in excess of their intrinsic worth as commodities (that is, pieces of paper) attests to a widely shared belief that they will continue to be valued in the future,[1] a belief that events typically bear out except in times of hyperinflation. Individuals, then, demand currency partly because it is a store of value just like loans; it is this motive for holding outside money that we explore in this chapter.

Currency is demanded not only because it resembles credit but for other reasons as well: it is, as we know from elementary economics, a universally acceptable medium of exchange, and a good buffer against unexpected fluctuations in a household's excess commodity demand which may arise from random shifts in the endowment or tastes of that household. The former motive for holding money is called the *transaction demand*; the latter motive is known as the *precautionary demand*.[2]

We will not discuss in detail any of these motives except to note that each of them is related to the "liquidity" of money, that is, to how quickly and at what transaction cost the owner of an asset can collect its maximum exchange value.[3] We defer until section 25.2 a discussion of why unbacked government liabilities are not completely displaced by interest-bearing private liabilities of like safety and liquidity, for example by the demand deposits of federally insured commercial banks or by interest-bearing liabilities of the treasury itself. Commodity money is introduced in questions IV.2 and IV.3 but does not receive systematic treatment in this text.

Part IV focuses primarily on economies in which fiat money either is the only store of value or is a perfect substitute for all other assets. The provision of circulating government liabilities by the central bank alone is an abstraction that is suited for some purposes but not for others. It permits us to study why unbacked government liabilities are valued, as well as a number of policy issues related to inflation finance. It does *not* permit us to explore in a fully satisfactory way the effect of open market purchases or sales for which one needs to define essential differences between currency and other forms of debt; sections 25.2 and 25.3 describe two alternative ways of exploring open market operations.

What expectations are consistent with competitive equilibria in which money has positive exchange value? In this chapter we discuss rational learning and study the short-term relationship between expectations and monetary equilibria. Chapter 24 examines the determinants of asset prices as well as the welfare properties of the resulting dynamical equilibria under the assumption of a perfect foresight. Chapter 25 identifies the special conditions under which the quantity theory of money holds, and discusses the optimum quantity of money.

Inflation finance is the subject of chapter 26. Here we examine how the printing of currency helps the government finance purchases but may cause hyperinflation if carried to excess; we also look at the equivalence of inflation to distortionary commodity taxation, and examine how inflation finance influences the accumulation of physical capital in the long run.

23.2   The formation of expectations

A movie is a collection of still photographs arranged sequentially. In approximately the same way, a dynamical equilibrium is a sequence of temporary competitive equilibria, that is, of single snapshots of an economy as it evolves over time. As one watches a movie partly to find out how it ends, so one studies dynamical equilibria to learn, among other things, where the economy is headed in the long run. Do things settle down to a stationary equilibrium or to a limit cycle? What policies will push an economy in a desirable direction or prevent it from going off on an undesirable path? What expectation schemes produce forecasts that experience tends to validate in the long run?

The last question is of interest because rational households will exploit time series of prices and other data in order to improve their forecasting ability. That this is in their own best interest is obvious from figure 23.1, which depicts the standard problem of intertemporal consumer choice. Suppose that p_t is the price observed at t, p_{t+1} is the true equilibrium price that will prevail at $t + 1$, and p_{t+1}^e is the forecast of P_{t+1} that household h makes at time t. From its own forecast budget set, the household chooses the bundle associated with point F, consuming $\hat{c}_{1h}$ in youth. Next period, however, the household will find out that the best available bundle is at some other point F', which is inferior to point E, the bundle that could have been attained if forecasting ability had been perfect.

Perfect forecasting ability is exceedingly rare among mortal men (both Pythia of Delphi and the Sibyl of Cumae, who reputedly used to possess this talent, were women) for it amounts literally to public knowledge of the true dynamical laws that govern the evolution of the economy. Such information is hard to accumulate for the same reason that a statistician cannot use a finite sample for an unknown probability distribution in order to infer the values of the parameters governing that distribution. Learning takes time, and economic structures often change before we become fully knowledgeable about them. No economy can be assumed to be forever stationary; endowments, preferences, population, and government policies change frequently and unexpectedly. The best dynamical information one can infer from a given economic structure must be based, of necessity, on time series of finite length.

Nevertheless, partial learning is possible and individually beneficial, even from a finite history; sections 28.4 and 29.2 furnish specific examples. As households learn, not

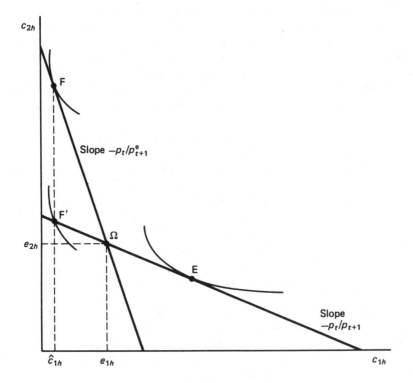

Figure 23.1 The private benefit from accurate forecasting.

only do they revise their forecasts in response to changes in the data, but also they seek to improve the *rules* that transform data into forecasts. In the snapshot analysis of temporary equilibrium, one is often justified in assuming, as we shall see in the section immediately following, that households possess a time-invariant rule by which they form expectations; forecasting rules in this case are among the data of the economy. Over longer periods of time, however, such rules form part of the initial conditions: they are a proper datum at most for the very first market date, not thereafter.

A logically coherent general theory of expectations formation is beyond our grasp at the moment. A large part of the blame for this belongs to a complication that we have not addressed so far – public knowledge of individual forecasting rules is not extensive. A Bayesian statistician would face this problem by letting each person *guess* the forecasts of all others: let us assign, for instance, to each individual member $h = 1,\dots, H$ of a given generation T a probabilistic model $f_h(T) = (f_{h1}(T),\dots, f_{hH}(T))$. The component f_{hj} of this model is a probability distribution assigning probability weights, subjectively held by household h at time T, to forecasts of p_{T+1} made by household $j = 1,\dots, H$ at time T.

What our statistician has in mind here is that each household will use its own model both to forecast and to make economic decisions; the aggregate outcome of all individual choices will feed into publicly observed prices and lead to a revision of the model $f_h(T)$ into $f_h(T + 1)$ by means of Bayes's rule. One may then study whether these models converge from some arbitrary starting specification. Is there a model f^* such that, as $t \to \infty$, $f_{hj}(t) \to f^*$ for all h and j?

Reasonable at this may appear in principle, it is not a meaningful exercise to pursue. The simple fact remains that, if an individual's own forecasting rule is not public knowledge, then neither is his or her model of the forecasting rules of others. Therefore, each household will attempt to forecast the models of all other households, since models of forecasts influence consumer choices. Because such second-round forecasts are not public knowledge either, individuals would benefit by building third-round models of them, and so on *ad infinitum*. This is the problem of *infinite regress*, a formidable obstacle standing in the way of a rational theory of expectations formation.[4]

Short of a complete theory, one is forced to make a convenient assumption about either the details or the outcome of the learning process. One such assumption, made often in the temporary equilibrium literature, is to allow a fixed length of past price history (say, T periods) to be reflected mechanically in price forecasts; this is done by assuming that there are time-invariant publicly known functions of the form

$$p_t^e = \psi^h(p_{t-1},\dots, p_{t-T}) \tag{23.1}$$

which describe the forecast of household $h = 1,\dots, H$.

When beliefs are given by such forecasting rules, the properties of equilibrium depend heavily on the properties of the functions $(\psi^1, \psi^2,\dots, \psi^H)$.[5] In fact, changes in beliefs are economically similar to, and operationally difficult to disentangle from, changes in preferences when our observations are points on household demand schedules. Figure 23.1 shows this plainly: point F' is the bundle chosen when expectations are $p_{t+1}^e \neq p_{t+1}$ and preferences correspond to the indifference curves already drawn in that figure. However, the same point could well be maximal in the true budget set if the indifference map were suitably changed.

At the other extreme, one may choose to specify neither the data from which forecasts are made nor the underlying computational mechanisms but, rather, the accuracy of the *outcome*. Suppose, for instance, that learning is completed, with all households having settled on the correct forecasting rule. This happy state of affairs is called *perfect foresight* and it holds, more precisely, when every household's forecasts are publicly known to be free of error. Perfect foresight is an enormous, if unrealistic, simplification of the forecasting process and it means that, for $t = 2, 3, \ldots$, we have

$$p_t^e = p_t \qquad (23.2)$$

We have already used this convention in Parts II and III and shall adopt it again throughout most of what follows. Equilibria with arbitrary forecasts are studied in section 23.3; we revert to the assumption of perfect foresight in chapters 24 through 27 and depart from it again in chapters 28 and 29 when we study learning.

23.3 Temporary equilibrium

Paper assets like currency and claims on currency are instrumental in the intertemporal exchange of perishable goods in dynamic economies. Many of these assets are liabilities of the government or the central bank and therefore are often widely accepted by households as stores of value because of their inherent "safety." The public institutions that issue such liabilities are generally regarded as trustworthy by lenders because their expenditure and income flows receive intense scrutiny in the press and the legislature; above all, governments are unlikely to become bankrupt for they are authorized to levy and collect taxes.

To accumulate paper assets like currency in an intelligent manner, individuals must forecast the future purchasing power of such assets more carefully than they would have to if all loans were denominated in commodity or "real" terms; the future value of money depends, roughly speaking, on unobserved future inflation rates. For example, an individual born at t and living through $t+T$ needs to observe p_t^m, the commodity price of money in period t, and then guess the T variables $(p_{t+1}^m, \ldots, p_{t+T}^m)$. If, as we have assumed all along, the life-cycle extends for just two periods and there is only one physical commodity, then *no price expectation* need be formed when value is stored in commodity-denominated loans, but *one* price expectation is still required to form consumption plans when fiat money is the store of value.

What expectations are consistent with competitive equilibrium? We reexamine the short-term working of the economy described in chapter 19 under the assumption that all debt, private and government, is denominated in the unit of account.

Suppose, in fact, that the central bank creates at $t = 1$ currency in the amount of M per capita, reckoned in arbitrary units of account, and distributes it as a gift to members of the very first generation, G_0. The per capita quantity of money remains constant at M, with the central bank paying interest to holders of *existing* money balances at a rate equal to that of population growth.

If money has no use value as a commodity or as a factor of production, yet possesses a positive exchange price every period, the stock of currency will be transferred from one generation to the next: from G_0 to G_1, from G_1 to G_2, and so on *ad infinitum*, as its holders exchange it for consumable commodities. The infinite horizon or, more precisely, the lack of certainty about a finite end to the world (see also section 29.1) is essential here: if the economy were to end for sure at some finite data T, however distant, then the commodity price of currency would certainly be zero after T. Hence, currency would surely be unacceptable in trade at $T - 1$ by anyone who expected the world to end at T; by the same token, it would not be accepted at $T - 2$ and so on – its price would be zero from the outset.

Dynamical equilibria, however, are not our present concern. We take instead a snapshot view of an economy at some period t: let $p_t = 1/p_t^m$ be the price of the consumption good in terms of money and p_{t+1}^e be a positive finite number representing the deterministic expectation of p_{t+1} held at t by every young household. More precisely, we assume that it is common knowledge that everyone expects the price p_{t+1}^e to prevail next period. Treating for the moment p_{t+1}^e as a parameter, we ask what combinations (p_t, p_{t+1}^e) are consistent with competitive equilibrium at t.

This issue is of considerable interest because we all know how anticipations of the future influence current decisions and therefore current prices; at the same time, price forecasts typically make heavy use of current and past prices.[6] Specifically, suppose that $D(p_t, p_{t+1}^e, M_t)$ is a well-defined aggregate excess demand function for commodities in period t or, equivalently, an excess supply function of real money balances. Then, for a given $M_t > 0$, any vector $(p_t, p_{t+1}^e) > 0$ such that

$$D(p_t, p_{t+1}^e, M_t) = 0 \qquad (23.3)$$

defines a *temporary* competitive equilibrium.[7] Temporary equilibria are called *monetary* (or outside money) if $p_t < \infty$, *autarkic* (or inside money) if $p_t = \infty$.

One may attempt to solve equation (23.3) by expressing p_t as a function of p_{t+1}^e; if that is possible, we say that a *backward-looking* equilibrium exists, that is, a positive price that clears the market at t, given expectations. On the other hand, any solution to (23.3) that yields p_{t+1}^e as a function of p_t means that a *forward-looking* equilibrium exists, that is, a positive finite expectation of p_{t+1} such that the market at t clears at the predetermined price p_t. As in Part I, a foward-looking equilibrium is so named because it unfolds forward from the present to the future whereas a backward-looking equilibrium unfolds backward from the future to the present.

The approach that has become standard in temporary general equilibrium theory is to begin with an arbitrary continuous *expectation function* ψ that maps price observations into price forecasts and to seek restrictions on this function which ensure that a temporary equilibrium exists at t, given the history of the economy up to $t - 1$. As we shall see below, all we need in order to guarantee the existence of equilibrium, besides the standard assumptions we have already made in Part II about preferences and endowments, is that price expectations should not be "too sensitive" to price history.

At time t, the per capita excess demand for commodities by members of the old generation is clearly M_t/p_t; by analogy with Part II, the per capita excess supply of commodities by members of the young generation is

$$s(R_t^e) = \frac{1}{H} \sum_{h=1}^{H} s_h(R_t^e) \qquad (23.4)$$

where s_h are individual savings functions and $R_t^e = p_t/p_{t+1}^e$ is the gross expected real yield on currency. The savings functions $(s_1, s_2, \ldots, s_H)$ are identical with the functions defined in Part II, that is,

$$s_h = \mathrm{argmax}_s\, u^h(e_{1h} - s, e_{2h} + Rs) \qquad (23.5)$$

Furthermore, it is fairly easy to demonstrate from the Slutsky equation for this problem (see also question IV.1(a)) that, for any R above household h's autarkic interest factor $\bar{R}_h$, the interest-factor elasticity of savings exceeds -1 for any household h that considers future consumption a normal good.

We may now define the per capita excess demand function for goods in equation (23.3) from

$$D(p_t, p_{t+1}^e, M) = \frac{M}{p_t} - s\left[(1 + n)\frac{p_t}{p_{t+1}^e}\right] \qquad (23.6)$$

where n is the nominal rate of interest on money balances, and conclude that D is homogeneous of degree zero in (p_t, p_{t+1}^e, M). Because D is also a continuous function, we can show in a way analogous to Part II that both forward and backward equilibria exist.

We begin with forward-looking equilibria, by fixing (p_t, M) and seeking a $p_{t+1}^e > 0$ that satisfies equation (23.6). We define $\bar{R}_1$ as the smallest individually autarkic interest factor and R^* from $s(R^*) \geq s(R)$ for all $R \geq 0$. Thus R^* is that factor which maximizes per capita savings over the non-negative real line. Suppose now that we fix p_t so that $p_t > M/s(R^*)$. Then clearly $D[p_t, (1 + n)p_t/\bar{R}_1, M] \geq M/p_t > 0$ because nobody wants to save when $(1 + n)p_t/p_{t+1}^e = \bar{R}_1$. Also, by definition, we have $D[p_t, (1 + n)p_t/R^*, M] = M/p_t - s(R^*) < 0$. A forward-looking temporary competitive equilibrium exists by continuity; as figure 23.2 suggests, however, this equilibrium need not be unique unless we place additional restrictions (for instance, gross substitutability)[8] on preferences that ensure the monotonicity of savings functions.

Continuing in the same vein, we look for backward equilibria by fixing (p_{t+1}^e, M) and seeking a $p_t > 0$ that satisfies equation (23.6). Here we employ a variant of the standard existence proof due to Grandmont (1983): we observe first that

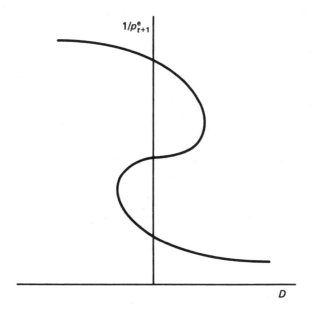

Figure 23.2 Forward-looking equilibrium.

$D(\bar{R}_1 p^e_{t+1}, p^e_{t+1}, M) = M/p^e_{t+1}\bar{R}_1 > 0$. Next we note from elementary consumer theory (see question IV.1(b)) that $Rs(R) \to \infty$ as $R \to \infty$. Hence

$$p_t D = M - p^e_{t+1}\left\{ \frac{p_t}{p^e_{t+1}} s\left[(1 + n)\frac{p_t}{p^e_{t+1}} \right] \right\} \to -\infty \text{ as } p_t \to \infty$$

and a temporary competitive equilibrium exists, again by continuity. This one is unique because (see question IV.1(c) and figure 23.3) the function D is decreasing in p_t at every temporary competitive equilibrium if goods are normal.

We sum up these results in the following theorem.

Theorem 23.1 Suppose that current and future consumption are normal goods. Then a unique backward-looking temporary competitive equilibrium exists. If the money price of current consumption is "not too large," then a forward-looking temporary competitive equilibrium exists as well, but is not necessarily unique.

Several expected prices, then, may be consistent with market clearing at a given current market price; to deliver a unique equilibrium we know that we need restrictions on preferences, like gross substitutability, familiar from Part II as well as from statistic general equilibrium theory. Figure 23.4 shows theorem 23.1 geometrically; because we have already encountered similar figures repeatedly in Part II, we explain this one in less detail. Readers who need more details on how to construct such diagrams may consult chapter 19, particularly section 19.2.

Each ray through the origin corresponds to a particular expected interest factor, and has slope equal to that factor if population is constant. The abscissa of any intersection between a ray and the graph of zero excess demand equals aggregate savings at the interest factor corresponding to the ray. Of course, not every ray intersects the graph $D = 0$; indeed the graph has an asymptote with slope equal to $\bar{R}$, the generationally autarkic interest factor, to remind us of the fact that aggregate saving is zero for $R = \bar{R}$.

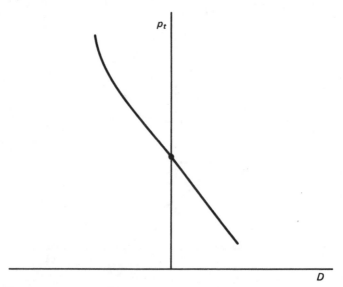

Figure 23.3 Backward-looking equilibrium.

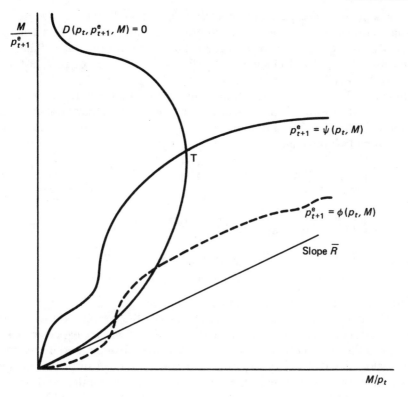

Figure 23.4 Temporary competitive equilibrium.

The graph of zero excess demand itself has the familiar shape of a *reflected offer curve*, that is, of an offer curve relating individually optimal quantities of excess supply for some commodity, measured on the horizontal axis, to the excess demand for another, measured along the vertical axis. The resemblance of the equilibrium frontier to an offer curve is not accidental for, if households are identical, the frontier *is* the offer curve.

Figure 23.4 verifies that a unique backward-looking equilibrium exists for any finite p_{t+1}^e, however large, because a unique non-negative flow of saving is associated with any interest factor, however large. By the same token, no backward equilibrium will exist if p_t is "too large," and more than one may appear if p_t is "not too large." The reason is obvious from consumer theory: the same flow of saving can very well be elicited at two different interest rates if the saving function bends backward, that is, if the intertemporal substitution effect is stronger than the corresponding income effect at low interest rates, and weaker at high interest rates.

The construction in figure 23.4 will turn out to be as powerful an analytic tool in Part IV as the corresponding national debt diagrams were in Part III: it will serve as a phase diagram with which to study dynamical monetary equilibria in chapter 24; and the government's monetary interventions will be captured in subsequent sections as vertical translations of the equilibrium frontier, as rotations of it about the origin, or as simple scale changes.

For the time being, however, we shall put that figure to good use in the standard existence problem of temporary equilibrium. We first connect forecasts and observations by a sequence of *expectation functions* $\psi_t \colon \mathbb{R}_+^2 \to \mathbb{R}_+$, mapping the stock of money and current price into an expected price. The time subscript on ψ means that past history is allowed to affect current predictions of future events. Nothing essential in what we study here will change if we allow a larger slice of past history to be reflected in the way future prices are forecast.

The functions ψ_t are endowed with the following properties: they are continuously differentiable, increasing in the price observation p_t, and they do not react too strongly to price history. We formalize this assumption of relatively "sticky" forecasts in the following two inequalities:

$$\lim_{p \to \infty} \psi_t(p, M) < \frac{1}{R} \qquad \text{for all } M \text{ and } t \tag{23.7a}$$

$$\psi_t\left(\frac{M}{s(1)}, M\right) \geq \frac{M}{s(1)} \qquad \text{for all } M \text{ and } t \tag{23.7b}$$

A temporary competitive equilibrium, then, is a $p > 0$ such that

$$D[p, \psi_t(p, M), M] = 0 \tag{23.8}$$

Geometrically, the equilibrium price is determined in figure 23.4 from the ordinate of point T where the equilibrium frontier intersects the graph of the expectation function. At least one such intersection exists if, at the origin, the expectation function is steeper than the asymptote of the zero excess demand frontier and if, in addition, it lies on or below the 45° line at $p = M/s(1)$. Continuity then ensures that the graph of the expectation function intersects the zero excess demand frontier, and a temporary competitive equilibrium exists.

Note that the existence of equilibrium does not require ψ to be differentiable. If, however, ψ is differentiable and, furthermore, goods are normal and the expected price always has elasticity less than unity with respect to current price, then one easily shows (see question IV.1(d)) that the excess demand function defined in equation (23.8) is decreasing in current price at every equilibrium, exactly as it is pictured in figure 23.3. This ensures the uniqueness of equilibrium. We summarize in the following.

Theorem 23.2 If the expectation functions $\psi_t(p, M)$ are continuous and increasing in p, then inequalities (23.7a) and (23.7b) are a sufficient condition for a temporary competitive equilibrium to exist. The equilibrium is unique if, in addition, goods are normal and ψ_t is differentiable with price elasticity everywhere less than unity.

Of course, inequalities (23.7a) and (23.7b) are not a necessary condition; equilibrium may very well exist even if this condition is violated, an example being the expectation function ϕ shown as a broken line in figure 23.4. Also worthy of note is the uniqueness of equilibrium which we have obtained here without employing the usual restriction of gross substitutes to ensure that the aggregate excess demand function is monotone. The required monotonicity is guaranteed, instead, by the assumption that price expectations be less than unitary elastic with respect to price observations. As we shall see later (in questions IV.5 and IV.6), this is just one instance of economic behavior that depends heavily on the nature of shared beliefs.

Inequalities (23.7a) and (23.7b) are relatively mild restrictions that conform with most well-known forecasting rules: they are satisfied automatically by *myopic expectations*, that is, by the rule

$$p_{t+1}^e = p_t \tag{23.9a}$$

Under some technical qualifications (see question IV.4(a)), the same inequalities are also satisfied by *adaptive expectations* schemes like

$$p_{t+1}^e = \theta p_t + (1 - \theta)p_t^e \tag{23.9b}$$

$$\log p_{t+1}^e = \theta \log p_t + (1 - \theta) \log p_t^e \tag{23.9c}$$

where $\theta \in [0,1]$ is an arbitrary constant representing the relative weight of the most recent observation.

Notes

1. This apparent paradox was brought to the fore by Hahn (1965); see also section 29.1.
2. A house or a financial asset with a distant maturity date are good examples of illiquid assets; realizing their maximal discounted value requires search, waiting, or both. See Kiyotaki and Wright (1989) for a recent search-based theory of the transactions demand for money.
3. Central governments in preclassical antiquity (especially in Egypt and China) had a strong precautionary demand for commodity money. Fairly large taxes in kind were levied in normal years to ensure that the ordinary expenses of the state, including upkeep of the armed forces, could be met even in periods of poor crops or famine. These precautionary "balances" were kept under armed guard in vast warehouses. The demand for money as a (relatively) safe component of asset portfolios is sometimes referred to as "speculative demand"; see Tobin (1958). A large empirical literature on the demand for money from the 1950s and 1960s is ably summed up in Laidler (1969).
4. In an interesting extended parametric example, Townsend (1981) shows how difficult it is to surmount the problem of infinite regress without assuming sufficient common knowledge. One shortcut is to follow Bray (1982) and Marcet and Sargent (1989b) who study convergence to rational expectations with least squares (as opposed to Bayesian) learning. See section 29.2 on least squares learning and DeGroot (1970) on Bayesian learning.
5. Cagan (1956) and Fuchs (1979) provide examples in this vein.
6. The importance for dynamical economies of links between the present and the future was well understood by the Austrians, by Wicksell (1906), and by the Stockholm school; the subject is treated with admirable clarity in Hicks (1946, chs 20–2).
7. The term is due to Hicks (1946), who also laid the early foundations. Temporary general equilibrium theory developed in the 1960s and 1970s with contributions by Drandakis (1966) and others. Much of this work is collected in Grandmont (1988).
8. See, for example, Arrow and Hurwicz (1958) and Arrow et al. (1959).

24 Asset prices – fundamentals and bubbles

24.1 Pure exchange with perfect foresight

The dynamical behavior of an economy with currency resembles closely that of an economy with national debt; after all, currency is a type of public debt that bears no interest. We postpone for section 25.2 an exploration of the essential differences between currency and debt,[1] and offer very little motivation for the transactions demand for money.

With this qualification in mind, we define a *dynamical competitive equilibrium with perfect foresight* to be a price sequence $(p_t)_{t=1}^{\infty}$ such that for $h = 1, \ldots, H$ and $t = 1, \ldots$ *ad infinitum* we have the following.

1. $e_{1h} - c_{1h}^t = s_h(p_t/p_{t+1})$

$$e_{2h} - c_{2h}^0 = \frac{M}{p_1}$$

$$e_{2h} - c_{2h}^t = \frac{p_t}{p_{t+1}} s_h \left(p_t/p_{t+1} \right)$$

2. $D(p_t, p_{t+1}, M) = 0$
   where D is defined in equation (23.6) and $M > 0$ is the stock of per capita currency.
3. The price sequence conforms to either an initial condition fixing p_1 or a terminal condition of the form

$$\lim_{t \to \infty} p_t = p_\infty$$

   with p_1 or p_∞ being no less than $\bar{p} = M/[\max_R s(R)]$.

An equilibrium clearly exists if the requirements (2) and (3) of this definition are met, that is, if we can find a price sequence that satisfies the first-order difference equation $D(p_t, p_{t+1}, M) = 0$ and conforms to the appropriate boundary condition; then part (1) fully describes equilibrium allocations for each generation of households.

Of these two types of possible boundary conditions, the initial condition fixing p_1 is suited to a forward-looking equilibrium, the terminal condition being more appropriate for a backward-looking equilibrium. Neither price can fall short of $\bar{p}$ because the value of real currency balances cannot surpass the maximal feasible flow of saving.

To study dynamical equilibria, we make use of the equilibrium price frontier $D = 0$ from figure 23.4, which is a weighted "average" of reflected offer curves for all households. Some of the many possible shapes of the resulting phase diagram are in figure 24.1, whose axes measure per capita *real currency balances* $m_t = M/p_t$. Because D is homogeneous of degree zero in (p_t, p_{t+1}, M), the equilibrium phase curve will not shift in figure 24.1 if the quantity of currency were to change. The first thing to notice in the figure is that, typically, the ratio $p_t/p_{t+1} = (1 + n)m_{t+1}/m_t$ is bounded away from zero at any competitive equilibrium. Furthermore, along an equilibrium path, $m_{t+1}/m_t \to \bar{R}/(1 + n)$ as $m_t \to 0$, where $\bar{R}$ is the autarkic interest factor.

There is a strong resemblance between figure 24.1 and the non-negative orthant of the diagrams in figure 19.3. As in Part III, there are *at most two* stationary equilibria: inside money is always one, supported by any interest factor $\bar{R}$ such that aggregate saving is zero. It is associated with a price system $p_t = \infty$ of permanently worthless fiat money, and allocations $c_{1h}^t = e_{1h} - s_h(\bar{R})$ for $t = 1, 2, \ldots$ and $c_{2h}^t = e_{2h} + \bar{R}s_h(\bar{R})$ for $t = 0, 1, \ldots$ The resulting *generational autarky* means a complete lack of trust in outside money which inhibits trade between generations. In fact, autarky is the *only* equilibrium, stationary or otherwise, in the classical case $\bar{R} \geq 1 + n$, as figure 24.1(c) clearly shows. On the other hand, for the Samuelson case, the phase curve intersects the 45° line *from below at exactly one point*,[2] as in figures 24.1(a), 24.1(b), and 24.1(d).

We conclude that, with the exception of the classical case, there is a second stationary equilibrium with valued money. The price system supporting this equilibrium is $p_t = M/s(1 + n)$ for all t, and the rate of interest is n.

Because the rate of interest equals the rate of population growth in this equilibrium, intuition and theorem 12.1 both suggest that the corresponding allocation is intertemporally optimal. Before we turn to dynamical issues, we sum up our results so far.

Theorem 24.1 Generational autarky is a stationary competitive equilibrium of the pure-exchange overlapping generations economy with a fixed amount $M > 0$ of per capita currency, supported at an interest factor $\bar{R}$ and an infinite price level. If the economy is classical, this autarky is the only competitive equilibrium, and it is intertemporally optimal. In the Samuelson case, a stationary monetary equilibrium exists in addition, supported at an interest rate n and constant price level $M/s(1 + n)$; the autarkic equilibrium is suboptimal in this case while the stationary monetary equilibrium is optimal.

Question IV.8 looks at economies with time-dependent structures in which preferences and endowments vary from one generation to the next; economies of that type do not possess stationary equilibria. We also recall from theorem 23.1 that a *forward*-looking equilibrium tells what conceivable futures are consistent with the present at any point in time. By the same token, a *backward*-looking equilibrium describes what conceivable past histories are consistent with the present. We now turn to figure 24.1(b), which confirms theorem 23.1 in answering the first question with "possibly many" and the second with "at most one." Unless we assume enough gross substitutability, as in figure 24.1(a), models of perfect foresight have difficulty in

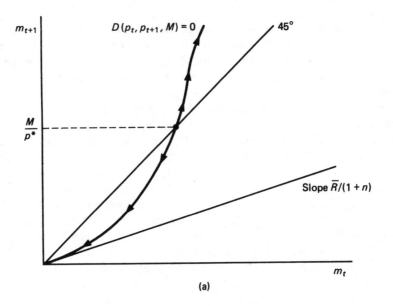

(a)

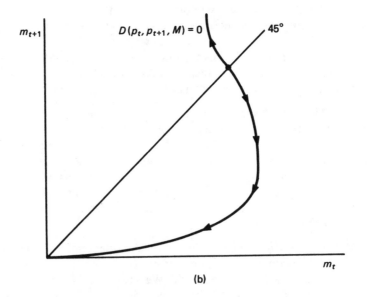

(b)

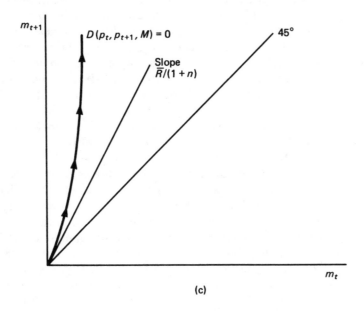

(c)

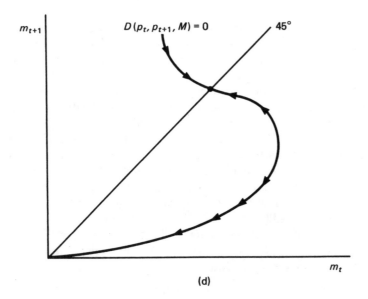

(d)

Figure 24.1 Perfect foresight equilibrium.

predicting the future from past history: a large number of future price paths may be consistent with a given price history. Readers who do question IV.5(b) will discover, as Cagan did in 1956, that adaptive learning and other forecasting rules with imperfect foresight avoid this difficulty. The reasons will become plainer later in this section.

The non-uniqueness of forward-looking perfect-foresight equilibrium becomes a problem if unalterable past decisions of households and the government bequeath to the present an economic state that must be taken as given. For instance, real values of such state variables as indexed national debt and the capital stock are inherited from the past and constrain current choices. We know from Part III that an economy that begins with a small capital stock or a large public debt may behave differently from one that does not share this predicament, everything else being the same. The appropriate equilibrium concept in all situations of this type looks forward.

What concept one should use for the monetary economy of this chapter is more debatable. Here we inherit from the past a state variable, the stock of currency, that is fixed in nominal terms, not in real terms. One of the things that the process of competitive equilibrium settles each period is the real value of money balances, picked by collective decisions that households make on the basis of what they expect prices will be in the future, not on the basis of what prices were in the past. This is precisely the concept we have termed a backward-looking equilibrium. It is most useful when prices are completely free of any residual ties to the past which appear inevitably with modest price "stickiness" or with even slightly imperfect foresight.

Imperfect foresight – whether it is Bayesian learning about an unknown environment or simply the *ad hoc* predictive rules of adaptive learning – exploits past history to forecast the future. Equilibria unfold forward because individuals look backward. This means that it is prudent to study both types of dynamical equilibria, and we return to figure 24.1.

We define $\epsilon(R)$ to be the interest-factor elasticity of aggregate savings and p^* to be the money price at the monetary stationary state, whenever it exists; and we look first at the classical case in figure 24.1(c). Here there are no forward- or backward-looking equilibria except the autarkic one at $p_t = \infty$ for all t. Autarky is then an unstable stationary equilibrium in the forward dynamics; it is sometimes called *determinate* because it can be reached only from one starting point – the stationary state itself.

An outside-money stationary equilibrium appears in all other panels of figure 24.1 in which $\bar{R} < 1 + n$. In each of these autarky is asymptotically stable of *indeterminate*; it can be reached from any nearby starting point. Indeterminacy permits a continuum of forward-looking and backward-looking equilibria that converge asymptotically to autarky and are indexed on the initial price $p_1 \geq p^*$. One such equilibrium is shown by arrows in figure 24.1(a), but similar ones exist in figures 24.1(b) and 24.1(d) as well. Section 28.5 contains additional material on indeterminacy.

From the definition of the excess demand function, we readily find that *the stationary outside-money equilibrium is asymptotically stable if, and only if, the elasticity $\epsilon(R)$ of aggregate savings satisfies*

$$\epsilon(1 + n) < -1/2 \tag{24.1}$$

that is, *if the intertemporal income effect is large enough relative to the intertemporal substitution effect to make the aggregate saving function bend backward sufficiently fast at the interest rate n*. Figure 24.1(d) meets this condition; figures 24.1(a) and 24.1(b) violate it. In figures 24.1(a) and 24.1(b), therefore, there are no forward or backward equilibria converging to p^* except the stationary one $p_t = p^*$ for all t.

Figure 24.1(d), on the other hand, has two stable (or indeterminate) stationary states and a great number of equilibrium sequences: in fact, there is again a continuum of forward-looking price sequences, converging asymptotically to the stationary monetary state. These are indexed on the initial price p_1 which lies in some neighborhood of p^*. We sum up in the following.

Theorem 24.2 Suppose there is a unique generational autarkic interest factor $\bar{R}$. If $\bar{R} < 1 + n$, then generational autarky is indeterminate and a continuum of dynamical equilibria exists, indexed by $p_1 \geqslant p^*$; all these converge asymptotically to autarky. The stationary monetary state is indeterminate too if, and only if, the intertemporal income effect of an interest rate change is sufficiently stronger than the corresponding substitution effect.

The welfare properties of dynamical equilibria may be studied exactly as in theorem 19.2 using the criteria we developed in Part II, especially the different variants of theorem 15.3. As before, we may evaluate competitive and other allocations by looking at the associated sequence of interest rates. These criteria apply directly here once we allow private loans; each household trades in a perfect credit market, that is, faces just one lifetime budget constraint.

Theorems 24.1 and 24.2 emphasize once again that the existence, stability, and optimality of pure-exchange equilibria in an economy of overlapping generations depend very much on the properties of the aggregate saving function. These properties reflect, in turn, a number of underlying factors. For instance, do individuals possess perfect foresight in real-world economies? Does the household sector actually tend to save or dissave in the aggregate when the real interest rate equals the growth rate? And how large is the interest elasticity of saving in those circumstances?

Readers who are content with a general "feel" for the range of parameters it takes to satisfy inequality (24.1) may wish to go through question IV.28 in some detail and conclude that the economies more likely to satisfy this are those with a *high* rate of time preference or a sufficiently *low* intertemporal elasticity of substitution in consumption. It is worth noting, in addition, that the ratio of net interest payments on debt by all governments in the USA (state, local, and federal) to the gross national product (GNP) has risen quite fast recently: from a traditional peacetime value of about 1 percent before the middle 1970s, to about 2.5 percent in 1989 (Council of Economic Advisers, 1990). The ratio of privately held federal debt to GNP was 15.7 percent in 1970 and 31.6 percent in 1989. Realistic estimates of elasticity of aggregate saving with respect to the after-tax real rate of return on capital are in the neighborhood of one-quarter to one-half; estimates come from time-series data [Boskin (1978)] and from simulations [O. Evans (1983)].

These estimates are suggestive but not very reliable, for they are based on data of questionable quality. Reported government debt, for instance, differs from the present value of all net private claims on the government sector because it ignores government-owned assets, like highways, of value to the private sector. One prudent conclusion one may draw from all this is that the evidence we have, even though it is not inconsistent with figure 24.1(a) (that is, a Samuelson-type economy with a monotone offer curve) comes from economies that are so complex relative to our overlapping generations structure as to invalidate direct empirical comparisons.

24.2   Adaptive learning

We turn now to the influence that forecasting rules may have on the determinacy of dynamical equilibrium, an issue that has concerned capital theorists since the mid-1960s.[3] To illustrate matters for pure-exchange overlapping generations economies, we go back to the excess demand function in equation (23.6) in which we fix $n = 0$ and $M = 1$ for convenience. Let us suppose, as one often does in the theory of temporary competitive equilibrium, that individuals form expectations at time t about the future price of money, $(p^m_{t+1})^e = 1/p^e_{t+1} = m^e_{t+1}$, by looking back at the two most recent realizations of that price, m_t and m_{t-1}.

We postulate a linearly homogeneous increasing expectation function $\Psi: \mathbb{R}^2_+ \to \mathbb{R}_+$, common to *all* households, which describes how price observations determine forecasts at each t:

$$m^e_{t+1} = \Psi(m_{t-1}, m_t) \tag{24.2}$$

This function satisfies $\Psi(m, m) = m$ for all $m \geq 0$. Exploiting its linear homogeneity, we obtain

$$\frac{m^e_{t+1}}{m_t} = \Psi\left(\frac{m_{t-1}}{m_t}, 1\right) \equiv \psi\left(\frac{m_{t-1}}{m_t}\right) \tag{24.3}$$

that is, a forecast of the expected yield on money based on the last observed yield. From the properties of Ψ it is obvious that ψ is an increasing function such that

$$\psi(1) = 1 \tag{24.4}$$

Given a constant stock of money, individuals forecast zero inflation next period if they have observed current inflation to be zero, positive inflation next period if they observe deflation this period, and deflation next period if they observe inflation now.

Combining the equilibrium condition $m_t = s(m^e_{t+1}/m_t)$ with the forecasting rule in equation (24.3) we obtain the following first-order difference equation:

$$m_t = s\left[\psi\left(\frac{m_{t-1}}{m_t}\right)\right] \tag{24.5}$$

Sequences (m_t) that solve this equation describe *dynamical competitive equilibria with adaptive learning*. It is easy to verify that $m_t = 0$ and $m_t = s(1)$ for all t are the only steady states of the adaptive expectations economy, exactly as they are in the perfect-foresight case.

Even though adaptive forecasting does not alter the set of steady states of a perfect-foresight economy, it affects their stability, or determiracy, quite a bit.[4] We define ϵ and γ to be the elasticities of the functions s and ψ respectively; clearly $0 \leq \gamma \leq 1$ by the assumptions we have made on the expectation function Ψ. Now, we differentiate (24.5) with respect to m_{t-1} and, after some algebra, we obtain

$$\frac{dm_{t+1}}{dm_t} = \frac{\epsilon_\gamma}{1 + \epsilon_\gamma} \tag{24.6}$$

at any positive steady state.

In a Samuelson pure-exchange economy with zero population growth, the autarkic interest factor $\bar{R}$ is below unity, and the demand for currency is well defined whenever the forecast yield on money satisfies

$$\psi\left(\frac{m_{t-1}}{m_t}\right) \geq \bar{R} \tag{24.7}$$

for all t. Since ψ is increasing, it has a well-defined inverse ψ^{-1}, and inequality (24.7) reduces to

$$\frac{m_{t-1}}{m_t} \geq \psi^{-1}(\bar{R}) \qquad \forall t \tag{24.8}$$

where $\psi^{-1}(\bar{R}) < 1$.

As (m_t, m_{t-1}) approach zero, equation (24.5) reveals that the ratio m_{t-1}/m_t must approach $\psi^{-1}(\bar{R}) < 1$ and hence

$$\lim_{m_t \to 0} \frac{m_{t-1}}{m_t} = \frac{1}{\psi^{-1}(\bar{R})} > 1 \tag{24.9}$$

Comparing equations (24.5) and (24.9) we quickly discover that the phase curve of (24.5) connects the two steady states $m = 0$ and $m = s(1)$, cutting the diagonal from below at $m = 0$ and from above at $m = s(1)$. Figure 24.2 illustrates. The exact slope of the phase curve depends on $\epsilon(1)$, the elasticity of saving with respect to the yield evaluated at the natural rate $R = 1$. In particular, if the relevant substitution effect dominates, then $\epsilon > 0$ and the phase curve is a monotonic and increasing line whose slope at $m = s(1)$ lies in the interval $(0, 1)$. This follows readily from equation (24.6) and corresponds to figure 24.2(a).

Similarly, if $\epsilon > 0$ and the income effect dominates, then the phase curve is no longer monotone; it rises initially and then falls through $s(1)$ with a slope that lies in the interval $(-1,0)$ if

$$-1/2\gamma < \epsilon < 0$$

Figure 24.2(b) illustrates this case.

The overall effect of forecasting schemes on the dynamical properties of competitive equilibrium becomes clearer if we compare the corresponding parts of figures 24.1 and 24.2. Adaptive expectations have a broad tendency to stabilize monetary equilibria whenever forecasts are not too sensitive to any particular price observation. Specifically, if current and future consumption are gross substitutes, the outside money steady state $s(1)$ is *unstable* (or determinate) *under perfect foresight, stable* (or indeterminate) *under adaptive learning*. The inside money steady state $m = 0$ has exactly the reverse properties. These cases are illustrated in figures 24.1(a) and 24.2(a).

If the income effect of an interest rate change dominates at the natural rate of interest, then the state $s(1)$ is stable in the forward perfect-foresight dynamics if $\epsilon(1) > -1/2$, and in the forward adaptive-learning dynamics if $\epsilon(1) > -1/2\gamma$. A look at figures 24.1(c) and 24.2(b) should convince you that an *unstable cycle of period 2* coexists with an asymptotically stable steady state $s(1)$ under perfect foresight; *a stable cycle of period 2* appears under adapative learning whenever the outside-money state loses stability.

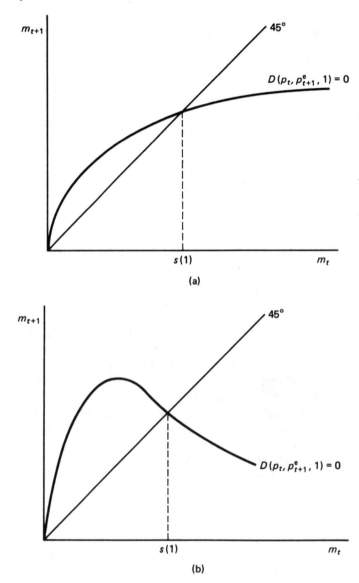

Figure 24.2 Adaptive learning dynamics.

24.3   Pricing productive assets

In earlier sections of this chapter, as well as in Part III, we explored the behavior of economies that contain two types of assets: rent-bearing inside assets like private loans or claims on physical capital, and intrinsically worthless outside assets like national debt or currency. The former assets typically represent some production technology and pay dividends to their owners, while outside securities are normally unproductive assets whose price measures intangibles like "speculation" or "trust."

We call these unproductive assets *bubbles*, and examine in this section the circumstances under which bubbles coexist with productive assets in private-asset portfolios.

Perpetually refinanced national debt is an excellent example of a pure bubble that contributes nothing to the stock of inputs in an economy, does not augment its production possibilities, and still may be valued in equilibrium even if the government should never redeem it. Like all bubbles, refloating national debt grows at the rate of interest and will eventually outgrow the entire economy if the rate of interest should exceed the long-term growth rate, that is, if equilibrium is dynamically efficient.

If that were to happen, the bubble could not be transferred between generations because the younger generation could not afford to buy it from the older generation. As we shall see below, dynamically efficient equilibria rule out asymptotic bubbles. A similar situation occurs if there is a productive infinitely lived asset that distributes a geometrically expanding stream of dividends. The pricing of these assets has been explored by Lucas (1978) in economies with a representative immortal household and by Tirole (1985) in economies with overlapping generations. The remainder of this section follows Tirole who amplified an earlier work by Wallace (1980).

If dividends grow at least as fast as the bubble (that is, if the rate of growth in rents is not below the equilibrium interest rate) then the productive asset will be infinitely priced and cannot be sold by one generation to the next. Hence, the bubble and the rent-producing asset cannot coexist in equilibrium, except perhaps for finitely many periods.

Let (p_t) be a sequence that describes the price evolution of an infinitely durable asset which produces a positive dividend sequence (d_t). If R_{t+1} is the yield on loans borrowed at t and repaid at $t + 1$, then arbitrage requires that the ex-dividend price of this rent-yielding asset satisfy

$$p_t = \frac{p_{t+1} + d_{t+1}}{R_{t+1}} \tag{24.10}$$

The term "ex-dividend" means that the asset is traded at the end of the period *after* the relevant dividend is paid out. Define $R(t_1, t_2)$ to be the product $\Pi_{s=t_1}^{t_2} R_s$, and iterate equation (24.10) forward to decompose the asset price

$$p_t = p_t^* + b_t \tag{24.11}$$

into a *fundamental value* p_t^* and a *bubble* b_t. Here

$$p_t^* = \lim_{T \to \infty} \sum_{s=1}^{T} \frac{d_{t+s}}{R(t + 1, t + s)} \tag{24.12a}$$

and

$$b_t = \lim_{T \to \infty} \frac{p_{t+T+1}}{R(t + 1, t + T + 1)} \tag{24.12b}$$

For any bounded dividend sequence (d_t), the decomposition (24.11) is valid if $\sum_{s=1}^{\infty} [1/R(t+1, t+s)]$ is finite. Furthermore, equation (24.12b) reveals that the bubble grows at the rate of interest, that is,

$$b_{t+1} = R_{t+1} b_t \tag{24.13}$$

To study the interplay of fundamental and bubble components in asset prices, we study below a pure-exchange economy of overlapping two-period-lived generations in which generation t has $N_t = (1 + n)^t$ identical members. This economy is endowed with a durable non-produced asset, such as land, which exists in fixed supply equal to 1 unit and yields a geometrically expanding flow of dividends $D_t = D_0(1 + g)^t$ where g is a constant. Let p_t be the price of the productive asset, and suppose that individuals may also hold a "bubble," that is, an unproductive intrinsically worthless paper claim that bears gross yield R_{t+1} payable at $t + 1$.

At any competitive equilibrium, the existing unitary stock of the productive asset must be owned by young individuals which means that

$$\frac{D_{t+1} + p_{t+1}}{p_t} \geq R_{t+1} \tag{24.14}$$

that is, the productive asset will yield at least as much as the bubble. The bubble will have no value unless equation (24.14) holds with equality, which is the assumption we shall maintain in the rest of this section. If we denote by $s(R)$ the savings function of the representative individual and by b_t the value of the bubble per capita, then competitive equilibrium requires that (i) aggregate financial wealth $N_t s(R_{t+1})$ should equal the market value $N_t b_t + p_t$ of the two assets; (ii) the arbitrage condition (24.14) should hold as an equality; (iii) the bubble should grow at the rate of interest; and (iv) $b_t \geq 0$, for otherwise the unproductive asset would be thrown away.

We write out these equilibrium conditions in the extensive form

$$N_t b_t + p_t = s\left(\frac{D_{t+1} + p_{t+1}}{p_t}\right) \tag{24.15a}$$

$$D_{t+1} + p_{t+1} = p_t R_{t+1} \tag{24.15b}$$

$$(1 + n)b_t = R_{t+1} b_t \tag{24.15c}$$

Denoting by $\pi_t = p_t/(1 + g)^t$ the price at time t of the rent-bearing asset per unit dividend, we may express the equilibrium conditions in intensive form:

$$b_t + \left(\frac{1 + g}{1 + n}\right)^t \pi_t = s\left[\frac{(1 + g)(D_0 + \pi_{t+1})}{\pi_t}\right] \tag{24.16a}$$

$$(1 + g)(D_0 + \pi_{t+1}) = \pi_t R_{t+1} \tag{24.16b}$$

$$(1 + n)b_{t+1} = R_{t+1} b_t \tag{24.16c}$$

The total value of each asset is bounded above by the youthful endowment. In particular, we have

$$\pi_t \left(\frac{1 + g}{1 + n}\right)^t \leq e_1 \qquad \forall t \tag{24.17}$$

We examine in some detail three cases which depend on how the population growth rate n compares with g, the rate of dividend growth.

Case 1: $g > n$

Since the value of the rent-bearing asset must be bounded, inequality (24.17) dictates that $\pi_t \to 0$ as $t \to \infty$. For any D_0, the yield on that asset, which equals $(1 + g)D_0/\pi_t$, must asymptotically tend to infinity. Note now from equation (24.16c) that this economy may admit the usual two types of stationary equilibria. One of them ($b > 0$, $R = 1 + n$) is a bubble that is identical to the outside-money equilibrium of section 24.1; the other is a fundamental equilibrium ($b = 0$, $R \neq 1 + n$) that resembles the inside money of Part II.

Bubbles must asymptotically vanish when rents grow faster than the population. Along any equilibrium path, yields become asymptotically infinitely large, which means that the bubble will disappear in the limit. At a stationary equilibrium the second term on the left-hand side of equation (24.16a) is constant and hence

$$\pi_t = p_0 \left(\frac{1+n}{1+g}\right)^t \tag{24.18a}$$

$$p_0 = \lim_{R \to \infty} s(R) \tag{24.18b}$$

Case II: $g = n$

The case $g = n$ is similar to the previous one. Bubbles, if they exist at all, will surely vanish again in the limit because the rent-bearing asset yields more than the rate of population growth in the steady state. Equations (24.16a)–(24.16c) become

$$b_t + \pi_t = s\left[\frac{(1+n)(D_0 + \pi_{t+1})}{\pi_t}\right] \tag{24.19a}$$

$$b_{t+1} = \frac{(D_0 + \pi_{t+1})b_t}{\pi_t} \tag{24.19b}$$

and admit only one steady state $b = 0$ and $\pi = \bar{\pi}$ where $\bar{\pi}$ is the unique fixed point of the equation

$$\pi_t = s\left[\frac{(1+n)(D_0 + \pi_{t+1})}{\pi_t}\right] \tag{24.20}$$

drawn in figure 24.3.

Case III: $g < n$

Allocations without bubbles are dynamically inefficient for $g < n$ because dividends grow too slowly relative to the population. At any stationary equilibrium, equation (24.18a) will hold again, $R = 1 + n$, and $b + p_0 = s(1 + n)$. Therefore, a bubble exists whenever the initial price of the productive asset satisfies

$$0 < p_0 < s(1 + n) \tag{24.21}$$

For any such initial price, stationary equilibrium allocations in a representative-agent economy are defined by the vector

$$(c_1, c_2) = (e_1 - s(1 + n), e_2 + (1 + n)s(1 + n))$$

All three cases refer to the pricing of capital assets employed as inputs in *linear* production technologies. What happens when dividends are not proportional to the

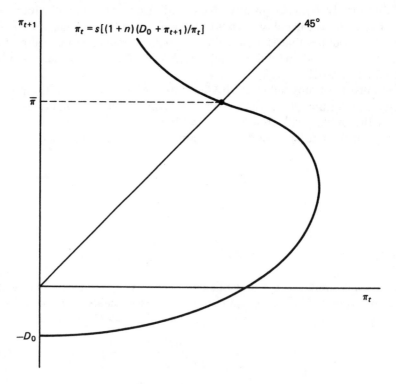

Figure 24.3 Pricing rent-bearing assets.

stock of capital in use? Questions IV.18–IV.20 deal with asset prices when the technology is convex.

Notes

1. In particular, restrictions of a legal nature will be helpful in explaining why currency is valued when it is dominated by debt in rate of return; see section 25.2.
2. Two or more intersections are not possible for they would imply that the aggregate saving function is set valued at the interest rate which obtains along the diagonal.
3. Morishima, for instance, found that slowly changing expectations would guarantee the asymptotic stability of the balanced growth path in the Hahn (1966) model of heterogeneous capital goods; that path is a saddle under perfect foresight. Similar phenomena arise in monetary growth theory: the steady state of the Sidrauski (1967) model is a saddle if foresight is perfect, a sink if forecasts are of the adaptive-learning variety. See Burmeister and Dobell (1970, pp. 183–9) and section 26.3 for more details.
4. Grandmont and Laroque (1986) explore this issue in greater detail.

25 The quantity of money

25.1 The neutrality of money

How equilibrium responds to changes in the stock of money has been one of the key issues in economics since its beginning as a distinct field of endeavor. There is an identifiable and influential "monetarist" school of economists, centered at the University of Chicago but extending well beyond it,[1] which regards this question as *the* central one in macroeconomics and monetary theory. Members of that school demonstrate an unusual concern for central banking, for they believe that central bank policy is the most important proximate determinant of the stock of money, and business cycles often arise from failures of the central bank to stabilize monetary aggregates.

The monetary origin of business cycles has been a working hypothesis ever since classical economists like Adam Smith (1776) and Henry Thornton (1802) observed a correlation between specie flows and aggregate economic activity. The idea is pursued forcefully, if inconclusively,[2] in the monumental work of Friedman and Schwartz (1963) who attribute the Great Depression itself to monetary factors.

Like many other broad questions, the one asked by monetarists is so incompletely specified that its pursuit is not entirely meaningful. One suspects immediately (and, as we shall see below, justifiably) that the outcome of a given increase in the stock of fiat money cannot fail to depend on the methods by which the money is created, and on the use to which it is put. It is not sufficient to ask what will happen if the government were to print 1 billion dollars unless one specifies as well what is to be done with it: Is it to finance current purchases of goods and services from the private sector? To purchase private debt or buy back part of the outstanding public debt? To make transfer payments? Or to pay interest on existing money?

The first question is examined in chapter 26. Here we confine ourselves to the last three questions, beginning with the very last.

Suppose that, at the beginning of each period t, the monetary authority augments or shrinks the currency holdings of all households in the *same* proportion by paying interest at the rate μ_t on all existing balances. So far in Part IV we have assumed that $\mu_t = n$ in order to keep constant the stock of money balances per capita; in the remainder of this chapter we permit μ_t to be any number greater than -1. If $\mu_t > 0$ is the rate applicable to period t, then whatever currency was accumulated by members of generation $t - 1$ is multiplied by $1 + \mu_t$. One may think of interest on money as a proportional subsidy if $\mu_t > 0$, a proportional tax if $\mu_t < 0$. To keep things as simple as possible, we assume that interest payments are financed by the costless printing of new currency, and tax revenue is destroyed, also at no cost. In the aggregate, of course, the rate of growth in the stock of currency per capita is $(\mu_t - n)/(1 + n)$.

The fact that we measure the nominal quantity of fiat money in arbitrary units means that we can redefine the unit of account as we please, without anything consequential happening to the equilibrium allocation of resources. This operation will change equilibrium only in the sense that (absolute) money prices will be expressed in different units. Paying interest on money amounts to exactly the same thing: a doubling of the stock of currency achieved by setting the interest rate at 100 percent is equivalent to defining a new unit of account equal to one-half the old unit, that is, to a 50 percent "devaluation."

It is very easy to demonstrate this claim formally; all we have to do is exploit the zero-degree homogeneity of excess demand functions. We define the positive sequence $(M_t)_{t=1}^{\infty}$ of per capita currency or, equivalently, its first element M_1 together with the positive sequence $(\mu_t)_{t=2}^{\infty}$ of interest factors, where $(1 + n)M_t = (1 + \mu_t)M_{t-1}$. For any household $h = 1, \ldots, H$ of generation t, the budget set is

$$\beta_h^t = (c_h^t | c_{1h} \in [0, e_{1h}], c_{2h} \geq 0, c_{1h} - e_{1h} + (c_{2h} - e_{2h})/R_t \leq 0) \quad (25.1a)$$

and the real interest factor is

$$R_t = \frac{p_t(1 + \mu_{t+1})}{p_{t+1}} = (1 + n)\frac{p_t M_{t+1}}{p_{t+1} M_t} = (1 + n)\frac{m_{t+1}}{m_t} \quad (25.1b)$$

Both expressions depend on (the sequence of) *real* currency balances alone, not on nominal balances, and all individual excess demand functions inherit this property. Thus, the aggregate excess demand in period t.

$$D_t = m_t - s\left[(1 + n)\frac{m_{t+1}}{m_t}\right] \quad (25.1c)$$

is independent of the sequence (M_t). The next theorem follows immediately from this.

Theorem 25.1 Suppose $(p_t^*, c_1^{t-1}(*), \ldots, c_H^{t-1}(*))_{t=1}^{\infty}$ is a competitive equilibrium for the currency sequence $(M_t)_{t=1}^{\infty}$. Then $(\hat{p}_t, c_1^{t-1}(*), \ldots, c_H^{t-1}(*))_{t=1}^{\infty}$ is a competitive equilibrium of the same economy for the currency sequence $(\hat{M}_t)_{t=1}^{\infty}$, where $\hat{p}_t = (\hat{M}_t/M_t)p_t^*$.

Several equivalent verbal explanations of this statement[3] are possible. The most precise of them is that *changes in either the stock of currency or its rate of growth do not alter the set of equilibrium allocations of resources.* Money in this case is both *neutral* and *superneutral,* and any changes in the stock of it simply redefine the unit of account. We shall see below that the neutrality property (that is, the invariance of the set of equilibrium allocations to a permanent change in the per capita stock of currency) is preserved, and superneutrality (that is, invariance to a permanent change in the *rate of growth* of per capita balances) is lost, when the combined stock of currency plus nominal public debt varies as a result of government spending. A corollary is that the set of all possible equilibrium real rates of intrest is not dependent on "monetary" factors, being completely determined by "real" ones like preferences and endowments.

A third, and somewhat looser, interpretation is that "systematic or fully anticipated monetary policy does not matter"; this simply means that a sequence M_t responding in a well-understood manner to past or anticipated future values of endogenous variables (for example the price level, real interest rate or real money balances) does not affect the set of equilibrium allocations that are associated with constant per capita money balances. However, to label "monetary policy" a choice for the stock of currency requires a good deal of poetic license. As we shall see later in this chapter, monetary policy is often concerned with the choice of the central bank discount rate or of reserve requirements. Most commonly, however, monetary policy consists of open market purchases of sales, that is, selecting the *proportion* of fiat money to public debt. Similarly, a pure fiscal policy defines over time the *sum* of the stocks of government liabilities without changing their proportions. When currency is the only asset, the term "monetary policy" is not quite meaningful.

What is the scope for "policy," however labeled, in this economy of interest-bearing money? It certainly cannot add to the set of equilibria; can it select *one* among the potentially infinitely many competitive equilibria? We analyse this issue in section 28.6. To see what the possibilities are, suppose the central bank announces at the beginning of time that, from time T onward, it will print whatever amount of currency is needed to ensure that per capita *real* balances are at their stationary monetary level, $s(1 + n)$. In other words, (M_t) satisfies.

$$M_t = p_t s(1 + n) \qquad t = T, T + 1, \ldots \textit{ ad infinitum} \qquad (25.2)$$

Given such a policy rule, the economy will settle down at the beginning of time to either the stationary monetary equilibrium, if the authorities are believed, or to an inside-money equilibrium, if households come to fear that outside money will become valueless. As we saw in Part II, a similar property holds in the Diamond model of national debt in which the number of equilibria is greatly reduced if we fix in perpetuity the real stock of debt. The same idea is explored by Grandmont (1985) in a currency model.

Any economy described by theorem 25.1 satisfies the *quantity equation*,[4] that is, $M_t = p_t y_t$, where M_t is currency in circulation; the income velocity of money is fixed by the technology of exchange at unity; and y_t is an index of the volume of exchange. In this chapter, y_t is merely net trade or aggregate saving and is exogenous to M_t. Whatever meaning one chooses to attach to theorem 25.1, one ought to keep in mind that it is only indirectly connected with real-world changes in the stock of currency. Currency bears little or no nominal interest, so that the only devaluations of it worth mentioning in a closed economy are *pure monetary reforms*. Monetary reforms in general are infrequent events, and they are rarely pure: they usually occur after hyperinflations as part of a more general stabilization program that includes fiscal measures as well.

The implications for "monetary" policy of theorem 25.1, then, are modest: policy does not change the set of equilibrium allocations, and changes in the unit of account by themselves are inconsequential. Substantially different conclusions would follow if currency were printed to finance government purchases, as in the following chapter, or to make transfer payments to households, as we shall discover immediately below.

Suppose, in particular, that the stock of currency grows geometrically at a constant rate $\mu \geq 0$, and newly printed money no longer finances interest payments on existing balances; it is instead distributed in equal per capita amounts to the members of the oldest generation alive. Does the set of competitive equilibria respond to changes in the policy variable μ, and if so how?

Let σ_t denote the per capita subsidy accruing at t to members of generation $t - 1$, n be the rate of population growth, N_t be the size of generation t, m_t be per capita real currency balances and $R_t = p_t/p_{t+1}$ be the real interest factor applicable to period t. Then we have

$$m_t = \frac{M_t}{p_t N_t} \tag{25.3a}$$

$$N_t = N_0(1 + n)^t \tag{25.3b}$$

$$M_t = M_0(1 + \mu)^t \tag{25.3c}$$

$$R_t = \frac{p_t}{p_{t+1}} = \frac{1 + n}{1 + \mu}\frac{m_{t+1}}{m_t} \tag{25.3d}$$

$$\frac{\sigma_{t+1}}{p_{t+1}} = \frac{M_{t+1} - M_t}{N_t p_{t+1}} = \frac{\mu(1 + n)m_{t+1}}{1 + \mu} \tag{25.3e}$$

We define $z_h(R,\alpha)$ to be the savings function that maximizes the utility of household h subject to the standard budget constraints

$$c_{1h} + \frac{c_{2h}}{R} \leq e_{1h} + \frac{\alpha + e_{2h}}{R} \tag{25.3f}$$

Here $z_h(R, 0) = s_h(R) \equiv \text{argmax}_s\, u(e_1 - s, e_2 + Rs)$, that is, the savings function z_h reduces to the standard function s_h whenever the real value α of the monetary subsidy is zero. Proceeding as before, we define $z(R, \alpha)$ to be the normalized aggregate savings function, and observe from equation (25.3e) that every competitive equilibrium is associated with a sequence $(m_t)_{t=1}^{\infty}$ of per capita money balances which satisfies

$$m_t = z\left[\frac{1 + n}{1 + \mu}\frac{m_{t+1}}{m_t}, \frac{(1 + n)\mu}{1 + \mu}m_{t+1}\right] \tag{25.4a}$$

The right-hand side of this equation is a decreasing function of μ if goods are gross substitutes and normal, because an increase in μ will reduce the yield on money and add to old-age income for given values of m_t and m_{t+1}. Saving is positive if the interest factor exceeds the individually autarkic factor $\bar{R}$, that is, if

$$\frac{m_{t+1}}{m_t} > \frac{\bar{R}(1 + \mu)}{1 + n} \tag{25.4b}$$

Dynamical equilibria are depicted in figure 25.1, which shows a monetary stationary equilibrium to exist whenever the money stock does not grow "too fast," that is,

$$1 + \mu < \frac{1 + n}{\bar{R}} \tag{25.4c}$$

If this inequality is violated, suggests figure 25.1, the phase curve of (25.4a) does not intersect the diagonal and no monetary equilibrium exists. One also sees readily from theorem 24.1 that the stationary monetary equilibrium, and every dynamical equilibrium converging to it, is dynamically inefficient for any $\mu > 0$ because it is associated

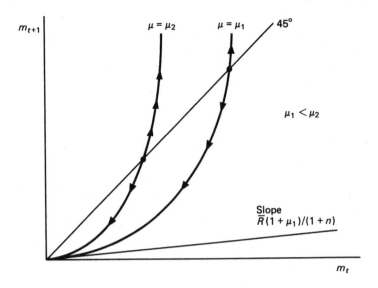

Figure 25.1 Inflationary finance.

with a rate of interest lower than n. The larger μ is, the lower is the real value of stationary per capita currency balances, and the higher the stationary inflation rate

$$\pi = \frac{\mu - n}{1 + n} \qquad (25.4d)$$

Per capita currency subsidies distort consumer choice in two ways: they redistribute resources first from large to small money holders and second from youth to old age. The second type of redistribution works like social security, reducing aggregate saving in equilibrium.

What policies does it take to ensure a good intertemporal allocation of resources? In a Samuelson-type economy, defined in inequality (25.4c), one has to avert the inefficiency that comes from inside-money equilibria. Given that inequality, we achieve intertemporal optimality for any non-negative rate of monetary growth $\mu \leq 0$, that is, by *not* issuing subsidies to the old. The golden rule allocation, which assigns zero weight to the transitional generation 0, obtains when $\mu = 0$ and the stationary rate of inflation equals $-n/(1 + n)$.

If we let the length of the trading period shrink relative to the lifespan, n becomes very small relative to unity; in the limit, trading takes place continuously and the stationary value of the rate of *deflation* becomes equal to the natural growth rate. Equality of these two rates is Milton Friedman's prescription for monetary policy, suggested in his *Optimum Quantity of Money* (1969). We summarize in the next theorem.

Theorem 25.2 If currency is created at a constant rate μ to finance equal per capita subsidies to old individuals, a monetary equilibrium exists if inequality (25.4c) holds. Dynamically efficient monetary equilibria are associated with non-positive rates of monetary expansion and with negative rates of steady state inflation. If goods are normal, then real per capita currency balances in the stationary state decrease in response to faster monetary expansion.

Whether money is neutral, then, depends theoretically on the precise manner in which the central bank injects high-powered money balances into the economy. The commonest way this is done is for the central bank to purchase from the private sector some of the outstanding stock of interest-bearing national debt. Open market purchases of this type are examined in the next three sections.

25.2   Open market operations: legal restrictions

The study of open market operations, that is, purchases and sales of circulating public debt by the central bank, requires an economy in which private asset portfolios contain both currency and interest-bearing national debt. Before we piece together such an economy, we must first explain why individuals would hold currency in their portfolios if they can purchase instead low risk liabilities issued by solvent governments or prudently managed firms yielding more than currency in every conceivable state of the world. As an asset, currency is *dominated in rate of return* by many other relatively safe assets; it is held by individuals for properties that other assets lack.

Two of these properties are of particular relevance for monetary policy: satisfying *legal restrictions* on asset portfolios and *facilitating transactions*. Below we explore each property in turn. This section, in particular, examines equilibria in an economy with a *reserve requirement* which ensures that the portfolios of commercial banks, and indirectly of all lenders, will keep a specified fraction of their value invested in government assets. Currency and central bank reserves are examples of such assets whose nominal rate of return is typically zero.

Capturing the transactions motive for holding money balances in a compact and logically appealing manner has turned out to be an enormously complicated task. Logically coherent models such as those proposed by Diamond (1982) and Kiyotaki and Wright (1989) tend to be so removed from neoclassical growth theory as to seriously hinder the job of integrating rigorous monetary theory with the rest of macroeconomics. What *does* fit compactly into existing dynamic structures requires unsatisfactory *ad hoc* assumptions about the exchange role of money. The most common of these assumptions is that currency is either a *consumption good* or a *unique medium of exchange* that must intermediate the buying and selling of certain commodities. We explore these two shortcuts in sections 25.3 and 25.4 respectively. In the remainder of this section we explore legal retrictions.

One of the several artificial ways we have for rationalizing why individuals hold a government liability that is dominated in rate of return is to impose a reserve requirement on lenders.[5] Following the work of Romer (1986), we use this requirement to keep the demand for high-powered money from falling to zero when the nominal interest rate is positive.

The same purpose is achieved by other legal restrictions (see Sargent and Wallace, 1982; Bryant and Wallace, 1984) or by a cash-in-advance constraint which defines money as a buffer stock that relaxes the coordination problems of sequential exchange (see section 25.4 below). Neither approach comes close to a fully worked-out model of how liabilities denominated in the unit of account facilitate the exchange process and why it is that some liabilities emerge as generally acceptable media of exchange. The artifact of fractional reserve requirements, however, is a good deal easier to analyze than other alternatives.

Reserve requirements support two different types of equilibria according to the stock of reserves held by lenders. One of them is an *excess reserve equilibrium* originally described by Wallace (1983). In this equilibrium, debt is a perfect substitute for currency, lenders hold greater reserves than they are legally required to, and the set of competitive allocations does not vary in response to local changes in any component of monetary policy; in fact, monetary policy is completely irrelevant. Excess reserve equilibria are typical outcomes of "loose" monetary policies; they correspond to the simple one-asset version of the overlapping generations model which we have studied in Parts III and IV.

The standard view of monetary policy is best illustrated by *required reserve equilibria*, a second type of equilibrium in which lenders hold exactly the minimum amount of reserves required. Here, as in elementary economics textbooks, reserve requirements alone determine the ratio of M_1 (that is, the stock of loans plus currency) to currency itself. Given certain technical conditions, looser monetary policies are associated with lower nominal interest rates, and the set of equilibrium allocations depends substantially on the monetary policy pursued by the central bank.[6]

To explore these equilibria, we describe in turn the operations of the government sector and the household sector, and we study the determination of nominal interest rates. "Government" here is an umbrella name for the treasury and the central bank: the treasury is charged with the responsibility of carrying out public expenditures and of collecting the revenue needed to finance these expenditures, either by taxing or by borrowing. In what follows, both taxes and government purchases are set equal to zero.

The central bank manages the structure of treasury liabilities to the private sector and regulates the behavior of the commercial banking system by choosing two policy parameters, $(z, \theta) \in [0, 1] \times \mathbb{R}_+$. Of these, z is a fraction that represents the reserve requirement on the portfolios of all lenders, and θ is a positive number that describes the central bank's open market policy. In particular, we suppose that

$$B_t/M_t = \theta \tag{25.5}$$

is the perpetual value of the ratio of interest-bearing public debt to currency. "Tight" monetary policies are associated with relatively high values of (z, θ); "loose" policies correspond to low parameter values.

At each time period t, the government has revenue $B_t + M_t - M_{t-1}$ from the sale of interest-bearing debt and the printing of currency; $R_{t-1}B_{t-1}$ is the expenditure needed to pay maturing public debt, where R_{t-1} is one plus the nominal rate of interest on both government and private loans. Given equation (25.5), the government budget constraint is

$$(1 + \theta)M_{t+1} = (1 + \theta R_t)M_t \tag{25.6}$$

The households in our economy come in two types, each with a life-cycle that spans two full periods. The first type, whom we call "lenders," has endowment vector $(e_1, 0)$ and consumes only in old age; the second type, called "borrowers," has endowment $(0, e_2)$ and consumes only in youth. Because endowments are different, no generality is lost by assuming that the two types exist in equal and constant populations.[7] Assume $e_1 > e_2$ to ensure that the economy is of the Samuelson type.

As we saw in Part III, reserve requirements affect the portfolios of borrowers and lenders in an asymmetric way, driving a wedge between the loan and deposit rates of interest. If $R > 1$ is the *nominal* gross yield paid by borrowers and R^D is the corresponding yield accruing to lenders, then

$$R^D = z + (1 - z)R \tag{25.7}$$

Equation (25.7) describes the yield on an asset portfolio which invests a fraction z of total resources in interest-free currency and the remainder in interest-bearing loans.[8]

Lenders will hold the minimum amount of currency required whenever the nominal yield on loans is positive but may keep *excess reserves* of currency if the nominal interest rate is zero. Total saving by lenders of generation t is e_1, held in debt and currency balances whose real values we denote by b_t^L and m_t^L, respectively. Specifically, we have

$$m_t^L + b_t^L = e_1 \tag{25.8a}$$

$$m_t^L \geq 0 \qquad b_t^L \geq 0 \tag{25.8b}$$

$$m_t^L \geq z e_1 \qquad (m_t^L = z e_1 \text{ if } R_t > 1) \tag{25.8c}$$

Borrowers, on the other hand, consume in youth the entire present value $e_2 \pi_{t+1}/R_t$ of their old-age endowment, where

$$\pi_{t+1} = p_{t+1}/p_t \tag{25.9}$$

is the inflation factor from time t to $t + 1$ and R_t/π_{t+1} is the *real* gross yield on loans. Dividing both sides of the government budget constant by p_{t+1}, we rewrite equation (25.6) in the form.

$$\frac{1 + \theta R_t}{\pi_{t+1}} = \frac{(1 + \theta)m_{t+1}}{m_t} \tag{25.10a}$$

where m is real money balances. In any stationary equilibrium with positively valued money, this expression defines a reduced-form relation

$$\pi = \frac{1 + \theta R}{1 + \theta} \tag{25.10b}$$

between the rate of inflation and the nominal rate of interest. Expressions like (25.10b) are named *Fisher equations* in monetary economics, after Irving Fisher who studied them seriously at the beginning of this century.

Stationary equilibria, in fact, are the only kind of equilibrium this economy admits; all dynamics is ruled out by our assumption of interest-inelastic saving. Required reserve equilibria, in particular, satisfy equation (25.10b) plus

$$m = z e_1 \tag{25.11a}$$

$$b = (1 - z)e_1 - e_2 \pi/R \tag{25.11b}$$

$$b = \theta m \tag{25.11c}$$

for some $R > 1$, given the policy choice (z, θ).

Excess reserve equilibria, on the other hand, are associated with a zero nominal rate of interest and hence no essential distinction between currency and other public liabilities. Given the policy choice (z, θ), these equilibria satisfy

$$\pi = R = 1 \tag{25.12a}$$

$$m + b = e_1 - e_2 \tag{25.12b}$$

It is easy to understand why excess reserve and required reserve equilibria are mutually exclusive: the former exist for "loose" monetary policies, the latter only for "tight" policy choices.

Substituting equations, (25.11a) and (25.11b) into (25.11c), we note that

$$(1 - z)e_1 - \frac{e_2\pi}{R} = \theta z e_1$$

Combine this and (25.10b) to obtain an equation in the nominal yield R:

$$\frac{(1 - z)e_1 - \theta z e_1}{e_2} = \frac{1 + \theta R}{(1 + \theta)R} \tag{25.13}$$

A required reserve equilibrium exists if equation (25.13) has a solution $R > 1$; a unique excess reserve equilibrium will exist otherwise.

The right-hand side of equation (25.13) is a decreasing function of R, equaling 1 at $R = 1$ and $\theta/(1 + \theta)$ as $R \to \infty$. Therefore, a required reserve equilibrium exists for monetary policies that satisfy

$$z(1 + \theta) > 1 - e_2/e_1 \tag{25.14}$$

Note that the right-hand side of (25.14) is a number in the interval $(0, 1)$.

Figure 25.2(a) illustrates the existence issue and figure 25.2(b) defines the types of policy which support required and excess reserve equilibria. Inequality (25.14), in particular, says that the nominal interest rate will be positive in equilibrium if the policy parameters z and θ are sufficiently high. Loose monetary policies, such as no reserve requirments ($z = 0$) or completely monetized public debt ($\theta = 0$), contribute to or ensure excess reserves and a zero nominal rate of interest. In fact, it is rather straightforward to demonstrate that real as well as nominal yields are low under a lax policy.

The tightness of monetary policy in this economy is measured by the product $z(1 + \theta)$. Up to some point, an expansionary open market policy may be used to counteract the effects of high reserve requirements and similar legal restrictions on private asset portfolios.[9] From a welfare standpoint, of course, tight monetary policies are undesirable: in any required reserve equilibrium the positive opportunity cost of holding currency exceeds the zero social cost of creating it. Furthermore, the terms of trade between present and future consumption depend on the sign of a trader's current excess demand.[10] Lenders are paid a deposit rate that is lower than the loan rate which applies to borrowers. Reserve requirements are the cause of this difference between the two rates, which measures the extent of interest rate discrimination against private liabilities in equilibrium.

25.3   Money in the utility function

The conclusions we reached in section 25.2 about the effect of open market operations extend to economies in which money is held for reasons other than legal restrictions. One case in point is when currency balances produce a flow of services that are directly related to the purchasing power of the real stock of money held by each household. You may think of these services as a description of the advantages of intermediated exchange: converting illiquid assets to purchasing power and arranging barter transactions are activities that consume time and resources.

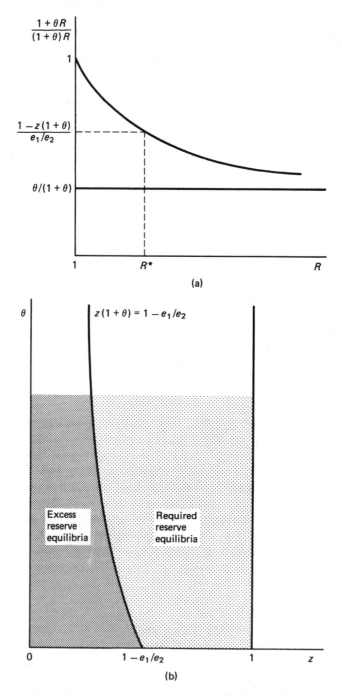

Figure 25.2 Reserve requirements: (a) required reserve equilibria; (b) the effect of monetary tightness.

Following Sidrauski (1967), we postulate that individual $h = 1, \ldots, H$ maximizes a utility function of the form $v^h(c_1^t, c_2^t, m_t)$, where $v^h: \mathbb{R}_+^3 \to \mathbb{R}$ represents a standard indifference map over three normal goods, with each pair being gross substitutes. The third argument in this utility function stands for real balances. We let $\omega^h = (e_{1h}, e_{2h}, 0)$ be the endowment vector for any household h born without cash balances; using the same symbols as before, we have the following budget constraints:

$$b_h^t + m_h^t + c_{1h}^t \leq e_{1h} \tag{25.15a}$$

$$c_2^t \leq e_{2h} + \frac{R_t}{\pi_{t+1}} b_h^t + \frac{m_h^t}{\pi_{t+1}} \tag{25.15b}$$

Here b_h^t, m_h^t are the real values of debt and currency balances held by trader h at the end of period t. Aggregating (25.15a) and (25.15b), we obtain the life-cycle budget constraint

$$c_{1h}^t + \frac{\pi_{t+1} c_{2h}^t}{R_t} + \frac{r_t}{R_t} m_h^t \leq e_{1h} + \frac{\pi_{t+1} e_{2h}}{R_t} \tag{25.16}$$

in which r_t is the nominal rate of interest.

For each individual who maximizes a utility function $v^h: \mathbb{R}_+^3 \to \mathbb{R}$ subject to this constraint, we may define two functions $\sigma^h: \mathbb{R}_+^2 \to \mathbb{R}$ and $\mu^h: \mathbb{R}_+^2 \to \mathbb{R}_+$ to express the demand for all assets and the demand for money, respectively, as functions of the real yield on loans and the nominal rate of interest. Specifically, we have

$$m_h^t + b_h^t = \sigma^h(R_t/\pi_{t+1}, r_t) \qquad r_t > 0 \tag{25.17a}$$

$$m_h^t = \mu^h(R_t/\pi_{t+1}, r_t) \qquad r_t > 0 \tag{25.17b}$$

It makes sense to assume a positive nominal interest rate; otherwise the demand for debt will go to negative infinity as consumers who are not satiated with money balances will arbitrage between useless debt and utility-producing currency. Normality and gross substitutability ensure that μ^h is decreasing in each argument while σ^h is increasing in R/π and decreasing in r. The same properties hold for the normalized aggregate asset demand functions

$$\mu = \frac{1}{H} \sum_{h=1}^H m_h^t \qquad \sigma = \frac{1}{H} \sum_{h=1}^H \sigma_h^t \tag{25.18}$$

Suppose again that the central bank maintains in perpetuity a constant ratio θ of interest-bearing public debt to currency. Then the government budget constraint from equation (25.10a) still applies to this economy; in addition, competitive equilibrium satisfies

$$(1 + \theta)m_t = \sigma(R_t/\pi_{t+1}, r_t) \tag{25.19a}$$

$$m_t = \mu(R_t/\pi_{t+1}, r_t) \tag{25.19b}$$

Using equation (25.10a) to eliminate π_{t+1} from these two equations leads to

$$(1 + \theta)m_t = \sigma\left[\frac{(1 + \theta)R_t}{1 + \theta R_t} \frac{m_{t+1}}{m_t}, r_t\right] \tag{25.20a}$$

$$m_t = \mu\left[\frac{(1 + \theta)R_t}{1 + \theta R_t} \frac{m_{t+1}}{m_t}, r_t\right] \tag{25.20b}$$

From these equations, it is fairly easy to ascertain the effect of open market operations on the nominal rate of return in stationary equilibrium. Dividing equation (25.20a) by (25.20b) we obtain

$$\frac{1}{1 + \theta} = h(r; \theta)$$

$$\equiv \frac{\mu[(1 + \theta)R/(1 + \theta R), r]}{\sigma[(1 + \theta)R/(1 + \theta R), r]} \qquad (25.21)$$

Recall that the function μ is decreasing in its first argument and σ is increasing; furthermore $(1 + \theta)R/(1 + \theta R)$ is decreasing in θ for each fixed R. Hence h is increasing in θ for each fixed r. In addition

$$h(0; \theta) = \frac{\mu(1, 0)}{\sigma(1, 0)} \geq 1 \qquad (25.22a)$$

because $\sigma(1, 0) > 0$ in a Samuelson economy, and the aggregate household demand for debt, $\sigma(1, 0) - \mu(1, 0)$, cannot be positive at a zero nominal rate of interest. Also note that the demand for money shrinks to nothing as the opportunity cost of holding it becomes very large. Formally,

$$\lim_{r \to \infty} h(r; \theta) = 0 \qquad \text{for all } \theta > 0 \qquad (25.22b)$$

From the intermediate value theorem and equations (25.22a) and (25.22b), we establish directly the existence of an equilibrium interest rate r for each value of $\theta > 0$. Figure 25.3 illustrates and suggests that r is an *increasing* function of the policy

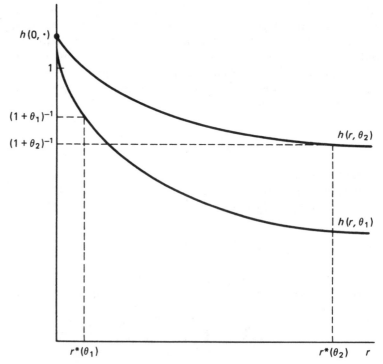

Figure 25.3 Open market operations.

parameter θ, just as it was in the legal restrictions model of section 25.2. In other words, there exists an increasing equilibrium map $r^*: \mathbb{R}_+ \to \mathbb{R}_+$, not necessarily a unique one, which describes the *stationary* nominal interest rate that corresponds to each value of the open market parameter θ.

25.4   Cash-in-advance constraints

A typical household sells (or indirectly contributes to the production of) an array of commodities that differs substantially from what the household itself consumes. Reconciling sales with purchases is a more complicated task than simply conforming to a life-cycle budget constraint. It requires some coordination between the purchasers and the sellers within an economic unit, because the rate at which buyers spend cannot permanently exceed the rate at which sellers collect revenue. This coordination is facilitated if the economic unit possesses a buffer stock of liquid assets that are generally acceptable in exchange.

Cash and related assets permit households and firms a degree of flexibility in planning their expenditure patterns that cannot be achieved by holding inventories of commodities. Clower's (1967) famous dictum "money buys goods and goods buy money; but goods do not buy goods" expresses this commonsense intuition succinctly.

One way to formalize this intuition is to emulate Lucas (1984) and suppose that there are two types of commodities: *credit goods* and *cash goods*. Excess demand for credit goods can be financed with loans, while the entire consumption of cash goods must be paid from existing money balances. However, the simplest way to describe cash-in-advance economies is to assume, as Clower (1967), Grandmont and Younès (1973), and Wilson (1979) did in their early work, that *all goods are cash goods*. Consider, for instance, a standard pure-exchange overlapping generations model with zero population growth and a representative household with endowment vector (e_1, e_2) and utility function $u: \mathbb{R}_+^2 \to \mathbb{R}$.

Households in this economy cannot consume their own endowment but desire the endowments owned by other persons which they regard as perfect substitutes in consumption at the ratio 1:1. Two markets open sequentially each period: first the credit market which trades cash for debt; after this market is closed, the goods market opens to facilitate the exchange of cash for the perfectly substitutable endowments of various households. Figure 25.4 illustrates.

A cash-in-advance economy differs from credit economies in that sales revenue from an individual's current endowment *cannot* finance current consumption. All that can be done in this regard is to borrow in advance the present value of one's future endowment and build up one's cash balances *before* the goods market opens, thus

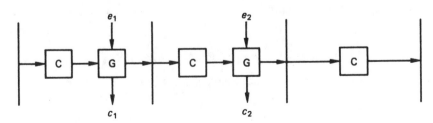

Figure 25.4 Sequential transactions in a cash-constraint economy.

avoiding the task of coordinating purchases and sales on the date the endowment accrues. Income from selling the endowment is then used to retire the household's accumulated debt.

To simplify the exposition, we allow households to participate in the credit market during their third period of life in order to settle debts. As shown in figure 25.4, a typical individual's life-cycle contains two trading dates for goods and three trading dates for credit. For each of these markets and dates, we need to write out a *separate* budget constraint.

Let I_i^t denote cash balances held *after* the closing of the goods market by an individual of generation t at stage $i = 1, 2, 3$ of the life-cycle; M_i^t and B_i^t denote the corresponding cash and debt balances held *before* the opening of the goods market and *after* the closing of the credit market. There are five budget constraints for this individual, one for each market in which he participates:

$$M_1^t = - B_1^t \geq 0 \tag{25.23a}$$

$$p_t c_1^t \leq M_1^t \qquad (p_t c_1^t = M_1^t \text{ if } R_t > 1) \tag{25.23b}$$

$$I_1^t \equiv M_1^t - p_t c_1^t + p_t e_1 \tag{25.23c}$$

$$M_2^t = I_1^t + R_t B_1^t - B_2^t \geq 0 \tag{25.24a}$$

$$p_{t+1} c_2^t \leq M_2^t \qquad (p_{t+1} c_2^t = M_2^t \text{ if } R_{t+1} > 1) \tag{25.24b}$$

$$I_2^t \equiv M_2^t - p_{t+1} c_2^t + p_{t+1} e_2 \tag{25.25a}$$

$$M_3^t = I_2^t + R_{t+1} B_2^t = 0 \tag{25.25b}$$

The first pair of these refer to period t: the individual sells debt to raise the cash he needs for his first-period consumption. If the interest rate is positive, the amount of cash balances borrowed will be *exactly equal* to the planned rate of youthful consumption; idle cash balances lower future consumption without raising current consumption.

The next pair of inequalities after the identity (25.23c) apply to the second period of life. In particular, (25.24a) says that balances carried over from youth are used to repay debts and are augmented by borrowing against old-age income. Inequalities (25.23b) and (25.24b) describe cash-in-advance constraints on youth and old-age consumption. Finally, equation (25.25b) says that the individual must carry over into the third stage of life enough cash to retire his second-stage indebtedness.

At first glance, equations (25.23a)–(25.25b) appear quite complicated, but in reality they are not very difficult to deal with. If all interest rates are possitive, for instance, we have

$$B_1^t = - M_1^t \qquad B_2^t = -p_{t+1} e_2 / R_{t+1} \tag{25.26}$$

and the budget constraints become

$$p_t c_1^t = M_1^t \tag{25.27a}$$

$$p_t c_2^t = M_2^t = p_t e_1 - R_t M_1^t + p_{t+1} e_2 / R_{t+1} \tag{25.27b}$$

When interest rates are positive, idle balances are zero, and hence

$$r_t (M_1^t - p_t c_1^t) = 0 \tag{25.28a}$$

$$r_{t+1} (M_2^t - p_t c_2^t) = 0 \tag{25.28b}$$

From these two equations and the original budget constraints, we easily derive the *life-cycle budget constraint*

$$c_1^t + \frac{c_2^t}{\rho_t} \leq \frac{e_1}{R_t} + \frac{e_2}{R_{t+1}\rho_t} \tag{25.29a}$$

where $\rho_t = p_t R_t/p_{t+1}$ is the real yield on debt.

The essential difference between a cash-in-advance economy and an ordinary credit economy emerges when we compare the previous inequality with the familiar budget constraint

$$c_1^t + \frac{c_2^t}{\rho_t} \leq e_1 + \frac{e_2}{\rho_t} \tag{25.29b}$$

From the vantage point of an *individual trader*, a cash-constrained economy with endowment vector (e_1, e_2) is similar to an unconstrained economy with a vector $(e_1/R_t, e_2/R_{t+1})$ which deflates endowments by the cost of holding cash.

This isomorphism does not necessarily extend to equilibrium behavior; the dynamical behavior of the two economies may be quite different. Readers who are interested in comparing equilibrium paths may consult the extensive survey by Woodford (1990b), who focuses on infinite lives. Alternatively, we can explore the dynamics of a cash-constrained overlapping generations economy by proceeding as in sections 25.2 and 25.3. Start with the consumption plans of the representative household we have just described, add a pair of market clearing conditions for money and credit

$$M_t = M_1^t + M_2^{t-1} \tag{25.30a}$$

$$L_t + B_1^t + B_1^{t-1} \geq 0 \qquad (L_t + B_1^t + B_2^{t-1} = 0 \text{ if } R_t > 1) \tag{25.30b}$$

and close the model with the usual government budget constraint

$$M_{t+1} - M_t = L_{t+1} - R_t L_t \tag{25.30c}$$

In these equations, L_t is *negative national debt*, that is, the stock of credit extended by the central bank to the private sector. In addition, one needs some description of government policy that pins down L_t or M_t. Readers who carry out this exercise are likely to confirm the main findings from sections 25.2 and 25.3: in stationary equilibrium looser monetary policies are associated with lower nominal interest rates and lower real interest rates as well.

Notes

1. Among the more prominent writers of this school are Fisher (1912), Simons (1948), and Friedman (1948, 1969).
2. Tobin (1970) and others have argued that the correlation between the money stock and aggregate economic activity may simply be a reflection of the banking system producing inside money to facilitate whatever level of economic activity is created by non-monetary factors: in this view, money is not the "cause" of economic activity, but a mere byproduct. Sims (1972) has run econometric tests of causality. Still others, like Kydland and Prescott (1982), Long and Plosser (1981), and Hamilton (1983) contend that business cycles have "real" rather than nominal causes: movements in money and output are themselves the

outcome of fluctuations in more fundamental characteristics of the economy, for example preferences, technology, endowments, and terms of international trade.

3. A transparent rendering of this theorem appears in Metzler (1951) and in Patinkin (1965, p. 41). Earlier writers like Haberler (1941) and Pigou (1943) were more opaque for they sought to establish that money was neutral (more precisely, that the quantity of money did not influence the real state of interest) without specifying how money was created or distributed. A modern treatment of this result appears in Balasko and Shell (1981).

4. Standard references on the quantity theory of money are Fisher (1912) and Friedman (1956). It is typical of quantity theorists to accommodate movements in real output by postulating that velocity and real income are exogenous to money in the "long" run.

5. Section 25.2 draws on an unpublished paper by Azariadis and Farmer (1987).

6. US financial statistics lend qualified support to this theoretical typology of equilibria. Excess reserves appear to have been substantial from 1933 to 1946 and borrowed reserves were negligible between 1947 and 1979. Correspondingly, the prime rate of interest (at which commercial banks lend their most creditworthy customers) was above but very close to the discount rate (at which commercial banks borrow reserves from the central bank) in 1917–32; it was near or below the discount rate from 1947 to 1979.

7. Clearly, we lose some generality by looking at boundary endowment and consumption vectors, but that turns out to be an enormous simplification to which the main results of this section are not very sensitive.

8. Another interpretation of (25.7) is that R^D is the breakeven loan rate charged by a commercial bank with no operating costs, cost of capital R, and reserve requirement $z \in [0, 1]$. At that loan rate, the commercial bank makes zero profits on each dollar lent out.

9. See Sargent and Wallace (1982) for a detailed study of this question.

10. In economies with completely interest-inelastic saving, interest rate differentials are not necessarily suboptimal, for they cannot affect any household's life-cycle distribution of consumption. Things change once we allow some intertemporal substitutability in consumption, for then a discrepancy between the loan and deposit rates leaves room for the usual static welfare gains.

26 Inflationary finance

The government's monopoly right to create fiat money has been a source of revenue ever since it was found that the exchange value of money exceeded its intrinsic worth as a commodity. Recent South American governments have been keen exploiters of this privilege whose abuse is intimately related by many to hyperinflationary episodes. But the practice goes far back in history. For example, Philip the Fair of France reportedly used to draw two-thirds of his total revenue in the thirteenth century by debasing the currency (Webber and Wildavsky, 1986, ch. 4). In this he was merely following established practice: the silver content of large-denomination Roman coins fell from 98 percent at the middle of the first century AD to about 40 percent by 250 AD, declining to a paltry 4 percent before the third century was out. Not every state succumbed so readily to inflationism; one prominent counterexample is the Byzantine gold "nomisma," the successor of the Roman "solidus." This coin, which retained its weight (4.48 grams) and gold title (98 percent) from the fourth to the eleventh century AD, circulated widely from England to Persia (Postan et al., 1971, vol. 3, appendix).

In this chapter we examine the consequences of financing deficits entirely by printing currency, that is, by using inflation to tax the holding of money. Some of these consequences were first worked out in the heyday of Keynesian economics by Mundell (1965), Tobin (1965), and other contributors to monetary growth theory who wanted to find out whether inflation could be used as an engine of economic growth. Their reasoning, a distant relation to the Phillips curve, went as follows: an increase in the rate of inflation drives down the real yield on money balances, and therefore encourages the demand for substitute assets such as claims on capital. As a result, the equilibrium stock of capital per worker will rise and the rate of return on capital will fall. This argument is pursued in section 26.2.

Section 26.1 focuses instead on pure-exchange economies, investigating more traditional issues like the relationship of inflation to money creation; how large a flow of resources the government can tax away by inflation; whether a hyperinflation may result from attempts to tax excessively; and the existence of the *Laffer curve* linking the revenue from inflation with the inflation rate in the stationary state. As a matter of precedent, we shall find that inflation finance is not unlike ordinary deficit finance; much of the analysis to follow has the flavor of chapters 19 and 20.

In sections 26.3 and 26.4 we examine the dynamics of inflation in a pure-exchange economy consisting of a representative immortal household; Brock (1974, 1975) was the original investigator of this economy. We explore, in particular, how inflation responds to money creation intended to finance transfer payments. Are there *speculative hyperinflations* during which the rate of inflation diverges away from the rate of money creation? *Speculative hyperdeflations* during which the price level collapses to zero? We also examine the possibility of endogenous cycles that occur when the inflation rate fluctuates about the rate of money growth.

26.1   Seigniorage

Let the government decide on the value of one policy tool per time period, the rate of growth $\mu_t \geq 0$ of the money stock. Newly created money is used to purchase goods from young sellers at the going competitive price p_t. Suppose, then, that (μ_t) is the policy and (g_t) is the implied sequence of real government purchases per head. The two sequences are related for all t by the equalities

$$M_t = (1 + \mu_t)M_{t-1} \tag{26.1a}$$

$$M_t - M_{t-1} = p_t g_t N_t \tag{26.1b}$$

where N_t is the size of generation t. Equation (26.1b) is the government budget identity which says that the change in the aggregate stock of currency equals the nominal value of *all* government purchases. Readers who find this state of affairs a bit unrealistic may think of g_t as the primary *deficit* rather than government purchases per head; in that event, all endowment vectors (e_{1h}, e_{2h}) should be interpreted as net of taxes. We assume, in addition, that government purchases do not influence the marginal rate of substitution between private consumption goods. Dividing (26.1a) through by p_t and rearranging, we obtain

$$\frac{p_{t-1}}{p_t} = \frac{(1 + n)m_t}{(1 + \mu_t)m_{t-1}} \tag{26.1c}$$

where m_t denotes per capita real balances.

Because this economy lacks interest-bearing assets denominated in the unit of account, the nominal rate of interest is zero by definition. The ratio p_{t-1}/p_t therefore does double duty: it is both the real interest factor R_t that accrues in period t and the inverse of the inflation factor π_t pertaining to period t. In other words,

$$\frac{p_{t-1}}{p_t} = R_t = \frac{1}{\pi_t} \tag{26.2}$$

Individual budget constraints are identical to those defined in chapter 25.

Given the sequence (μ_t), we define a competitive equilibrium with perfect foresight by analogy with section 24.1: it is a price sequence $(p_t)_{t=1}^{\infty}$ and a real balance sequence $(m_t)_{t=1}^{\infty}$ together with a sequence of consumption vectors $(c_1^t, c_2^t, \ldots, c_H^t)_{t=0}^{\infty}$ such that for $h = 1, \ldots, H$ and $t = 1, \ldots$ equation (26.1c) holds and, in addition,

$$e_{1h} - c_{1h}^t = s_h\left(\frac{p_t}{p_{t+1}}\right) \tag{26.3a}$$

$$c_{2h}^t - e_{2h} = \frac{p_t}{p_{t+1}} s_h\left(\frac{p_t}{p_{t+1}}\right) \tag{26.3b}$$

$$m_t = s\left[\frac{(1 + n)m_{t+1}}{(1 + \mu_{t+1})m_t}\right] \tag{26.3c}$$

Equations (26.3a) and (26.3b) in this definition describe individual behavior; equation (26.3c) says that excess supply per member of the young generation equals the excess demand of the old generation plus the demand of the government. The initial condition m_1 may be interpreted as the real value of money holdings by generation-0 households, with government purchases being zero in period 1.

The per capita excess demand function under inflation finance

$$D^I(m_t, m_{t+1}, \mu_{t+1}) = m_t - s\left[\frac{(1 + n)m_{t+1}}{m_t(1 + \mu_{t+1})}\right] \tag{26.4}$$

is very similar to the excess demand function $D(p_t, p_{t+1}, M)$ defined in equation (23.6). In fact, for all (m_t, m_{t+1}) we have

$$D^I(m_t, m_{t+1}, 0) = D\left(\frac{1}{m_t}, \frac{1}{m_{t+1}}, 1\right) \tag{26.5}$$

In other words, if we were to draw the phase curve implied by equation (26.4) in the space of real currency balances, it would be identical to the parts of figure 24.1 whenever $\mu_{t+1} = 0$. Furthermore, if $\mu_{t+1} = \mu > 0$, for all t, the frontier $D^I = 0$ is simply that of $D = 0$ rotated counterclockwise about the origin; this is shown in figure 26.1(a).

The monopoly right to print currency enables the government to remove resources from the private sector in order to finance public spending plans, exactly as a counterfeiter taxes his fellow citizens when he operates his clandestine printing press without detection; the amount of resources appropriated by inflation finance is called *seigniorage*. How much revenue can the government raise on a sustained basis by debasing the currency? We call *maximum seigniorage* the greatest constant flow of real government purchases that can be financed by the issue of new currency in a steady state.

Maximum seigniorage is a meaningful concept, being the monetary counterpart of the maximal sustainable primary budget deficit studied in chapter 19. From equation (26.1b) we obtain the following expression that relates seigniorage to the rate of monetary expansion in any stationary equilibrium:

$$g = \frac{M_t - M_{t-1}}{p_t}$$

$$= \frac{M_t}{p_t} - \frac{M_t/p_t}{1 + \mu}$$

$$= \frac{m\mu}{1 + \mu}$$

From this equation and equation (26.3c) we obtain

$$g(\mu) = \frac{\mu}{1 + \mu} s\left(\frac{1 + n}{1 + \mu}\right) \tag{26.6}$$

which says two interesting things. First, the tax revenue from inflation is a function of the rate of monetary expansion, that is, the steady state inflation rate. Second,

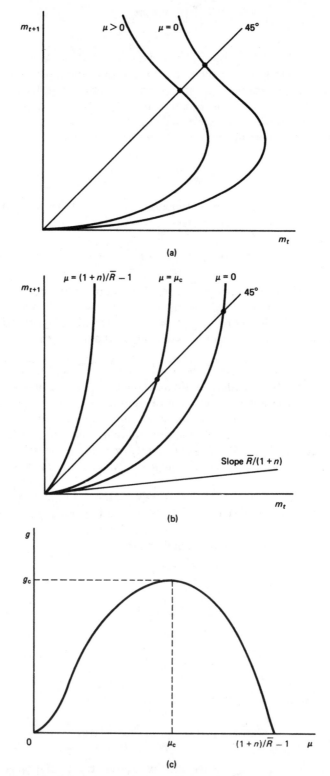

Figure 26.1 Seignorage in pure-exchange economies.

seigniorage is the product of the tax base $s[(1 + n)/(1 + \mu)]$ and the effective inflation tax rate $\mu/(1 + \mu)$. This tax rate equals the ratio of the rate of growth in money balances divided by $1 + \mu$.

When the rate of monetary growth is zero, every Samuelson economy with a unique inside-money equilibrium possesses a phase curve with slope $\bar{R}/(1 + n) < 1$ at $m = 0$, where $\bar{R}$ is the unique solution to $s(R) = 0$. The phase curve is shown in figure 26.1(b) to cross the diagonal at the golden rule point; the corresponding real seigniorage is zero because the *tax rate* is zero. The same diagram shows seigniorage to be zero again when the *tax base* (that is, the value of real money balances) shrinks to zero in response to an inflation tax $\bar{\mu} = (1 + n)/\bar{R} - 1$ that is large enough to discourage the holding of any money balances. Therefore, the intermediate value theorem dictates that there should be a rate $\mu = \mu_c$ at which stationary real seigniorage is maximal. Figure 26.1(c) illustrates this.

Denote by $\epsilon(R)$ the elasticity of the aggregate saving function evaluated at R. The precise rate μ_c at which seigniorage is maximal is located with the help of the formula

$$\frac{1}{\mu_c} = \epsilon \left[(1 + n)(1 + \mu c) \right] \tag{26.7}$$

due to Auernheimer (1974). To derive this formula, we use the first-order condition for a maximum of the function $g(\mu)$ defined in equation (26.6), rearrange terms and obtain equation (26.7). An example illustrates immediately below.

Example 26.1 (Seigniorage in an exchange economy) Suppose population is constant and households are identical with endowment vector $(2, 1)$ and utility function $c_1 c_2$. An inside-money equilibrium occurs at $R = 1/2$. The saving function is $s(R) = 1/2\,(2 - 1/R)$, and the rate of return is $1/(1 + \mu)$ in the stationary state. As a function of the growth rate μ in the stock of money, real seigniorage is given by

$$g(\mu) = \frac{\mu}{1 + \mu}\, s\left(\frac{1}{1 + \mu}\right)$$

$$= \frac{\mu}{1 + \mu} \left(1 - \frac{1 + \mu}{2} \right)$$

$$= \frac{\mu}{1 + \mu} - \frac{\mu}{2}$$

This function vanishes at $\mu = 0$ and $\mu = 1$; it is maximal at $(1 + \mu)^2 = 2$, that is, at $\mu_c = \sqrt{2} - 1$ whose approximate value equals 0.414. At this point, real seigniorage equals $1.5 - \sqrt{2} = 0.086$, which amounts to approximately 30 percent of all net trading.

Note also from $s(R) = 1 - 1/2R$ that $\epsilon(R) = 1/(2R - 1) \Rightarrow 1/\epsilon(R) = 2R - 1$ which equals $2/(1 + \mu) - 1$ at $R = 1/(1 + \mu)$. The Auernheimer formula immediately yields $\mu = \sqrt{2} - 1$.

We study next dynamical competitive equilibria associated with constant rates of money growth in the interval $[0, \mu_c]$. Figure 26.1(b) shows that there is only one outside-money equilibrium, which may or may not be stable. This means that there is also a continuum of dynamical equilibria indexed on first-period real balances m_1; some of these converge asymptotically to the inside-money stationary state.

The welfare properties of equilibria are easy to establish when $\mu > 0$. Any inflationary finance equilibrium is associated with a normalized single-period interest factor $R_t/(1 + n) = m_{t+1}/[(1 + \mu)m_t]$. The relevant multiperiod interest factor $R^t = \Pi^t_{s=1}[R_s/(1 + n)]$ therefore satisfies

$$R^t = (1 + \mu)^{-t} \frac{m_{t+1}}{m_1} \leqslant (1 + \mu)^{-t} \frac{e_1}{m_1} \qquad (26.8)$$

where e_1 represents the aggregate resources of the young. For any $\mu > 0$, the infinite sequence R^t is summable, and equilibrium is dynamically inefficient. The inefficiency is not surprising, for it appeared under similar circumstances when we analyzed deficit finance in chapter 19. Inflation, in particular, is a tax that discourages the use of money balances, driving down the real rate of interest on loans whose nominal yield is by definition zero. We collect results in the following theorem.

Theorem 26.1 Suppose $\bar{R} < 1 + n$ and $\mu \in [0, \mu_c]$. Then there is a continuum of dynamically inefficient competitive equilibria indexed on m_1, the initial value of real balances.

A fully informed social planner could raise a given real revenue g per capita by lump-sum taxes, avoid the distortion of the inflation tax, and make *every* household better off. Governments, however, are typically not fully informed about the individual characteristics of taxpayers, and virtually always resort to raising revenue by distortionary means like the income tax or the inflation tax.

Real balances per head are constant at each stationary equilibrium, which means that the rate of inflation equals $(\mu - n)/(1 + n)$, roughly the rate of money creation less the rate of growth (see also question IV.35). Therefore, each feasible flow of per head government purchases in the interval $[0, g_c]$, where g_c is maximum seigniorage, can be financed in the stationary state at two or more distinct rates of inflation: a high rate that corresponds to a rate of monetary expansion in the interval $[\mu_c, (1 + n)/\bar{R} - 1]$; and a low rate that corresponds to a rate of monetary expansion in the interval $[0, \mu_c]$.

Outside the stationary state, the relation between the inflation and money creation rates is more complicated. Figure 26.1(a) shows that real balances may cycle over time for any dynamical equilibrium that converges to the monetary steady state. Along all such paths, therefore, the rate of inflation must be *smaller* than $(\mu - n)/(1 + n)$ in, say, odd periods and *bigger* in even periods.

Here is a digest of what we have covered in the last few paragraphs.

Theorem 26.2 Suppose again that $\bar{R} < 1 + n$. Then each constant level of per capita real government purchases below maximum seigniorage can be achieved by two or more rates of monetary expansion, one above μ_c and the other below μ_c. If $n = 0$, then the rates of inflation and money creation are equal to each other in the steady state, unequal outside the steady state.

The functional relationship between the inflation rate and real seigniorage is illustrated in figure 26.1(c) for an economy with constant population. Diagrams like figure 26.1(c) are known as *Laffer curves* after Arthur Laffer, a Southern California economist who popularized the concept in the 1970s to demonstrate that excessive tax rates weaken incentives to produce and trade, and depress total tax revenue because they shrink taxable income rapidly. The ideas of Laffer, and others who favored lower tax rates to stimulate supply and raise tax revenue in one fell swoop, became known as "supply-side" economics in the late 1970s.

Whatever one thinks of that doctrine, figure 26.1(c) fits it to a tee. Zero government seigniorage is consistent with two equilibrium inflation factors: $(1 + n)^{-1}$ corresponding to the outside-money steady state, and $1/\bar{R}$ corresponding to the inside-money state. Any seigniorage in the interval $[0, g_c]$ may be obtained at either a high or a low rate of inflation and also of money creation. [1]

The content of theorems 26.1 and 26.2, particularly the number of stationary equilibria and comparative dynamics results, depends to a certain extent on the choice of policy instrument, that is, on exactly what feature of government purchases one regards as exogenous. We chose in this section to fix the rate of currency growth and then purchase with the resulting amount of newly created currency whatever resources competition permitted. Instead, we could have fixed real government expenditure (as we did when we analyzed deficit finance in Part III) and found out how much currency one would have to print in equilibrium.

What is quite independent of the policy instrument we choose is the distortion caused when money creation pays for public consumption. The intuitive reasons for this, pointed out in theorem 26.1, are well understood ever since Bailey (1956) stressed the loss in consumer surplus that results from inflationary finance. In the framework of this chapter, equation (26.7) suggests that the debasement of currency is exactly equivalent to an excise tax on commodity sellers equal to the equilibrium fraction $\mu/(1 + \mu)$ of net trades absorbed by public consumption. See question IV.14 for details.

26.2 Inflation and growth

In this section we examine how inflationary finance influences the accumulation of physical capital. The economic intuition for that influence was outlined at the beginning of the chapter; here we formalize it within the overlapping generations model of growth. The analysis that follows will bear more than a passing resemblance to the material on deficit finance in growing economies contained in section 20.2: inflation finance, after all, is simply deficit finance pursued with the specialized instrument of monetary expansion.

Assuming for simplicity that physical capital depreciates immediately on use and that the saving rate is a constant $s \in [0, 1]$, we denote by (M_t) and (m_t) the sequences of nominal and real balances *per capita* and by (g_t) the sequence of real government purchases per capita. Suppose, as before, that government purchases do not affect anybody's marginal rate of substitution between private goods.

We take the policy again to be the rate $\mu > 0$ of growth in the *aggregate* money stock, which is constant for all time. The government budget identity consists of the equations

$$p_t g_t = M_t - \frac{M_{t-1}}{1 + n} \qquad (1 + n)M_t = (1 + \mu)M_{t-1}$$

Combining these two, we obtain once more

$$g_t = \frac{m_t \mu}{1 + \mu} \qquad\qquad (26.9a)$$

The inflation factor from period t to period $t + 1$ is again the inverse of the gross yield on money in period t, that is,

$$\pi_{t+1} = \frac{p_{t+1}}{p_t} = \left[\frac{1 + n}{1 + \mu} \frac{m_{t+1}}{m_t} \right]^{-1} \tag{26.9b}$$

Equilibrium here satisfies two equations:

$$\frac{(1 + n)m_{t+1}}{(1 + \mu)m_t} = f'(k_{t+1}) \tag{26.10a}$$

$$(1 + n)k_{t+1} + m_t = sw_t \tag{26.10b}$$

The first of these is a portfolio balance relation that equates the rates of return of the two existing assets (currency balances and claims on real capital) and hence removes all gains to arbitrage between them. The second equation balances the aggregate supply and demand for assets.

Recalling that the wage rate in a competitive labor market satisfies $w_t = w(k_t) = f(k_t) - k_t f'(k_t)$ if returns to scale are constant, we define equilibria of this economy as positive solutions (k_t, m_t) to the dynamical system

$$(1 + n)m_{t+1}/m_t = (1 + \mu)f'(k_{t+1}) \tag{26.11a}$$

$$(1 + n)k_{t+1} + m_t = sw(k_t) \tag{26.11b}$$

Before we explore this economy further, we suppose that it is a Samuelson economy with a unique positive inside-money steady state $\bar{k}$. In particular, we assume that

$$\lim_{k \to \infty} f'(k) = 0 \qquad \lim_{k \to 0} w'(k) > \frac{1 + n}{s} \tag{26.12}$$

and

$$sw(k^*) - (1 + n)k^* > 0 \tag{26.13}$$

where the golden rule capital–labor ratio k^* solves the equation $1 + n = f'(k)$.

Under these assumptions, the dynamical system (26.11a)–(26.11b) possesses the usual three steady states: two inside-money ones $(k, m) = (0, 0)$ and $(\bar{k}, 0)$, and an outside-money steady state $(k_I(\mu), m_I(\mu))$ such that k_I and m_I satisfy

$$f'(k) = \frac{1 + n}{1 + \mu} \tag{26.14a}$$

$$m = sw(k) - (1 + n)k \tag{26.14b}$$

for each $\mu \geq 0$.

The vector field of this economy is fairly straightforward. Note from (26.11b) that

$$k_{t+1} \geq k_t \qquad \Leftrightarrow sw(k_t) - m_t \geq (1 + n)k_t$$

$$\Leftrightarrow m_t \leq sw(k_t) - (1 + n)k_t \tag{26.15a}$$

Similarly, equation (26.11a) says that

$$m_{t+1} \geq m_t \quad \Leftrightarrow \quad (1 + \mu)f'(k_{t+1}) \geq 1 + n$$
$$\Leftrightarrow \quad f'(k_{t+1}) \geq f'(k_I)$$

$$\Leftrightarrow k_{t+1} \leq k_I$$
$$\Leftrightarrow sw(k_t) - m_t \leq (1 + n)k_I$$
$$\Leftrightarrow m_t \geq sw(k_t) - (1 + n)k_I \qquad (26.15b)$$

The constant-capital and constant-money phaselines $KK = \{(k, m) | k \geq 0, m \geq 0, m = sw(k) - (1 + n)k\}$ and $MM = \{(k, m) | k \geq 0, m \geq 0, m = sw(k) - (1 + n)k_I\}$ are very similar to the corresponding lines in figure 7.4(c) of Part I; in fact the entire vector field of this dynamical system looks very much like that of the planar overlapping generations model we studied in chapter 7. Figure 26.2 illustrates.

Inflationary finance is meaningful only when money holdings are positive, that is, as long as the rate μ of monetary expansion keeps k_I *short* of $\bar{k}$. There is a critical value $\bar{\mu}$ such that $k_I(\bar{\mu}) = \bar{k}$, that is,

$$1 + \bar{\mu} = \frac{1 + n}{f'(\bar{k})} \qquad (26.16)$$

The demand for money vanishes if $\mu \geq \bar{\mu}$. For any $\mu \in [0, \bar{\mu})$, however, the outside-money steady state (k_I, m_I) is a well-defined saddle while the inside-money states $(0, 0)$ and $(\bar{k}, 0)$ are a source and a sink respectively. These conclusions are easily verified from the Jacobian of the dynamical system (26.11a)–(26.11b).

As the parameter μ increases in the interval $[0, \bar{\mu}]$, the KK line remains unchanged while the MM line shifts downward by some given vertical distance. This occurs because none of the parameters in equation (26.15a) depends on μ whereas k_I in equation (26.15a) is an increasing function of μ. As $\mu \to \bar{\mu}$, $k_I \to \bar{k}$, $m_I \to 0$, and a saddle-node bifurcation occurs. Seigniorage vanishes.

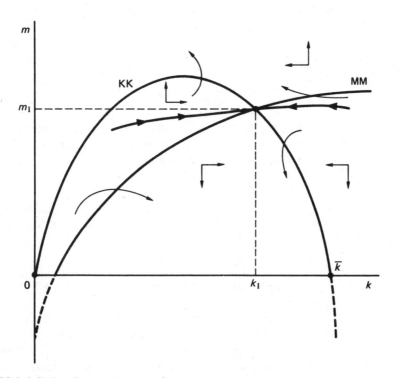

Figure 26.2 Inflation finance in a growing economy.

What is the Laffer curve of an economy with production? One way to gain some insight is to generalize the Auernheimer formula of the previous section to production economies or work out an example with empirically plausible parameters. Question IV.11 asks readers to do just that.

Figure 26.2 sums up the conclusions one should draw about the connection between inflation and economic growth in a closed economy. Faster money creation reduces the steady state yield on capital and raises the capital–labor ratio in any stationary outside-money equilibrium *provided that the economy is already dynamically efficient,* that is, whenever $k_1(0) < k$. Note from eq. (14a) that, at $\mu = 0$, the value $k_1(0)$ of the steady-state capital-labor ratio equals the golden rule. However, if $k_1(0)$, the demand for money vanishes and so does the revenue for inflation.

Another important limitation on inflation as an engine of growth is that claims on domestic capital, however broadly defined, are not the only substitute to money balances as we have assumed in this section. Gold, foreign currency, and claims denominated in foreign currency are assets with almost worldwide availability. If recent experience in South America is any guide, a determined inflationist policy seems more likely to increase capital outflow or domestic holding of foreign assets than to encourage domestic investment.

26.3   Infinite lives: unique equilibrium (*)

This section is an extension of the material in section 25.1 to a pure-exchange economy that consists of identical infinitely lived households born at $t = 0$. We study once more the neutrality of money under the assumption that newly printed money is transferred in lump-sum fashion, and in equal amounts, to all living households. These households have a flat endowment sequence $e_t = y$ for all $t = 0, 1, \ldots$; their preference order over infinite sequences (c_t) of the consumer good and (m_t) of real-money balances is captured by the discounted value of the utility stream

$$W = \sum_{t=0}^{\infty} \beta^t w(c_t, m_t) \tag{26.17a}$$

where $\beta \in [0, 1]$ is a discount factor and $w: \mathbb{R}_+^2 \to \mathbb{R}$ is an instantaneous utility function endowed with the usual smoothness, monotonicity, and concavity properties. Of special interest, is the *additive instantaneous utility* case,

$$w(c, m) = u(c) + v(m) \tag{26.17b}$$

in which $u: \mathbb{R}_+ \to \mathbb{R}$ and $v: \mathbb{R}_+ \to \mathbb{R}$ are again smooth, monotone, concave functions. We suppose throughout this section that consumers never become satiated with any finite amount of money balances, that is,

$$\lim_{m \to \infty} w_m(c, m) = 0 \tag{26.17c}$$

for all $c > 0$, where the marginal utility of money w_m is positive for all finite (c,m).

Pure exchange economies with money-holding infinitely lived households have been extensively studied in macroeconomics, first by Brock (1974, 1975), and later by Obstfeld and Rogoff (1983), and many others. All these economies are special cases of the *optimal growth model with money* due to Sidrauski (1967) which permits the consumption good to be produced under constant returns to scale from physical capital and labor.

In what follows we ignore capital accumulation, production, and interest-bearing public debt. We assume instead that the central bank expands the per capita stock of money by a constant rate each period, that is,

$$M_{t+1} = (1 + \mu)M_t \qquad \mu > 0 \qquad (26.18a)$$

using newly printed money to pay at t a lump-sum transfer H_t to each household. Hence

$$H_t = \mu M_{t-1} = \frac{\mu M_t}{1 + \mu} \qquad (26.18b)$$

The representative household picks (c_t, m_t) to maximize the lifetime utility function W subject to the flow budget constraint

$$p_t(m_t + c_t) \leqslant p_t y + H_t - p_{t-1} m_{t-1} \qquad (26.19a)$$

and a transversality condition due to Brock (1975)

$$\lim_{T \to \infty} [\beta^T (p_t/p_{t+T}) w_c(c_{t+T}, m_{t+T})] = 0 \qquad \forall t \qquad (26.19b)$$

which rules out permanent utility gains from temporary adjustments in money balances. This condition is derived and discussed later. From the first-order conditions for a maximal consumption sequence we readily obtain

$$w_c(c_{t+1}, m_{t+1}) = \frac{\pi_{t+1}}{\beta} [w_c(c_t, m_t) - w_m(c_t, m_t)] \qquad (26.20)$$

where $\pi_{t+1} = p_{t+1}/p_t$ is the inflation factor and (w_c, w_m) are partial derivatives of the flow utility function.

Equation (26.18a) implies as usual that

$$\pi_{t+1} = \frac{p_{t+1}}{p_t} = \frac{M_{t+1}}{M_t} \frac{m_t}{m_{t+1}} = (1 + \mu) \frac{m_t}{m_{t+1}} \qquad (26.21)$$

Dynamical competitive equilibria come about if $c_t = y$ for all t; hence every equilibrium sequence must satisfy equation (26.20) once we replace c_t by y, and π_{t+1} by the expression on the right-hand side of equation (26.21). In other words, every (m_t) that is associated with an equilibrium is a solution to the following first-order difference equation:

$$m_{t+1} w_c(y, m_{t+1}) = \frac{1 + \mu}{\beta} [w_c(y, m_t) - w_m(y, m_t)] m_t \qquad (26.22)$$

If we rule out corner solutions to the consumer's problem, sequences (m_t) that converge to zero cannot be competitive equilibria, except in one unusual case noted later. It follows that stationary equilibria $\bar{m} > 0$ solve

$$w_m(y, m) = A w_c(y, m) \qquad (26.23a)$$

where

$$A = \frac{1 + \mu - \beta}{1 + \mu} \in (0,1) \qquad (26.23b)$$

For each fixed $y > 0$ and $A > 0$, the expression $w_m(y, m) - Aw_c(y, m)$ is a *decreasing* function of m if money is a normal good; for each fixed $A > 0$ and $m > 0$, the same expression is an *increasing* function of y. Hence a unique stationary solution $\bar{m} > 0$ to equation (26.22) exists if the following relation holds for all $A \in [1 - \beta, 1]$:

$$\lim_{m \to 0} [w_m(y, m) - Aw_c(y, m)] > 0 \qquad (26.24a)$$

$$\lim_{m \to \infty} [w_m(y, m) - Aw_c(y, m)] < 0 \qquad (26.24b)$$

At this equilibrium we have $\pi = 1 + \mu$. Furthermore, it is easy to check that $\bar{m}$ is an increasing function of y and of the discount rate β, and a decreasing function of μ. We sum up in the following theorem.

Theorem 26.3 Suppose that inequalities (26.24a) and (26.24b) hold. Then the difference equation (26.22) has a unique positive steady state $\bar{m}$ which is an increasing function of income and the discount rate, a decreasing function of the rate of monetary growth. The stationary inflation rate equals the rate of money creation.

Before we explore the stability properties of this steady state, we recall that the right-hand side of equation (26.22) is an increasing function of m_t if money balances are a normal good, and note that the left-hand side is *not necessarily* an increasing function of m_{t+1}. *For very small values of m_t*, therefore, inequality (26.24a) says that the right-hand side of equation (26.22) must be negative and this equation cannot hold for any $m_{t+1} \geqslant 0$. In either case the implicit function theorem guarantees the existence of a map $J \colon \mathbb{R}_+ \to \mathbb{R}_+$ such that $m_t = J(m_{t+1})$ solves equation (26.22).

The uniqueness of the steady state $\bar{m}$ suggests that there are two possible ways we can draw the time map of equation (26.22). If $mw_c(y, m)$ is an increasing function of m for each y, as it would be in the additively separable case described by equation (26.17b), then the solution of equation (26.22) is the monotone time map J^{-1} shown in figures 26.3(a) and 26.3(b). Figure 26.3(a) is drawn for the case $\lim_{m \to 0} [mw_c(y, m)] > 0$ and 26.3(b) for the case $\lim_{m \to 0} [mw_c(y, m)] = 0$. If, on the other hand, $mw_c(y, m)$ is *locally a decreasing function of m for each y*, then the time map J^{-1} is not uniquely defined and may have the backward-bending shape of figure 26.3(c).

In the first case, exhibited in figures 26.3(a) and 26.3(b), the steady state $\bar{m}$ is unstable[2] and the only perfect-foresight equilibrium turns out to be $m_t = \bar{m}$ for all t, given some mild technical conditions. In the second case, shown in figure 26.3(c), the *steady state may be asymptotically stable* and attract sequences from its immediate neighborhood; periodic cycles and chaotic equilibria are also possible here as Wilson (1979) conjectured long ago and Matsuyama (1991) demonstrated with several robust parametric examples.

We begin with the monotone time map case: suppose that $mw_c(y, m)$ is an increasing function of m for each $y > 0$. Can sequences (m_t) starting below $\bar{m}$ be competitive equilibria? If so, say figures 26.3(a) and 26.3(b), m_t must be a decreasing sequence corresponding to a *speculative hyperinflation* for it will support an inflation rate, $(1 + \mu)m_t/m_{t+1} - 1$, which diverges from the rate of money creation μ. Figures 26.3(a) and 26.3(b), however, rule out such speculative inflations because they require, in almost all cases, that money balances become *negative* in finite time. The only exception is in 26.3(b) where sequences starting by coincidence at $\hat{m}_1$ converge to $m_t = 0$ in one step and therefore are legitimate competitive equilibria, even if they remain unlikely events.

What about *speculative hyperdeflations*, that is, increasing sequences (m_t) which start above the steady state? Are these competitive equilibria if the time map is monotone? To see why inflation rates permanently below the rate of money growth cannot be competitive equilibria, we need to discuss the transversality condition (26.19b). We recast the first-order condition in equation (26.20) in the form

$$w_c(c_t, m_t) = \frac{\beta}{\pi_{t+1}} w_c(c_{t+1}, m_{t+1}) + w_m(c_t, m_t)$$

and iterate forward T periods to obtain

$$\frac{1}{p_t} w_c(c_t, m_t) = \sum_{s=0}^{T-1} \frac{\beta^s}{p_{t+s}} w_m(c_{t+s}, m_{t+s}) + \frac{\beta^T}{p_{t+T}} w_c(c_{t+T}, m_{t+T}) \qquad (26.25a)$$

Equation (26.25a) describes the gain in current utility that accrues to a household at t from reducing money holdings by a small constant amount for T consecutive periods starting at t. Permanent gains from lowered balances will be possible, and hence strong incentives will exist *to hold no money* unless, for each t, we have

$$\lim_{T \to \infty} (\beta^T/p_{t+T}) w_c(c_{t+T}, m_{t+T}) = 0 \qquad (26.25b)$$

Equation (26.19b) is a constant multiple of this one.

To derive an equilibrium version of the transversality condition (26.19b), we use the market clearing condition $c_t = y$ for all t, and the definition of inflation in equation (26.21):

$$\frac{p_{t+T}}{p_t} = \pi_{t+1} \cdots \pi_{t+T} = (1 + \mu)^T \frac{m_t}{m_{t+T}} \qquad (26.26)$$

Then equation (26.19b) becomes

$$\lim_{T \to \infty} \left[\left(\frac{\beta}{1 + \mu} \right)^T \frac{m_{t+T}}{m_t} w_c(y, m_{t+T}) \right] = 0 \qquad \forall t \qquad (26.27)$$

for a general utility function, and simplifies further to

$$\lim_{T \to \infty} \prod_{s=1}^{T-1} \left[1 - \frac{v'(m_{t+s})}{u'(y)} \right] = 0 \qquad \forall t \qquad (26.28)$$

if the instantaneous utility function is additively separable, as in equation (26.17b).

From the fundamental difference equation (26.22), any competitive equilibrium satisfies

$$\frac{m_{t+1}}{m_t} = \frac{1 + \mu}{\beta} \frac{w_c(y, m_t) - w_m(y, m_t)}{w_c(y, m_{t+1})}$$

Iterating this relation forward, we obtain

$$\left(\frac{\beta}{1 + \mu} \right)^T \frac{m_{t+T}}{m_t} = \prod_{s=t}^{T-1} \frac{w_c(y, m_s) - w_m(y, m_s)}{w_c(y, m_{s+1})} \qquad (26.29)$$

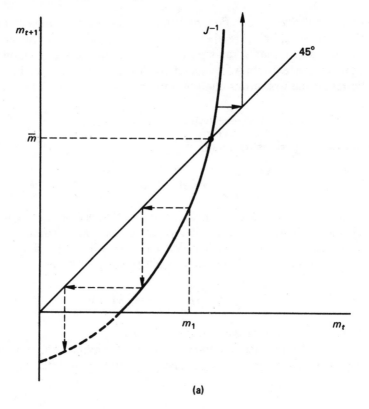

(a)

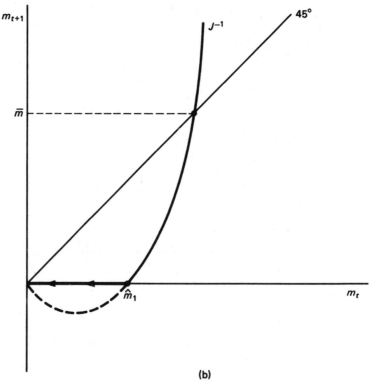

(b)

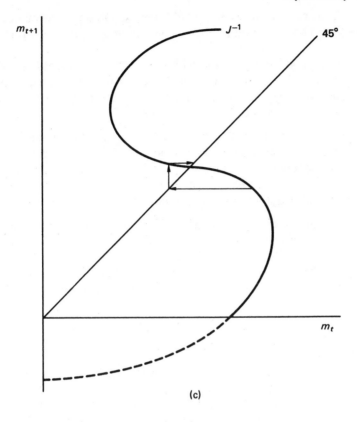

(c)

Figure 26.3 Monetary dynamics with infinitely lived households:
(a) $\lim_{m \to 0} mw_c(y, m) > 0$; (b) $\lim_{m \to 0} mw_c(y,m) = 0$.

Hyperdeflationary sequences (m_t) that start at $m_1 > \bar{m}$ allow money balances to grow without bound. For sufficiently large t, this explosive growth satiates the representative household, driving the marginal utility of money to zero as assumed in equation (26.17c). Equation (26.29) then yields for any large t

$$\left(\frac{\beta}{1 + \mu}\right)^T \frac{m_{t+T}}{m_t} = \prod_{s=t}^{T-1} \frac{w_c(y, m_s)}{w_c(y, m_{s+1})}$$

$$= \frac{w_c(y, m_t)}{w_c(y, m_T)}$$

This equation implies that the left-hand side of equation (26.27) equals $w_c(y, m)$ for sufficiently large m and therefore

$$\lim_{T \to \infty} \left[\left(\frac{\beta}{1 + \mu}\right)^T \frac{m_{t+T}}{m_t} w_c(y, m_{t+T}) \right] = \lim_{m \to \infty} w_c(y, m)$$

for large t. The transversality condition (26.27) then denies hyperdeflationary sequences (m_t) the property of competitive equilibrium if, for each $y > 0$,

$$\lim_{m \to \infty} w_c(y, m) > 0 \qquad (26.30)$$

In other words, if the representative household is not satiated with consumption goods as its money holdings become infinite, then an unbounded sequence (m_t) cannot be an equilibrium.

As an example, consider a household with the additively separable instantaneous utility of equation (26.17b). Here $w_c(y, m) = u'(y) > 0$ satisfies inequality (26.30), ruling out all competitive equilibria other than the steady state itself. We summarize our results in a statement essentially due to Brock (1974, 1975).

Theorem 26.4 Suppose that the representative consumer's utility function satisfies the boundary conditions of equation (26.27) and inequality (26.30) and, furthermore, that $mw_c(y, m)$ is an increasing function of m for each $y > 0$. Then neither hyperinflationary nor hyperdeflationary equilibria exist; the unique steady state $\bar{m}$ described in theorem 26.3 is the only competitive equilibrium.

All solutions to the difference equation (26.22) other than the stationary one diverge towards the *infeasible range* of negative money balances or towards an *explosive path* that violates the transversality restriction (26.27). What economic mechanism causes these solutions to diverge? Recall the definition of the inflation factor from the marginal rate of substitution between consumption at two successive dates; then

$$\rho_t = \frac{w_c(y, m_t)}{\beta w_c(y, m_{t+1})} \tag{26.31}$$

Using equations (26.21) and (26.31), we rewrite equation (26.22) as follows:

$$w_c(y, m_t) = R_t[w_c(y, m_t) - w_m(y, m_t)] \tag{26.32}$$

where $R_t = \pi_{t+1}\rho_t$ is the *nominal* interest factor. This equation suggests that the equilibrium marginal rate of substitution between current consumption and money balances is

$$\frac{w_m(y, m_t)}{w_c(y, m_t)} = 1 - \frac{1}{R_t} \tag{26.33}$$

Assuming that money is a normal good and inequalities (26.24a) and (26.24b) hold, the left-hand side of equation (26.33) is a decreasing function of m which varies in the interval $[0, 1]$. Hence we may solve equation (26.33) by expressing the demand for real balances as a function of the nominal interest rate:

$$m_t = L(R_t) \tag{26.34}$$

where L is a decreasing function mapping the interval $[1, \infty]$ into positive numbers. At the steady state we have

$$\bar{m} = L(\bar{R}) \quad (\bar{R}) \equiv \frac{1 + \mu}{\beta} \tag{26.35}$$

Suppose now that the economy finds itself at $m_t < \bar{m}$. Because L is a decreasing function,

$$m_t < \bar{m} \Leftrightarrow R_t > \bar{R}$$

$$\Leftrightarrow \frac{1 + \mu}{\beta} < (1 + \mu)\frac{m_t \rho_t}{m_{t+1}}$$

$$\Leftrightarrow m_{t+1} < \beta\rho_t m_t$$

$$\Leftrightarrow m_{t+1}w_c(y, m_{t+1}) < m_t w_c(y, m_t) \qquad \text{from equation (26.31)}$$

$$\Leftrightarrow m_{t+1} < m_t \qquad \text{if} \quad mw_c(y, m) \text{ is increasing in } m.$$

Hence $m_t < \bar{m}$ implies $m_{t+1} < m_t$ and the solution (m_t) diverges. A similar argument shows that $m_t > \bar{m}$ leads to $m_{t+1} > m_t$.

What should we conclude from theorem 26.4? The circumstances for which it holds are so restrictive as to exclude all genuinely dynamical equilibria. Dynamical equilibria, however, exist in the larger-dimensional state space of economies with production. The Sidrauski model, which analyzes the joint processes of holding money, consuming, and accumulating capital, possesses a unique saddle and a nontrivial stable manifold; questions IV.16 and IV.17 introduce readers to this model.

26.4 Infinite lives: multiple equilibria (*)

Wilson (1979) suggested another way to enlarge the set of equilibria in a monetary pure-exchange economy with a representative immortal household: drop the assumption that the function $mw_c(y, m)$ is increasing in m. This permits a locally decreasing solution $m_{t+1} = J^{-1}(m_t)$ to the difference equation (26.22), as illustrated in figure 26.3(c), which, in turn, raises the possibility of an asymptotically stable steady state or of periodic equilibria about $\bar{m}$. We illustrate what is possible here with an example due to Matsuyama (1991).

The starting point of the example is an instantaneous utility function of the form

$$w(c, m) = \frac{(c^{1/2}m^{1/2})^{1-\sigma}}{1 - \sigma} \qquad \sigma > 0, \quad \sigma \neq 1 \tag{26.36}$$

in which the parameter σ is the reciprocal of the intertemporal elasticity of substitution between current and future values of the commodity "aggregate" $(cm)^{1/2}$. For this specification, equation (26.22) of the previous section simplifies to

$$m_{t+1}^{-\alpha} = \frac{1 + \mu}{\beta} m_t^{-\alpha}\left(1 - \frac{y}{m_t}\right) \tag{26.37a}$$

In this equation we restrict the parameter σ to exceed 3 or, equivalently, we assume

$$\alpha \equiv (\sigma - 3)/2 > 0 \tag{26.37b}$$

Next we define the normalized variable $x_t = y/m_t$ and rewrite equation (26.37a) in the form

$$x_{t+1}^{\alpha} = \frac{1 + \mu}{\beta} x_t^{\alpha}(1 - x_t) \tag{26.37c}$$

which resembles a logistic equation more closely than we might at first suspect. This equation has a unique positive steady state

$$\bar{x} = 1 - \frac{\beta}{1 + \mu} \in (0, 1) \tag{26.38}$$

Substituting equation (26.38) into (26.37c) and taking roots we obtain the map

$$x_{t+1} = x_t \left(\frac{1 - x_t}{1 - \bar{x}}\right)^{1/\alpha} \equiv f(x_t) \tag{26.39}$$

The map f is defined only for $x_t \in [0, 1]$ and satisfies $f(0) = f(1) = 0$; it is a *unimodal* or single-peaked map, increasing in the interval $[0, \hat{x})$, attaining a maximum at $\hat{x} = (\sigma - 3)/(\sigma - 1)$, and decreasing in the interval $(\hat{x}, 1]$. Its slope exceeds unity at $x = 0$, is less than unity at the fixed point $\bar{x}$. After a little algebra, we can show that

$$f(\hat{x}) \leq 1 \Leftrightarrow \frac{(\sigma - 3)^{\sigma-3}}{(\sigma-1)^{\sigma-1}} \leq \left(\frac{1 - \bar{x}}{2}\right)^2 \tag{26.40}$$

Given this inequality, the function f maps the interval $[0, 1]$ into itself, exactly like the logistic map. In fact, f *is* the logistic map if $\sigma = 5$ which means $\alpha = 1$. Figure 26.4 illustrate some of the possibilities which are familiar to us from Part I.

The dynamical behavior of trajectories in the neighborhood of $\bar{x}$ depends on the size and sign of the derivative.

$$f'(\bar{x}) = 1 - \frac{\bar{x}}{\alpha(1 - \bar{x})} = 1 - \frac{1 + \mu - \beta}{\alpha\beta} \tag{26.41}$$

In particular, we check straightaway that

$$\begin{align}
f'(\bar{x}) \in (0, 1) \quad &\Leftrightarrow \quad 1 + \mu - \beta < \alpha\beta \tag{26.42a} \\
f'(\bar{x}) \in (-1, 0) \quad &\Leftrightarrow \quad \alpha\beta < 1 + \mu - \beta < 2\alpha\beta \tag{26.42b} \\
f'(\bar{x}) < -1 \quad &\Leftrightarrow \quad 1 + \mu - \beta > 2\alpha\beta \tag{26.42c}
\end{align}$$

Using the definition of α in equation (26.37b) we rewrite these inequalities in terms of the fundamental parameters μ, β, σ:

$$\begin{align}
f'(\bar{x}) \in (0, 1) \quad &\Leftrightarrow \quad 1 + \mu < \beta(\sigma - 1)/2 \tag{26.43a} \\
f'(\bar{x}) \in (-1, 0) \quad &\Leftrightarrow \quad \beta(\sigma - 1)/2 < 1 + \mu < \beta(\sigma - 2) \tag{26.43b} \\
f'(\bar{x}) < -1 \quad &\Leftrightarrow \quad \beta(\sigma - 2) < 1 + \mu \tag{26.43c}
\end{align}$$

Figure 26.5 shows the relevant parameter ranges. For moderate values of μ and large σ, the steady state is a stable node of the type shown in figure 26.4(a). As we move northwest in figure 26.5, we raise μ relative to σ; $\bar{m}$ becomes at first a stable spiral of the sort depicted in figure 26.4(b) and then loses stability along the line $1 + \mu = \beta(\sigma - 2)$ in figure 26.5. Once across that line, the economy undergoes a series of period-doubling bifurcations while spiral equilibrium trajectories, repelled by $\bar{m}$, are attracted by periodic cycles of increasingly larger periodicity. Sufficiently rapid monetary growth combined with relatively small values of σ (high intertemporal elasticity of substitution) results in cycles of period 3 and the emergence of chaotic trajectories. The "chaotic range" that appears in figure 26.5 is a rough approximation of true parameter values.

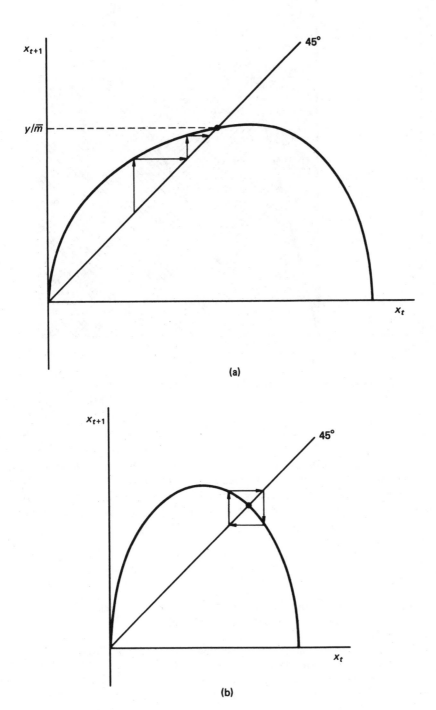

Figure 26.4 Multiple equilibria.

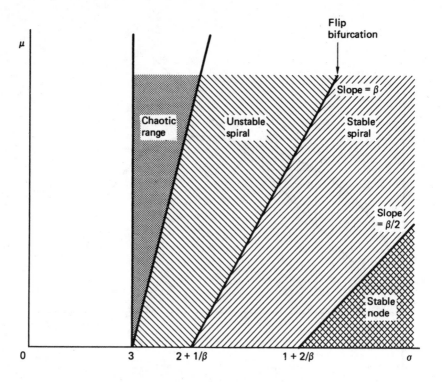

Figure 26.5 Bifurcation diagram for monetary dynamics.

Oscillatory and periodic equilibria are possible in this extended example because the logic of divergence that underlies theorem 26.4 does not apply when $mw_c(y, m)$ is locally a decreasing function of m. Readers who retrace the steps following equation (26.35) will find that $m_t < \bar{m}$ now implies $m_{t+1} > m_t$ rather than $m_{t+1} < m_t$. If, in fact, $mw_c(y, m)$ is a *strongly* decreasing function of m in the neighborhood of $\bar{m}$, then $m_t < \bar{m}$ will lead to $m_{t+1} > \bar{m}$ and to equilibria with damped or periodic fluctuations in the value of real balances.

Notes

1. The existence of a Laffer curve with two branches seems to be consistent with experience during the 1980s from hyperinflationary economies like Bolivia in which real seignorage became negligible.
2. If μ were to be raised from, say, μ_1 to μ_2, the time map in figure 26.3(a) would shift upward, and the transition from the steady state $\bar{m}$ to a lower one $\hat{m} > \bar{m}$ would involve a once-and-for-all *jump* in the inflation factor from the original $(1 + \mu_2)$ to $(1 + \mu_2)(\bar{m}/\hat{m})$ before inflation settled down to its new equilibrium at $(1 + \mu_2)$.

27 Rational expectations

Chapters 27 and 28 explore the impact of uncertainty on outside-money equilibria in pure-exchange economies. Uncertainty about the future forces individuals to make decisions based on forecasts, that is, guesses illuminated by the best information decision-makers can muster. In this chapter and the next, forecasts cease to be point estimates, as they were in chapters 23–26, and become more complicated objects.

Following the seminal work of John Muth (1961) and Robert Lucas (1972), we regard predictions to be random variables whose subjective probability distributions are built from the ground up: they are derived by the forecaster from a *model* of the economy that he or she believes to be in, that is, from a mathematical description of all the factors which, in the opinion of the forecaster, are relevant to the future course of the exogenous variables that he or she needs to predict.

We call *rational expectations* any beliefs that conform to models of rational economic behavior; expectations of this sort extend the concept of perfect foresight to economies with uncertainty. Much of the early work in this area, such as that of Sargent and Wallace (1975), explored the mechanism by which monetary disturbances influence economic activity. The focus of research has since changed towards the economics of information.

Our exploration takes up two chapters for it reflects the two main sources of randomness that economists are interested in: the first is *intrinsic* or *objective* uncertainty about such fundamental economic parameters as preferences, endowments, technology, or economic policy. The second, *extraneous* or *subjective* uncertainty, refers to market psychology and other nonfundamental parameters which may influence current decisions because they condition beliefs about the future.

The distinction between objective or fundamental uncertainty, on the one hand, and subjective or psychological uncertainty, on the other, is a convenient pedagogical device without much operational significance. Neither theory nor practice permits us neatly to categorize exogenous disturbances into two mutually exclusive groups. For example, we do not know how to decompose a movement in stock prices into a revised dividend forecast, which would tend to change the "fundamental" component of a stock price index, and a change in market optimism; there are no reliable and generally available indices of either future dividends or market psychology. Neverthe-less, we divide the material on uncertainty somewhat artificially into two parts: in this chapter we examine objective uncertainty, and the next chapter takes up subjective uncertainty.

Section 27.1, in particular, introduces the concept of rational expectations and reviews the intertemporal theory of choice under uncertainty for finitely lived agents. Section 27.2 defines dynamical rational expectations equilibria in a monetary economy and examines the informational content of prices, that is, their ability to convey new information to traders fully and accurately. In section 27.3 we review the extent to which the neutrality-of-money results derived in section 25.1 under perfect foresight extend to environments with uncertainty, and conclude with a look at economies in which prices are noisy signals transmitting to traders only a fraction of new information.

27.1   Uncertainty

The economy within which we frame our discussion of rational expectations is a stochastic extension of the standard deterministic overlapping generations model of pure exchange with outside money that we have studied extensively in Part IV, most recently in section 25.1. We suppose, in addition, that both population and the rate of money creation are independent identically distributed discrete random variables with probability distributions that are publicly known and do not change over time. In keeping with section 25.1, we assume that currency is injected into this economy in the most neutral possible manner – as interest payments on existing money balances.

Let L_t, the size of generation t, be a discrete random variable with mean unity and a stationary probability distribution; similarly the aggregate stock of currency M_t satisfies

$$M_t = x_t M_{t-1} \tag{27.1}$$

where x_t is also a discrete random variable with mean $\mu > 0$ and a stationary probability distribution. This variable stands for both the gross nominal interest yield on loans and the gross rate of money creation. Following a well-known convention from early search theory (Phelps, 1970), we suppose that traders do not directly observe the currently realized values of these two random variables. In particular, individuals know all *past* realizations of prices, population, and the stock of money, as well as the current money price of the consumption good, which they may use to make inferences about the unobserved *current* values of population and the stock of money.

Early search theory did not mean to deny that advanced industrial economies possess precise information about monetary aggregates or reliable census figures. Rather, the informational conventions we adopt in this section reflect the fact that reliable current information is more expensive to obtain than is dated information. The only source of current information we allow households here is whatever is contained in the price signals which they freely observe in competitive equilibrium.

The old generation does not have to decipher this price message; they simply give up their cash balances in return for as much consumption as the competitive goods market will allow them. Young people have the luxury of learning from the Walrasian auctioneer the price at which trade will occur and *then* deciding how much they wish to save. Any interior solution to the problem of maximizing expected lifetime utility, conditional on the current price, will equate the marginal utility of current consumption with the expected marginal utility of future consumption, conditional again on observed price.

To see why, suppose that p_t is today's realized price for the consumption good, p_{t+1} is a random variable that represents tomorrow's price, and x_{t+1} is another random variable representing tomorrow's proportional currency transfer. Then a young individual who saves an amount s_t at t faces the standard budget constraints

$$c_1^t + s_t = e_1 \qquad c_2^t = e_2 + R_t s_t \qquad (27.2)$$

where $(e_1, e_2) \in \mathbb{R}_+^2$ is a deterministic endowment vector and $R_t = p_t x_{t+1}/p_{t+1}$ is a stochastic rate of return. To choose the value of saving, individuals will maximize the expected value of an additive lifetime utility function $u(c_1^t) + v(c_2^t)$, endowed with the usual smoothness and monotonicity properties. The second term of that function is a *von Neumann–Morgenstern cardinal utility index* that represents choices over consumption lotteries, that is, probability distributions of old-age consumption.[1]

To compute the expected value of lifetime utility

$$u(e_1 - s_t) + \sum_{i=1}^{J} \pi_t^i \, v\,(e_2 + R_t^i s_t)$$

the consumer needs estimates of the probability distribution of the unknown rate of return R_t, that is, the entire array $(R_t^1, \dots, R_t^J)$ of possible realizations together with associated probabilities $(\pi_t^1, \dots, \pi_t^J)$ which must sum to unity. Armed with these estimates, the household chooses a maximal consumption plan from the first-order condition

$$u'(e_1 - s_t) = \sum_{i=1}^{J} \pi_t^i \, R_t^i v'(e_2 + R_t^i s_t) \qquad (27.3)$$

as we guessed two paragraphs ago.

How does a household or firm estimate future rates of return? Where do the probability estimates come from? A key insight of John Muth (1961), destined to become the foundation of the theory of rational expectations, was to postulate that households derived estimates of future prices from a structural model which described the interaction of future supply and demand. In the saving problem of equation (27.3), individuals need to know how p_{t+1}, the future price of the consumption good, interacts with the current price p_t and the future proportional currency transfer variable x_{t+1}.

Suppose, for the time being, that the consumer has learned the joint probability distribution of the random variables (p_{t+1}, x_{t+1}) conditional on all information I_t publicly available at time t which he or she considers relevant to this forecast. Then we may rewrite the first-order condition (27.3) in the form

$$u'(e_1 - s_t) = E\left[\frac{p_t x_{t+1}}{p_{t+1}} \, v'\!\left(e_2 + \frac{p_t x_{t+1}}{p_{t+1}} s_t\right) \middle| I_t\right] \qquad (27.4)$$

where E is a mathematical expectation taken over the variables (x_{t+1}, p_{t+1}) and conditional on the information set

$$I_t = \{I_{t-1}, L_{t-1}, x_{t-1}, p_t, \theta_t\} \qquad (27.5)$$

This set describes the entire history of the economy up to time $t - 1$ plus all information that enters the public domain at t, that is, the values (L_{t-1}, x_{t-1}) of the structural random variables realized at $t - 1$, the current price of the consumption good, plus a vector θ_t of all *other variables the consumer believes will influence future prices*.

To close this model of rational expectations we need to specify the conditional probability distributions held by each household and require that the asset market clear in each state of nature, that is, for each possible value of the information set. The simplest way to do this is to limit ourselves to an economy with a representative household on which we impose a *common-knowledge assumption*. Not only are households identical in endowments and indifference maps but, in addition, it is public knowledge that all of them base their forecasts on some common information set I_t.

Define real per capita currency balances to be

$$m_t = \frac{M_t}{p_t L_t} \tag{27.6a}$$

and observe that the real gross yield on money is

$$R_t = \frac{p_t x_{t+1}}{p_{t+1}} = \frac{m_{t+1}}{m_t} \frac{L_{t+1}}{L_t} \tag{27.6b}$$

A competitive equilibrium satisfies the condition

$$m_t = s_t \qquad \text{for all } I_t \tag{27.7}$$

Substituting this relation into (27.4) we obtain the equation

$$u'(e_1 - m_t) = E\left\{ \frac{m_{t+1}}{m_t} \frac{L_{t+1}}{L_t} v' \left(e_2 + m_{t+1} \frac{L_{t+1}}{L_t} \right) \middle| I_t \right\} \qquad \forall I_t \tag{27.8}$$

Solutions to equation (27.8) are called rational expectations equilibria. A large literature has emerged over the last twenty years[2] analyzing the existence, unique-ness, and other properties of such equilibria in stochastic dynamical macroeconomic models. Among the most interesting of these properties are that (i) some information about the unknown realizations of intrinsic random variables like m_t, L_t, x_t can be extracted by observing the contemporaneous price p_t; and (ii) to some extent equilibrium prices seem to respond not only to objective random variables that define the structure of the economy but also to subjective or psychological variables that need not be directly relevant to economic behavior. We take up these issues in the following two sections.

27.2   The information content of prices

Equation (27.8) of the previous section appears to be a rather straightforward extension of the corresponding relation that prevails under perfect foresight. If, for instance, we were to remove all uncertainty from the economy of the previous section and set $L_{t+1} = (1 + n)L_t$ for all t, then equation (27.8) would reduce to equation (25.1c) of section 25.1 whose zeroes describe the perfect-foresight dynamics of a pure-exchange economy with outside money.

Yet to "solve" equation (27.8) turns out to be a much more difficult undertaking than the study of equation (25.1c). The latter is an ordinary first-order difference equation with a well-known set of solutions and, in particular, a uniquely defined backward solution. Rational expectations equilibria are more complicated objects: they are not sequences of *numbers* but, rather, sequences of *functions*

$$\phi_t: H_t \rightarrow \mathbb{R}_+ \tag{27.9}$$

mapping the set of all possible histories into positive numbers that represent commodity prices. The set H_t of all possible histories contains I_t, that is, all public information up to date t deemed by households to be of economic relevance. Since I_t may contain realizations of random variables from the distant past, the order of the stochastic difference equation (27.8) could easily be higher than one.

Instead of attempting to study *all* sequences of random variables that satisfy (27.8), we focus in what follows on *particular* solutions that make compelling economic sense. To identify such solutions, we must begin with a clear specification of the information set on which individuals condition their forecasts. Lucas (1972) understood this connection early on when he explored stochastic stationary equilibria associated with the information set

$$I_t^* = (I_{t-1}^*, L_{t-1}, x_{t-1}, p_t) \tag{27.10}$$

constructed from equation (27.5) by dropping the vector θ_t of "other relevant variables." One way to simplify the set I_t^* even further is to note that the supply of real balances per capita

$$m_t = \frac{M_t}{p_t L_t} = \frac{M_{t-1}}{p_t} \frac{x_t}{L_t} \tag{27.11}$$

depends on the two random variables acting on the economy through their ratio $z_t \equiv x_t/L_t$ alone. It stands to reason then that price observations will convey information on this ratio; if the commodity price p_t is a monotone function of z_t, then price observations will reveal to traders the *exact value* of the ratio x_t/L_t from which they can infer a conditional probability distribution for either x_t or L_t.

This observational equivalance of p_t and z_t reduces the information set that conditions economic predictions to

$$I_t^0 = \{(L_s, x_s)_{s=1}^{t-1}, x_t/L_t\} \tag{27.12}$$

Solutions to equations (27.8) are then price functions $J_t: \mathbb{R}_+^2 \rightarrow \mathbb{R}_+$ mapping each pair (M_{t-1}, z_t) into commodity prices. Because the set of equilibria does not depend on deterministic changes in the units which measure the stock of currency, we restrict each J_t to be linearly homogeneous in M_{t-1} and write

$$p_t = M_{t-1} \phi_t(z_t) \tag{27.13a}$$

Equivalently, we define $z/\phi_t(z) \equiv \psi_t(z)$ and rewrite (27.13a) in the form

$$p_t = M_{t-1} z_t/\psi_t(z_t) \tag{27.13b}$$

This formulation implies that $m_t = \psi_t(z_t)$ and simplifies equation (27.8) to

$$\psi_t(z_t)u'[e_1 - \psi_t(z_t)] = E\left\{\frac{L_{t+1}}{L_t}\psi_{t+1}(z_{t+1})v'\left[e_2 + \frac{L_{t+1}}{L_t}\psi_{t+1}(z_{t+1})\right]\Big| z_t\right\} \tag{27.14}$$

for all realized values (L_t, x_t). On the right-hand side of equation (27.14) we note that the random variables (L_{t+1}, x_{t+1}) are distributed independently of z_t but the distribution of the unobserved variable L_t may be heavily conditioned on z_t. In particular, a relatively high z_t would typically mean that the conditional expectation of L_t should be *below* its unconditional expected value of unity.

To solve equation (27.14) we need a sequence of real-valued functions $\psi_t: X \to [0, e_1]$, each one of them mapping some subset $X \subset \mathbb{R}_+$ into positive numbers less than e_1. The subset X may be finite, if z is a discrete random variable, or the real line if z is continuous. A conveniently simple form of equation (27.14) is displayed in the following example.

Example 27.1 (Quadratic utility) Suppose as in Azariadis (1981b) that $u(c) = e_1 c - 1/2\, c^2$ and $v(c) = c$. Then equations (27.8) and (27.14) become, respectively,

$$m_t^2 = E\left\{\frac{m_{t+1} L_{t+1}}{L_t}\middle| I_t\right\} \tag{27.15a}$$

$$[\psi_t(z_t)]^2 = E\left\{\psi_{t+1}(z_{t+1})\,\frac{L_{t+1}}{L_t}\,\middle|\, I_t\right\} \tag{27.15b}$$

These two equations are mathematically tractable. We shall take another look at them when we study noisy price equilibria later.

Proceeding with our investigation of rational expectations equilibria, we shall now verify the conjecture that there exists a sequence (ψ_t) of monotone functions that satisfy equation (27.14) and contain useful information about the ratio $z = x/L$ of the unobserved structural random variables. To understand how information is extracted from price signals, we place ourselves in an economy free of monetary uncertainty. Accordingly we assume that the currency transfer variable is deterministic, that is, $x_t = \mu$ with probability 1 for each t, and that L_t is a discrete random variable whose probability distribution is $(L_1, \ldots, L_J)$ with associated probabilities $(\pi_1, \ldots, \pi_J)$. This means that the random variable $z = \mu/L$ has support $(z_1, \ldots, z_J)$ where $z_i = \mu/L_i$ for $i = 1, \ldots, J$.

We seek a stationary solution $\psi_i \equiv \psi(z_i)$ to equation (27.14) which we rewrite in the form

$$u'[e_1 - \psi(z_i)] = E\left\{\frac{\psi(z')}{\psi(z_i)}\,\frac{z_i}{z'}\,v'\left[e_2 + \frac{z_i}{z'}\psi(z_i)\right]\middle|\,z_i\right\} \qquad \forall z_i \tag{27.16}$$

Here z' is the unknown future value of z and z_i is the observed current value. Since z and $\psi(z)$ are *discrete* random variables,[3] equation (27.16) simplifies to

$$\psi_j u'(e_1 - \psi_j) = \sum_{i=1}^{J} \pi_i \psi_i \frac{z_j}{z_i} v'\left(e_2 + \psi_i \frac{z_j}{z_i}\right) \qquad \forall j \tag{27.17}$$

This expression describes compactly a system of J equations in J unknowns $(\psi_1, \ldots, \psi_J)$; a solution $\psi^* = (\psi_1^*, \ldots, \psi_J^*)$ typically exists in which all components of the vector ψ^* are distinct, except for "rare" combinations of endowments and utility functions termed *nongeneric* in general equilibrium theory.[4] Recalling that $p_t =$

$M_{t-1}z_t/\psi(z_t)$, we normalize beginning-of-time currency balances at unity and obtain equilibrium prices

$$p_t^i = \mu' z_t^i / \psi_i^*$$ (27.18)

for the consumption good in state $i = 1, \ldots, J$ at date $t = 1, 2, \ldots$.

What can an inhabitant of this economy learn by observing the equilibrium prices described in equation (27.18)? It is easy to show (see question IV.22) that p_t^i cannot be independent of the state z_i; therefore the consumption good price *fully reveals* the unknown size of the young generation to all traders. Situations of this sort are idealized examples of actual market economies in which price movements carry valuable information about factors determining supply and demand.

When prices convey all relevant information to traders, they are called *sufficient statistics* for the underlying unobservable variables. How a particular price comes to aggregate all the information that is available in a market is an issue of considerable interest in the literature on rational expectations. Actual markets comprise informed and less informed traders, the former being specialists or large volume dealers who expend time and other resources to gather pertinent information from private sources and published reports. If an uninformed agent can learn all there is to know instantaneously by the mere act of trading or even observing quoted prices, what incentive does anyone have to collect information at a cost? What returns are there to acquiring information in the first place?

One way out of this quandary is to admit that prices are *noisy* information signals containing less than perfect information about underlying random variables. Uninformed agents who possess coarser information about these variables than do informed agents gradually become more knowledgeable in the course of trading but pay the "penalty" of earning lower profits.[5] Section 27.3 looks at partly revealing equilibria which convey through prices only a fraction of the total available information.

Before we move on, it is instructive to compute an explicit parametric example of the fully revealing equilibrium displayed in equations (27.17) and (27.18). One parameterization that comes easily to mind is the quadratic utility economy of example 27.1.

Example 27.2 (Quadratic utility, continued) In the economy of example 27.1, suppose that, for all t, $x_t = 1$ with probability 1, and $L_t = L_i$ with probability $\pi_i \in (0, 1)$ for $i = 1, \ldots, J$. We seek a stationary solution to equation (27.15b):

$$\frac{[\psi(z_i)]^2}{z_i} = E\left\{\frac{\psi(z')}{z'}\right\} \qquad \forall i$$ (27.19)

where z' is the future value of the variable $z = 1/L$. Since z is serially uncorrelated, the expected value of the right-hand side of equation (27.19) is independent of z_i. Hence the solution to (27.19) is of the form

$$\psi(z) = \lambda z^{1/2}$$ (27.20a)

for some constant $\lambda > 0$. The value of that constant is found by substituting (27.20a) into (27.19), that is, $\lambda^2 = E(\lambda z^{1/2}/z) \Rightarrow$

$$\lambda = E(z^{1/2})$$ (27.20b)

Equation (27.18) then suggests that the equilibrium price function is

$$p_t = (z_t)^{1/2}/\lambda \qquad (27.21)$$

Inverting this expression, we obtain the formula $L_t = (\lambda p_t)^{-2}$ which infers the size of the young generation of traders from the equilibrium price at which they are willing to exchange currency for the consumption good. A price observation in this economy is informationally equivalent to an accurate census of population!

27.3   The neutrality of money revisited

In this section we explore whether theorem 25.1 and related neutrality-of-money results derived at the start of chapter 25 extend to pure-exchange economies in which the stock of currency is stochastic. The uncertainty we have in mind is of a rather special nature: we fix the population of the economy in section 27.1 to be a deterministic constant normalized to unity and assume that the central bank expands the stock of outside money by paying interest at the gross rate $x_t > 0$ on existing balances. The interest factor x_t, which also equals one plus the rate of monetary growth, is again an independent, identically distributed random variable with mean $\mu > 0$.

Since population is constant, the unobserved random variable x_t may be inferred in any fully revealing equilibrium from the consumption good price p_t. Does a revealing equilibrium exist here? To answer this question, we return to equation (27.14) which reduces to

$$\psi_t(x_t)u'[e_1 - \psi_t(x_t)] = E\{\psi_{t+1}(x_{t+1})v'[e_2 + \psi_{t+1}(x_{t+1})]|x_t\} \qquad (27.22)$$

for the economy at hand. A rational expectations equilibrium is a sequence of functions $\psi_t: [0, e_1] \to \mathbb{R}_+$ which represent per capita real money balances in equilibrium.

As we shall see below, equation (27.22) turns out to have infinitely many solution sequences (ψ_t) even if we fix the initial values of x and ψ. Proportional currency transfers will be neutral in some equilibria and not in others. Not all of these equilibria are equally relevant for economic policymakers or equally compelling in terms of common sense. To discuss them intelligently we need the following definition.

Definition 27.1 Money is neutral relative to a particular solution (ψ_t^*) of equation (27.22) if each ψ_t^* is independent of all realized values of the currency transfer variables up to time t.

For any rational expectations equilibrium with neutral money, both sides of equation (27.22) must be independent of x_t. Since the left-hand side of equation (27.22) is clearly an *increasing function* of ψ_t, all neutral solutions are simply sequences of real numbers, that is, they satisfy

$$\psi_t(x_t) = m_t \qquad \forall t \qquad (27.23)$$

A quick inspection of equation (27.22) suggests that the set of all rational expectations equilibria with the neutrality property is the one we have already described in sections 24.1 and 25.1; it consists of non-negative sequences (m_t) that solve the equation

$m_t = s(m_{t+1}/m_t)$ where s: $\mathbb{R}_+ \to [0, e_1]$, the representative household's saving function, attains positive values for any interest factor that exceeds the autarkic value

$$\bar{R} \equiv u'(e_1)/v'(e_2) \tag{27.24}$$

Stochastic money transfers support the same set of allocations as in the corresponding deterministic-transfers economy of sections 24.1 and 25.1. Currency uncertainty has no allocative side-effects here. Are there any rational expectations equilibria in which monetary uncertainty causes, or at least is correlated with, allocative uncertainty?

One example of non-neutral equilibria of this type is when real balances attain a high value if money transfers exceed some critical value $\bar{x}$, and a low value otherwise. The intuition for this conjecture is the pure-exchange counterpart of the cliché that "businesses invest when money and credit are plentiful, and hold back when money is tight." To simplify matters, let us conjecture an extreme rational expectations equilibrium of the form

$$\begin{aligned}\psi_t &= 0 &&\text{if } x_s < \bar{x} \text{ for some } s = 1, \ldots, t\\&= \bar{m} > 0 &&\text{if } x_s \geqslant \bar{x} \text{ for all } \quad s = 1, \ldots, t\end{aligned} \tag{27.25}$$

The conjecture is that, if the currency transfer variable were to fall below a critical value $\bar{x}$ in some period, then the economy would revert to an inside-money equilibrium in perpetuity. As long as the transfer variable stays above $\bar{x}$, real balances per capita remain fixed at $\bar{m}$.

The pair $(\bar{x}, \bar{m})$ is a rational expectations equilibrium if the sequence (ψ_t) of step functions defined in equation (27.25) satisfies equation (27.22) for all t. To find a suitable pair, note that $\bar{R} < 1$ for any Samuelson economy of the general type we are exploring in this chapter. Now choose an arbitrary fraction $\pi \in [\bar{R}, 1]$ and observe that, for each π, the equation

$$\frac{u'(e_1-m)}{v'(e_2+m)} = \pi \tag{27.26}$$

has a unique solution $\bar{m}(\pi)$ in the interval $[0, s(1)]$ where $s(1)$ is the amount saved by the representative household when the gross yield on loans equals unity. To complete the description of the equilibrium, define the initial value $\bar{x}$ from the equation

$$\pi = \text{prob}(x \geqslant \bar{x}) \tag{27.27}$$

Are the step functions in equation (27.26) indeed a rational expectations equilibrium? Substituting equations (27.25) and (27.27) into (27.22) we obtain

$$\bar{m}u'(e_1 - \bar{m}) = \pi\bar{m}v'(e_2 + m)$$

which is a simple recasting of equation (27.26). We conclude that *there is a continuum of these equilibria, one for each value of the free parameter* π. Question IV.23 asks readers to prove that all outside-money equilibria $(\bar{x}, \bar{m})$ converge almost surely to an inside money equilibrium and money becomes asymptotically worthless.

This particular rational expectations equilibrium does not invite or deserve a closer look; the step function in equation (27.25) makes scant economic sense compared with the neutral solution that preceded it in this section. It does, however, make a compelling metaphor about the power of beliefs that are spread wide among economic decision-makers. Stochastic injections of currency are not neutral in the equilibrium of equation (27.25), even though they are simple interest payments on existing balances, because of a *coordinated belief* that they are not neutral.

We conclude with an example of a rational expectations equilibrium in which prices transmit to uninformed traders only a fraction of the information that is relevant to their welfare. This is typically the case when households trade in a commodity space of lower dimension than the vector of exogenous random variables that influence prices; consumers observe fewer endogenous variables than the number of unknown parameters that they are interested in inferring from these observations. Consequently, prices are not sufficient statistics, revealing to the public only *part* of the information that society as a whole possesses.

Example 27.3 (Partially revealing equilibria with quadratic utility)   In the economy of example 27.1 suppose that (θ_1, θ_2) are two distinct positive numbers such that $\theta_1 < 1 < \theta_2$ and $\theta_1 + \theta_2 = 2$. Let also (L_t, x_t) be identically and independently distributed random variables with the same probability distribution, that is, $x_t = \theta_1$ with probability $1/2$, $x_t = \theta_2$ with probability $1/2$, for all t. Then the ratio variable $z = x/L$ has the distribution $z = \theta_1/\theta_2$ with probability $1/4$, $z = 1$ with probability $1/2$, $z = \theta_2/\theta_1$ with probability $1/4$. Conditional on the value of z, we have

$$L_t = \begin{cases} \theta_2 \text{ with probability 1 if } z_t = \theta_1/\theta_2 \\ \theta_1 \text{ with probability 1 if } z_t = \theta_2/\theta_1 \\ \theta_1 \text{ with probability } 1/2, \theta_2 \text{ with probability } 1/2, \text{ if } z_t = 1 \end{cases} \tag{27.28}$$

We seek a stationary function $\psi(z)$ that satisfies the equilibrium relation (27.15b):

$$[\psi(z_t)]^2 = E\left\{\psi(z_{t+1})L_{t+1}\left(\frac{1}{L_t}\right)\Big|z_t\right\} \qquad \forall z_t \tag{27.29}$$

Since L_t is the only term on the right-hand side of this equation which depends on z_t, we may define a function

$$[M(z)]^2 \equiv E\{(1/L)|z\} \tag{27.30a}$$

and rewrite equation (27.29) in the form

$$[\psi(z_t)]^2 = [M(z_t)]^2 \, E\{\psi(z_{t+1})L_{t+1}\} \qquad \forall z_t \tag{27.29)'}$$

The solution to this equation is clearly proportional to $M(z)$, that is, $\psi(z) = \lambda M(z)$ in which we choose the constant λ to satisfy equation (27.29)'. Then we have the following equilibrium expression for real money balances per capita:

$$\psi(z) = \lambda M(z) \qquad \lambda = E_{x,L}\{LM(z)\} \tag{27.30b}$$

From equation (27.28) it is easy to check that

$$M^2\left(\frac{\theta_1}{\theta_2}\right) = \frac{1}{\theta_2} \qquad M^2(1) = \frac{1}{\theta_1\theta_2} \qquad M^2\left(\frac{\theta_2}{\theta_1}\right) = \frac{1}{\theta_1} \tag{27.31}$$

Therefore $p_t = M_{t-1}z_t/\psi(z_t)$, the equilibrium price of the consumption good in period t, satisfies

$$\frac{p_t}{M_{t-1}} = \frac{\theta_1}{(\theta_2)^{1/2}} \qquad \text{if } z_t = \frac{\theta_1}{\theta_2}$$

$$= (\theta_1\theta_2)^{1/2} \quad \text{if } z_t = 1 \tag{27.32}$$

$$= \frac{\theta_2}{(\theta_1)^{1/2}} \quad \text{if } z_t = \frac{\theta_2}{\theta_1}$$

Prices are *partly revealing* in this example because of what happens at $z_t = 1$. Observing that event conveys *no* information whatsoever about the realized values of (x, L). The probability distributions of (x, L) conditioned on $z = 1$ are simply the unconditional distributions. On the other hand, $z = \theta_1/\theta_2$ reveals that $(x, L) = (\theta_1, \theta_2)$ with probability 1, and $z = \theta_2/\theta_1$ similarly implies that $(x, L) = (\theta_2, \theta_1)$ with probability 1.

Noisy-price equilibria like that in example 27.3 have a property of some historical interest: they feature positively correlated movements between indices of inflation and economic activity that resemble a *Phillips curve*.[6] Question IV.24 asks the reader to compute such a correlation in the economy of example 27.3. Providing a theoretical justification for the Phillips curve was a major objective of early search theory, as one quickly finds by perusing the volume edited by Phelps (1970), and also an inspiration to much of the research on rational expectations throughout the 1970s.

Notes

1. Kreps (1990, ch. 3) describes the contribution and properties of this index and discusses its limitations.
2. See the survey by Grossman (1981) and the two-volume collection of articles edited by Lucas and Sargent (1981).
3. If z is a continuous random variable, recovering the function $\psi(z)$ from equation (27.16) becomes a more complicated affair which generally requires proving that equation (27.16) maps bounded continuous functions $\psi: [0, e_1] \to \mathbb{R}_+$ into bounded continuous functions. Then Schauder's fixed-point theorem ensures the existence of a continuous function ψ^* which solves equation (27.16). For a statement of that theorem, see Stokey and Lucas (1989, p. 520).
4. Radner (1979) and Allen (1981) prove the generic existence of rational expectations equilibria in atemporal general equilibria with finitely many commodities.
5. This argument is due to Grossman and Stiglitz (1980). Other key papers on information aggregation are surveyed in Radner (1982).
6. Named after the New Zealand engineer and economist T. W. Phillips (1958) who uncovered that British data before 1939 displayed a negative correlation between the unemployment and wage inflation rates. Similar correlations were found later in many other countries and time periods, but the correlation proved to be unstable in the 1960s and 1970s.

28   Market psychology

28.1   The role of shared beliefs

Celestial objects move through the sky on orbits determined by their gravitational interaction with other bodies. The resulting motion often displays remarkable regularity and predictability, conforming in many cases to the fairly simple systems of differential equations one studies in classical mechanics. The solutions of these equations enable astronomers to predict many years hence the position of a particular planet relative to the Earth. Why are economists unable to forecast the capital–labor ratio, per capita gross national product (GNP) and other state variables for dynamic economies as far into the future and as confidently as astronomers predict the stars?

One obvious reason is that the external forces acting on an economy are far less regular and fathomable than the gravitational field within our solar system. To make *unconditional* predictions of per capita GNP for, say, Bangladesh in the year 2020 requires guessing a large number of parameters which, as a first approximation, may be regarded as completely random: population growth, emigration, monsoon patterns in the Bay of Bengal, actions of the national government or its main trading patterns. As a practical matter, none of these factors is predictable far in advance.

It seems fairer to compare the forecasting ability of celestial mechanics with *conditional* economic predictions made under specific numerical assumptions about the future course of the relevant exogenous variables. One way to proceed is to insert whatever values of these exogenous variables were observed over some time period into a particular structural econometric model and measure how well that model fits time-series data from the same period. A particular case in point is recent empirical work on stock market prices.[1]

Starting with the seminal work of Shiller (1981), empirical research in financial markets has built up a substantial body of evidence that casts some doubt on the *efficient markets* hypothesis.[2] Loosely speaking, this hypothesis states that asset prices fully reflect all publicly available information relevant to portfolio holders, especially information about future returns. Asset prices, however, tend to fluctuate considerably more than one would expect from the volatility of their fundamental determinants; by one of Shiller's measures stock prices very five times as much as one might expect from fluctuations in dividends and interest rates.

What causes this overaction, or "excess volatility," of asset prices to changes in fundamentals? One explanation of the evidence is that asset prices contain a volatile but not necessarily explosive bubble term that may be driven by market psychology. The idea can be traced to Pigou (1929) who conjectured that half the amplitude of observed cyclical fluctuations was due to psychological factors and autonomous changes in the quantity of money. Since then we have learned that common stock returns are positively correlated at high frequencies and that their bubble component or "excess return" (that is, the difference between the price of a stock and the expected discounted value of the relevant dividend sequence) is weakly negatively correlated with, and hence helps predict, future stock returns.[3] None of these findings conforms to the theory of efficient markets which requires rational price predictions to be uncorrelated with forecast errors.

According this body of empirical evidence the weight it seems to deserve leaves in a quandary economists who like "structural" explanations of short-term fluctuations. If market sentiment indeed controls the bubbles that drive asset price fluctuations, what lies behind swings in market sentiment? The financial markets literature is at a loss before this question which appears at first blush to belong in the field of group psychology. Shiller (1989, p. 1), for instance, suggests that prices change because the public capriciously changes its mind. Others rely on irrational trading by small "fringe" investors to sustain measured volatility in asset prices.[4] Here the financial markets literature reflects Keynes (1936), especially the discussion on "the state of long-term expectation" contained in chapter 12 of the *General Theory*.

Keynes coined this phrase to describe the confidence businessmen put in their own forecasts and, in particular, to capture the likelihood of a large forecast error. Confidence in forecasts was low in volatile or abnormal times of rapid changes in the economic environment during which business decisions became sensitive to what Keynes called "waves of pessimism and optimism." In such times, economic prediction was conducted as a beauty contest with each judge voting not for the contestant they deemed most eligible but, rather, for the one they think will attract the votes of *other* judges. Keynes believed that investment decisions were often driven by "animal spirits" rather than sober calculations of profitability, and rejected forecasts based on mathematical expectations because he thought that the future was not measurable.

As we shall see in the remainder of this section, as well as in sections 28.3 and 28.4, excess volatility in prices or quantities is not hard to reconcile with traditional postulates of rational prediction and maximizing behavior, especially under realistic assumptions about demography and market structure. The easiest way to fathom excess volatility in a fully specified economic environment is to think of it in its most extreme form: an endogenous stochastic fluctuation in asset prices that takes place even though market fundamentals remain unchanged.

Unforced oscillations of this general type are by now familiar to the reader under such names as "periodic" and "chaotic" equilibria but remain virtually unknown in finance.[5] They are best understood as fluctuations about an unstable steady state or as recurrent random movements between several deterministic equilibria. The following paragraphs review some examples of stochastic endogenous fluctuations in a fairly standard pure-exchange overlapping expectations economy. All these examples, and the ones in the remaining sections of this chapter, are dynamical rational expectations equilibria which satisfy a vector difference equation of the form

$$E\{x_{t+1}|I_t\} = f(x_t, \mu_t) \qquad (28.1)$$

In equation (28.1) μ_t is the realization of the possibly random parameter vector drawn from a well-defined unchanging parameter space; x_t is the value of the state vector realized at t; f is an appropriately defined continuous nonlinear map; and the left-hand side is the mathematical expectation of the state vector at $t + 1$ conditional on a common information set I_t. This set captures the entire history of the economy up to $t - 1$, contains x_t and is publicly known to be the set on which all forecasts are based.

For a while economists hoped, somewhat mysteriously, that expectations formed according to the true laws of motion of an economy would eliminate whatever degrees of freedom were contained in arbitrary prediction and help pin down the equilibrium uniquely. As has already been demonstrated in section 26.3, these hopes were not justified. Among the first to question them was Taylor (1977) who pointed out in an early paper that, given the history of an economy up to time t, equation (28.1) determines only the expected value of the state vector at $t + 1$, leaving higher amounts indeterminate. Suppose for instance that ε_t is an arbitrary random variable independently and identically distributed on a narrow interval $[-a, a]$ about zero, with zero mean. Then infinitely many solutions to equation (28.1) exist with the general form

$$x_{t+1} = f(x_t, \mu_t) + \varepsilon_{t+1} \tag{28.2}$$

If the economy described in (28.1) has a stationary deterministic structure of population, endowments, preferences, and production sets, then the parameter vector μ_t is a constant. Any randomness remaining in the solution (28.2) must come from extraneous or psychological factors for which David Cass and Karl Shell (1980) have invented the convenient name "sunspots." The name is borrowed from Jevons (1884) who used it for quite a different purpose: he believed that solar activity influenced climate conditions and hence affected farm output.

For a simple demonstration of a dynamical sunspot equilibrium we return to example 27.1. Assuming that population is a deterministic constant, say $L_t = 1$ for all t, and that the information set I_t contains the current real value of money m_t, we simplify equation (27.15) to

$$m_t^2 = E\{m_{t+1}|m_t\} \tag{28.3}$$

Any sequence $(\tilde{m}_t)$ of random variables defined on the interval $[0, e_1]$ and satisfying equation (28.3) is a rational expectations equilibrium. Among these we count sequences of positive real numbers that solve the deterministic difference equation

$$m_t^2 = m_{t+1} \tag{28.3'}$$

Readers who recall the material on the neutrality of money from section 27.3 will recognize deterministic solutions to (28.3) as those that prevent interest payments on money from having any influence on equilibrium allocations.

One class of sunspot solutions to equation (28.3) is due to Peck (1988) and Azariadis and Guesnerie (1986). Starting with two arbitrary numbers $\theta \in (0, 1)$ and $q_1 > 1$, define the scalar sequences $(q_t)_{t=2}^{\infty}$ and $(\pi_t)_{t=2}^{\infty}$ recursively from the equations

$$q_{t+1} = \frac{q_t^2}{\theta} \qquad \pi_{t+1} = \frac{1-\theta}{q_t^2-\theta} \tag{28.4}$$

Note that $q_{t+1} > q_t > 1 > \theta$ for all t, which implies $\pi_t \in (0, 1)$ for $t = 1, 2, \ldots$. Then it is easy to verify that the sequence $(\tilde{m}_t)$ of random variables with realizations

$$m_t = 1 \qquad \text{if } m_{t-1} = 1$$

$$m_t = \begin{cases} 1/q_t & \text{with probability} \quad 1 - \pi_t \\ 1 & \text{with probability} \quad \pi_t \end{cases} \quad \text{if } m_{t-1} \neq 1$$

is a sunspot equilibrium, that is, a stochastic solution to equation (28.3). This solution converges to the outside-money steady state $m = 1$ with some probability $Q \in (0, 1)$, and to the inside-money steady state $m = 0$ with probability $1 - Q$.

Another class of dynamical equilibria, due to Cass and Shell (1983), regards a sunspot equilibrium as a *lottery on multiple deterministic equilibria*. A typical instance is an outside-money equilibrium in an economy with a representative household whose offer curve bends backward like the phaseline in figure 24.1(d). Here the quadratic utility function that underlies equation (28.3) is of no use for it is associated with a monotone offer curve. Instead, we should think of a more general deterministic difference equation

$$m_t = s(m_{t+1}/m_t) \tag{28.5}$$

which has a unique backward-looking solution but not a unique forward-looking one.

Suppose, in particular, that two or more solution sequences to equation (28.5) are associated with the *same* initial condition: $(m_1, m_2, m_3, ...)$ and $(m_1, m'_2, m'_3, ...)$ both satisfy that equation and $m_s \neq m'_s$ for some $s > 1$. Then it is easy to verify that a third solution sequence exists as well, $(m_1, \tilde{m}_2, \tilde{m}_3, ...)$, which just mixes the first two. For any $t \geq 2$, $\tilde{m}_t$ is a random variable with realizations

$$\tilde{m}_t = \begin{cases} m_t & \text{with probability} \quad \pi \\ m_t^1 & \text{with probability} \quad 1 - \pi \end{cases}$$

where $\pi \in [0,1]$ is an arbitrary probability.

To see why the mixture is indeed an equilibrium, let $u(c_1, c_2)$ be the utility function of the representative consumer and (e_1, e_2) be the corresponding endowment vector. Since m_1 is the equilibrium flow of saving by generation 1 when the competitive gross rate of return is $R_1 = m_2/m_1$ as well as $R'_1 = m'_2/m_2$, it follows that one number, $s = m_1$, solves two distinct consumer problems:

$$m_1 = \underset{0 \leq s \leq e_1}{\text{argmax}} \; u(e_1 - s, e_2 + R_1 s) \tag{28.6}$$

$$= \underset{0 \leq s \leq e_1}{\text{argmax}} \; u(e_1 - s, e_2 + R'_1 s)$$

By the same token, m_1 must also maximize *any* convex combination of the two utility functions that appear on the right-hand side of (28.6), that is,

$$m_1 = \underset{0 \leq s \leq e_1}{\text{argmax}} \; [\pi u(e_1 - s, e_2 + R_1 s) + (1 - \pi)u(e_1 - s, e_2 + R'_1 s)] \tag{28.7}$$

for any $\pi \in [0,1]$. Hence m_1 is an equilibrium flow of saving consistent with the following rational expectations of future returns:

$$\tilde{R} = R \text{ with probability } \pi, \; \tilde{R} = R' \text{ w.p. } 1 - \pi$$

where $R = m_2/m_1$ and $R' = m'_2/m_1$.

Sunspots in this example are the random factors that choose one specific realization from the underlying deterministic equilibria. Because the number π is arbitrary, there is a continuum of sunspot equilibria.

To maintain some discipline on the great variety of possible equilibria, we ignore dynamical sunspot equilibria in what follows. We concentrate instead on a particular type of strongly regular equilibria that resemble stochastic periodic orbits.

28.2   Stationary sunspot equilibria

The reasons we are interested in sunspot equilibria range beyond excess volatility in asset prices into speculative and business cycle phenomena in which prices and economic activity fluctuate randomly even if there is very little discernible movement in the fundamentals of the economy.[6] Evidence on the economic influence of psychological factors predates recent empirical work on asset prices by serveral centuries; the Dutch "tulip mania," the South Sea bubble in England, and the collapse of the Mississippi Company in France are three well-documented cases of speculative price movements which economic historians regard as unwarranted by fundamental conditions.[7]

In this section we study stochastic equilibria driven by market sentiment in which the effect of beliefs that individuals hold about their environment does not vanish asymptotically, as it does when price bubbles burst; we call these "stationary" sunspot equilibria. Specifically, we explore economies whose random state variable has a Markov structure with two states of nature; a random variable has the Markov property if its probability distribution is conditional on its realization last period but otherwise remains independent of events in the more distant past. Stationarity in this extended sense is worth our attention because (i) stationary beliefs are likely to be the asymptotic outcome of many well-defined learning processes like those surveyed in section 28.4; and (ii) it helps us understand how the set of stationary equilibria is enlarged by the sunspot hypothesis.

The framework we shall use is the familiar deterministic overlapping generations pure-exchange economy of the Samuelson type with outside money: it contains a constant nominal stock of currency (normalized to unity), a constant population of identical two-period-lived households endowed with a vector $e = (e_1, e_2)$ of the single nonproduced consumption good, a standard well-behaved utility function $u: \mathbb{R}_+^2 \to \mathbb{R}$, and an autarkic interest factor $\bar{R} = u_1(e)/u_2(e) < 1$. All the fundamental building blocks of this economy are deterministic.

Sunspot equilibria are perfectly correlated with stochastic natural events that do not affect the endowment or indifference map of any individual. Consider a random variable θ that takes on two values: either sunspot activity (a) or absence of sunspot activity (b). The occurrence of a and b is governed by a Markov process with the following stationary transition probability matrix:

$$\Pi = \begin{pmatrix} \pi_{aa} & \pi_{ba} \\ \pi_{ab} & \pi_{bb} \end{pmatrix} \tag{28.8}$$

For $i = a, b$ and $j = a, b$, an element π_{ij} of this matrix denotes the probability that sunspot activity will be i tomorrow given that it is j today.

Suppose now that all households believe in a perfect and stationary correlation of future prices with sunspot activity: in other words, all individuals forecast future price to be $p = \phi(i)$, for $i = (a, b)$, if i occurs tomorrow. A stationary sunspot equilibrium (SSE) is a rational expectations equilibrium in which the forecast is validated by actual price behavior. Before we proceed to define this concept, let us describe savings plans for households facing stochastic rates of return.

Recall first the deterministic savings function

$$s(R) = \text{argmax}_s \, u(e_1 - s, e_2 + Rs) \qquad (28.9)$$

and define its stochastic extension

$$z(R, \pi) = \text{argmax}_z \, [\pi u(e_1 - z, e_2 + z) + (1 - \pi)u(e_1 - z, e_2 + Rz)] \qquad (28.10)$$

which describes the amount saved by a household when the gross yield is 1 with probability π and R with probability $1 - \pi$. The stochastic saving function z is a simple deformation of its deterministic counterpart s; in fact, $z(R, 0) = s(R)$ for all $R > 0$, and $z(R, \pi)$ lies between $s(R)$ and $s(1)$ for all R and π.[8]

The two savings functions are related also through their interest elasticities. Letting $\epsilon(R)$ denote the interest factor elasticity of the saving function s and $\eta(R,\pi)$ be the corresponding elasticity of the function z, then we obtain (see question IV.29) the relation

$$\eta(1,\pi) = (1 - \pi)\epsilon(1) \qquad (28.11)$$

The existence of stationary sunspot equilibria

A stationary sunspot equilibrium (SSE) is a quadruple $(p_a, p_b, \pi_{aa}, \pi_{bb})$ of positive numbers with the property that the probabilities π_{aa} and π_{bb} lie in the open interval $(0, 1)$; the state-contingent commodity prices $p_a \neq p_b$ are distinct; and the excess demand for the consumption good is zero for each current state, that is,

$$D^a \equiv \frac{1}{p_a} - z\left(\frac{p_a}{p_b}, \pi_{aa}\right) = 0 \qquad (28.12a)$$

$$D^b \equiv \frac{1}{p_b} - z\left(\frac{p_b}{p_a}, \pi_{bb}\right) = 0 \qquad (28.12b)$$

An SSE obtains with respect to a given matrix Π if the numbers π_{aa}, π_{bb} in our definition are diagonal elements of the matrix Π. If event a (respectively b) occurs in the present period, p_a (respectively p_b) is actually the equilibrium price by equations (28.12a) and (28.12b). The beliefs $p_a = \phi(a)$, $p_b = \phi(b)$ are then self-fulfilling.

Note also that the definition requires both $p_a \neq p_b$ and $\pi_{aa} \in (0, 1)$, $\pi_{bb} \in (0, 1)$. If $p_a = p_b$, an SSE degenerates to a stationary equilibrium of the golden rule type. Another type of degeneracy obtains when certain transitions are ruled out in the matrix Π. In particular, when $\pi_{aa} = 0$, $\pi_{bb} = 0$, the event a (respectively b) today ensures the occurrence of b (respectively a) tomorrow. In other words, the equilibrium prices p_a and p_b *necessarily* succeed each other. An SSE then reduces to a two-cycle, as we can see from equations (28.12a) and (28.12b): two-cycles thus appear as *degenerate sunspot* equilibria associated with a degenerate 2×2 matrix Π that has zeros on the diagonal.

What is a set of conditions sufficient to ensure the existence of an SSE? To find out, we put $w = p_a/p_b$ and define the following continuous single-valued function:

$$F(w, \pi_{aa}) = wz(w, \pi_{aa}) - z(1/w, \pi_{bb}) \qquad (28.13)$$

An SSE exists if, and only if, F has a positive root $w \neq 1$ for some $\pi_{aa} \in (0, 1)$ and $\pi_{bb} \in (0, 1)$. This is so because any SSE satisfying (28.12a) and (28.12b) for some $p_a \neq p_b$, also satisfies $1/w = z(w, \pi_{aa})/z(1/w, \pi_{bb})$, and therefore $F(\bullet) = 0$. Moreover, for any positive root $w \neq 1$ of F, we can find two positive numbers p_a and p_b such that (28.12a) and (28.12b) hold true. For each $(\pi_{aa}, \pi_{bb}) > 0$, $w = 1$ is obviously a root of F; somewhat less obviously (see question IV.30) we have

$$\lim_{w \to \infty} F = \infty \qquad (28.14a)$$
$$F < 0 \text{ for small enough } w > 0 \qquad (28.14b)$$

Armed with these properties of the function F, it is easy to see that F has a root other than unity, and hence an SSE exists, if F is negatively sloped at $w = 1$. Figure 28.1 illustrates. Using equation (28.11) we obtain the relevant partial derivative evaluated at $w = 1$:

$$\begin{aligned} F_w(1, \pi_{aa}, \pi_{bb}) &= s(1)[1 + \eta(1, \pi_{aa}) + \eta(1, \pi_{bb})] \\ &= s(1)[1 + \epsilon(1)(2 - \pi_{aa} - \pi_{bb})] \end{aligned}$$

Hence,

$$F_w(1, \pi_{aa}, \pi_{bb}) < 0 \text{ if } (2 - \pi_{aa} + \pi_{bb})\epsilon(1) < -1 \qquad (28.15a)$$

Both inequalities are violated if $\epsilon(1) \geq 0$. Then (28.15a) directly implies the following sufficient condition for the existence of a two-state SSE.[9]

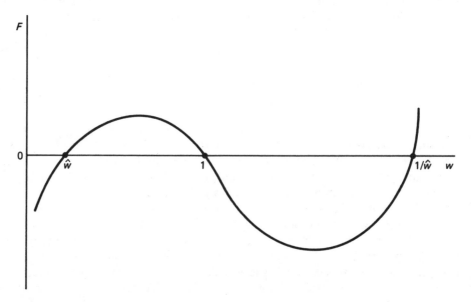

Figure 28.1 Existence of sunspot equilibrium.

Theorem 28.1 Suppose that the utility function satisfies regularity assumptions on differentiability, concavity, and boundary behavior. Then a sufficient condition for the existence of a sunspot equilibrium with respect to a given Markovian transition probability matrix Π is

$$\epsilon(1) < 0 \qquad \pi_{aa} + \pi_{bb} < \frac{1}{|\epsilon(1)|} \qquad (28.15b)$$

This theorem applies directly to the existence of two-cycles which are degenerate SSEs with zeros on the diagonal of the transition matrix Π. The outcome is a restatement of what we already know from chapter 9: a two-cycle exists if the outside-money steady state loses stability in the backward sense or gains stability in the forward sense.

Corollary If $\epsilon(1) < -1/2$, then there exists a periodic equilibrium with period 2.

From the definition of the function F we note that its roots appear in pairs: if $\hat{w}$ solves $F = 0$, then so does $1/\hat{w}$. SSEs then must occur in pairs as well; in particular,

$$\left(\frac{1}{p_a}, \frac{1}{p_b}\right) = \left(z(\hat{w}, \pi_{aa}), \ z\left(\frac{1}{\hat{w}}, \pi_{bb}\right)\right) \qquad (28.16a)$$

is one SSE, and

$$\left(\frac{1}{p_a}, \frac{1}{p_b}\right) = \left(z\left(\frac{1}{\hat{w}}, \pi_{aa}\right), \ z(\hat{w}, \pi_{bb})\right) \qquad (28.16b)$$

is another.

Theorem 28.1 identifies a subset of all two-state transition probability matrices for which SSEs exist. This subset is marked by the shaded area in figure 28.2, where

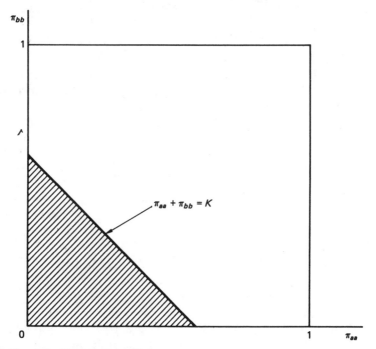

Figure 28.2 The set of sunspot equilibria.

$K = 2 - 1/|\epsilon(1)|$. The whole set of these matrices coincides with the unit square, and the origin represents the degenerate matrix associated with deterministic two-cycles. It seems obvious now that some connection should exist between strictly periodic equilibria and stationary sunspot equilibria which are, after all, stochastic periodic orbits.

Sunspots and cycles

Since periodic equilibria with period $p \geq 2$ are a degenerate special case of an SSE with p states, common sense suggests that an economy with a periodic equilibrium should also admit an SSE with the corresponding number of states, but the converse should not hold. In other words, we cannot expect an economy that has an SSE with $p \geq 2$ states necessarily to possess a periodic equilibrium with period p. This intuition is formalized in a result due to Guesnerie (1986).

Theorem 28.2 Stationary sunspot equilibria with $p \geq 2$ states generically exist in the neighborhood of a periodic orbit with period p.

A proof of this proposition relies on continuity; periodic orbits of the general form $(x_1, \dots, x_p)$ are SSE whose $p \times p$ transition probability matrices have rows with all but one entries equal to zero and a single entry equal to unity. The general form of these matrices is

$$
\tilde{\Pi} = \begin{pmatrix}
0 & 1 & 0 & \dots & 0 \\
0 & 0 & 1 & \dots & 0 \\
\cdot & \cdot & & \dots & \cdot \\
\cdot & \cdot & & \dots & \cdot \\
\cdot & \cdot & & \dots & \cdot \\
0 & 0 & & \dots & 1 \\
1 & 0 & & \dots & 0
\end{pmatrix}
\tag{28.17a}
$$

This form does not change appreciably if we replace some, or all, of the zeros in each row with infinitesimal quantities and correspondingly reduce the non-zero element, thereby transforming Π into

$$
\tilde{\Pi} = \begin{pmatrix}
\epsilon_{11} & 1 - \epsilon_1 & & \dots & \epsilon_{1p} \\
\epsilon_{21} & \epsilon_{22} & 1 - \epsilon_2 & \dots & \epsilon_{2p} \\
\cdot & \cdot & & \dots & \cdot \\
\cdot & \cdot & & \dots & \cdot \\
\cdot & \cdot & & \dots & \cdot \\
\epsilon_{p-1,1} & & & 1 - \epsilon_{p-1} & \\
1 - \epsilon_p & \epsilon_{p2} & & & \epsilon_{pp}
\end{pmatrix}
\tag{28.17b}
$$

where each row sums to one. This will happen if for $j = 1, \dots, P$ we have

$$
\epsilon_j = \Sigma_{k \neq j+1} \, \epsilon_{jk}
\tag{28.17c}
$$

If $\tilde{\Pi}$ is not too different from Π, then the continuity argument asserts that any economy admitting the degenerate SSE $(x_1, \dots, x_p; \Pi)$ should also admit a proper SSE $(\tilde{x}_1, \dots, \tilde{x}; \tilde{\Pi})$ in the neighborhood of the degenerate one.

Sunspots and cycles are even more tightly related in the special case $p = 2$ for which the converse of theorem 28.2 applies. Azariadis and Guesnerie (1986) prove the following proposition which does *not* extend to $p \geq 3$.

Theorem 28.3 Given standard assumptions on preferences and strict normal goods, a stationary sunspot equilibrium with two states exists if, and only if, a periodic equilibrium with period 2 exists.

Proof The "if" part is a simple technical reformulation of the intuitive argument immediately preceding this theorem. The reciprocal is not trivial and is sketched below.

Assume accordingly that there exists a sunspot equilibrium, that is, three positive numbers $(\bar{w}, \pi_{aa}, \pi_{bb})$ such that $\pi_{aa} < 1$, $\pi_{bb} < 1$ and $F(\bar{w}) = \bar{w}z(\bar{w}, \pi_{bb}) - z(1/\bar{w}, \pi_{bb}) = 0$. We shall demonstrate that a deterministic two-cycle necessarily exists. To that end, we define the sets $\Omega_1 = \{w | s(w) \geq s(1)\}$, $\Omega_2 = \{w | s(w) \leq 1\}$ and prove successively the following four statements:

(S1) $\psi(w) \equiv wz(w, \pi_{aa}) < s(1)$ for $w < 1$.
(S2) There is no $w > 1$ such that $w \in \Omega_1$ and $F(w) = 0$.
(S3) There is no $w > 1$ such that $1/w \in \Omega_2$ and $F(w) = 0$.
(S4) If $F(\bar{w}) = 0$ for some $\bar{w} > 1$, then $\bar{w}s(\bar{w}) - s(1/\bar{w}) \leq 0$.

(S1) For the first statement, we recall from the properties of the function z that $s(w) \geq z(w, \bullet) \geq s(1)$ in Ω_1, and $s(w) \leq z(w, \bullet) \leq s(1)$ in Ω_2. Therefore, if $w \in \Omega_2$ then $z(w, \bullet) \leq s(1)$ and $\psi(w) = wz(w, \bullet) \leq ws(1) < s(1)$ for any $w < 1$. If $w \in \Omega_1$, on the other hand, then $s(1) \leq z(w, \bullet) \leq s(w)$ by the definition of Ω_1; therefore $\psi(w) \leq ws(w)$. However, our normality assumption implies that $ws(w)$ is an increasing function of w, that is, $ws(w) < s(1)$ for $w < 1$. Hence $\psi(w) < s(1)$ for $w \in \Omega_1$ subject to $w < 1$. This completes the proof of (S1).
(S2) $F(w) = 0$ implies $z(w, \pi_{aa}) = (1/w)z(1/w, \pi_{bb})$. For $w > 1$, the right-hand side of this equality is smaller than $s(1)$, which implies $z(w, \pi_{aa}) < s(1)$ for $w < 1$, or $s(w) < s(1)$. By definition this cannot happen for any $w \in \Omega_1$, and the proof of (S2) is complete.
(S3) This is shown in the same manner as (S2).
(S4) From (S2) we have that $\bar{w} \in \Omega_2$ and $z(\bar{w}, \bullet) > s(\bar{w})$; hence $\bar{w}z(\bar{w}, \bullet) > \bar{w}s(\bar{w})$. From (S3), on the other hand, it follows that $1/\bar{w} \in \Omega_1$, so that $z(1/\bar{w}, \bullet) \leq s(1/\bar{w}, \bullet) \leq s(1/\bar{w})$ and $-z(1/\bar{w}, \bullet) > -s(1/\bar{w})$. Hence, (S2) and (S3) together yield $F(\bar{w}) > \bar{w}s(\bar{w}) - s(1/\bar{w})$, which completes the proof of (S4).

Next we make two additional observations. First, from the symmetry of the roots of F noted earlier, we may assume without loss of generality that the root $\bar{w}$ of $F(w)$ exceeds unity (possibly after inverting events a and b). Second, the function $ws(w) - s(1/w)$ becomes positive as $w \to +\infty$. Therefore, the continuous function $ws(w) - s(1/w)$ is non-positive at $\bar{w} > 1$, and becomes strictly positive as $w \to +\infty$; it will have at least one finite real root greater than unity.

The existence of stationary sunspot equilibria with many states

Generalizing from theorem 28.1, readers may wish to know sufficient conditions for the existence of SSEs with $k \geq 2$ states of nature. The answer requires the study of solutions to systems of n nonlinear equations in n unknowns for which index number theorems are available from differential topology.[10] A particularly useful instrument is the Poincaré–Hopf theorem employed by Chiappori and Guesnerie (1989) to generalize theorem 28.1 in the following manner.

Theorem 28.4 Suppose $f: \mathbb{R}_+ \to \mathbb{R}_+$ is a smooth inverse map of a standard deterministic pure-exchange economy with outside money whose equilibria are solutions to the first-order equation $m_t = f(m_{t+1})$. Let $T = f'(m^*)$ be the slope of this map evaluated at the unique outside-money steady state, and assume that $T < -1$. Then, any $p \times p$ Markov matrix Π that has an odd number of real eigenvalues below $1/|T|$ is associated with a stationary sunspot equilibrium with p states.

It is easy to recover theorem 28.1 as a corollary of this. The matrix Π defined in equation (28.8) has two eigenvalues, 1 and $\pi_{aa} + \pi_{bb} - 1$. The economy to which the earlier theorem applies obeys the well-known difference equation $m_t = s(m_{t+1}/m_t)$, with $\epsilon(R)$ being the interest-yield elasticity of the savings function s. From this difference equation, we easily obtain

$$1 - \frac{1}{|T|} = \frac{1}{|\epsilon(1)|} \tag{28.18}$$

whenever $\epsilon(1) < -1/2$. Then the sufficient condition (28.15b) in theorem 28.1 follows directly from (28.18) and the requirement that the smallest eigenvalue, $\pi_{aa} + \pi_{bb} - 1$, of the matrix Π should not exceed $1/|T|$. Specifically

$$\pi_{aa} + \pi_{bb} - 1 < \frac{1}{|T|} = 1 - \frac{1}{|\epsilon(1)|}$$

leads directly to inequality (28.15b).

Guesnerie (1986) and Chiappori and Guesnerie (1989) have shown an even more general proposition that applies to smooth higher-dimensional dynamical systems of the form $m_t = f(m_{t+1})$ in which $f: \mathbb{R}^n \to \mathbb{R}^n$. We state this proposition without proof below and then move on to the volatility of asset and commodity prices.

Theorem 28.5 Assume that the smooth time map $f: \mathbb{R}^n \to \mathbb{R}^n$ describes competitive dynamical equilibria in some overlapping generations economy that possesses a unique nontrivial steady state $m^* \neq 0$ and satisfies certain additional regularity conditions.[11] Let also T be the Jacobian matrix defined in theorem 28.4.

(a) If T has at least one real eigenvalue with modulus above one, then for each $p \geq 2$ there exists a Markov matrix Π with p states and a stationary sunspot equilibrium associated with the matrix Π.

(b) Let R_T and R_Π, respectively, be the sets of real eigenvalues of the matrices T and Π. If the products

$$P_T = \prod_{t \in R_T} (1 - t)^p \qquad P_\Pi = \prod_{\substack{t \in R_T \\ \pi \in R_\pi}} (1 - \pi t)$$

have opposite signs, then there is a stationary sunspot equilibrium with p states associated with the matrix Π.

28.3 Price volatility and price rigidity

In this section we explore the psychological sources of price movements. Do all price changes necessarily reflect some intrinsic volatility in the structure of the economy, that is, in the tastes of consumers, the technology of the producers, or the economic policies of governments? Or is it at least partly the case that price fluctuations reflect and perpetuate whatever beliefs economic agents happen to hold at the moment about the factors affecting future prices? Can prices be "excessively" or "inadequately" responsive in the short run to changes in economic fundamentals?

Evidence exists on both sides of this question. From the financial markets literature we mentioned briefly in section 28.1 come measurements suggesting, but not establishing conclusively, that the prices of common stocks and other assets fluctuate too much relative to movements in the underlying fundamentals. From the labor and intermediate product markets, on the other hand, we have a wealth of data[12] suggesting that, whenever the underlying rate of inflation is moderate, money wages and product prices show quite a bit of short-term rigidity. Both union contracts and supply agreements on intermediate products are free from cost-of-living clauses and similar escalator features that protect the seller against unexpected rises in the cost of providing the good or service in question.

Wage rigidity, in particular, has been an observed regularity of the labor market for so long that it has become a fundamental *assumption* in Keynesian macroeconomics; it is an essential ingredient in both the fix price quantity-rationing approach popularized by Malinvaud (1977) and in the macroeconomic contracting models of Fischer (1977), Taylor (1980), and Okun (1981) as well.[13] This entire line of work is concerned with economies which accommodate exogenous disturbances by quantity adjustments in the short run and by joint price–quantity changes in the long run.

Like financial market analysts who are without a satisfactory explanation of the sources of the excess asset price volatility they observe, Keynesian macroeconomists have little to say about the sources of nominal rigidity in product prices and wages, and therefore about price change in general. This paucity of good stories about the factors that influence the rate of exchange between currency and commodities suggests that we need to delve into the mechanism which transforms random disturbances in the fundamental characteristics of a monetized economy into price and quantity adjustments. What does a rational expectations model of the type we studied in chapter 27 say about the transmission of, say, random policy shocks through money to nominal prices, relative prices, and allocative decisions?

One convenient vehicle for this exercise is the stochastic extension of the inflationary finance model we studied in section 26.1 for a determinstic pure-exchange economy. To simplify matters somewhat, suppose that all generations are of equal size and consist of identical risk-averse individuals. Each individual is endowed with a deterministic commodity vector $(e_1, e_2) \in \mathbb{R}^2_+$ and maximizes the expected value of utility function of the form $u(c_1^t) + v(c_2^t)$, where (c_1^t, c_2^t) is the consumption of a typical member of generation t. The functions $u: \mathbb{R}_+ \to \mathbb{R}$ and $v: \mathbb{R}_+ \to \mathbb{R}$ are smooth, increasing, concave, and satisfy

$$u'(e_1) < v'(e_2) \tag{28.19}$$

In other words, the deterministic variant of this economy is Samuelson.

Real per capita government purchases are an independent and identically distributed random variable $\tilde{g}_t$, with expected value $\mu > 0$ and a probability measure defined over the interval $G = [a, b]$, with $a > 0$. We assume $b < e_1$, that is, government purchases never exceed the endowment of the young, which provides an upper bound on saving.

If M_t is the nominal stock of money in period t and $m_t = M_t/p_t$ is real balances, the government budget constraint is of the familiar form

$$p_t g_t = M_t - M_{t-1} \qquad \frac{p_{t-1}}{p_t} = \frac{m_t - g_t}{m_{t-1}} \qquad (28.20)$$

As in section 27.1, all traders, including the government, are price takers. Commodities purchased by the government are used up with no effect on any household's marginal rate of substitution between private goods.

Public information in this economy is the *history* $H_t = (g_0, g_1, \dots, g_t)$ of realized government consumption from the beginning of time to date. The vector H_t is an element of the product space $G^{t+1} = G \times G \times \dots \times G$. A rational expectations equilibrium is then a complete description of all prices, net trades, and consumption that correspond to each individual history. Somewhat more formally, a rational expectations equilibrium is a sequence of functions $(p_t, m_t, c_1^t, c_2^t)_{t=0}^{\infty}$, each of them mapping G^{t+1} into $\mathbb{R}_+$ or G (whichever is appropriate), such that for each $t = 0$, 1, ... and each realization $H_t \in G^{t+1}$ we have that (i) individual expected utility is maximized subject to the appropriate budget constraint at given prices; (ii) the asset market clears at each H_t; and (iii) the government budget constraint in equation (28.20) holds for each H_t.

The stock of real balances, m_t, is once again the state variable for this economy, but it is now a random variable rather than a scalar. Exactly how do real balances evolve over time? Combining the market clearing condition $e_1 - c_1^t = m_t$, the government budget constraint in (28.20), and the first-order condition for the representative consumer's problem

$$u'(c_1^t) = E\left\{ \frac{p_t}{p_{t+1}} v'(c_2^t) | H_t \right\} \qquad (28.21)$$

we obtain the stochastic difference equation[14]

$$u'(e_1 - m_t) = E\left\{ \frac{m_{t+1} - g_{t+1}}{m_t} v'(e_2 + m_{t+1} - g_{t+1}) | H_t \right\} \qquad (28.22)$$

Every rational expectations equilibrium must justify equation (28.22). Conversely, every solution to (28.22) that satisfies

$$g_t < m_t \qquad \forall (t, H_t) \qquad (28.23)$$

is a rational expectations equilibrium. All such equilibria are probability distributions of m_{t+1} on the interval $[0, e_1]$ conditional on the realized value of H_t.

As an example, we consider the case $u(c) = c$, $v(c) = \beta c$ for some $\beta > 1$, that is, risk neutrality combined with perfect substitutes in consumption. Then the difference equation (28.22) reduces to

$$E\{m_{t+1} | H_t\} = \mu + (1/\beta)m_t \qquad (28.22)'$$

For this very special economy there are interior equilibria $(c_1^i, c_2^i) \in \mathbb{R}^2_{++}$ that satisfy (28.22)' as well as corner equilibria of the form $c_1^i = 0$ or $c_1^i = e_1$ that violate equation (28.22)'.

Slow quantity adjustment

We examine first equilibria with *flexible prices and predetermined net trades*. These equilibria, which allow current events to be fully reflected in contemporaneous prices but not in contemporaneous net trades, satisfy inequality (28.23) plus the deterministic analog of the difference equation (28.22):

$$u'(e_1 - m_t) = E\left\{\frac{m_{t+1} - g}{m_t} v'(e_2 + m_{t+1} - g)\right\} \tag{28.24}$$

This is an ordinary difference equation in (m_t) in which the expectation is taken over the random variable g alone. Real balances here are independent of the *entire history* of public consumption.

Suppose now that the offer curve of the representative household is monotone or, what amounts to the same thing, saving is an increasing function of the rate of return. Since g is always in the interval $[a, b]$, a moment's additional thought should convince readers that equation (28.24) admits a solution of the form $m_t = F(m_{t+1})$. Here the function F is increasing and satisfies the inequality

$$s\left(\frac{m_{t+1} - b}{m_t}\right) < m_t < s\left(\frac{m_{t+1} - a}{m_t}\right) \tag{28.25}$$

in which $s(R)$ is the saving function of the representative household expressed in terms of the gross rate of return R.

As we know from chapter 26, equations of the form $m_t = s[(m_{t+1} - g)/m_t]$ are the standard description of competitive perfect-foresight equilibria in overlapping generations models of inflation finance, when g is real government consumption. Such equilibria are known to exist whenever government purchases are "not too large." Figure 28.3 reminds us that there are typically two stationary values (m^1 and m^2) of real balances corresponding to each g, plus a continuum of dynamic solutions indexed on the beginning-of-time value m_0.

An equilibrium with predetermined net trades is a solution of equation (28.24) that satisfies $m_t < b$ for all t. Therefore, if government consumption is "not too large" on average, there are two stationary equilibria, which correspond to intersections of the 45° line with the frontier labeled C in figure 28.3.

For each equilibrium, stationary or dynamic, net trades and youthful consumption are completely predetermined by initial conditions, preferences, endowments, and the probability distribution of public spending. *Actual* government purchases affect the price level and old-age consumption, which they displace one for one. Thus, the main allocative effect of *unexpected* government expenditure in these equilibria is completely to crowd out consumption by holders of money balances by raising the inflation tax instantaneously.

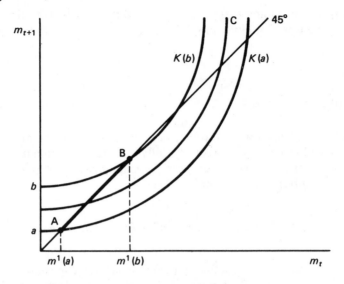

Figure 28.3 Invariant set in the' Farmer–Woodford model.

Slow price adjustment

At the opposite extreme from predetermined net trades are solutions to equation (28.22) associated with *predetermined prices and flexible net trades*. These solutions have a distinct Keynesian flavor but it is worth emphasizing that all of them are bona fide rational expectations equilibria; *the price rigidity property we are about to study neither assumes nor implies quantity rationing of any kind.* Predetermined price equilibria satisfy the stochastic difference equation

$$m_t = s[(m_{t+1} - g_{t+1})/m_t] \qquad (28.26)$$

a special case of equation (28.22) whose solutions have the property that $m_{t+1} - g_{t+1}$ depends only on events realized in period t and earlier.

From the government budget constraint in equation (28.20) it follows that the price ratio $p_t/p_{t+1} = (m_{t+1} - g_{t+1})/m_t$ should be independent of events that occur at time $t + 1$ or later; hence every solution to equation (28.26) has p_{t+1} fully determined *one period in advance.* Solutions of this type, suggests figure 28.3, are obtained if the upper support b of government purchases is not too large. In fact, equation (28.26) describes a family of two-dimensional curves, one for each possible value of g, in the interval $[a, b]$. The extreme members of the family, labeled $K(a)$ and $K(b)$, correspond to extreme values of government spending.

Stationary predetermined price equilibria do not exist in the usual deterministic sense. However, figure 28.3 shows that the interval $[m^1(a), m^1(b)]$ is an *invariant set* for real balances; m_t will stay in the interval with probability one if it starts there. Farmer and Woodford (1984) exploit this property to demonstrate that real balances will tend asymptotically towards a stationary probability distribution defined over this invariant set.

Unlike the predetermined net trades in the above section, predetermined price equilibria allow public consumption to have a strong influence on net trades and consumption by the young, but no impact whatsoever on contemporaneous prices or consumption by the older generation. Since government spending does not affect the short-run rate of inflation in this type of equilibrium, the usual inflation tax works with a lag: public consumption displaces the private consumption of *future* money holders, not of current ones. Crowding out thus smites the young generation rather than the old one.

A good example of the differences between the two polar kinds of equilibrium we have just surveyed is the perfect-substitutes case in equation (28.22)'. Here interior predetermined net trade equilibria are associated with solutions of the equation

$$m_{t+1} = \mu + m_t/\beta \qquad (28.27a)$$

in the interval $[b, e_1]$; interior predetermined price equilibria correspond to solutions of

$$m_{t+1} = g_{t+1} + m_t/\beta \qquad (28.27b)$$

in the interval $[0, e_1]$.

The geometry of figure 28.4 shows that equilibria of the former type exist if

$$b < \frac{\beta\mu}{\beta - 1} < e_1 \qquad (28.27c)$$

and converge monotonically to $\beta\mu/(\beta - 1)$. For the latter kind of equilibria, on the other hand, equation (28.27b) says that

1. the rate of price inflation is independent of history and, in particular, $p_{t+1} = \beta p_t$, for all t;
2. the time path of real money balances,

$$m_t = \beta^{-t}m_0 + \sum_{s=1}^{t-1} \beta^{-s}g_{t-s} \qquad (28.28a)$$

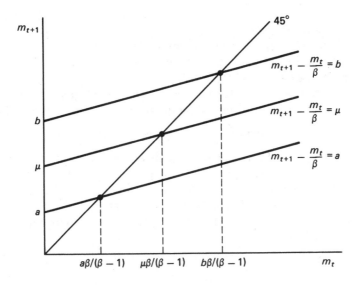

Figure 28.4 Equilibria with predetermined prices of net trades.

stays in the interval $[a\beta/(\beta - 1), b\beta/(\beta - 1)]$ if it begins there. Therefore, an equilibrium with predetermined prices exists if

$$\frac{b\beta}{\beta - 1} \leqslant e_1 \qquad\qquad (28.28b)$$

Both types of equilibria refer to the same economy, and yet they differ substantially in their qualitative properties, especially in what they predict to be the consequences of aggregate demand shocks. The situation is further complicated when one realizes that the set of rational expectations equilibria associated with equation (28.22) is much larger: typically, there is a *continuum* of equilibria.

To understand why this is so, suppose that we have found two distinct solutions to (28.22), that is

$$m_{t+1} = F^1(g_{t+1}, m_t) \qquad m_{t+1} = F^2(g_{t+1}, m_t) \qquad (28.29)$$

Here we assume that (F^1, F^2) are functions of the form $F^i : [a, b] \times [b, e_1] \rightarrow [b, e_1]$ for $i = 1, 2$. Then we can construct another function F^θ such that $m_{t+1} = F^\theta(g_{t+1}, m_t)$ also is a rational expectations equilibrium. To that end, we define F^θ from

$$(F^\theta - g_{t+1})v'(e_2 + F^\theta - g_{t+1}) = \theta(F^1 - g_{t+1})v'(e_2 + F^1 - g_{t+1})$$
$$+ (1 - \theta)(F^2 - g_{t+1})v'(e_2 + F^2 - g_{t+1}) \qquad (28.30)$$

for an arbitrary $\theta \in (0, 1)$.

Next we observe that F^θ lies between F^1 and F^2 for all (g_{t+1}, m_t), provided that the offer curve is monotone. Therefore, F^θ maps $[a, b] \times [b, e]$ into $[b, e_1]$ and satisfies equation (28.22) by definition for all $\theta \in [0, 1]$. This makes F^θ a rational expectations equilibrium for each θ, and implies that there is a continuum of such equilibria.

The volatility of asset returns

What do we learn from the equilibria of the last two sections about the issue of volatile asset returns raised at the beginning of this chapter? To understand what is at stake, let us compute the one-period-ahead variance of the yield on loans $R_{t+1} = (m_{t+1} - g_{t+1})/m_t$ conditional on the history of the economy up to time t. This is easiest to accomplish in the perfect-substitutes risk-neutral economy of the linear equation (28.22)′ but the argument extends easily to the nonlinear equation (28.22).

Consider the following fairly general family of solutions to equation (28.22)′:

$$m_{t+1} = \mu + (1/\beta)m_t + \epsilon_{t+1} \qquad (28.31)$$

where $\beta > 1$ and ϵ_t is an independent random variable with zero mean, identically distributed on the interval $[a_0, b_0]$ where $a_0 + \mu > 0$. By analogy with figure 28.4, it is easy to check that any sequence of random variables that satisfy equation (28.31) have as an invariant set the interval $[\beta(\mu + a_0)/(\beta - 1), \beta(\mu + b_0)/(\beta - 1)]$. Each of these random variables is a proper rational expectations equilibrium if $m_t < e_1$ with probability 1, that is, if

$$\frac{\beta(\mu + b_0)}{\beta - 1} < e_1 \qquad (28.32)$$

From the general solution (28.31) we obtain equilibria with predetermined net trades if ε_t is deterministic for each t, equilibria with predetermined prices if $\varepsilon_t = g_t$ for each t, and all sorts of other equilibria as well. For all of these, the yield on loans is

$$R_{t+1} = \frac{m_{t+1} - g_{t+1}}{m_t}$$

$$= \frac{1}{\beta} + \frac{1}{m_t} (\mu - g_{t+1} + \varepsilon_{t+1}) \qquad (28.33)$$

Hence the one-period-ahead conditional expectation of R_{t+1} is

$$E\{R_{t+1}|H_t\} = 1/\beta \qquad (28.34a)$$

for *every* rational expectations equilibrium.

The one-period-ahead conditional variance of the yield on loans is

$$\sigma^2(R_{t+1}) = \frac{1}{m_t^2} [\sigma_g^2 + \sigma_\varepsilon^2 - 2 \text{ cov}(g, \varepsilon)] \qquad (28.34b)$$

where $(\sigma_g^2, \sigma_\varepsilon^1)$ are the variances of the identically and independently distributed random variables g and ε respectively. In particular $\sigma^2(R_{t+1}) = 0$ at a predetermined price equilibrium (ε_t and g_t have perfect positive correlation); it is σ_g^2/m_t^2 under predetermined net trades (at which ε_t and g_t are uncorrelated); it could in principle *exceed* σ_g^2/m_t^2 if the random variable ε_t were negatively correlated with g_t. We conclude that the set of rational expectations equilibria in stochastic economies of the sort we are considering displays a *whole range of asset return volatilities* for any given structure of economic fundamentals. The family of solutions indexed by (28.31), for example, permits the conditional variance of the gross asset return to be anywhere in the interval $[0, 2\sigma_g^2/m_t^2]$.

It is a rather daunting prospect to contemplate a continuum of rational expectations equilibria. How is a particular equilibrium supposed to prevail in this economy anyway? The next two sections take up this question: section 28.4 postulates some rules that govern how households learn to forecast prices and isolates the equilibria that tend to survive under a variety of learning rules; section 28.5, on the other hand, deals with multiple equilibria as a policy problem of particular concern to the central bank, exploring government policies and operating procedures that reduce the set of equilibria or exclude some particularly undesirable outcomes.

28.4 Learning and stability

In this section we briefly survey a number of informal and formal criteria for selecting or excluding some equilibria when many are possible. Many of these criteria reject a particular rational expectations equilibrium if it cannot be reached asymptotically as the limit of some learning process by households who do not know the actual law of motion governing their economic environment. Other selection criteria choose rational expectations equilibria on the simplicity of the underlying state space, on the welfare properties of the resulting allocation, and on several other considerations.

Policy invariance of forecasts

A particularly simple criterion, proposed by Farmer (1991), selects equilibria consistent with autoregressive forecasting rules that are invariant to some changes in economic policy. The aim here is to put credence on those equilibria associated with time maps that are not "too policy sensitive." To grasp this idea, let us return to the economy described in the previous section, and specifically to equation (28.22).

That equation is a deterministic solution of the form $m_{t+1} = F(m_t)$ called a rational expectations equilibrium with predetermined net trades; the function F is increasing (if consumption goods are gross substitutes) and depends on the utility function of the representative household, its endowment vector, *and* on the probability distribution μ_g of government purchases. Any household with full knowledge of this function may use the government budget constraint in equation (28.20) to make rational autoregressive price forecasts according to the rule

$$p_{t+1} = \frac{p_t m_t}{F(m_t) - g_{t+1}} \qquad (28.35)$$

Closer inspection of the stochastic difference equation (28.22) indicates that *almost all* its equilibria must be supported by forecasts that are sensitive to the "policy instrument" μ_g.[15] The sole exception is the predetermined-price equilibrium which satisfies $m_t = s(p_t/p_{t+1})$. If the saving function is monotone, households may invert it to forecast future prices by the rule

$$p_{t+1} = p_t/s^{-1}(m_t) \qquad (28.36)$$

All that is needed to employ equation (28.36) is a knowledge of the function s, that is, of the representative household's indifference map and endowment vector. The probability measure μ_g does not affect equation (28.36) which predicts equally well for *any* technically feasible distribution of government purchases and remains immune to unexpected swings in economic policy.

This particular form of policy invariance is a desirable property that equation (28.36) does not possess against other types of policy. A social security scheme, for instance, like those we discussed in Part III, would shift equation (28.36); unexpected or undetected swings in social security benefits or taxes, or in debt-financed government deficits, would inject clear biases into forecasts made from either equation.

Welfare and complexity criteria

A second selection criterion suggests that we should exclude all equilibria that are Pareto inferior to others on the grounds that the economy will *somehow* gravitate toward undominated equilibria. This proposal has certain attractive features: it rules out both stationary and dynamical sunspot equilibria of the type examined in sections 28.1 and 28.2, because spurious random variables like sunspots introduce undesired uncertainty in equilibrium allocations. (Question IV.31 asks readers to verify this statement.)

Undominatedness will rule out many indeterminate outside-money equilibria that we think are completely legitimate, for example those converging to the inside-money steady state in the pure-exchange economies of section 24.1. The same token excludes empirically relevant monetary steady states of inflation finance which lie on the downward-sloping "wrong" side of the Laffer curve in, say, figure 26.3.

Inflation finance is a good illustration of the limited usefulness that welfare criteria have in selecting among multiple equilibria, even those that just involve sunspots. The addition of the spurious allocative uncertainty that a sunspot equilibrium represents is not necessarily harmful in a second-best situation in which the underlying funda-mental (or nonsunspot) allocations are themselves distorted away from Pareto optimality by inflation and other taxes of by market imperfections. In addition, equilibrium selection on welfare grounds weakens the distinction between competitive equilibria and social optima to the point of rendering meaningless all welfare comparisons of alternative economic policies.

McCallum (1983) proposes another informal device, called the "minimum state variable" approach, to screen out some rational expectations equilibria. Among all possible laws of motion that may describe a given dynamic economy, this criterion picks the one with the smallest-dimensional state space. Taken at face value, this criterion rules out all bubbles, including currency and unbacked national debt, from overlapping generations models: instead of looking for solution sequences $(k_t, b_t)_{t=1}^{\infty}$ to the *planar* overlapping generations model, one could simply ignore outside money and focus on inside-money equilibria in the corresponding *scalar* economy.

To understand how this criterion works under uncertainty, we narrow our attention to a family of stationary rational expectations equilibria of the form

$$p_t = \phi(x_t, s_t) \tag{28.37}$$

not unlike those we encountered in section 28.3. Without much loss of generality, we assume that equation (28.37) represents a class of equilibrium price functions that describe the stationary response of prices to two types of exogenous forcing variables: x describes fundamental influences like preferences, endowments, and economic policy; s stands for psychological variables such as sunspots. All three variables are governed by vector Markovian stochastic processes; the map ϕ is possibly set valued and known to all agents.

The minimum state variable rule does not say how one should choose among a family of equilibria, like solutions to equation (28.22), all of which respond to fundamentals. It does not guide our choice between predetermined net trade and predetermined price allocations; it does, however, instruct us to delete s_t from the right-hand side of equation (28.37) which would be a workable prescription if we had a tight distinction between fundamentals and sunspots. Section 28.1, however, suggests that sunspots may be thought of as just a randomizing device over multiple fundamental equilibria. Suppose, for example, that ϕ is single valued and s_t takes scalar values in the finite set $S = \{1, 2\}$. Next we replace (28.37) with the equation

$$p_t = \psi^s(x_t) \tag{28.38}$$

in which ψ^s is a set-valued map from fundamentals into prices such that, for all x,

$$\phi(x, 1) = \psi^1(x) \qquad \phi(x, 2) = \psi^2(x) \tag{28.39}$$

The unique sunspot equilibrium of equation (28.37) is now metamorphosed into two fundamental equilibria.

Another undesirable feature of this criterion is that it lacks continuity with respect to parameters. It denies psychological variables any allocative role but permits in principle *small* perturbations in some fundamental parameter to induce *very large* movements in endogenous variables, even though sunspot equilibria come arbitrarily close to being disproportionate economic responses to small structural changes.

Evolutionary stability

A more traditional way of selecting among dynamical equilibria uses asymptotic stability as a yardstick. Particular stationary, periodic, or Markovian rational expectations equilibria are selected from a larger set of consistent competitive outcomes if they are rest points of a particular adaptive or statistical learning mechanism. Individuals who feed observed data into one of these mechanisms learn about the true structure of the economy, converging from an arbitrary initial model of their environment to a rational forecast and, in more elaborate cases, to the true law of motion itself.

Sections 23.1 and 23.2 have already dealt with the simplest cases of adaptive learning and built up an economic intuition that carries over to the more complicated settings studied by Grandmont and Laroque (1986), and many others. The building blocks are a deterministic time map

$$p_t = F(p_{t+1}^e) \tag{28.40a}$$

connecting the state variable p_t with its expected value p_{t+1}^e one period ahead; and an equally deterministic adaptive-learning rule

$$p_{t+1}^e = \psi(p_t, p_{t-1}, \dots, p_{t-L+1}) \tag{28.40b}$$

formalizing how forecasts are made from a sample of finite length containing the last L observations on the state variable.

Combining these two equations, one obtains an ordinary difference equation of order $L-1$ whose solution will reveal whether stationary states p^* or periodic equilibria $(\bar{p}_1, \dots, \bar{p}_k)$ are reachable from other points in their immediate neighborhood as households accumulate data. A particular case of equation (28.40b), which permits Guesnerie and Woodford (1991) to examine the evolutionary stability of periodic cycles, is

$$p_{t+1}^e = p_{t+1-k}^e + \theta(p_{t+1-k} - p_{t+1-k}^e) \tag{28.40c}$$

for some fixed parameter $\theta \in [0,1]$ and an integer $k \geq 1$. In this expression forecast errors are partially corrected with a lag of k periods because agents already know that the equilibrium is of period k.

In the presence of uncertainty, the time map (28.40a) becomes stochastic with the general form

$$p_t = F(p_{t+1}^e) + \varepsilon_{t+1} \tag{28.41a}$$

where ε_t is an independent and identically distributed random variable with compact support. The adaptive-learning rule may be replaced by an ordinary least squares regression of p_t on p_{t-1}, that is, by

$$p_t = ap_{t-1} + b \tag{28.41b}$$

run on the entire sample of available observations. Convergence to the steady state p^* occurs if the slope a converges to zero and the intercept b converges to the fixed point p^* of the map F, as the sample size goes to infinity. We return to the issue of least squares learning in chapter 29.

Midway between adaptive and least squares learning is the statistical learning approach of Lucas (1986) and Evans and Honkapohja (1990) which produces adaptive forecasts of a state variable p_t from the sample mean of all past observations by the formula

$$p_{t+1}^e = p_t^e + \frac{1}{t}(p_t - p_t^e) \tag{28.42}$$

As $t \to \infty$, forecasts settle down at a value that is independent of forecasts made at the beginning of time.

A related learning mechanism is used by Woodford (1990a) to describe how individuals slowly accumulate knowledge about their optimal response to psychological state variables in the pure-exchange overlapping-generations setting of section 28.2. In the resulting dynamical learning process, the outside-money steady state is unstable; even if households start with the belief that sunspots do not have much of an effect on their own actions (and hence do not have appreciable influence on equilibrium allocations), what they observe will steer their views away from the deterministic outside-money steady state toward one of the two stationary sunspot equilibria. With probability 1 beliefs will asymptotically settle on one of the two available sunspot equilibria.

Expectational stability

Adaptive learners seek to uncover regularities in the behavior of state variables by observing samples of them. More ambitious forecasters may attempt, in the spirit of Muth (1961) and much of the early rational expectations literature, to learn the actual time map governing the dynamical structure of the economy. Can households learn the law of motion F in equation (28.40a) if they start with a slightly different model f that is "close" to F in the space of continuous functions?

Learning in this context means choosing at $t = 0$ some initial member f_0 in a particular parametric class of models Φ and then going through the procedure outlined in section 23.1. We forecast state variables at $t = \Delta t$ on the basis of f_0; insert these forecasts into the actual time map to generate the true values of the state variables at Δt; revise f_0 into another model $f_1 \in \Phi$ on the basis of the discrepancy between predicted and observed values of the state variables; and keep going in this way until the discrepancies at $2\Delta t$, $3\Delta t$, ... asymptotically vanish. If all goes well, we shall end up with the actual model F as the fixed point of the map T that leads from perceived to actual models.

Iterations over models $f \in \Phi$ need not take place in real time but could also occur in fictitious or notional time as individuals construct laws of motion to fit progressively larger spans of existing time-series data. It is most useful to regard the set Φ as containing all the perfect-foresight or rational expectations equilibria of a fixed economic structure. A particular law of motion $F \in \Phi$ is called *expectationally stable* if it is an asymptotically stable fixed point of the nonlinear map T. Originally due to Lucas (1978) and DeCanio (1979), the concept of expectational stability (or E-stability) has seen extensive use as a selection device for rational expectations equilibria – notably in work by G. Evans (1983, 1989) surveyed in the remainder of this section.

The notion of expectational stability most relevant for our purpose is that of *weak E-stability*. Suppose, in particular, that the process of model revision takes place in continuous time and is limited to a predetermined parametric family Φ of possible solutions. Then the model $f^* \in \Phi$ is weakly E-stable if it is an asymptotically stable stationary solution of the initial value problem

$$f'(t) = T(f(t) - f(t)) \qquad f(0) = f_0 \qquad (28.43)$$

for a given value of f_0 and $f(t) \in \Phi$ for all t.[16]

We reexamine next the expectational stability of the monetary steady state and of two-state SSEs in a suitably parametrized version of an overlapping generations model with production due to Azariadis (1981a). This one is identical to the familiar pure-exchange economy most recently analyzed in chapter 27 in all but two respects: (i) individuals are not directly endowed with the consumption good but, rather, with the vector of leisure $(e, 0)$ part of which they must expend to produce the consumption good by the technology "output equals labor input;" and (ii) individuals consume leisure only in youth and the consumption good only in old age. A representative household in generation t has a utility function of the form $u(c_{t+1}) - v(n_t)$ with

$$u(c) = \frac{c^{1-\sigma}}{1 - \sigma} \qquad v(n) = \frac{n^{1+\varepsilon}}{1 + \varepsilon} \qquad (28.44)$$

where $\sigma \geqslant 0$ and $\varepsilon \geqslant 0$ are given parameters, and the youthful leisure endowment satisfies

$$e > 1 \qquad (28.45)$$

In any competitive equilibrium with a fixed nominal stock of money M, the supply of real balances must equal real saving by the young, that is, the entire labor supply of the economy. Since $R_{t+1} = p_t/p_{t+1}$ as usual, and $p_t = M/n_t$, we have $R_{t+1} = n_{t+1}/n_t$. Combining this with the usual first-order condition for the consumer, one obtains a stochastic nonlinear differences equation of the form

$$v'(n_t) = E_t\{R_{t+1} u'(n_{t+1})\} = E_t\left\{\frac{n_{t+1}}{n_t}u' (n_{t+1})\right\} \qquad (28.46)$$

Except for the obvious changes in notation and minor differences in structure, this equation is what equation (28.22) reduces to when government purchases are identically zero.

For the functional forms contained in equation (28.44), the previous difference equation readily simplifies to

$$n_t^{1+\varepsilon} = E\{n_{t+1}^{1-\sigma}|I_t\} \qquad (28.47)$$

where I_t is the set of all information that households use at time t to predict future variables. Stationary solutions to equation (28.47) are the outside-money steady state $n^* = 1$ and the inside state $n = 0$. Note that the inside state does *not* solve this equation for $\sigma \geqslant 1$ because of the boundary endowment vector $(e, 0)$, but still remains a corner equilibrium.

To ascertain the expectational stability of deterministic stationary equilibria, we start with the perceived law of motion $f_0 \colon n_t = n$ where n is a parameter that can be set arbitrarily close to any constant solution. This law implies a price level $p_t = 1/n$, if the normal stock of money is normalized to unity, and a yield or loans $R_{t+1} = p_t/p_{t+1} = 1$. Substituting $R_{t+1} = 1$ into equation (28.46) we obtain the second-round solution $f_1: n_t = 1$ once we use the functional forms in equation (28.44). The mapping from perceived to actual solutions is then $T(n) = 1$ for all $n \in [0, e]$.

A stationary solution to equation (28.47) is defined as weakly E-stable if it is a stable restpoint of the differential equation

$$\dot{n} = 1 - n \qquad (28.48)$$

Clearly the outside-money state $n^* = 1$ is such a point while the inside state $n = 0$ is not. What about sunspot solutions? From equation (28.47) we note that an SSE with two natural states exists if there are probabilities (π_{aa}, π_{bb}) and two distinct numbers (n_a, n_b), each in the interval $[0, e]$, which satisfy the following two equations:

$$n_a^{1+\varepsilon} = \pi_{aa} n_a^{1-\sigma} + (1 - \pi_{aa}) n_b^{1-\sigma} \qquad (28.49a)$$

$$n_b^{1+\varepsilon} = (1 - \pi_{bb}) n_a^{1-\sigma} + \pi_{bb} n_b^{1-\sigma} \qquad (28.49b)$$

An SSE will exist if the sufficient condition (28.15b) holds at the monetary steady state, that is, if the elasticity of saving $\eta(R)$ accords with the inequalities

$$\eta(1) < 0 \qquad \frac{1}{|\eta(1)|} < 2 \qquad (28.50)$$

From the first-order condition for the consumer's deterministic optimum we obtain

$$n = R^{(1-\sigma)/(\varepsilon+\sigma)} \Rightarrow \eta(R) = \frac{1-\sigma}{\varepsilon+\sigma} \quad \forall R$$

In view of this equation, the two sufficient conditions for a two-state SSE merge into one, that is,

$$\sigma > 2 + \varepsilon \qquad (28.51)$$

Next we need the map from perceived to actual laws of motion in the presence of a sunspot variable $s_t \in \{a, b\}$. As in the certainty case, we hypothesize a solution of the form $f_0: n_t = n_a$ if $s_t = a$, $n_t = n_b$ if $s_t = b$. Any competitive equilibrium satisfies $R_{t+1} = n_{t+1}/n_t$ so that the distribution of R_{t+1}, conditional on $s_t = i$, under the perceived law of motion is n_j/n_i with probability π_{ij} for each $i = a, b$ and each $j = a, b$. Faced with this probability distribution of returns, a young consumer whose actions are described by equation (28.46) will choose to supply in state $i = a, b$ an amount of labor

$$n_i^* = \left[\sum_{j=1}^{2} \pi_{ij} \left(\frac{n_j}{n_i} \right)^{1-\sigma} \right]^{1/(\varepsilon+\sigma)} \qquad (28.52)$$

Equation (28.52) describes how the perceived rational expectations equilibrium (n_a, n_b) is mapped into the actual one (n_a^*, n_b^*). In particular, an SSE $(\pi_{aa}, \pi_{bb}, n_a, n_b)$ is weakly E-stable if (n_a, n_b) is an asymptotically stable steady state of the dynamical system

$$\dot{n}_a = \left[\pi_{aa} + (1 - \pi_{aa}) \left(\frac{n_b}{n_a} \right)^{1-\sigma} \right]^{1/(\varepsilon+\sigma)} - n_a \qquad (28.53a)$$

$$\dot{n}_b = \left[(1 - \pi_{bb})\left(\frac{n_a}{n_b}\right)^{1-\sigma} + \pi_{bb} \right]^{1/(\varepsilon+\sigma)} - n_b \qquad (28.53b)$$

From the Jacobian of this system one may prove (see also question IV.32) the following theorem.

Theorem 28.6 If $\sigma > 2 + \varepsilon$, there exists a weakly E-stable stationary sunpot equilibrium with two states of nature.

   In the overlapping generations economy we are studying, this result holds not only for the stationary sunspot variable $s_t \in \{a, b\}$ but also for any binary psychological variable for which the probabilities (π_{ab}, π_{ba}) of switching states are sufficiently large. In other words, explicit learning dynamics may lead this economy to *any one of a large number of belief-driven equilibria*. One corollary of this syllogism is that SSEs cannot be strongly E-stable because the economy has no way of judging the relative importance of subjective variables and selecting one psychological equilibrium over another. The second, and farther reaching, conclusion is that dynamical learning mechanisms cannot be relied on to rule out sunspot equilibria, to select among a potentially large number of rational expectations equilibria, and even less to reassure us that asymptotically a unique fundamental solution will emerge in a dynamic economy.

   Adaptive, statistical, and other simple learning processes offer valuable insights about the robustness of several interesting types of equilibria by requiring each one to be stable when we perturb the underlying economic parameters. But efforts to deliver unique equilibria in dynamic economic models by stability, minimum state space, and related selection criteria inspired by the natural sciences are not very likely to bear fruit because interactions among humans are fundamentally different from those of physical objects and chemical particles. Economic policy offers a set of institutional mechanisms set up to regulate interactions among individuals and, hence, indirectly to guide the economy towards those outcomes that policymakers may deem in the interest of some social group.

28.5   The problem of multiple equilibria

In this section[17] we begin by summing up some of the more common categories of multiple equilibria, found in Part IV and elsewhere in this text, discuss why they exist, review some of the empirical evidence for them, and conclude with several detailed examples of economic policies that help select desirable equilibria or manage to rule out undesirable ones. Policies in this section are viewed in the traditional manner as stabilizing devices that insulate the economy from the allocative consequences of volatile beliefs.

   Anyone who looks at the set of possible rational expectations solutions to equations like (28.12a), (28.12b) or (28.22), even at the subset of solutions that are stable under some explicit learning process, may be inclined to ask with a reasonably straight face if almost everything is a rational expectations equilibrium. If almost everything is, one could be forgiven the opinion that sunspots, periodic cycles, indeterminacies, and other forms of multiple equilibria are an intellectual curiosity with no empirical content, a property of economic models that lack a commonsense prescription of how one equilibrium actually emerges among several candidates.

Readers who sympathize with this view should feel most comfortable with dynamical structures that possess unique or locally unique equilibria like the optimal growth model with complete markets. Given enough regularity assumptions about preferences, endowments, and production sets, economies with unique equilibria provide unequivocal answers to the standard comparative statics questions of economic theory, to forecasting exercises conducted in structural econometric models, and to the policy simulations that are the bread and butter of economic consultants. What logically compelling reasons have we found so far in this textbook, and in the literature at large, to take multiple equilibria seriously? What empirical regularities do we know of which are easy to illuminate with multiple equilibria but hard to explain with models possessing locally unique equilibria?

Multiple equilibria: a recapitulation

Consider in discrete time a dynamic economy with deterministic autonomous fundamentals: it is inhabited by a sequence of agents whose preference orderings, endowments, and production sets are known and time invariant. The laws of motion for an economy of this type are typically expressed by a vector difference equation of the form

$$x_{t+1} = f(x_t, \mu) \tag{28.54}$$

where $x_t \in X \subseteq \mathbb{R}^n$ is the vector of state variables; $\mu \in M \subseteq \mathbb{R}^m$ is a vector of parameters that affect the structure of the economy; f is a continuously differentiable function; and $t = 0, 1, \ldots$ is a time subscript. The spaces X and M are often Euclidean but on occasion may become probability spaces.

Dynamical equilibria are solutions of equation (28.54) that start with a historically predetermined vector of initial conditions $x_0 \in X$. In formal terms, an equilibrium is a sequence

$$\gamma^+(x_0) = \{f^t(x_0): t = 0, 1, \ldots\} \tag{28.55}$$

defined for each value of the parameter vector μ and called "the positive orbit through x_0"; it is unique by the Cauchy–Peano theorem. The symbol f^t denotes the tth iterate of the function f formed according to the usual definitions $f^0(x) \equiv x$, $f^1(x) \equiv f(x)$, $f^2(x) \equiv f[f(x)], \ldots, f^t(x) \equiv f[f^{t-1}(x)]$.

Multiple equilibria occur if the orbit $\gamma^+(x_0)$ is not uniquely defined and the Cauchy–Peano theorem somehow does not apply. What causes these deviations from uniqueness? One useful way to think about them is to identify the technical reasons for the implied departure from the basic uniqueness results of dynamical systems: *missing initial conditions; subjective state or parameter spaces; and such "peculiarities" of the time map as sensitive dependence on initial conditions or lack of homeomorphism*. The first two of these causes arise from institutions and interactions peculiar to economics, and perhaps other social sciences as well; the last one is also valid in classical mechanics and the natural sciences. Let us review briefly all three classes of deviations.

The logic of multiple equilibria

Newtonian mechanics describes the motion of a particle or planet in a finite-dimensional coordinate system as the unique solution to a vector differential equation which conforms to the location of the object at some particular point in time. *Initial conditions* of this sort are not always meaningful in economics because history does not predetermine all state variables of interest; some of them are set instead in forward-looking markets on the basis of expectations people hold about future events.

What history does predetermine in dynamic economies are the aggregate stocks of physical capital, human capital, and other assets denominated in purchasing power (say, indexed national debt); history also fixes the initial distribution of wealth among households, and describes past consumption in situations where an individual marginal rate of substitution between current goods depends on inherited consumption patterns.[18] This still leaves the prices of consumption goods, the prices of factors of production, as well as the purchasing power of nominal assets (currency, unindexed public debt) to be settled by current interactions between buyers and sellers.

Missing initial conditions are responsible for *indeterminate equilibria*, the best known and most thoroughly studied form of multiplicity. If $\mathbb{R}^m$ is the state space of the dynamical system (28.54) and history predetermines only $j < m$ initial conditions, then any positive orbit that conforms to historical data has in principle up to $m-j$ degrees of freedom. Suppose, in particular, that (28.54) admits a steady state $\bar{x} \in \mathbb{R}^m$ that has no eigenvalues with modulus one and $i \leqslant m$ eigenvalues with modulus less than one; then there is a stable manifold (that is, a higher-dimensional analog of a surface) in $\mathbb{R}^i$ that includes $\bar{x}$, and any orbit that starts in that manifold converges to $\bar{x}$.

Given j initial conditions, the actual degrees of freedom for solutions to equation (28.54) are $d = \max(i-j, 0)$ which is a positive number whenever the number of stable eigenvalues exceeds the number of predetermined variables. For any initial conditions that place the economy in the stable manifold of $\bar{x}$ there is a *continuum* of equilibria, that is, a d-dimensional family of orbits converging to $\bar{x}$.

Some illustrations from earlier chapters should be helpful here. Competitive equilibria in one-sector neoclassical growth models are a special case of the dynamical system (28.54) which we studied extensively in Parts I and II; there $\bar{x}$ denotes the stock of physical capital k_t, $X = \mathbb{R}_+$, and the parameter space M reflects the specifics of technology, endowments, and demographic structure in use. Indeterminacy is impossible here because, in typical situations, $i = j = 1$; other forms of multiplicity are very rare.[19]

This logic does not extend to the two-sector growth models we studied in chapter 15 in which capital is only one of two state variables; the other is a price, typically the wage–rental ratio ω_t, that history does not determine. The system (28.54) is two dimensional, and equilibrium is indeterminate with one degree of freedom if (28.54) has an asymptotically stable steady state $(\bar{k}, \bar{\omega}) \in \mathbb{R}_+^2$. This is generally the case if the consumption good is more capital intensive than the investment good.

One well-known source of indeterminate equilibria is the overlapping generations model, with and without currency. As Samuelson (1958) observed early on, pure-exchange economies of this type have a pervasive tendency towards fewer market clearing equations than unknown prices. The simplest way to display the indeterminacy is in an economy like the one we examined in section 24.1: it is inhabited by two-period-lived households who choose portfolios of two perfectly substitutable assets: liabilities of other households (inside money) or liabilities of the central bank (currency).

If current and future consumption are gross substitutes for all consumers, and the stock of fiat money per capita is fixed, then the resulting dynamical equilibria are expressed in the space of real money balances by a time map that corresponds to the curve drawn in figure 24.1(a). This economy has two stationary equilibria: an attracting inside-money state $m = 0$ and a repelling outside-money state at $m^* = M/p^*$. History does not specify the initial value m_0 of real money balances which depends on p_0^m, the market-determined purchasing power of money at the beginning of time. For each setting of p_0^m there is a different value of m_0 and hence a different solution of equation (28.54). It is easy to see from figure 24.1(a) that there is a continuum of solution sequences indexed on $m_0 \in [0, m^*]$; all but one of them converge to the origin.

Why should this multiplicity of equilibria cause any concern? After all, once the initial value m_0 is set *somehow* in the interval $(0, m^*)$, does not the continuation of equilibrium become pretty determinate from that point forward? To see why it is not, consider a pure-exchange economy that changes structure once and for all at $t = T$. For concreteness, suppose that the parameter μ, which describes preferences and endowments, has the value μ_1 from $t = -\infty$ to $t = T - 1$ and switches forever to μ_2 at $t = T$ in a direction that strengthens the demand for central bank liabilities at any given real yield. Figure 28.5 illustrates how the time map f shifts, forcing equilibrium sequences to jump onto the rightmost phaseline.

A moment's notice will convince you that the position of this economy before the structure change does *not* dictate its evolution afterward, as it would if the state variable were physical capital rather than money. For instance, $m_t = m^*(\mu_1)$ for $t \leqslant T - 1$ does not imply that $m_T = f[m^*(\mu_1), \mu_2]$; in fact m_T may be any number in the interval $[0, m^*(\mu_2)]$. As a Sargent and Wallace (1973) pointed out, the price of money may rise sufficiently at T to support the new outside-money equilibrium state $m^*(\mu_2)$, or it may rise less in which case the economy slides down the new phaseline into the origin.

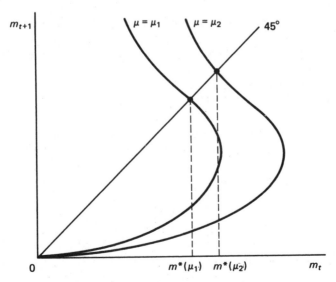

Figure 28.5 Indeterminacy from policy change.

For a while the profession thought that indeterminacy and other types of multiple equilibria were an artificial property of economies with intrinsically useless assets like fiat money, and one which would evaporate in the presence of arbitrage between currency and "productive" assets. We now know from Calvo (1978a) that interest rates may be indeterminate in overlapping generations economies with productive land, and from Kehoe and Levine (1985, 1990) that this indeterminacy applies even to pure-exchange economies *without* outside money.[20]

A familiar example of indeterminate equilibrium in an economy with production is the one-sector overlapping generations model of capital accumulation with currency or perpetually refinanced public debt that we explored in chapter 7. This two-dimensional application of equation (28.54) has one initial condition (capital) set by history, two state variables (capital and public debt), and three steady states: a trivial state $(0, 0)$ with two unstable eigenvalues; the golden rule outside-money state (k^*, b^*) with one unstable and one stable eigenvalue; and the inside-money state $(\bar{k}, 0)$ with two stable eigenvalues.

Figure 7.4(c) reminds us that equilibria converging to the golden rule state are determinate while those approaching the inside-money state are not. For each initial value k_0 of physical capital in the neighborhood of k^*, there is only one initial value b_0 of public debt that will put the economy on the stable manifold of (k^*, b^*); on the other hand, *any* initial value (k_0, b_0) in the neighborhood of $(\bar{k}, 0)$ defines equilibrium sequences leading to the inside-money state.

What does indeterminacy mean for the standard comparative statics and dynamics exercises we need for econometric prediction and policy evaluation? As Kehoe and Levine (1990) stress elsewhere, the fundamental difficulty with indeterminate equilibria is that they require so much coordination among economic agents as to undermine the very concept of perfect foresight. For a simple example of the coincidence needed to select any perfect-foresight solution, we return to the structural change depicted in figure 28.5; the economy will not jump from, say, m^* (μ_1) to $m^*(\mu_2)$ at $t = T$ unless it is public knowledge that *everyone* expects precisely this change to occur. Our models are silent on the economic mechanisms that will focus public opinion so sharply.

Missing initial conditions, however, turn out to be the least worrisome source of multiplicity even if they permit a continuum of equilibria to exist. To the extent that all equilibrium sequences converge to the *same* steady state, the impact of initial conditions weakens over time especially if the stable eigenvalues associated with the steady state have moduli far below one. In that case, forecasts of state variables will prove reasonably accurate in the medium run even if they are wide of the mark in the short run.

Of more immediate concern are the belief-driven equilibria that we have studied throughout this chapter because they produce a large range of outcomes consistent with rational predictions and market clearing. Because of the subjective nature of individual beliefs, the appropriate parameter spaces that define excess demand functions are somewhat arbitrary as are the state spaces in which we seek to express our solutions.

As we saw in section 28.1, we may occasionally, but not always, think of individual beliefs themselves as forecasts about which one of several locally unique temporary equilibria will prevail next period, given a vector of forecasts about events in the more distant future. This happens whenever an economy has a set-valued law of motion or a set-valued excess demand correspondence; in either case coordinated beliefs may act as an equilibrium selection device whose inner working we have no way of predicting.

Multiplicity-generating mechanisms

Why do non-unique equilibria appear so often in dynamical models of rational economic behavior? We saw already how the existence of forward-looking markets for productive inputs and nominal assets contributes to indeterminate outcomes in economies whose state space contains competitive prices. Other common reasons for multiplicity are the assumptions of externalities and of incomplete or missing markets. These two common departures from the familiar Arrow–Debreu and optimal growth paradigms are meant to strengthen the descriptive power of general equilibrium models and extend their range of applicability.

Externalities, in particular, establish strategic or technological links between one agent's payoff and the actions of another and therefore tend to condition any individual's behavior on how he or she expects others will act. The end product of externalities, especially the strong local ones that have become known in the literature as *strategic complementarities*, is often a large number of pure strategy or perfect-foresight equilibria in competitive markets, any one of which may prevail if beliefs are coordinated in a specific manner. [21]

Incomplete markets, too, contribute to non-uniqueness by raising the number of restrictions that define the budget sets of individuals, reducing the number of independent market clearing conditions below the dimension of the vector of goods and asset prices, and thus enlarging the set of equilibrium allocations. Readers who are interested in how this is done in an atemporal general equilibrium setting should consult the surveys by Geanakoplos and Polemarchakis (1986) and Magill and Shafer (1991).

Missing markets are intimately related as well to the existence of *payoff-relevant* sunspot equilibria, that is, of random allocations that affect the utility of economic agents. This connection, developed in a fundamental contribution by Cass and Shell (1983), begins with the observation that sunspot allocations like those supported by the SSEs of section 28.2 are Pareto dominated by the corresponding non-sunspot outcomes because the sunspots inject spurious noise in an economic environment whose fundamental structure may very well be quite stable. Since competitive equilibria are necessarily Pareto optima in, say, an Arrow–Debreu framework with complete markets for contingent claims, sunspots and similar indices of consumer sentiment cannot affect equilibrium allocations whenever all the standard assumptions of the Arrow–Debreu model apply.

Nontrivial sunspot equilibria presuppose that at least *one* of the standard assumptions of finite competitive general equilibrium fails. The specific assumption that most investigators have focused on [for example Mas-Colell, (1989)] is the *insurability of sunspots*. "Sunspots" may stand for a subjective state of mind whose realization will be hard to establish in the eyes of a disinterested third party, or they may describe a publicly verifiable and easily measurable event like an index of consumer sentiment. In either case it is unrealistic to suppose that complete markets exist for insuring individuals against all possible natural events. Even if the sunspot realization s_t at time t were indeed public knowledge, a truly complete market structure should permit each individual by definition to trade securities contingent on any possible history $H_t = (s_1, \ldots , s_t)$ of natural events. This is impossible in overlapping generations economies whose demographic structure rules out trading by unborn or deceased individuals.

Households may very well desire to engage in trading at times they are not "alive" or legally entitled to transact for one simple reason: the natural states and prices they face over their lifespan are in principle correlated with what took place before their birth and with what is predicted to take place after their death. These demographic realities prevent many agents from participating beneficially in markets in which they would have traded if their life were longer. The resulting *incomplete market participation* is a key reason why payoff-relevant sunspot equilibria may exist even if all relevant securities markets are physically open at all times.

Empirical evidence

Readers who suspect that externalities and missing markets will remain prominent features of economic models in the foreseeable future must learn now how to cope with multiple equilibria: they need to understand the situations in which such equilibria are likely to be present, develop criteria that permit them to judge the robustness of each equilibrium, and study the mechanisms by which a particular equilibrium is selected. But why should such an esoteric set of questions hold any interest for anybody not engaged in pure research? What practical relevance does it have for economists who work in business organizations, regulatory agencies, and policy-advising units?

Economic volatility and the seigniorage Laffer curve are two among many policy-related questions that are difficult to analyze in the context of economies admitting unique equilibria. We discussed the volatility of asset prices at the very beginning of this chapter, and later found in section 28.3 how the excess volatility of asset returns may be a consequence of nonfundamental random factors. Below is a thumbnail sketch of seigniorage drawn in large part from chapter 26.

When observers discuss the root causes of the persistent inflation rates experienced in Argentina, Brazil, and elsewhere, much of the blame falls on excessive public sector deficits and the rapid creation of bank reserves. The Laffer curve in figure 26.1(c) reminds us that any constant flow of per capita government deficit in some bounded interval $[0, g_c]$ may be financed in the steady state at two different rates of inflation or per capita money creation: a rate below the maximal seignorage tax μ_c and another above μ_c.

The two equilibrium rates of inflation endow Laffer curves with two sides: a "good" side of relatively modest inflation taxes and high real monetary base, and a "bad" side with the opposite configuration. Equilibria on the bad side are inferior to those on the good side; switching sides lowers the distortion from the inflation tax on the allocative decisions of households without lowering government revenue.

Even though the two types of stationary equilibria are Pareto ranked, we continue to observe both of them in practice, for example, in the large fluctuations of inflation rates and the succession of stabilization plans that mark the economic history of Latin America. In this regard, it is useful to compare the inflationary experience of Latin America with that of Southern Europe. Perusing back-issues of *International Financial Statistics* for the 1980s, we find that the public sector borrowing requirement has averaged about 4 percent of GNP in Brazil, 10 percent in Italy, and 15 percent in Greece. The corresponding expansion in government liabilities occurred at annual inflation rates of roughly 8 percent in Italy, 16 percent in Greece, and a *monthly* rate of 10 percent in Brazil.

A successful switch from the "wrong" side to the "right" side of the seigniorage Laffer curve amounts to a free lunch with all gainers and no losers. How to coordinate expectations in order to engineer this jump from one equilibrium to another is an issue that has constantly preoccupied, and often eluded, policymakers in many countries around the world for some time now. Plans designed to keep an inflating economy on the acceptable branch of the Laffer curve are likely to remain a key policy concern as long as inflation does.

Stabilization policies with feedback

If cyclical fluctuations arise in part from arbitrary changes in market psychology, governments and central banks may be able to coordinate beliefs by committing themselves to courses of action, that is, to specific fiscal and monetary policies, which are consistent with a particular set of beliefs about future state variables but do not conform with other possible forecasts of them. Policies chosen with care and some knowledge of the underlying economy can guide the private sector toward a specific perfect-foresight or rational expectations equilibrium, or steer the economy away from undesirable outcomes. Public actions of this type will be taken seriously by markets if they are *credible*, that is, if individuals judge that the government is motivated to maintain its announced course. As of this writing, we do not have a well-defined theory of government behavior and hence we lack a good yardstick with which to judge the credibility of government plans.

To advance our discussion of economic policy, we suppose provisionally that governments do commit themselves to whatever technically feasible course they choose to announce, and explore to the remainder of this chapter two classes of policies: with feedback and without feedback. The former require a lot of information; the latter are simple operating rules that appeal to central bankers.

A policy with feedback is in general a sequence of rules $\pi_t: \mathbb{R}^{ts} \to \mathbb{R}^n$ that describe how each of the n instruments set by the policymaker at time t reacts to the history $H_t \in \mathbb{R}^{ts}$ of the economy up to that time; history generally consists of all values realized by an s-dimensional vector of state variables from time 1 up to t.

To demonstrate the potential effectiveness of feedback rules, we return to equation (28.22)′, which describes the rational expectations equilibria of an economy with inflation-financed random government purchases and perfectly substitutable dated goods. As we saw in equation (28.27b), that economy admits a predetermined price equilibrium of the form $p_t = p_0\beta^t$ and $m_{t+1} = g_{t+1} + m_t/\beta$, with $\beta > 1$. If the central bank wishes to validate *this particular* equilibrium to the exclusion of all others, then its policy has to specify that money be printed to finance government purchases at a constant rate of inflation equal to $\beta - 1$. Specifically, money supply must follow the rule

$$M_t = M_0 + \sum_{i=1}^{t} p_i g_i = M_0 + p_0 \sum_{i=1}^{t} \beta^i g_i \qquad (28.56)$$

which assigns greater influence on the current stock of money to more recent government purchases.

Similar considerations apply to other solutions of (28.27b), and the argument easily extends outside the perfect-substitutes case. In general, we suppose that, for $t = 1, \ldots$, a sequence of price functions $p_t^*: \mathbb{R}_+ \to \mathbb{R}_+$ is associated with a particular equilibrium. Then a central bank that knows this sequence, and controls with pinpoint accuracy the stock of money, can implement the equilibrium by applying the rule

$$M_t = M_0 + \sum_{i=1}^{t} p_i^*(H_i) \, g_i \qquad (28.57)$$

where $H_i \in \mathbb{R}^{i+1}$ is the history of the economy from $t = 0$ to $t = i$.

To see how the argument applies beyond the perfect-substitutes case, we look at the set of rational expectations equilibria associated with the more general equation (28.22). Dropping government purchases from this equation, we obtain another equation

$$u'(e_1 - m_t) = E\left\{ \frac{m_{t+1}}{m_t} \, v'(e_2 + m_{t+1}) | H_t \right\} \qquad (28.58)$$

This equation is isomorphic to equation (27.22): it describes a pure-exchange economy without any fundamental uncertainty but allows for changes in the stock of outside money engineered by (possibly random) interest payments on existing currency balances.

Equation (28.58) has a number of deterministic perfect-foresight equilibria, the details of which appear in chapter 24, plus a number of nonstationary sunspot equilibria; we saw some of these in the examples of sections 27.3 and 28.1. In addition, equation (28.58) will have stationary sunspot solutions if the representative consumer's preference ordering satisfies the sufficient condition (28.15b) for some two-state Markov process on sunspots.

To eliminate the undesirable allocative noise associated with SSEs, the central bank may attempt to support a particular deterministic equilibrium or, more generally, to prevent random solutions of equation (28.58) from becoming equilibrium outcomes. Consider the general class of feedback rules for money supply

$$\frac{M_{t+1}}{M_t} = \frac{p_{t+1}}{p_t} \, \pi\left(\frac{p_t}{p_{t+1}} \right) \qquad (28.59)$$

proposed by Grandmont (1986). All these rules pay currency holders interest on money at a rate that depends on current inflation and on past inflation; the past influences current actions through the function $\pi: \mathbb{R}_+ \to \mathbb{R}_+$.

If individuals believe that the central bank will stick with the rule (28.59), then real balances become predetermined one period in advance; we rewrite (28.59) as

$$m_{t+1} = m_t \, \pi\left(\frac{p_{t-1}}{p_t} \right) \qquad (28.59)'$$

and substitute into (28.58) to obtain the *deterministic* difference equation

$$u'(e_1 - m_t) = \pi\left(\frac{p_t}{p_{t-1}} \right) v'\left[e_2 + m_t \pi\left(\frac{p_{t-1}}{p_t} \right) \right] \qquad (28.60)$$

Taken together, equations (28.59)' and (28.60) are a dynamical system with state variables $(m_t, p_t/p_{t-1})$; this system has no random solution. If the policymaker sets $\pi = 1$ for all p_t/p_{t-1}, then the *golden rule is the only positive equilibrium*.

Both of the examples in this section have been economies in which the central bank cannot affect the set of equilibrium allocations but still retains considerable influence on the actual choice of equilibrium within that set. With enough detailed knowledge of the economy and sufficiently precise monetary controls, the central bank "guides" the economy to any equilibrium allocation simply by reacting to events in a particular way, that is, by picking the appropriate policy rule.

What if the central bank has insufficient understanding of the economy and/or inaccurate control of money supply? How does a policymaker convince the private sector that the government means business when the policy itself, a complicated object like equations (28.57) or (28.59), may be difficult to explain? These questions need not be answered if central banks follow plain operating procedures whose implementation does not make heavy use of past data. We examine next the stabilizing properties of policies based on simple targets like the price level or the stock of money.

Stabilization policies without feedback

When monetary economists and central bankers debate the conduct of monetary policy, they often do so by trying to figure out the implications of adopting a particular central bank operating rule on certain key prices and on equilibrium outcomes. The handful of rules discussed typically target some easily measured index of government liabilities, prices, or economic activity: central bankers may focus on nominal interest rates, the inflation rate, the growth of monetary aggregates, or even foreign exchange rates. Arguments are heard aplenty on whether policy should peg interest rates or regulate the growth in commercial bank reserves: fix exchange rates, let them float freely, or follow some intermediate course of action; separate through legal measures the issuing of money from the granting of credit; and a host of related issues.[22]

It is instructive to formalize these arguments somewhat. We explore next the consequences for stabilization policy of targeting some key monetary indices and taking whatever action is needed to keep them on the targeted path. What impact do some of these targets have on the set of equilibrium allocations? Which operating procedure is most effective in controlling the indeterminacy of equilibrium or in eliminating fluctuations driven by beliefs?

These are traditional concerns of monetary policy: the enactment of legislation by the British Parliament in 1844 separating the issue of money from credit was motivated in part by fear that both price-level instability and cyclical fluctuations would be encouraged if the issue of exchange bills by commercial banks were not regulated. To identity conditions under which some of these concerns are justified, we study the mixed overlapping generations economy due to Smith (1990a, b) with a constant population of identical households.[23] Each household in generation t is endowed with a well-behaved utility function $u: \mathbb{R}_+^2 \to \mathbb{R}$, and a vector $(w, 0)$ of consumption goods; it receives a vector of real lump-sum transfers (τ_1^t, τ_2^t) from the government and owns a constant-returns-to-scale production technology which transforms k_t units of the consumption good at t into Ak_t units at $t + 1$. The government does not produce any goods.

The two dated consumption goods are gross substitutes for the representative household, and the technological scale factor A is generally (but not always) assumed to exceed unity. In this general case, households will typically prefer to store value in capital than in money balances except in the unusual case of a sufficiently large permanent deflation. To motivate the holding of currency when it is dominated in rate of return by another asset, we resort to a reserve requirement on saving of the type we briefly studied in section 25.2. Each saver is legally obligated to hold in his or her portfolio an amount of currency balances greater than or equal to a fraction $\theta \in [0, 1]$ of the entire portfolio.

Denoting by m_t real currency holdings, we write individual budget constraints in the form

$$c_1^t = w + \tau_1^t - (k_t + m_t) \tag{28.61a}$$

$$c_2^t = \tau_2^t + Ak_t + (p_t/p_{t+1})m_t \tag{28.61b}$$

$$m_t \geqslant \theta(k_t + m_t) \tag{28.61c}$$

The equilibria we are concerned with are those for which the reserve requirement is binding: it holds as an equality whenever

$$A > p_t/p_{t+1} \tag{28.62}$$

that is, if physical capital dominates money in rate of return. Then all portfolios have the minimal fraction θ of currency, $1 - \theta$ of capital, and an average rate of return

$$R_{t+1} = \theta p_t/p_{t+1} + (1 - \theta)A \tag{28.63}$$

Whenever inequality (28.62) holds, then individual portfolio decisions are

$$m_t = \theta q_t \tag{28.64a}$$

$$k_t = (1 - \theta) q_t \tag{28.64b}$$

If prices are deterministic, individual saving is

$$q_t = s(R_{t+1}, w + \tau_1^t, \tau_2^t) \tag{28.65}$$

where the function $s(R, y_1, y_2)$ specifies again what the representative household saves when the portfolio yield is R and the net endowment vector is (y_1, y_2). Transfer payments to individuals are made in money issued by the government. The relevant budget constraint is

$$M_t = M_{t-1} + p_t(\tau_1^t + \tau_2^{t-1}) \tag{28.66}$$

for each $t \geqslant 1$, with M_0 given. For each specification of government policy, perfect-foresight equilibrium consists of a sequence (M_t, p_t, q_t) that satisfies equation (28.63), (28.65), and (28.66) at each t.

Suppose, for instance, that $\tau_1^t = \tau_2^t = 0$ for all t and money supply is forever predetermined at $M = 1$. Then equations (28.63) and (28.65) simplify to the first-order difference equation

$$q_t = s[\theta q_{t+1}/q_t + (1 - \theta)A, w, 0] \tag{28.67}$$

which describes the dynamic response of this economy to *a fixed money supply rule*. There is a unique determinate steady state. Figure 28.6(a) illustrates this (see also question IV.33). Setting $\theta = 1$ means 100 percent reserve requirements, which

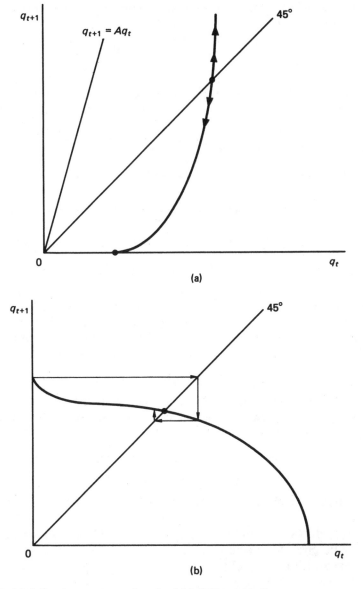

Figure 28.6 (a) A fixed money supply rule; (b) inflation targeting.

prevents all legal investment in physical capital and converts this production economy into one of pure exchange of the sort we studied in section 24.1. In either case, the assumption of gross substitutes rules out both periodic equilibria and SSEs.

Dropping the money supply target in favor of a *price level target* raises the chances for endogenous fluctuations. Suppose, for example, that the central bank chooses to peg the inflation rate at some value such that

$$p_t/p_{t+1} = \rho < A \tag{28.68a}$$

This is equivalent to fixing the portfolio yield at

$$\bar{R} = \theta\rho + (1 - \theta)A \tag{28.68b}$$

To achieve these targets, the government makes lump-sum transfers exclusively to old individuals, that is, sets

$$\tau_1^t = 0 \qquad \tau_2^{t-1} = \frac{M_t - M_{t-1}}{p_t} \tag{28.69}$$

When the policy target is a constant inflation rate, a perfect-foresight equilibrium is a sequence (M_t, p_t, q_t) that satisfies at each t equations (28.68a), (28.69), and the asset-market clearing condition

$$M_t/p_t = \theta s(\bar{R}, w, \tau_2^t) = \theta q_t \tag{28.70}$$

From equations (28.68a) and (28.69), we quickly obtain

$$\tau_2^t = \frac{M_{t+1} - M_t}{p_t} = m_{t+1} - \frac{\rho M_t}{p_t} = m_{t+1} - \rho m_t = \theta(q_{t+1} - \rho q_t) \tag{28.71}$$

Substituting (28.71) into (28.70) yields a first-order difference equation

$$q_t = s(\bar{R}, w, \theta q_{t+1} - \theta \rho q_t) \tag{28.72}$$

in the state variable q_t.

The normality of consumption implies that saving is a decreasing function of net old-age income with a partial derivative $s_2 = (\partial/\partial y_2)s$ in the interval $(-1, 0)$. Together with standard regularity assumptions on the consumer's utility function, normality guarantees that, for each q_t, equation (28.72) has a unique solution

$$q_{t+1} = Q(q_t) \tag{28.72}'$$

This solution has a unique fixed point q^*; uniqueness is easy to establish from equation (28.72) if $\rho \leqslant 1$, somewhat less easy to prove if $\rho \in (1, A)$. In either case, the slope of the time map Q

$$Q'(q) = \rho - \frac{1}{\theta|s_2|} \tag{28.73}$$

is a negative number unless the government chooses to deflate prices at a truly stupendous rate.

Figure 28.6(b) draws the time map of equation (28.72) and shows how periodic equilibria may be possible as a result of a flip bifurcation that occurs whenever the policy parameters (θ, ρ) satisfy $Q'(q^*) = -1$ or

$$\rho = \frac{1}{\theta|s_2|} - 1 \tag{28.74}$$

The possibility of endogenous fluctuations under an inflation or interest rate target are illustrated in the following example due to Smith (1990b).

Example 28.1 Suppose the representative agent has utility function $\log c_1 + \beta \log c_2$ with $\beta \in (0, 1)$, and endowment vector $(1, 0)$. Then

$$s(R, y_1, y_2) = \frac{\beta}{1 - \beta} y_1 - \frac{1}{(1 + \beta)R} y_2$$

A fixed money supply rule supports the perfect-foresight equilibria described in equation (28.67), that is,

$$q_t = \beta y_1/(1 + \beta) \qquad \forall t \qquad (28.75a)$$

On the other hand, an inflation targeting policy generates the equilibria of equation (28.72) which, in this example, become

$$q_t = \frac{\beta w}{1 + \beta} - \frac{1}{R} \theta(q_{t+1} - \rho q_t)$$

Solving this equation for q_{t+1} and using (28.68b) we obtain the linear time map

$$q_{t+1} = \alpha - \frac{1 - \theta}{\theta} q_t \qquad (28.75b)$$

where

$$\alpha \equiv \frac{\beta w [\rho + (1 - \theta)A/\theta]}{1 + \beta} \qquad (28.75c)$$

A fixed money supply rule excludes all but the stationary equilibrium of equation (28.75a) while an inflation or interest rate target is much more permissive: it supports the steady state $q^* = \alpha\theta$, a continuum of damped oscillatory equilibria that converge to q^* if $\theta > 1/2$, and at $\theta = \frac{1}{2}$ it spawns periodic two-cycles. Equilibrium is determinate (at $q_t = q^*$ for all t) under an inflation target only if the reserve requirement is *sufficiently small*, that is, if $\theta < 1/2$

What makes one policy regime immune to indeterminacy and endogenous fluctuations while another is so prone to them? The logic clearly has something to do with the removal of the substitution effect by inflation targeting. When the dated goods are gross substitutes, changes in interest rates exert a stabilizing influence on individual plans; fixing money supply facilitates that influence while inflation targeting pegs the rate of interest and annihilates the substitution effect.

Oscillations in output under inflation targeting have their economic roots in fluctuating beliefs by producers which this policy regime tends to validate. Specifically, if young producers are optimistic about the future they will save and invest large amounts of goods against which they are legally required to hold large currency reserves. These reserves are supplied by the central bank via lump-sum transfers to the old generation. As equation (28.71) suggests, an inflation targeting regime will provide in equilibrium a fluctuating stream of real transfers to successive generations of retirees. By keeping reserves constant, a fixed money supply regime prevents producers from anticipating price fluctuations.

Arguments formalized in theorem 28.2 lead us to believe that SSEs may well exist for any economy in which deterministic periodic orbits are possible. To investigate whether SSEs occur in an inflation targeting regime, we start as in section 28.2 with the transition probability matrix Π in equation (28.8) defined over two natural events $s \in \{a, b\}$. Let $M_t(s)$ be the stock of money at time t in state s and assume that the government still clings to the deterministic inflation target of equation (28.68a). Then the subsidy accruing at time $t + 1$ and in state s' to an individual born at time t and state s is given by the government budget constraint

$$\tau_2^t(s,s') = \frac{M_{t+1}(s') - M_t(s)}{p_{t+1}} \qquad (28.76)$$

Individuals born at (t, s) maximize the expected value of their utility function $u[c_1^t(s), c_2^t(s, s')]$, over the old-age natural event s', subject to the budget constraints

$$c_1^t(s) = w - k_t(s) - m_t(s) \tag{28.77a}$$

$$c_2^t(s, s') = \tau_2^t(s, s') + Ak_t + \rho m_t(s) \tag{28.77b}$$

$$m_t(s) = \theta[k_t(s) + m_t(s)] \tag{28.77c}$$

which hold for all s and s'. Assuming that the reserve requirement is binding in every state and that the yield on money is pegged at $\rho < A$ by the inflation targeting procedure, individuals choose a saving plan for each $s \in \{a, b\}$. Because the natural state of birth is known at the time that consumers formulate these plans, saving is deterministic but reflects the random nature of the transfer variable τ_2^t which depends on the state prevailing at $t + 1$. To see this we rewrite equation (28.76) in a way analogous to equation (28.71), that is,

$$\tau_2^t(s, s') = m_{t+1}(s') - \rho m_t(s) \tag{28.78}$$

Denote again total saving in state s by $q_t(s)$ and observe from (28.77c) and (28.78) that

$$c_1^t(s) = w - q_t(s) \tag{28.79a}$$

$$\begin{aligned}
c_2^t(s, s') &= \tau_2^t(s, s') + [A(1 - \theta) + \rho\theta q_t(s) \\
&= \theta[q_{t+1}(s') - \rho q_t(s)] + [A(1 - \theta) + \rho\theta]q_t(s) \\
&= \theta q_{t+1}(s') + A(1 - \theta)q_t(s) \tag{28.79b}
\end{aligned}$$

These simpler budget constraints reveal that saving $q_t(s)$ is an optimal consumer response to a deterministic yield $\bar{R}$ and an exogenous lifetime income vector $(w, \theta q_{t+1}(s') - \rho\theta q_t(s))$ whose second element is random.

To study SSEs, we postulate that, for each t, $q_t(s)$ takes two possibly distinct values in the interval $[0, w]$. Specifically, let

$$q_t(a) = q_a \qquad q_t(b) = q_b \tag{28.80}$$

For a fixed yield R and first-period income y_1, let $z(R, y_1, y_2^a, y_2^b; \pi)$ be saving by the representative consumer if his old-age income is y_2^a with probability π and y_2^b with probability $1 - \pi$; note that z is independent of π if $y_2^a = y_2^b$. Given the budget constraints (28.79a) and (28.79b), then, the equilibrium conditions satisfied by all two-state SSEs are

$$q_a = z[R, w, \theta(1 - \rho)q_a, \theta(q_b - \rho q_a); \pi_{aa}] \tag{28.81a}$$

$$q_b = z[R, w, \theta(1 - \rho)q_b, \theta(q_a - \rho q_b); \pi_{bb}] \tag{28.81b}$$

An SSE relative to the Markov process Π defined in equation (28.8) exists if equations (28.81a) and (28.81b) have a solution (q_a, q_b) in $(0, w) \times (0, w)$ such that $q_a \neq q_b$. To simplify matters, we assume that $\rho \leqslant 1$ and $\theta \in (0, 1)$ which means that we can invert (28.81a) to obtain $q_b = f_a(q_a)$ and (28.81b) to obtain $q_b = f_b(q_a)$. For $s = a, b$, both functions f_s are smooth, increasing and admit as a fixed point the perfect-foresight steady state q^* of the inflation target regime. Do these schedules intersect off the diagonal, at some point other than $q_a = q_b = q^*$? Question IV. 34 asks you to demonstrate that an SSE exists if q^* is an asymptotically stable state.

Notes

1. The remainder of this section, as well as parts of section 28.5, is based on material drawn from Azariadis (1992).
2. Many of the relevant publications, from Shiller (1981) and LeRoy and Porter (1981) to Poterba and Summers (1988), are reviewed in Shiller (1989), ch. 4.
3. This empirical regularity is called "mean reversion." In a study of serial autocorrelations for a variety of asset prices in 13 industrial countries, Cutler et al. (1991) find statistically significant monthly autocorrelations of prices that range from 0.02 for gold and 0.07 for foreign exchange to 0.10 for common stocks and 0.27 for industrial metals.
4. Called "noise" or "feedback" traders, these investors are supposed to follow mechanical trading strategies that enhance their survival probability but are not rational in any easily definable sense; see, for example, Kyle (1985) and DeLong et al. (1990).
5. One notable exception is the work of Diamond and Dybvig (1983) on banking panics.
6. This section is based in part on material contained in Azariadis (1981b) and Azariadis and Guesnerie (1982, 1986).
7. See, for example, Garber (1989) who lists an extensive bibliography.
8. From the first-order conditions implied by equation (28.10), it is easy to verify the more general result that for each $R > 0$ and $\hat{\pi} \in (0, \pi)$, $z(R, \hat{\pi})$ lies between $z(R, 0)$ and $z(R, \pi)$.
9. The earliest proofs of this result are due to Azariadis and Guesnerie (1982) and Spear (1984).
10. Many of these are reviewed in Milnor (1965).
11. These regularity conditions include hyperbolicity of the dynamical system, distinct eigenvalues, a diagonalizable Jacobian matrix at m^*, and the existence of a bounded rectangle that includes the state m^* at whose boundary the sector field points inwards.
12. See Carlton (1986) on industrial product prices and Cousineau and Lacroix (1981) on money wages.
13. The remainder of this section is based in part on material drawn from Farmer and Woodford (1984) and Azariadis and Cooper (1985). The narrative here follows Azariadis (1989).
14. Two good references on rational expectations solutions to stochastic linear difference equations are Blanchard and Kahn (1980) and Gouriéroux et al. (1982).
15. This syllogism, due to Lucas (1976), is widely known as the "Lucas critique."
16. If f^* continues to be a stable stationary solution to (28.43) when we permit the parametric class of models Φ to exceed the minimum dimension defined by the parameters of f^*, then f^* is called a *strongly E-stable* solution.
17. Much of this section is based on Azariadis (1992).
18. One case of this type arises when utility indices over dated consumption goods are not intertemporal additive separable.
19. One exception is the familiar scalar overlapping generations growth model when it is endowed with a large income effect from interest rate changes. We recall from chapter 13 that this model will support unstable periodic equilibria about a stable steady state, as in figure 13.2(c).
20. Kehoe and Levine (1990) examine inside-money equilibria in pure-exchange economies with overlapping generations of three-period-lived households and show that indeterminate interest rates occur when the dated consumption goods are sufficiently complementary.
21. Cooper and John (1988) review thoroughly how strategic complementarities may cause multiple Pareto-rankable equilibria; the literature originates with Bryant (1983).
22. See Sargent and Wallace (1982) and Smith (1991).
23. This narrative owes much to recent work by Bruce Smith (1990a, 1991) a reading of which stimulates interest in issues of stabilization policy.

29 Advanced topics

This chapter deals with three somewhat heterogeneous questions: section 29.1 starts where section 24.1 left off: it examines how the price of fiat money is affected by the expectation that currency will be valued in the future. The main result, due to Weil (1987), is that individuals will not accept money unless they have sufficient "faith" in its future purchasing power.

Least squares learning is the subject of section 29.2 which extends some of the material we covered in section 28.4. The exposition, based on Marcet and Sargent (1989a), focuses on the stability of a steady state when agents use existing observations to estimate the regression coefficients of an autoregressive law of motion. Stability in the sense of learning dynamics means local convergence of the estimated coefficients to their perfect-foresight values. Marcet and Sargent show that, roughly speaking, this convergence occurs if the steady state is determinate under perfect foresight.

Section 29.3 concludes with a brief survey of some interesting laboratory experiments of overlapping generations economies which test inside- versus outside-money equilibria, multiple equilibria in inflation finance, and a variety of other hypotheses.

29.1 Money and trust

In chapter 25 we saw how a currency economy admits a continuum of inflation equilibria, almost all of which begin at a price of money below its stationary value and converge asymptotically to an inside-money state. That situation, shown clearly in figure 24.1(a), corresponds to a widely shared erosion of trust in currency as an asset: the value of money drops asymptotically from $1/p^*$ to zero. On the expectation that the purchasing power of money will keep declining, households are willing to exchange it for physical goods at rates that are more and more attractive to commodity sellers; the resulting inflation fully validates the inflationary expectations that set it off in the first place.

The inflationary equilibrium paths of figures 24.1(a) are in example of inflation not caused by money creation or by adverse shifts on the supply side, but driven instead by the shared belief of continued inflation. Starting from an idea of Cass and Yaari

(1966), Philippe Weil (1987) investigates how trust helps determine the value of money, not only in dynamical equilibrium but in the steady state as well. Suppose, suggests Weil, that households are unsure about whether money will have *any* positive value at all in the future. In particular, if the price level p_t is finite at t, everyone expects it to be finite, say p_{t+1}, in period $t + 1$ with some fixed probability $q \in [0, 1]$, and infinite with probability $1 - q$. On the other hand, if money has no value at t, everyone expects it to have no value at $t + 1$; this situation is similar to that described in the example following equation (28.4). The price level here follows a Markov process with two states (outside money and inside money), with inside money being an "absorbing" state in which the economy remains forever once it is there.

With "trust" neatly embodied in the parameter q (which we assume to be fixed for all time), we may now ask how q influences the equilibrium value of currency. For that we return to the standard overlapping generations model of pure exchange in which we allow for the *possibility* of valueless money by expressing consumer preferences over risky consumption vectors. Once more we assign each household an additive cardinal von Neumann–Morgenstern utility index

$$v^h(c_h^t) = u_h(c_{1h}^t) + \beta_h u_h(c_{2h}^t) \tag{29.1}$$

where $\beta_h > 0$ is the discount factor. Since this index is defined up to an increasing linear transformation, without loss of generality we may set $u_h(e_{2h}) = 0$ for all h. For each household, we define in the usual way autarkic interest factors $\bar{R}_h$ and saving functions $s_h(R)$ under certainty which describe completely individual behavior when $q = 1$, that is, under full trust in currency.

Partial trust means that $q < 1$, in which case households maximize the expected value of v^h. Because money has positive value with some probability, the yield on saving is p_t/p_{t+1} with probability q and 0 with probability $1 - q$. Let $z_h(R, q)$ denote saving by household h when the gross rate of return is R with probability q and zero with probability $1 - q$. Clearly, the saving function for uncertain yields is related to that for sure yields; specifically z_h is increasing in q and such that

$$
\begin{align}
z_h(R, 1) &= s_h(R) & \forall R \tag{29.2a} \\
z_h(0, q) &= -\infty & \forall q \tag{29.2b} \\
z_h(R, 0) &= -\infty & \forall R \tag{29.2c}
\end{align}
$$

Equilibria are fully described by the evolution of the non-negative state variable m_t, the real value of money balances conditional on positively valued currency. For a given $q \in (0, 1)$, the asset market clears if

$$m_t = z(m_{t+1}/m_t, q) \tag{29.3}$$

has a non-negative solution sequence (m_t). The function z in equation (29.3) is simply the aggregate of the individual schedules summed over all households. For $q = 1$, this equation reduces to the familiar relation $m_t - s(m_{t+1}/m_t) = 0$ of chapter 24; for $q = 0$, it has no solution because the right-hand side is negative infinity by equation (29.2c) and the left-hand side is non-negative by definition.

How does the trust parameter q affect the equilibrium value of money in economies with positively valued currency? A quick look at equation (29.1) should suffice to convince you that a reduction in q is similar to a reduction in β_h; with probability $1 - q$, individuals forgo all income from saving and consume their own second-period endowment whose utility we have normalized to zero. Consequently, less confidence is similar to less patience on the part of consumers, and a tendency toward less saving.

The intuitive effect of less confidence is money, then, is that it reduces the private sector's demand for currency at any given yield, and accentuates the "classical" character of a given economy. It may well be that an economy of the Samuelson type at $q = 1$ becomes classical at some lesser q. Equation (29.3) validates this intuition (because it is decreasing in q and equals $-\infty$ at $q = 0$), and figure 29.1 illustrates it with phaselines of equation (29.3) drawn for different values of q.

For $q = 1$ we have the standard full-confidence saving function $s(R)$ which produces an inside-money equilibrium at some $\bar{R} < 1$. As q falls, inside-money equilibria occur at progressively higher yields if dated goods are gross substitutes; inside-money yields for each q are defined implicitly from the equation

$$z(R, q) = 0 \qquad (29.4)$$

Meanwhile, the value of currency in a stationary outside-money equilibrium is a monotone increasing function of q:

$$m = z(1, q) \qquad (29.5)$$

If q fell below a critical value q_c defined from the equation

$$z(1, q_c) = 0 \qquad (29.6a)$$

then outside-money equilibria would disappear. Comparing (29.6a) with the definition of the full-confidence inside-money yield $\bar{R}$, that is, with

$$z(\bar{R}, 1) = 0 \qquad (29.6b)$$

we conclude that $q_c < \bar{R}$. We sum up the essentials of this section in the following theorem.

Theorem 29.1 Let $\bar{R} < 1$ be the inside-money yield of a pure-exchange economy of the Samuelson type. There is a critical value $q_c < \bar{R}$ of the trust parameter q below which there is no competitive equilibrium with valued money; furthermore, the value of money in stationary equilibrium is an increasing function of q for any $q \in [q_c, 1]$.

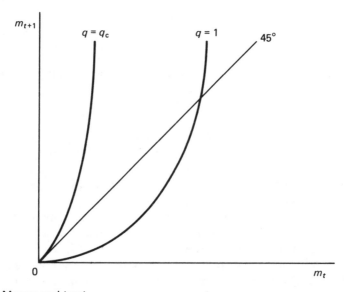

Figure 29.1 Money and trust.

Weil's extension of the standard overlapping generations model then accomplishes three things: (i) it elucidates in a simple and attractive parametric manner the relationship of valued money to trust; (ii) it points out that money cannot have any value unless individuals believe that there is a sufficiently good chance that it will continue to be valued in the future; and (iii) it relates the equilibrium price of money to individual beliefs about events, like inside-money states, which are not observed in equilibrium. In fact, Weil's model has a continuum of stationary monetary equilibria indexed on the off-equilibrium belief parameter $q \in [q_c, 1]$.

Multiple equilibria generated by disequilibrium beliefs are quite common in repeated games of asymmetric information (see Kreps and Wilson, 1982). One useful extension of Weil's idea would be to allow the confidence parameter to change over time, reflecting continued observations of positively or highly valued currency.

29.2 Least squares learning

In section 28.4 we discussed learning mechanisms as a criterion for selecting among perfect-foresight and rational expectations equilibria. The idea was to endow individuals with some means of gradually learning from observations something about the true structure of the economy, of studying the interaction between individual forecasts and actual data, and of seeing whether they converge to each other. A particular steady state, cyclic equilibrium, or stationary sunspot equilibrium that proves to be the rest point of some sensible learning process has a legitimate claim on our attention if it attracts nearby dynamical equilibria at which the initial beliefs of individuals differ somewhat from stationary perfect-foresight forecasts or stationary rational expectations beliefs.

One relatively simple learning mechanism is the notional adjustment process of equation (28.43) which lies at the heart of the expectational stability criterion. Learning typically involves the use of data in real, not notional, time and therefore introduces into dynamical economics *additional* state variables that describe the evolution of forecasts over time. In order to judge the validity of alternative equilibria in a given perfect-foresight economy, we must embed that economy in a larger state space in which forecasts are perfect only in an asymptotic sense. A typical example is the adaptive-learning forecast of equation (23.1) which uses a fixed-size sample of the T latest price observations to forecast next period's price.

From an econometric point of view, it is more efficient to utilize the entire data sample by, say, running an autoregression of the form

$$p_{t+1} = \alpha p_t + \omega_{t+1} \tag{29.7}$$

where ω is an identically and independently distributed random variable with zero mean. Suppose α_t is the least squares estimate of the coefficient α that we obtain from the sample $(p_0, \ldots, p_t)$ of observations. Then an unbiased forecast of p_{t+1} as of time t is

$$p^e_{t+1} = \alpha_t p_t \tag{29.8}$$

and α_t is a state variable for our economy. This approach to learning in dynamical economic models was pioneered by Marcet and Sargent (1988, 1989a,b) and applied to forecasting schemes more general than equation (29.7). The exposition here follows Bullard (1991).

To see how formal learning methods work, we augment the pure-exchange model of seigniorage in section 26.1 with the autoregressive forecasting scheme of equation (29.7). The complete economy consists of one asset-market equilibrium condition, a description of government policy, and a specification of the least squares forecast. Denoting by $\pi_{t+1}^e = p_{t+1}^e/p_t$ the one-period-ahead forecast of the inflation rate, and by $\mu > 1$ the gross rate of growth in the stock of currency, we have

$$m_t = s(1/\pi_{t+1}^e) \tag{29.9a}$$

$$M_{t+1} = \mu M_t \tag{29.9b}$$

for the asset market and government policy. New currency issue at $t + 1$ is $(\mu - 1)M_t$; it is spent to purchase goods and services at market prices without affecting individual indifference maps.

With equation (29.7), autoregressive learning generates an estimate of the expected inflation rate

$$\pi_{t+1}^e = \alpha_t = \frac{1}{\beta_t} \sum_{s=1}^{t-1} p_{s-1} p_s \tag{29.10a}$$

from the price sample $(p_0, \ldots, p_{t-1})$ where

$$\beta_t \equiv \sum_{s=1}^{t} p_{s-1}^2 \tag{29.10b}$$

When this prediction interacts with consumer tastes and endowments, the end result is the community demand for real money balances described on the left-hand side of equation (29.9a). Equilibrium then determines the price p_t, and the whole process is repeated one more time with a larger price sample.

To avoid high-order difference equations, we note that $\beta_t = \beta_{t-1} + p_{t-1}^2$ and rewrite equation (29.10a) in the recursive form

$$\pi_{t+1}^e = \pi_t^e + \frac{p_{t-2}(p_{t-1} - p_{t-2}\pi_t^e)}{\beta_{t-1}}$$

$$= \pi_t^e + \frac{p_{t-2}^2}{\beta_{t-1}} \left(\frac{p_{t-1}}{p_{t-2}} - \pi_t^e \right) \tag{29.10c}$$

However, we note that

$$\frac{p_{t-1}}{p_{t-2}} = \frac{M_{t-1}/m_{t-1}}{M_{t-2}/m_{t-2}} \qquad \text{by definition}$$

$$= \frac{\mu m_{t-2}}{m_{t-1}} \qquad \text{by equation (29.9b)}$$

Using the asset-market clearing condition (29.9a) we obtain

$$\frac{p_{t-1}}{p_{t-2}} = \frac{\mu s(1/\pi_{t-1}^e)}{s(1/\pi_t^e)} \tag{29.10d}$$

Taken together, equations (29.10c) and (29.10d) lead to the expression

$$\pi_{t+1}^e = \pi_t^e + \gamma_t \left[\frac{\mu s(1/\pi_{t-1}^e)}{s(1/\pi_t^e)} - \pi_t^e \right] \tag{29.11a}$$

where

$$\gamma_t \equiv \frac{p_{t-2}^2}{\beta_{t-1}} = \frac{p_{t-2}^2}{\sum_{s=1}^{t-1} p_{s-1}^2} \tag{29.11b}$$

Equation (29.11a) says that next period's expected inflation rate is equal to this period's expected inflation rate plus a small fraction of the difference between this period's actual and expected rates of inflation. It is also a second-order *non-autonomous* difference equation in which the coefficient $\gamma_t \in (0, 1)$ is the time-varying element. To remove this source of variability, we need to express γ_t recursively in terms of lagged values of the state variables γ and π. When we do that, we shall be left with a third-order autonomous dynamical system. Starting from equation (29.11b), we have successively

$$p_{t-1}^2 = \gamma_{t+1} \sum_{s=1}^{t} p_{s-1}^2$$

$$= \gamma_{t+1} \left(p_{t-1}^2 + \sum_{s=1}^{t-1} p_{s-1}^2 \right)$$

$$= \gamma_{t+1} \left(p_{t-1}^2 + \frac{p_{t-2}^2}{\gamma_t} \right)$$

which we divide through by p_{t-1}^2 to obtain

$$\frac{1}{\gamma_{t+1}} = 1 + \frac{1}{\gamma_t (p_{t-1}/p_{t-2})^2} \tag{29.12}$$

Dynamical equilibria are sequences (γ_t, π_t^e, p_t) that satisfy equation (29.10d), (29.11a), and (29.12). To express these equations more compactly we define a new variable x_t to be the right-hand side of equation (29.10d), substitute equation (29.10d) into (29.12), and rewrite everything in terms of the state vector (γ_t, π_t^e, x_t):

$$\gamma_{t+1} = \frac{\gamma_t x_t}{1 + \gamma_t x_t} \tag{29.13a}$$

$$\pi_{t+1}^e = (1 - \gamma_t)\pi_t^e + \gamma_t x_t \tag{29.13b}$$

$$x_{t+1} = \frac{\mu s(1/\pi_t^e)}{s\{1/[(1 - \gamma_t)\pi_t^e + \gamma_t x_t]\}} \tag{29.13c}$$

This is an autonomous dynamical system in $\mathbb{R}^3$ with a unique outside-money steady state

$$(\gamma, \pi, x) = (1 - 1/\mu, \mu, \mu) \tag{29.14}$$

which has the same equilibrium allocations as the corresponding perfect-foresight state. In particular, both states have inflation rates equal to the rate of money creation. To understand why this is so, note that equation (29.11a) has a steady state $\pi_t^e = \mu$ for all t if γ_t does not approach zero.

The main issue one investigates in learning models of this sort is whether the unique steady state of the dynamical system (29.13a)–(29.13c) is asymptotically stable, and, if not, what is it that attracts orbits that start in the vicinity of the steady state. To keep the set of potential attractors relatively small *we assume that the saving function s is monotone*, thereby excluding periodic equilibria in perfect foresight as well as stationary sunspot equilibria under rational expectations.

We compute next the Jacobian of the dynamical system and evaluate it at the steady state, obtaining as a result the 3×3 matrix of partial derivatives

$$J = \begin{pmatrix} 1/\mu & 0 & A \\ 0 & 1/\mu & 1-1/\mu \\ 0 & -(1-1/\mu)\epsilon & \epsilon \end{pmatrix}$$

where ϵ is the elasticity of saving evaluated at the yield $1/\mu$. The element A is the partial derivative of γ_{t+1} with respect to x_t and is an expression we shall not need. The characteristic polynomial of J is of the third order, namely

$$p(\lambda) = \left(\frac{1}{\mu} - \lambda \right) \phi(\lambda) \tag{29.15a}$$

where

$$\phi(\lambda) = \lambda^2 - \left(\epsilon + \frac{1}{\mu} \right) \lambda + \epsilon \left[\frac{1}{\mu} + \left(1 - \frac{1}{\mu} \right)^2 \right] \tag{29.15b}$$

These equations suggest straightaway that the Jacobian has one stable eigenvalue $\lambda_0 = 1/\mu \in (0, 1)$ plus two others – the roots of $\phi(\lambda)$. The discriminant of ϕ,

$$\Delta = \left(\epsilon + \frac{1}{\mu} \right)^2 - 4\epsilon \left(1 - \frac{1}{\mu} + \frac{1}{\mu^2} \right)$$

is the difference of two positive terms and may be of either sign depending on the size of the positive parameters ϵ and μ. For example, at $\epsilon = 0$ we have $\Delta = 1/\mu^2 > 0$ while at $\epsilon = 1$ we have $\Delta = -3(1/\mu - 1)^2 < 0$. Also $\Delta > 0$ if ϵ and $\mu - 1$ are very small positive numbers, whereas $\Delta < 0$ if ϵ and $1/\mu$ are very small positive numbers.

The prudent conclusion to draw from all these numerical examples is that the Jacobian matrix may have either one or three real eigenvalues in the relevant parameter space for the pair (ϵ, μ) which, roughly speaking, satisfies

$$0 \leqslant \epsilon \leqslant \mu \tag{29.16}$$

If the polynomial ϕ has two real roots, they are both positive and on the same side of unity because the constant term in ϕ is positive for all (ϵ, μ) that satisfy (29.16); furthermore we check easily that

$$\phi(1) = \left(1 - \frac{1}{\mu} \right) \left(1 - \frac{\epsilon}{\mu} \right) > 0$$

What if ϕ has complex roots? Then their modulus is the square root of the constant term in ϕ, and cannot exceed unity if the saving function is monotone. Therefore, J has three stable eigenvalues if

$$\epsilon \left(\frac{1}{\mu^2} - \frac{1}{\mu} + 1 \right) < 1 \tag{29.17}$$

that is, if the constant term in ϕ is in the interval $(0, 1)$; one stable and two unstable eigenvalues if inequality (29.17) fails.

For any $\mu > 1$, the term within parentheses on the left-hand side of (29.17) is in the interval $[3/4 , 1]$. Hence the steady state described in equation (29.14) is asymptotically stable for all $\epsilon \in [0, 1]$, that is, *whenever the aggregate saving function is not too sensitive to changes in yields*. In that event learning tends to stabilize outside-money steady states, just as adaptive learning did in section 24.2. We recall, from figures 26.1–26.3 for instance, that a monotone saving function means that monetary steady states are *unstable* in the usual forward-looking perfect-foresight dynamics.[1]

We shall need to discuss the fate of trajectories starting near the steady state when inequality (29.17) is reversed. Do such sequences converge to the inside-money state, simply diverge, or are they attracted by a closed, periodic, or quasi-periodic orbit? Does the dynamical system admit a Hopf cycle in some range of μ if ϵ is sufficiently large? Bullard (1991) looks at this question in detail. As we know from theorem 8.5, we should expect a closed orbit to emerge around the steady state if we can find values (ϵ, μ) such that the polynomial ϕ has a negative discriminant and a unitary constant term. In other words, we seek a solution to

$$\epsilon\left(1 - \frac{1}{\mu} + \frac{1}{\mu^2}\right) = 1 \tag{29.18a}$$

$$\epsilon + \frac{1}{\mu} < 2 \tag{29.18b}$$

which also satisfies inequality (29.16). Two examples of such critical solutions are $(\epsilon_c, \mu_c) = \{(64/49, 8/3), (68/49, 8/5)\}$.

Bullard gives simulation results for a similar model with a constant elasticity of substitution utility function in which equilibrium sequences in the vicinity of the steady state converge to $\pi = \mu$ if $\mu \in (1, \mu_c)$ but are attracted to a closed orbit if $\mu > \mu_c$, that is, for sufficiently rapid monetary expansion. This attractor is a cycle that gross substitutability rules out under perfect foresight; it is generated by the learning process itself.

29.3 Laboratory experiments with monetary economies

How does a group of traders predict future prices in an actual economy? What outcomes are selected in circumstances that permit indeterminate or multiple equilibria? In this section we review some data from two series of recent experiments conducted with undergraduate students in laboratories at Carnegie-Mellon University by Marimon and Sunder (1990) and at the California Institute of Technology by Aliprantis and Plott (1990). All these experiments replicate pure-exchange economies with overlapping generations and without a known terminal date. Each economy consists of repeated sessions ("time periods") of trading among alternating subgroups of students drawn from a group of individuals that is fixed at the start of each experimental sequence. Typically, groups of four to eight people play for two periods and the economy runs for 5–20 periods before the experiment ends "unexpectedly."

Individuals live two "periods" and are endowed with a given vector of "chips" (that is, consumption goods); the old also receive stocks of "script" money denominated in some arbitrary unit of account often called the "franc." After traders have a chance to exchange francs for chips, they are left at the end of each period of their life with a number of chips; their end-of-period commodity vector influences the rate at which the experimenter converts their holdings into US dollars. The actual rule by which chips are translated into dollars is known to each participant in the play and is supposed to define for each one a lifetime utility function.

Prices are set either by an actual auction or by a Walrasian auctioneer, that is, by an experimenter who elicits written excess demand schedules from all participants and then selects that price at which community excess demand vanishes for each good. The aggregate stock of "francs" changes over time because the experimenter buys each period a fixed and publicly known amount $g \geq 0$ of chips at market prices. This experimental economy is therefore one of inflationary finance with a fixed budget deficit; similar economies are explored in question IV.13 under perfect foresight, and in section 29.2 under least squares learning.

Dynamical equilibria in these economies are compactly expressed by three elements: an asset-market clearing condition, a "central bank" (or experimenter) budget identity, and a forecasting rule. The relevant equations for each $t = 1, 2, \ldots$ are

$$m_t = s(p_t/p_{t+1}^e) \tag{29.19a}$$

$$M_{t+1} = M_t + p_{t+1}g \tag{29.19b}$$

$$p_{t+1} = p_{t+1}^e \tag{29.19c}$$

if foresight is perfect. A least squares prediction mechanism replaces (29.19c) by an autoregressive forecast like that of equations (29.10a) and (29.10b).

All evidence from laboratory experiments suggests that exchange prices converge fairly rapidly to a narrow neighborhood of some steady state, and measured expectations quickly gain in predictive accuracy. What is most interesting is the *particular* steady state to which virtually all competitive equilibria converge in these laboratory economies: it is the low-inflation high-real-balances state that lies on the "good" side of the seigniorage Laffer curve depicted in figure 26.3 rather than the high-inflation low-real-balances state that occupies the "bad" side. Readers who do question IV.13 will discover that, if consumption goods are gross substitutes, the high-inflation state is asymptotically stable under perfect foresight while the low-inflation state is not. This is already implied by the phase diagram in figure 24.1(a).

Figure 29.2 illustrates a typical laboratory experiment from Marimon and Sunder (1990): exes show the perfect-foresight path from given initial conditions, zees trace equilibria with least square forecasts, and dark balls denote actual data. The two stationary inflation rates are shown by solid horizontal lines. Experimental evidence then tends to reverse the perfect-foresight predictions of figure 24.1(a) about the stability properties of the high- and low-inflation steady states; it is more in tune with the adaptive-learning material in section 24.2 and figure 24.2(a) which predicts that an inflationary pure-exchange economy will converge to the low-inflation steady state if dated consumption goods are gross substitutes.

Another interesting feature of laboratory experiments is that individual predictions do not differ appreciably from least squares forecasts after a few periods of play, except that convergence is more haphazard in the laboratory than in an ideal least squares environment; as figure 29.2 suggests, the experimental economy ends up fluctuating randomly in a slowly narrowing band *about* the steady state even though there is nothing stochastic in its fundamental structure.

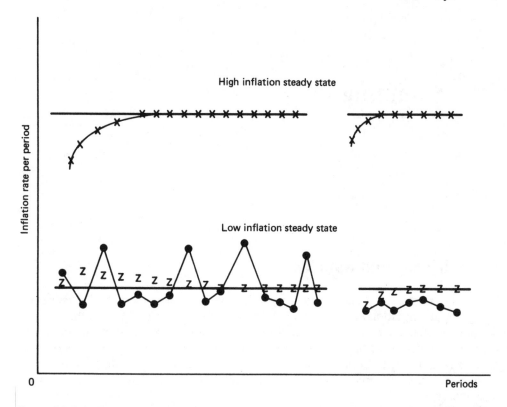

Figure 29.2 Laboratory experiments: x, rational expectations path; z, least squares learning path; •, actual economy's path.

Note

1. In a slightly different setting, Marcet and Sargent (1989b) prove a stronger result: under certain technical assumptions the steady state (γ, π, x) is asymptotically stable under least squares learning if the corresponding outside-money steady state is unstable (or determinate) in the perfect-foresight dynamics.

30   Summing up

30.1   Money and bubbles

In Part IV we studied a fairly large number of topics: money and bubbles, monetary policy and the inflation tax, expectations and sunspot equilibria. Most of the time we did so under the assumption of perfect foresight or rational expectations; on occasion, however, we discussed how people learn to anticipate the future both in theoretical models and in structured laboratory experiments. It is time to recapitulate our key findings and collect some of the issues that are uppermost in the minds of active researchers.

The word "money" in Part IV has meant almost exclusively outside money, that is, a collection of assets with positive exchange price and zero intrinsic worth or "use" value. More generally, an asset has a "bubble" component if its exchange value exceeds its "fundamental," that is, the present value of the services or dividends it yields over its economic life. To each equilibrium in which asset bubbles are positive corresponds an underlying fundamental equilibrium in which the bubble component bursts to zero. We have learned from Wallace (1980) and Tirole (1985) that bubbles occur only if two preconditions are satisfied: the lifespan of the asset must be potentially infinite and the underlying fundamental equilibrium must be dynamically inefficient.

Good examples of bubbles are fiat money, national debt, and other long-lived assets whose prices are affected by speculative considerations, for example land, common stocks, and foreign exchange. What does one gain or lose by regarding fiat money as a bubble? The chief advantage is that we allow the price of that asset to reflect public "trust" which loosely captures how much faith current asset holders have in the future value of their holdings. In symmetric fashion, the chief disadvantage of that view is that the value of money reflects *nothing but* trust and fails to recognize the transactions role of an exchange medium that permits traders to solve the "double coincidence of wants" problem. Consequently, economic models in which money is a bubble cannot explain easily how currency coexists with interest-bearing assets like loans, claims on capital, and national debt.

To discuss monetary policy, in particular, we need to understand why the asset portfolios of households and commercial banks contain both interest-bearing securities and lower-yielding assets such as currency or bank reserves. At present we have three ways, all of them somewhat artificial, of ensuring that individuals will hold currency and debt simultaneously. One is to impose legal restrictions on asset holdings, much as central banks do on commercial bank portfolios, which require that a specified minimum fraction of each portfolio should consist of currency or reserves. Two, we may simply assert that money is a service commodity, like haircuts, which happens to allow traders to economize on the time they spend in transacting other commodities; individual tastes to consume and save time are transformed into preferences over consumption goods and money balances. The end result is to put money in the representative household's utility function.

The most popular way to justify the holding of money comes from cash-in-advance constraints which appeal directly to money's function as a medium of exchange. One starts from the observation that credit is of little use in purchasing goods like newspapers, fleamarket items, and the like – these goods are sold strictly for cash and anyone who demands them must hold money. All three approaches to the demand for money draw broadly similar conclusions about the effects of open-market operations, and each of them yields special insights about certain instruments of monetary policy.

What is missing from all these stories of the demand for money are the underlying reasons for that demand. None of the available theories will explain why credit cards, electronic banking, and similar instruments have so successfully displaced money in the exchange process nowadays to the point that our societies are about to become cashless. To understand what drives the demand for money, it would be helpful – and perhaps necessary – to know something about circulating media of exchange. Why is it, for instance, that central bank liabilities like dollars and Deutschmarks are accepted on a global scale, some credit cards are honored all over the world, personal checks are accepted at most within a narrow geographical area, and personal IOU's are refused almost everywhere?

To put the question somewhat differently, suppose that an exchange economy consists of many different individuals, dates, states, and locations, that an individual may trade only in one location at each date, and that the itinerary of each person is public knowledge. How will the liabilities of each household be priced at each (date, state, location) triple? Whose IOU's will be widely accepted, that is, sell at a positive and fairly uniform price at many locations? What individual characteristics are responsible for broadly traded liabilities? Townsend (1980) and Townsend and Wallace (1987) have made interesting progress on these questions, but much work remains to be done.

30.2 Quantity issues

Perhaps the oldest issues in monetary theory concern the relationship of the stock of money to economic activity. How do changes in money supply and, more generally, in monetary policy affect the set of equilibrium allocations? How fast should the monetary authority permit banks to expand money and create credit? We found that the first question does not have a simple answer because there is no uniquely defined relationship between money and "economic activity." Equilibrium allocations, as one might suspect from first economic principles, are less influenced by the amount or the rate of change in the stock of an intrinsically worthless liability and more by the *manner* in which the aggregate stock of paper money is distributed over households at each (state, date) pair.

At one extreme we may go through the conceptual experiment of augmenting the quantity of money by paying all currency holders a uniform rate of interest on their balances; this operation does not change a whit the set of equilibrium allocations and preserves the neutrality of money. Other ways to create money involve lump-sum transfers to retired individuals, a lowering of reserve requirements on commercial banks, debasing the currency to finance government deficits, open market purchases of public debt, and several others. *Except in unusual or trivial cases, each of these operations alters the prevailing equilibrium in some essential way*. Faster monetary expansion that augments old-age subsidies, for instance, lowers real balances in the steady state and so, up to some point, will lower reserve requirements. Within certain bounds, looser monetary policies tend to depress nominal yields and to lower real returns as well.

The inflationary finance of government deficits is of independent interest because of its historical relevance to economic events in nations with profligate public sectors – from Imperial Rome to present-day Eastern Europe. We learned that modest government deficits may be paid for by inflationary means *in perpetuity* and how this is accomplished in two different ways: a low inflation tax levied on large money holdings or, alternatively, a high inflation tax on relatively small aggregate balances. The former solution is preferable to the latter on pure welfare grounds (it distorts the economy less), but high inflation seems quite persistent in countries with a record of insincere or failed attempts to bring price instability under control. It seems that the credibility of monetary authorities is an essential element of successful stabilization plans. Why governments choose to undermine their own reputation and that of their successors is a key issue in the "new political economy," a field that analyzes government policy as a rational response of policymakers to given resource constraints and electoral realities.[1]

In an ideal economy without distorting taxes, informational restrictions, or governments of ill repute, monetary authorities need not be concerned with seigniorage. If money is an asset that competes on equal terms with private loans and physical capital in individual portfolios, then the correct monetary policy is to ensure that money yields exactly as much as competing assets – neither more nor less. This typically means that one should follow the Friedman prescription, setting the rate of *deflation* equal to the economy's natural rate of interest, that is, to either the growth rate or the rate of time preference.

30.3   Expectations and business cycles

In chapters 27 and 28 we learned about two types of randomness, *intrinsic* or *objective* and *extraneous* or *subjective*, which affect economic equilibria. The first type refers to uncertainty about fundamental economic parameters such as preferences, endowments, technology, or economic policy; the second type is concerned with market psychology and how current decisions may reflect "optimistic" or "pessimistic" beliefs about future events.

The theory of rational expectations, developed in the 1960s and 1970s, was an attempt to analyze the role of anticipations in an objective way, that is, as statistical forecasts drawn from a correct structural model of an industry or an entire economy. When information about current values of economic variables is private or restricted, rational expectations models permit traders to extract from price observations valuable knowledge about the realized values of unobserved variables.

Separating uncertainty into subjective and objective components has not turned out to be a productive undertaking for what is the "correct" structural model of an economy often comes to depend substantially on what forecasters believe the correct answer to be. For instance, paying interest on existing money balances preserves the neutrality of money in the sense of the previous section if traders hold the view that monetary expansions are neutral; the same policy maneuver will have real consequences if traders come to believe that the quantity of money is an important determinant of economic activity.

In the same vein, Farmer and Woodford (1984) have shown that money-financed random variations of modest size in government purchases may be transmitted to prices and production by a continuum of possible mechanisms. At one extreme, prices adjust immediately and production responds with a lag; at the other extreme, prices are initially rigid and the burden of adjustment falls on production. There are all sorts of intermediate possibilities whose realization depends on public beliefs, that is, on what variables individuals consider to be salient for economic prediction. Provided that variations in government purchases are relatively small, many forecasting rules turn out to be consistent with rational expectations and each one supports an equilibrium that allocates a distinct random consumption bundle to each consumer. We call these allocations payoff-relevant sunspot equilibria; we have learned something about the precise conditions under which stationary sunspot equilibria exist.

At a broader level, sunspot equilibria are closely connected with missing markets for contingent securities. This connection, developed by Cass and Shell (1983), begins with the observation that sunspot allocations are Pareto dominated by the corresponding non-sunspot outcomes because the sunspots inject spurious noise in an economic environment whose fundamental structures may very well be quite stable. Since competitive equilibria are necessarily Pareto optima in, say, an Arrow–Debreu framework with complete markets for contingent claims, sunspots and similar indices of consumer sentiment cannot affect equilibrium allocations whenever all the standard assumptions of the Arrow–Debreu model apply.

Nontrivial sunspot equilibria presuppose that at least one of the standard assumptions of finite competitive general equilibrium fails. The specific assumption that many investigators have focused on is the *insurability of sunspots*. "Sunspots" may stand for a subjective state of mind whose realization will be hard to establish in the eyes of a disinterested third party, or they may describe a publicly verifiable and easily measurable event like an index of consumer sentiment. In either case it is unrealistic to suppose that complete markets exist for insuring individuals against all possible natural events. Even if the sunspot realization s_t at time t were indeed public knowledge, a truly complete market structure should by definition permit each individual to trade securities contingent on any possible history $H_t = (s_1, \ldots, s_t)$ of natural events. This is impossible in overlapping generations economies whose demographic structure rules out trading by unborn or deceased individuals.

Households may very well desire to engage in trading at times when they are not "alive" or legally entitled to transact for one simple reason: the natural states and prices they face over their lifespan are in principle correlated with what took place before their birth or with what is predicted to take place after their death. These demographic realities prevent many agents from participating beneficially in markets in which they would have traded if their life were longer. The resulting *incomplete market participation* is a key reason why payoff-relevant sunspot equilibria may exist even if all relevant securities markets are physically open at all times.

Many economists are disconcerted, and rightly so, by the large number of equilibria produced by models of rational expectations. One reason for this concern is that sensible economic prediction and meaningful policy evaluation require equilibria to be locally unique; and one implication of it is that economic research needs to pay closer attention to mechanisms that narrow down the number of equilibria.

Learning processes are a particularly interesting device that selects among all rational expectations or perfect foresight equilibria those which turn out to be the outcomes of some intuitively plausible learning rule. A number of adaptive or statistical learning rules, for example, least squares learning, exist in the literature which are well suited for this purpose. Each one specifies how actual state variables interact with their predicted values over time and describes the circumstances under which forecast errors vanish asymptotically.

Equilibria that are robust under a learning rule will prevail even if individuals do not fully understand the working of the economy from the start or cannot make an accurate forecast at any finite date. This form of robustness is an equilibrium requirement of considerable descriptive value but it may not work well as a selection device. Learning processes that exclude some non-robust perfect foresight equilibria may spawn others and compound whatever indeterminacy already existed under perfect foresight. Adding forecasts to the state space of an economy could easily increase the number of eigenvalues associated with any steady state without changing the number of initial conditions determined by history.

If we take seriously the traditional intent of stabilization policy, then it is natural to think of monetary and fiscal instruments as filters that may help guide a dynamic economy away from equilibria displaying endogenous fluctuations, extraneous uncertainty, and other welfare-reducing phenomena. One promising class of policies, explored by Smith (1990), consists of simple operating rules that do not use much information, seeking instead to achieve target values for a key relative price (that is, the inflation rate, the nominal interest rate) or some monetary aggregate. Each of these policies alters the set of equilibria in some fundamental way; Smith provides an example of a monetized overlapping generations economy in which inflation-targeting policies eliminate the substitution effect and thereby open the door to periodic fluctuations, stationary sunspot equilibria, and other cyclical equilibria. Fixing the money supply rules out all these endogenous fluctuations.

These examples are not comprehensive prescriptions of how to dampen or eliminate spurious fluctuations in the familiar paradigms of dynamical macroeconomics, but they do illustrate convincingly that selecting the most desirable, or excluding the least desirable, item in a list of equilibria remains one of the key tasks of stabilization policy. This task is not one that economists understand well: a rich harvest of results is likely to reward further research in this area.

In the end, what and how much policymakers want to stabilize depends critically on the sources to which we attribute business cycles. The case for smoothing out fluctuations is weak in economies with a representative infinite-lived household and constant returns-to-scale production if cyclical behavior is a competitive response to technological disturbances of the sort that predominate in real business cycle theory.[2] The reason is that competitive equilibria are typically Pareto optimal in these stochastic variants of the optimum growth model; smoothing out cycles in these circumstances is an interesting exercise only if the policymaker possesses a social welfare function that ranks Pareto-optimal allocations.

Sunspot equilibria in overlapping generation economies make a stronger case for stabilization policy. To formulate policy proposals that reach beyond the interesting theoretical abstraction to something of practical significance, researchers need to accomplish two tasks. One is to construct models of sufficient realism to mimic in sufficient detail the aggregate time-series behavior of actual economies. The other is to articulate the events, institutions, and mechanisms that focus the expectations of households, firms, and financial institutions on one particular equilibrium when many (oftentimes, infinitely many) are possible. Much work is now under way on each of these lines of research, with interesting results likely to follow.

Notes

1. An excellent introduction to this field is the monograph by Persson and Tabellini (1989).
2. See the reference in note 2, ch. 25; also consult Hansen (1985) and Rogerson (1988) for issues relating to employment.

Bibliography

Further Reading

Two classic introductions on the exchange value of money are Wicksell (1906, part IV) and Hahn (1965). Calvo (1978) and Wallace (1980) provide good starts for the literature on bubbles.

Fisher (1912), Friedman (1956), and Patinkin (1965) give concise statements of early work on the quantity theory of money; a good survey of recent work is in Woodford (1990b).

Cagan (1956), Brock (1975), and Wilson (1979) are three lucid expositions of inflation finance, listed in order of increasing technical sophistication; for a good example of empirical work on seignorage, see Alogoskoufis and Christodoulakis (1990). The literature on long-lived overlapping generations models is still quite thin but research in this area is picking up rapidly. Among theoretical papers Aiyagari (1988) and Kehoe et al. (1991) stand out; Auerbach and Kotlikoff (1987), Rios-Rull (1991), and Bullard (1992) have put together parametric examples that may become useful in simulating real-world economies.

Standard references for the existence of rational expectations equilibria are Radner (1979) for atemporal economies with many physical goods, and Spear (1985) for overlapping generations settings. Guesnerie and Woodford (1991) provide an extensive survey of recent advances on sunspot equilibria; the unpublished related work of Farmer and Woodford (1984) is an early classic on price stickiness and price volatility. Finally, Evans and Honkapohja (1992) provide a readable general introduction to the stability of learning processes.

References

Aiyagari, R. 1988: Nonmonetary steady states in stationary overlapping generations models with long lived agents and discounting. *Journal of Economic Theory*, 45, 102–27.

Aliprantis, C. and Plott, C. 1990: Competitive equilibria in overlapping generations experiments. Mimeo, California Institute of Technology.

Allen, B. 1981: Generic existence of completely revealing equilibria for economies with uncertainty when prices convey information. *Econometrica*, 49, 1173–99.

Alogoskoufis, G. and Christodoulakis, N. 1990: Fiscal deficits, seigniorage and external debt: the case of Greece. Discussion Paper 468, CEPR.

Arrow, K. and Hurwicz, L. 1958: On the stability of competitive equilibrium. *Econometrica*, 26, 522–52.

——, Block, H., and Hurwicz, L. 1959: On the stability of competitive equilibrium, II. *Econometrica*, 27, 82–109.

Auerbach, A. and Kotlikoff, L. 1987: *Dynamic Fiscal Policy*. Cambridge: Cambridge University Press.

Auernheimer, L. 1974: The honest government's guide to the revenue from the creation of money. *Journal of Political Economy*, 82, 598–606.

Azariadis, C. 1981a: A reexamination of natural rate theory. *American Economic Review*, 71, 944–60.

—— 1981b: Self-fulfilling prophecies. *Journal of Economic Theory*, 25, 380–96.

—— 1989: Rational expectations equilibria with Keynesian properties. *Finnish Economic Papers*, 2, 99–105.

—— 1992: The problem of multiple equilibrium. Mimeo, University of California at Los Angeles.

—— and Cooper, R. 1985: Nominal wage–price rigidity as a rational expectations equilibrium. *American Economic Review (Papers and Proceedings)*, 75, 31–5.

—— and Farmer, R. 1987: Fractional reserve banking. Mimeo, University of Pennsylvania.

—— and Guesnerie, R. 1982: Prophéties créatices et persistence des théories. *Revue Economique*, 33, 787–806.

—— and —— 1986: Sunspots and cycles. *Review of Economic Studies*, 53, 725–37.

Bailey, M. 1956: The welfare cost of inflationary finance. *Journal of Political Economy*, 64, 93–110.

Balasko, Y. 1983: Extrinsic uncertainty revisited. *Journal of Economic Theory*, 31, 203–10.

—— and Shell, K. 1981: The overlapping generations model, II: The case of pure exchange with money. *Journal of Economic Theory*, 24, 112–42.

Bewley, T, 1980: The optimum quantity of money. In J. Kareken and N. Wallace (eds), *Models of Monetary Economies*, Minneapolis, MN: Federal Reserve Bank of Minneapolis.

—— 1986: Dynamic implications of the form of the budget constraint. In H. Sonnenschein (ed.), *Models of Economic Dynamics*, New York: Springer.

Blanchard, O. and Kahn, C. 1980: The solutions of linear difference models under rational expectations. *Econometrica*, 48, 1305–11.

Boskin, M. 1978: Taxation, saving and the rate of interest. *Journal of Political Economy*, 86, S3–27.

Braudel, F. 1981: *Civilization and Capitalism, 15th–18th Century, vol. I, The Structures of Everyday Life*. New York: Harper and Row.

Bray, M. 1982: Learning, estimation and the stability of rational expectations. *Journal of Economic Theory*, 26, 319–39.

Brock, W. 1974: Money and growth: the case of long-run perfect foresight. *International Economic Review*, 15, 750–77.

—— 1975: A simple perfect foresight monetary model. *Journal of Monetary Economics*, 1, 133–50.

Bryant, J. 1983: A simple rational expectations Keynes-type model. *Quarterly Journal of Economics*, 98, 525–9.

—— and Wallace, N. 1984: A price discrimination analysis of monetary policy. *Review of Economic Studies*, 51, 279–88.

Bullard, J. 1991: Learning equilibria. Mimeo, Federal Reserve Bank of St Louis.

—— 1992: Samuelson's model of money with N-period lifetimes. Working Paper, Federal Reserve Bank of St Louis.

Burmeister, E. and Dobell, R. 1970: *Mathematical Theories of Economic Growth*. London: Macmillan.

Cagan, P. 1956: The monetary dynamics of hyperinflation. In M. Friedman (ed.), *Studies in the Quantity Theory of Money*, Chicago, IL: University of Chicago Press.

Calvo, G. 1978a: On the indeterminacy of interest rates and wages under perfect foresight. *Journal of Economic Theory*, 19, 321–37.

—— 1978b: On the time consistency of optimal policy in a monetary economy. *Econometrica*, 46, 1411–28.

Carlton, D. 1986: The rigidity of prices. *American Economic Review*, 76, 637–58.

Cass, D. and Shell, K. 1980: In defense of a basic approach. In J. Kareken and N. Wallace (eds), *Models of Monetary Economies*, Minneapolis, MN: Federal Reserve Bank of Minneapolis.

—— and —— 1983: Do "sunspots" matter? *Journal of Political Economy*, 91, 193–227.

—— and Yaari, M. 1966: A re-examination of the pure consumption–loans model. *Journal of Political Economy*, 74, 353–67.

Chiappori, P.-A. and Guesnerie, R. 1989: On stationary sunspot equilibria of order *k*. In W. Barnett, J. Geweke, and K. Shell (eds), *Economic Complexity*, Cambridge: Cambridge University Press.

Clower, R. 1967: A reconsideration of the micro-foundations of monetary theory. *Western Economic Journal*, 6, 1–9.

Cooper, R. and John, A. 1988: Coordinating coordination failures in Keynesian models. *Quarterly Journal of Economics*, 103, 441–64.

Council of Economic Advisers 1990: *Economic Report of the President*, Washington, DC: US Government Printing Office.

Cousineau, J.-M. and Lacroix, R. 1981: *L'Indéxation des Salaires*. Montreal: University de Montréal.

Cutler, D., Poterba, J., and Summers, L. 1991: Speculative dynamics. *Review of Economic Studies*, 58, 529–46.

DeCanio, S. 1979: Rational expectations and learning from experience. *Quarterly Journal of Economics*, 93, 47–58.

DeGroot, M. 1970: *Optimal Statistical Decisions*. New York: McGraw-Hill.

DeLong, B., Schleifer, A., Summers, L. and Waldmann, R. 1990: Noise trader risk in financial markets. *Journal of Political Economy*, 98, 703–38.

Diamond, D. and Dybvig, P. 1983: Bank runs, deposit insurance, and liquidity. *Journal of Political Economy*, 91, 401–19.

Diamond, P. 1982: Aggregate demand management in search equilibrium. *Journal of Political Economy*, 90, 881–94.

Drandakis, E. 1966: On the competitive equilibrium in a monetary economy. *International Economic Review*, 7, 304–28.

Evans, G. 1983: The stability of rational expectations in macroeconomic models. In R. Frydman and E. Phelps (eds), *Individual Forecasting and Aggregate Outcomes*, Cambridge: Cambridge University Press.

—— 1989: The fragility of sunspots and bubbles. *Journal of Monetary Economics*, 23, 297–317.

—— and Honkapohja, S. 1990: Convergence of recursive learning mechanisms to steady states and cycles in stochastic nonlinear models. Mimeo, London School of Economics.

—— and —— 1992: Adaptive learning and expectational stability: an introduction. Mimeo, London School of Economics.

Evans, O. 1983: Tax policy, the interest elasticity of saving, and capital accumulation. *American Economic Review*, 73, 398–410.

Farmer, R. 1991: Sticky prices. Mimeo, University of California at Los Angeles.

—— and Woodford, M. 1984: Self-fulfilling prophecies and the business cycle. Mimeo, University of Pennsylvania.

Fischer, S. 1977: Long-term contracts, rational expectations and the optimal money supply rule. *Journal of Political Economy*, 85, 191–205.

Fisher, I. 1912: *The Purchasing Power of Money*. New York: Macmillan.

Friedman, M. 1948: A monetary and fiscal framework for economic stability. *American Economic Review*, 38, 245–64.

—— (ed.) 1956: *Studies in the Quantity Theory of Money*. Chicago, IL: University of Chicago Press.

—— 1969: *The Optimum Quantity of Money and Other Essays*. Chicago, IL: Aldine.

—— and Schwartz, A. J. 1963: *Monetary History of the United States, 1867–1960*. Princeton, NJ: Princeton University Press.

Fuchs, G. 1979: Is error learning behavior stabilizing? *Journal of Economic Theory*, 20, 300–17.

Gale, D. 1973: Pure exchange equilibrium of dynamic economic models. *Journal of Economic Theory*, 6, 12–36.

Garber, P. 1989: Tulipmania. *Journal of Political Economy*, 97, 535–60.

Geanakoplos, J. and Polemarchakis, H. 1986: Existence, regularity and constrained suboptimality of competitive allocations when markets are incomplete. In W. Heller, R. Starr, and D. Starrett (eds), *Essays in Honor of Kenneth Arrow*, vol. III, Cambridge: Cambridge University Press.

Gouriéroux, C., Laffont, J.-J. and Montfort, A. 1982: Rational expectations in dynamic linear models: analysis of the solutions. *Econometrica*, 50, 409–25.

Grandmont, J.-M. 1983: *Money and Value*. Cambridge: Cambridge University Press.

—— 1985: On endogenous competitive business cycles. *Econometrica*, 53, 995–1045.

—— 1986: Stabilizing competitive business cycles. *Journal of Economic Theory*, 40, 57–76.

—— (ed.)(1988): *Temporary Equilibrium*. San Diego, CA: Academic Press.

—— and Laroque, G. 1986: Stability of cycles and expectations. *Journal of Economic Theory*, 40, 138–51.

—— and Younès, Y. 1973: On the role of money and the existence of a monetary equilibrium. *Review of Economic Studies*, 39, 355–72.

Grossman, S. 1981: An introduction to the theory of rational expectations under asymmetric information. *Review of Economic Studies*, 48, 541–59.

—— and Stiglitz, J. 1980: On the impossibility of information efficient markets. *American Economic Review*, 70, 393–408.

Guesnerie, R. 1986: Stationary sunspot equilibria in an *N*-commodity world. *Journal of Economic Theory*, 40, 103–28.

—— and Woodford, M. 1991: Endogenous fluctuations. Mimeo, DELTA.

Haberler, G. 1941: *Prosperity and Depression*, 3rd edn. New York: Columbia University Press.

Hahn, F. 1965: On some problems of proving the existence of an equilibrium in a monetary economy. In F. Hahn and F. Brechling (eds), *The Theory of Interest Rates*, London: Macmillan.

—— 1966: Equilibrium growth with heterogeneous capital goods. *Quarterly Journal of Economics*, 80, 633–46.

Hamilton, J. 1983: Oil and The Macroeconomy since World War II. *Journal of Political Economy*, 91, 228–48.

Hansen, G. 1985: Indivisible labor and the business cycle. *Journal of Monetary Economics*, 16, 309–27.

Hicks, J. 1946: *Value and Capital*, 2nd edn. Oxford: Clarendon Press.

Jevons, W. 1884: *Investigations in Currency and Finance*. London: Macmillan.

Kehoe, T. and Levine, D. 1985: Comparative statics and perfect foresight in infinite horizon economies. *Econometrica*, 53, 433–53.

—— and —— 1990: The economics of indeterminacy in overlapping generations models. *Journal of Public Economics*, 42, 219–43.

——, ——, Mas-Colell, A. and Woodford, M. 1991: Gross substitutability in large square economies. *Journal of Economic Theory*, 54, 1–25.

Keynes, M. 1936: *The General Theory of Employment, Interest, and Money*. London: Macmillan.

Kiyotaki, N. and Wright, R. 1989: On money as a medium of exchange. *Journal of Political Economy*, 97, 927–54.

Kreps, D. 1990: *A Course in Microeconomic Theory*. Princeton, NJ: Princeton University Press.

—— and Wilson, R. 1982: Sequential equilibrium. *Econometrica*, 50, 863–94.

Kydland, F. and Prescott, E. G. 1982: Time to build and aggregate fluctuations. *Econometrica*, 50, 1345–70.

Kyle, A. 1985: Continuous auctions and insider trading. *Econometrica*, 53, 1315–35.

Laidler, D. 1969: *The Demand for Money*. Scranton, PA: International Textbook.

LeRoy, S. and Porter, R. 1981: The present value relation: tests based on variance bounds. *Econometrica*, 49, 555–84.

Long, J. and Plosser, C. 1981: Real business cycles. *Journal of Political Economy*, 91, 39–69.

Lucas, R. 1972: Expectations and the neutrality of money. *Journal of Economic Theory*, 4, 103–24.

—— 1976: Econometric policy evaluation: a critique. In K. Brunner and A. Meltzer (eds), *The Phillips Curve and Labor Markets*, Carnegie-Rochester Conference Series on Public Policy 1, Amsterdam: North-Holland.

—— 1978: Asset prices in an exchange economy. *Econometrica*, 46, 1429–45.

—— (1984): Money in a Theory of Finance. *Carnegie Rochester Conference Series on Public Policy*, 21, 9–46. Amsterdam: North Holland.

—— 1986: Adaptive behavior and economic theory. *Journal of Business*, 59, S401–26.

—— and Sargent, T. (eds) 1981: *Rational Expectations and Econometric Practice*. Minneapolis, MN: University of Minnesota Press.

Magill, M. and Shafer, W. 1991: Incomplete markets. In W. Hildenbrand and H. Sonnenschein (eds.), *Handbook of Mathematical Economics*, Amsterdam: North-Holland.

Malinvaud, E. 1977: *The Theory of Unemployment Reconsidered*. Oxford: Blackwell.

Marcet, A. and Sargent, T. 1988: The fate of systems with "adaptive" expectations. *American Economic Review (Papers and Proceedings)*, 78, 168–72.

—— and —— 1989a: Least squares learning and the dynamics of hyperinflation. In W. Barnett, J. Geweke, and K. Shell (eds), *Economic Complexity*, Cambridge: Cambridge University Press.

—— and —— 1989b: Convergence of least squares learning mechanisms in self-referential economic models. *Journal of Economic Theory*, 48, 337–68.

Marimon, R. and Sunder, S. 1990: Indeterminacy of equilibria in a hyperinflationary world: experimental evidence. Mimeo, Carnegie-Mellon University.

Mas-Colell, A. 1989: Three observations on sunspots and asset redundancy. Mimeo, Harvard University.

Matsuyama, K. 1991: Endogenous price fluctuations in an optimizing model of a monetary economy. *Econometrica*, 59, 1617–32.

McCallum, B. 1983: On non-uniqueness in linear rational expectations models: an attempt of perspective. *Journal of Monetary Economics*, 11, 139–68.

Metzler, L. 1951: Wealth, saving and the rate of interest. *Journal of Political Economy*, 59, 93–116.

Milnor, T. 1965: *Topology from the Differentiable Viewpoint*. Charlottesville, VA: University of Virginia Press.

Mundell, R. 1965: Growth, stability and inflationary finance. *Journal of Political Economy*, 73, 97–109.

Muth, J. 1961: Rational expectations and the theory of price movements. *Econometrica*, 29, 315–35.

Obstfeld, M. and Rogoff, K. 1983: Speculative hyperinflations in maximizing models: Can we rule them out? *Journal of Political Economy*, 91, 675–87.

Okun, A. 1981: *Prices and Quantities*. Washington, DC: Brookings Institution.

Patinkin, D. 1965: *Money, Interest and Prices*, 2nd edn. New York: Harper and Row.

Peck, J. 1988: On the existence of sunspot equilibria in an overlapping generations model. *Journal of Economic Theory*, 44, 19–42.

Persson, T. and Tabellini, G. 1989: *Macroeconomic Policy, Credibility and Politics*. Chur: Harwood Publishers.

Phelps, E. (ed.) 1970: *Macroeconomic Foundations of Employment and Inflation Theory*. New York: Norton.

Philipps, A. 1958: The relation between unemployment and the rate of change of money wages in the United Kingdom, 1861–1957. *Economica*, 25, 283–99.

Pigou, A. 1929: *Industrial Fluctuations*, 2nd edn. London: Macmillan.

—— 1943: The classical stationary state. *Economic Journal*, 53, 343–51.

Postan, M., Rich, E. and Miller, E. (eds) 1971: *The Cambridge Economic History of Europe*. Cambridge: Cambridge University Press.

Poterba, L. and Summers, L. 1988: Mean reversion in stock prices: evidence and implications. *Journal of Financial Economics*, 22, 26–59.

Radner, R. 1979: Rational expectations equilibrium: generic existence and the information revealed by price. *Econometrica*, 47, 655–78.

—— 1982: Equilibrium under uncertainty. In K. Arrow and M. Intriligator (eds), *Handbook of Mathematical Economics*, vol. II. Amsterdam: North-Holland.

Rios-Rull, V. 1991: Life cycle economies and aggregate fluctuations. Mimeo, Carnegie-Mellon University.

Rogerson, R. 1988: Indivisible labor, lotteries and equilibrium. *Journal of Monetary Economics*, 21, 3–16.

Romer, D. 1986: A simple general equilibrium model of the Baumol–Tobin model. *Quarterly Journal of Economics*, 101, 663–86.

Samuelson, P. 1958: An exact consumption–loan model of interest with or without the social contrivance of money. *Journal of Political Economy*, 66, 467–82.

Sargent, T. and Wallace, N. 1973: The stability of models of money and growth. *Econometrica*, 41, 1043–8.

—— and —— 1975: Rational expectations, the optimal monetary instrument, and the optimal money supply rule. *Journal of Political Economy*, 83, 241–54.

—— and —— 1982: The real bills doctrine versus the quantity theory: a reconsideration. *Journal of Political Economy*, 90, 1212–36.

Shiller, R. 1981: Do stock prices move too much to be justified by subsequent changes in dividends? *American Economic Review*, 71, 421–36.

—— 1989: *Market Volatility*. Cambridge, MA: MIT Press.

Sidrauski, M. 1967: Rational choice and patterns of growth in a monetary economy. *American Economic Review*, 57, 533–44.

Simons, H. 1948: *Economic Policy for a Free Society*. Chicago, IL: University of Chicago Press.

Sims, C. 1972: Money, income and causality. *American Economic Review*, 62, 540–52.

Smith, A. 1776: *The Wealth of Nations*. Reprinted by Pelican Books (1973).

Smith, B. 1990a: Legal restrictions, "sunspots" and Peel's Bank Act. *Journal of Political Economy*, 96, 3–19.

—— 1990b: Efficiency and determinacy of equilibrium under inflation targeting. Mimeo, Cornell University.

—— 1991: Interest on reserves and sunspot equilibria: Friedman's proposal reconsidered. *Review of Economic Studies*, 58, 93–105.

Spear, S. 1984: Sufficient conditions for the existence of sunspot equilibria. *Journal of Economic Theory*, 34, 360–70.

—— 1985: Rational expectations in the overlapping generations model. *Journal of Economic Theory*, 35, 251–75.

Stokey, N. and Lucas, R. 1989: *Recursive Methods in Economic Dynamics*. Cambridge, MA: Harvard University Press.

Taylor, J. 1977: Conditions for unique solutions in stochastic macroeconomic models with rational expectations. *Econometrica*, 45, 671–84.

—— 1980: Aggregate dynamics and staggered contracts. *Journal of Political Economy*, 88, 1–23.

Thornton, H. 1802: *An Enquiry into the Nature and Effects of Paper Credit in Great Britain*. Reprinted by Kelley, New York (1965).

Tirole, J. 1985: Asset bubbles and overlapping generations. *Econometrica*, 53, 1499–528.

Tobin, J. 1958: Liquidity preference as behavior towards risk. *Review of Economic Studies*, 25, 65–86.

—— 1965: Money and economic growth. *Econometrica*, 33, 671–84.

—— 1970: Money and income: post hoc ergo propter hoc? *Quarterly Journal of Economics*, 75, 301–17.

Townsend, R. 1980: Models of Money with Spatially Separated Agents. In J. Karellen and N. Wallace (eds), *Models of Monetary Economics*. Minneapolis: Federal Reserve Bank of Minneapolis.

—— 1981: Forecasting the forecasts of others. *Journal of Political Economy*, 91, 546–88.

—— and Wallace, N. 1987: A Model of Circulating Private Debt. In E. Prescott and N. Wallace (eds), *Contractual Arrangements for Intertemporal Trade*. Minneapolis: University of Minnesota Press.

Wallace, N. 1980: The overlapping generations model of fiat money. In J. Kareken and N. Wallace (eds), *Models of Monetary Economies*, Minneapolis, MN: Federal Reserve Bank of Minneapolis.

—— 1983: A legal restrictions theory of the demand for "money" and the role of monetary policy. *Federal Reserve Bank of Minneapolis Quarterly Review*, 7, 1–7.

Webber, C. and Wildavsky, A. 1986: *A History of Taxation and Expenditure in the Western World*. New York: Simon and Schuster.

Weil, P. 1987: Confidence and the real value of money in an overlapping generations economy. *Quarterly Journal of Economics*, 102, 1–22.

Wicksell, K. 1906: *Vorlesungen über Nationalökonomie*, vol II. translated as *Lectures on Political Economy*, London: Routledge (1934). Reprinted by Kelley (1977).

Wilson, C. 1979: An infinite horizon model with money. In J. Green and J. Scheinkman (eds), *General Equilibrium, Growth and Trade*, New York: Academic Press.

Woodford, M. 1984: Indeterminacy of equilibrium in the overlapping generations model: a survey. Mimeo, Columbia University.

—— 1986: Stationary sunspot equilibria in a finance constrained economy. *Journal of Economic Theory*, 40, 128–37.

—— 1988: Expectations, finance and aggregate instability. In M. Kohn and S. C. Tsiang (eds), *Finance Constraints, Expectations and Macroeconomics*, Oxford: Oxford University Press.

—— 1990a: Learning to believe in sunspots. *Econometrica*, 58, 277–307.

—— 1990b: The optimum quantity of money. In F. Hahn and B. Friedman (eds), *Handbook of Monetary Economics*, vol. II, Amsterdam: North-Holland.

Questions

Unmarked questions are the easiest to do while starred questions relate to advanced material. Other questions are labeled (T) if they are primarily technical and (C) if they require some creative thinking.

IV.1 (T) Suppose household h has a twice continuously differentiable strictly concave utility function $u^h: \mathbb{R}_+^2 \to \mathbb{R}$, an individual saving function $s^h: \mathbb{R}_+ \to \mathbb{R}$, and an individually autarkic interest factor $\bar{R}_h$. All households consider youthful and old-age consumption to be strictly normal goods.

    (a) For any interest factor $r > \bar{R}_h$, show that the interest-factor elasticity of saving exceeds -1. (*Hint*: Use the Slutsky equation of consumer theory.)

    (b) Prove that $Rs_h(R) \to \infty$ as $R \to \infty$. (*Hint*: Use the first-order conditions to the consumer's maximum problem.)

    (c) Demonstrate the uniqueness of the backward-looking equilibrium. (*Hint*: Show that aggregate excess demand is a decreasing function of p_t at any backward equilibrium.)

    (d) Show that the excess demand function in equation (23.8) is decreasing in current price at every equilibrium if the expected price always has elasticity less than unity with respect to current price.

IV.2 In an economy with constant population, suppose that the only store of value is commodity inventories with constant proportional depreciation rate γ.

    (a) Investigate the existence and intertemporal efficiency of competitive equilibrium when $0 < \gamma < 1$.

    (b) Is competitive equilibrium optimal if $\gamma = 0$, that is, when storage is costless?

    (c) Discuss whether your conclusion in part (b) is in accordance with the Phelps–Koopmans theorem.

IV.3 An economy with constant population has two stores of value: currency, of which there is a constant stock M per capita, and commodity inventories which can be stored according to the diminishing-returns technology $x_{t+1} = f(k_t)$. Here k_t is the amount put in storage at time t and x_{t+1} is the amount available to every consumer at time $t+1$. The function f is increasing, concave, and such that $f(0) = 0$.

    (a) Describe how the introduction of storage changes the set of competitive equilibria available to a pure currency economy. In particular, what happens to the steady states pictured in figure 24.1 if $f(k) = \alpha k$ for some parameter $\alpha > 1$?

    (b) Are there competitive equilibria, stationary or otherwise, in which both stores of value are in use? Only one is in use? Assume now that f is nonlinear.

IV.4 (T) Reexamine the existence and stability of the dynamical equilibria we analyzed in section 24.1 *without* the assumption of perfect foresight. In particular:

(a) Assume it is common knowledge that all households predict future prices via the rule

$$\log p^e_{t+1} = \lambda \log p_t + (1 - \lambda) \log p_{t-1} \qquad 0 < \lambda < 1$$

(b) How do your results differ from those of perfect foresight? Can you find parametric examples of preferences for which the forward-looking equilibrium is unstable with perfect foresight, but asymptotically stable under the expectation function of part (a)?

IV.5 In an overlapping generations economy with zero population growth, M is the stock of money, all households are identical, and there are no endowments of consumable commodities. Each household is endowed in youth with $e > 1$ units of divisible leisure which it can transform into a perishable consumption good by means of the stationary technology $y = L$, where y is output and $L \in [0, e]$ is labor input. Work can only take place in youth and consumption occurs exclusively in old age. The utility function common to all households and all generations (except G_0) is

$$u(c'_2, L'_1) = c'_2 - 1/2 \, (L'_1)^2$$

(a) Construct the excess demand function for this economy and derive a difference equation describing dynamical equilibria, assuming (common knowledge) that forecasts are universally made by the *adaptive rule*

$$\hat{p}^e_{t+1} = (1 - \lambda)\hat{p}_t + \lambda\hat{p}^e_t \qquad 0 < \lambda < 1$$

where $\hat{p}_t$ is now the *logarithm* of the money price of the consumption good.
(b) Demonstrate the existence of a stationary equilibrium of the form $\hat{p}_t = \hat{M}$, where $\hat{M}$ is the logarithm of the money stock.
(c) What, if anything, can you say about dynamical equilibria in this economy? In particular, can you express equilibrium prices in terms of initial conditions? Are these equilibria asymptotically stable?

IV.6 (T) Suppose $(p_t)^\infty_{t=1}$ and $(\hat{p}_t)^\infty_{t=1}$ support two distinct outside-money equilibria of the same Samuelson economy, both converging monotonically and asymptotically to the unique inside-money equilibrium. Show that the outside-money equilibrium with the higher starting price (lower starting real balances) is Pareto inferior to the other.

IV.7 (*) In a pure-exchange economy with identical households and zero population growth, the endowment vector is $(2, 1)$ and the utility function is $\log c_1 + \log c_2$. Explore how the value of money in the stationary state depends on Weil's confidence parameter q. What is the minimum value of that parameter if money is to be accepted in exchange?

IV.8 (a) Study an economy with the following time-dependent structure: the aggregate savings function is $Z_1(R)$ in odd periods and $Z_2(R)$ in even ones; Z_1 and Z_2 are increasing functions such that $0 < Z_1 < Z_2$ at every $R > 0$. Does this economy possess a stationary monetary equilibrium? A periodic one? Does it admit an intertemporally optimal monetary equilibrium?
(b) Suppose now that the aggregate saving function of a pure-exchange economy is Z_1 for $t = 1, \ldots , T$ and Z_2 for $t = T + 1, \ldots$ *ad infinitum*; again it is the case that $0 < Z_1(R) < Z_2(R)$ for $R > 0$. Describe the set of monetary equilibria for this economy and show that at least one of them is dynamically efficient.

IV.9 (T) Show that any perfect-foresight equilibrium of a Samuelson economy converging asymptotically to the outside-money stationary state is intertemporally optimal.

IV.10 (D) Suppose the stock of currency grows at a constant proportional rate $\mu \geq 0$ and that newly printed money is distributed exclusively, in equal per capita amounts, to households of the oldest generation alive. Population is constant and consists of identical households with utility function $c_1 c_2$ and endowment vector $(1, 0)$.

(a) Write down the standard consumer problem. Study competitive equilibrium and find out how it is affected by changes in μ.
(b) What values of μ are consistent with dynamically efficient equilibria?
(c) Suppose, instead, that the rate of money creation is not set once and for all but is reset each period t in order to promote the welfare (maximize the lifetime utility) of those generations that are alive at t. What equilibria are supported by this "myopic" monetary policy?

IV.11 (C) (a) Generalize and interpret the Auernheimer formula for maximum seigniorage to the production economy of section 26.2.
(b) As an independent check on the formula you derived in part (a), suppose that $f(k) = k^{1/4}$ and the saving rate s is sufficiently large for the economy of section 26.2 to be of the Samuelson type. Compute the maximal seigniorage as a function of the parameter s. What rate of money creation achieves this maximum?

IV.12 A pure-exchange economy with constant population consists of identical households with endowment vector $e = (1/2, 1/2)$ and utility function $u = c_1' + b[c_2' - 1/2 (c_2')^2]$, where $b > 0$. There is a constant stock of currency $M = 1$.

(a) For what values of b is this economy of the Samuelson type? Of the classical type?
(b) Compute and draw the saving function. Find the inside money interest factor $\bar{R}$. Show that saving attains a unique global maximum when the interest factor equals $2\bar{R}$. What happens to saving when the interest factor tends to zero or infinity?
(c) Calculate the real value of currency balances at a golden rule equilibrium.
(d) Discuss the stability of stationary equilibria. Show that the golden rule equilibrium is stable in the Samuelson case if $\bar{R} < 1/3$.
(e) For what values of the parameter b does this economy admit periodic cycles of order 2?
(f) Design a system of lump-sum transfer between generations to eliminate *all* periodic cycles. What is the smallest transfer that will accomplish this? Describe intuitively why your scheme works.

IV.13 This question looks at inflationary equilibria in a pure-exchange economy in which government does not directly fix the rate of money creation, as in section 26.1. Rather, policy chooses a constant per capita deficit $g \in [0, g_c]$, printing whatever amount of currency is needed to finance that deficit at market prices. Assume all taxes are zero and that dated consumption goods are gross substitutes.

(a) For an economy with constant population, show that equilibria satisfy a difference equation of the form

$$m_t = s[(m_{t+1} - g)/m_t]$$

(b) What happens to your equation at $g = 0$? At $g = g_c$?
(c) How many steady states does this equation have? Are they asymptotically stable?
(d) Compare your expression with the one illustrated in figure 26.1(a) or equation (26.3c). What are the main similarities and differences of equilibria under a constant deficit policy from those under a constant rate of money creation?

IV.14 Explore the tax equivalence of inflation finance. In particular, prove that any competitive equilibrium associated with inflation finance of constant government purchases

$g \in [0, g_c]$ may be supported by an appropriate excise tax on commodity sellers.

IV.15 For the pure-exchange economy described in example 26.1 derive an algebraic expression for the Laffer curve, that is, the relation between the real government deficit and the rate of money creation in the steady state.

IV.16 (The Sidrauski model): An economy consists of a single infinitely lived individual who supplies 1 unit of labor inelastically each period. There are two dated goods: a consumption good denoted c_t and produced under constant returns from capital and labor; and real money balances denoted m_t and created (or destroyed) by the government through lump-sum transfers (or taxes). Time is discrete, capital does not depreciate, and the individual maximizes an objective function of the form

$$\sum_{t=0}^{\infty} \beta^t w(c_t, m_t)$$

where $\beta \in (0, 1)$ and $w: \mathbb{R}_+^2 \to \mathbb{R}$ is a standard utility function.

(a) Suppose that the government changes the stock of nominal money at a constant rate, that is, $M_{t+1} = \mu M_t$ for all t and some $\mu > \beta$. Show that all equilibrium sequences (k_t, m_t, c_t) satisfy the following equations:

$$\beta R_t w_c (c_t, m_t) = w_c(c_{t-1}, m_{t-1})$$

$$w_m(c_t, m_t) = [1 - (m_{t+1}/m_t)(1/\mu R_t)]w_c(c_t, m_t)$$

$$c_t = f(k_t) + k_t - k_{t+1}$$

where $R_t = 1 + f'(k_t)$ and (w_c, w_m) are marginal utilities. (*Hint*: Add production and capital to the consumer problem at the beginning of section 26.3. Derive the first-order conditions, and use the appropriate government budget constraints to express everything in terms of the sequence (k_t, m_t, c_t).)

(b) Show that the dynamical system defined in part (a) has *at most one* steady state $(\bar{k}, \bar{m}, \bar{c})$, if all goods are normal. Find sufficient conditions guaranteeing that *exactly* one steady state exists. (*Hint*: Assume that the instantaneous utility function w is additively separable. What happens if it is not?)

(c) Does the rate of money creation affect income or consumption in the steady state? The value of real balances $\bar{m}$? Compare your answers with those of the overlapping generations model in section 26.2. Explain any discrepancies you find between the overlapping generations and Sidrauski models.

IV.17 (The Sidrauski model continued): Continuing to assume that w is additively separable in question IV.16, look at the original dynamical system in part (a). What can you say about the asymptotic stability properties of the steady state $(\bar{k}, \bar{m}, \bar{c})$? Is it a saddle and, if so, what is the dimension of its stable manifold? (*Hint*: Linearize the system about the steady state and find how many eigenvalues of the relevant Jacobian lie within the unit circle.)

IV.18 This question will help you explore the pricing of a nondepreciating non-reproducible asset like land. Consider, in particular, an overlapping generations model of growth with constant population, inelastic labor supply $N_t = 1$, and a fixed amount of capital $K_t = 1$ for all t. A single perishable consumption good is produced under constant returns from labor and capital. Capital is infinitely durable; it cannot be produced or consumed. There is no currency or any other outside asset.

(a) Denote by p_t the price of capital, by u_t its rental rate, and by R_t the interest factor on private loans, all expressed in terms of the consumption good. Show that if individual asset portfolios include both loans and land at time t, then

$$u_t = p_t R_t - p_{t+1}$$

(b) Compute the wage and rental rates at any competitive equilibrium, and prove that they are constant over time.

(c) Write down a first-order dynamical system whose solution jointly determines the equilibrium sequence (p_t, R_t). (*Hint*: Use the arbitrage condition from part (a) together with the requirement that aggregate saving equals the value of the capital stock.)

IV.19 (T) Suppose that the aggregate saving function in question IV.18 is increasing in the loan yield R. Prove that the dynamical system you wrote in part (c) has a unique steady state $(\bar{p}, \bar{R})$. Is that state asymptotically stable? Dynamically efficient?

IV.20 (C) Investigate the holding of national debt in the land economy of question IV.18. Consider, in particular, a constant-flow policy of perpetually refinanced per capita debt. Taxes and government purchases are zero.

(a) Write down a dynamical system that consists of the arbitrage condition in question IV.18(a) plus the requirement that aggregate saving should equal the value of land plus the value of public debt. Draw the relevant vector field.

(b) Is there a stationary equilibrium with positive public debt? Explain the economic intuition behind your answer.

(c) Is there a dynamical equilibrium such that the stock of public debt vanishes asymptotically?

IV.21 Describe periodic equilibria and stationary sunspot equilibria in a pure-exchange overlapping generations economy with a fixed stock of fiat money in which the representative individual has a Leontieff indifference map of the form $u(c_1, c_2) = \min(c_1, ac_2)$ for some constant $a > 0$. In particular:

(a) Derive a first-order difference equation that is satisfied by all deterministic equilibria. Define the values of the parameters for which two-cycles appear.

(b) Are there any deterministic three-cycles in this economy?

(c) Define the set of all possible stationary sunspot equilibria with two states of nature.

II.22 (*) Prove that the equilibrium prices of the economy analyzed in section 27.2 are fully revealing. In particular, let $(\psi_1^*, \dots, \psi_J^*)$ be a solution vector to equation (27.16) and suppose that it consists of distinct elements. Show that the associated price function of equation (27.18) takes a distinct value in each state. Specifically:

(a) Suppose that $\psi_i^* = \lambda z_i$ for some $\lambda > 0$ and all $i = 1, \dots, J$ and obtain a contradiction with equation (27.16).

(b) Suppose now that $\psi_i^*/z_i = \psi_j^*/z_j$ for two distinct states i and j, and show that this violates equation (27.16) if youthful and old-age consumption are gross substitutes. (*Hint*: Part (b) is not easy. Readers may find Lucas (1972) particularly helpful here.)

IV.23 (*) Investigate how long currency stays positively valued in the non-neutral currency equilibrium $(\bar{x}, \bar{m})$ of section 27.3. In particular, pick a value $\pi \in (\bar{R}, 1)$ and show that the duration of an outside-money equilibrium is a discrete random variable with a known probability distribution. Compute the expected value of that duration.

IV.24 (*) (a) In the economy of example 27.3 write out two equations that describe how per capita real balances m_t and the inflation factor $\pi_t \equiv p_t/p_{t-1}$ depend on the variable z_t.

(b) Compute the correlation coefficient for the pair (m_t, π_t).

(c) Eliminate z_t from the relationships you wrote out in part (a) and attain a *reduced-form* equation that expresses m_t as a function of π_t and other variables. What "other variables" are involved in this relationship?

IV.25 Examine how a cash-in-advance constraint changes an otherwise standard optimal growth model whose representative household maximizes a discounted sum of utilities

$\Sigma_{t=0}^{\infty}\beta^t u(c_t)$ subject to the usual resource constraint and an additional liquidity constraint of the form $p_t c_t \le M_t$ where M_t are money balances accumulated at the end of period $t-1$, and A_t is the corresponding stock of interest-bearing assets. Each household consists of a shopper and a worker: the shopper finances consumption purchases each period out of pre-existing cash balances without access to the labor and capital income earned within the period. The worker supplies one unit of labor inelastically, is paid in cash, and all earnings are added at the end of the period to the household's cash balances.

Between shoppers and workers are a number of producing firms which sell consumption goods for cash and pay out factors of production, also in cash. A typical household's balances of currency and earning assets evolve according to the relation

$$A_{t+1} + M_{t+1} = M_t - p_t c_t + p_t w_t + R_t A_t$$

where R_t is the interest factor on loans and wt is the real wage rate. Suppose that the aggregate stock of currency is constant.

(a) If $(\bar{k}, \bar{c})$ is the unique positive steady state of the standard optimal growth model, show that $k_t = \bar{k}$, $c_t = \bar{c}$, $m_t = \bar{c}$ is a steady state of the cash-constrained economy in which m_t denotes real balances.

(b) (T) Assume that physical capital depreciates fully on use. Prove that equilibrium sequences (k_t, c_t, m_t) of the augmented economy, for which the cash constraint is binding each period, satisfy the following relations:

$$m_t = f(k_t) - (m_t/m_{t+1})k_{t+1}$$
$$m_t u'(m_t) = \beta f'(k_t) m_{t+1} u'(m_{t+1})$$
$$\beta m_{t+1} u'(m_{t+1}) \le m_t u'(m_t)$$

(*Hint*: You do not need these conditions to do part (a). If you need help to derive them, consult Wilson (1979) or Woodford (1988).)

IV.26 (*) This question and the next one, drawn from Bewley (1980, 1986) and Woodford (1986), explore how dynamical equilibria are influenced by the presence of sequential budget constraints, that is, borrowing constraints like those of section 11.3 or cash-in-advance constraints such as those of section 25.4. Starting with the pure-exchange economy with infinitely lived households, described in section 15.2, we suppose that there are two types of agents, indexed by $h = 1, 2$. Both have a utility function of the form $\Sigma_{t=0}^{\infty}\beta^t u(c_t^h)$. Agent 1 has endowment e_1 in odd periods and $e_2 < e_1$ in even periods; agent 2 has the reverse pattern with e_1 in even periods and e_2 in odd ones. We assume that

$$u'(e_1)/u'(e_2) < \beta < 1$$

(a) Suppose there is a perfect credit market, as in section 15.2. Show that there is a unique inside-money equilibrium at which $\beta R_t = 1$ for all t and that both consumption profiles are flat in equilibrium. Which agent has the higher consumption?

(b) Assume now that agents *cannot borrow* from each other and are obliged, instead, to finance all consumption in excess of their endowment from pre-existing currency balances. Write down a period-by-period budget constraint for this problem (this should not require the holding of money for consumption *within* one's current endowment), and derive the first-order conditions for an optimum consumption plan.

(c) Show that, at each competitive equilibrium, the entire stock of currency, $M_t = 1$, will be held by individuals whose current endowment is e_1. Suppose there are no taxes or transfers of money.

(d) Prove that the sequence (m_t) of real balances satisfies

$$u'(e_1 - m_t) = \beta(m_{t+1}/m_t)u'(e_2 + m_{t+1})$$
$$u'(e_2 + m_t) \geqslant \beta(m_{t+1}/m_t)u'(e_1 - m_{t+1})$$

at any competitive equilibrium. Explain the intuitive meaning of the inequality.

(e) Compare the equilibrium consumption profiles of parts (a) and (d). Does the steady state in part (d) permit agents a completely smooth consumption profile?

IV.27 (*) Compare the borrowing-constraint economy in part (d) of the previous question with a standard pure-exchange overlapping generations economy with currency consisting of two households with a common utility function $u(c_1) + \beta u(c_2)$ and endowment vectors (e_1, e_2) and (e_2, e_1) respectively. Suppose that private loans are prohibited.

(a) Define $s(R, y_1, y_2) = \text{argmax}_s \, [u(y_1 - s) + \beta u(y_2 + Rs)]$ and prove that the two dynamical equilibrium conditions in the previous question are equivalent to

$$m_t = s(m_{t+1}/m_t, e_1, e_2) \qquad s(m_{t+1}/m_t, e_2, e_1) \leqslant 0$$

(b) Draw a phase diagram for these two relations and explain geometrically how the inequality in part (a) restricts equilibrium dynamics.

IV.28 This question will help you identify the class of economies which satisfy inequality (24.1). All these economies possess stationary outside-money equilibria that are asymptotically stable in the forward dynamics and periodic equilibria that are not stable. In particular, consider the class of economies indexed by the parameter vector (α, β, σ) where $\alpha \in (0, 1)$, $\beta \in (0, 1)$, and $\sigma > 0$, $\sigma \neq 1$. These parameters refer to standard pure-exchange overlapping generations economies with a constant population of representative households endowed with an additive isoelastic utility function $u(c_1, c_2) = c_1^{1-\sigma} + \beta c_2^{1-\sigma}$ and an income vector $e = (1, \alpha)$. The parameter σ is the reciprocal of the intertemporal elasticity of substitution in consumption.
  Denote by R the interest factor on loans and let $\pi \equiv (\beta R)^{1/\sigma}$

(a) Use the first-order condition for the consumer problem to show that the representative saving function is

$$s(R) = \frac{\pi - \alpha}{\pi + R}$$

(b) Prove that the interest-factor elasticity of saving at the golden rule equilibrium is

$$\epsilon(1) = \frac{\alpha - \pi + (1 + \alpha)(\pi/\sigma)}{(1 + \pi)(\pi - \alpha)}$$

(c) From the expression above, show that $\epsilon(1) \leqslant -1/2$ if, and only if,

$$\alpha \leqslant \frac{\pi(1 - \pi - 2/\sigma)}{2\pi/\sigma + 1 - \pi}$$

(d) Conclude that inequality (24.1) holds for some parameter vector (α, β, σ) if there exist $\beta \in (0, 1)$ and $\sigma > 0$ that satisfy

$$\beta < (1 - 2/\sigma)^\sigma \qquad\qquad (*)$$

(e) Can you find numerical values of β and σ that are consistent with (*)? What are the general features of utility functions for which (*) holds true? What types of indifference maps violate (*) and why?

IV.29 (T) Prove equation (28.11) by differentiating with respect to the yield R the first-order conditions for the two-household saving problems (deterministic yield, stochastic yield), evaluating the resulting two expressions at $R = 1$, and comparing the two outcomes.

IV.30 (T) Prove the relations in (28.14a) and (28.14b) (*Hint:* For (28.14a) use the fact that $ws(w) \to \infty$ as $w \to \infty$ if old-age consumption is a normal good; then use (28.14a) to demonstrate (28.14b).)

IV.31 (a) Suppose that stationary sunspot equilibria exist in the economy of section 28.2. Prove that they are Pareto inferior to the outside-money steady state in the sense that the transition from one allocation to the other will improve the *expected* lifetime utility of some generation without an expected utility reduction to any other generation.

(b) What can you say about the welfare properties of dynamical sunspot equilibria like those of equations (28.3) and (28.4)? (*Hint:* For a general statement, consult Balasko (1983).)

IV.32 (T) Prove theorem 28.6 (*Hint:* In case of difficulty, consult Woodford (1990a).)

IV.33 (a) Explain why the phaseline of equation (28.67) does not pass through the origin.

(b) Prove that, under a fixed money supply rule, this equation has a unique determinate steady state $\bar{q} > 0$.

(c) Is this steady state optimal?

(d) What about explosive equilibria converging to $q = 0$? Show that there is a countable infinity of them.

IV.34 (T) Suppose that the perfect-foresight steady state q^* of the inflation targeting regime described in equation (28.72) is an orientation-reversing sink. Show that a stationary sunspot equilibrium with two natural states exists for the stochastic economy of equations (28.81a) and (28.81b).

IV.35 Write out the fundamental difference equation of inflation finance under perfect foresight in a pure-exchange model using as a state variable the inflation rate rather than per capita real balances. Specifically, if μ is the rate of money creation and n the rate of population growth, show that equation (26.3c) may be rewritten in the form

$$\frac{1 + \mu}{1 + n} = \frac{s\,(1/\pi_{t+1})}{\pi_t s\,(1/\pi_t)}$$

What do you conclude from this equation about the inflation rate in an outside-money steady state?

IV.36 Are least squares predictions unbiased forecasts in the learning model of section 29.2? In particular, how are forecast errors correlated with past inflation rates?

Index of Names

Index of Subjects